The Collected Sermons of

William
Sloane
Coffin

The Riverside Years

The Collected Sermons of

William Sloane Coffin

The Riverside Years

———

VOLUME ONE

———

William Sloane Coffin

Westminster John Knox Press
LOUISVILLE • LONDON

Scripture quotations taken from *The New English Bible* are © The Delegates of the Oxford
University Press and The Syndics of the Cambridge University Press, 1961, 1970. Used by
permission. Scripture quotations from *The Holy Bible, New International Version,* are copyright
© 1973, 1978, 1984 International Bible Society. Used by permission of Zondervan Bible
Publishers. Scripture quotations from The New King James Version are copyright © 1979,
1980, 1982, Thomas Nelson Inc., Publishers and are used by permission. Scripture quotations
from the Revised Standard Version of the Bible are copyright © 1946, 1952, 1971, and 1973
by the Division of Christian Education of the National Council of the Churches of Christ in
the U.S.A. and are used by permission. All other biblical quotations are the author's.

Every effort has been made to determine whether texts are under copyright. If through an oversight
any copyrighted material has been used without permission, and the publisher is notified of this,
acknowledgment will be made in future printings.

See Acknowledgments, p. xv, for additional permission information.

Book design by Drew Stevens
Cover design by Lisa Buckley
Cover photograph: © *Bettmann / CORBIS*

First edition
Published by Westminster John Knox Press
Louisville, Kentucky

This book is printed on acid-free paper that meets the American National
Standards Institute Z39.48 standard. ∞

PRINTED IN THE UNITED STATES OF AMERICA

08 09 10 11 12 13 14 15 16 17—10 9 8 7 6 5 4 3 2 1

Library of Congress Cataloging-in-Publication Data
Coffin, William Sloane.
  The Collected sermons of William Sloane Coffin : the Riverside years /
William Sloane Coffin ; introduction by Martin E. Marty.—1st ed.
    p. cm.
  ISBN-13: 978-0-664-23299-3 (v. 2: alk. paper)
  ISBN-13: 978-0-664-23244-3 (v. 1: alk. paper)   1. Presbyterian
Church—Sermons.   2. Sermons, American.   I. Title.
  BX9178.C58C65   2008
  252'.051—dc22   2007039284

Dear Reader,

Before he was unable to do so any longer, Bill always made the morning coffee. He would bring it to me in bed and there we would have our best talks of the day; fresh, sharp, intimate, challenging, and of course, all the "to-dos" that come with living together. Often he would talk around the sermon he was working on, or bring a new quote, like a treasure, that he was going to use to brighten a moment in a sermon. One Valentine's Day morning four or five years ago, he brought me this note with my coffee, and I give it to you, who also try.

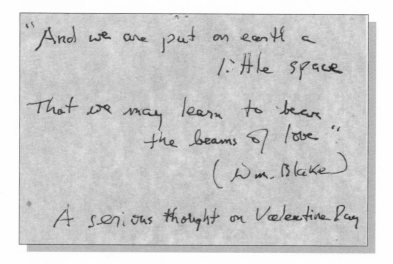

"And we are put on earth a
little space
That we may learn to bear
the beams of love"
(Wm. Blake)

A serious thought on Valentine Day

It is my hope that you will find courage and hope for your own work in these sermons, that you will see how Bill found his way, and that he may help you find yours.

With all my best wishes,
Randy Coffin

Contents

1980

1981

1982

Thank You

These sermons could not have been published without first and foremost the dedication of Bill's longtime editor, Stephanie Egnotovich at Westminster John Knox Press, and its former senior editor, Davis Perkins, who encouraged the project at the very beginning, and Julie Tonini, also of WJK. Thanks to folks at The Riverside Church to James Forbes, Thomas Stiers, Victor Jordan, and Robert Lundberg; and at Yale University to Thomas Hyry, William Massa, Diane Kaplan, Nancy Lion, Laura Tatum, and John Lindner. And to David Coffin particularly for help at Yale, to Amy Coffin, Jessica Tidman, Tom Scull, Wil and Jill Tidman, Sperry Wilson, Caroline Steele, Kate Siepmann, and Ruth Whybrow for the sustaining encouragement you gave to me throughout. Thank you! I am ever grateful to you all.

Randy Wilson Coffin

Acknowledgments

Excerpt from "Stopping by Woods on a Snowy Evening" from *The Poetry of Robert Frost* edited by Edward Connery Lathem, published by Jonathan Cape. Copyright © 1923, 1969 by Henry Holt and Company. Copyright © 1951 by Robert Frost. Reprinted by permission of Henry Holt and Company, LLC, and The Random House Group Ltd.

From *A Thousand Clowns* by Herb Gardner, copyright © 1961, 1962 by Herb Gardner and Irwin A. Cantor, Trustee. Used by permission of Random House, Inc.

From *Our Town* by Thorton Wilder Copyright © 1998 by Harper Perennial Classics. Used by permission of The Barbara Hogenson Agency, Inc.

From "Stopping by Woods on a Snowy Evening" from *The Poetry of Robert Frost* edited by Edward Connery Lathem, published by Jonathan Cape. Reprinted by permission of The Random House Group Ltd.

From *Straw for the Fire: From the Notebooks of . . .* by Theodore Roethke, Selected & Arranged by David Wagener, copyright © 1972 by Beatrice Roethke. Used by permission of Doubleday, a division of Random House, Inc.

The Art of Living by Wilferd A. Peterson (Simon & Schuster, 1961). Permission granted by Lilian A. Thorpe and the Heacock Literary Agency, Inc.

The lines from "you shall above all things be glad and young." Copyright 1938, © 1966, 1991 by the Trustees for the E. E. Cummings Trust. The lines from "after all white horses are in bed." Copyright 1926, 1954, © 1991 by the Trustees for the E. E. Cummings Trust. Copyright © 1985 by George James Firmage, from *Complete Poems:1904–1962* by E. E. Cummings, edited by George J. Firmage. Used by permission of Liveright Publishing Corporation.

Wilder, Thorton. *Our Town*. New York: Harper Perennial Classics, 1998. Used by permission of The Barbara Hogenson Agency

Introduction

"Come off it!" Praise the Reverend William Sloane Coffin too extravagantly, as many did in his hearing, using hyperbole to describe his works and ways, and they would be dismissed with a smile, a shrug, and a posture which suggested: "Now that *that's* out of the way, let's get down to business."

Moved as I am by the Riverside sermons and tempted as I am to praise the preacher and author lavishly, I hear his virtual "Come off it." So I will, out of respect and in his honor. This means that hyperbole will have no place, though here and there I might express some awe. To get to the point, I will concentrate first on what this chapter is not:

It is not a song of praise. We've already settled that.

It is not a biography. There is a commendable one: *William Sloane Coffin Jr., A Holy Impatience* by Warren Goldstein (Yale, 2004).

It is not an exegesis of the sermons in this book, though it is an introduction to the world out of which they issued and a peephole into the world of the sermons themselves.

It is not a snippet of a personal memoir by the author of this introduction. While I frequently saw, heard, read, and conversed with Coffin, hundreds of people who knew him at Yale, Riverside Church, or elsewhere, have better credentials for reminiscing than I. So I'll get to the assigned business at hand, introducing a book of sermons which represent only one element—though an extremely important one—in his ministry.

It is not a history of Riverside Church, where these sermons were preached through a decade of Coffin's ministry there. For the detailed context its numerous authors provide, see *The History of the Riverside Church in the City of New York*, by Peter J. Paris and seven other authors—big churches demand big casts of characters—(New York University Press, 2004). Leonora Tubbs Tisdale wrote the chapter on the Coffin decade, 1977–1987.

It is remarkable, first off, that anyone cares about sermons preached from one pulpit, far away from all but New York readers, up to thirty years before their publication here, namely 1977 to 1987. There are so many sermons preached each week, and most preachers, however high they aim in faith, are realistic enough to know that most are ephemeral. If we count one homily or sermon per congregation each weekend, almost half a million messages get preached each Friday night, Saturday, or Sunday in the United States. Many of these forms of witness are quite effective, life-giving—some hearers would even say life-saving—alongside the many more that are less effective, vibrant, or memorable. Most of them achieve their goal if they help situate the hearers in the experienced presence of God, are instructive, and inspire the congregation to leave the pulpit and pew behind in order to put the message to work for the next seven days. Only a wildly egocentric preacher could envision seeing all of his or her messages in print, or at least in print that was intended for more than the local membership. Local hearers often can pick up the previous week's messages at the door as they leave the house of worship.

What becomes of these sermons? Are some of them folded and crafted into paper airplanes for children's play; are they piled up on bedroom reading tables; do they nourish passengers on commuter trains or transform the lives of some of those who could not be present for the preaching? If this sounds dismissive of preaching, an act commanded by the Jesus of the Gospels and an honored form of communication through twenty centuries of Christian meeting, it is not intended to be. Rather, it reflects something about the ephemeral character of human achievements, even those which reflect sacred intentions, and also shows awareness of the limits of human memory.

As for the substance of sermons, a British theologian asked an audience of regular worshipers: *Try to bring to mind five sermons you have heard in your lifetime.* Most of those who were challenged to do so were stumped. They might remember a funeral sermon, something said on a special occasion, or an occasional stunner. Most are forgotten. After they came up with a few, the theologian went on: *Now try to bring to mind five people through whom the hand of God was laid upon you.* Instantly, everyone came up with such.

Not a few of those described as God's agents were preachers remembered from childhood or through long years of the pastoral care they offered. From all evidences of his popularity and the demand for published versions after decades, Dr. Coffin would be one of those few whose sermons were remembered and cited by hearers and readers after many years. He would also be one that a generation of Yale students, Riverside members, and guests remember. They could say, "The hand of God was laid upon us" by him. If they would choose to follow up on this metaphor, they would likely go on to say that that figurative hand of God in the case of Coffin's sermons was one that could lift people up when they were down, push them back when they were proud, and impel them into action. I envision a new generation of readers of these works from the Coffin years and ministry feeling that hand of God and hearing whispers of the divine call afresh. Those who might consider that sentence to be hyperbolic and its expectation too extravagant are asked to read a few of the sermons here and see whether my vision is realistic or not.

Regard these sermons first as what Christian sermons should all be: testimonies. One definition of preaching, tired-sounding but full of promise, is that of the great Boston preacher Phillips Brooks: "Truth through personality." The personality of preacher Coffin is evident on every page. That is why the many subscribers to his sermons years ago soon learned that from them they could probe more deeply into biblical texts; learn what Coffin did with a text and how he did it; and pick up a line full of insight here and there. But they soon discovered that they could not simply reproduce and then preach his sermons effectively. I am told that an Episcopal priest in California was caught simply lifting one of his homilies. Such plagiarism was easy to discern.

Truth through personality—the idea pushes us into the realm of a more complex concept: that to understand the act of preaching we have to become aware of the "hermeneutics of testimony." That is a phrase of the French philosopher Paul Ricoeur, who pondered what happens when we reject "absolute knowledge of the absolute," or, in Pauline terms, we recognize that "our knowledge is piece-work" or partial (1 Cor. 13). Yet the preacher who wishes to address and impart the things of God cannot simply surrender all notions that "the absolute," or, in Johannine terms, "the Truth" is accessible and can be partly imparted.

Testimony, for Ricoeur, first involves the "claim to have experienced something." Second, as with testimony in court, we have to judge the truth of the witness. Whoever has been in court is likely to agree that the testimony cannot be grasped absolutely. It does deal strongly with "the probable." Ricoeur recognizes testimony could be false, and some preaching turns out to be such. We call it "inauthentic," if not deceiving. A commentator on Ricoeur puts all this well: "Witnesses must back their beliefs. Commitment does not guarantee the veracity of a belief, but lack of commitment undermines it." In

Ricoeur's terms, this means that "testimony is also the engagement of a pure heart and an engagement to the death." To the death?

Martin Luther King Jr., for instance, was a credible witness because those who testify on the basis of conscience and risk death become especially attractive and believable to those whose consciences are stirred. Members of audiences were aware that enemies of his message and cause might kill him at any moment, and his audiences and congregations knew it. That is why, even when on some occasions and in some modes he preached the gospel in terms that a comfortable suburban pastor might use, his message rang truer and was more compelling. It sealed the relation of the hearer with the speaker and behind them, "the Absolute" or in biblical terms, "the Truth." Lest the reference to the suburban pastor is taken as a slap against preachers who enjoy apparent security, let me say that it does not exclude the witness of those who are not at the edge of the zone where the violent would kill. "Testimony" is compelling when the middle-class, comfortable preacher is fighting a shattering disease, or is facing a psychological battering. Such can come when the preaching parent is frustrated in efforts to be reconciled to an alienated child, or when existential doubt is plaguing.

It is at this point that one can hear a haunting, chiding whisper: "Come off it." Bill Coffin would squirm or kick if he thought we thought that anything he did put him in a "quasi-martyrial" situation. The label "martyr" applies to St. Stephen, or Steve Biko in South Africa or Dietrich Bonhoeffer in Germany, or some murdered civil rights workers in the American South. True, Bill was hated, lividly, by those who could never forget the activities he undertook and instigated at Yale and elsewhere to protest the American adventures in the Vietnam War. It is also true that he was hated for his participation in civil rights and disarmament causes. Many a pastor-preacher will identify with Coffin, who engaged in ominous tangles with some influential membership blocs and even some obstructionist staff members at Riverside Church. Yet whatever the scale of threat and jeopardy a preacher feels, or however nagging the personal and up-close temptations might be, they serve to force the preacher to think through what truth he or she is to convey, and with what degree of self-reference he does so in the sermon.

Coffin retains authenticity because his references to conflicts afar, conflicts near, conflicts within, are always brief, as readers will soon find. They are, if anything, understated and told in such a way that they display no traces of narcissism. I do not mean by that last comment to suggest that Coffin was a virtuoso at self-deprecation, modest to a fault, or someone who felt compelled to remind us how insignificant he is. Part of the "hermeneutics of testimony" in Christian preaching is that the witness manifests enough sense of self-worth—thanks to the genes and Jesus—to show the guts to commend "the Absolute"="the Truth" of God in Jesus Christ and to ask others to join in the wager, the one that deals with the "probability" of the resurrection of Christ, the decisive point of witness for Paul, Paul Ricoeur, and Bill Coffin.

Paul Ricoeur, on a theme that perfectly matches the stand and outlook of Coffin, continued with analysis of the biblical or "sacred" meaning or context for testimony when it uses extraordinary expressions. "What separates this new meaning of testimony from all its uses in ordinary language is that the testimony does not belong to the witness. It proceeds from an absolute initiative as to its origin and its content." To bring testimony, says the philosopher, is different than cinching the deal through philosophy: "To attest is of a different order than to verify in the sense of logical empiricism." (On the hermeneutics of testimony and comment on it see Dan R. Stiver, *Theology after Ricoeur: New Directions in Hermeneutical Theology* [Westminster John Knox Press, 2002], 196–202).

Whoever wants to test the testimony of Bill Coffin as father need only read "Alex's Death," his most famous and revered sermon from the Riverside years or all his life. Note also the sermons that chronologically follow "Alex's Death." They are cries of the heart, revelations of bewilderment, exorcisms of temptations to turn against God but, significantly, they show that the signals of a more profound faith and impulse to exercise ministry comes from them. After suffering the loss of a child during those Riverside years, all the rest was put in perspective. He faced criticism and rejection even by many Riverside stalwarts. Some of them were reached by adversarial television and newspapers, for his stand against nuclear armament and, after showing some signs of timidity, support for homosexual rights and the enhancement of understandings on this troubling issue. Even further in the background are the nagging tensions over Riverside church administration, which was not his chosen or favorite field of action, or one in which he excelled.

Now for some lower level but perhaps relevant personal testimony of my own: I had not expected to read so much Coffinesque Christian orthodoxy as one finds on so many pages. Before I was personally acquainted with him or had read him, back in his Yale years, I only knew that he was described as the most prominent standard-brand or liberal Protestant. Those were the years when the concept of a Protestant mainline was being marketed. Often it was used invidiously against those who were not in the evangelical/evangelistic or Pentecostal ranks and certainly against those who were forming a religio-political New Christian Right. In polemical portraits of these, "liberal Protestants" were faithless Christ-deniers who got their signals from Soviet communism or secular humanism, and then spoke and acted while applying only a biblical-sounding Christian veneer to their preaching and preachments. William Sloane Coffin was supposed to be "Exhibit A" to represent the faithless.

During the intervening years, when I began to read Coffin's books and occasional sermons, I was jolted into the need to make reappraisals or, should I say, first-time appraisals. Far from muffling the voice of the Gospels and serious Christian theologians through the ages, Coffin was a witness to the acts of God in Christ, one ready to profess faith in the Trinity, one at home with the relevant voices of Christian traditions. True, you will find here no discussions of modalistic monarchianism, patripassionism, or semi-Pelagianism. However, as their author employs fresh language, Coffin's sermons are clear and draw their power from the basics. When it came to politics, he may have seemed to be, to polarizers in the parish and the media, "on the left." My hunch is that his biblical testimony must have sounded as if it was coming not "from the right" but from the mainline of the mainline. I'd call it the "moderate" middle, but Coffin did not believe that Christian prophecy, judgment, or gospel, could ever be "moderate."

The immediate impression one receives from any page of these sermons is that preacher Coffin had internalized a dictum of top theologian Karl Barth, one which had almost been reduced to cliché by the 1970s, but which was still to the point: "Take your Bible and take your newspaper and read both. But interpret newspapers from the Bible." Today I suppose Barth would have to urge preachers to google internet signals in order to know what is going on in the minds of YouTube and MySpace addicts in the pew. Here, again, standard-brand Protestants of the sort who established Riverside Church and many from African-American church traditions that were cherished and assertive on Morningside Heights in the Coffin decade might have expected preacher Coffin in his sermons to become enslaved by a passion for the moment. He certainly did have an awareness of performance and attracting the media. But he did not become addicted to it, and he did not have to become obsessed with a passion for relevance.

Something needs to be said about the situation of Riverside Church. It was founded in the 1920s in a merger of a Baptist and a Congregational Church. With the backing of immensely wealthy John D. Rockefeller Jr., they built cathedral-size modern-Gothic appearing Riverside. It towered and towers over Morningside Heights near Columbia University, Union Theological Seminary, and any number of educational institutions. A succession of great preachers, most notably fighter-against-fundamentalists Harry Emerson Fosdick in the 1920s, led it to become well known for liberal theology and its powerful agencies for making change in New York City. Massive though the walls were, the church with its programs and personalities had always been fragile. Fosdick and Rockefeller, who admired each other, regularly tangled, especially when Fosdick would preach about social policies offensive to the man of wealth.

Morningside Heights became a neighborhood of turmoil, and Riverside had to react to shocks as both rich and poor, black and white, liberal and moderate, and, by Coffin's day, gay and straight people were in tense relations with each other. The cumbersome polity of the church was Baptist-style writ large—it stressed the autonomy of the local congregation. It was heavily bureaucratic, difficult to administer. As years passed, funding itself became a major problem, and Coffin had to attend to financial affairs, not always adeptly. For all the tremors and traumas affecting the foundations of that church and the people who worshiped in it, Riverside became no doubt the most prominent pulpit in American Protestantism. The press and radio and television knew where to focus on issues of the day, and found them in the Coffin pulpit. Tourists and guests knew where to come for great preaching and the music for which the church was also famed. By the time Coffin came to the scene, relations between the large black caucus and some other elements in the membership of the staff were tense. Coffin had to address them.

In addition to the description of the location and the physical circumstances of the church, we need to pay some attention to the place of preaching in such a pulpit, circa 1977. In church and society, a kind of therapeutic revolution was continuing. One of the features of its "feeling movements" was the sowing of distrust of the spoken word. In these years the public was experiencing the high prime of Marshall McLuhan, priest of the media revolution, who called into question messages and even the concept of messages in a critique. The electronic revolution was focused on television and devoted to imagery. Often advocates of this medium dismissed oral communication. Seminaries attracted students who felt a call to ministry, but many of them wanted to avoid anything as drab and boring as preaching, then seen as an outmoded form. They were told that embrace, gesture, drama, and pictures were the ways to communicate the sense-revolution. Preaching, discourse by one to many, was declared to be dying out.

Yet at the same time, new movements were arising. And every one of them—whether they existed in support of civil rights or in causes such as dealing with the environment, war and peace, identity movements of ethnic or interest groups, the understanding of gender—was led by people who used words well. The pioneers of the women's movements possessed no guns, no ships, and meager funds. But they had words, and their speeches rallied newcomers to the cause and fortified those already in it. In other words, they were secular preachers. In religion, there had been new stirrings for twenty years. Heads of the black movement for those two decades had been "Reverends." Among all these activists was Bill Coffin, preaching and gaining followings mainly through sermons. He believed in the spoken word. Without instruments of government, the military, big business, or advertising firms, he had virtually no source of power beyond his spoken words. He had used his feet during protests at Yale and was ready to use them now, but they were relatively unimportant when compared to this voice box and his words that issued from it.

A third event or trend that should have worked against Coffin at Riverside was the relative decline of churches that came to be called "mainline," ironically at the time this putative mainline was seen to be losing its place. Others were on the rise. Barriers which had once set quotas on Jews in the academy were down. Nonwhite Protestants, tending to the city, were producing headlines and celebrities unmatched in the then still prevalent Protestant style. Preaching was being rediscovered, most significantly among African Americans. Significantly, Coffin's successor at Riverside was to be James Forbes, who, like Coffin, was often pointed to as the most prominent preacher of the day.

In the midst of this colorful cast was Coffin, whose very name recalled the days when Anglo-Saxonhood meant so much. The Reverend Doctor William Sloane Coffin Jr., rooted in WASPdom, was now a prophet against some of its practices and an evangelist who would heal people within the old Protestant nexus. Others took confidence from his example.

One learns from the record of Coffin at Riverside how hard it is for even the most eloquent and wisely admired spiritual leaders to move complex institutions. In fact, as one reckons with the causes to which he gave support, it was clear that few were prospering. During those years the electorate took a turn to the right with the election of Ronald Reagan. More and more investment of funds and faith went to armament. Priorities in the nation favored the rich and led to neglect of the poor. In almost every sermon here there is a reference to some in-church or beyond-church matter that needed address, but for which there were no resources in pocketbook, mind, or heart to turn things around easily. So, since the nation and church were losing so much, was Coffin himself a loser? Hardly. Realistic as he was about his own fallibility—his marital record, for instance, had disturbed some on the calling committee at Riverside—he was generous in his appraisal of faults of others. His critical voice was never whiny. He once chuckled during a University of Chicago visit which included a stop in my office where there was a sign "No Whining." I don't think he noticed my other wall decoration, Walt Kelly's Pogo saying: "We have faults we have hardly used yet." His sermons suggest that he would have acclaimed it.

The reason he could be angry but not sullen, disappointed but not despairing, was because he believed in the Christian gospel, with its accent on the triumph that came with suffering, the power that issued from the weak, the victory that was the seal of the loving sacrifice unto death of Jesus on the cross. The theology was moving to those who heard it, and should be so to readers of these sermons. They were not covered by the media as much as were his demonstrations against racism and nuclear armament, or as had been his counseling of conscientious objectors to the Vietnam War draft in the years before he came to Riverside. Yet devotion to that gospel of weakness was the secret of his power, or the power of that in which he believed. To test that, one has to sample the sermons, or, in due course, to read them all with a highlighter or colored pen for underlining in hand.

Pastor William Sloane Coffin, in times of such unrest, tried to "interpret the newspapers" in the light of the Bible. He could preach some landmark sermons, one of which we will sample: The occasion was Martin Luther King Jr.'s fiftieth birthday. Coffin used the occasion to celebrate King's ability to shake things up in general.

> Even as Blacks are breaking up all-white patterns, so women are upsetting the patriarchal structures of America. And this bodes well for the Gay liberation movement, as historically only societies that subordinate women are harsh in their treatment of homosexuality—male homosexuality, that is. Interestingly enough, with the exception of one vague passage in St. Paul, there is not a single mention of lesbianism in all the Bible. (Someday we'll deal with the gross misinterpretations of Scripture on the part of those who, for their convenience, forget that the Nazis put over 200,000 homosexuals to death.)

That is the typical Coffin who loads up several causes within a few lines. A few lines later he pointed to those who put no friendly hand on the shoulders of teenagers in Harlem and other ghetto sites. Still a moment later he could ask: "Isn't the arms race getting ahead of the arms control process?" Old military veteran Coffin almost lost it whenever he came to current military affairs and war:

> As Martin well knew, the church is called to be the Bride of Christ, not the whore of Babylon. She cannot bind herself to the Prince of Peace and go awhoring after the gods of war. She cannot proclaim the gospel of Christ while officiating at the altars of anticommunism. She cannot stand for peace while lying prostrate before the shrine of "national security."

Soon he was announcing Riverside Church's organizing of an anti-arms race initiative, crediting King's spirit.

What is more striking than those comments, which almost became boilerplate among Christian critics of racial injustice and the arms race, is the incidental way Coffin would reach beyond the moment:

> What the prophets teach us to believe and what the world regards as belief are not the same. . . . Prophets recognize that revelation always has to be worked out, that there is a progressive nature to moral judgment. So they criticize what is, in terms of what ought to be. They judge the darkness of the present by the light of the future. And they reject what is narrow and provincial, in the name of what is universal. Prophets know that just as all rivers finally meet in the sea, so all individuals, races and nations meet in God.

Coffin quoted Galatians 3:28 after those lines which summarize as well as any what being prophetic in his time meant, though he was embarrassed when people called him a prophet as he himself was addressing the agenda he had just outlined.

The reader will find many variations on this prophetic theme, which he handles with care. In a sermon preached soon after there was a poignant reference to the presence of the powerful in the case of Nelson Rockefeller, whose funeral at Riverside drew the wealthy and the mighty. Almost immediately in the sermon, Henry Kissinger was the focus. Here was another illustration of a preacher who had that newspaper in his one hand. On the global scene, Iran and Iraq became regular topics in the year when Iranian leaders took some Americans hostage.

Sometimes pastors in large and endowed congregations are envied because their main task is preaching, so they have all week to prepare for the pulpit. It happens that prominent pulpits are usually the main means of outreach of a congregation and the chief means of nurturing the adults, and, one hopes, often the children. This connecting task inevitably forces administrative tasks on the leader of the pastoral staff, usually the preacher. Coffin saw to it that he did set aside plenty of hours for study and the writing-out of his sermons. But anyone who reads the history of Riverside covering his years knows that he was forced to face tensions and crises, sometime financial, sometimes in staff battles, and most of all when his participation off the premises in causes that not all members found congenial took great expenditures of time. He used the tensions as energizers for the act of speaking.

Sometimes his allusions are so dense that the reader, finding it difficult to follow, has to have empathy for the congregation. Still, the people stuck with him, looked forward to his sermons, quoted them, and sometimes testified that they tried to live by what they learned. Here is a sample of an overladen allusion-rich paragraph that is still worthy of unpacking:

> Descartes was wrong. *Cogito, ergo sum?* ("I think, therefore I am.") We are not detached brains, nor do we establish who we are by thinking alone. Self-knowledge through self-contemplation is self-defeating. In his *Memoirs*, the British philosopher A. J. Ayre writes, "The self seethes, and philosophy analyzes. An abacus is substituted for the sinew of human mystery, and wit for passion."

One hopes that the hearers "got it," for it encapsulates so much of what I found to be central to Coffin in Ricoeur's "hermeneutics of testimony." For the French philosopher and here for an English one thrown in, analysis is not testimony. One can stand back during analysis. My teacher of preaching sixty years ago planted an idea that has never left my classmates or me. He posed eighteen questions that dealt with the quest for effective preaching. Coffin would have breezed through such a test. But the eleventh question was elusive and plaguing. We were to read other people's sermons and ask, "Does this preacher *describe* God or *offer* God?" Offering God meant testifying that "the Absolute"—no, translate that to "the Truth" in Jesus

Christ—is an offering of God's presence which expects response. Philosophy, like the abacus, is then on the shelf, while the self seethes and the sinew of human mystery has to be reached.

Coffin moved on to disturb the peace of the antirationalist romantics who were coming to such prominence in the church and world in 1978. These were the romantics who dodged the reach of God by saying *sentio, ergo sum* ("I feel, therefore I am"). If Coffin could have appraised such "feeling" as a mere fad in middle-class therapy and the discourse of the time, he would have dropped the matter; but he found that something was at stake. He feared that people would end their quest for or response to God with nothing but feeling. Those who wanted to be closer to God, he urged, had to go deeper. For deeper than thinking, deeper than feeling, is caring. I care, therefore I think. I care, therefore I feel. I care, therefore I wish, therefore I will. I care, therefore I am. Coffin discerned an ontological and biblical grounding for this depth: "We have passed out of death into life, because we love the [sisters and brothers]" (1 John 3:14). If one was to care, he or she had to get rid of grievances, in the manner of Jesus the "plant from the stem of Jesse," who never allowed his soul to be cornered into despair; who needed no enemies to tell him who he was; who never counted what was unworthy of his suffering.

In a time when people were beginning to be "spiritual but not religious," or who found the church and ministry irrelevant, Coffin found a way to confront them by asking questions, even by quoting questions.

> I have a friend—very successful—who in the fifties toyed with the idea of becoming a minister. When he came to see me at Yale Divinity School I introduced him to my teacher, Richard Niebuhr. . . . Afterwards my friend told me of their conversation. He said to Dr. Niebuhr, "I believe in God all right, and Jesus and the Christian life, but somehow the church and its ministry seem a bit irrelevant, not part of the 'big show'" as he put it. He wanted himself to be part of the big show. Finally Dr. Niebuhr said, "Tell me, Mr. Jones, what is the big show?"

That exchange prompted a new inspection of Nicodemus, the successful ruler who came to Jesus at night. Soon he was speaking against the concept of machismo which did not allow the powerful to have to ask questions or be questioned.

I cannot conclude this beginning of a book without citing a typical Coffin sermon. Typical, you might think? It's the one he preached the Sunday after his son Alex's death in an auto accident in 1983. The agony was more deep, no doubt, than that the preacher felt over the deaths of children far away. His theological blast at people who were too sure they knew the will of God in the accident was more furious than it might have been when other well-meaning people misspoke theologically. But it all comes close to the heart of his preacherly theology:

> And of course I know, even when pain is deep, that God is good. "My God, my God, why hast thou forsaken me?" Yes, but at least, "My God, my God"; and the psalm only begins that way, it doesn't end that way. As the grief that once seemed unbearable begins to turn now to bearable sorrow, the truths in the "right" Biblical passages are beginning once again, to take hold. . . . "The light shines in the darkness, and the darkness has not overcome it" (John 1:5).

Coffin regularly preached about victory over death and the triumph of resurrected life. So he could conclude of this accident, "If a week ago last Monday a lamp went out, it was because for him at least, the Dawn had come. So I shall—so let us all—seek consolation in that love which never dies, and find peace in the dazzling grace that always is."

Authors of introductions to books don't usually end with an "Amen," but sermons by William Sloane Coffin Jr. make up a different kind of book, so I end with: Amen.

Martin E. Marty
Emeritus, The University of Chicago

1977

The Spirit of Power and Love

NOVEMBER 6, 1977

"for God did not give us a spirit of timidity, but a spirit of power and love . . ."

2 Timothy 1:7

At this point in the service I imagine a few personal words are in order. So to all members of Riverside Church let me say that I am totally disposed to cherish, nurture, and love each and every one of you in the sure hope that you will do the same for me—as so many of you have done already! Among the problems of the church, I see none that are insoluble. To bring relief to the far-flung misery of New York City is obviously more complicated. The human rights about which we speak so often do not exhaust the Gospel, but they are an essential part of it. Therefore, complex as these city problems may be, we cannot throw in the towel, until there is food for all, housing for all, work for all, education and decent medical help for all. And finally, in the pursuit of my new duties, I promise that I will try always to heed the advice of whoever it was who said, "Take yourself lightly, so that, like angels, you may fly."

Now let us return to our text—"for God did not give us a spirit of timidity,"—or "craven spirit" as some of the translations read—"but a spirit of power and love." And let us also turn to the none too gentle words of our Lord and Saviour—"to every one who has, will more be given; but from him who has not, even what he has will be taken away."

It is hard to believe that this parable (Matt. 25:14–29) is as cruel as it sounds. It is hard to believe that Jesus is actually saying what the world seems so intent on proving, that the big-time always wins and that small-fry always lose. Is Jesus really joining the already all too numerous citizens of almost every nation who are intent on attacking the vulnerable instead of the powerful? Or is he simply trying, once again to break through our defenses in order to unearth something that most of us would much prefer to keep buried?

My own conclusion is that this parable is harsh, but also strangely hopeful. New Yorkers live in an enormous city, and we are gathered here in a building that is, shall we say, intimidating in its size. But all people everywhere are feeling a bit overwhelmed by bigness, and thoughtful people concerned with how human beings arrange their lives are beginning to see that the very scale of organization is an independent and primary problem. Bigness has a special relationship to pollution. Bigness has a special relationship to genocide, to suicide too, to terrorism—and to fatalism—to name but a few ailments highly contemporary. So in such a time it is surely comforting to hear what I take to be the deep-down message of this parable: *small is beautiful. God loves one-talent people.* That's why he made so many of us! And that's why His son comes down so hard on this particular one-talent person—because he refuses to believe it. What can you do with someone who refuses to believe that he or she is loved?

We Americans are today rightly suspicious of those in high office, for the events of recent years have shown us more than we have wanted to know about the arrogance of power. But we tend to forget the degree to which the inertia of the powerless makes possible the powerful. We tend to forget that in God's eyes self-obliteration is just as wicked as self-exaltation. And as this parable makes clear, both stem from the same fateful error of confusing a person's talents with a person's value.

To one he gave five, to a second two, and to a third he gave one. To each he gave not according to his value, but according to his ability. You remember that the two-talent man entered into the same joy of his master as the five-talent man. (That's a lovely phrase, isn't it—"enter into the joy of your master.") What the parable is saying is that though our talents differ, our value is the same. And the reason for this equality of value, proclaimed on almost every page of the Old and New Testament, is a cornerstone of the Christian faith: God's love does not seek value; it creates it. Our value is a gift, not an achievement. It is not because we have value that we are loved, it is because we are loved that we have value.

I've always loved the story of the beggar in the sixteenth century in Paris, desperately ill, who was brought to an operating table of a group of doctors who said in a Latin they were sure he would not understand, "*Faciamus experimentum in anima vile.*" ("Let us experiment on this vile fellow.") Whereupon the beggar, actually an impoverished student, later to become a world-renowned scholar, Marc Antoine Muret, asked from the slab on which they had laid him out, "*Animan vilem appelas pro qua Christus non dedignatus mori est?*" ("Will you call 'vile' one for whom Christ did not disdain to die?")

What Muret understood so movingly was that on the cross, God's son laid bare his father's heart for all to see. "This is my body broken for you," "this is my blood shed for you"—"for each and every one of you because whether you believe it or not, my love for you is greater than any telling of it."

Now why is that so hard to believe? Is it because it is too good to believe—we being strangers to such goodness? But before asking that, let's go on with the parable. After disbursing the talents the master goes off on a long journey. This too sounds cruel, as if he were some kind of absentee landlord. But here again I think we are dealing with another cornerstone article of the Christian faith: God is a good father—which is to say, he is not paternalistic. (*Pater noster non est paternalistic!*) As all of us who strive to be good parents know, love is self-restricting when it comes to power. We cannot exercise our power in such fashion as to restrict the freedom of our children, the freedom to become the independent, mature people God meant them to be. So it is right that the master should have left his servants freedom of choice.

And now I think we have arrived at the heart of the parable, the harsh heart, the part that unmasks what we would rather conceal. Most Americans think that the greatness of our democracy is that it offers us freedom of choice. I believe that too. But what that statement overlooks is the present tragedy of American democracy. The present tragedy of American democracy is that although we are offered freedom of choice, most of us, to a startling degree, have lost the ability to choose. I have in mind those who sit in the seats of Congress as well as those who walk the desolate streets of the South Bronx. And I think this is true of our private as well as our public life. The tragedy of our country today is that most of us do not believe that we are loved by God—not really. If we do think so, we don't think so emotionally. Consequently our much vaunted individualism is selfish instead of selfless.

Rather than accepting our value as a gift, we think we have to prove it. We think it derives from the jobs we hold, from the places where we live, from our status and reputation. So unlike the five-, unlike the two-talent person, and unlike the blessed saints, whom on this All Saints' Sunday we call to remembrance, we take no chances—not for God's sake. Like the one-talent man, we play it safe, adopting what might be called the protective strategy of deliberate failure. If you don't place any bets, you won't lose any money. If you sleep on the floor, you will never fall out of the bed.

Actually, for all his having only one talent, this fellow is shrewd. Deciding that the best defense is offense, he says, "Master, I knew you to be a hard man, reaping where you do not sow and gathering where you do not winnow." In effect, what he's saying is, "You see, Master, you shouldn't be like that. Look where it gets you. Now of course if you had slipped me five, or even two talents, things might now be different."

Psychiatrists among you might well call this person a passive-aggressive, a passive-aggressive with a punishing instinct. Overcome by fear, he digs, shall we say, his own hole, then tries to punish the master for putting him in it and for not rescuing him from it. When you stop to think of it, it's really surprising that he didn't present the master with a bill for the shovel!

"For God did not give us a spirit of timidity, but a spirit of power and love." What I love about that line is the beautiful implied understanding of our all too human inclination to feel overwhelmed; an understanding that there are always plenty of outer reasons for our inner defeats. At the same time, the text ruthlessly insists that what is understandable is also inexcusable. We need not be defeated and we won't be defeated if instead of colluding with our fears, we have the courage of our conviction that God has more love for us than we will ever have hearts ready to receive. That's the choice—everyday, almost every hour, and in almost every decision. Will we collude with the fears that tell us, "No, I can't," or with our conviction, hard as it may be to believe, that we are loved with an absolutely overwhelming love? It's a little like this building: either we can feel overwhelmed by its size, or we can allow it to lift up our spirits until we feel with the psalmist, "we are a little lower than the angels."

Finally, it is perfectly true to say, "to everyone who has will more be given." For what are we being given? It's not money, it's love. Love begets love; it's power, more power. The greatest reward of love is the opportunity to love more.

So dear friends—old and new—the next time you feel overwhelmed by a sense of your own insignificance, don't reach for the shovel. Remember that God's love doesn't seek value, but creates it. Remember that small is beautiful, that God loves one-talent people. In fact, if our poor wretched earth is ever going to be saved from its present misery, and from the flames that threaten to engulf us, it is going to be rescued by one-talent people like the twelve disciples and all the saints. They became saints very simply because they acted on the belief that there is a divine unquenchable spark in each and every one of us. So, instead of digging, let's start singing: "This little light of mine, I'm going to let it shine—Let it shine, let it shine, let it shine."

November 6, 1977

It's Easier to Be Guilty

NOVEMBER 13, 1977
Reading: Mark 6:25–34

When St. Teresa, that great Spanish saint, finished St. Augustine's *Confessions*, she is reported to have sighed and said, "I see myself there reflected." And who wouldn't see herself or himself reflected in one who prays, "Oh God, make me a Christian, but not quite yet."

To reveal us to ourselves is, of course, a characteristic of all great literature, so it is hardly surprising that on almost every page of the Bible we see ourselves reflected. For example, we see ourselves in Adam's excuses, "the woman you gave me," in Jacob, donning his Gordon Liddy-like disguise in order to deceive his father as a first step up the rung of financial success; or in Saul, the moment he hears the chant go up from the crowd—"Saul has killed his thousands but David his ten thousands." And doesn't Saul's jealousy mirror our own perversity? When you stop to think of it, jealousy is the only one of the so-called seven deadly sins, which unlike lust, gluttony and all the rest has no immediate satisfaction whatsoever. Yet there is not one among us who can totally resist this totally pleasureless vice.

In the New Testament we can see ourselves reflected in promise-making, promise-breaking Peter, or in the pathetic figure of the paralytic, quite literally scared stiff, or if you will, scared to death, his life one long suicide. But can we see ourselves reflected in the New Testament lesson, the story in Mark which comes shortly after the story of the paralytic, the story of the woman who for twelve years was bleeding internally? For twelve years she sought unsuccessfully a cure, which makes it hard for us today not to believe that her illness wasn't in part emotional, particularly as in those days to hemorrhage in this fashion was thought to be unclean. So we can say for twelve years, invisible to the public eye, she suffered her weakness, her secret guilt.

I think it would be fairly easy to say "of course we see ourselves reflected there." All of us have secret guilts, and they don't all stem from infantile fantasies either; rather they are a product of an adult understanding of reality. For it is perfectly true that we have fallen short as parents. As American citizens we have strewn the world with our blunders. Lord knows we fail often enough in our vocations, and if we are women these days we may think that we are a failure because we do not have a vocation. And because to an extraordinary degree we are our memories, that is, our memories shape us more than our genes, the memory of what we have done and what we have neglected to do, like the woman's hemorrhaging, has enormous secret power over us, draining our lives of vitality and joy.

As I say, I think it would be fairly easy to say something like that. But to leave it at that would be to miss the point of the story. For the story is not about the woman's sickness, the story is about her cure. She hears what people are saying about Jesus, she says to herself, "If I touch even His clothes I shall be cured." She makes her way through the crowd pressing around him, touches his clothes and instantly is well again.

Now I do not doubt that like the woman, all of us, shall we say, are bleeding. Nor do I doubt that most of us know it, although I think that you will agree with me that some of our wounds are so deep we neither know how nor want to examine them. But what I suspect is that we can see ourselves reflected more in the crowd than in the woman. We are pressing around Jesus all right, in fact so much so that some people out there, like the disciples in the story, think we are actually touching Jesus. But he knows differently. No power has gone out of him. He knows we are keeping our hands to ourselves. In short, unlike the woman who, after all, despite many setbacks, for twelve long years continued to seek a cure, we, after perhaps a comparable number of years, have come to terms with our bleeding. Our wounds are now familiar. In fact, we are rather comfortable with them. Some of us have even learned how to coerce others with them. Having reached a truce with our guilt, we now don't want to touch Christ. We fear the cure more than the illness.

Have you ever heard yourself or anyone else say sentences something like the following?

"No, I think I'll just keep my mouth shut and endure my marital problems."

"Oh, some day I suppose I'll sit down and have a good long talk with the kids."

"I know my job is boring and certainly isn't useful to anyone, but I guess these days you are lucky to have any job at all."

"Too bad the rest of the world doesn't have America's wealth, but I guess we just have to hope for the best."

These sentences are symptoms of an advanced state of a disease recently called by Ashley Montague "psychosclerosis," a hardening, not of the arteries as in arteriosclerosis, but of the spirit. As a result, the mind cannot see and embrace new ideas, the heart cannot stay vulnerable. Sufferers of psychosclerosis deaden themselves against life in order to go on living. They sell their freedom as the price of their self-perpetuation. It is a very common disease, and people who contract it are far from dumb. In fact, they are very smart. It is smart to fear the cure more than the illness. Didn't the woman herself almost die of fright when she grasped what had happened? Isn't forgiveness terrifying? It may be Hell to be guilty but isn't it worse to be responsible, response-able, able to respond to the love of God?

God's love casts out fear. The opposite of love is not hate; the opposite of love is fear. So faith means courage. Forgiveness means freedom. To be healed means to have the courage and freedom not to endure marital problems, that is easy; but to face and resolve them; to talk to the kids right now; perhaps to change jobs; and certainly to seek to redistribute the nation's wealth and power at home and abroad.

So why be healed when love is so costly? One reason is because it is so boring to be sick. Fearful people are boring people. Their fear of failure makes them miss out on some of the best things in life. So they are boring to themselves, boring to others. And the same is true of guilt-ridden people. They are too driven, too self-preoccupied to be fun. In fact, not to feel too badly about themselves they make sure they don't feel too good about anything. For them, life has no heights, no depths. It is all flattened out.

The trick in life is to die young as late as possible. But sufferers of psychosclerosis, spiritually speaking, seek to die old as soon as possible. But life is too short to be boring. Furthermore for Christians at least, it is dishonest to go on living in fear and guilt as if within our very reach the cure wasn't there.

Some Christians love to berate atheistic communism. But the heresy of rejecting Christ is small potatoes compared to the heresy of remaking Christ into something he never was, still isn't, and never will be. We cannot say we are Christians and pretend that Christ isn't a healer. He came precisely so that, like this woman, we might touch Him, that power might go out of Him and into us. And what a moving picture that is—power coming out of Christ in order to staunch her bleeding, a prefigurement of the Cross.

This is such a rich story that one could go on talking about it far too long. So let's only note two points more. While it is true that without Christ the woman could not have been healed, what the woman did she did entirely on her own. She didn't tell him what she was going to do, she didn't ask his permission, and she wasn't planning to tell him afterwards what she had done. In other words, she made herself totally responsible for her own cure, which is why she was cured. That is to say, we are healed by God, but only when we choose to be healed. Christ didn't say, "My power has healed you." He said, "Your faith has cured you." His power was there, but she had to want it, she had to take it, and as to take it took such courage, it is small wonder that he wheeled around to see who had touched Him.

The second point is this: In St. Luke's version, after Christ has turned around, when the woman explains why she touched him and how she had been instantly cured, in that sentence the Greek word for "crowd" changes to the word for "people" or community. By her willingness to become deeply human, this woman humanized all around her, changing a faceless multitude into a community of warm human beings. To touch Christ is to be put in touch with one another. His power is there, but we have to want it, we have to take it. God grant that there may be among us men and women of sufficient courage to do so and in so doing transform us all into a loving, caring community.

Sophocles said of Athens that it was people not stones. May the same be said of Riverside.

A World Fit for Children

NOVEMBER 20, 1977

For the last two Sundays, I have been saying things like "faith means courage," emphasizing courage because the virtue of courage is that it makes all other virtues possible. Anwar Sadat's visit is a dramatic example of that today. And I have been saying, "forgiveness means freedom," "God loves one-talented people," "we should not fall victims to psychosclerosis," the hardening of the spirit. In other words, for the last two Sundays we have been talking of ourselves as individuals, which is perfectly all right as long as we remember that as Christians we do not believe in the cult of the individual ego. That cult is as bloody as the Aztecs'; it feeds on victims.

As Christians we do not believe in the Gospel of private salvation—"Not my father, not my mother, not my deacon, not my city, not my nation, not my world, just me and Thee, O Lord." No. Salvation is for everyone—including me. That is the Christian understanding of salvation. It's a package deal. It cannot be untied or negotiated. It includes everyone and everything, politics and economics, the past, the present, and particularly the future. The God we worship is a God ahead of us, as much as above us or within us. And what are our dear children, if not living signposts pointing to the future? "*Los niños son la esperanza del futuro del mundo*," said the great José Martí—"Children are the hope of the future of the world," and in so saying, he implied that they could use a little help from their friends. Let us recall too the words of A. J. Muste, "We need a foreign policy fit for children."

So on this golden morning let us think big thoughts. Let's make our hearts as wide as God's universe, and to get us started, let us call to mind the story in the thirteenth and fourteenth chapters of the Book of Numbers. After a long and tear-stained trek, the children of Israel finally reach the borders of the Promised Land. Spies are sent out, and when they come back there is a majority report and there is a minority report. The minority report, submitted by Joshua and Caleb, is prophetic, saying in effect, "We can go ahead, we can do God's will, if only we don't lose hope," which we can translate as a passion for the possible. The majority report, as one might expect, is pragmatic. The prudence it counsels only thinly veils the cowardice of those submitting it. It speaks of "giants in the land"—the sons of Anak, literally the long-necked one. "And we seemed to ourselves like grasshoppers and so we seemed to them" (Num. 13:33).

Predictably, the children of Israel accept the majority report, and we read that "all the congregation raised a loud cry and the people wept that night; and all the people of Israel murmured against Moses and Aaron. The whole congregation said to them, 'Would that we had died in the land of Egypt.' . . . And they said to one another, 'Let us choose a captain and go back to Egypt.'" And then when Aaron and Moses remonstrate, and Caleb gets up once again, and Joshua, and say, "The Lord is with us," the congregation said to stone them (Num. 14:1–10).

I recall this story because that line "We seemed to ourselves like grasshoppers" seems to reflect the constant problem, "We have nothing to fear but fear itself." The story shows us that while love seeks the truth, fear seeks safety. And fear distorts the truth, not by exaggerating the ills of the world, which would be difficult, but by underestimating our ability to deal with them. "We seemed to ourselves like grasshoppers." As in the story of the one-talent man, we see again the protective strategy of deliberate failure, only with two added wrinkles: if you think other people make you into a failure—"giants in the land"—then you don't have to feel badly about being one. And if you think that those trying to wean you from your sense of failure—the Joshuas and the Calebs of the world—are only trying to push you around, then you can stone them with a good conscience.

Now I do not think there is a Promised Land for anybody any more, but I recall this story because I believe there is a Promised Time for everybody. After a far longer and even more arduous trek, the three hundred odd billion of us who inhabit this planet are in fact on the very borders of that time promised in Scripture—"and it shall come to pass in the latter days"—a time when quite literally, if we do not lose our passion for the possible, we might indeed create a world without borders, a world without famine, a world at one, a world at peace.

But instead of pressing forward, God's children once again are holding back. Instead of "seizing the time," we are losing our grip; and some of us seem eager to elect captains to lead us back to the flesh-pots and spiritual slavery of Egypt.

It is understandable. We have been through tough disillusioning times. Who was it who said, "I used to be an incurable optimist, but now I'm cured." And understand why we are fearful. Ahead *are* giants. But what are giant obstacles if not brilliant opportunities brilliantly disguised as giant obstacles? And aren't we Christians to say with Camus, "Even in deep darkness of winter I know in my heart an invincible summer"?

The best definition of patriotism that I know is the one offered by the ancient Roman Tacitus. "Patriotism," he said, "is entering into praiseworthy competition with our forefathers." So let me suggest that we enter into praiseworthy competition with the children of Israel and with our nation's Revolutionary forefathers. They declared their independence, one from Egypt, the other from England. Let us declare our interdependence with all people. Let us dare to see pragmatically that the survival unit in our anguished time is no longer an individual nation or an individual anything. The survival unit in our time is the whole human race plus its environment.

It used to be that we worried about this part of the globe not being able to protect itself against that part. Now it is the whole that cannot protect itself against the parts. Therefore, we can no longer say that an individual nation-state is the principal focus for thought and action. Responsible national citizenship has to give way to international citizenship. And that pragmatic view is, of course, only the ancient prophetic view. According to this view, all of us belong one to another, all three billion odd inhabitants of this planet. That's the way God made us. Christ died to keep us that way. So our sin is that we are always trying to put asunder what God himself has joined together. I am not my brother's keeper, I am my brother's brother. That is something again that Sadat seemed to understand as he talked to the Israelis this morning. In other words, to Christians, territorial discrimination is as evil as racial. "God cares for all, as if all were but one."

But God also "cares for each as if he had naught else to care for." Do you remember how Jesus says, "Are not five sparrows sold for two pennies?" He is referring to the practice of sacrifice, and to the poor who couldn't afford bullocks. They would buy two sparrows for a penny, and if they bought two pennies' worth—four sparrows—a fifth was thrown in. God cares for that fifth sparrow! And he goes on to say, "Are you not of more value than many sparrows" (Luke 12:6–7).

It is not enough then to talk of interdependence. Many people have been doing that for some time: Henry Kissinger, for one. And presidents of multinational corporations are quick to say that national boundaries are no more interesting to them than the equator. But the powerful of the world tend naturally to see themselves as the village elders of the global village. They tend to see a unity based on the present order rather than on greater justice for the poor and the powerless. Their greater concern for disorder over injustice inevitably produces more of both. And while we are saying harsh things, let us recognize the degree of truth in that accusation frequently launched against us Christians that we have a vested interest in unjust social structures because they produce victims to whom we can then pour out our charity.

I am a great believer in charity. I think it is such a wonderful thing that even the poor should have a chance to engage in it. I think it is a wonderful thing that all this food was brought this morning to the altar. But every outpouring of charity is also a signpost to a deficiency in justice. So while in myriad programs here at Riverside we try as we must try to pour out our hearts in charity to the victims of society, we must never cease asking, "Why must we have these victims?"

We need then to talk not only of a global but of a just and global future, the only one worthy of the children we honor today.

In closing let me just say one word to the rich and powerful among you, and to all of us who are citizens of a rich and powerful nation. The message of the prophets is that judgment of the rich spells mercy for the poor, judgment of the powerful spells mercy for the powerless. The message is summed up in the words of the Magnificat:

> He has put down the mighty from their thrones
>   and exalted those of low degree;
> He has filled the hungry with good things,
> And the rich he has sent empty away.
> Luke 1:52–53

But it is often forgotten that judgment of the rich spells mercy for the rich as well. Judgment of the powerful spells mercy for the powerful as well. The rich should not be left to the mercy of their riches any more than the poor should be left to the mercy of their poverty. There are two ways to be rich. One is to have lots of money, the other is to have few needs. In the United States, the second option is rarely weighed. But the Bible promotes it all the time, suggesting moreover that dwindling economic resources may allow spiritual resources to grow.

Consider this: The United States, with only 5.8 percent of the world's population, currently consumes about 35 percent of the world's resources. Were we Americans profoundly happy, I suppose it could be argued (though certainly not by me) that such is the price the rest of the world must pay for American happiness. But we are not a profoundly happy people. Our affluence has not bought morale. In fact, it has brought a great deal of loneliness and emptiness as our acquisitiveness has disrupted our sense of community. So if the wealth of rich Americans must be redistributed at home in order to eliminate our monstrous inequalities, if the wealth and power of America must be redistributed abroad, if to some degree austerity is called for, God be praised. All is well. We need not view austerity as a necessary evil, only as a necessary ingredient for that sense of community of which we see all too little among our own people, and among the nations.

So, dear friends, let us continue with good heart our exodus from the old time to the new. The road is hard but the future is bright. The Promised Time is there ahead. Already we can dimly view its contours. The spies are back, the prophetic ones among them announcing that the Promised Time will be much better than the good old days! So, enough of this "back to Egypt" talk. Enough of this talk about seeming to ourselves like grasshoppers. We, too, can become giants, Anaks—by sticking out our necks! We have created a world for some of us. Let's make one for all of us.

Born to Set Thy People Free

DECEMBER 4, 1977

The text for the morning's sermon on this second Sunday in Advent is the well-known verse from the Gospel of John as recorded in the New English Bible,

> So the Word became flesh; he came to dwell among us, and we saw his glory, such glory as befits the Father's only Son, full of grace and truth. (John 1:14)

I can't recall the exact spot, but somewhere in the writings of Kazantzakis, he describes a dream that disturbs the sleep of the old monk, Father Joachim. In the dream a troubled Mary brings her 12-year-old Jesus to him for help.

"What's the matter?" asks Father Joachim.

"I don't know," says the boy. "I seem to roam the streets, wrestling."

"With whom are you wrestling?"

"With God, of course. With whom else would you wrestle?"

Then Father Joachim takes the boy to his house, teaches him carpentry, takes him for long walks during which he talks to him of God as if God was some kind of neighbor who might stop by for a chat on a long summer's evening when he was sitting out on the steps. After about a month, the boy is cured; he goes home. Many years later Father Joachim hears he is doing fine, in fact, he is the best carpenter in Nazareth. Instead of saving the world he becomes the best carpenter in Nazareth!

If that dream doesn't make you squirm a bit it should, for by every blessed saint in heaven, almost all of us give up wrestling with God to become splendid splinters. Full of self-confidence, perhaps, in what we are doing, we are also full of self-contempt for doing more. And it is not really a question of doing more; it is a question of being more, thinking more, thinking about things that really matter. We know so little about things that really matter.

I once asked a group of Yale faculty if they thought the existence of God a lively question. Said a political scientist, "It's not even a question, Bill, let alone a lively one." That he didn't believe in God didn't bother me that much. After all, that was his problem and fortunately for His continued existence, God doesn't depend on our proving it. Moreover, the important question is not who believes in God but "in whom does God believe?" As betwixt Christians and atheists I imagine it is about even steven. There are as many sheep without the fold as there are wolves within!

But what did trouble me was this: I can see doubting the quality of the bread, but I can't see kidding yourself that you are not hungry—unless of course your soul has so shrivelled that you have no appetite left for all that elicits astonishment, awe, and wonder. It's this shrivelling up that is so disturbing. What's so boring at universities is not that scientists specialize, it's that specialists generalize, insisting that not only in their particular area, but in all areas of life the only truths that matter are the truths that can be proved, mysteries that can be explained. They see only those truths they can dominate. They have no truck with those to which one can only surrender. Their minds are both powerful and frighteningly narrow. No wonder there is a widespread withdrawal from wisdom in universities today.

Not that we churchgoers have great cause for smugness. We believe religion is a good thing like social security and regular exercise, but we don't want to overdo it. It might affect the heart!

But enough of such angry comments. They probably make me feel better but serve no other cause. The point I wish to make is the obvious one: Answers demand questions, and the bigger the answers the bigger the questions. The main reason why people don't believe in God is that they don't wrestle with such questions, sometimes even denying their validity. And when you stop to think of it, there is nothing as irrelevant as an answer to an unasked question.

But the text begs us today to ask big questions, for it speaks of "The Word," not many little words. *The* Word, *The* answer to *The* question! "What's it all about?" All the tears and laughter of our lives—what do they amount to? How are we to conduct our lives?

Now I hesitate to turn to the answer which you remember St. Paul calls folly. I suppose that if it is hard to wrestle with a big question, it may be harder to accept the form the big answer takes: "The Word became flesh." It certainly is unusual, to say the least, that the greatest truth should become as ordinary as we, that the "King of Kings" should be born to Joseph and Mary, that "the bread of life" for human beings should be laid in the feedbox of animals.

Let me tell you another Christmas story, courtesy of the rich imagination of Søren Kierkegaard. Once upon a time, there was a king who fell in love with a maid. Whereupon he summoned his wisemen together to advise him on how he was to declare his love. "What could be simpler," they answered in one voice. "Your majesty has but to appear in all his glory before her humble abode and instantly she will fall on her knees and be yours."

But that was precisely what was troubling the King. He didn't want his glorification, he wanted hers. His love, freely offered, wanted hers, freely returned. So, night after night he walked the corridors of his palace alone, pondering his dilemma, and what a dilemma it was, when not to declare his love was the death of love, and to declare it was the death of his beloved. Finally, the King saw love's truth, that freedom for the beloved demands equality with the beloved. So, late one night when all his courtiers and wisemen had retired, he stole out the side door of his palace and appeared before the abode of the maid dressed as a servant.

It is a lovely story, isn't it, the kind that makes the heart melt, the eye fill? Or is it? I think if I had been the maid I would have wanted to know more about this stranger. What about his future, and mine? Were we two going to be stuck together in this miserable hovel all the rest of our lives? In fact, this solution so satisfactory to Kierkegaard and to the King, I wouldn't have found satisfactory at all. I would rather he had been more honest. I don't mind marrying a King!

The fact of the matter is, "The Word became flesh" is not only astonishing, it's offensive. We want God to be God. Why does he want to be human? We want God to be strong, so we can be weak; but he wants to be weak, so that we can be strong. We want God to prove himself. But He answers, "What do you want—proof or freedom? I know what you are looking for—evidence to make an intelligently selfish decision. You'll never find it."

What Kierkegaard is so correctly insisting, is that God is known devotionally, not dogmatically. If as Scripture says "God is love," then the revelation is the relationship. Christianity is not clearing up old mysteries; it's the disclosure of new mystery. It is not a truth that you can master; it's only one to which you can surrender. Faith is being grasped by the power of love.

"Divine folly is wiser than the wisdom of man, and divine weakness stronger than man's strength" (1 Cor. 1:25). So at Christmas the Word became silent, a song without words, knowledge without articulation. The Christ Child in the manger is like the grown man before Pilate—wordless truth. At Christmas as on Good Friday, God does not give us an answer. He gives us Himself.

I said there are truths we can master and truths to which we can only surrender. (And Lord knows we must constantly strive to know the difference.) We now have to grasp the paradoxical truth that in surrendering lies freedom. I don't think it is that hard. When you say that you were "captivated" by a great book or a great painting, aren't you saying that you somehow felt free? "Enthralled" by the singing of the choir and the playing of the organ, aren't all of us liberated, including the choir members and the organist himself? We need make no bones about it, we need to be liberated, released, delivered, saved from our egocentric preoccupations, our endless niggling worries, our fears of failure and of dying. We need to be freed *from* fear *for* love, *from* self *for* God. For God is not seeking to convert us from this world to some other but from something less than life to the possibility of full life itself. We come to church not to prepare ourselves for the worst but to prepare ourselves for the best, not to become splendid splinters but to save the world by becoming as those who know that love is the expression of our aliveness, that to live and to love are to do the same thing.

So, come, thou long expected Jesus, born to set thy people free. Come, take our minds and think through them, take our lips and speak through them, and take our hearts and set them on fire. Amen.

A Sign That Is Spoken Against

DECEMBER 18, 1977

"... that thoughts out of many hearts may be revealed"
Luke 2:35

About this time of year there is generally a mild hubbub about the dangers of a commercialized Christmas. In my own opinion, a commercialized Christmas may be in wretched taste but, at least, it doesn't pretend to be anything else. What is really dangerous is a sentimentalized Christmas, sentimentality being an emotion that does not arise out of the truth but which is poured on top, diluting, distorting.

Let me give you an example. The smallest street in Paris leads off from the left bank of the River Seine not far from the Cathedral of Notre Dame. It goes by the quaint name of "The street of the cat that fishes" (La rue du chat qui pêche). It is so narrow two bicycles could barely pass, and it extends no further than a quarter of a normal city block. Year after year hundreds of tourists strolling down the quay stop for a moment to peer down it, to look at the street sign, and to exclaim "Oh, how picturesque." Few, however, venture down the street, let alone into the dank, dark rooms that pass for habitation. If they did they might conjecture that for over five hundred years that street probably contributed more to the tuberculosis rate in Paris than any other street in the city. The unsentimental truth about the street of the cat that fishes is that it is better suited for cats than for humans. It is picturesque all right; it is also horrible.

The same is true of the manger scene. Bending low over the Christ child, the ox and ass add a tender touch. But they are not guests. This is their home. "There was no room for him in the inn" only because the innkeeper, knowing his guests, knew that like him none would be inclined to move over for a pregnant woman. The unsentimental truth about Christmas is that he who is to be bread of life for humans is laid in the feedbox of animals.

The Gospel of John, being very unsentimental about these things, suggests that our inhumanity to one another may only be exceeded by our inhumanity to God. "He was in the world and the world was made through him, yet the world knew him not. He came to his own home, and his own people received him not" (John 1:10–11). At Christmas as on Good Friday, human beings come off badly.

But why insist on this? To be a killjoy? On the contrary, to bring the real joy of Christmas to life, the real joy, not the frills and froth, the real joy that sadly enough won't be available to the eager readers of those best sellers promoting the notion that the good life is the painless life. Their writers want to do away with the sensation of pain rather than examine and change the situations that cause it. Deep down, they are shallow!

But not old man Simeon. He saw the true joy of Christmas: "Mine eyes have beheld thy salvation which thou hast prepared in the presence of all peoples" (Luke 2:30–31). But he also foresaw how prohibitive this salvation would be to those who want their happiness cheap. Mind you, I am not saying that God doesn't want to make us happy. I am only saying that while God would like to please us He would much rather save us!

Listen again to Simeon. "Behold this child is set for the fall and rising of many . . . a sign that is spoken against . . . that thoughts out of many hearts may be revealed" (Luke 2:34–35). That makes Christmas sound pretty terrifying, doesn't it?

Before looking at these words more closely, let us look for a moment at the old man himself. We read that Simeon is "just," "upright," "righteous," and "devout"—to use all the words in all the translations—which makes him sound admirable but not necessarily sympathetic. For highly principled people can be remarkably insensitive to frailty and suffering. But then we read, "He looked forward to Israel's comforting." That's lovely! First of all, as an old man should, he looked forward. Simeon is the New Testament's first example of the fact that the senior years are the formative years, years when one sees the fundamentals of life with fresh clarity and urgency, when the imminence of death makes the preciousness of life so clear. (I heard a scientist the other day say that science has pretty well determined that there is no more life in our galaxy, and certainly has established the fact that before us and after us there is no one like us. What a statement about the preciousness of every human life!)

But back to Simeon. Looking forward, he was old and fresh. You are only old and stale when dreams are replaced by regrets. Or perhaps we should say you are old and stale when you look forward only to be able to say, "I told you so, but you wouldn't listen to me."

Simeon, however, has no need to prove himself. He is ready, even eager to die. He is aging "toward the light." But he wants to hang around long enough to see the promised consolation of those he will leave behind. He must have been a dear man.

Now to his words—"that thoughts out of many hearts may be revealed." I am impressed that the Bible locates thoughts not in the mind but in the heart. So does the prayer book: "Cleanse the thoughts of our hearts by the inspiration of Thy Holy Spirit." It's as if there is a difference between what we think with our minds and what we feel in our hearts. And I'm impressed by the strong suggestion in Simeon's words that if, so to speak, the Christ child is to be born in the chambers of our hearts, and not forced out into some manger, we are going to have to dislodge some of the thoughts presently residing there.

"That thoughts out of many hearts may be revealed." It's rough going to be confessional—no sentimentality allowed—but let's try in order to be properly prepared for next week. While in our minds we know everyone else is as important as we are, in our hearts we don't feel it that way, do we? In our minds we know that all human beings are created equal, but our hearts don't always feel the monstrosity of inequality. Our minds tell us to rejoice in the fact that this congregation is genuinely interracial, but there is a fear in the hearts of some of us that it is becoming too black.

I think we should not feel anxious if such prejudicial thoughts are revealed, only if they are repressed. I assume that I can't be born white in the United States without being antiblack at some level of my being. And I assume that every black person I meet at some level of his or her being must feel "Whitey can't be trusted." How could it be otherwise in a country—let's not be sentimental—which is at one and the same time a great nation and the only nation born in the blood of ten million Indians and developed in the sweat of forty million slaves?

But if we reveal and do not suppress these prejudiced thoughts deeply lodged in our hearts, if we genuinely want to be liberated from their power, God be praised we have Jesus Christ and one another. We can refuse to become the enemies that our prejudices want to make us. We can grow into the conviction that in Christ Jesus we all are one. And brothers and sisters in Christ, is it not the case that no salvation, no consolation, no joy is comparable to that of people determined no longer to be enemies who then embrace one another? Isn't that the joy we are seeing day after day in our newspapers reflected upon the faces of countless Egyptians cheering the

Israeli delegation in the midst of Cairo? As one Egyptian reporter said, "I'm seeing it, but I can't believe it!"

If Christ is born anew in our hearts this Christmas, I'm confident that by next Christmas this church will have found many ways to confront and to confound our prejudices, so that we can proudly claim on the bottom of our order of worship that not only are we interdenominational, interracial, and international, but deeply interpersonal.

Now what about that "international"? Frankly, I think class may be a tougher nut to crack than race; and the toughest of them all may be national prejudice. But surely we do have to confront it if there is to be room in our hearts for the Prince of Peace.

At the present rate of weapons procurement, it takes the nations of the world only two days to spend the equivalent of the annual budget of the UN and all its specialized agencies. This tragedy is compounded by the irony that the arms race is rapidly destroying the one thing arms are supposed to provide—national security. Then there is a further irony. World security is probably threatened less by relations between nations than by the relation of all of us to our environment. I have in mind the dwindling reserves of oil, the pollution of the air and of the sea.

So while in our minds we think it's national security we are after, in our hearts we worship military power. In our minds we may believe that all nations are created equal, but in our hearts most Americans feel about the United States the way Muhammad Ali talks about himself: "I'm the greatest." And the greatest not in terms of decency, but in terms of power.

"You corrupted your wisdom for the sake of splendor" (Ezek. 28:17). The Bible takes a jaundiced view of national power. But we love it. We cheer it as we cheer the power of Muhammad Ali, or the power of the bat of Reggie Jackson, and we never cheer louder than when a president warns that the United States "must not become a pitiful and helpless giant"—at the very moment it is becoming a mindless and heartless one. (In our congregation this morning sits the man who had the decency in Geneva to apologize for what the United States had done in Chile. But believe me, the State Department for once in its life acted with alacrity in informing him that powerful nations do not apologize for what they have done to small nations. We occasionally apologize to other big nations, for bullies are always weak on the tough and tough on the weak.)

"For unto us a child is born, unto us a son is given; and the government shall be upon his shoulder" (Isa. 9:6). If that kind of a child is to be born in our hearts we shall first have to remove our irrational love of loveless power. We shall have to see that arms control is not enough; it doesn't work, and it validates the arms that remain. Disarmament is the only answer. This spring the United Nations General Assembly will convene a special session on disarmament. So my second hope for next Christmas is that we will then be able to look back and say of ourselves and of the religious community generally, that not only did we pray, we worked for peace, we struggled for peace, we suffered for peace.

"And his name shall be called Wonderful, Counsellor, The mighty God, The everlasting Father, The Prince of Peace." When you stop to think of it, all the armies that ever marched, all the navies that ever sailed, all the air forces that ever took to the air, in terms of influence can't hold a candle to this one man born in a manger whose sole possession at death was a robe. So let us not say we are powerless in the face of loveless power. Let us prepare ourselves so that with Simeon we may say that our eyes have seen, not some cheap easy selfish happiness, but "thy salvation which thou hast prepared in the presence of all peoples." Let us cleanse the thoughts of our hearts with the inspiration of the Holy Spirit so that we may mean it when we sing "O come to my heart Lord Jesus; there is room in my heart for Thee." Amen.

Power Comes to Its Full Strength in Weakness

DECEMBER 25, 1977
Reading: John 1:1–14

May I wish you all a Merry Christmas, particularly you children in the congregation, and you old folks among our radio listeners. Some of your lives are not as full as once they were with people you loved dearly. So to you our special wish that Christ be with you today.

To the reading of John's Christmas story, let us add these words of St. Paul: "God was in Christ reconciling the world to himself, no longer holding men's misdeeds against them" (2 Cor. 5:19); and these words also, "Three times I begged the Lord to rid me of it,"—a sharp pain in his side—"but his answer was: 'My grace is all you need. Power comes to its full strength in weakness.' I shall therefore prefer to find my joy and pride in the very things that are my weakness. And then the power of Christ will come and rest upon me. Hence I am well content, for Christ's sake, with weakness, contempt, persecution, hardship and frustration; for when I am weak, then I am strong" (2 Cor. 12:9–10).

I once was told of a man who arrived at the Canadian border north of Detroit on his bicycle. Behind him on the rack, he had a box full of sand.

"What have you got in there?" asked the customs official.

"Nothing."

"Well, let's just check it out."

The customs official raked his fingers through the box of sand. Finding nothing he waved him on.

A few days later the man was back again, with the same box of sand behind his seat, on the bicycle.

"Well, what have you got this time?"

"Same thing, nothing."

This time the official took the bicycle and turned it upside down, shook it out, took the box apart, but still he found nothing. For weeks the scene was re-enacted, each time the customs official certain he was going to find whatever it was this man was smuggling through. But he never did.

Several years later, the customs official, now retired, was having himself a few beers in a bar in Detroit. Suddenly he spied the erstwhile cyclist coming through the door. Hailing him, he bought him a drink and said, "Look, it doesn't mean anything to me now that I am retired, but I am curious; what was it you were smuggling all that time?"

"Bicycles."

I suppose that is something of a Christmas story. Certainly it never occurred to Herod to search a stable for the threat to his world that God was smuggling into it on that first Christmas. And ever since, the Herods and wisemen, the foes and friends alike of Christ have never ceased marvelling at the form God's revelation takes at Christmas.

Here are some lines from an unknown fifteenth-century writer:

> Thou shalt know him when he comes
> Not by any din of drums,
> Nor by the vantage of his airs,
> Nor by anything he wears,
> Neither by his gown
> Nor his crown.
> For his presence known shall be
> By the Holy Harmony
> That his coming makes in thee.

I like that verse because my passions need harmonizing. I like it too because it reminds me that God's revelation is like a stained-glass window: from the outside one sees nothing; only insiders see the radiance. And I like it because it is another reminder that never are we going to be helped by God's power, at least not as the world judges power. We are only going to be helped by God's weakness. At Christmas we can say that God undertakes a Sadat-like initiative[*] to change the premises of human relations—which the experts, of course always see as immutable! But compared to God's, Sadat's initiative is as the lightning bug to the lightning, for God undertakes to bring peace to the whole hostile world. He wants worldwide disarmament, politically and spiritually. And to break through our defenses, he arrives utterly defenseless. Nothing but unguarded goodness in that manger!

I suppose some would call it perverse to make too much of a tragedy out of something so inevitable, but the lengths to which we humans go to protect our tender egos never ceases to appal me, although I can't help being fascinated by the variety and subtlety our defenses take. For instance, the other day I met a man who came across as one of the friendliest fellows I have met since coming to this proud provincial town. Listening to him I had the impression that he had lowered the drawbridge of his castle, so to speak, and was inviting me over. But even as he pumped my hand and told me how happy he was to see me, I realized that he himself had rushed over the bridge to make sure I never set foot on it.

Need I say it? He was a fellow minister. We ministers have the most invulnerable way of making ourselves vulnerable!

But at least we try. You doctors, particularly you lawyers, you professors . . . but what's the point of singling out any of us? No sooner are we out of diapers than almost all of us are into suits of armor. Then, isolated by the fear we feel and the fear we inspire, we get lonely and become even more anxious and uncertain. So we erect even stronger defenses against the threat of even larger defeats. Then we attach ourselves to powerful institutions whose prestige we hope will protect us. Then to powerful nations whose arms we hope will defend us. I have never yet met a man who believed in a high military budget who wasn't himself incredibly defensive.

Some of you may protest: "The problem is that the only thing the other side understands is force." But the problem with that position is

[*]Coffin is referring here to the 1977 diplomatic initiative of Anwar Sadat, president of Egypt. Sadat openly expressed his willingness to negotiate peace with Israel. His action led to the 1978 Camp David Accords. Sadat won the Nobel Peace Prize for his work, which he shared with Israeli Prime Minister Menachem Begin.

that you then have to act as if the only thing *you* understand is force. There is nothing Sadat-like in that position; nothing Christ-like either. God enters the world utterly defenseless. Nothing but unguarded goodness in that manger.

One of the reasons we love to hold babies, or puppies or kittens for that matter, is that they don't threaten us. They respond to that yearning in all of us to be disarmed, which may be why to the most heathen among us Christmas is so appealing. Our isolation is killing us. We are tired of this clanking armor, of bumping masks with one another. Living on the outside of everyone and everything, we long for substantial relations.

Suppose you were given the Christ child to hold. I'm serious. Close your eyes and pretend for a moment that Mary has taken Jesus from her breast, has turned to you and said, "Here, hold the child for a moment, will you?" Wouldn't that undo you, to hold in your arms all God's love for you? I can't think of anything that would undo me more. And that, I suspect, is precisely God's Christmas plan for each of us: to undo us.

"Three times I begged the Lord to rid me of this weakness, but his answer was, 'My grace is all you need. Power comes to its full strength in weakness.'"

It's all right to be weak. It's only wrong to pretend we are not weak. It's all right to be full of doubts. All feelings are valid. Not all behavior, but all feelings are valid. Now I know how terrifying it is to lay down our arms, to step out of our armor. "What will they say when they see me as I really am?" But it is the only way to live—as defenseless as the baby Jesus. "Power comes to its full strength in weakness."

We all know that the greatest expenditure in our personal defense budgets are caused by guilt. The same may be true, I suspect, of our national defense budget, but let's leave consideration of that little subject for another time. Let's stay, for a moment, with this harassing question of guilt, for what in our imaginations we were holding in our arms just now is God's forgiveness in person on earth. So, how guilty are we? How badly do we need God's forgiveness?

For many of the crimes we think we have committed we don't need forgiveness at all; we need exoneration. I am sorry to report this but we never committed most of the crimes we like to think we committed. I'm thinking particularly of wrongs we think we have done our parents. Children take note: Nine out of ten times, if anyone's to blame, it's the parents.

But it is convenient to think that we committed these wrongs, for they detract us from our real sin. From our real sin we generally take refuge in a jungle of scruples, inhibitions, and totally inconsequential sins. (A priest friend of mine once described hearing the confessions of nuns. "It's like being stoned to death with popcorn.")

For instance, our real sin here at Riverside may be that although we belong to a big church, we don't think big thoughts. Our membership is incredibly talented, but New York hasn't been saved. We haven't even saved the Hudson—let alone the world!

In other words, guilt is important to quicken our imagination, to enlarge and sensitize our hearts, to show us how much we need the grace of God. But after that its usefulness is over. Christians are not sinners; they are forgiven sinners. The rejection of forgiveness is as wicked as the denial of sin.

Particularly on this Christmas Day do not say the confession and refuse the assurance of pardon. To do that would be to come to this church to make your last stand against God. Guilt is the last stronghold of pride. For guilt is your opinion of yourself. Forgiveness is God's opinion. Are you too proud to give up your opinion? to allow God to do for you what you can't do for yourself?

"God was in Christ reconciling the world unto himself not holding our misdeeds against us." By entering the world utterly defenseless he disarms us. By forgiving us he relieves us, not of the consequences of our sins but of the consequences of being sinners. With no fear of condemnation we can now make ourselves vulnerable, which is what we are yearning to be—honest, sensitive, compassionate, courageous. No longer isolated by the fear we feel and the fear we inspire, we are ready now for substantial relations with one another and with God.

But one thing more. "God was in Christ reconciling the world." We don't start with ourselves and then "work out." We start with the world, which includes us. We start with the understanding that all human beings are created equal. If you follow that word all the way down to its Greek root you will find the word for oneness. All human beings are created one. Human unity is not something we are called on to create; it is something we are called to recognize. And Christ at Christmas enters this world to reconcile its warring factions, to say to us, "will you stop putting asunder what God himself has joined together."

Allowing our guilt to quicken our imaginations, we might be able to turn the sin to good use. If all the nations are not one in love, at least they are one in sin, and this is no mean bond, for it precludes the possibility of separation through judgment. "Judge not that ye be not judged," that's the meaning of that phrase. Suppose at their first meeting, Sadat were to start out, "My dear brother Begin, you have no idea how we Egyptians have sinned against you . . ." And Begin would answer "You think that's bad, Anwar? Listen . . ."

We laugh, but isn't that how you make peace, whether between individuals, or between nations? "My grace is all you need; power comes to its full strength in weakness." What appears to be psychological defeat is spiritual victory, for again we are talking of honesty, sensitivity, compassion, courage. We are talking of a strength greater than the strength of the strong, as the world judges strength. Were the nations to vie in "weakness" then we would see the power of God at work. For God's strength is victory over the self. It is the sense of conquest without the humiliation of the conquered.

So, our work once again is cut out for us. God's Sadat-like initiative, His coming utterly defenseless into our hostile world has changed the premises of human relations. We have only to recognize it. And we can, because we are not experts, we're Christians. So let's let go our defenses, which only make for war, and let God create in their stead that Holy Harmony of which the fifteenth-century writer spoke so simply.

Last night the choir sang another verse, a prayer to the Christ child, which might well stand as our Christmas prayer today:

> Love in that stable was born
> Into our hearts to flow;
> Innocent dreaming babe,
> Make me thy love to know.
> Amen.

1978

"They Returned Home Another Way."

JANUARY 8, 1978
Reading: Matthew 2:1–12

There is, in the experience of parachuting at night, one perfectly glorious moment. It follows an inglorious one when, leaping out of the plane, the jumper is seized by the wind rushing by the open door at some 135 miles per hour. Mercilessly buffeted, he feels helpless in the midst of chaos. Then abruptly the parachute opens. As the plane by this time is some distance hence, all is quiet. The stars appear to be lower than the jumper on the horizon. At first there is no sensation of falling. So for one perfectly glorious moment, he hangs suspended among the stars. It is a time to say with Faust, "Moment, ah still delay. Thou art so fair." But of course the moment will not delay. Inexorably the stars begin to recede upwards and soon, with a rude jolt, the jumper is returned to earth, to business as usual.

That's a pretty fair reflection of life, isn't it? Unless of course your life never gets off the ground. Christmas was just such a high moment, certainly for many of us, certainly for me, particularly during the many services of this church, all of which I am free to say because I personally had so little to do with them. But now it's January the eighth. The lives of most of us have returned to their routine. Perhaps it was inevitable.

> "Go, go, go," said the bird.
> "Humankind cannot bear very much reality."
> T. S. Eliot

As we see in the lives of the apostles and of so many saints, from St. Paul all the way to Dorothy Day, Christmas or any dramatic encounter with Christ, can radically alter the routine of our lives. Some of your "own" have been so altered, and all of us must be open to the possibility, even when we are as old as Abraham. But in contrast, those who first beheld Christ went back to what they were doing. The shepherds, you remember, went back to their sheep, which for the sheep was probably a good thing. And of the wisemen we read, "They returned home another way."

But was it to business as usual? Granting that T. S. Eliot is right—"Humankind cannot bear very much reality"—doesn't Christmas, doesn't an encounter with Christ, significantly redeem the routine?

Obviously, it does, if only by renewing our sense of wonder. The world is so much more wonderful if it belongs to God and if God is eminently present in it. "The world," said G. K. Chesterton, "does not lack for wonders, only for lack of wonder." And with this renewed sense of wonder goes, too, a very peculiar serenity. This week, one of you thinking—mistakenly of course—that like so many New Yorkers I was moving too fast, sent me "A Prayer For the Hurried."

> Slow me down Lord!
> Ease the pounding of my heart by the quieting of my mind.
> Steady my hurried pace with a vision of the eternal,
>   not the temporary.
> Give me, amidst the confusion of my day, the calmness
>   of thine own peace.

And this lovely line, "Teach me to take minute vacations." A lovely gift, even if sent to the wrong person!

What else can we say about redeeming the routine? "They returned home another way." That was, you remember, because they were warned in a dream to avoid Herod. As Gene Laubach, last Sunday, was pointing out, there is an important contrast to be made between the authority of Christ and the power of Herod, or perhaps we should say, the authoritarianism of Herod. Spiritual authority has the power of conviction. Authoritarianism has the power of coercion. Whenever the church tries to coerce, it robs itself of spiritual authority.

As we all know, coercion can take very subtle forms. (The most coercive person I know is a woman who says, "Nobody pays any attention to me.") So, let me ask you, do you think we are living in an authoritarian society? I'm not thinking of dictators, secret police. I am thinking now of the power of the institutions of our society—and of others as well—the power of these institutions to tell us who we are, to define human beings in inhuman ways. Let me illustrate: When I was chaplain of Yale University it was natural that a great many undergraduates should ask me to write for them letters of recommendation to various graduate schools. And if I may say so, I wrote superb letters. For instance, to deans of admission of such law schools as Columbia or Harvard, I would frequently begin, "This student will undoubtedly be in the bottom quarter of your class." (You see, momentarily, I bought their definition of "top" and "bottom.") Then I would go on "But I am sure you will agree with me that the bottom quarter should be as carefully selected as the top. And for what should you be looking in the bottom quarter if not for the sterling extra-curricular qualities so eminently embodied in this particular candidate?"

When I showed the students what I had written, invariably they were hurt. Never mind that I said they were dedicated, conscientious, decent, caring, concerned people. No, they bought permanently the university's definition of top and bottom. If they didn't have academic prowess, then they didn't rate. Christ tells them, you are human beings who happen to be students. The university tells them, you are students who then happen to be human beings.

In a large business, you have a functional definition. If you are poor and on welfare, you are defined as a problem to be solved. You see what I am getting at. To redeem the routine not only for ourselves but for others, each Christian within the institutions of our society must herself or himself become an institution, embodying at all times and in all places, the humanity we see in the face of Christ. It is Christ who defines us, not Herod. To redeem the routine we have to return home another way. We are always far more and far beyond what society conceives as our beloved nation. To me there is something pathetic about the figures of the senators we see, standing on the banks of the Panama Canal, their brows furrowed, trying to figure out how the United States can hang on to the Panama Canal so that they can hang on to their right-wing constituency. Where is their historical memory that would tell them that a society which seeks to live like an empire will die like one? We don't want the United States to be given over to the wind.

"They returned home another way." Christ redeems the routine first and foremost by telling us not what to do but how to be—full of wonder, peace, care, and concern for one another, eager even as God is eager to make humanity more human. I can't tell you how important I think this is. Things are going to get worse, and when things get worse we have to get better.

But the personal discovery of how to be leads almost immediately to unpredictable discoveries of what to do. "Behold, I create a new heaven, and a new earth." God is always creating; it's really exhausting. For just as God can only suffer for his world through the suffering bodies of his creatures, so God can only create through the creative energies of his creatures. So we mustn't poop out.

I see 1978 as a tremendously creative year for Riverside Church. And I'd like to be quite specific. Remembering that the redemption of the routine begins at home, we must first be certain that all staff members and volunteers are receiving maximum appreciation and support. Mrs. Ruth Herrmann and her volunteers need space for the clothes they so diligently collect and distribute to the poor. Emily Dunlap is such a devoted social worker that she could use some volunteer help. Then for some church secretaries and other staff members, it may be more convenient to work from 10 to 6, which is perfectly all right as there is nothing sacrosanct about 9 to 5. Nor is there anything sacrosanct about having one job. Some staff members may prefer one in the morning, another in the afternoon. I mention the latter two not as problems for all of you to solve, but as possibilities to be considered wherever it is you work.

Beyond that, we must organize our large congregation so that pastorally we take better care of one another. It is really shocking that once a year we know quite a bit about each other's pocketbook, but on a weekly basis we really don't know that much about each other's health, each other's soul. That's a matter to which I hope the deacons will address themselves. Then we must rid ourselves of one or two practices that simply belie our faith. This week newspapers carried the story of the daring escape of Donald Woods, the South African editor banned from his newspaper for five years by the government in Pretoria. His escape was a reminder that the same day, October 19, on which he was banned, an equally distinguished editor was arrested and imprisoned. The reason for the different treatment is that Mr. Qobozo is black, as are most readers of his newspaper, *The World*. Mr. Woods has escaped, Mr. Qobozo is still in prison, still uncharged, and *The World* remains shut.

Yet, this week every member of the Riverside staff was paid with a check from Citibank, one of several U.S. banks that provides loans to the same government that banned Mr. Woods and imprisoned Mr. Qobozo. The bank was originally selected purely for reasons of convenience, which simply shows that to be a Christian is not always convenient. But it has put the entire Riverside staff in a morally intolerable position. I am confident that at tomorrow night's meeting the trustees will hear our plea for help. Meanwhile, we'll continue to use our checks as bookmarkers!

Then I hope the deacons of the church might consider open hearings, mostly for the members of this church, on what Riverside might do for the city. We are not doing badly now, and thanks to George Thomas and some very devoted laity, soon we will be doing a lot more. But I suspect God would be well pleased to see this church turn itself inside out for the sake of *His* city—for New York belongs to God before it belongs to the institutions that govern it. I think God wants us to become a religious constituency for those who have no political constituency. Open hearings I see as a way for our members to express their creative thoughts, to put talent in touch with talent. Maybe lawyers want to get together. Doctors might work as a team with people on welfare. There are really endless possibilities for those who, like the wisemen we recall today, follow a star. The wisemen were wise because they had a cat-like ability to see in the dark, to see in the night a bright light of hope. "They returned home another way." God grant that we too after Christmas may return home another way. To business as usual? No, to business as never before!

"Moses, Moses . . . Here I Am"

JANUARY 15, 1978

After the first of several sermons that Martin Luther King Jr. was to deliver at Yale—this was in 1959—a black undergraduate said, "That man makes us Blacks proud to be black," to which a Southern white student immediately added, "and us Whites proud to be human beings." They could as easily have said, "and us Americans proud to be Americans" and "us Christians proud to be Christians." At a time of greater anguish than promise, what finer blessing could one human being bestow upon his fellows than to give them a legitimate pride in their race, their species, their nationality, and their faith? I and many others across the country will always bless this Church because in 1967 it saw fit to provide a dignified forum in which Dr. King could say, in effect, you cannot bow the knee to Caesar and at the same time worship a convicted criminal as your Lord and Saviour. Even in wartime, it is the faith that dictates the terms of national life, never the other way around. So, on what should have been his 49th birthday, let us keep Brother Martin in mind as we consider once again the well-known story of the call of Moses.

I readily confess that the word "call" has always bothered me. Whenever ministers go to a new church, they are "called"—generally at a slightly higher salary. But why can't you be called to Chase Manhattan Bank? And don't teachers and lawyers have a calling? What about the calling of motherhood and fatherhood? What is it we are really talking about when we talk about a call?

In the good old days of vaudeville, every show invariably included a magic act. Dressed fit to kill, with cages and boxes, saws, wands and scarves, the magician with a few extra hats on his head would lurch to the center of the stage where, after putting down all his gear, he would start to warm up the audience with jokes deserving of respect only because they were as old as he was. Then suddenly the magician would point and say, "Would the gentleman sitting on the end of the row please come forward." And you would chuckle again and look around to see whom he had gotten this time.

"No, no, you, the gentleman looking around. Would please come forward?" And you would realize to your horror that this time he had gotten you. If you weren't a natural comic or show-off, you'd be embarrassed, even angry, and legitimately so. You had not paid your money for this. You had paid to be a spectator, and now that man on the stage was calling on you to take part in the act.

Admittedly, it is a crude analogy, but perhaps a helpful one, for God's call often seems to come to people playing essentially a spectator's role. Certainly this was the case with Moses. Oh, in his early youth he had briefly been part of what might have been called "the movement," but only impulsively, without any deep commitment. And when you remember he killed an Egyptian, he beat a hasty retreat, or as we would prefer to say today, he entered "a period of consolidation." He went to Midian, he married, had a fine boy, entered his father-in-law's business, he settled down. Suddenly in the midst of that serenity and security he hears, "Moses, Moses, come, I will send you to Pharaoh"—right back into the thick of everything he had been trying so hard to get away from.

We can be more precise. Listen again to some of the words Moses heard. "Then the LORD said, 'I have seen the affliction of my people who are in Egypt, and have heard their cry because of their taskmasters; I know their sufferings and I have come down to deliver them out of the land of the Egyptians'" (Exod. 3:7–8). Tending the sheep of his father-in-law Jethro, at a time when he never had it so good, far away in the land of Midian—even there Moses could not totally turn a deaf ear to the cry of his own people. (After all, he had called his son Gershom, which means "I live as a sojourner in a foreign land.") His feet were in Midian but his heart was in Egypt land. In other words, the call of God was deeply embedded in a cry of pain. And it was a call to alleviate that pain by sharing it.

The same is true of the call that came to Samuel, to Elijah, Amos, Isaiah, Jeremiah, and even to Jesus himself, who rose on that day in the synagogue to quote Isaiah:

The Spirit of the Lord is upon me, because he has
anointed me to preach good news to the poor.
He has sent me to proclaim release to the captives
and recovering of sight to the blind. (Luke 4:18)

When Moses heard his call, did he fall on his knees? No, he reared
up on his hind legs. "Who am I that I should go to Pharaoh, and bring
the sons and daughters of Israel out of Egypt?" (Exod. 3:11).

I love that cry of protest from Moses. I feel it so strongly myself and
feel that it is one of the most honest religious sentiments, for if there is
no arguing, no anguish in our relationship to God, there is precious little
honesty either. If there is one thing I hold against fundamentalists it is their
failure to recognize that too ready a submission to the will of God is but
a facade for repressed rebellion. No wonder so many are so hostile.

During my time in New Haven, I frequently used to take what was
euphemistically called "The Express" to New York. If you weren't desperately poor, it was easy, watching Fairfield County and Westchester
County go by, to remain a relaxed spectator. Outside the window, life
looked pretty good. Then the train pulled in to the 125th Street station.
Now as you looked out the window at all that frustrated, embittered
life, you began to feel yourself being drawn out of yourself, pulled out
of your spectator's role, being brought under some kind of strange
judgment, as you began to feel your own complicity in the very evil that
you abhorred. And so it was a real relief when, instead of all that truncated, embittered life, you saw through the window your own face
reflected back to you as the train, thank God, entered the tunnel.

"Who am I, that I should go to Pharaoh?" We should be comforted
to know that most of the prophets initially resisted their call. "Ah
Lord God," said Jeremiah, "Behold I do not know how to speak, for I
am only a youth"; words Brother Martin himself might well have
repeated, for he was all of 27 years old when "Rosa Parks sat down
and the world stood up."

But if there are reasons initially to resist, there are deeper ones
ultimately to accept God's call. "But I will be with you," said God.
Could God have stayed with Moses? Could he have been with him in
the same way had Moses elected to stay in Midian? Could Moses have
become Moses? If Jeremiah had refused to speak could he ever have
become a prophet? Could Jesus have been the Christ had he not
agreed that some things worth living for are also worth dying for?

In other words, as the call of God is deeply embedded in a cry of
pain, so the acceptance of God's call is at one with our self-fulfillment.
Seen in this light, the call of God is less a call to action than it is a call

into being. For what makes human beings human is not their capacity to create serene, secure surroundings. It is not even what the great Descartes claimed: "*Cogito, ergo sum*"—"I think, therefore I am." What nonsense! "I love, therefore I am" (*Amo, ergo sum*). For love is the ultimate expression of our aliveness. Caring is the greatest thing, caring matters most. There is no smaller package in this world than a person all wrapped up in himself. What made Martin such a giant was that he unwrapped himself, made himself vulnerable, alleviated the pain of the nation by sharing it, first in his imagination and in his heart, and finally by absorbing it into his own body.

I love, therefore I am. The call of God is simply a call to be what we were made and meant to be. But we can go on, "We love, therefore by God's grace, we are the church." What finally defines the church, what brings the church to its fulfillment is not the purity of its dogma but the integrity of its love.

The church's enemy is not disagreement, but indifference, including a determined indifference caused by fear of disagreement. Listen to these words of Brother Martin addressed from jail to the church leaders of Birmingham: "I see the church as the body of Christ. But oh how we have blemished and scarred that body through social neglect and through fear of being nonconformists. So often (the church) is the arch defender of the status-quo. Far from being disturbed by the presence of the church, the power structure of the average community is consoled by the churches' silent and often even vocal sanction of things as they are."

And finally we have to say, "We love, therefore we do not hate." We hate the sin, but not the sinner. Or perhaps we can put it this way: if you love the good, you have to hate evil, or you're sentimental. But if you hate evil more than you love the good, you will become a damned good hater. No man I've ever known understood better than Martin how to oppose sin in the name of salvation, evil in the name of the good. He opposed the government in the name of the country, American practices in the name of our ideals, the present in the name of the future—"I have a dream." That was why he was so profoundly nonviolent.

> Through violence you may murder the liar but you cannot murder the lie, nor establish the truth. Through violence you may murder the hater, but not the hate. Returning violence for violence multiplies violence, adding deeper darkness to a night already devoid of stars. Darkness cannot drive out darkness; only light can do that. Hate cannot drive out hate, only love can do that.

Nobody understood as Martin did that it was true for the church as well as for individuals: we love, therefore we do not hate.

But have we answered that question about a call to Chase Manhattan? And what about the calling of an artist, and the calling of motherhood and fatherhood? Does God ever call you to stay in Midian?—which I suppose we can roughly translate as Tenafly, N. J.!

If, when we talk about a call we are talking about a call into being, a call to love and not to hate, a call away from indifference and into participation, then it would seem that such a call could be answered in almost any place, at any time, in any vocation. But only if we see our professional as well as our personal lives as love in search of form. It takes imagination for a doctor to say of the medical profession that it is love in search of form; for a lawyer to say of the legal profession that it is love in search of form. It certainly takes rare imagination to move ourselves to the creative edge of whatever state we happen to be in, as well as a constant readiness to sacrifice something big for something good.

Then if we see how God calls not only individuals but communities into being, we are free to be and to do so much more, helping one another in so many different ways. Remembering Martin Luther King Jr., we have to think of social action. But social action is still only a special concern for special times and maybe only for special people, not the vocation of everyone. And when we fight for justice, for what are we fighting if not for more opportunities to offer more people the chance to hear great music and to see great art? For great art and music, like Martin Luther King Jr. himself, remind us of the grandeur that lies ignored within us.

"Moses, Moses." "Mary, Mary." "Riverside, Riverside." The air is full of calls, coming to us all times, in unexpected places. How many times will we hear it this week? And how many times, after some stout resistance, will we find the grace to answer, "Here am I," "Here we are"?

On Changing Water to Wine

FEBRUARY 5, 1978
Reading: John 2:1–11

This story, to say the least, has several puzzling aspects. Why, for instance, does Jesus talk to his mother in this fashion: "O woman, what have you to do with me?" (Or as some translations say: "Your concern is not mine.") "My hour has not yet come." But the most troubling question to most people is, did Jesus really turn the water into wine? A fundamentalist—or perhaps we should say a "literalist"—would say, "Of course he did. The Bible doesn't err. The hand that held the pen was held by God."

When, as is the case, everything is up in the air, there is something very attractive about an answer that settles things. And Lord knows once we do begin to pick and choose in the Bible, we end up believing true the things we so long to believe true. We all do that anyhow, the literalists included. Complacent people always read the passages on forgiveness, while the guilt-stricken make haste to find those that begin "Thus saith the Lord."

But for all its attractiveness the answer is unsatisfactory, at least to those who with St. Augustine "believe in thinking and wish to think in believing." And, we might add, it is confusing to say the least, that those who think Jesus *did* turn the water into wine so often refuse to touch a drop—on religious principles.

What about the answer then of the factory worker who said, "I don't know whether Jesus turned the water into wine. All I know is that in my house he turned beer into furniture, and that's miracle enough for me." I like that answer. First of all it suggests what is profoundly true, that the greatest miracles in this world take place there where people say, "I don't see anything so miraculous about that." And it gets at the real evil in so much drinking—that drinking drains income and energy which should be invested elsewhere.

But in a general way, isn't there something helpful one might say about Biblical miracles, to someone who is a serious reader of the Bible but not a literalist? Let me try an analogy. Several years ago, driving south through Virginia, I crossed the mighty Rappahannock River. Amazed at its width, I couldn't help concluding that George Washington's throwing arm must have been comparable to Reggie Jackson's if he hurled, as he reputedly did, the silver dollar from one bank clear across to the other. Suppose one day modern scholarship should establish that the silver dollar splashed. Would George Washington no longer be father of his country? Obviously not, because George Washington is father of his country not because he hurled a dollar clear across the Rappahannock or because he could not tell a lie about that fallen cherry tree—what choice did he have?—but because he was commander of the Revolutionary forces and the first president of the United States. So with Jesus. He is not Lord because he turned the water into wine but because those who claim him as Lord believe that he was God's love in person on earth.

In other words there are stories that constitute a basis of faith and others that represent an expression of faith. Like the factory worker,

I personally don't know whether Jesus changed the water into wine. But I do know that to me at least the story is more an expression than a basis of faith, the kind of story the disciples would love to tell after their faith in Christ had been established on very different grounds.

All of which is not to say that the story isn't important for it certainly is. Like most New Testament stories it tells us simultaneously a lot about Jesus and just as much about ourselves.

Mardi Gras, the festival that is celebrated these days just before Lent, mostly in Catholic quarters, is frequently downgraded by dour Protestant detractors. But at heart, in its intent, is Mardi Gras not a rather religious festival? I'm struck that in the Gospel of John, Jesus first visits people not in their sorrow, but in their joy. What does that say to gloomy Christians? Mind you, I am not suggesting that all, or even most of the assorted sourpusses of the world are to be found in the churches. But there are an awful lot who seem to forget that if only one tenth of what we Christians believe were true, we still ought to be ten times as excited as we are.

So why are so many so joyless?

I think it is because so many Christians instead of loving the Lord their God with all their heart, mind, and strength, instead of deifying God, they deify their own virtue. Theirs is a religion of respectability. They never think, or at least say anything outrageous. They never do anything a little bit wild. They are never caught off guard. And it has always saddened me, because it seems to me out of character with Christianity that our churches should have so many more Victorians than Elizabethans.

And it is no laughing matter. For people who strive so hard to be respectable, people who are straitlaced, people who are repressed, become themselves repressive. We see that in the Boers in South Africa, we see it among the people who live in what is euphemistically called the Bible Belt. Why in some quarters today are homosexuals so mercilessly attacked, if not because when a homosexual comes out of the closet, sex comes out of the closet, and that's the last thing repressed Victorians want to see happen. Now I don't know whether God loves homosexuality, but I do know that God loves homosexuals. And I know exemplary Christians who happen to be gay. Are they to be attacked for something over which they had so little choice? Before rushing in with easy judgments, it would seem to behoove those of us who are not gay to listen very carefully to what our fellow Christians who are have to say about the matter.

What is true of sex can also be true of drinking. I think it fair to say that the Bible is pro-drink, anti-drunkenness, although this particular story makes me wonder about the latter. For in true Mardi Gras spirit, Jesus is here doing something really outrageous. We don't know how many guests there were at the wedding. But we read that the jars numbered six, each holding from 20 to 30 gallons. That's anywhere from 120 to 180 gallons of wine, not counting the original amount provided by the groom. So the story suggests that Jesus had a healthy disrespect for respectability. It is as if on this particular occasion he wanted the guests—as he always wanted the Pharisees—to loosen for just a moment their white-knuckled grip on their own sense of virtue. These guests weren't drinking alone—a dangerous pastime; nor were they drinking to forget—a futile pastime. They were drinking together, and drinking to celebrate. In other words, when literally or figuratively Jesus turns water into wine it is surely blasphemous for us to turn the wine of life into water. Life is to be celebrated. In all its God-given wholeness it is to be enjoyed.

Some of the most poignant lines in all the Psalms are the ones we heard earlier:

> By the waters of Babylon, there we sat down and wept,
>   when we remembered Zion.
> On the willows there we hung up our lyres.
> For there our captors required of us songs,
>   and our tormentors, mirth, saying,
> "Sing us one of the songs of Zion!"
>
> Ps. 137:1–3

And then comes one of the most touching questions in all Scripture:

> How shall we sing the LORD's song in a foreign land?
> 137:4

How shall we celebrate life when we are crippled, or in personal pain, or when we are put down, exiled from the mainstream of American life?

It is comforting to remember that the Jesus who turned the water into wine knew as much about human misery as any welfare recipient in New York City today. And because Christ never tolerated the intolerable he would have cried out against the wholly unnecessary sadness and pain caused by our inhuman welfare system. Yet because he was the son of God he never allowed his soul to be cornered into despair. And for that matter, neither did the psalmist, for he went on:

If I forget you, O Jerusalem, let my right hand wither!
Let my tongue cleave to the roof of my mouth, if I do
   not remember you,
If I do not set Jerusalem above my highest joy.
137:5–6

Just as freedom of speech is a right that must be most highly prized when its exercise is most offensive, so the love of God must be most deeply celebrated when all around seems to deny its existence. We cannot hand over our high morale to the United States government, or to a welfare system, or to any other system that seeks to repress our God-given joy. Better than most, Blacks have known this truth: "Sometimes I feel discouraged and think my work's in vain, but then the Holy Spirit revives my soul again."

And Jesus is our balm in Gilead, the physician who makes the wounded whole—by his own wounds. He who, at the beginning of his ministry, turned water into wine for the guests at a wedding, at the end turns his own blood into wine for the salvation of all. But don't look for the miracle in the noun. What's divine is in the verb: this is my body *broken*, this is my blood *shed*. Doesn't so outrageous an outpouring of self shame our stuffy respectability? Doesn't courage such as this enable us to keep fighting even when the day goes hard, and cowards steal from the field?

"This cup is the new covenant in my blood. Drink all ye of it." He kept the best wine until the end. With grateful hearts let us keep the feast.

Lincoln's Religion*

FEBRUARY 12, 1978

In that rare year when Lincoln's birthday falls on a Sunday, it seems right that sermons be given recalling him who, perhaps more than any other American, stands at the spiritual center of American history. I say this not because Lincoln's knowledge of the Bible far exceeded the content-grasp of most present-day clergy, although it most certainly did, but for two other reasons. No American president, before

*This sermon was greatly inspired and informed by William S. Wolf's paperback, *Lincoln's Religion*.—WSC

or since, has been more attuned to the pain and sorrow tearing at the life of his people; and no American *citizen*—and I say this mindful of theologians from Jonathan Edwards to Reinhold Niebuhr—no citizen of this country has interpreted more eloquently this sorrow and this pain in the light of biblical motifs of judgment, punishment, justice, mercy, and reconciliation.

"The sins of the fathers are visited upon the sons and unto their children's children" (Exod. 34:7). *Life is consequential.* The world swings on an ethical hinge. Loosen that hinge and all of history and even nature will feel the shock. Individuals and nations do not break the ten commandments so much as they are broken on them. "God is not mocked." All this Abraham Lincoln knew better than any of us, and he said it without the least trace of pomposity—which of course has nothing to do with the faith; and with maximum humor, which has a considerable amount to do with the faith. Let's put it this way: Faith is for the ultimate incongruities of life; humor does very nicely for the immediate ones. No, we can say more: humor, by destroying the illusion of our control over life, opens us up to the realization of God's governance.

In case you hadn't guessed it, I'm very fond of Abraham Lincoln; in fact so much so, that in the sixties and early seventies when like many of you I went, time and again to Washington to protest the war, feeling for all the world like a sensitive grain of wheat going up against a millstone, at day's end I never lost the opportunity to steal away for just a moment to the Lincoln Memorial. For Lincoln, too, had protested a war, calling the war against Mexico "unnecessary and unconstitutional," words which cost him his seat in the House of Representatives.

I love that memorial. Unlike so many other statues in the capital, Lincoln is not astride some rearing stallion; he's in an old armchair. He is not even standing like Jefferson, he's just sitting. Yet all the depth and grandeur are there, all the greatness that was his after he had grown from an average self-centered small-town politician— albeit one of unsuspected talents—to a statesman of world stature.

Let's start right there—with Lincoln's amazing capacity for growth. Undoubtedly it had a lot to do with his humility, for without some humility none of us can grow very far. But there was more to it than that. Two days ago I was in Robert E. Lee's church, St. Paul's Episcopal Church in Richmond. There a friend told me that when he thinks about Abraham Lincoln—and southern whites think quite a bit about Abraham Lincoln, more than some of us Yankees imagine—he remembers the old story of the boy asking the pilot of a Mississippi River boat how long he had been at his job.

"Twenty-six years."

"O, then you know where all the rocks are, all the shoals and sandbars."

"No," said the pilot, "But I know where the deep waters are."

There was something monumentally untrivial about Abraham Lincoln. That's why he was able to dig through the sands of sectarianism, so loveless and unfortunately so characteristic of the churches of his day—dig through the sands of sectarianism to the bedrock of biblical faith, our Savior's life and teaching. That's why also he was able to cut through all arguments in support of slavery to lay bare the injustice of governing another without that other's consent, of earning one's bread in the sweat of another person's face. And that was why, when the Civil War was drawing to its close, Lincoln came out so cleanly for amnesty. Like any sensible man he feared anarchy on the one hand as he did despotism on the other, and his legal training enhanced his reverence for the law. Yet the wisdom of compassion allowed him to grasp the biblical insight that human relations are finally not contractual but human. Just as "the Sabbath belongs to man not man to the Sabbath," so Lincoln understood the law to be a good servant but a bad master. Therefore, not a single soldier or officer who wore the grey—not even those like Robert E. Lee who once wore the blue—not a one was punished for breaking the law. Of the states that had seceded he said, "Finding themselves safely at home, it would be utterly immaterial whether they had ever been abroad." "With malice towards none; with charity for all." Would that more recent Republican presidents had been able to recall to their people that biblical understanding of human relations.

Humility, an ability to see in depth the big issues he faced—these certainly aided his growth. And so, too, did a capacity related to seeing the big issues in depth, that is, Lincoln's unrelenting willingness to doubt, to question. I think it fair, and in a church important to say, that because Lincoln doubted some religious dogmas he became more acutely aware of the biblical realities behind them. Listen to these words written as a young man and see if they don't reflect a deeply religious spirit:

> Probably it is to be my lot to go on in a twilight, feeling and reasoning my way through life, as questioning doubting Thomas did. But in my poor, maimed way, I bear with me as I go on a seeking spirit of desire for a faith that was with him of olden times, who, in his need, as I in mine, exclaimed, "Help thou my unbelief."

Because he refused to be dogmatic, and because he knew how desperately selfish we human beings are, Lincoln abhorred self-righteousness. After several dispatches from General McClellan, all of which began "Headquarters—in the saddle," Lincoln remarked to his cabinet members, "It's strange how the general keeps his headquarters where most people put their hindquarters." Even more trying than the generals was the self-righteousness of the clergy who visited him in droves. After the departure of a particularly obnoxious delegation, Lincoln turned to an aide to tell him the story of a small black boy who, out of mud, had sculpted a beautiful church replete with pews and pulpit. When asked, "Where's the preacher?" he replied, "I ran out of mud."

The clergy was pressing for the immediate abolition of slavery, an institution Lincoln too had detested since childhood. But what was he to do, when as president he had taken an oath of office to uphold the Constitution which provided for slavery in the original states? Because there was no possibility of a Constitutional amendment, he eventually released the Emancipation Proclamation, but considered it an unconstitutional act justified only because not to do so would imperil even more the Union.

Because of his willingness to maintain the tension, no matter how painful, in a dilemma, Lincoln was remarkably sensitive to the dilemmas of others, such as the dilemma tormenting the Quakers. What were *they* to do, opposed as they were to both war and oppression, when only war seemed to be the way to abolish the oppression?

Now we come to what I suggested at the beginning, Lincoln's unique contribution to his country. Aware though he was of the complexity of historical processes, and of the mixture of human motivation, and of our seemingly insurmountable self-righteousness, Lincoln never for a moment doubted the word of the psalmist that "the judgments of the Lord are true and righteous altogether." Although he doubted that these judgments could be mechanistically applied from outside, as suggested by the clergy, he was certain that they would always be enacted organically within history, for God is not mocked.

To read the Lincoln-Douglas debates is to hear Lincoln begin to expound our history as a biblical prophet, the plumb line being morality rooted in the righteous will of God. He appreciates the fact that the founders of the Republic also faced dilemmas: unity with slavery, or the abolition of slavery and no Republic, at least not of thirteen states. Choosing unity, as our forefathers did, they did not solve the dilemma, for they left a moral poison in the bloodstream of American life. By prohibiting the extension of slavery in the Northwest Territories, however, by the Ordinance of 1787, they had at least put slavery, as Lincoln put it, "in course of ultimate extinction," a principle he argued that had remained intact despite the Missouri Compromise of 1820, reaffirmed in 1850.

But now Senator Douglas wanted to break that principle. Douglas was offering, as Lincoln saw it, moral indifference as a calculated policy to political slavery there; the question was to be resolved by the settlers through self-determination. That, said Senator Douglas, was the democratic way. Answered Lincoln, "This declared indifference, but as I must think, covert real zeal for the spread of slavery, I cannot but hate. I hate it because of the monstrous injustice of slavery itself." As to the argument for self-government he said: "If the negro is *not* a man, why in that case, he who is a man may as a matter of self-government, do just as he pleases with him. But if the negro *is* a man, is it not to that extent a total destruction of self-government, to say that he too shall not govern himself? When the white man governs himself, and also governs another man, that is more than self-government—that is despotism. . . . No man is good enough to govern another man, without that other's consent. I say this is the leading principle—the sheet anchor of American republicanism."

To guard against self-righteousness he describes the problem as national, not sectional. "They"—southern whites—"are just what we would be in their situation. If slavery did not now exist amongst them, they would not introduce it. If it did now exist amongst us, we should not instantly give it up. This I believe of the masses North and South." Because in these debates Lincoln spoke to the generous self in so many Americans, in part at least, for this reason, he was elected President.

Then came the Civil War. You remember how prophetically he interpreted that event in his Second Inaugural:

> Quoting from the 18th chapter of Matthew he says, "Woe, unto the world because of offenses! For it must needs be that offenses come; but woe to that man by whom the offense cometh!" If we shall suppose of those offenses that American Slavery is one of those offenses which, in the providence of God, must needs come, but which, having continued through His appointed time, He now wills to remove, and that He gives to both North and South, this terrible war, as the woe due to those by whom the offense came, shall we discern therein any departure from those divine attributes which the believers

in a Living God always ascribe to Him? Fondly do we hope—fervently do we pray—that this mighty scourge of war may speedily pass away. Yet if God wills that it continue until all the wealth piled by the bond-man's two hundred and fifty years of unrequited toil shall be sunk, and until every drop of blood drawn with the lash shall be paid with another drawn with the sword, as was said three thousand years ago, so it must be said again "the judgments of the Lord, are true and righteous altogether."

With malice toward none; with charity for all; with firmness in the right, as God gives us to see the right, let us strive on to finish the work we are in; to bind up the nation's wounds; to care for him who shall have borne the battle, and for his widow, and his orphan—to do all which may achieve and cherish a just, and a lasting peace, among ourselves, and with all nations.

I hope a great many Americans will today think of the pain and sorrow still tearing at the life of our nation, for life *is* consequential, and we have strayed from the spiritual center of our history. But maybe we shall one day fit the wonderful description Lincoln gave of us as "God's almost chosen people" by building our national and personal lives, as he built his life, on the bedrock of scriptural faith.

The Wounded Healer

FEBRUARY 19, 1978
Readings: John 7:53–8:11; Luke 23:39–43

Many people have just enough religion to make themselves miserable. If they come to church, they pray the General Confession but don't believe the Absolution. And because misery loves company, they inevitably become killjoys. Like Mencken's Puritan, they are haunted by the fear that somewhere someone might be happy.

In a city far from benign, and in a mass society characterized by banality and barbarism, cheerfulness becomes a form of asceticism; just as in a corrupt world, resignation to that corruption becomes the subtlest form of corruption. So not because we are resigned or gloomy, but only because we wish to be realistic, let us talk this morning about sin. What does the church mean by the myth of Original Sin, the truth of a myth being a truth that is and always will be, no matter how much we try and say it was? (The story of Adam and Eve is not literally true, only eternally true.) And how does the church understand that solemn word, atonement?

The New Testament story just read indicates at least three very positive things that can be said about sin, the first being that if nothing counts against you, nothing counts. There is an intimate relationship between sin and meaning. It is no accident that the General Confession always comes toward the beginning of every service, in our own right after the opening hymn, the call to worship, the invocation, the introit, Jesus' summary of the law, all of which speak of the truth, goodness and beauty of God, the amazing grace that fills every corner of the universe with meaning. Yet even as we gaze with wonder at the height of the mountains, so to speak, we cannot help but become aware of the floor of the valley on which we stand. So the mood of the service moves swiftly and naturally from praise and thanksgiving to repentance.

To confess sin then is to reaffirm meaning. To say what's wrong with the world is to recall what's right. And I think we can hear the two poles of right and wrong and the tension between them in these wonderful words spoken by Jesus to the woman caught in adultery: "Neither do I condemn thee; go and sin no more."

Now some folks these days might be inclined to say, "Shucks kid, sleeping around with every man in town doesn't make a nice clean kid like you into a whore. Neither do I condemn you; go and sin some more." Only it isn't sin; it isn't anything. And that's the point: no sin, no nothing. So the first positive thing to say about sin is that to confess it is to reconfirm that the world has meaning.

There is a second positive thing to be said. When the scribes and Pharisees brought the woman to Jesus it was to say, "Teacher, this woman has been caught in the act of adultery. Now in the law Moses commanded us to stone such. What do you say about her?" The answer has to be one of the memorable lines of scripture: "Let him who is without sin among you cast the first stone"; and they all disappeared.

If we are not bound one to another in love, at least we are one in sin, and that is no mean bond, for as the story shows us, it precludes the possibility of separation through judgment. "Let him who is without sin among you cast the first stone." The knowledge that we are all sinners should not only cultivate forbearance; it should forge among us a fantastic bond of understanding and compassion. For instance, those who work in fine office buildings are often tempted to sell their souls for the sake of the security that money can buy. Shouldn't that knowledge help them understand the woman on 42nd Street selling her body for some of the same security? Or knowing how tempted we will all be in the coming weeks, if we have sophistication, education, money and power, to fudge just a bit on the income tax form— shouldn't such knowledge help us to understand those who precisely because they have no sophistication, no education, no money and no power, hold up liquor stores? Mind you, I'm not condoning any of this. I think we should take each other to task for our slippery ways. But only on the sound assumption that it takes a sinner to catch a sinner.

Let's stop here for just a moment, because the rationalizations that we can find for our slippery ways are really fascinating. For instance, contrary to what we generally believe, I think most good behavior is due to the weakness of our passions rather than the strength of our virtues. And every time I hear old people bemoan the sins of their youth, I think I am hearing a complaint that they are no longer able to commit them. In 1974, one of the Watergate defendants who seventeen years earlier at Williams College had taken my course in Social Ethics [sic!], said to me, "You have to understand, Bill, we didn't set out to break the law. I mean we're not like bank robbers." For a moment he had me confused until I remembered that bank robbers, too, don't set out to break the law. They set out to get money, and if they want to badly enough they'll break the law to get it. So with the Watergate defendants; whatever it was they wanted, they wanted it badly enough to break the law to get it. The only difference was that a bank knows when it is robbed!

To confess sin is to reaffirm meaning; to confess sin is also to tap into an unending source of understanding and compassion. And thirdly, is it not an enormous relief to know that you are not expected to be a boy scout or a girl scout? Some people think the passage from childhood to youth is marked by the discovery of one's sexual awareness, but I think far more important is the discovery of one's capacity for evil. (That is why I so like John Knowles' *A Separate Peace*, a story built on Kant's axiom that there is something about the misfortune of even our best friends which is not altogether disagreeable.) I think maturity begins with the recognition that paradise is lost, that there is no reentry into that garden. The same myth instructs us that there is an angel with a flaming sword barring the way. That means that the only real sin is the denial of it, the only real danger, a pretension to innocence. Let us never forget that we Americans had the very best of motives for intervening in Vietnam, which is why perhaps the best book about our involvement there was one written before that involvement began. I have in mind Graham Greene's *The Quiet American* which concludes "innocence should wander the world wearing a leper's bell."

Sin is a mystery. But one thing we know: it is too inevitable not to happen. In the sullied stream of human life, not innocence but holiness, is our only option. And when we remember that the words whole and holy have the same root we can better see that sin is essentially separation. It is probably a mistake to talk about sins in the plural, for sin is a state of being, a state of being in which we are separated from God, from one another and from our true, i.e., loving self.

Earlier I was suggesting that we were closet criminals. Goethe once said that no crime had ever been committed of which he didn't feel himself capable. I certainly have no trouble whatsoever identifying with the greatest criminal of them all—the hero of *Crime and Punishment*. His name, Raskolnikov, is carefully chosen, for in Russian a "raskolnik" is both a split personality and a heretic. It was Dostoyevsky's profound insight to see that heresy is a psychological matter, not an intellectual one. Heresy is rooted in pride. And it was Dostoyevsky's genius to see that crime is only superficially breaking the law. At a much deeper level it is rending the bond of love. And the punishment for crime is experiencing the bond of love rent; not the isolation imposed by barred windows and prison walls so much as the isolation imposed by the hardening walls of the heart. Separated from God, separated from each other, locked into our own hearts is to experience the punishment of sin. And it is a form of suffering with which I think all of us are acquainted.

Now let us turn once again to that scene in Calvary, to the words exchanged between the criminal and Christ. If we use our imaginations we can say that the criminal is on his cross because he has rent the bond of love. Christ is on his because he cannot but love. The criminal is experiencing the agony of sin, Christ the cost of devotion. Then he who is guilty hears the one who of all people is the victim of injustice pray to God for the forgiveness of his own executioners. Such love was too much. His own hard heart melts. He cries out "Jesus remember me," and Christ performs his last healing miracle on his cross.

In portraying the myth of creation, Michelangelo pictures the bond of love as it was first established—so easily, so naturally, God, surrounded by cherubim and seraphim, reaches out from heaven, and Adam on earth reaches up his arm to God. But the bond, once rent, is not so easily restored. Sin has its price and so has forgiveness. Restoration takes place on two crosses, when a human being in his or her agony reaches out his or her hand to Christ, and Christ on his cross stretches out his hand in reply. That's what atonement is all about.

Atonement—at-one-ment—spells the end of our imprisonment in our own hearts, the beginning of renewed communications with God. We are released from prison to share deep feelings, hard truths with one another, to pour out our hearts once again to end the banality and barbarism that besets our society. "He was wounded for our transgressions, bruised for our iniquities: the chastisement of our peace was upon him and with his stripes we are healed" (Isa. 53:5). All praise and thanksgiving to Christ our wounded healer.

"Tempted of the Devil"

FEBRUARY 26, 1978
Reading: Luke 4:1–13

R eligion," said the philosopher Whitehead, "is what people do with their solitude." I wonder if he didn't have this particular story in mind. It is the Holy Spirit, you remember, that led Jesus into the wilderness to be tested, to find out what was really in the bottom of his heart, knowledge that he could only come by after he had been eyeball to eyeball with the Devil. Solitude, in other words, is where you have it out, where you decide the basic issues of your life. What, for example, are you going to do with your loneliness, for everyone of us finally is alone? We are born alone, we die alone, and in between we stumble along in the footsteps of lonely literary prototypes, the likes of Abraham, Ulysses, Faust. Solitude is also where you decide how you are going to be with other people. Said another philosopher, "Hell is other people." I don't believe it, but he had a point. Solitude is where you decide how much money you *don't* need, where your instincts for self-preservation go up against your convictions about self-sacrifice. Solitude, in short, is scary; in fact so scary that only infrequently do we stop to pay calls on ourselves, and even then we are lucky to find anyone at home.

But going back to the story: "The devil said to him, 'If you are the Son of God, command this stone to become bread.'" As in a congregation of this size there are always two or three people who don't believe in the devil, before going further I want to describe to them this person I myself know so well. The Devil is a person because he/she—if anyone is androgynous it's the Devil—the Devil is a person because evil is experienced as an intensely personal power. The Devil is a person also, not because evil exists outside of us, but because evil is experienced as something within us but greater than us; hence it's separate existence. And the most important thing to say about the Devil is that he is a fallen angel. One of the dumbest ideas that people have ever come up with is the notion that evil arises in our so-called "lower" nature. The Devil doesn't ask Jesus how he feels about sex, nor does Jesus put that question to anybody else, for both know that evil arises in our "higher" nature, in that which is most god-like in us—our freedom. This is not to say that our higher nature can't use our lower nature for evil purposes, but the source of evil is in our freedom. The Devil is always advising us how to use our freedom, and although he's subtle, his advice is always the same. "I'll tell you what to do with your freedom," says the Devil, "sell it."

I said the Devil was subtle. Notice the way he begins, "*If* you are the Son of God." What makes him so devilish is that he attacks where we are most vulnerable—at the point of our identity. Those of you who were here Wednesday night may remember that I said lack of clarity about who we are is not as innocent as other forms of ignorance. It muddies the waters at their source. If we're confused about who we are, we'll be confused about all manner of things further downstream, so confused in fact that the Devil may successfully tempt us to prove that we are human beings by doing something inhuman. "If you are a human being, get what's yours and forget about everyone else." As if what's yours wasn't already God's, and as if getting it had anything to do with the essential humanity of human beings. And of course he does even better with our collective confusion. "If you are a great nation, don't send wheat to the hungry Vietnamese whose cropland you destroyed, hang on to the Panama Canal instead"—as if that had anything to do with the greatness of a nation.

Fortunately Jesus knows well that to be the Son of God means you don't turn stone into bread. "Man does not live by bread alone." To make material well-being the end-all of life is the surest way to lose your freedom. Look at our own beloved land, at the number of our citizens losing their freedom of thought and action. Alarmed at the prospects of dwindling economic resources, they are running scared, limiting their liabilities, trying desperately to avoid all risks. This is true even of our businessmen who no longer show the old American entrepreneurial spirit; most of them are mere managers. Labor's even worse, showing precious little interest in organizing the unorganized, the ones who really need organization. And what about our intellectuals? How many tenured professors say things they would not dare to say had they not been given tenure? There was a time when tenure protected controversial ideas; now it protects jobs. And of course our snobbish insistence on educational credentials makes it doubly difficult for our ghetto teenagers to get jobs. It's nonsensical to insist on high school degrees. Look at our own American history, which shows that immigrants went for jobs first; schooling came later. And how un-American as well as unchristian is this insurance mentality that wants life to be safe, predictable, reliable. Why, to avoid surprises, tourist agencies are now offering pre-packaged vacations which assure you on any given day one museum, one scenic tour, two cocktails with dinner, and after dinner a bus ride through the red-light district. No one, of course, gets off the bus; that would be too risky.

In the churches too the Devil is successfully persuading people to be Christians in Galilee but not to set their faces towards Jerusalem. Have you ever noticed how the nails never graze the palms of those busy saving their souls? We're not supposed to save our souls. We're supposed to transcend ourselves and save the world. Christianity teaches that life is a moral venture symbolized by the cross. The cross is still in our churches, but it is fast disappearing from the lives of our members.

The sad thing is that this insurance mentality won't pay off for anybody. Our unlived lives will poison our existence. We'll end up with more regrets than pleasures.

Well, enough of that gloomy temptation. On to the next one which, if not as gloomy, is unfortunately twice as frightening. (I'll be glad when the Lenten season is over and we can really get to Resurrection again!) "And the Devil took him up, and showed him all the kingdoms of the world in a moment of time, and said to him, 'To you I will give all this authority and their glory; for it has been delivered to me, and I give it to whom I will. If you, then, will worship me, it shall all be yours.'"

I suppose that is about as clear a statement as you can find in scripture that imperialism and despotism are the works of the Devil. And once again we are talking of loss of freedom. But in this temptation, whose freedom is being threatened—those over whom Jesus would rule, or his own freedom? "And Jesus answered him, 'It is written, you shall worship the Lord your God, and him only shall you serve.'"

"Him only shall you serve" whose service is "perfect freedom." By freedom, the Bible doesn't mean merely freedom of choice, which St. Augustine, rather scornfully, called the "*libertas minor*." The big freedom—"*libertas maior*"—is to be able to follow through on your good choices, that is to fulfill yourself as a loving child of the same kind of

God who for that very reason we address as father. In God's service then, the one thing we cannot give up is love. In the Devil's service, the one thing we must have is power. And in the dictatorship the Devil was offering Jesus, in any dictatorship for that matter, the ultimate form of power is the power to kill.

Now let me tell you what came to my mind as I reread this second temptation. Suppose, as a preventative measure against murder, the police of New York City were to announce that they would kill all the family members and all the friends of anyone who committed murder. Although such a policy would be an effective deterrrent, I think we'd be horrified at such a commitment to kill on the part of the police, especially as the hostages, the family and friends of the murderer, would probably have little if anything to do with the decision to commit murder. I think we'd feel that against the threat of murder the police were threatening an equally immoral response. We'd say "that's police power run amok."

Yet what I have just described is, I think, an exact analogy for our present policy of nuclear deterrence, except that nuclear deterrence represents a hostage system on a massive scale. How many of the millions of Soviet citizens we are presently prepared to kill in reprisal will have had anything to do with the decision to attack us? And how many of us, for that matter, will have anything to say about the decision to retaliate? Against the threat of an immoral attack are we not threatening an equally immoral response?

Many of us who fought in World War II thought Hitler had to be some kind of a devil to bomb an open city like Rotterdam, unmilitary targets like Coventry. Yet by war's end, where once fists shook, shoulders shrugged; the unacceptable slaughter of civilians had become totally acceptable. In that sense Hitler won the war. Now the unthinkable has become thinkable, and we kid ourselves if we don't think the undoable was also doable. Instead of offering one man all the kingdoms of the world in a moment of time, the devil is now proposing to destroy all the kingdoms of the world in a moment of time, and we are listening, because the one thing we cannot give up is power.

And finally the Devil "took him up to Jerusalem and set him on the pinnacle of the temple, and said to him, 'If you are the Son of God, throw yourself down from here; for it is written, He will give his angels charge of you, to guard you'" . . . And Jesus answered him, "It is said, 'You shall not tempt the Lord your God.'"

I suppose this is the kind of temptation that comes to a person who has renounced the struggle for worldly security, the struggle for worldly power. Instead he has committed himself to God, only with the secret expectation that God will now do all the work. So much spirituality is superficiality, pure laziness, reminiscent of the story of the priest who went golfing with the rabbi. Before putting the priest crossed himself. By the ninth hole he was nine strokes ahead. Said the rabbi, "Father, do you suppose it would be all right if before I putted I too sort of crossed myself?"

Said the priest, "Of course, rabbi. But it won't do you any good until you learn how to putt."

There are so many lazy people in the church, who want to cop out on all the responsibilities that go with freedom, who want selfishly to ask God to take care of them when they are supposed to be out taking care of the world. They come to church but they don't *leave*. They do church work but not the work of the church.

I suppose the one thing the Devil learned from his meeting with Jesus was that it is not very smart to engage in direct confrontation. Don't let people get alone with themselves, keep them busy with each other, members of a mass society. For smart man that he is, the Devil must have noticed that it is the isolated consciences in history that have best stood for the universal conscience, not the mass mind. "It is the solitary person," Thomas Merton wrote, "who does humankind the inestimable favor of reminding it of its capacity for maturity, freedom, and peace."

And so, dear friends, let us confound the Devil by confronting him. Let us not be afraid to go into our own wilderness, to have it out, eyeball to eyeball with him on all the basic issues of our lives. Do we really want to sell our freedom for material well-being? Do we as individuals or as a people, want to sell our capacity to love for loveless power? Do we really want to ask God to take care of us where we should be caring for others?

In Matthew's account of the story we read, "Then the Devil left him, and behold, angels came and ministered to him." There are still angels around ready to do no less for us. Amen.

A Gesture of Reconciliation

MARCH 5, 1978

Yesterday, with several of you, I was in Houston, Texas, where the weather was so cold that the distinguished senator from Iowa, Richard Clark, had to put on his overcoat, something all politicians have hated to do since the days of John F. Kennedy. But it was a heartwarming address that he delivered, and everything else was heartwarming, too, from the dancing of the young women, the giant puppets led by the Goddess of Wheat, the singing of the gospel choir, to the mighty praying of the president of the National Council of Churches, William Thompson. All these took place in a service dedicated to the sending of ten thousand metric tons of wheat to the people of Vietnam.

Most moving to me was the moment the farmers and their families came forward to pour a portion of their donated grain into a giant container. Said the five-year-old daughter of one, "I am pouring my grain because all children of the world are friends."

Some Americans, of course, are vigorously opposed to this action. Others are abstaining, fearful to come down on either side of what they conceive to be a hotly debated issue. And most, I fear, are indifferent to this first ship in three years to sail from the shores of the United States to Vietnam. For this indifference, our government is doubtlessly grateful, because since the days of President Ford a total embargo has been imposed on trade and aid, including all food and all medicine. A special permit was difficult to obtain for this particular shipment.

The State Department always likes to take a very complicated view of its own efforts. But the first thing to be said about this shipment of wheat is something very simple. The story of the Good Samaritan says that if it is possible to do good without risk or great cost we ought to do good. So, what we celebrated there yesterday and here today, is no big thing. The shipment of wheat is an act of minimal decency, from a people still committed to a moral world. They are hungry, and we are not; it's as simple as that. And the fact that "they" are Vietnamese has nothing to do with it. If civilians are not a legitimate target in wartime why should they be in peacetime? If, during the war, we tried to spare civilians bombs and bullets, why should we, in peacetime, try to kill them through starvation? It makes neither moral nor logical sense, which is why practically every major power in the world, and endless small countries, are helping reconstruct a country devastated by war and recently pounded by two typhoons. But the one power most present at the destruction is conspicuously absent at the reconstruction. Why?

Had we openly declared war on the Vietnamese, had we fought it as cleanly as possible, had we won it fairly and squarely, I would imagine our government today would be demonstrating a generosity that would make 10,000 tons of wheat look like pittance. Magnanimity becomes a victor, generosity is the vanity of giving. Surely those reasons would obtain. But it is also true that our country has a long tradition of generosity going all the way back to words spoken in 1630 by John Winthrop while still on board the *Arabella,* "We must abridge ourselves of our superfluities for the supply of others' necessities." Because we would be at peace with ourselves, we would be making peace with the Vietnamese.

We are still waging war with the Vietnamese today because we are still at war with ourselves. Our nose is out of joint because we didn't win; because our army went to pot—in all senses of that word; because many more soldiers killed many more officers than the army officially recognizes; and because we extricated ourselves from the war as callously as we waged it. But what we should be trying to understand, we are desperately trying to forget. That's why we alone are not at the reconstruction of Vietnam, why we have changed the famous dictum of Carl von Clausewitz around and made politics the extension of war by other means.

Ten thousand metric tons of wheat. For those of you who wonder why it is not rice, let me say that the request came from the Vietnamese themselves. After the long occupation of the French and the more recent American occupation of the south, Vietnamese tastes have changed. They requested wheat milled into bread and noodles. Ten thousand metric tons of wheat will supplement the diet for 200,000 Vietnamese for a year. But just think what 10,000 metric tons of wheat might do for American souls. Were we to search them to seek the errors of our ways, were we to seek peace in our own hearts, we would become peacemakers. The Old Testament prophets preached doom, but only to sinners who denied their sin, to nations whose pride-swollen faces had closed up their eyes. The moment the people heard what the prophets were saying, the moment they saw what the "se-ers" saw—for love is not blind but visionary—at that very moment the prophets began to preach hope, deliverance, peace, reconciliation.

Democracy is a way of distributing responsibility. American Christians have a special responsibility to lead their nation to repentance. What right did we have to decide who lived and died and ruled in Vietnam? To withdraw from one country we had to invade two and bomb three. I myself saw the contents of some of these bombs—twenty thousand little pellets, which could be released silently eighteen miles away from the victims; and in North Vietnam, I saw what these pellets can do to the entrails of small children. But the war is over. Therefore it is time we ended it, in our own hearts, so that we might reach out the hand of friendship to our former enemy. We don't have to approve their form of government. We are not asking our government to send their government arms—that's over. We are only asking that our government send food and medicine. Do you realize that "the starving Indians" have sent 300,000 tons?

A companion, quite literally, is a sharer of the loaf. Soon we ourselves will once again become companions, one of another, by sharing the bread, the body of Christ. But the Vietnamese, too, are our companions, which is why it is quite proper that their pictures should today adorn the church. They are our companions as ultimately everybody on this planet is a companion. There is only one race—the human race. And the history of that race is a long struggle against all restrictions, a long struggle to affirm that God made us one, that Christ died to keep us that way, so that our sin is only that we are constantly trying to put asunder what God himself has joined together. "For in Christ, all the fulness of God was pleased to dwell, and through him to reconcile to himself all things, whether on earth or in heaven, making peace by the blood of his cross" (Col. 1:19–20).

During the war in Vietnam I could not escape the feeling that Christ was between heaven and earth, between the lines, absorbing in his body every pellet and every bullet. And he still is making peace with his blood, until we stop the enmity that divides us, until we fill the hollow in the heart where love should be.

When American troops landed in France during World War I, almost 150 years after the American Revolution, General Pershing said, "Lafayette, we are here." Lafayette is remembered far more in this country than he is in France. The same is true of Morrison, the man who outside the Pentagon poured gasoline on himself, lit a match and turned himself into a blazing signpost pointing to the horrors of the war. Here there is no memorial for Morrison. But in Hanoi, a whole broad avenue is named in his honor.

In 1945 as a liaison officer on the frontier between the Russian and the American zones, I watched the Iron Curtain descend. It was cruel. But long after access to the east had been denied all groups, one group could still get through. I had only to say the word "Quakers" and the curtain went up. Every Soviet citizen remembered what the Quakers did to help their starving people in the 1920s. May Church World Service be so remembered in Vietnam.

I am glad we are breaking bread with Christ, with each other, and with the Vietnamese today. "For in Christ Jesus, all the fullness of God was pleased to dwell, and through Him to reconcile to Himself all things whether on earth, or in heaven, making peace by the blood of His Cross. . . . This is my body broken for you, this is my blood shed for you. Come, let us keep the feast." Amen.

Jonah

MARCH 12, 1978

Some weeks ago, you may remember, I suggested that we could see ourselves reflected on practically every page of the Bible: in Adam's excuses, in Jacob, elbowing his way up the ladder of financial success; in the New Testament story of the paralytic, a man literally scared to death, his life one long suicide; in promise-making, promise-breaking Peter. And who can't see himself or herself reflected in Jonah, who, the moment he hears, "Arise, go to Nineveh," hotfoots it to Joppa, to take a slow boat to Tarshish.

One has to admire Jonah's persistence. So determined is he not to get involved, that when a mighty storm arises he goes to sleep. And when the captain wakes him, he comes up with an even better idea, and one that would have worked had the Lord not arranged to have a whale meet him as he came over the side.

Hasn't Jonah tremendous appeal? Who needs Nineveh? Who needs the Middle East? Who needs Rhodesia? South Africa? Uganda? The Panama Canal? Who needs New York with all its pollution and poverty? Who needs a world of urgent problems? Nobel prizewinner, Albert Szent-Györgi, was right; in a world governed by a terrible strain of idiots only fornication and drugs will serve. So here's to Jonah, and to a world of non-urgent non-problems, where the word of the Lord falls with the force of a snowflake.

There is only one drawback, as Jonah found out, and probably knew all along: you can't get away with it. This makes Jonah all the more appealing. He's no psychotic who thinks two and two make five. He's like most of us, a good neurotic who knows that two and two make four—but Oh God, how he hates it.

You can't get away with it. We could say grandiloquently with Charles Williams, "Shall our tremors measure the omnipotence?" or with the psalmist, "Whither shall I flee from thy presence?" But, in the mood of the story, let's underplay it and say simply, if it is trouble to care, it's more trouble not to. And more trouble than it's worth. For finally, as the story of Jonah tells us, either you care, or you go off the deep end where only the Lord can help you. In this world, you care or you die.

All of which reminds us once again that Descartes was wrong. *Cogito, ergo sum?* ("I think, therefore I am.") We are not detached brains, nor do we establish who we are by thinking alone. Self-knowledge through self-contemplation is self-defeating. In his *Memoirs*, the British philosopher, A. J. Ayre, writes, "The self seethes, and philosophy analyzes. An abacus is substituted for the sinew of human mystery, and wit for passion."

On the other hand, it makes no more sense to say with the romantics, *Sentio, ergo sum* ("I feel, therefore I am."). For deeper than thinking, deeper than feeling, is caring. I care, therefore I think. I care, therefore I feel. I care, therefore I wish, therefore I will. I care, therefore I am. If I can be scholarly for one more moment, Heidegger was closer than Descartes in perceiving that human beings are ontologically constituted by care, and in so seeing he was only reflecting the Bible. "We pass out of death into life because we love the sisters and brothers." The call of God is simply the call to care. It is because people are hurting that the call comes. "Arise, go to Nineveh," "Go to Pharaoh, Go to Ahab, Go to Nashville, Go to Washington. Stay in New York."

I care, therefore I am. One proof is the price we pay for not caring. We live in a different world from Jonah. But what differentiates our world from his is technology, which has not so much solved as internalized our problems. We are better cared for, but we have more cares. And for the basic reason that we ourselves don't care, not enough for ourselves, not enough for each other, not enough for our community, our world. And let's be quite clear: we are not limiting care to preaching à la Jonah, or even in political commitments, for life offers possibilities for fulfillment far richer than its political expressions.

So the first thing this story reminds us is that if it is complicated to care, it is simply more complicated not to. If it is complicated to have intimate relations with each other, it is more complicated to have no intimate relations whatsoever. If it is complicated to bring about the changes that alone can avert violence in New York City, it is not so complicated as trying to deal with the violence caused by no change. To care, or not to care. And finally, is it a question, when in our heart of hearts we know that we are never freer than when captivated?, never more in control of ourselves than when lost in each other?

Meanwhile, back at the whale, Jonah has decided that Spinoza was right: freedom is the recognition of necessity. So he decides to cooperate with the inevitable. He decides to start caring. He goes to Nineveh, and starts a citywide crusade. "Yet forty days and Nineveh will be overthrown."

Surely Jonah is Billy Graham's idol, for after only one day, and after his having been in only one-third of the city, the entire city repents, the king included. The Lord, of course, is delighted and immediately suspends sentence. But Jonah is miffed. It is as if God had suddenly removed his whole raison d'être. And in this moment Jonah resembles nothing so much as half a million people in the peace movement ten years ago to the month, the day after President Johnson announced his resignation.

Who am I without my enemy? Who am I if my minority views prevail? Why, just think what it would have meant to have read in the morning papers that the banks of New York City had not only refused to invest further in apartheid but also had foresworn redlining, the practice of taking the money of local depositors and investing that money in suburbs and in the Sun Belt of the southwest. Suppose we had read that the giant landholdings throughout America were going to be divided so that farming could be more efficient, and our cities no longer have to bear the social costs of agro-business. Suppose Carter and Brezhnev had concluded that the arms race was madness. What a depressing discovery, to realize that our enemies were no longer enemies, that our own best efforts were no longer needed!

I remember reading with fascination of a Japanese top sergeant on trial in 1945 for committing war crimes against American prisoners of war. His defense rested on three contentions: he had killed no one; he had little or no control over the miserable conditions in the camp; and given the conditions in the camp, many prisoners of war would have died had he not sustained them by the hatred for him which his words and actions engendered. It was a powerful argument. Hatred and defiance can motivate human beings to great things, and not only for themselves but for justice as well. A defiant person has not only fury and determination, but often moral credibility. There is no question about it: the fury of blacks in this country has served the cause of American justice.

But having one's will motivated essentially by defiance is essentially willfulness, not freedom. And it has two drawbacks. One's identity is always at the mercy of the enemy: Nineveh for Jonah, Whitey for Blacks, communists for anti-communists, men for defiant women. And secondly, defiance means you are against something more than you are for something. You hate evil more than you love the good. Therefore, you cannot get justice and mercy into decent alignment, which was Jonah's second problem. After Jonah began to care, he cared about many things, but not about the people of Nineveh; at least not for their sake. He became a champion of justice, but an enemy of mercy, and so ended up unjust.

At a time when more and more of our church members are getting involved in the politics of this city and of this nation, and when it is so easy to participate in politics of defiance, it is worth remembering that there is only one decent commitment, and that is the commitment to reduce human suffering. That's what caring is all about. That's what this church should be all about—to reduce human suffering.

The story ends with Jonah pouting under a plant, feeling betrayed, once again wanting to die. Here we can make our third and last identification with Jonah, for our lives too are saturated with grievances. One of Arthur Miller's characters cries out: "Oh God, why is betrayal the only truth that sticks?" Do you ever notice how you occasionally wake up in the morning?, how before ever opening your eyes you remember that garden of grievances? And you reach for the rake and hoe, and the watering-pot. I think that if you want to avoid God and your neighbor, that is, if you want to avoid caring, the best thing to do is to concentrate on health, wealth, and status; but most of all, concentrate on your grievances.

At this time of year we should be helped by the remembrance of that other plant from the stem of Jesse, who never allowed his soul to be cornered into despair; who needed no enemies to tell him who he was; who never counted the world unworthy of his suffering. There is still time to give up something for Lent. Let me suggest our grievances. Without them, without defiance, we can live freely by caring deeply.

The Things That Make for Peace

MARCH 19, 1978

L ending drama to the overall excitement of the Palm Sunday scene is an extraordinarily high level of conflict. In fact, with the obvious exception of Calvary, there is, in the whole Bible, no other event in which the participants have more conflicting ideas about what is going on. In Matthew, we read that the multitudes of disciples carried palms—certainly better than spears—and that they were praising God. Yet they were hailing a King, which makes you wonder what mixture of spiritual and earthly hopes they might have been entertaining. Some no doubt remembered the prophesy of Zechariah: "Behold your King is coming to you . . . humble and riding on an ass" (9:9). But the majority, it is likely, had in mind Saul and Solomon. They were cheering a new national leader, one to help them throw off the hated Roman yoke—hardly "a lamb upon his throne."

With different perceptions go different emotions. The crowd is ecstatic. But instead of smiling and acknowledging the cheers, the King weeps, and not for what he has predicted will befall him, which would be poignant enough, but for what he is sure is about to befall the city because of the blindness of its citizens. In Matthew is one of the most heart-rending statements in all the Gospels: "O, Jerusalem, Jerusalem, killing the prophets and stoning them who are sent to you. How often would I have gathered your children unto me as a hen gathers her brood under her wings, and you would not. And now, you are forsaken and desolate" (23:37–38). And in Luke, you remember, Jesus says of the city: "Would that even today you knew the things that make for peace" (19:42).

Finally, just to bring us folks of 1978 into the picture a little more, doesn't that word "peace" raise a host of conflicting perceptions and emotions? "Peace in our time," cried Neville Chamberlain, as he capitulated to Hitler. We all know what happened to "atoms for peace." "Food for peace" went to friendly countries only. And carrying on a long tradition President Carter on Friday proclaimed, in effect, "armaments for peace." I don't doubt his sincerity but I do wonder how we are ever going to institute peace while we keep a war system intact. It's a little like trying to humanize slavery while keeping slaves. And just to complete the week's confusion, in the name of security the State Senate of New York reinstated capital punishment, and the Israelis shall we say, did the same in invading Lebanon. All the experts in Albany and recent Middle Eastern history have testified that these deterrents don't work. They only make a point Jesus must have had in mind: in the pursuit of an illusory security we willingly sacrifice our most precious beliefs. "Would that even now you knew the things that make for peace."

Well, let's begin with ourselves, for peace like charity obviously begins at home. Obviously to be at peace with the world you have to be at peace with yourself. But it is also an obvious, if much overlooked, fact that to be at peace with yourself, you have to have a self. Three days ago, a college chaplain visiting me described college students as confused and not a little bit frightened. "They are no longer certain how in the job world they are going to make it up the ladder of conventional American success." When I asked: Had they some self-contempt for being so eager, to do so? he said, "Bill, they don't have enough self to have self-contempt."

I understand those students, and how they got that way. In the first place they are not all as described. Professor Donald Kennedy, once a scientist at Stanford, and now head of the Food and Drug Administration, credits his students with being what he called "a corrupting influence," shifting his interest from hard science toward public policy questions. Last year he said to them, "You seduced me into that dreadful scientific error, the substitution of important unanswerable questions for unimportant answerable ones."

"Certain questions," said Tolstoy, "are put to human-kind not that we should answer them, but that we should forever wrestle with them." That's how you get a self—by wrestling with important unanswerable questions. What is just? Is that beautiful? Is this true? The travesty of higher education is that it spends most of its time training its students to answer unimportant answerable questions.

"They haven't enough self to have any self-contempt." The chilling thing about that statement is its widespread applicability. Apply it, for instance, to the Palm Sunday scene, and probably you could conclude that lack of self accounts for the horrendous fact that those who cried, "Hosannah" on Sunday, by Friday were shouting "Crucify." You have to have a self to take a stand, to say with Luther, "Here I stand; I can do no other." And if you don't stand for something, you will fall for anything.

Turning again to our own country, is not our landscape strewn with people in the prone position? One year they vote out the death penalty and the next year they vote it in. We are not talking of the banality of evil, we are talking of the evil of banality. Deep down, we are shallow.

So, too, was Jacob shallow, conniving, cunning, until he began to wrestle with God. Then he got himself a self; a name. And one not only for himself but for a whole nation, for nations, too, have to have a self. Like individuals, they have to wrestle with important unanswerable questions, questions of justice, mercy, and peace. All of us, individuals and nations alike, have to look to something above us or we will sink to something below us. That is the tragedy of Israel today. Instead of wrestling with God, it wonders how it can deny a homeland to three and a half million homeless Arabs. Israel has become Jacob again. Mind you, it takes a sinner to catch a sinner. For years, our government tried to deny the existence of the National Liberation Front in South Vietnam and thought it could end its terrible terror—the weapon of the weak—by killing many times more people by aerial bombardment. "Would that even now you knew the things that make for peace." In the pursuit of an illusory security, we sacrifice our most cherished beliefs.

Maybe the Palm Sunday crowd sensed in Jesus such royalty because he had such a small ego and such a large self. The two really are opposites. As the self grows, the ego diminishes. As Israel flourishes, Jacob shrivels and dies. Constituted in the image of God, the self is fearless, unafraid of generosity, of the magnanimity that history has proven a better safeguard than myopic military thinking. But with no higher identity, the ego is cowardly, seeking always its own invulnerability.

When the Senate reinstated capital punishment, isn't that the ego reasserting itself, at the expense of the self? When we kill the killer, it is at bottom, fear pitted against fear. Love, freedom, have nothing to do with that transaction.

The same is true of Israel's attack on the Palestinians. National ego is asserting itself against national self. And I would say the same of our efforts to retain some control over the Panama Canal, and Mr. Carter's sabre rattling on Friday.

"Would that even now you knew the things that make for peace." Security, whether individual or national, rests on justice and faith. One of the great Jews of this city wrote recently: "How can we talk of human rights and ignore them for Palestinian Arabs? How can Israel talk of a Jewish right to a homeland and deny one to the Palestinians? How can there be peace without some measure of justice? And of our own government, we have to ask not only how can we abolish weapons when we continue to rely on them for security?" We have also to ask, "How in the name of justice can we ask weaker nations to abstain from developing nuclear weapons without pledging to them our willingness to surrender our own?"

But finally security rests on faith: "A mighty fortress is our God." Finally there is no security in this world. That's a statement the self can accept, but never the ego.

I suppose on this Palm Sunday there are probably as many conflicting views of Christ as there were on that first Palm Sunday. So, let me urge you not to throw away the symbols of peace, the palms the children put in your hands. We have future plans for those palms. But this Holy Week, put them in some prominent place, spend a few minutes every day looking at your palm. Ask yourself, "For what kind of a King do I wave this symbol of peace? Is my self large enough and my ego small enough to follow him into a city of violence? What are the things that make for peace?"

And now as a special gesture of peace, may I ask you all to rise, to take one another's hand, as I read the prayer of St. Francis.

> Oh Lord, make me an instrument of your peace;
> Where there is hatred, let me sow love,
> Where there is injury, pardon,
> Where there is doubt, faith,

Where there is despair, hope,
Where there is darkness, light,
And where there is sadness, joy.
Oh, divine Master, grant that I may not so much seek
to be consoled, as to console;
to be understood, as to understand;
to be loved, as to love;
for it is in giving that we receive,
it is in pardoning that we are pardoned,
and it is in dying that we are born to eternal life. Amen.

Our Resurrection, Too

MARCH 26, 1978

I am sure this freezing morning that none of us need the reminder found in Haydn's *Seasons*: "As yet the year is unconfirmed, and oft-returning winter blast the bud and bloom destroy." But never mind, April is on its way. Soon the robins will join the pigeons, the branches will bud, the sky will be filled with the thunder of the sun. Soon overhead, underfoot, and all around we shall see, hear, feel the juice and joy of spring.

But suppose for a moment we knew that April would never arrive. For one terrible moment, pretend that somehow the earth had swung out of orbit and was headed toward the immensities of space, there to be gripped forever in the cold of winter. That, according to St. Paul, would be a fair presentation of the human world without Easter. "For if Christ has not been raised, your faith is futile and you are still in your sin; those who have fallen asleep in Christ have perished" (1 Cor. 15:17–18). No doubt about it: St. Paul puts all his eggs in one Easter basket.

And rightly so. For Christianity is a religion of resurrection, and we shall have to talk about the resurrection event, the empty tomb. But not 'til later, for it is a common and tragic mistake to view Easter in too narrow, too individualistic a light. St. Paul makes it abundantly clear that Easter is concerned essentially not with one man's escape from the grave, but with a cosmic victory of seemingly powerless love over loveless power. The lamp of the resurrection doesn't swing over some narrow, empty grave, but rather over the thick darkness covering the whole earth.

On Good Friday the darkness was all but complete, the message clear: fear and hatred kill. And let us not be sentimental; ours is still a Good Friday world. Goodness incarnate stretched out on a cross bequeathing its spirit to the oncoming night is still an apt symbol for a century that has planted more senseless crosses than any other in history, and for a nation which recently planted more than its fair share of such crosses. Today as then we are fearful of living as we are of dying, that is, of thinking boldly, caring deeply, and loving passionately. And when we see someone who is truly alive our instinct is not to emulate his life but to take it from him. Never would we have crucified the best among us had we not first crucified the best within us.

But by the light of Easter morn we read through the darkness a "yes, but" kind of message. Yes, hate kills, but love ultimately never dies, never dies with God, never even with us. Love is stronger than death. So the Easter message says essentially that all that tenderness and strength, all that beauty and goodness that on Good Friday we saw scourged, buffeted, and stretched out on a cross, all that goodness incarnate is once again alive. "And lo, I am with you always til the close of the age." Until all eternity Christ will be alive, now in the form of a Holy Spirit trying not only to bring about our resurrection but through us, to assail and overpower all the demonic forces that corrupt life and bring ruin to the earth. That's why Easter is so decisive an event.

"If Christ has not been raised, your faith is futile." If it's only a Good Friday world, then truth will forever be on the scaffold, wrong forever on the throne. College students, go ahead, take your law boards, play it safe. Christians, retreat from the giant issues of the day into the pygmy world of private piety.

But, says St. Paul, Christ *has* been raised from the dead. Some of you will say, "Well, can you prove it?" To which I am happy to respond, God will never supply evidence to help us make intelligently selfish decisions. In this case it's proof or freedom; the choice for Christ is a free, not a selfish one.

But if the resurrection cannot be proved, it can be known, experienced, and it can be trusted. Faith anyhow is not believing without proof; it's trusting without reservation. The resurrection faith is a willingness on the basis of all that we have heard, all that we have observed, all that we have thought deeply about, and experienced at a level far deeper than the mind ever comprehends—faith is a willingness to risk our lives on the conviction that while we human beings kill God's love we can never keep it dead and buried. Jesus Christ is risen, today, tomorrow, every day.

There is nothing sentimental about Easter. Resurrection is a demand as well as a promise. Picture, if you will, the disciples shortly after Good Friday. Surely they were grief stricken. But doubtlessly, too, they were experiencing that sense of relief that comes with resignation from the struggle. "Well, we tried hard, but the Establishment was too powerful. He wasn't elected King. So it's back to fishing, to business as usual." And then comes the word, "He's back."

"Oh no, not again."

Easter is a demand not for sympathy with the crucified Christ, but a demand for loyalty to the resurrected one. It is a travesty that so often Christians show sympathy for their crucified Christ and at the same time continued loyalty to the institutions that crucified Him. Easter, then, is the day to break that loyalty, to say there can be no sympathy without a changed loyalty. The new loyalty must be that of Peter after Jesus' death, the loyalty that made him ten times the person he was before; the same loyalty that made Stephen under the rain of death-dealing stones cry out, Christlike, "Father, forgive"; the loyalty of other martyrs who with their blood watered the seed of the church until it became the acorn that broke the mighty boulder that was the Roman Empire.

There used to be an annual sunrise service on the rim of the Grand Canyon. As the scripture line was read from Matthew, "And an angel of the Lord descended from heaven and came and rolled back the stone," a giant boulder was heaved over the rim. As it went crashing down the side of the Canyon, thousands of feet below into the Colorado River, a two-thousand voice choir burst into the "Hallelujah Chorus." Too dramatic? Not if St. Paul is correct: we live in an Easter, not a Good Friday world.

But let's move on. The second consequence Paul draws from the resurrection is that we are no longer tied to our sin. I am sure you have all heard of, and many of you have probably read the best seller *I'm OK, You're OK*. Well, one day there is going to be another best seller: *I'm not OK, and You're not OK and That's OK*. Human beings are never finished products. And we are not perfected because we are not perfectible. Those who think we are simply show how little they have ever tried to live out their convictions. It's healthy, it's a sign of freedom to feel guilt about our failures as parents, or as children, or as inhabitants of this city, or as citizens of our nation and world. The only thing that is unhealthy is our failure to believe that there is more mercy in God than sin in us. "Father, forgive them for they know not what they do." That same forgiveness is alive and well today. So let us not live as sinners, but as forgiven sinners, and what a world of difference there is.

Now we can live gratefully, joyfully, not as permanently defeated folk whose contrition has drained all the joy out of their hearts, not to mention the iron out of their spines. So let us give that boulder in the Grand Canyon a second meaning. Let it stand for the burden of guilt which, in Bunyan's *Pilgrim's Progress*, Christian carries on his breaking back up the hill until at last he reaches the cross. There it falls off, and rolls down the hill faster and faster until it disappears into the empty tomb.

And now perhaps we can deal with the empty tomb, the resurrection event. As I am sure many of you know, St. Paul was the earliest New Testament writer. And it is clear that his resurrection faith, like the faith of the disciples, was not based on the negative argument of an empty tomb, but on the positive conviction that the Lord had appeared to him. It is also clear that Christ's appearances were not those of a resurrected corpse, but much more akin to intense visionary experiences.

The apostles after Jesus' death were ten times the people they were before; that's irrefutable. It was in response to their enthusiasm that the opposition organized; and it was in response to the opposition, so many scholars believe, that the doctrine of the empty tomb arose, as a consequence not a cause of the Easter faith. The last chapter of Matthew may be literally true—I don't want to dispute it—but don't let it hang you up indefinitely. The chances are it is an expression of faith rather than a basis of faith.

Convinced by his appearances that Jesus was a living Lord, the disciples had really only one category in which to articulate this conviction, and that is the doctrine of the resurrection of the dead. To Paul, the events of the last days had been anticipated, and God by a mighty act had raised Jesus from the dead. To Paul, the living Christ and the Holy Spirit are never differentiated so that when he says, "Not I, but Christ who dwells within me," he is talking about the same Holy Spirit that you and I can experience. I myself believe passionately in the resurrection of Jesus Christ because in my own life I have experienced Christ as a presence, not as a memory. So today on Easter, we gather not to close the show with Bob Hope's "Thanks for the Memory," but rather to reopen the show because "Jesus Christ is risen today. Alleluia."

There remains only to say a word about the third consequence Paul draws from the resurrection. "If Christ has not been raised then those also who have fallen asleep in Christ have perished. If only in this life have we hope in Christ, we are of all people most to be pitied." What then are we to say of those who now "rest from their labor"? What are we to say as we anticipate our own death?

The Bible is at pains to point out that all life comes to an end. But the Bible also says that not only is God in this world; the world is in God. "He's got the whole world in His hands," which means that our lives run "from God, in God, to God again. Alleluia." Life is eternal, and love is immortal, and death is only a horizon, and a horizon is nothing save the limit of our sight. We do not know what lies beyond, but we do know *who* is beyond the grave. And Christ resurrected links the two worlds, telling us that we really live only in one. Actually, as St. Paul sees it, if spiritually speaking we now die to ourselves and are resurrected in Christ, before us lies only a physical counterpart to this death. And physical death need not be a lifelong terror if fear of the unknown, fear of final condemnation—these fears lie not before us but behind us. Then we can say with that marvelous freedom of St. Paul, "Whether we live, or whether we die, we are the Lord's." "Death, where is thy sting? Grave, where is thy victory? Thanks be to God who givest us the victory through our Lord, Jesus Christ."

He is risen. He is risen, indeed. And so hopefully are we, for did we not sing "Made like him, like him we rise. Ours the cross, the grave, the skies"? So, "Bloom, frozen Christian. April stands before thy door."

Whether We Live or Whether We Die

APRIL 9, 1978
Reading: 2 Corinthians 4

At the end of the Easter sermon, I had the distinct and unhappy impression that I had treated death solely as an enemy. To be sure, "Death where is thy sting; grave where thy victory?"—these defiant words of St. Paul imply that death is a threat. But elsewhere Paul speaks differently. Remember what we just heard: "For this slight momentary affliction is preparing for us an eternal weight of glory beyond all comparison." In the first chapter of Philippians he writes, "My desire is to depart to be with Christ, for that is far better" (v. 23). And in the fourteenth chapter of Romans we read "No one lives to himself alone and no one dies to himself alone. If we live, we live unto the Lord, and if we die, we die unto the Lord. So, whether we live or whether we die, we are the Lord's" (vv. 7–8). These words imply what certainly is true, that death is not the enemy we generally make it out to be.

Often in hospitals, outside the operating room, I have heard surgeons say as they emerge, "We lost her." But did they have her to lose? Back in the '50s Joe McCarthy used to say, "We lost China" as if China had ever been ours to lose. Doctors, be of good cheer. If you don't kill us, you don't fail us. It is enough that you do your best. Our lives are not yours to lose, for "whether we live or whether we die, we are the Lord's."

Death is far more friend than foe. Suppose we lived forever; we wouldn't live at all. I could imagine my taking two hundred years to decide whether or not to come to Riverside. I can imagine every Trustees' meeting lasting at least a month. When you stop to think of it, without death, life would be interminable! Like that little bit of Ireland a Spanish priest once told me about. It reminded him of home, so de-accelerated was the pace. He asked an Irish friend if in Gaelic there was an equivalent for "mañana." Answered the friend: "Oh, yes, we have several expressions like that, but none carry the same sense of urgency as mañana."

I have a private nightmare. We'll live for hundreds of years sitting in armchairs, hooked up to an Empire State building of extra kidneys and hearts and livers. No, no, it is part of the Good News that life is short. Death brings us to life. So let us address death as would St. Francis: "brother death," "sister death."

We can say more. As our common destiny, Sister Death enhances our life together. It is often said that death is a great equalizer. But let's be clear: death is an equalizer not because it makes us equal, but because death mocks all our pretensions to be anything else.

In this regard, death is like something else. "It is a good thing," writes Werner Pelz, "that the King has to take off his crown, that the bishop has to divest himself of his cope and mitre, when they go to bed with their wives. It is a good thing that the great general has to unpin his many decorations, and undo the many layers of glory, even before the slip of a girl that happens to be his mistress. . . . It is a good thing that even the very poor may sometimes take off their shabby clothes to offer themselves to each other in all the richness of any king or queen." Before the passion of a man or a woman, as before death, the distinctions of nationality, race, color, ideology become known as the futile and artificial things they finally are.

Death and desire both point to our ultimate human destiny which is complete and unreserved togetherness. The most beautiful cemeteries in the United States are Indian cemeteries and Moravian cemeteries. I remember years ago in Bethlehem, Pa., at day's end, late in the fall when the leaves were falling, much like in the last act of Cyrano, walking through a Moravian cemetery. I could see all the way across it, because all the tombstones were flat. No pyramids to individual egos there. And when I started to read the names, I found Mr. Schmidt in one row, and Mrs. Schmidt two rows back. When I asked, it was explained, "Oh, yes. When you die you are buried next to the person who died before you." What a way to be buried. What a way to live!

So, thanks be once again to God, who gives us Sister Death to remind us that in life, as in death, we all have more in common than in conflict.

But now let us turn to matters more complicated. Death is also an enemy, but one that can be befriended. In the twelfth chapter of John we find Christ's words, "Truly, truly I say to you, unless a grain of wheat falls into the earth and dies, it remains alone. But if it dies, it bears much fruit" (v. 24). Christ never urged anyone to die, but rather to live; but to live for something worth dying for, and to die for it if necessary. Certainly that is the complete story of His life, and the most important part of the life of every martyr from Socrates to Martin Luther King Jr.

Try for a moment to imagine how impoverished our lives would be were there no cause worth dying for, or had no one died for such a cause. (Perhaps for the latter to obtain, we would all have to be less sinful, which would be all right.) But the point is this: until by the grace of God we are sinless, where in the world are we poor sinners going to derive inspiration and strength to contend against our sin, and the sin of the world, if not from the deaths of the likes of Martin Luther King Jr.? What makes this springtime so hard to bear is not the remembrance that ten years ago they shot Martin Luther King and Bobby Kennedy. It's that our lives are not bearing the fruits of their deaths. We are sorry for their deaths, but we are not loyal to their lives. We say we loved them, but we fear to be like them. If we consider the last part of Bobby's life—his days in rural Mississippi, South Africa, his time with Cesar Chavez—we can say of him, as we can of King, "they fought for the poor"; surely a cause worth dying for. But instead of carrying on the struggle, we are seizing their crosses by the other end, turning crosses into swords, and attacking the very people they sought to protect.

Were we loyal to King and Kennedy, not to mention God Himself, the cry today would be "Jobs, not jail." But it's "jail, not jobs." Capital punishment, crime on the streets—once again these are becoming the big electoral issues. Do you realize that we citizens of the richest nation in the world lock up more people per capita than any other industrialized nation in the world, including South Africa? Did you know that the people of Lake Placid could get federal funds for the Olympic Games only by agreeing to allow the Olympic Village that will house the athletes of the world to be turned into a federal prison the moment the athletes depart? From symbol of peace to Gulag! The people of Lake Placid accepted the deal because they were assured five hundred recession-proof jobs. And you can be sure the majority of the inmates will be our people, blacks and other minorities from New York City. Once again, urban minorities will be guarded by rural whites; another Attica in the making.

The seeds of discord, the roots of crime, lie in the very inequalities we promote in defiance of the great equalizer death. We lock people up largely because we are scared to death of death. That's why we have to befriend the enemy. Of course, we should be scared of crime, but scared to life, to the realization of "jobs, not jails." And until such time as we deal with the true seeds of crime, we must not panic. Whether we live, or whether we die, whether we are mugged or whether we are not mugged, whether we are robbed or not robbed, yes, whether we are raped or whether we are not raped, we are the Lord's. King died that our fear of death would be decreased, not increased.

I hope we can learn, in this violent city, to befriend death. For only when death is befriended does life become human.

I said that death brings us to life, and as our common lot it enhances our life together. Let me finally say a word about how death affects our life with God. It is a strange thing that those closest to God, those who most intensely feel His presence in every place and moment, these devout people feel the best is still ahead. So Bach writes one of his most beautiful arias, "Come, sweet death." And a black slave writes, "I looked over Jordan and what did I see? a band of angels coming after me, coming for to carry me home." "My desire is to depart and be with Christ, for that is far better."

I'll tell you what Heaven is going to be like. A Dutch theologian once told me. His name is Henri Nouwen. He told me that every time his airplane landed in some airport, he had a fantasy that there would be a voice in the crowd saying "Hey, Henry." There would be some-body who knew him. Each time he would wait for the voice and each time he would be disappointed. But then he would say to himself, "It's all right. When I get home my friends will be there." Nevertheless, the fantasy persisted. Every time he landed at a new airport, he would wait for the "Hey, Henry." Each time he'd be disappointed, but then he would remember that when he got home his friends would be there. "So," said Henry, "Heaven is going to be like that. God will be there, and he will say 'Hey, Henry, how was it? Let's see your slides.'"

"No one lives to himself alone and no one dies to himself alone. If we live, we live unto the Lord, and if we die, we die unto the Lord. So, whether we live or whether we die, we are the Lord's" (Rom. 14:7–8). That understanding allows us to befriend death. And fundamentally, we can embrace death as a brother or sister. Then we can be about the all-important task of finding things worth living for that are also worth dying for.

Nature and Nature's God

APRIL 30, 1978

This sermon is about ecology, the church and the university and owes a great debt of thanks to Theodore Roszak's *Where the Wasteland Ends*.

To get us started, let us take as a text these mystifying verses from the thirty-first chapter of the book of the prophet Jeremiah:

> Thus says the LORD
> who gives the sun for light by day
>   and the fixed order of the moon
>   and the stars for light by night,
> who stirs up the sea so that its waves roar—
>   the LORD of Hosts is His name:
> "If this fixed order departs
>   from before me, says the LORD,
> then shall the descendants of Israel cease
>   from being a nation before me for ever."
> Thus says the LORD:
> "If the heavens above can be measured,
>   and the foundations of the earth below can be
>   explored,
> then I will cast off all the descendants of Israel
>   for all that they have done,"
> says the LORD.

Once upon a time the university and church were wed. Then they were divorced, the university pleading mental cruelty. And the university was right. Not the great theologians, nor the great musicians, nor the great artists, but the little inquisitors of Europe, and the little inquisitors of Puritan America were diminishing and deadening life. They were guilty of what psychiatrists call in a nice phrase, "premature closure." They wanted order, but at the expense of splendor. They wanted to help, but like most people in power they would rather be responsible for, than responsive to the people they wanted to help. Most of all, I think they wanted control.

No wonder then that Newton and Galileo and Francis Bacon cried out "more room." These first scientists of the Enlightenment and their philosophic champions were not atheists, they weren't even anti-ecclesiastical. And they were not, in idolatrous fashion, worshiping their new-found scientific methodology. On the contrary, the new methodology was to serve ancient and high purposes—to combat ignorance and superstition, to release the bottled up genie of imaginative human energy. Bacon, I imagine, would have agreed with the later philosopher Renan: "The main contribution of science will be to deliver us from superstition, not to reveal ultimate truth."

All these strains, we can catch, in the preface to the second edition of Newton's great *Principia Mathematica*, written by Robert Coates. "The gates are now set open, and by the passage Newton has revealed we may freely enter into the hidden secrets and wonders of natural things. . . . Therefore, we may now more nearly behold the beauties of Nature, and entertain ourselves with the delightful contemplation; and, which is the best and most valuable fruit of philosophy, be thence incited the more profoundly to reverence and adore the great Maker and Lord of all. He must be blind who from the wisest and most excellent contrivances of things cannot see the infinite wisdom and goodness of their almighty Creator, and he must be mad and senseless who refuses to acknowledge them."

Mr. Coates, I imagine, would find a lot of us mad and senseless. But let us not denounce the godless, but rather ask, "Where has all the grandeur gone?" Why is it that the descendants of the Enlightenment seem to be walking in gross darkness? Why is it that students are still deeply alienated? Could it be that the University is now diminishing and deadening life, bottling up the genie of imaginative energies, putting on all of us what Blake once called "mind-forged manacles"?

I think we can trace an important progression from the Enlightenment to now. Newton, Galileo and Bacon did not separate Nature from Nature's God. But their successors quickly divorced them, and the divorce left Nature without any animating purpose. Nature still held its beauty, but the greedy eyes of human beings focussed more on the riches in the warehouse than the beauty in the shop. "We shall become the masters and possessors of Nature," said Descartes. So a qualitative view of Nature gradually gave way to a quantitative view. Nature was seen as neutral, essentially a machine. And a machine has no purpose, only a function. It was obvious that Nature's function was to serve us human beings, the only purposeful creatures around. So over the centuries, as Descartes had predicted, we have become powerful, mastering and possessing Nature.

But the price of power is always communion. (That's why love is self-restricting when it comes to power.) If, for instance, you want to dominate natives, as in colonialism, you cannot communicate with them. If you want to dominate emotions, as in Victorianism, you cannot communicate with your emotions. In other words, if to know means to dominate and to objectify, then the very act of knowing becomes an act of alienation. That's why there is so little humility in the academic world, and so little love in this kind of knowledge. And imagination and vision are rarely called upon. (Let us remember that love is not blind but visionary.)

So e.e. cummings wrote

> I would rather learn from one bird how to sing
> Than teach ten thousand stars how not to dance.

So William Blake vigorously opposed what he called the "single vision" of scientific methodology, and wrote on the title page of *Vala* these words of St. Paul: "For we contend not with flesh and blood, but with dominion and authority, with the world ruling powers of this dark age, with the spirit of evil in heavenly places" (Eph. 6:12).

Blake foresaw that scientific methodology, once a servant at the service of loving masters, would become a loveless master, a "world-ruling power in this dark age." Blake was prophetic, for the scientific method has won us over, lock, stock, and barrel, to its conception of truth. Do you want to know what's real? It's what's objectively real. Do you want to know how this butterfly works? Tear the wings off. Analyze the parts. Get down to the hard facts.

Of course, there are still some good old human values lying around, but they are worn like a faded flower in the lapel of hard facts. So the progression from the Enlightenment to this day goes like this: once the stars were seen as parts of a machine it was only a step—a psychological step—to view animals as machines, as did

Descartes; then to view human society as a machine, as did Hobbes; to view the human body as a machine, as did La Mettrie; to view human behavior as machine-like, as did Pavlov, Watson, and most recently and notoriously Professor Skinner. And need we add that if you can objectify and depersonalize human beings under a microscope, you can do it the more easily under a bombsight.

Charles Gillespie said, "The scientific act of knowing is an act of alienation." It seems to me that as long as political scientists and sociologists and philosophers and literary critics, yes even teachers of the faith—as long as all these non-scientists take their standard of intellectual respectability primarily from the sciences, as long as they believe that the objective route is the only respectable access to reality, then every act of knowing will be an act of alienation. The more we objectify knowledge, the more, as Roszak says, "We force experience out and away from our personal grip."

Let me make a mean remark just to be provocative. Most professors don't want to visit the place, they'd rather read the map. It is not the experience that's real, it's the explanation of the experience.

So from whence come the mind-forged manacles of today? From the drive to objectify, to depersonalize, which stems, once again, from premature closure. Again it is the drive for order at the sake of splendor. We are contending with a "more objective than thou complex," and I say "complex" advisedly, for the objective mode of consciousness pushed to the extreme is a psychological rather than an epistemological stance. The objective mode of consciousness has more to do with a way of feeling—or of not feeling—than with a way of knowing. To be "tough-minded" spares us the vulnerability that comes of being tender-hearted. It allows us the more easily to master, to dominate, to control—and deem unimportant what cannot be mastered, dominated, and controlled.

Where the churches were once the great promoters of petty orthodoxy, now it is the universities. Knowledge for power at the expense of love and humility. (Where does the heart go to school in higher education?)

It is small wonder then that so many students feel that under the academic hand life has been diminished and deadened. For to view life impersonally is to see life that is shallow, inexperienced, academic; and in this way of looking there is finally more blindness than seeing.

"Circumcise yourselves to the LORD and take away the foreskins of your hearts," says Jeremiah (4:4). The Bible does not enjoin us to be tender-minded, but it does insist that we be tender-hearted. The Bible does not claim that faith is a substitute for thought. It insists that faith is what makes good thinking possible—something the Roman Catholic Church recognized when it made the first cardinal virtue *prudentia*, which basically means good thinking.

But back to the text now, which is perhaps beginning to make more sense. "Thus says the LORD who gives the sun for light by day and the fixed order of the moon and the stars for light by night . . . If this fixed order departs from me then shall the descendants of Israel cease from being a nation . . . If the heavens above can be measured, and the foundations of the earth below can be explored, then I will cast off all the descendants of Israel for all that they have done."

In a last ditch effort to save the world from complete depersonalization, most secular humanists today set up two cultures—one for things and one for persons. According to this scheme things can be known rationally, but human beings cannot. Human beings cannot be objectified and dissected without being destroyed. Human beings are a mystery and hence our deepest knowledge of human beings comes through communion. Communion is possible for there is something in each of us that we can recognize in our neighbors.

Good luck! For as Theodore Roszak for one points out, while the intention is noble, "it is apt to cut no ice with the hardnosed behaviorists who will wonder why this particular conglomeration of molecules and atoms and electrochemical circuitry called a human being should indeed be regarded as different, special, unique."

Therefore, instead of trying to defend against the encroachments of the objective mode, what about trying to expand the area of subjectivity, to expand the mode of subjective consciousness? Suppose for a moment that we might find some mysterious deep kinship not only with each other, but with animals and flowers, with all of Nature? Suppose we were to re-wed Nature to Nature's God?

It is at this point ecologists have made their most profound contributions. For while some ecologists are merely asking for caution, lest we exhaust our natural resources and kill ourselves in the process, others are asking for reverence. And why reverence? Because Nature has animating purposes of its own.

How threatening to many academics these ecologists are one can quickly pick up. Here's a paragraph on ecology in the latest Encyclopedia Britannica:

> The wholistic emphasis implied by the very idea of
> human ecology has been a continual threat to the
> unity of the discipline. Comprehensive treatises on
> the subject typically represented expressions of

social philosophy rather than empirically grounded statements of scientific theory. Indeed, numerous commentators have put forth the view that human ecology must remain a philosophic view point rather than aspire to the status of a systematic discipline.

Catch that "aspire to the status"!

Now let me read you another statement on ecology: "Among the Iroquois the bear was highly esteemed. When the hunted bear was confronted, the kill was preceded by a long monologue in which the needs of the hunter were fully explained, and assurances were given that the killing was motivated by need and not by a wish to dishonor." (It is a bit difficult to picture the bear waiting around all this time, but what's being said is very important and very beautiful!) "The hunter who believes that all matter and actions are sacramental and consequential will bring deference and understanding to his relations with the environments. He will achieve a steady state with his environment; he will live in harmony with Nature and survive because of it" (Ian McHarg).

Now I think we can understand the text. Jeremiah is telling us that once Nature is separated from Nature's God, the whole human structure will begin to collapse. Perhaps this is a word not only ecologists but the Church might gently whisper to the University. Certainly if we wish to know not only more, but to know deeper, we shall need more love and humility and communion. And I dare say it might even be more fun to "learn from one bird how to sing than to teach ten thousand stars how not to dance."

Amen.

A Certain Man Had Two Sons

MAY 7, 1978

The word of the Lord hits the world with the force of a hint. Could anything be more frustrating? We want God to be God; but He wants to be a still small voice, a babe in a manger. We want God to be all-powerful, so that we can be weak and dependent; but He wants to be all-loving, so that we can be strong. We want God to prove His existence; but He wants us to prove our freedom, to be able to act wholeheartedly without absolute certainty. "God is love" means God is known devotionally, not dogmatically. So the word of the Lord has to hit the world with the force only of a hint.

The story of the prodigal son is a parable about all this, about an all-loving father who precisely because he is all-loving has to restrict his power, for love is self-restricting when it comes to power. As the story has a happy ending we cheer the father. But suppose the boy had gotten knifed in a brothel, had died of hunger; or, on the contrary, had become a powerful ruler dictating the deaths of hundreds of his fellow citizens. Wouldn't we then have complained! "How could you let it happen?"

But that's the risk. The father could have said "nix" to any dividing of any estate, and kept the boy at home. But he could not have kept him filial. God, I suppose, could keep us all "at home," in the brute calm of servitude. But because love is the name of the game, he releases us into the storms of freedom, and then stands on the road trembling with concern.

Now a parable, as opposed to an allegory, seeks to make only one point. But this story is so rich it is hard—no, it's impossible—to leave it alone after it has made its one point about a father whose caring never ceases. For instance, it is clear that the older brother could no more handle his freedom than could the younger son. The story is really of two journeys, for the older son ends up as distant in spirit from his father as did his brother. Why, we can only speculate, but this much we know: the older brother's brand of moralism and legalism— "I never once disobeyed your orders . . . this son of yours" (notice he doesn't say "my brother")—this brand of moralism and legalism is almost always born in anxiety and nourished in more of the same.

Maybe he envied his younger brother's easy good looks, high spirits, and, feeling inferior, projected that the father's love for him must be inferior, too. In any case, instead of trusting his father's love and becoming himself loving, he seeks instead to become virtuous—"I never disobeyed your orders," "I slaved for you all these years." And we can state categorically, that he who seeks virtue no longer seeks God or his neighbor. For the search for virtue is too self-enclosing, too self-seeking, too self-justifying to be loving. We catch this at the end of the story. While the father sees the boy from afar, the older brother sees him from above. The father wants him restored, the older brother wants him punished. The father seeks what is good in the situation and tries to develop it, the older brother has clearly decided about what is evil in this world, so that he will not have to come to grips with what is really good.

I think the older brother beautifully reflects something in all of us, the portion of our nature that seeks to develop an ethic rooted not in wickedness but in virtue, but in virtue not in love. Like the older brother we do not trust the love of a loving father. So instead of expressing ourselves in love, we try to prove ourselves in virtue. And of course we can only prove ourselves by "disproving" someone else, for pride is not accidentally but essentially competitive.

And reflections of the older brother are everywhere to be seen in our country. We see him in the Anita Bryants, the Woman's Christian Temperance Union, in "law and order" people, in foreign policy officials, in "leading citizens," clergy and "pillars of the church," in short, wherever people see themselves as islands of virtue in a sea of wickedness.

"*All* have sinned and fallen short," says St. Paul. We are flawed, all of us, and when we're honest we know that is true, which is why from one another we need so little judgment and so much love. It is often said, disparagingly, that the church is a crutch. Of course the church is a crutch. What makes you think you don't limp?

Those who think of themselves as virtuous are like giraffes, lofty up front, but dragging a bit behind.

There's something else. Berdyaev once wrote of his fellow Russian: "There is something demonic in Tolstoy's moralism,"—this was after Tolstoy's conversion—"something that would destroy all the richness of life." Maybe it was the hypocrisy and suffocating moralism of the older brother that finally drove the younger one away; much as the virtuous portion of our own nature constricts the freedom loving portion. For we love our freedom and the richness of this world. We don't want to deny either. Like trees and flowers we want to bloom. Behind the bars of our ribs there is a bird waiting to burst into song. In the heart of every one of us there's someone who wants to dance naked in the sun, grow like corn in the rain. So inevitably, from time to time, we feel we must take leave of our virtuous self in order to seek our freedom.

But the freedom we seek is often merely anti-establishment, anti-virtue; a freedom from, not a freedom for. Basically it's aimless. And while aimless freedom is admittedly heady and exhilarating, it quickly becomes decadent, as we see in this story and can hear in these words of Theodore Roethke:

> Deliver me from myself:
> My journeys are all the same, Father,
> I can't find my life

I'm lost in my name
I must be more than what I see. O Jesus,
Save this roaring boy riding the devil's blast.

It's a bit too simple to put it this way, but I think basically it's true: in each of us dwell the older brother *and* the younger brother, just as both live in our land in the form of a rather moralistic establishment and a rather chaotic anti-establishment. And what is needed, within and without, is not only that they should confront each other, but that they should confront a reconciling father.

An individual is not one who separates himself from others. An individual is one undivided within. Isn't that what we see in Jesus in such compelling form? From the outer periphery to the inner core and back again, he's all of a piece. And had anyone asked him, "Jesus, do you consider yourself part of the establishment or part of the anti-establishment?" he probably would not have recognized the question because he never recognized the authority of the establishment in the first place. To Jesus, truth was his authority, not some authority his truth. And because his truth was a love transcending earthly divisions he was able to heal them. Remember how with equal freedom he ministered to Nicodemus and Mary Magdalene.

So, today, why don't we let the still small voice of reconciliation reach deep inside each of us? To the virtuous portion of our nature God is saying, "Why so tense? You are all right. My love doesn't seek value; it creates it. You don't have to prove yourself; I've taken care of all of that. You have only to express yourself." What a world of difference there is between proving ourselves and expressing ourselves!

Then to the wayward portion God says: "Though your sins are as scarlet they shall be white as snow. You are forgiven, your value has been restored, and because your life is valuable, don't throw it away."

Freedom is given not that we should throw but give our lives away, and for the same high purpose for which Christ gave his. Christ will not ascend on high on this Ascension Sunday unless we hear deep in our hearts, "This is my body broken for you"—broken that you might be united, you with yourself, you with everyone else in this world.

And so let our prayer be to our Lord:

O Jesus, save these warring boys;
warring within, warring without. Confound
the virtuous and save the wayward by filling
the hollow in the heart where love should be.
In thy name we pray. Amen.

Fire or Fire

S ome people believe that Mother's Day is a conspiracy of the greeting card people. They just might be right. But whatever its origins, the fact that Mother's Day has become a national institution
proves that "time cannot wither nor custom stale" the veneration in
which we hold our mothers and their great wisdom in bringing us
into the world! So, on this your nationally designated day, gentle
women, we salute you. May the Lord bless you. May you forgive us
our myriad failures. Enjoy our better portions and remember that
gratitude for all that you have done for us expresses itself mostly in
all the things we try to do for our children.

As with Mother's Day, so with the day of Pentecost. If its origins
too are shadowy, its persistence as an important day in the church cal-
endar is even more impressive. If you ask what happened, what really
happened, the answer I imagine is, "Who knows?" We cannot pretend
to a degree of precision to which the story itself doesn't admit. But,
finally, who cares? For this is a story about the spirit that giveth life,
and not about the letter that killeth. Like the singing of the choir
or the rolling of the organ, the outpouring of the Holy Spirit can
be experienced on levels far deeper than the mind can comprehend.
This much we can say: that the disciples who since the crucifixion
had been waiting and watching, now began to be moved and used by
God. In some mysterious way they were transformed. To observers
there was fire in the air that day, and fever in the blood of Peter and
Andrew and John and all the other disciples, and also women, including Mary the mother of Jesus. In fact, so great was the outpouring of
the Holy Spirit, so hot and fast was the rush of words, that many
thought them drunk. Then the tower of Babel itself was overturned,
as the disciples began to speak in tongues of devout people from
every nation under heaven.

The Spirit is potent stuff—more Dionysian than Apollonian. So
this is not a day to embrace the calm of the emotionless stoic, not a
day to starve our dreams and deny our hopes. Rather this is a day for
hot love and living hope, burning honesty, a day for enthusiasm which
quite literally means "in God." In short this is a day to release impulses
as creative and varied as the Biblical imagery is wild.

Several years ago, when Ted Fiske switched from Religion Editor
to the Education Desk of *The New York Times*, I had the temerity to

write James Reston, suggesting a small committee of Jews, Catholics, and Protestants to help the *Times* select a new Religion Editor. To my surprise, Mr. Reston replied that he couldn't understand Mr. Fiske's decision. "I used to think," he wrote, "that education was our best hope. Now I am inclined to think that if we are going to be rescued from the flames of impending destruction, we had better look more to the religions of the world."

It was not that Mr. Reston was being anti-intellectual. He had simply reached the conclusion, I imagine, that a rational mind is no match for an irrational will; also that what needs most to be cleansed are not errors of the mind so much as impurities of the heart. Even the most intellectual poet of our time talked of sin as well as error, and insisted that the flames of impending destruction can only be fought with the Pentecostal fire of the Holy Spirit.

> The dove descending breaks the air
> With flame of incandescent terror
> Of which the tongues declare
> The one discharge from sin and error.
> The only hope, or else despair
>   Lies in the choice of pyre or pyre—
>   To be redeemed from fire by fire.
>   T. S. Eliot

But how many of us Christians would Mr. Reston or Mr. T. S. Eliot consider aflame with faith? The trouble with the church is that too many Christians mean well feebly. They believe that to do evil in this world you have to be some kind of a Bengal tiger, when in fact it's enough to be a tame tabby, a nicely packaged citizen, safe, polite, obedient and sterile. St. Paul, who knew what the Holy Spirit was all about, enjoined the Ephesians, "Be angry, but do not sin." And Ernest Hemingway wrote of Francis Macomber, "He always had a great tolerance which seemed the nicest thing about him, if it were not the most sinister."

Tolerance is sinister when it reflects indifference; anger is good when it reflects concern. When you stop to think of it, our Lord and Savior was angry about fifty percent of the time: "Woe to you who neglect justice." "Woe to him by whom temptations come." "Woe to you, scribes, Pharisees, hypocrites." He never tolerated the intolerable. And, neither did Peter, when on that Pentecostal day, filled with the Holy Spirit, he cried out to his hearers, "Save yourselves from this crooked generation."

As the crooked has not yet been made straight, what should be our honest Christian feeling, when, for example, on entering this church we see posters announcing the special U.N. session on Disarmament and Development, and remember that the session was demanded by the non-aligned small nations of this world, insisting that there be "no annihilation without representation"? What should our feelings be when we remember that Defense in our country is a top-level, high-priority, well-staffed operation of senior Cabinet rank, while disarmament is a low-level, underbudgeted, understaffed invisible subdivision in the policy hierarchy? The Pentagon has over 1,000 fully paid full-time public information officers. The Arms Control and Disarmament Agency has five.

As Christians shouldn't we also feel angry with our National Council of Churches, which with a budget of some $15,000,000, has twice this year refused to appoint even a single person full-time for disarmament work? And, what about a city of Westways and giant office buildings and all the appurtenances of wealth that can't even find decent classrooms for Manhattan Community College? What about a culture that exploits rather than satisfies the wants of its people? a nation that is at once sex-saturated and sex-starved? Only, I believe, in America do people want sex at one and the same time to be stripped down, impersonal, clickety-click computer style, *and* so romantic that a Lord Byron would be all shook up. Sometimes I wonder if that Peter deVries character wasn't speaking for the entire USA when he said, "Way down deep in the depths of me I am pretty shallow."

The Holy Spirit is first of all a dis-comforter. Yes, God must afflict the comfortable before he can comfort the afflicted. "Save yourselves from this crooked generation." "Be angry . . .

". . . but do not sin." And there's the trick, isn't it? God hates sin only because He so loves us sinners. True, we must fight fire with fire, but only the healing fire of Pentecost can overcome the flames of impending destruction. For if there is one lesson we have learned and relearned, it is that while it is difficult to overcome evil with good, it is impossible to overcome evil with evil.

So, on this day of Pentecost, let me suggest two things. First, in our own personal lives, let us not fear the holy fire. Truth is error burnt up. Truth is only possible after our make-believe world is in ashes. Truth can reign only after the power of the Holy Spirit has overturned our beloved self-protecting lies, has rejected the secret flatterings of self-importance, has pulled the rug from under ambition's tower of blocks. Then let us seek to allow the Holy Spirit, in this church, to make of us a community of the power and magnitude of the one formed in Jerusalem on that first day of Pentecost. Banding together, let us say in one tongue, that the cruelty and indecency we see around us must have no place among us. And, when, as we must, we side with the oppressed against the oppressor, let us do so in the context of a struggle for a world in which there will be no master-slave relationships. When, as we must, we oppose our political and religious leaders, let us do so with the understanding that if by God's grace His Spirit is alive in us, it needs only liberation in them. Accepting the outpouring of the Holy Spirit, let us become twice as tough and twice as tender—as only the truly strong can be tender.

Eliot was right, the choice is clear: "We only live, only suspire / consumed by either fire or fire."

Warring Madness

MAY 21, 1978

In Browning's *The Ring and the Book*, Pompilia says of her friend, "Through such souls alone, God stooping shows sufficient of his light for us in the darkness to rise by."

It is marvelous that in every generation God raises up men and women with visions larger than their times. These are people who are for truth, no matter who tells it; for justice, no matter who's against it. Like God himself, they carry on a lover's quarrel with the world. It is not a grudge fight, mind you. If they are against evil it is only because they so love the good. And if they say the present situation smells to heaven, it is only because they hold such a bright view of the future. It is not surprising then that we should find that their knowledge still lights our path, their faith lives on in our hearts, and that their tasks have fallen to our hands.

One such person was Harry Emerson Fosdick. To that I can attest because I have read his sermons. But I envy those of you who heard them preached. Sermons are to be heard, rather than read. Preaching is "truth through personality," as Phillips Brooks once described it. I can imagine God's truth through Fosdick's personality Sunday by Sunday, deepening, stretching—sometimes painfully—always enlarging never diminishing the minds and hearts of his hearers. In fact, rereading this week some sermons, it struck me that Fosdick never entertained a diminishing thought or emotion. Oh, I suppose a few came to visit, but I'll bet he never invited them to dinner.

It is wonderful to have so many of you "Fosdick-members" with us today. But I doubt if even the most hoary-headed among you heard the sermon, "Shall The Fundamentalists Win?" This was the one that embroiled him first in public controversy, and it was delivered 56 years ago to the day, on May 21, 1922. It was an hour both delicate and dangerous for the church, and Fosdick rose to plead the cause of liberality and tolerance. He said:

> I would, if I could reach their ears, say to the funda-
> mentalists about the liberals, what Gamalial said to
> the Jews: "Refrain from these men and let them
> alone, for if this council or work be of men it will be
> overthrown, but if it be of God ye will not be able to
> overthrow them, lest haply ye be found even to be
> fighting against God."

Against the fundamentalists he stated his belief that "finality in the Bible is ahead. We have not reached it, we cannot yet compass all of it." And he ended, where he generally did, at the human crux of the matter:

> These last weeks in the minister's confessional, I
> have heard stories from the depths of human lives,
> where men and women were wrestling with the ele-
> mental problems of misery and sin; stories to put
> upon a man's heart a burden of vicarious sorrow
> even though he does but listen to them. Here was
> real human need, crying out after the living God
> revealed in Christ. Consider all the multitudes of
> men and women who so need God, and then think
> of Christian churches making of themselves a cock-
> pit of controversy, when there is not a single thing at
> stake in the controversy on which depends the salva-
> tion of human souls.
>   That is the trouble with this whole business. So
> much of it does not matter. But there is one thing
> that does matter more than anything else in the
> world, that people in their personal lives and in their
> social relationships should know Jesus Christ.

Fifty-six years later, we still have the intellectual problem, of how to incorporate the latest thinking into the old faith, or as Fosdick put it, "how to believe both in abiding stars and changing astronomies."

But more importantly, as then, so even now, we need to seek the grace of magnanimity, the ability to differ and yet love, for if we fail in love we fail in all things else. And it was Fosdick's insight to see the ethical perversion underneath the theological one.

Since coming to Riverside only last November, I have heard many wonderful tales about life in the '30s and '40s, and, in all candor, some not so wonderful. Wealth wielded a lot more influence in those days. Most of the blacks in the church apparently manned the elevators; yet there were more blacks in the congregation than women among the trustees, deacons, and ushers. And who knows, our membership might still be very much the same had not so many affluent whites in the 1950s been carried off into suburban captivity. (I still think the most enduring feature of the Eisenhower administration will be his federal highway building program.)

But let us not judge the past in terms of the present. In the '30s and '40s there was only one national civil rights organization, and that one founded for the advancement, not the equality of blacks. And I can remember when I first went to Yale in 1958, 13 years after Dr. Fosdick had retired, there were, in the entering Freshmen class at Yale, all of four black students. As for the women, they received the right to vote only fourteen years before the completion of this building.

Dr. Fosdick would find us poorer in things but richer in soul for the changes that have taken place. He would have been pleased this week to hear Bob Polk, the first black preacher of Riverside, say that he thought that Riverside Church today was probably the most important interracial voluntary association in the City. But let us thank Dr. Fosdick for preparing the way. Time and again he stated that racial discrimination was the most evil thing in the world. It was in response to the depression that he established the Arts and Crafts program here. And he worried about the church. "I fear," he once said, "for a church like this, where from the pulpit to the pew, we come from privileged backgrounds, when I remember how often in history the underdog has been right."

To honor the memory of so great a person we need some great undertaking. But before describing that undertaking, I want to read to you from another sermon. Bear in mind that only two days from now, the United Nations will convene its first special session on disarmament. This sermon is an Armistice Day sermon, one of the first Dr. Fosdick delivered in this church. It is entitled, "The Unknown Soldier." In it, Dr. Fosdick recalls his own role in World War I, and how war, in fact, does elicit the best in human beings.

They sent men like me into the camps to awaken his idealism, to touch those secret holy springs within him, so that with devotion, fidelity, loyalty, and self-sacrifice, he might go out to war. Oh, war, I hate you most of all for this: that you do lay your hands on the noblest elements in human character with which we might make a heaven on earth, and you use them to make a hell on earth instead. If war were fought simply with evil things like hate, it would be bad enough, but when one sees the deeds of war done with the loveliest faculties of the human spirit, he looks into the very pit of hell.

He ends up,

Oh, Church of Christ stay out of war, withdraw from every alliance that maintains or encourages it. It was not a pacifist, it was a field marshal, Earl Haig, who said "it is the business of the churches to make my business impossible." Oh, my soul, stay out of war. At any rate I will do my best to settle my account with the unknown soldier. I renounce war. I renounce war because of what it does to our own men. I have watched them come in gassed from the front line trenches. I have seen the long, long hospital trains filled with their mutilated bodies. I have heard the cries of the crazed and the prayers of those who wanted to die and could not; and I remember the maimed and ruined men for whom the war is not yet over. I renounce war because of what it compels us to do to our enemies, bombing their mothers and villages, starving their children by blockades, laughing over our coffee cups about every damnable thing we have been able to do to them. I renounce war for its consequences, for the lies it lives on and propagates, for the undying hatreds it arouses, for the dictatorships it puts in the place of democracies, for the starvation that stalks in its wake. I renounce war and never again, directly or indirectly, will I sanction or support another. Oh, unknown soldier, in penitent reparation, I make you that pledge.

Dr. Fosdick would be greatly heartened by the U.N. Special Session on Disarmament—as heartened, as he would be disheartened by the fact that neither President Carter nor Mr. Brezhnev plan to attend. He would also be disheartened by the fact that the only proposal the United States ever made since World War II for general disarmament—that was 1962—that proposal is today out of print. And he would be disheartened by the fact that not a single person in the United States government today is charged with the responsibility for thinking about how to end or to reverse the arms race. All they think about in Washington is arms control, which hasn't worked, and, more importantly, validates the arms which remain.

You don't have to be a pacifist, as was Dr. Fosdick, you can be as anticommunist as Senator Barry Goldwater; still you can be convinced that each escalation of the arms race provides less and not more security for the peoples of both the United States and the Soviet Union. There is no more military security in military might alone. When national military security has come to depend basically on the reliability with which we do *not* use nuclear weapons, then the "experts" are the experts on human nature.

We are courting disaster. If a nuclear holocaust takes place, not only will millions of innocent civilians here and in the Soviet Union and elsewhere be slain, the ozone layer will be affected, radiation will come through the atmosphere, crops will be poisoned, beasts, such as remain, will eat them, and those who survive the holocaust can be assured of dying of cancer.

And ten years from now we needn't expect terrorists like the Red Brigade to be kidnapping former prime ministers. They will be holding an entire city like New York City hostage with a suitcase bomb.

"Son of Man, I have appointed you as sentry to the House of Israel. When you hear a word from my mouth, warn them in my name" (Ezek. 3:17). To honor the memory of Dr. Fosdick and the hopes that we all share for the United Nations special session, the Deacons of Riverside have unanimously endorsed a national undertaking. For too long, disarmament has been the concern of the anti-establishment. It is time to make it the business of the establishment. To do this, Riverside Church has employed for one year one of the best organizers in this country, Cora Weiss. She was the one who, for Church World Service, organized the shipment of 10,000 tons of wheat to Vietnam. With the help, I am sure, of many church members, Cora Weiss will organize three convocations under the Riverside roof. To the first, we shall invite all the mayors of the United States and the mayor of Moscow. The subject: Cities or the Arms Race?

To the second we shall invite labor and industrial leaders. The subject: Jobs or the Arms Race? (The arms industry is so capital-intensive that it takes more jobs than it provides. For one billion dollars, you can employ 58,000 people in the arms industry and 145,000 in the Job Corps, not to mention 73,000 firemen.)

To the third convocation we shall invite the religious leaders of this nation.

I hope you will all agree that it is right that this church should undertake an educational task of such magnitude. Frankly, I give it about a forty percent chance of success. But let others worry about enterprises that have eighty percent chance of success. We must dream visions larger than our times.

We don't want to cut into the capital of this church: that's other people's money. We want to dig into our own pockets. I am confident that by the end of this week we shall have enough money to launch this program, enough money to ask for matching funds from elsewhere. Already we have received two anonymous gifts of $1,000. All cannot give $1,000, but all can give. And I'll tell you a secret. One of these anonymous donors told me that it was the largest contribution that he was making to charity this year. All of us can match that! In the name of Harry Emerson Fosdick, we can all try to change the arms race into a peace race.

We, too, must carry on a lover's quarrel with the world, so that when, like Harry Emerson Fosdick, we depart this life, we leave behind a little more truth, a little more justice, a little more peace, a little more beauty, than would have been there had we not cared enough about the human race to quarrel with it, not for what it is, but for what it yet might be. On this day, let our prayer be: Oh, God, take our minds and think through them, take our lips and speak through them, and take our hearts and set them on fire. Amen.

The Ships

JULY 2, 1978

Several years ago driving south through Virginia, I had occasion to cross the mighty Rappahannock. Taking in its awesome width, I couldn't help wondering whether George Washington had indeed sailed that silver dollar from one bank clear across to the other. Then

I went on to muse: suppose modern scholarship should one day establish that the dollar, in fact, splashed. Would that mean George Washington was no longer father of his country? The answer, of course, is no. That story is an expression of faith, not a basis of faith. Like the story of young George, the hatchet and the cherry tree, it's the kind of story followers of George Washington committed to him on other grounds would just love to tell about him.

And so with Jesus. If he never walked over the surface of the sea of Galilee, still he is Lord. His Lordship is not based upon his breaking the laws of physical nature in some Houdini-like fashion. Rather he is Lord because he transcended the limits of human nature—loving as no one else could love unless he were the Son of God, God's love in person on earth. So let's not worry overly about whether this story is literally true. It is eternally true, as I think we shall see, and that is enough. And, in fact, it's a perfect three-act drama for a Fourth of July sermon. For all the action takes place in and around a ship, calling to mind not only the best feature of the bicentennial—the tall ships— but also what most of us learned in school:

> Thou, too, sail on, O Ship of State!
> Sail on, O Union, strong and great!
> Henry Wadsworth Longfellow

As the first act opens, we see the disciples boarding a boat for what appears to be a very routine crossing. But some furlongs from the shore, they suddenly find themselves buffeted by an unexpected and terrible storm. Their ship begins to sink, not only because the winds are high and against them, but, as we later find out, because Jesus is not there.

Well, 202 years ago this Tuesday our ship set sail. To many—not blacks and Native Americans to be sure—but to many others, the journey looked promising. And almost 100 years later we still seemed to be more or less on course. Lincoln called us "God's almost chosen people," "the last best hope of democracy." In the decades that followed his death we were a haven to Europe's "huddled masses longing to breathe free." And as recently as World War II, Churchill sent Roosevelt a telegram quoting Longfellow:

> Thou, too, sail on, O Ship of State!
> Sail on, O Union, strong and great!
> Humanity with all its fears,
> With all the hopes of future years,
> Is hanging breathless on thy fate!

But thirty-odd years later, no one sends us telegrams like that anymore. Like the disciples' ship ours too has lost headway and maybe even direction. Like them we find ourselves buffeted by storms seemingly beyond our power to control. And we are forced to ask—simply because it is our Christian duty to see that this question never ceases to be asked—is Jesus with us?

Among some highly questionable things Solzhenitsyn, the other week at Harvard, said some true and good ones. Personally I thought it too bad that he focused on the discontents of the rich rather than the sufferings of the poor. Still he was correct in saying that "happiness is today being defined in a morally inferior way." He also caught the psychological result of pursuing such happiness: "The constant desire to have still more things and a still better life, and the struggle to obtain them imprints many faces with worry and even depression—although it is customary to conceal such feelings." And he was certainly correct in saying that "two hundred or even fifty years ago it would have seemed quite impossible in America that an individual could be granted boundless freedom simply for the satisfaction of his instincts or whims."

To most of our revolutionary forebears freedom didn't mean simply the opportunity to say what you wanted and the opportunity to become rich. Freedom meant taking advantage of the high level of human possibilities opening up in a new land. In fact, freedom was practically synonymous with virtue, as it obviously was later for Lincoln when he called for "a new birth of freedom."

As regards our foreign policy I think Solzhenitsyn was categorically wrong in linking our failure to pursue the war in Vietnam with a failure of nerve. Our main problem has been quite different, I think, and it came home to me the other day in dramatic fashion. The first speaker on a U.N. panel rose to say: "I come from a country that in all its history has never threatened another country." I couldn't believe it, until he announced he came from Malta, the island which received its independence I believe in 1964. Then it hit me. When my turn came I started out: "I come from a country that since World War II, has intervened militarily, or in a major CIA effort, in the internal affairs of small countries on an average of one every eighteen months." It seems incredible, doesn't it? But let's go through the list: 1948–Greece; 1953–Iran; 1954–Guatemala; 1958–Lebanon and Indonesia; 1960–Laos; 1961–Cuba; 1964–the Congo and British Guiana; 1965–the Dominican Republic; and since 1965–Vietnam, again Laos, Cambodia and Chile.

Our ship of state is floundering today because in the words of Ezekiel, "we corrupted our wisdom for the sake of our splendor."

Instead of inspiring the world by fulfilling our own promises to our own people, and particularly to our poor, we sought to impose our rule on others. So our ship, like that of the disciples, is losing headway and direction not only because the winds are high and against us, but because Christ is not in our midst.

Well, on to Act II which opens with a picture of one person preparing to abandon ship. And can't you hear the cries—there are so many of them in every sinking ship: "For God's sake Peter, sit down, you're rocking the boat!" Now what do you suppose moved Peter, and not the others, to abandon ship? I think it is easier to live with fear, yes even to accept the burden of guilt, than to face something that requires us to grow. But in our honest moments some of us are willing to face the shallowness of our lives, the superficiality of our culture, what Solzhenitsyn properly called "the calamity of a dispiritualized and irreligious consciousness." And when in the fourth watch of the night, that miserable 2 a.m.–6 a.m. shift, when we are most alone with ourselves, Jesus bids us come to him across the water, some of us, like Peter, are ready for the leap of faith.

Now Peter, you remember, almost immediately began to sink, and modern scholarship may one day establish that Jesus called him "the rock" then, not for his foundational but for his sinking properties! And when you stop to think of it, why not? "In my weakness is my strength" said St. Paul. It is only when we realize that we can no more trust our own buoyancy than we can the buoyancy of the ship we have just abandoned, that we truly give ourselves to Christ. Then the true miracle takes place, the one that makes this story eternally true. Peter cries out, "Lord, save me" and Jesus does. Isn't that the central miracle of so many lives? When sinking in our own fears, when sinking in our own guilt, when sinking in our own sense of helplessness, we see with incredible clarity a love greater than we ourselves can ever express, a truth deeper than we ourselves can ever articulate, a beauty richer than we ourselves can ever contain—when seeing that we cry out "Lord, save me," Christ's divine truth, divine love, divine beauty rescues us from the calamity of a despiritualized, irreligious consciousness. Ask only for a thimbleful of help and you receive an oceanful in return.

Many people wish the story ended with Act II. For what is more beautiful than self-abandonment? What greater relief to an unhappy soul than to find stability in a world of turmoil, certitude in a world of doubt, contentment amidst pain? But self-abandonment is not the name of the Biblical game. The Biblical quest is to vindicate the human struggle of which all of us are a part. It is the struggle to redeem history—to find what Martin Marty called "a usable future."

Peter doesn't say to Jesus, "Now that you have saved me Lord, let's just walk off—you and me—into the sunrise of a new day for me and forget about all those fellows in the sinking ship." No, having abandoned the sinking ship for Jesus, Peter now returns with Jesus.

There is our Fourth of July example for shining patriots who call themselves Christians. "America, love it or leave it"—do you remember the slogan? Actually it meant "America, obey it or leave it." But let's think up a new one for today: "America, love it *and* leave it." Leave it for Jesus, for America's sake as well as for your own, and then return with Jesus. That's how to love America these days—with Christ's wisdom, with Christ's compassion, with a transcendent ethic which can renew "the patriots' dream, that sees beyond the years, her alabaster cities gleam, undimmed by human tears!"

It's a time of incomparable danger and incredible opportunity. We can still fulfill the hopes of John Quincy Adams: "Whenever the standard of freedom and independence has been or shall be unfurled, there will be America's heart, her benedictions and her prayers. But she does not go abroad in search of monsters to destroy."

When Peter returned to the boat with Jesus the winds abated. I think our own ship could once again recover headway and its direction if more Americans followed Peter's example. We really do love America. Two hundred and two years after our birth most of us still feel the way Longfellow did. So let's give him the last words of this Fourth of July sermon:

> Sail on, nor fear to breast the sea!
> Our hearts, our hopes, are all with thee.
> Our hearts, our hopes, our prayers, our tears,
> Our faith triumphant o'er our fears,
> Are all with thee,—are all with thee!

"Born Again"

JULY 9, 1978
Reading: John 3:1–15

"Rabbi, we knew that thou art a teacher come from God:
for no person can do these miracles thou doest, except God
be with him."

John 3:2

Among the many miracles reported to Nicodemus one was never mentioned. Jesus made the blind to see, the lame to walk; he cleansed lepers, he even brought Lazarus back from the dead. But he never made an old person young again. Apparently that was not part of God's plan.

"All mortal flesh is as the grass." That's not only a grim statement about the grim reaper. That's saying length is not the most important dimension of life. That's saying life is so beautiful—properly lived—that we who are among the living should be willing to step aside and let others have a chance to enjoy it too. Moreover, the senior years can be the formative years, so why pass them up? Old age cannot destroy beauty. "Though our outer nature is wasting away, our inner nature is being renewed every day." A merely pretty face can become mysteriously beautiful when its wrinkles manifest the history of a splendid personality. Did anyone ever suggest to Whistler that he should have painted his mother ten years earlier?

But if we can't be young again we can be born again—can, and should be. "Verily I say unto Thee, except a person be born again, he [or she] cannot enter the Kingdom of God." When Jesus said this to Nicodemus, Nicodemus didn't dispute the need. He only said it wasn't practical. "How can a man be born when he is old? How can he enter a second time into his mother's womb?"

Most Christians judge Nicodemus harshly. They say, "He was pretty obtuse, wasn't he?" Well I don't judge him harshly and I don't think he was obtuse at all. I think he was stalling. I think he was defending himself. I think he understood perfectly well—all too well, as a matter of fact—what Jesus was talking about. The very fact that he, a member of the Sanhedrin, one of the rulers of the people, came at all to Jesus, bespeaks a sensitive, troubled person; a seeker, albeit a furtive one. My guess is that, like most of us, Nicodemus was hoping that his salvation might be accomplished by merely tinkering with his life. Instead, he hears talk of rebirth. Remember now, he's not among the lame, the halt and the blind; he is a success, as the world measures success. So any suggestion that he might have to start all over again must have been threatening. It is to any "successful" person.

One of the most interesting phenomena any university chaplain could observe in the sixties was the need for failure on the part of children of successful parents. It was a nuisance because it often meant that antiwar student protesters organized badly and behaved worse. But psychologically, their behavior was understandable. They were doubting the terms of success and failure. It was also under-standable that their hardworking fathers who had knocked themselves out getting their families into the suburbs, so that they now had to get up an hour earlier and return an hour later from work—it was understandable that such hardworking papas were driven up the wall by remarks such as, "You have to grow up in Scarsdale to know how bad it is."

But that's what being born again is all about: to recognize the possibility that every word of congratulation you receive upon the success of your life may represent that pat on the back that sends you deeper into the quicksand. I'll bet Nicodemus heard Jesus saying that to be born again means to re-examine old questions as though they had never been asked before, to make sure that what is of utmost importance occupies the important place in your life.

I have a friend—very successful—who in the fifties toyed with the idea of becoming a minister. When he came to see me at Yale Divinity School I introduced him to my teacher, Richard Niebuhr, who incidentally had the most beautifully lined face I have ever seen. Afterwards my friend told me of their conversation. He said to Dr. Niebuhr, "I believe in God all right, and Jesus and the Christian life, but somehow the church and its ministry seem a bit irrelevant, not part of the 'big show'" as he put it. He wanted himself to be part of the big show. Finally Dr. Niebuhr said, "Tell me, Mr. Jones, what is the big show?"

Because, like Nicodemus, he was sensitive and intelligent, like Nicodemus he departed without giving any cheap, easy answer.

Years later he grieves that he has never been able to do what he really wanted to. Now he's no longer being intelligent. He's simply being sentimental. He thinks it's a question of not being able. The fact is it's a question of not really wanting to. Few of us really want what we think we want. It just makes us feel better about ourselves to think we do.

To be born again is no easy thing. It is possible only when one is convinced that Christianity *is* the big show, the only yardstick by which we can measure success and failure. "Although I speak with the tongues of men and angels and have not love—I am nothing." I admire Nicodemus. He recognized the seriousness of what Jesus was talking about.

Let's go on. Not only was Nicodemus successful; he was a ruler—and male. Probably in his day as in ours masculinity was not just a fact of biology but something that had to be proved, and reproved, a continual quest for some ever-receding male Grail. As for what it took then, and takes now, to be a ruler—well, let me recall a famous scene, again from the sixties: In the winter of 1967, to his great credit, another ruler, Secretary of Defense McNamara, and also a religious man like Nicodemus, went to Harvard to explain his war policies. When he was set to leave and got into his car, he found himself surrounded by milling Harvard students, furious at what they took to be his plastic explanations. Suddenly Secretary McNamara got out of the car again and the next day newspapers showed him standing on the hood shouting, "I was tougher than you are then (in World War II) and I'm tougher than you are now."

What made the scene so poignant was Mr. McNamara's inability to see that the students were not doubting his machismo. It was his humanity they were questioning.

In rebirth what comes first—humanity or machismo? We know the answer. But it's not an easy one to live out, if, like Nicodemus, you're a ruler and male.

During our all-day session on disarmament this Tuesday evening we're going to have to ask, "Why is toughness, defined as being comfortable with violence, so admired a character trait and so essential to reputation in the national security bureaucracy?" But today let us ask: are we ourselves willing, personally, to be disarmed? How many of us would rise and say, to the world, "I am a disarmed person"? That's what's demanded, for "Unless you turn and become like children, you will never enter the kingdom of heaven."

"That which is born of the flesh is flesh; and that which is born of the Spirit is spirit." This week I was reading a fascinating book by a woman named Barbara Kraft. It is about the peace ship that sailed from America to Europe in 1915 laden with Americans filled with hope that somehow they could get the neutral nations of Europe to stop the horrible bloodletting of World War I. The whole expedition was financed by Henry Ford. Ms. Kraft describes Ford as an American folk-hero in those days. "He was revered worldwide, college students voted him the third greatest man ever to have lived, after Napoleon and Christ." And then comes this sentence: "The legend that his advertising office and his own pronouncements created fed the needs of those anxious to obtain the good life through material wealth, *but unwilling to lose their sense of innocence*. Henry Ford proved to them that a man could make millions without losing his conscience or the exalted values of the American dream."

Nicodemus probably realized that to be born again meant that he would have to become as vulnerable as a child but not innocent as a child. On the contrary, he would have to see the sullied stream of human life with greater clarity than ever before; he would have to see his own complicity in the very evils he abhorred; and he would have to dedicate himself as never before to their eradication even if it meant that like the Son of Man he might be "lifted up."

But most of the so-called "twice-born" in America don't want to be vulnerable as children; they want to be innocent as children, and loved as children. They see Jesus as something to be added to their life, not as a person who will transform it from top to bottom. They want a personal conversion but no change in their vocational lives, no change in their social attitudes. Unwilling to lose their sense of innocence they are really seeking to enter a second time into the womb, to be born of the flesh, not of the spirit. And as innocence, like misery, loves company, they are vigorously out to make converts, but converts not disciples. Few will be lifted up.

And finally they do not realize that "the spirit bloweth where it listeth"—sometimes, yes, within the church, but often outside, for God can always believe in those who have very little understanding of how really deeply they believe in Him.

Let me end with a story I heard recently of a man who *was* lifted up, a young man, a singer, imprisoned with thousands of others in the National Stadium in Santiago when the Salvador Allende government of Chile was overthrown. As he stood among the frightened and demoralized prisoners, he began a solitary song. A guitar was passed to him, the spirit began to blow. Soon thousands were singing with him. As usual, the authorities were threatened by the power of the spirit moving so freely and blatantly. So they seized the young man and took him away. When he returned not only had his guitar been smashed; all ten fingers had been cut off. Horrified, his fellow prisoners drew back. But he walked into the empty space they had created, lifted his bloody hands and again began to sing. Once more the spirit began to move, the people took up his song, and predictably the guards moved in again. This time when he came back there was blood trickling from his mouth. They had cut out his tongue. Many wept. Everyone was watching. For a while he stood motionless. Then he began simply to sway. Some thought he was fainting. But then they realized his graceful, silent swaying was a dance. And soon they were all swaying silently with him. This time when the guards came back, they shot him dead in front of all the people. But the spirit continued to blow.

We shouldn't be surprised at this story. Didn't St. Paul tell us that "while we live we are always being given up to death for Christ's sake so that the life of Jesus may be manifested in our bodies" (2 Cor. 4:11)?

Nicodemus appears briefly again in the Gospel of John. When Peter panics and runs, Nicodemus stands his ground against his fellow pharisees. And finally, after his Lord had been lifted up, he was there with ointment to embalm the Lord's body.

God, grant that we might at least see as clearly and care as deeply as did that sensitive, intelligent man.

The Twenty-third Psalm

JULY 16, 1978

Contrary to what a great number of people rather automatically assume, the really great sentences in the Bible are not in the imperative mood; they are in the indicative. To say that is in no way to slight the great "Thou shalt's" and the great "Thou shalt not's," the Ten Commandments and all the other ringing, ethical imperatives of the Bible. They are stunning and they are stirring. But the greatest sentences are in the indicative. Here they are—just a few of them:

"God so loved the world that He gave His only begotten Son, that whosoever believeth in Him should not perish but have eternal life." (John 3:16)

"God is love, and he who abides in love abides in God and God abides in him." (1 John 4:16)

"God is our refuge and strength, a very present help in trouble." (Ps. 46:1)

"The LORD is my shepherd, I shall not want." (Ps. 23:1)

Not surprisingly they are all about God and His never ceasing love for us. And if God's love for us is the first and greatest thing that we can say about Biblical faith, then the primary religious emotion is gratitude not duty. Duty calls when gratitude fails to prompt. So the great imperatives have to take second place. They are the signposts of faith. The indicatives are the hitching posts.

"The LORD is my shepherd; I shall not want. He maketh me to lie down in green pastures." Albert Camus once said: "For rich people the sky is just an extra, a gift of nature. The poor, on the other hand, can see it as it really is: an infinite grace."

A green pasture is not only a July meadow, it is any one of God's infinite graces. For us urban folk it is more likely to be a view of the river, Tosca, or Shakespeare in the park; maybe our jobs, certainly the food with which our labors are repaid, hopefully our husbands, wives, our children, our friends; the memories our forebears have left us, the earth in which they repose—anything or everything that nourishes us, all are an infinite grace. The suffering of the innocent, terrible and awesome as that mystery undoubtedly is, is as nothing compared to the mystery of undeserved good. "The Lord is my shepherd, I shall not want. He maketh me to lie down in green pastures."

It's too bad we reserve grace for meals alone. How about saying just before opening a great novel, or before a concert—yes, even before a Red Sox-Yankee's Series—"For what we are about to receive, Lord, make us truly thankful."

Let's go on. The psalm is dominated by the metaphor of God as a shepherd. So let me ask you where in relationship to the sheep do you usually picture the shepherd? Unless I am very much mistaken, your answer will be, "Behind, of course," where shepherds are generally depicted in Western paintings. But listen again: "The LORD is my shepherd . . . He leadeth me beside the still waters. . . . He leadeth me in the paths of righteousness for His name's sake."

Maybe it's significant that Eastern shepherds lead where their Western counterparts delve. In any case, God, as we see in the person of Christ, leads more than he drives. Jesus says: "follow me," and always, everywhere, himself goes first. It's a beautiful thought, isn't it? But let's not be sentimental: that's what makes the faith so difficult. It's easier to have someone tell you what you want and drive you toward it. It's harder to be in the church than in the army.

"He leadeth me beside the still waters. . . . He leadeth me in the paths of righteousness." If green pastures refer to everything that nourishes us, perhaps paths of righteousness are those that lead around prickly bushes and perilous pitfalls to our greater humanity. Isn't Christ always trying to make human beings more human?

But do we want to follow? In our cities, the poor, God knows, live in physical ghettos. But God also knows that the rest of us usually live in psychological ghettos, philosophical and moral ghettos. And where the poor can't break out, we don't want to. Most of us want to get educated—which means quite literally "led forth"—but only in order to get the degree and then sink back into the little we have learned. We don't want to know better, deeper and more, to keep thinking all the time. We don't want to feel more deeply, more tenderly. It's more comfortable not to—even though it's ten times as boring. So we stay in our ghettos seeking not so much physical comfort as that psychological comfort founded on continuing insensitivity. That's why when they seek to lead us out, the great pathfinders, like Christ himself, find themselves very much alone. Remember Galileo, or the pioneer painter, Manet? They told the public of new things they had discovered, not the time-worn things the public already knew and wanted to hear again. So the public was offended.

And the public was offended again this week by another independent spirit. Let us agree that the political trials in Russia are morally revolting. Let us also grant that Andy Young should have said "economic" rather than political prisoners when referring to the hundreds of American poor who are in jail today more because they are poor than because they are bad. But he said so little in reminding us that we should not seek to justify ourselves by relying on others' crimes. He said so little, but oh how they screamed, those souls out of touch with any moral landscape, those who for decades have been using communist dirt to make soap to wash clean their own hands.

When ghettoized souls see someone who has broken out their instinct is not to emulate him but to take his freedom from him. So Christ is crucified, Galileo is persecuted, Manet's paintings are not hung, Andy is called on to recant if not to resign.

Perhaps now we can better see what the psalmist had in mind when after "He leadeth me in the paths of righteousness" he wrote "Yea, though I walk through the valley of the shadow of death." Instead of a natural death maybe he was thinking of freedom's price.

But let's continue that sentence. "Yea, though I walk through the valley of the shadow of death, I will fear no evil." We are back again to the beginning, to the great indicatives: "God is our refuge and our strength, a very present help in trouble."

But note the beautiful device the psalmist now uses to underscore his certitude of God's never ceasing love. Up to now God the shepherd has been referred to in the third person singular. "The LORD is my shepherd. . . . *He* leadeth me beside the still waters. . . . *He* restoreth my soul. . . . *He* leadeth me in the paths of righteousness." But watch the change when the psalmist refers to life's most devastating moments. "Yea, though I walk through the valley of the shadow of death I will fear no evil, for *thou* art with me." How beautiful is that little switch from the third person singular to the second person! And he goes on with the second person: "Thy rod and thy staff they comfort me. Thou preparest a table before me in the presence of mine enemies. Thou anointest my head with oil; my cup runneth over."

Do you know what's going on? The reference here is to a desert law of hospitality. Were I fleeing my enemies and came to your campsite, you would be obliged to take me in for two nights and the day intervening while my enemies remained outside the circle of light cast by your campfire.

The psalmist ends by contrasting this limited hospitality with the hospitality we can expect from God: "Surely goodness and mercy"—as well as enemies—"will follow me all the days of my life; and I shall dwell in the house of the LORD"—not for two nights and a day intervening—but "forever."

Let me end on a personal note. With each passing month this psalm gains meaning. I have no more idea of how and where to intervene to save this city than I had when I first arrived some eight months ago. Many of you who have been here far longer feel exactly the same way—I know that. And I know that when Proposition Thirteen or its equivalent gets on every state ballot where it is constitutionally permitted to be, our cities are going to suffer far more.* But I also know that when things get worse we are going to have to get better. As misery deepens and violence rises, we are going to have to gain in decency and lucidity. We are going to have to move out of our spiritual ghettos on the high paths of righteousness, in the footsteps of our Lord. And all this will be quite possible—if not easy—because of the great indicatives of the Bible. "The LORD is my shepherd; I shall not want. . . . Yea, though I walk through the valley of the shadow of death, I will fear no evil." For, with St. Paul, "I am persuaded that neither death nor life, nor principalities, nor powers, nor things present, nor things to come, nor powers, nor height, nor depth, nor anything else in all creation, will be able to separate us from the love of God which is in Christ Jesus our Lord" (Rom. 8:38–39).

"Except We Be as Children"

JULY 23, 1978
Reading: Matthew 18:1–11

On the first page of what he calls his "Anti-memoirs," André Malraux writes of meeting a priest in the underground Resistance during World War II. "Tell me, Father," he asks. "What have you learned after listening all these years to all these confessions?"

Replied the priest: "I have learned that people are not as happy as they appear to be, and that none of us, finally, really grows up."

I love that answer. There is something tender yet tough in what the priest was saying, something not only true but very wise, wisdom

*Proposition 13 was a 1978 California ballot initiative that resulted in a cap on property tax rates.

being rooted in compassion. And, of course, he could have gone on to say that the two were not unrelated—our unhappiness and our failure to grow up. For instance, in the story just read, the disciples come to Jesus obviously to settle a childish dispute which must have been causing them considerable pain. They ask "who is the greatest in the Kingdom of Heaven?"

Had I been Jesus, I think my heart would have sunk at hearing such a question from the lips of my own disciples. Isn't it bad enough to covet and compete for the choice places in the Kingdom of earth? Must we drag all this competition and envy into the Kingdom of Heaven?

Of course it's just possible that the disciples had a foresight of things to come. The other day I heard the story of a doctor (doctors, you will forgive me!) who upon arrival in heaven found a long line waiting at the gate. "Well," he thought to himself "as on earth so in heaven, lines are for patients not for doctors." So he went to the front and proposed to St. Peter that he simply proceed on in.

"Listen," said Peter, "Doctor, lawyer, merchant, chief—there is no difference up here, just get in line." Chastened, the doctor took his place. After about an hour he heard someone whistling to himself, and, looking around saw to his amazement a surgeon all dressed in green from his floppy pants to his little green hat. A little white gauze mask hung jauntly around his neck. As he passed St. Peter the surgeon waved and went on in.

"My word," said the doctor, "they must have changed the rules." So he returned to the front and proposed once again that he be allowed to proceed.

When Peter got angry he held his ground. "You let the other doctor in." "What doctor?" said St. Peter. "The one right there," said the doctor pointing to the receding figure of the surgeon.

"Oh," explained Peter. "That's not a doctor, that's God. He likes to play doctor."

(If you want to know the truth, God is a Protestant minister!) "When I became a man, I gave up childish ways." That statement of St. Paul is one of aspiration only to most of us. As the priest said "none of us finally really grows up." So why in answer to the disciples does Jesus call a child into their midst saying, "Unless you turn and become like children you can never enter the Kingdom of Heaven"? (And the Kingdom of Heaven can never enter you!) Maybe Jesus is pointing out the difference between being childish and childlike. To the childish arguments about who is the greatest he is saying childlikeness is the only greatness.

A few moments ago we had a small child in our midst being presented for baptism. Mark Ryan is only a few weeks old. What's his greatness? It seems to me that one at least of the great things about Mark Ryan is that he is totally honest about his dependence on the love of his parents. He is very "up front" about it. He is "objective," if you will, and humility is being objective. St. Paul was merely being objective when he said "not I, but Christ who dwells within me." St. Paul had many gifts and he was free to enjoy them all because he didn't have to take credit for any. How free we all would be from the tireless competition and envy that gives us pain if, with Mark Ryan, we had a childlike dependence on our heavenly parents; if with St. Paul, we could recognize that whatever is of good is of God. "Not I, but Christ who dwells within me."

"Truly I say to you, unless you turn and become like children, you will never enter the Kingdom of Heaven." Jesus is talking about what we might call "the grace of dependence." There is nothing obsequious about being dependent, nothing weak. Christ wasn't obsequious, and he was the strongest man ever to have lived. So why hesitate to become like children—children of God, childlike, not childish! It can only cause us much happiness. And, maybe, we'd finally grow up!

Humility is not the only characteristic note of childhood, although it is the one that Jesus emphasized in this story. But while we are on the subject we might as well mention at least two others, deeply religious in nature. One is a sense of wonder. Chesterton wrote: "The world does not lack for wonders only for a sense of wonder." Children are full of wonder. They are always wide-eyed. They are always squealing in amazement or in delight. The only good thing about this infernal heat is that all over the city you can hear the ecstasy of the water squeal. And when the hydrants are turned off you can watch children going about the serious business of puddle gazing—wondering how so much sky and earth could be captured in such small bodies of water. Our spiritual health depends on our continual capacity to say, "Isn't that amazing." This last Thursday in Central Park I was saved from incipient depression by singing in the chorus of Verdi's *Requiem*. Halfway through the really boisterous "Sanctus" I remembered something Beethoven said because it applied to the *Requiem*. In a statement as rash and noble as any of his works Beethoven said, "He who understands my music can never know unhappiness again." Marvelous! And when you think that Beethoven broke all the rules and turned out pieces of breathtaking rightness—it's amazing!

"The world begins with wonder," said Aristotle. He should have gone on, "And ends with wonder too."

Also, faster than anyone, children can spot a phony. You who are parents: how many of your guests have been ungraciously unmasked by your children? No search committee looking for a new minister or for a college president, or for the president of any company, should be without a child of about nine years old. After all it was just such a child in Anderson's fairy tale who pointed out, "the emperor has no clothes."

So cry hosanna for the children—their humility, their sense of wonder and their candor. Except we become as they, the Kingdom of Heaven can never be ours.

But we can't leave the story without measuring in the harshness of Jesus' words, the depth of his concern for the well-being of children. Verse 6 as you remember reads: "But whoever causes one of these little ones who believe in me to sin, it would be better for him to have a great millstone fastened round his neck and to be drowned in the depth of the sea." That means drowned with such a weight that you could never be brought up for a decent burial.

The sin of causing others to sin—one of the worst in the world. Years ago in East Harlem I knew a juvenile delinquent who refused to say The Lord's Prayer. He had had enough of fathers, he said. His own on earth had deserted him. Most juvenile delinquents are like that; they are delinquent because they have never really been juvenile. They have never had the care, protection, and love they needed. They are like the young birches that you can see at this time of year in any New England forest—twisted and all bent over. The storms of winter hit them before they were ready. Now, no amount of warmth and sunshine can ever straighten them out again.

But we cannot blame alone the vanished fathers, the mothers with no room in their lives for their kids, when the parents themselves are the victims of a twisted social order. In the sixties we preferred to put one man on the moon rather than millions of our fellow citizens on their feet. The babies of that decade are today teenagers. Not surprisingly many are delinquent. But instead of seeing that our love for children, like God's love for the world, is communal in scope, not merely personal, instead of assuming responsibility for the sin that causes others to sin, we are trying to insulate ourselves in childish fashion from our responsibilities. We have just passed in New York state legislation that makes it possible to put thirteen-year-olds away for life. We are clamoring for our own safety rather than for more compassion and imagination of the kind Peter Edelman has courageously displayed as director of New York State's division for youth. And in an election year where crime is already an issue as hot as the weather, not unsurprisingly our fears are being exploited by certain politicians weak in courage but strong in cunning.

Of course the public deserves protection. That's why we are trying to reverse the arms race! But if we love our children we have to take chances. Christians in particular should understand this. Aren't we always being called upon to risk something big for something good?

"See that you do not despise one of these little ones; for I tell you that in heaven their angels always behold the face of my Father who is in heaven." Let's hope their guardian angels will soon have better things to report. May Christians at least assume their responsibility for the sin that causes others to sin.

"I have learned that people are not as happy as they appear to be, and that none of us, finally, really grows up." But if we ceased to be childish, and became childlike, we just might!

The Wages of Grace

SEPTEMBER 24, 1978
Reading: Matthew 20:1–16

On first hearing this parable, before applying any insight or foresight, few, if any of us identify with the owner of the vineyard— though we might be as rich and even as generous as he. And few of us identify with those who stand idle, most of the day, in the marketplace—though our undeserved misfortune, too, may be unemployment. Initially, the great majority of us ally ourselves with the day-long workers. Their protests ring true. Why should those who have borne the heat and burden of the day be paid exactly the same as those who came in at the eleventh hour and never even worked up a sweat?

It's interesting that we should identify ourselves so quickly with those who labored the hardest. A reporter once asked John XXIII, "How many people work here in the Vatican?" to which the dear old Pope said, "Oh, about half, I guess." Well, how many of us work in the vineyard of the Lord?

But, wait, let's hold such mean questions for later. Suffice it at this point to state the text for this Homecoming Sunday: "For it is by His Grace you are saved, through trusting Him. It is not your own doing. It is God's gift, not a reward for work done. There is nothing for anyone to boast of, for we are God's handiwork, created in Jesus Christ to devote ourselves to the good deeds for which God has designed us" (Eph. 2:8–10).

The action in the parable takes place at exactly this time of year—the last week in September. In ancient Palestine, as in Israel today, it is at this very moment that the grapes finally mature. Soon the rain will fall with devastating effect, so, with a heavy harvest at stake, the race against time becomes serious. All workers are welcome, even those who can only give an hour. The pay in the parable is one denarius or about eight cents. It was normal but only sufficient. The workers came from the lowest economic class. They were much like our own migrant workers. (This week I heard a story of a child of a migrant worker family who went to school for the first time in her life, thanks to an enterprising social worker who found her picking apples with her parents in an orchard not far from the school. On the first day of school, the teacher asked the children to say where they were born. When it came the turn of the migrant worker's child, she said "I was born in the beans." The other children laughed, but the teacher understood it was no joke. The child's birthplace, the child's home, were beans, apples, lettuce—wherever it was her parents happened to be picking at the time.)

In ancient Palestine, the marketplace was the hiring hall. So the idle workers weren't there to gossip. The fact that they remained all day was an indication of how desperately they wanted to work, for if they went unemployed for even one day they went home to worried wives and hungry children.

Clearly it was this injustice that so touched the heart of the owner of the vineyard. The injustice of equal pay for unequal work was as nothing compared to the justice of giving "to each according to his need." Marxists, incidentally, only picked up that slogan after the church had dropped it. (Marx only became anti-Christian after he perceived the church as inhuman, and not that much has changed, has it? The Gospel is still the answer and the church is still part of the problem.)

When you stop to think of it, the owner of the vineyard was concerned with the two basic rights at the heart of the charter of every working person: the right to work and the right to a living wage. This is hardly the point of the parable, but in our times when unemployment is undermining the right to work and inflation the right to a living wage, and when both are largely caused by an arms buildup that is credible neither to the heart nor to the intellect—in such times that in all honesty we should call "evil" because we could do something about them, it is well to remember the intelligent, large-hearted concerns of this employer. God is like him. God cannot bear to see the unemployed. He sees the worried mothers and the hungry

kids. God pities the poor, and God is outraged at their plight, particularly in a country where poverty can no longer be termed a private
tragedy; it's a public crime.

Now let us turn, or return, to the main point, to the heart of the
parable which is really at the very heart of the Gospel itself. You
remember that the day-long workers cry "Unfair." But "things are seldom what they seem," and, knowing that, the owner said to one of
them, "My friend, I am not being unfair to you. You agreed on the
usual wage for the day, so take your pay."

No one was getting less than a subsistence wage, and the workers
got what they bargained for. So there is no unfairness there. No, what
the workers were grumbling about, what the older brother in The
Prodigal Son was complaining bitterly about, was something that
haunts each one of us: it is the fear that somewhere, someone might
be getting away with something. The grumblings of the workers and
the complaints of the older brother reflect the profound truth that
when we demand justice for ourselves, nine times out of ten it's envy
masquerading as justice. Freud once remarked, "The demands of justice are but a modification of envy." So quite properly the owner
asked, "Why be jealous because I am kind?"

But envy still is not what this parable is essentially about. The parable really opposes two deep-seated views of human existence, two
worlds, if you will, between which we go back and forth like a shut-
tlecock on a loom. They are the world of merit and the world of grace.
The full-day workers lived, or at least worked, in the world of merit.
They believed in a quid pro quo. They believed in the merit system.
And like most believers in a merit system, they considered themselves
meritorious, deserving of their reward. For some people to feel
deserving, others obviously have to be undeserving. In the parable,
they are the other workers. So in the eyes of the day-long workers, the
owner's graciousness becomes injustice. Instead of seeing themselves
as self-centered, they see the landowner as unfair. And the tragedy is
that they estrange themselves from the source of graciousness. The
point of the parable is not that while some get by on merit others need
grace. The parable explains why some people never receive it.

By contrast, in the world of grace, we pray for mercy not for justice. We know we don't earn or deserve what God has given us. We
don't worry about someone getting away with something, for we
ourselves are getting away with something—something for nothing.
And oh, how joyful life becomes when you understand that in this
world salvation is a gift, not a reward for work done. I can't remem-

ber whether or not I have told this story; if I have, forgive me, but listen, because it is a good one.

When I was a seminarian and living and working in East Harlem, I tried one day in my youthful eagerness to talk a bookie out of his chosen vocation. He listened, I must say, very patiently and then he said, "Son, one of these days you are going to be a preacher, aren't you?" I said, "Yes, why?"

"You believe in grace then, don't you?"

I said, "Yes, why?"

"I'll tell you why, son. You believe in grace and I believe in gambling, and that means both of us believe life is good, when it's something for nothing."

I don't know about gambling. Like Dostoyevsky, I think many gamblers may really want to lose, but the bookie was right about grace. It makes winners out of human beings—something for nothing. So you can live gratefully. And while in the world of merit we estrange ourselves from God, in the world of grace we are at home with God.

There's the message for Homecoming Sunday. We come to Riverside to find that our home is with God. Here on earth we have no abiding place, as Scripture reminds us. We are like migrant workers, only instead of being born in the beans, we are born in the Spirit, nurtured in Grace, and always at home with God. "Keep me, God, for in Thee have I found refuge. In Thy presence is the fullness of joy; in Thy right hand pleasures for evermore" (Ps. 16:1, 11).

At home with God, we are of course at home with one another. So, let us on this Sunday pledge ourselves to take better care of one another. Let each of us pray for a heart that never hardens, a touch that never hurts. Let us be generous with one another as the landowner was generous, and let us trust each other a little bit more. There are really two ways you can go through life: being wary, and trusting. Trusting, you will probably get hurt more often, but you will miss none of the action which includes a great deal of loving.

At home with God, at home with one another, we are of course at home with all the world which belongs to God. So let us also pray to God that these walls will never get so thick as to cut out the sound of the city's anguish. More than ever we must tutor the illiterate and feed the hungry and clothe the naked, and always with an eye on the goal, which is not to alleviate the results of poverty but rather to eliminate its causes. And, finally, through our disarmament project, we must convince the nation that patriotism is not so much protecting the land of our fathers, as conserving the land of our children.

So, on this golden day, there is much to do and we shall do it. And we will be paid with the wages of grace. "For it is by His grace you are saved, through trusting Him. It is not your own doing. It is God's gift. Not a reward for work done. There is nothing for anyone to boast of, for we are God's handiwork, created in Jesus Christ, to devote ourselves to the good deeds for which God has designed us."

Happy Homecoming. In the world of Grace, God waits to embrace each and every one of us. Amen.

On Winning Defeats

OCTOBER 1, 1978

The text for this morning's sermon is from St. Paul, his second letter to the Corinthians, "All this is from God, who through Christ reconciled us to himself" (2 Cor. 5:18).

What I have to say this morning will be more in the form of a meditation than a regular full-length sermon, and to start us off I'd like, if I may, to speak rather personally. A minister such as myself, with two marriages that eventually failed, was hardly the natural choice for the selection committee last year seeking a new senior minister. For myself, while I knew intellectually that no sin in God's eyes is beyond the pale of forgiveness, still emotionally I was having a hard time appropriating the knowledge. The burden of these failures was great. So when the selection committee invited me, it was as if a great yoke had been lifted. I knew the members of the committee couldn't overlook my failures, nor certainly condone them. What they could not approve, they could only forgive. And I experienced their forgiveness in the only way possible—as a gift, sheer and beautiful. Since then, I have been working here with what one might call the "zeal of gratitude."

I mention this experience because Communion is very like it. It is not a meal for the righteous. The invitation reads "Come unto me all ye who are weary and heavy-laden," and whereas the words might refer to those heavy-laden with the works of the Lord, they certainly refer also to those burdened with failures of many kinds. I knew a young woman who, quite distraught, stood up in the middle of a Communion service, and started for the door only to run into the outstretched arms of an old man. Taking her gently by the hand he pulled her into the pew and down next to him, saying, "Don't run my child, it's for the likes of you and me."

But if it is not a meal for the righteous it is also not a meal for mourning. It is a feast of joy, called early on in church history "a eucharist" (from the Greek word for "thanksgiving"). Communion is an invitation to be reconciled to God, to each other, and to ourselves, and it is an invitation as wide open as the outstretched arms of Christ on the cross. Of course there is pain; forgiveness is costly. But what Christ feels as blood we taste as wine.

"And He took a cup, and when He had given thanks He gave it to them, and they all drank of it. And He said to them 'This is the blood of the covenant which is poured out for many.'" But which covenant, the old or the new? It used to be that Christians, rather unfairly, presented the Old Testament—or covenant—as the law of God; and the New Testament—or covenant—as the love of God. But that is not fair, because both covenants are in the Old Testament. Listen again to these words of Jeremiah:

> Behold, the days are coming, says the LORD, when I will make a new covenant with the house of Israel and the house of Judah, not like the covenant which I made with their fathers when I took them by the hand to bring them out of the land of Egypt, my covenant which they broke, though I was their husband, says the LORD. But this is the covenant which I will make with the house of Israel after those days, says the LORD: I will put my law within them, and I will write it upon their hearts; and I will be their God, and they shall be my people. And no longer shall each man teach his neighbor and each his brother, saying, "Know the LORD," for they shall all know me, from the least of them to the greatest, says the LORD; for I will forgive their iniquity, and I will remember their sin no more. (Jer. 31:31–34)

It is hard to find more touching lines in the Old Testament. Clearly Jesus poured out his blood to seal that kind, that is, the New Testament. The Old was based on law, the New on love. The old demanded obedience, the new could only prompt overwhelming gratitude. The new doesn't do away with the old, but adds to it, insisting that we stand not only under the law of God but always *within* the love of God.

Don't worry now about transubstantiation or consubstantiation—how Christ is present in the bread and in the wine. Christ is in the verbs, not the nouns. "This is my body *broken*," "This is my blood *shed*." The whole thing is an act of grace taking place in *his* presence. We remember our Crucified Lord in the presence of our Risen Lord.

Today is Worldwide Communion Sunday, so let us note that no act in the Christian life is more universal. A Communion service always removes us from the loneliness of our egos to find us a home in the community; and the community is world-wide. When Christ said "This is my blood poured out for many," the "many" is not exclusive. It doesn't mean "many, but not all." It means "the totality, which is many." The Communion service, as no other act in the church, reminds us that we all belong one to another, every last single member of the human race. That's the way God made us. Christ died to keep us that way, our sin being that we are always putting asunder what God himself has joined together.

But at the same time no act is more intensely personal. So let us end where we began, on a more intimate note. God cares for all as if all were but one, but also for each as if he had naught else to care for. His gifts are given to us one by one.

There is a story which is really an Easter story, but I want to tell it now because each Communion service means our own resurrection. A certain man was travelling on a train in the hill country of West Virginia. Next to him, by the window, was another man who seemed unusually distraught. When the first asked if there was something wrong, the second explained, though rather diffidently and hesitatingly, that for the last ten years he had been a prisoner in a federal penitentiary. Now he was heading for home. As he and his family were practically illiterate, there had been little communication between them during the last ten years. But a week before, he had dictated a letter saying that he would understand if they did not want him home again. If they *did*, they were to tie a white ribbon around the bough of the last apple tree in the orchard, which he knew was visible from the tracks. If there was no ribbon, he would go right on into the station and continue on his way, and they wouldn't have to worry about him again. Now as the train drew nearer and nearer he, understandably, was getting more and more nervous. So the first man volunteered to watch for him. They switched seats. As the train rounded the next to the last curve, the ex-convict heard his new friend sing out, "Look, look." He did. And the whole tree was white with ribbons.

In life it is easy to win victories. What is hard is to win defeats, especially self-defeats. But God makes it possible. "All this is from

God, who through Christ reconciled us to himself." I hope that each of you, through the Communion service today, may experience God's forgiveness as this convict did through his family, and as I was lucky enough to do last year through the search committee.

Triumphantly Normal

OCTOBER 8, 1978

Shortly after that strong and gentle man, Steve Biko, was murdered by South African police, an admirer said of him, "There was about Steve an air of triumphant normality." It was a beautiful tribute to one who was full of laughter, to one who could think in fun because he so felt in earnest. As used by this woman, the word "normal" did not mean "average," but "that which operates according to the norm." Steve Biko was that rarest of human beings; he lived as he was supposed to live. In a sick society, he was health incarnate. In a world of death, he was a living reminder of all that makes for life. He fit St. Paul's description: "Afflicted, in every way, but not crushed; perplexed, but not driven to despair; struck down, but not destroyed; always carrying in the body the death of Jesus, so that the life of Jesus may also be made manifest in our mortal flesh" (2 Cor. 4:8–10).

Might it be helpful to suggest that Sunday by Sunday we come to church to encounter the norm, Jesus Christ, the norm himself, the one who, more even than all the blessed martyrs, shows us that love is the only valid human purpose—our only choice, or the soul's death? And we come here because there, outside the church, our society like that of Biko's land, is given over to the exercise of power, more than to the exercise of love. And even were it more normal, as God grant someday it will be, still the everydayness of life would still tend to drag us below normality, freeze our emotions, corrupt out intellects, so that we would still be yearning to be made normal again. And a church is the right place, because faith doesn't convert us from this life to some other; it converts us from something less than life to the possibility of full life itself.

Properly understood, the liturgy, in dramatic fashion, seeks to do exactly that: to convert us from something less than life to the possibility of full life itself. So, I propose that we follow it today, at least all the way from the Processional hymn through the Absolution, or as we call it here, the Assurance of Pardon.

My life is made easy by the fact that Fred Swann always picks the hymns. I review them, but I have yet to make a change. Because he is such a good theologian, Fred knows that the opening hymn is always about the greatness and goodness of God. Therefore it is always full of praise and thanksgiving. This morning we sang, "O Worship the King"—worship deriving from "worthship," the worthship of God—"O worship the King, all glorious above; O gratefully sing His power and His love." This isn't sung lightly. We are not mindless believers. Faith, Lord knows, for a sensitive seeker is hard to find, and in a society geared to deny it, even harder to keep. But if we have kept the faith this week, think of what we proclaimed already in those two lines alone. No, the world is not meaningless, it's only in a meaningless state. The world is cold and dark, yes, but even in the deep darkness of winter, we know in our heart an invincible summer. The world is lined with shadows, but what are shadows finally if not proof of the light? These are the sorts of things we sing at the very beginning when we stand up and face the central symbol of our faith, when the choir and clergy move forward to take their places where the church should always take its place, at the foot of the Cross of Christ.

"O gratefully sing." We have to sing; we have no choice. We are dealing with a mystery that can only be celebrated, never explained. And we have to sing because joy is the primary religious emotion. Never forget, duty calls only when gratitude fails to prompt.

The opening sentences, or the "call to worship" as it is sometimes called—these sentences, whether they are Biblical or personal, continue the mood of exaltation, as do the Invocation and the Choral Introit, although in the latter two, the mood already begins to change.

Powerful emotions are like deep currents; they move rapidly. So inevitably, in the service, the moods change fast, and from exultation inevitably to contrition. How could it be otherwise? Once you view the mountaintop, you become acutely aware of the floor of the valley on which you stand. So in only a short time we are ready for what is called the General Prayer of Confession.

It is a well-worn truth, but one that wears well, that confession is good for the soul. One reason is that its opposite, repression, is so bad for the soul. Modern psychiatry has only demonstrated more scientifically what we have known intuitively all along, that the subconscious has no digestive track. What goes down has to come up again, and usually does so in the form of displaced hostility. We impute unto others what rankles in ourselves. Repression cannot exorcise. Confession can, and let's face it: we have much to confess. None of us fill all that well the space and time allotted to us. Called on to be creative, most of us by the age of 40 are as set in our ways as trolley cars. Were we normal, we'd be free, loving, cheerful, fearless; yet much of the time we run around like cornered rats trying not to be clubbed.

And our collective lives are worse. Not only in South Africa but here in America, whites won't reckon with racism, not until the collective force of the opposition gives us no choice. As for blacks— well, let blacks confess for themselves. If we are men, we won't liberate the woman most in need of liberation—the woman in every man. If we are rich, we court disaster by clinging inordinately to privilege. If we are Americans, instead of living out our rich heritage we are content merely to enshrine it.

But, I say all this, not to depress us. If you remember only one thing from this sermon, remember the phrase I am now about to utter. *Guilt is to save us, not to destroy us*. It saves us by keeping us honest, and by pointing us toward forgiveness. It destroys us when through repression it mars our perception, and when, in our arrogance, we refuse forgiveness. Yes, guilt is the last stronghold of pride. For guilt represents my opinion of myself; forgiveness yours, or God's. And I just may be too proud to allow you to do for me what I can't do for myself. You know, sometimes it's more blessed to receive than to give; at least it takes more humility. And that is why I think the hardest, truly the most difficult part of the whole service is the Assurance of Pardon. Anybody can confess, but who can receive forgiveness?

There is another reason why it is so difficult to accept God's forgiveness. I used to wonder why people went so regularly to church, when church going was regularly so dull. Then I had an insight. When you know you are a sinner, your first instinct is to escape judgment; and the best way to escape judgment is to seek punishment. Judgment demands a new way of life, but punishment, by assuaging a bit the guilt, makes the old bearable anew. So the churches, I figured, were filled with people with too much conscience not to be punished, but with not enough conscience to accept judgment. So, the duller the service, the more it suited their purposes.

Forgiveness *does* entail judgment. Remorse without reform, is merely self-pity. It stands to reason, for if from God we receive good for evil, then we will repay evil with good. If, when we were enemies, God loves us, then we will love our enemies. If Christ came to bind up the wounds of the world, we cannot claim to be Christians without opposing human misery. In other words, to accept forgiveness is to be made normal again, to be able to live the way we are supposed to live. To us, no more than to Steve Biko then, can life be a dull affair. It is a moral venture, played for high stakes. How can people be devout without being daring? It is criminal that so many churches draw the settled and comfortable, and repel the venturesome, when the New Testament was precisely the opposite.

But the demands of forgiveness are not the whole story. If we live as we are supposed to live, we shall find the rewards to be as great as promised by the prophets. Life for Biko was a hazardous and straining enterprise, and it was short; but it was full, and peculiarly satisfying.

So the liturgy as far as we followed it, sets forth a thesis, if you will, an antithesis, and a very difficult synthesis: God's love, of which we sang; our sin, which we confessed, and the words of assurance that God's love is greater than our sin. Spoken to the hearts of sinful people, words of forgiveness should be as pure oxygen on dying embers. Therefore, God grant that we too, in a sick society, may bless with health the lives we touch; in a world of death, become living reminders of all that makes for life. By God's grace, may we too become triumphantly normal. Amen.

Access

OCTOBER 22, 1978

Today is the first day in what is being announced as the "first annual human rights week for persons with disabilities." In large part the organizing work has been done by Riverside's *Mainstream*, a group headed by that indefatigable modern missionary, Betty Knapp, whose wheelchair figuratively and perhaps literally has covered more ground than the feet of ten able-bodied persons.

If we measure progress by how far we have come there is cause for rejoicing. In the United States today deaf people are far better off than they were in 1817 when the first school for the deaf opened in Hartford, Connecticut. The same can be said of the blind, since 1832, when the Perkins Institute for the Blind opened in Boston; and even the emotionally disturbed are better cared for in our public institutions today than they were in 1854, when President Franklin Pierce vetoed the first bill to provide federal funding for mental hospitals. Science and medicine have wrought wonders for the disabled, and thanks to their own inspired protests, landmark legislation on accessibility has just now been passed by HEW and the Congress, although the struggle for compliance and implementation has only just begun.

But how are we to measure progess: by how far we have come, or by how far we might be if only we cared more?

Imagine yourself for a moment in a wheelchair trying to get up the steps of the 125th Street and Broadway subway station; or trying to go down the steps at 116th and Broadway; or into a bus anywhere in New York City; or into the balcony of a theatre for a play, or a class-room on the second floor of almost any public school, or Columbia University; or for that matter imagine yourself in a wheelchair trying to get into most of the city's churches. And I blush myself to realize that I have arrived Sunday after Sunday at the front door of Riverside and have never noticed, until Betty told me, that we don't even have a sign for disabled tourists indicating that accessibility is on the Clare-mont Avenue side.

Or, imagine yourself a blind person in the elevator of a New York office building, trying to find the right button to push; or, once you emerge on the right floor, trying to find the right office door, when the doors are shut and none, as in the elevator, have numbers that are raised so a blind person could feel them.

And how many movie theatres provide hearing aids for the hard of hearing? On and on we could go listing obstacles that wittingly or unwittingly, have been placed in the path of what now amounts to 36 million American citizens, who to some degree are physically or emotionally disabled. And, by the way, what about our little people, what about the thousands of children in this city who live in high-rise apartments who are simply too short to reach the elevator button that will carry them to their homes?

Christians in particular will have much to think about—and do—this week, especially as we remember how much time our Lord spent trying to relieve the suffering of the lame, the halt, the blind, and the emotionally disturbed.

It all boils down to how we view one another. Why else would physical access to so many places be denied so large a minority of our citizens if not that they have been denied access to the hearts of the able-bodied majority? And I can't help thinking that the button pan-els in our elevators would be further down if we sought to support our children more, and to dominate them less. (It helps to remember that children are loaned treasures. They belong to God before they belong to their parents.)

Let me tell you a story about John Silber, the current president of Boston University, who is a short man from Texas and, as if that weren't bad enough, his right arm is only a withered stump. Years ago I knew Silber as an instructor of philosophy competing fiercely with another instructor, Chet Lieb, for that first rung on the ladder leading to academic success. Silber in particular was aggressive, and to the point that one day Lieb couldn't take him any longer. "Silber," he said, "I'm inviting you outside."

"What," said Silber, "you'd fight a man with only one arm?"

"For a man with only one arm you've got too big a mouth. Come on, let's go."

Telling me the story, Silber ended it, "You know, if I had had two arms, I would have embraced him. He treated me as a human being, not as an aberration."

People in wheelchairs will tell you they are smiled at more than anyone else, that even their dumbest opinions meet nodding agreement on the part of people who don't believe a single word of what they are saying. Blind people who work in offices will tell you they always receive the loudest "hello" in the morning, until they remind people that there is nothing wrong with their ears.

Why can't people be just different—not different up, or different down? Why can't the disabled be just folks, natural and normal, only with specific limitations?

I think I know the answer. When I was a college undergraduate I found myself one sunny morning in lower Manhattan, where a bunch of Bowery winos were slumped up against the wall enjoying the sunshine. They looked up at me, but I had trouble looking down at them, because that is exactly what I was doing, in more ways than one. For their looks said to me, "You think you are pretty smart with your college education, don't you," and I had to admit, "Yes, I think I am pretty smart." Their looks said to me, "You think you are hot stuff because you are young and healthy, while we are old and beat up, don't you?" And I had to admit to the truth of that, too. Those winos, having given up their responsibilities had also given up their pretensions. But I had about ten pretensions for every responsibility.

The poor unmask the pretensions of the rich—that their money somehow makes them superior. The old unmask the pretensions of youth—that their youth somehow makes them superior. And youth unmasks the pretensions of middle age—that somehow middle age makes them superior. The uneducated unmask the pretensions of the college crowd, and the disabled the pretensions of the able-bodied. The poor, the elderly, the uneducated, the disabled—they threaten the status quo of all pretentious people who are seeking status elsewhere than in the sight of God. Ah, if only we could stop judging ourselves in relationship to each other and start judging ourselves and others in relationship to God! Then we would be of one heart and soul, united in one Lord whose love is not blind but visionary and perceives behind the wheelchair, behind the braces, the leather, the dog, human beings created in the image of God.

And of course, the disabled have to view the able in the same light, which may be even harder. I love the words we heard earlier from the thirty-seventh Psalm, because they obviously come from such a struggle against bitterness:

> Fret not yourself because of the wicked,
> Be not envious of wrongdoers . . .
> Trust in the Lord, and do good;
> So you will dwell in the land, and enjoy security.
>
> Ps. 37:1; 3

It must have cost the psalmist a lot to say that.

To live from morning to evening the bitterness of one's grievances is no way to live. "To pity oneself," wrote Weatherhead, "is the most weakening of all emotions," and all of us have had experience with that. "Jealousy," wrote Cervantes, "sees with opera glasses, making little things big, dwarfs into giants, suspicions into truths." None of us are victims only of others, never of ourselves. And grievances beget grievances. If ever the wolf is to lie down with the lamb it won't come about because of the grievances of the lambs. It will come about because all see, with St. Paul, that "none is righteous, no, not one," and that all are redeemed by the love of God, made members one of another in one sacred family.

So during this week let us remember the size of our true family, and how we have rent its fabric by denying rights to the disabled among us. Spiritually speaking, none of us are that able, are we? We all need access, most of all to each other's heart. Maybe that's a right too. In any case we shouldn't be loathe to grant such access when we remember how accessible God has made his own heart to all of us.

The Gift without the Giver Is Bare

OCTOBER 29, 1978

Would that today were Reformation Sunday only; but alas it is Budget Sunday also. And while it can, of course, be true of any given Sunday it is peculiarly true of Budget Sunday: sermons can be deadly. They can be flat as soufflés that won't rise; as stale and comfortless as last night's beer; worse yet, they can be theologically poisonous. That those who have listened to such sermons have so considered them for a long time, and in countries other than our own, is indicated by this little rhyme from ancient England, sung to the tune of the Doxology:

> God save us from these raiding priests
> Who seize our crops and steal our beasts,
> Who pray "Give us our daily bread"
> And take it from our mouths instead.

I could point out that in this church it is the Trustees and the Deacons who set the annual goal for the Every Member Canvass. But that would be a weasely sort of thing to do! So instead, let me start with three things I want to avoid, three things that would indeed poison theologically any Budget Sunday sermon.

The first is the often implied assumption that to meet the financial demands of a church is automatically to do the will of God. The "Body of Christ" is the whole church, not every particular church. Surely God must wish some churches dead, so inefficient are they, or so blatant is their unfaithfulness. Said St. Augustine, "There are as many sheep without the fold as there are wolves within." Therefore, to give to an efficient secular organization dedicated to humanist goals may be altogether as pleasing in God's sight as to give to any particular church.

The second thing I want to avoid concerns tithing. Tithing is giving ten percent of your income to a church. I want to defend and commend it as a disciplined means of supporting a church. But in no way do I want to present tithing as some kind of payment-tribute to God—pay it and you're squared away with God. "Woe to you, scribes and Pharisees, hypocrites! for you tithe mint and dill and cummin, and have neglected the weightier matters of the law, justice and mercy and faith" (Matt. 23:23). What Jesus is saying is that merely to tithe is straining out a gnat and swallowing a camel. Merely to tithe is like the army chaplain who ten years ago said with considerable righteousness, "If it weren't for some of us Army Chaplains in Vietnam who do you think would look after the orphans?" The answer was simple: if you want to do something for the orphans, stop killing their fathers and mothers. (I often wonder if there is anything in this world quite as irrelevant as irrelevant righteousness. We don't transcend pharisaical righteousness by doing more of what the pharisees do!)

And finally, among the things I don't want to do this morning is to talk indirectly about what we are talking about—money. Money may be the hardest thing to redeem, but whether or not we give determines whether or not we are practical atheists. The Lord is only served by generosity.

Let's listen again to these words from Deuteronomy: "When you come into the land which the LORD your God gives you for an inheritance, and have taken possession of it, and live in it, you shall take some of the first of all the fruit of the ground, which you harvest from your land that the LORD your God gives you, . . . and you shall go to the place which the LORD your God will choose" (Deut. 26:1–2). The ancient Israelites gave the first fruits of the harvest not as a bleak but unavoidable duty. Rather they did it out of sheer gratitude, and for a simple reason: Why shouldn't God share in the harvest God himself made possible? "The earth is the Lord's and the fullness thereof." That understanding leaps from almost every other page of the Old Testament. The Israelites might take possession of the Promised Land, but they knew they could never claim ultimate title.

Actually, the Israelites were not only more aware than we are of the ultimate source of their bounty; they were also more sensitive to the question of how much everyone should share in the fruits of the labor who took part in the labor. Not even the animals were excluded. How much should the beasts of burden receive? The answer is buried among those 613 often tedious laws in the Deuteronomic Code. How's this for a tender Commandment: "Thou shalt not muzzle the ox when he treads out the grain."

So not only God, but the animals too, were invited to share in what both make possible. So also were the widows and orphans, and the strangers. But they were invited not as a matter of charity; they came simply because God's gifts are for all, not some. In giving to the needy, the Israelites were, in a sense, only giving what was theirs already. No noblesse oblige here; only responsible stewardship. As I said last month, "to each according to his need" is a Biblical form of justice far more basic than "to each according to his work."

And finally let's recall that all this giving on the part of the Israelites took the form of a great festival with lots of food and strong drink. From beginning to end, it was a joyous affair.

Now let's turn to ourselves and this question: How many, do you suppose, of those Californians who voted for Proposition 13 took the first fruits, the first part of the money that was saved by the reduction in their property tax and gave it to their ultimate landlord; how many shared the savings with the poor whose services were so threatened by the passage of Proposition 13? The fact that it's an odd kind of question to ask simply shows how far we have strayed from the ancient understanding. Forgetting God, most of us Americans consider ourselves ultimate property owners, with the government as a sort of mafia to be paid off in taxes in return for protection. To give or not is therefore a question for us alone to decide, and as our charitable instincts dictate, not as justice demands. Worse, we have made our possessions an object of faith. We are what we own. We are what we consume. We are more when we reach a higher standard. In short, we have given our hearts to the status and security our possessions afford, and therein lies the danger of wealth to salvation. Didn't Jesus make crystal clear that you cannot worship both God and mammon?

Let's see if we can be as clear as possible about what Jesus did say regarding money. He did not ask us to renounce all possessions, only the spirit of possessiveness. He is for poverty, not penury. (Lady Poverty is not Dame Destitution.) He asks us to give up luxuries, not necessities. He himself was a carpenter, not a beggar. He didn't separate the "haves" from the "have-nots" so much as he separated the "have too much" from the "have enough." He wants us not to detach ourselves from worldly goods but to use them lovingly. True he sent his disciples forth without possessions, but I think he did so because he wanted all who met them to understand beyond a shadow of a doubt that they were free from all bondage to possessions.

So we have three good reasons to give generously and joyously. First, we give to God because She gave us all things. "All things come of thee, O Lord, and of thine own have we given thee" (1 Chr. 29:14). Secondly, we give to the needy because God's gifts are for all, not some. We only give to the needy what is theirs already. And thirdly, what is to their benefit is also to ours, for in giving we free ourselves from bondage to our possessions.

If we believe in the work of this church we have a fourth reason. Thanks to the initial contribution of Mr. Rockefeller, most of our gifts go to benevolence, to the church's programs, not to her upkeep; and I ask you to consider how many church members in this country can count themselves so fortunate?

I confess that when the deacons and trustees decided to ask $50,000 more of us this year, I winced. Now, however, I rejoice. It's a lot—14 percent more than last year. We would have had to raise 7 percent more, given the rate of inflation, just to stay even. But why double that percentage? Because hard times are good times for Christians to behave in proper Christian fashion.

There is a mood of disaffiliation in the land. The middle class is in revolt, seeking security rather than the public good. Individuals and families seem bent on becoming sanctuaries from society, not tributaries to it. And while many "new-born" Christians are affirming in their private lives much that is true, good, beautiful and human, they are refusing to cope with what is untrue, not good, unlovely and inhuman in our corporate life. This is irresponsible. We are rapidly making modern day lepers out of the poor and neediest among us.

So, there is no doubt that our first fruits, our gifts, are desperately needed! As I said at the beginning, I myself find practical value in tithing as a disciplined means of giving support. I commend it to you. But the only safe example is the example of the widow to whom Christ called the attention of his disciples. The widow proved that the really loving gift is not something extracted from a person, however large it may be, but something which is given in the overflow of the heart, no matter how small it may be. The widow gave more than she could spare. She gave until she felt the pinch. She gave until she felt the hurt. No, she gave until it felt good! How much should we give? The only safe rule is to give more than we can spare. For only then do we finally give ourselves. The poet was right:

> Not what we give, but what we share,
> The gift without the giver is bare.
> James Russell Lowell

"For When I Am Weak, Then I Am Strong."

NOVEMBER 5, 1978

Twenty years ago I heard a distinguished theologian say, "Ministers are like manure: spread out in the field they have a certain usefulness. But when brought together in a heap, well, the odor gets pretty strong."

Twenty years ago I heard another person say, "Behind every successful minister stands a member of the National Rifle Association."

The trouble was we ministers were all desperately trying to be successful, and as everyone knows, that enterprise is not accidentally but essentially competitive. When together, instead of enjoying, finding comfort in one another's company, we competed. Each put forward what he or she—mostly "he" in those days—deemed his best foot—never mind that the other needed the attention. (It's odd, isn't it, how we always keep putting our best foot forward when it is the other that needs the attention?) So, the Presbyterian ministers would give you bits of last Sunday's sermon; the Episcopalians would give you their worldly sophistication; the Methodists would become oppressively hearty; and don't ask me what the Baptists would do because I saw little of them in those days.

But those days, as I said, were twenty years ago. Now everything has changed. No one knows any more what it means to be a successful minister. And the hulking figure of failure darkens the doorway of many a pastor's study. At the recent Convocation, one pastor said to me, "No matter how old I get, I can't reach the median age of my congregation. The young don't want to be only with the old, just as the old wouldn't want to be only with the young. So as the median age in my congregation rises, the number attending Sunday by Sunday decreases. I'm a failure, no doubt about it, as the world measures these things."

But how are things measured in the divine dispensation? At least among losers, who are overt about their losses, there is less competition, fewer pretensions. Among people who acknowledge their hurt there is more honesty, and if their hurt isn't merely that of a bruised ego, which can't put you in touch with anyone else's hurt, then there is more compassion. I think ministers today feel the suffering and sorrow of the world far more keenly than we did twenty years ago. Successful ministers today are those who have allowed their defeat at the hands of the world to become an occasion for the victory God always had in mind for them. For "God's power is made perfect in weakness." "When I am weak, then I am strong."

I have been talking of ministers, but as I am sure you have recognized, I have been talking about a profound human experience shared by almost all of us. When we are young we dream of glory. We are going to dance like Patricia McBride, sing like Luciano Pavarotti. We are going to have the lashlike left arm of Ron Guidry, a pen that writes like that of Saul Bellow, or a courtroom career like that of F. Lee Bailey. It's all very hot and heady. Then—say at thirty-five or forty—comes the cold shower, the often brutal contrast between the dream of our youth and what became of it.

It's a traumatic moment with which those people cope well who recognize at long last a profound truth: life is limitation. Just as a stream has no possibility of running deep until it finds its banks, so we, until we discover our limits, haven't a chance of being profoundly honest, compassionate, understanding. Like the ministers of whom we were speaking earlier, these people too allow their defeats at the hand of the world to become an occasion for the victory God always had in mind for them. How often in this place we have heard John Morrison sing, "If you cannot sing like angels, if you cannot preach like Paul, you can tell the love of Jesus, and say he died for all." You can take your pain to Christ. You can allow your pain to widen your sympathies, and so make of your pain a balm in Gilead to make other wounded whole.

But while some cope, no few mope. At thirty-five or forty, they suffer the defeat, but they have no taste of victory. They begin to feel vaguely inferior, but instead of courageously confronting the cause, they go on futiley trying to win marks of esteem from a society that is constantly attacking their self-confidence. It's sad to see them become defensive, to hear their bitter words, "If you don't expect anything from life, you'll never be deceived." That of course is true. But it's also true that if you stop breathing you'll never swallow germs.

You *have* to expect something from life. You have to believe that you're a somebody, that there is a place and purpose for you in this world, a certain calling, even a mission for your life. *And there is*, only it may not be the one defined in our expectations.

It's crucial that we make the switch. It's a central act of Christian faith to allow God to turn our defeats into victories. The cross itself, a central symbol of our faith, can be seen as a minus—our minus— turned by God into a plus. I know how hard it is to make the switch, but if we stay mired in our disappointments, if we allow grievances to be the only truth that sticks in our lives, then believe me not only will all the vital juices drain from our lives; we shall become a bane rather than a blessing to others.

Once, when the bottom dropped out of my life, I went to see a friend I knew was a wonderful counsellor. "I'm feeling miserable," I said. "Good," he answered. "Can you stay with the feeling?" I was shocked. I thought I had come for comfort. He thought I had come for greater honesty, no matter what the pain in attaining it. Fortunately he won. He made me realize that if I was disillusioned it was my fault for having illusions in the first place. Who in the world ever gives any of us the right to have illusions? He even pulled out of his wallet one of those Salada tea bag sayings, which he handed over to me and said, "Here, I carry this around for people like you." I looked at it, and it read: "Don't complain about the way the ball bounces if you are the one who dropped the ball."

Although I swore at him, he smiled knowing that at heart I was deeply grateful. He was a true friend, one who risks his friendship for the sake of his friend.

Well, I would like to risk my friendship for the sake of some of you, dear friends. Some of you have been deeply disappointed in life; you have been hurt. But you haven't acknowledged it with the honesty of which you are capable, with the strength which God gives you precisely for this purpose. How do I know? Because I am your pastor and I see your hidden agendas. Every pastor observes people working in the church in a way that obviously reflects an effort to compensate for failures outside. As a result of the hidden agendas, individuals and groups compete, when there should only be cooperation among them. There is too much jockeying for position, not enough trust; too much whining, not enough good honest fighting; too little of the anger of the kind that clears the air, too much of the hostility that pollutes it.

We all have hidden agendas. They spring up like weeds in the soil of unacknowledged disappointment. And I am not excluding myself. But that's why we need each other in the church—to help each other gently but firmly to acknowledge these hidden agendas, not to become victims of them. For it is hidden agendas that erode the fabric of human relations, whether at home, or in an office or factory, or in the church.

Remember that just as you cannot find God without finding yourself guilty of betraying him on a thousand occasions, so you cannot have expectations without being disappointed by them. But just as God grants us mercy for our sins, so he gives us strength for our disappointments. Remember too that society doesn't tell you who you are. Maybe an individual is measured in relationship to society, but a person is defined in relationship to God. In God's sight every one of us is precious. For every one of us, She has a place, a purpose, a calling, a ministry. For we all are ministers, *after* our defeats have become occasions for God's truth to triumph through us. For God's power is made perfect in weakness. "When I am weak, then I am strong."

Martin Luther once said, "God can carve the rotten wood and ride the lame horse." Oh, what excellent company we are going to become one for another when we can translate that truth into the life of Riverside Church.

"And the Greatest of These"

NOVEMBER 19, 1978

One of the things I like most about Ann Landers' column—aside from her common sense—is the way her correspondents sign off: "Miserable in Memphis" or "Perplexed in Peoria." If you are either of these, or perhaps "Yearning in the Yukon," "Happy in Harlem," or "Hopeless in Hackensack"—it makes no difference—the Bible is for you. It is also for atheist psychiatrists, who leap to read the insights on human nature contained therein. For example, our Savior has declared that "a man will leave his father and mother and cleave unto his wife." That means the wife, when she marries the husband, is not supposed to marry his father too. And what about "Let the dead bury the dead!" That means, let the dead bury the dead—and not the living.

The Bible is also for poets who know both the inexplicable joy and the intolerable pain of beauty. There's even more in the beauty of holiness.

The Bible's for the young who want to know what the world will be like when all the surprises are over, and it's for the old who want to remain unwrinkled in heart.

I heard of a prisoner once who, feeling utterly abandoned, decided that he would hang himself in his cell. But before climbing up on his cot his eye fell on a scribbled message left there by a former inmate. It read Isaiah 43:1–3 Unable to die without satisfying his curiosity, he asked for a Bible, and he read:

> Fear not, for I have redeemed you; I have called you
> by name, you are mine. When you pass through the
> waters I will be with you; and through the rivers,
> they shall not overwhelm you. . . . For I am the LORD
> your God.

Well, he's still alive. The Bible can comfort the afflicted. It can also afflict the comfortable, bring down the mighty from their thrones. In fact, the Bible can do almost anything for anybody. But we don't worship a book, which in fact is many books—*biblia* in Greek means many books. We worship the main character of all the books, God, who is unbelievably stern and at the same time excruciatingly tender.

So, don't read the Bible for helpful hints, for a little light to brighten your way. No, read the Bible for something big: to find out about what God has done for all of us through the prophets, through the history of Israel, through the life of Christ. The best way to find out about yourself is to read the Bible. Self-knowledge through self-contemplation is self-defeating. You just stew in your own juice. But if you study the Bible you will find yourself revealed and the whole world with you. And furthermore, you will see what it all might be were we to achieve the condition described by the poet as one of "complete simplicity costing not less than everything."

Nowhere is this condition more lyrically described than in the thirteenth chaper of First Corinthians, whose first paragraph has to be one of the most radical statements in all literature: "Though I speak with the tongues of men and angels but have not love, I am a noisy gong"—I am nothing but noise, no music. "And though I have all knowledge, and faith sufficient to move mountains, and though I give my body to be burned"—the very stuff of heroism—"and have not love, I am nothing."

The first paragraph of that chapter says in effect, we are what we eat, in part, because we are part animal. We are as we think, in part, because the life of the mind is a very important part of the human life. But most of all, we are as we love, for if we fail in love, we fail in all things else. There is no smaller package in the world than that of a person all wrapped up in himself.

So look out preachers who dangle your hearers over the flames of hell. You may scare them but you can't save them, and you probably can't save yourselves either, for it sounds as if you hate evil more than you love the good. And if that's true you'll only end up very good haters.

Look out scholars whose truths are not rooted in compassion. You may be very clever but you'll never be wise.

Look out patriots. Though American blood be shed, that doesn't make the cause one whit more sacred, for in and of itself sacrifice confers no sanctity. "Though I give my body to be burned. . . ."

Look out parents, more interested in discipline than in good old body warmth. And look out, kids. You may have been abused by your parents; you may have been hurt by discrimination, unemployment, gang warfare, teachers—you name it. You don't hurt back. Not if you know who you are. For we are as we love, as we are able to make a gift of ourselves to others, as Christ made a gift of himself to us.

A condition of complete simplicity, costing not less than everything. Who says Christianity has been tried and found wanting? It's been tried and found difficult. Only the very strong can be tender.

The second paragraph lists fifteen characteristics of love. Let's take a brief look at just a few. The first, "Love is patient," sounds pretty passive, doesn't it? Why should we knock ourselves out when no one seems to respond?

The answer to that is that God seems to have the very same problem with all of us. Harry Emerson Fosdick once pointed out that no one treated Abraham Lincoln with more contempt than Edwin Stanton. He called him "a low cunning clown." He said that a man named Du Chaillu was a fool to wander about Africa trying to capture a gorilla when he could have found one so easily at Springfield, Illinois. Lincoln said nothing. He made Stanton his war minister because he was the best person for the job. The years wore on. Then came the fatal evening when Lincoln was assassinated. In the little room to which they carried Lincoln's body stood the same Stanton, his face now bathed in tears. Looking down on the rugged silent face of Lincoln, he blurted out, "There lies the greatest ruler of men the world has ever seen." The patience of love had done its work. "Love is patient and kind" just as God is patient and kind with us.

The paragraph continues: "Love is not jealous." What makes envy so irresistible, I think, is that jealousy is associated with loss of power. If you are annoyed because your wife has looked at another man, or won't tell you what someone else said, it's not only because you fear losing your wife; what you also fear is losing power over her. But love doesn't need that kind of power. It's secure. And for that reason it is not boastful either, boastfulness always reflecting insecurity.

St. Paul makes nice linkages: "Love is patient and kind; love is not jealous or boastful." Further on we read, "Love does not insist upon its own way" or, as in some translations, "Love does not insist upon its rights." That again sounds a little passive. If you are a woman, or if you are Black, or if you are Puerto Rican, or if you are a homosexual, of course you must insist upon your rights when they are denied. But you must do so as a matter of justice, in the name of God, for the sake of the person oppressing you altogether as much as for your own sake. It's not good for people to oppress. In fact it's worse to oppress than to be oppressed.

The trick is not to hand over your identity to others. Some people— too many in fact—need enemies to tell them who they are. One of the beautiful characteristics of Martin Luther King Jr. was that he did not. His identity was a matter between God and himself; white folks didn't enter in. Therefore King was free to love white folks because he didn't have to hate them. He was free to rejoice in the right. You rejoice in the wrong only when you need enemies to tell you who you are.

And at the end of the paragraph we read, "Love bears all things, believes all things, hopes all things, endures all things."

Well, if there is one thing we learn from Christ and one thing we have to learn well as we watch our barbaric progress towards ever sicker cities, and ever higher military budgets, it is the importance of endurance. Love is a long distance runner. Love has a longer wind than any of the other contestants in the race. In fact, says St. Paul, beginning the last paragraph of the chapter, "Love never ends." When all the other things in which we glory and pride ourselves have passed away, love will still stand.

You remember what the prisoner read—"when you pass through the waters I will be with you; and through the rivers they shall not overwhelm you . . ."? That same water metaphor appears frequently in Scripture. "Many waters cannot quench love, neither can the floods drown it."

Love alone is safe against all the assaults of the world, and love is safe against the assault of death itself. "God is love and he who abides in love abides in God and God abides in him." Death cannot separate us from the love of God. In another lyrical chapter Paul writes, "For I am persuaded that neither death nor life, nor principalities nor powers, nor things present nor things to come, nor heights nor depths, nor any other creature can separate us from the love of God which is in Christ Jesus our Lord" (Rom. 8:38–39). So, "Death, where is thy sting? Grave, where thy victory?" Our lives run from God, in God, to God again. The abyss of love is deeper than the abyss of death.

Well, dear fourth graders, there are many things in that big thick book which today you have received, and which probably ought to have a red cover rather than one so severe. The Bible's not grim. There are many things in that book that you don't understand now. And if you are like most of us there are some things you will never understand. But don't worry about the things you don't understand. Stay with the things you really do understand. Remember God tells you who you are. God tells you you are an infinitely precious person. And God has sent you Jesus as a Savior not a destroyer, somebody to look out for you, not somebody who is supposed to scold you and discipline you and all those things all the time. Learn by heart some of those passages which will stand you in good stead in Memphis, or in Peoria, or in Harlem, or Hackensack. And maybe some day you will want to learn an entire psalm, like the Twenty-third Psalm in the Old Testament, or this entire chapter in the First Letter to the Corinthians. In any case, learn the last sentence, learn it and recite it to your parents before you go to bed tonight. As you can see it says, "Now abide faith, hope, love, these three, but the greatest of these is love."

November 19, 1978

"Be on the Watch"

The text for today's sermon is "I say to all—be on the watch" (Mark 13:37).

One reason there is so little excitement in standard brand Protestant churches is that there is so little sense of expectation. The expectation of something new has either died in skepticism born of bitter experience, or has emigrated to cults, aspects of the human potential movement, the peace movement—which includes many religious people—or to certain political revolutionary movements. It is more than sad, it's a shame to state this, for the New Testament is nothing if not a testament of the new. It speaks of a new heaven and a new earth; it describes a new Jerusalem. It anticipates a new song, new wine. It describes the "new being" that all of us Christians are supposed to become, and winds up at the end of the book of Revelation praising a God who says, "Behold, I make all things new."

And at the beginning, describing Advent, the New Testament declares that we shall have what our faith expects—a Messiah.

The historical Jesus, however, is not automatically the Christ of our personal faith. As in Biblical times so in ours, the Savior can't save you—not from the listlessness, the banality, maybe even the cruelty of your daily life; he cannot save you unless you expect to be saved, unless you yearn for the unexpected, unless you are convinced, as it were, that life is too short to waste on daily living. So, let this first Sunday in Advent be full of expectations, and let the message read something like this: unless you say, "There must be something more," you're living something less than life. Unless you say, "There must be some mistake," you *are* mistaken. Unless you say, "Wake, awake, the night is flying," you'll never see the dawn of a new day, neither in your personal life nor in the life of this nation. In other words, unless you say, "There is hope" you're hopeless!

We shall have what our faith expects. But we have to yearn for it—

> Like the deer that yearns
> For running streams
> So my soul is yearning
> For you, my God.

(Nobody could yearn like the psalmist!)

My soul is thirsting for God
The God of my life;
How can I enter and
See the face of God?

Psalm 42:2

When thou sayest, Seek ye my face; . . .
Thy face, LORD, will I seek.

Psalm 27:8

In my experience, those who most yearn to seek the face of God are dying people. Let's say a woman who is both wife and mother is living her last days. She can generally see and talk to, and enjoy the company of her husband, her children, and her friends who come to visit. (Don't forget that in dying everything isn't sad, just as in living everything isn't glad.) But then the time comes, if she is a believer, when she must seek the face of God and his alone. Her eyes may be open but she no longer sees John and Mary and the children around the bedside. Her eyes are clearly on something inward. It is the last moment of life, the time to heed the admonition. "Don't die with the others, die with Christ."

But clearly we need Christ to live a good life, not just to die a good death. In times of such insecurity as ours, people are clinging to their possessions for the security they think their possessions afford. It's a terrible mistake. When we are secure in Christ's love we don't need all these things—except to enjoy them all the more for the wonderful gifts of God that they are. There's such a difference between clinging to and enjoying. Blake caught it—

He who bends to himself a joy
Doth the winged life destroy,
But he who kisses a joy as it flies
Dwells in eternity's sunrise.

More than ever we need to yearn to see God's face. Cluttered though it may be, Advent is a time when we simply must clear space fervently to pray "Veni Emmanuel, Come Lord Jesus, take possession of my life, that I may loosen my white-knuckled grip on my possessions. Make me as vulnerable, Lord Jesus, as thou wast on the day when thou wast born."

Many of you will know what I am talking about when I say that, around a dying person, family members know an intimacy rarely before enjoyed. The reason is simple. Death is a great truth, and in the presence of a great truth, we ourselves become more truthful.

How much more in the presence of the living Christ should we be open and vulnerable, at ease one with another. Yes, we shall have what our faith expects. In Christ's birth we ourselves shall be born again to a more loving, truthful, joyous life. That is God's Advent promise. But we have to yearn for it. "When thou sayest, Seek ye my face; . . . Thy face LORD, will I seek."

But great expectations are not selfish ones. The expectation of change is not for us alone but for all people, and especially for those whose hopes for peace and a crust of justice have been so long and inexcusably deferred. It is interesting how, already before his birth, it was clearly understood by rulers such as Herod, that the Messiah was coming to the poor. In those days Jesus belonged to the poor, and the rich were properly nervous. Today it is blithely assumed that Jesus belongs to the rich; and the poor sometimes wonder where their friend has gone.

In that first Advent it was equally clear that the Messiah would signal peace on earth—and not through preparation for war either. Now, it is blithely assumed that our coming Savior comes champagne bottle in hand to break over the latest aircraft carrier proposed by the Pentagon. What's happened that we should have gotten everything upside down? Will the clay say to the potter, "I made you"; will the thing made say to its maker, "You don't understand, you are naive"?

To yearn for Christ is not to pray "Thy Kingdom come" and tomorrow bar its way. To yearn for Christ is not to pray for peace and pay for war. To yearn for Christ is not to empty our pocketbooks for the biggest ballistic binge the world has ever known.

When I consider the terrible events of Guyana, I keep returning to one question: when at two in the morning, they were going through the Kool-aid drill for a simultaneous suicide, didn't someone understand the possibility of what might happen? Suppose someone had said, "This is crazy. I'm not going to take this drink. We're not going through with a mass suicide, ever, so why the drill?" That, at least, would have brought home some reality.*

I suppose they took the drill, many feeling, "Well, it can't happen." If it seemed a little much, "Well, you have to take the bad with the good." Besides "Rev. Jones is a real Dad to us. He makes us feel good, he has given us security, he has provided direction for our lives."

---

*Coffin is referring here to the mass suicide of more than 900 members of the Peoples Temple group in Jonestown, Guyana, in November 1978.

Today the Pentagon is Rev. Jones. Once an honorable institution, it is showing signs of the same paranoia and meglomania that afflicted Jones in his last months. Like Jones it has conditioned us, in our case by ever rising military budgets, against which we have not protested, so that we are in the same danger as Rev. Jones' followers of passively giving over to the Pentagon the power to cause our own destruction. The proposed civil defense is the Kool-aid drill without the cyanide, a preparation for mass suicide of unthinkable proportions—what of the millions who won't be included in the drill? Of course it is called a test of patriotic loyalty to prove that we are willing to die for our country.

Isn't it time for somebody to refuse the drill? Isn't it time for somebody to say "This is crazy"? And who should refuse to drink from the giant vats of the Pentagon, if not those who take the cup of salvation with their Lord and Savior? Those who are made strong by the blood of Christ can have nothing but contempt for the poison proffered by the Pentagon. In the name of our coming Savior, the Prince of Peace, we refuse it.

Advent is the season to yearn for Him who was nothing but goodness and decency, sweet reason, God's love incarnate. It is his face alone that we must seek, even if it means we must turn for a while from public life, and even if it means we must turn for a while from the faces of those we love. Never before have we needed our Savior more. We shall receive what our faith expects—but only if we prepare the way, only if our expectation is great. Thus "I say to all, 'Be on the Watch.'"

The Courage of Hope

DECEMBER 10, 1978
Reading: Luke 1:46–55

On this the second Sunday in Advent, let's talk for a few minutes about hope. But let's not talk about hope as a noble quality of heart which stoically endures despite everything. Rather lot us talk about hope as it is understood biblically. Let us talk about hope as it rings so clearly and rightly in the words of Mary in the Magnificat: "My soul magnifies the Lord, and my spirit rejoices in God my Savior."

We can start by noting that hope has nothing whatsoever to do with optimism. In fact, the man who said "I used to be an incurable optimist, but now I'm cured"—that man is ready for hope. For hope is what's still there when all your worst fears have been realized.

Advent is a dramatic time. It anticipates Christmas, which can be seen as a mammoth struggle between God's light and human darkness, both desperate to overcome the other. The darkness mustn't be overlooked. We must recognize that today some, at least, of our worst fears are going to be realized. This nation is on the brink of a major economic collapse, and on the brink of an energy crisis of enormous magnitude. Nor do I think we can prevent World War III, not as long as we continue to nourish a "win" mentality in a "no win" situation.

These ills have moral roots. The trouble with this country is that it misses Richard Nixon. The trouble with this country is that to be a good American you no longer have to be a good person. Sensitive secularists recognize the selfishness of the age. David Bell speaks of a "neo-hedonism," Christopher Lasch of "the narcissistic personality of our time." Tom Wolfe bemoans a "me generation," and Richard Sennett what he calls "the Fall of public man."

And do not say "Well, we still have one another, our families, islands of intimacy in an increasingly choppy sea." Poor families at least cannot withstand the assaults of unemployment and inflation. Two days ago on 125th Street I stood beside a car which the night before had rammed into a lamppost so hard that the lamppost now stood inches from the steering wheel. Wondering how it happened, I found myself recalling words of the poet Vladimir Mayakovsky, his last before he took his life:

> And now, as they say, the incident is closed,
> Love's boat has smashed against the daily grind.

"I used to be an incurable optimist, but now I'm cured. I see the selfishness. I don't want to hear anymore of self-awareness, self-realization, self-actualization, self-fulfillment as if all these 'selves' finally didn't amount to the worst form of deception, self-deception. I now see that optimism is for the proud, hope for the humble; optimism is human, hope divine. And I see that human affairs are too important to be left to human beings alone."

"All glory to the creator, man, the maker and master of all things?" No, Mr. Swinburne.

> My soul doth magnify the Lord,
> And my spirit rejoices in God, my Savior.

Notice that hope always stands in contradiction to what we are presently experiencing. Mary was convinced she would never have a child; and God gave her the baby Jesus. Sarah, Abraham's wife, was certain that she was barren, and she bore Isaac. And one more thing: "My soul magnifies the Lord." Mary is not rejoicing in what she has done, but in that which is going to be done by the child she bears within her. So, likewise, St. Paul rejoices: "Not I, but Christ who dwells within me."

We have to be convinced that we ourselves are barren, before we can become expectant. To make room for the Messiah, we have to be rid of all our messianic complexes. To make room for the Savior, we have to be rid of all illusions that we can save ourselves or anyone else in this world. For hope to be born, optimism must die.

Let's go on.

> He has shown strength with his arm,
> He has scattered the proud in the imagination of their
>   hearts. [what a line!]
> He has put down the mighty from their thrones,
> And exalted those of low degree;
> He has filled the hungry with good things,
> And the rich he has sent empty away.

How can we dare to hope for all that? Because the world swings on an ethical hinge. Loosen it and all history and even nature will feel the shock. We don't break the commandments; we are broken on them. We aren't punished for our sins so much as we are punished by them. Show me a happy murderer, a deeply contented thief! The bad news of today is part of the eternal Good News of the Gospel: God is not mocked. Affluence can't buy morale. You can't grind the faces of the poor into the dirt and get away with it forever. Nixons come, but Nixons go. And at this moment, the Shah of Iran, that modern day armed-to-the-teeth John Wayne, is about to take his terminal ride into the sunset, no doubt on board the latest American fighter jet. Yes, pride goes before a fall. Anyone who needs more than God as his witness is too ambitious.

In other words, the world denounces itself as it were; we can't get away with anything. But beyond denunciation is also annunciation: the coming of Emmanuel, "God with us." Marx saw God as a coward's excuse. He failed to see God as a brave man's hope. Courage is the inseparable companion of hope. And the virtue of courage is that it makes all other virtues possible.

Earlier I talked of the evil of presumption. Now let me point out that presumption has a twin—equally evil—despair. Presumption is the premature anticipation of fulfillment, despair the premature anticipation of non-fulfillment. And they do go together. Mayakovsky, ten years before his suicide, was describing the Russian revolution as the second flood which would wash clean all the cities of the world. And after "All glory to the creator man, the maker and master of all things," Swinburne ended up writing:

> From too much Love of living, from too much hope
>   set free,
> We thank with brief thanksgiving whatever Gods may be
> That no life lives forever, that dead men rise up never.
> That even the longest river winds somewhere out to sea.

Presumption and despair. At the turn of the century we were threatened by Prometheus, but not far behind comes Sisyphus to haunt us at century's end.

Presumption and Despair. These evil twins can be defeated by Hope and her twin Courage. We don't have to suffer history, we can make history. We don't have to be destroyed by the predictable future, we can create a preferable one. But only if we fall to our knees out of a sense of no other place to go. So let us declare ourselves barren that we may become expectant. Like Mary let us bear the Christ Child, each of us. With Mary let us sing, "My soul magnifies the Lord," rejoicing not in anything we have done, but in that which will be done by the Child we bear within us. With St. Paul let us say, "Not I, but Christ who dwells within me." Amen.

"Rejoice in the Lord Always"

DECEMBER 17, 1978

Last week, as some of you may be kind enough to remember, I spoke of hope as it is understood biblically. I said that hope had nothing whatsoever to do with optimism. I said that even after your worst fears have been realized, hope can survive, a flame in the night, for while optimism is human, hope is divine. I think I even said "When optimism dies, hope is born."

Well, in somewhat the same vein we can perhaps talk today of joy. Biblically understood, joy is that which still stands firm when the last shreds of happiness have been scattered on the winds like thistledown. Joy is that which still blazes when the sorrows of the world sweep over you like a sea; for while happiness is human, joy is divine. Therefore, as of love so it can be said of joy: many waters cannot quench it, neither can the floods drown it.

Living with me this week is an Argentinian friend, an exile, who tells me that at Christmas he cannot go to church because to do so would be too painful a reminder of the happy times spent with his now absent family. It would also be too painful a reminder of his fiancée who was arrested, tortured, and probably put to death, unless, as he says, she was sold as a prostitute to some Arab country, a fate, he claims, not uncommon to political prisoners in Argentina. What he feels and says I can well understand. But I find it sad that when he most needs God's comfort, he pulls back because he cannot separate the joy that is of God from human happiness, because he hasn't yet experienced that which teaches that finally it is easier to unite pain with joy, than superficial pleasure with joy.

But my friend Juan might well say to me, "And what right do you have, amigo, to be joyful when as a professed Christian your conscience must be anxious. You know that the present ambivalence of the church in Argentina, vis-à-vis oppression only reflects the characteristic stance of the church in every country, in every generation, in almost every instance of oppression?"

We all know how the church waffled on slavery. We all know how even after 1,900 years not a single woman, not even a St. Teresa, has been allowed to enter the sacred orders of the Roman Catholic clergy. And shall Protestants boast? It was, I believe, Antoinette Louisa Brown who was the first ordained seminary graduate in the United States. That ordination was in a Congregational Church in Wayne County, New York in the year 1853. So great was the hostility from both clergy and laity that one year later she, herself, requested dismissal.

And if we don't know it already, we certainly should learn the Church record on anti-Semitism. Three hundred Jewish communities were destroyed in the German Empire in 1348. Jews were expelled from England even earlier, in 1290; from France in 1394; from Spain a hundred years later—98 to be exact; and in 1497 all Jews were expelled from Portugal.

What right have we to be joyful this Christmas, when we remember that the Christian church has probably killed more martyrs than it has produced? Joy is not automatically every Christian's just deserts. And how poignant that truth becomes when we remember that our inhumanity one to another is only exceeded by our inhumanity to God. What makes it so hard for me to go to church at Christmas is the painful reminder that he who was to be bread of life for human beings is laid in the feedbox of animals.

And yet we sing "Joy to the world," and properly so—the louder the better—for "the Lord is come," not as a reward, but as the most gracious gift a loving father could make his erring children. "Rejoice in the Lord always, and again I say rejoice," because while happiness may be human, joy is divine.

But let us be clear. Last week I opposed hope to optimism, but this week let us not oppose divine joy to human happiness. *Joy is not the denial but the foundation of happiness.* Joy enhances worldly pleasures infusing them with more meaning than they could possibly have were they not parts of God's creation. And by pleasures I mean every last one of them that doesn't represent an escape from reality. The Messiah we await is not a John the Baptist dedicated to locusts and honey in the desert. Jesus will be called "a glutton and a drunkard." In the Gospel that depicts Christmas so starkly—"He came unto his own home, and his own people received him not"—in that same Gospel our Lord and Savior first visits human beings not in their sadness but in their happiness, at a wedding feast at Cana. Whether you believe he turned the water into wine is not as important as your understanding that Jesus comes down on the side of human happiness. Jesus is not "uptight," or as we say in the church, "upright." No, he is full of passion, full of love, full of sorrow mingled with tears of joy, for the more one is capable of joy the greater one's capacity for sorrow. Believe me, if we are heavy and gloomy it's not because we're Christians; it's because we are not Christian enough. It's probably because, afraid of accusations too harsh, we avoid joys too intense. It's a sort of boring bargain we make with ourselves: in order not to feel too badly about some things we won't feel really good about anything. But emotional mediocrity is not the Good Life.

"Rejoice in the Lord always; and again I say rejoice . . . The Lord is at hand, in nothing be anxious." What an incredible statement, that last, but it's true; it's all this fretting about our insecurity and our inadequacy which produces all this emotional, and we should add, "intellectual and spiritual" mediocrity. You know what that son of a Protestant preacher, Friedrich Nietzsche said about Christ's followers? "His disciples should look more redeemed." He's right. "Rejoice in the Lord always; again I say rejoice."

But if joy does not deny pleasure, neither does it oppose pain, except those forms of pain that like so many pleasures constitute an escape from reality. People escape reality through pain as much as they do through pleasure. All of us are crisis-prone, I am convinced of that. But the way we avoid the major and proper crises of life is to get embroiled in the wrong ones. And the only answer to that kind of pain and suffering is "Stop it. It's too boring. Get on to the real crises!"

I said at the outset that it is easier to unite pain with joy than superficial pleasure with joy. What I meant was that it is not really pain that is unbearable. What is really unbearable in this world is meaninglessness. God, while He doesn't explain everything—far from it—in every seemingly meaningless situation can help us fashion a purposeful response. In concentration camps there are always two kinds of inmates: the majority who feel that meaning depends upon the possibility, no matter how slim, of survival; and a minority who insist that meaning be affirmed in the context of no survival. I'm with the latter. I think meaning has to be affirmed in the face of death—which means no survival. I think meaning has to be affirmed in the face of tragedies we cannot possibly fathom, and in the face of human stupidities we can understand all too readily. It is meaning that finally provides joy, a joy that is more profound than either happiness or unhappiness. That's why many waters cannot quench joy.

And finally there is a related kind of joy which is inseparable from pain. St. Paul describes it eloquently and convincingly, in the chapter before the one from which I read. "Whatever gain I had I count as loss for the sake of Christ. Indeed I count everything as loss because of the surpassing worth of knowing Jesus Christ my Lord. For His sake I have suffered the loss of all things and count them as refuse in order that I may gain Christ and be found in Him, not having a righteousness of my own based on law, but that which is through faith in Christ, the righteousness from God that depends on faith. . . . Not that I have already obtained this, or am already perfect; but I press on to make it my own because Christ Jesus has made me His own" (Phil. 13:7–9).

Have you ever had that sense of undeserved integrity which comes with being in the right fight! That is what Paul is here describing. "Rejoice in *the Lord*"—not finally in anything else. A dollar bill may seem more real than Christ, the most real of all realities. But don't short-change yourself. Rejoice finally and always in the Lord, and you will know that sense of undeserved integrity.

Advent is the time to organize your life unobtrusively and yet decisively according to the life and spirit of our coming Savior. It won't always be easy. In fact it will often be hard, for faith has its night as well as its day, and most of the world is dark around us. But the joy of faith cannot be stifled by the suffering we experience within us. The joy of faith cannot even be stifled by the suffering we see around us, nor by the doubts from which we cannot escape. We believe in the sun even when it isn't shining. We believe in love, and especially so when we feel only the anguish of its absence. So we believe in God even in the inevitable moments when we do not feel his light and his love.

So I say "Rejoice in the Lord always; again I say rejoice." The fire of the Spirit blazes unquenchable. "In nothing be anxious, but in everything by prayer and supplication let your requests be made known unto God, and the peace of God which passes all understanding shall keep your hearts and minds in Christ Jesus."

"Joy to the world, the Lord is come." Amen.

The Fear of Christmas

DECEMBER 24, 1978

On Wednesday of this week, writing on the Op Ed page of the *New York Times*, a Princeton historian, Theodore Rabb, recalled John Matthys and John of Leyden, the two charismatic founders of a religious sect that quite literally took over the city of Münster, Germany, in 1534 and 1535. After describing the mind-control exerted by these leaders—non-believers were put to the sword, believers submitted to torment in the name of religion—Rabb explained why it is we are gripped by such bizarre events. Whether in Münster in the sixteenth century, or in Guyana in the twentieth, these events become landmarks because, more than all other events, they challenge our comfortable assumptions about ourselves. They pose disturbing questions: "Are those people so different from me that I don't have to worry about the limits of my sanity? Or is it just possible, under certain conditions, that I, you, all of us, might become equally homicidal and suicidal?

In other words, it is not the prosaic and recurrent events of history but the unique and the bizarre which remain, as Rabb put it, "the best proving grounds for our conclusions about human nature, society, and the temper of a particular time and place."

I found myself in agreement with Rabb's conclusions but dissatisfied with the incompleteness of the presentation. He failed to note the unique and the bizarre on the "positive" side, shall we say, of human history. Sure, it's the crazies who show us a darkness we would prefer to ignore. But it is also true that "it is the cracked ones who let in the light." It is the unique consciences of bizarre characters, like Amos, Ezekiel, Jeremiah—people you wouldn't automatically think of inviting to Christmas dinner—it is these unique consciences, as opposed to the mass mind, that best reflect the universal conscience of humankind. The prophets as well as the demented citizens of Münster are "the best proving grounds for our conclusions about human nature, society, and the temper of a particular time and place."

You can see where I am heading: of all the unique and bizarre events of history, the one that most seriously challenges our comfortable assumptions about ourselves is neither Münster nor Guyana; it is Christmas. It is Christmas that poses questions of the most disturbing order: "Is that small child so different from me that all I have to do is to enshrine him but not follow him? Or, is it just possible that under certain conditions of discipleship, that I, you, all of us could become ever so much freer, more loving, more courageous than we are?"

It's interesting: we fear Guyana, but not Christmas. We're afraid, but not of God. We fear everything except the one great unique event of which we should properly be afraid—the revelation of God. And therein lies not only the key to any profound interpretation of the nature and temper of our time and place but also its tragedy. For as already 50 years ago Karl Barth viewed it: "Christmas without fear carries with it fear without Christmas."

We read of the shepherds, that "they were sore afraid," and inasmuch as it is night about us, so are we. Almost daily, I am impressed by what I sense to be an overriding fear in our time and place—the fear of being reduced. It seems almost to have a life of its own inside each one of us. Economic inflation plays into this spiritual fear of being reduced. And so does unemployment, crime on the streets, and fear of the heightened destructiveness of succeeding generations; and of course the fear of becoming old and lonely. These are all real fears, as I don't have to tell you; fears of uncertainty, fears of the night. Over all hovers death, which threatens to reduce us spiritually more than physically. Tolstoy once said, "Is there any meaning in my life that the inevitable death awaiting me does not destroy?" He understood that it's not extinction, but extinction without significance that is so threatening.

But let us return to the shepherds whose fears are undergoing a radical transformation. If earlier, perhaps, they had feared the night, now, suddenly, their fear of darkness is as nothing compared to their fear of the light. You've seen the pictures, you heard the text. "And the glory of the Lord shone round about them, and they were sore afraid." Suddenly their fears of all kinds of uncertainties are effaced by the awe they experience in the presence of one great certainty. Instead of death they start to fear life. It must have been a fantastic conversion experience; instead of many uncertainties, one certainty; instead of many little fears, one great fear.

To return to us: isn't our trouble that we are a bundle of small terrors, sometimes overwhelming? We have so many little fears, but no great fear. About this and that and the other, we have many little questions, but rarely do we pose the all-important question: does God exist, and if so how are we to fill the time and space allotted us? We put down our roots in flowerpots and expect to grow and flourish like great oak trees!

We fear Guyana, but not Christmas. We're afraid, but not of God. In fact we are so concerned, most of us, with darkness instead of light, with death instead of life, that the great comforting command addressed to the shepherds, "Fear not," which if heeded could take care of all fears including the one great fear—that command we don't even hear.

"Christmas without fear carries with it fear without Christmas." It's Barth's contention that Christmas has become a carnival, a time in which to put aside for the moment your fears instead of that unique bizarre event which attacks all fears at their roots.

"Fear not, for unto you is born this day"—not a stern judge of all our pathetic fears, but "a savior." Can you believe it? Heaven is touching earth with healing. God is humanizing the heavens and spiritualizing the earth, welding the two in one inseparable unit.

"Fear not, for unto you." For your sake, God is not content to be God but has willed to become a human being. For you he has emptied himself so that you might not be reduced, but exalted. God doesn't want His glorification, he wants your glorification. To you, he has given himself in love that you might in love be drawn to him. It's all for you, for you regardless of who you are, for all of us; not a single one is found wanting. "For God so loved the world that he gave his only begotten son that whosoever should believe in him should not perish, but have eternal life."

And finally, "Fear not, for unto you is born this day." Not tomorrow, not next week, not next year. Now. Now is the time to decide, and for us to decide. God is not a charismatic leader demanding that we give over to him our freedom of choice. He only insists that we exercise the freedom of choice which he has given us. So, friends, what is going to grip you: Guyana or Christmas? Nine hundred tragic dead, or one small child born in Bethlehem? What do you choose to fear, death or life? darkness, or the light that "shines in the darkness and the darkness has not overcome it"?

"And the glory of the Lord shone round about them and they were sore afraid." May the glory of the Lord shine around us this Christmas and scare us—to life. Then may we hear the comforting command, "Fear not," which I imagine should help us decide, as did the shepherds, to go "even unto Bethlehem and see this thing which has come to pass."

1979

Some Thoughts on Martin's Fiftieth

JANUARY 14, 1979

L et not the foreigner who has joined himself to the LORD say: 'The LORD will surely separate me from his people' . . . Thus says the Lord GOD, who gathers the outcasts of Israel, 'I will gather yet others to him besides those already gathered'" (Isa. 56:3, 8).

"There is neither Jew nor Greek, there is neither slave nor free, there is neither male nor female, for you are all one in Christ Jesus" (Gal. 3:28).

And to these words of Isaiah and Paul let us add these: "Procrastination is still the thief of time. Life often leaves us standing bare, naked and dejected with a lost opportunity. . . . Over the bleached bones and jumbled residue of numerous civilizations are written the pathetic words: 'Too late' . . . We still have a choice today: non-violent co-existence or violent co-annihilation. We must move past indecision to action."

Had he lived, the author of those last words would tomorrow have been fifty years old. Martin Luther King Jr. was killed before he reached forty. Yet his prophetic life and martyr's death changed all who knew him, all who only heard and saw him. Indeed we can say until the very end of American history this nation will never again be the same because of him. Yet who today is ready "to move past indecision to action"?

After his conversion to Christ a farmer once cried out: "Even my chickens know I'm different." But that's a rare kind of conversion, isn't it? If truth be told, most of the tributes today and tomorrow will be spoken and heard by those who would rather enshrine than follow Martin Luther King Jr. It's a familiar story. When that great man Pope John XXIII died, how many Protestants were eager to join the throngs saying: "This is the one person the world can least afford to lose." Yet saying that in no way affected their basic anti-Catholicism. Never mind that he was only the Pope! And the same is eminently true of our Lord and Savior: him especially we would rather keep *in vitro*— safe under the glass—than *in vivo*, alive among us, asking of us as he did of Peter, "Do you love me?" And if so, then "Feed my sheep."

There are good reasons. What the prophets teach us to believe and what the world rewards as belief are not the same. Martin preached that gentleness takes more courage than violence. How many in the world are ready to be that courageous? Martin preached that human compassion is more valuable than any ideology. Tell that to a communist—or to an American anticommunist. Martin preached that we should be governed by our dreams and not by our fears, that having the ability to fight is as nothing compared to having something worth fighting for. Well, the largest peacetime buildup of military power in the history of the planet belies that belief. What then shall we say? We shall say that we honor, that we love our martyrs—but only after we have slain them as prophets. For what they teach us to believe and what the world rewards as belief are always two different things.

"Thus says the Lord GOD, who gathers the outcasts of Israel, 'I will gather yet others to him besides those already gathered.'" Prophets recognize that revelation always has to be worked out, that there is a progressive nature to moral judgment. So they criticize what is, in terms of what ought to be. They judge the darkness of the present by the light of the future. And they reject what is narrow and provincial, in the name of what is universal. Prophets know that just as all rivers finally meet in the sea, so all individuals, races and nations meet in God. "There is neither Jew nor Gentile, there is neither bond nor free, there is neither male nor female; for you are all one in Christ Jesus."

In a memorable moment in an extraordinary saga of World War II—I am speaking of Herman Wouk's *War and Remembrance*—Captain Henry, a U.S. naval officer, is brought into a bullet-ridden building in Stalingrad. Behind a plank desk he sees a tough-looking grey-headed man in uniform, his face lined with fatigue. He doesn't look friendly. It is 1943, and more and more Soviets are beginning to be convinced that the British and Americans are prepared to fight to the last Russian, that they are never going to open up a second front in Europe. For their part, the British and Americans are leery lest the Russians, exhausted by the war, revert to their ancient truce with Hitler and make a separate peace with the Germans, as they had in World War I. So the American too is reserved. Behind the desk the Soviet official raises thick eyebrows at his compatriot, General Yevlenko, who has brought this man to Stalingrad. In response Yevlenko puts the one remaining hand that a German explosive has left him—puts this good hand on the shoulder of the American and says "Nash"—"ours," and in an instant the word has worked magic. All suspicion on both sides is erased.

How many human problems would resolve and dissolve themselves if all those who are in reality one in God—Americans and Russians, black and white, here or in South Africa; and let's not forget the yellow and the red, the starved and the stuffed, the male and the female—if all were to put hands today on one another's shoulders and say "Nash!," "ours." And it is precisely to that kind of practical utopia that we have here to rededicate ourselves if we are to prove true to him who said, "We still have a choice today: non-violent co-existence or violent co-annihilation."

All in this world is not urgency and anguish. Whenever possible, we should take time out to be proud of the human race. Progress has been made since the sixties because that was a decade of ethical unrest, which to our convenience we call "student unrest." Dr. King would be pleased that black enrollment in colleges increased 275 percent from 1966 to 1976, from 282,000 to 1,062,000. About 11 percent of all collegians are now black as opposed to 4.5 percent in 1966. And when they graduate, few of these students will go back to the streets from which so many of them came—streets of Harlem, Bedford-Stuyvesant, Roxbury, East Detroit, Watts. And in fairness to whites, they will meet more curiosity than hostility in the newly integrated neighborhoods and jobs.

Even as Blacks are breaking up all-white patterns, so women are upsetting the patriarchal structures of America. And this bodes well for the Gay liberation movement, as historically only societies that subordinate women are harsh in their treatment of homosexuality—male homosexuality, that is. Interestingly enough, with the exception of one vague passage in St. Paul, there is not a single mention of lesbianism in all the Bible. (Someday we'll deal with the gross misinterpretations of Scripture on the part of those who, for their convenience, forget that the Nazis put over 200,000 homosexuals to death.)

But what of those streets of Harlem, Bedford-Stuyvesant, Roxbury, East Detroit, St. Louis, and Watts? Who today puts a friendly, as opposed to a rough, hand on the shoulders of those teenagers? Are they "Nash" or do they prove that class is a tougher nut to crack than race? And isn't the arms race getting ahead of the arms control process? Aren't we then ourselves in danger of honoring King as a martyr while trampling on what he stood for as a prophet, as long as we fail to say "ours" to the poor and the foreigner? And King himself saw the connection: "A nation that continues year after year to spend more money on military defense than on programs of social uplift is approaching spiritual death."

Today we are far nearer that death, and it is time for Christians who would honor their fallen prophet to take note. For, as Martin knew well, the church is called to be the Bride of Christ, not the whore of Babylon. She cannot bind herself to the Prince of Peace and go awhoring after the gods of war. She cannot proclaim the gospel of Christ while officiating at the altars of anticommunism. She cannot stand for peace while lying prostrate before the shrine of "national security." If she is to be the church, then she must stand against the drift toward militarism, proclaiming that there is no security in arms alone, that in fact, ironically, the more destructive, the more vulnerable and insecure we become. It is status we are seeking, not security and the "present danger" lies less in the Russians than in the arms race itself. With more nuclear weapons than either we or the Russians will ever need except to obliterate the entire planet, it is time to reverse the arms race, not to propel it to ruinous lengths.

This Wednesday evening, this church is holding a public hearing to see what modest things all of us might do to help alleviate the problems of New York City. I have a suggestion. To honor the centennial of Harry Emerson Fosdick, this church launched a nationwide "reverse the arms race" program. Why not, in honor of the fiftieth birthday of Martin Luther King Jr., send some 75 or 100 or 150 of us to churches throughout this city as a step toward the formation of a citywide religious coalition. The eventual goal of the coalition will be to protest as effectively as possible the President's proposed annual 3 percent increase in the arms budget while cutting human services to the bone.

I cannot help recalling that Martin Luther King Jr. chose this pulpit to denounce the war in Vietnam. That same night, also in opposition to President Johnson, he declared that the choice was between guns and butter. He got roasted, not only by government officials, but other civil rights leaders as well, and of course by *The New York Times*. But he was right. His was one of the great prophetic speeches of American history.

It was King's insight to realize that those furthest from the seat of power are often nearer to the heart of things. It was King's compassion that led him consistently to make common cause with sufferers. And it was King's genius to be able to take a Christian message out of the sanctuary of a church and into the corridors of power. Remember, he was leading a Poor People's March on Washington when he was assassinated.

Something like that needs to be undertaken again. So let us today and tomorrow think about this prophet and martyr who said we should be governed by our dreams, more than our fears; who said that Compassion was more valuable than any ideology; who could lay a hand on anyone's shoulder and say "ours" because he knew that the

Lord "will gather yet others to him besides those already gathered." More than any other human being I ever met, Martin knew that "there is neither Jew nor Greek, there is neither bond nor free, there is neither male nor female; for (we) are all one in Christ Jesus." Amen.

Revelation from 9 to 5

JANUARY 21, 1979
Readings: 1 Samuel 3:1–18; 1 Corinthians 7: 17–24

It was Louis Pasteur, I think, who said, "Chance favors the mind prepared." To bear him out, just think of how many apples fell from how many trees, over how many years, without anyone noticing anything more than falling apples. But when Newton saw the apple fall he saw that all the motions of the universe are expressed in the formula that bodies attract each other in proportion to their masses, and inversely as the square of the distance between them. Yes, indeed. Chance favors the mind prepared.

When Ramanujan, the genius Indian mathematician, lay dying, he was visited by his English and no less brilliant colleague, G. M. Hardy. Always a bit inept, apparently, at introducing any conversation—let alone one to a dear friend on his deathbed—Hardy began, "The number of my taxicab was 1729. It seemed to me rather a dull number."

"No, no, Hardy," replied Ramanujan, his spirit momentarily reviving. "It is a very interesting number. It is the smallest number expressible as the sum of two cubes in two different ways."

When the Pittsburgh Steelers say that they are ready for the game this afternoon, we know they haven't been sitting around on their duffs. And neither have we, when we say we're ready to practice law or medicine. In fact, in every realm other than the religious we train to gain insight. We know it's necessary, if we are to see more than falling apples and dull numbers. But when it comes to a word from the Lord, we expect God to do all the work. He's supposed to minister to us. Yet of young Samuel, we read—and this mind you, before his revelation—he was "ministering to the Lord," in the temple. Just think; the kid went to church in order to help God! I feel ashamed. I work reasonably long hours. But I go home at night to bed. But home to Samuel was the temple, and we read that he slept next to the ark where in some mysterious way the Lord himself was supposed to live. No wonder "the Lord came and stood forth to him." Like chance, revelation favors the mind—and heart—prepared.

Not that all revelations come in temples. Moses' bush was about as far removed from any organized place of worship as Newton's apple. But the point is that all seers—literally those who see—train to be perceptive. Elizabeth Barrett Browning wrote:

> Earth's crammed with heaven
> And every common bush afire with God
> But only he who sees takes off his shoes—
> The rest sit around and pluck blackberries.

I guess that makes most of us a bunch of blackberry pickers, compared, at least, with Moses and Samuel, and their secular counterparts like Newton and Ramanujan. Revelation favors the mind and heart prepared. You have to train to gain insight.

You can remember there was a judgment in Samuel's vision. In fact, it was this ethical note that authenticated the message as coming from God in the mind of Samuel's tutor, the old man Eli. And then comes the truly tender moment. Though the judgment is rendered against Eli himself, and comes through his own pupil, the old man accepts it. At his prompting, "Samuel told him everything and hid nothing from him." The boy gave the old man the undecorated truth. And did Eli overflow with excuses? No, his goodness shining through his humility, he says, "It is the Lord; let him do what seems good to him."

Let me say I have trouble with that "forever" stuff in Samuel's message, as I have trouble with all Biblical "forevers" that pertain to God's judgment. I simply have to rule out of court any conception of God's love which comes out as something less than human love as we know it at its best. But this I do understand: Eli is a man of faith, who understands that life is consequential. Through forgiveness, we can be spared the consequences of our sin. God's justice is tempered by mercy. God's justice is not diluted in mercy.

Now with these points from this story in mind, let us turn to our own "calling," our own "vocation," the word, as most of you know, from the Latin vocation which means literally "a call." That from most of our vocations we can't wait to take a vacation probably indicates to what degree the life of faith has been suspended during working hours. In our time, as in Samuel's, the word of the Lord is rare; there are no frequent visions. But can we, like Samuel, use these hours to minister unto the Lord? Is it possible for us to hear the word of God in a 9-to-5 job? And what is the ethical note that authenticates such a word?

I think it helps to recall that the Bible sets forth two views of work, both in the early chapters of Genesis. Before he took a bite from the only apple more famous than Newton's, Adam is pictured as a happy gardener, tilling and tending Eden. But any change in our vertical relationship with God affects all our relationships on a horizontal level. So the consequences of Adam's fall affect even his work, about which God now says to him in his vision, "in the sweat of your face you shall eat bread" (3:19).

Whether we view our work as that of a steward in God's garden or as a necessary evil, will depend in large part on whether or not we take to heart these words of St. Paul: "For he who was called in the Lord as a slave is a freedman of the Lord. Likewise he who was free is a slave of Christ." I love these words. I read them as preaching the essential democracy of all vocations. All vocations are created equal, as it were. Therefore all comparisons are odious. St. Paul seems to be saying that you cannot enhance your self-esteem by comparing yourself as a freedman to a slave, or, shall we say, as a doctor to a nurse, a college professor to a public school teacher. And vice-versa. If you are a janitor you have no right to compare yourself negatively with the boss whose office you clean after he goes home.

Last month we heard a lot about the shepherds. Well, that was low-down work keeping watch over those flocks by night, and no doubt there are a lot of people who considered them low-down folk. Yet a multitude of the heavenly host appeared unto them, as opposed to a single star to the wise men! And after they had seen the Christ-child, did the shepherds run off and become lawyers and doctors? No, they went back to tending their sheep, and a good thing for their sheep they did, not to mention the people who needed the wool.

So what is the word of the Lord for those who have ears to hear? "Work does not make us holy, we must make work holy" (Meister Eckhart). Our work does not give meaning to our lives. It is meaningful lives that confer meaning upon work. It's simple enough. If in your 9-to-5 job you are looking for status, then you cannot, like Samuel, minister unto the Lord between 9 and 5. You are ministering unto yourself. If instead of the satisfaction of achievement you're looking for the vindication of your pride, then your work is still a consequence of the fall, a necessary evil. And, like Adam, you will earn bread without pleasure, through the sweat of your face, because pride in achievement always outstrips the achievement itself, even crippling the faculties necessary for achievement. So the authenticating note of judgment is pretty clear, isn't it? So many of us Americans are unhappy because we are putting all the eggs of our self-vindication into one basket of vocation. We have become slaves of status, not freed people of Christ. And just think of how many "heaven-sent mechanics in this country have been turned into doctors to the public danger because of the false status given to the professions" (Alexander Miller).

"Work does not make us holy, we must make the work holy." But can all work be made holy? How do you sanctify the sale of heroin? Or the sale of your body? The sale of armaments? How about being a salesperson trying to persuade people they need things they obviously don't? And what about work in a company where the profits of the employer are ever so much more important than the welfare of the employees?

You all agree with me I am sure; those are tough questions. And I don't propose to answer them. But I do want to insist that no Christian serious about his or her faith can avoid them. I think it a travesty that in the church we are so concerned with how people spend their money and so indifferent as to how they make it in the first place.

Wrestling with these questions is training to gain insight. If Revelation favors the mind and heart prepared, then wrestling with these questions is the kind of preparation necessary if ever we are to hear a word from the Lord between 9 and 5. Let me offer only this guideline from St. Paul. In Romans he enjoins us to be *in* this world but not *of* this world. If then in our jobs we make all the compromises the world demands, then we are in this world and we are also of this world. We have suspended our faith during working hours. If on the other hand we refuse all compromises and withdraw we may end up not *of* this world, which is fine, but also not *in* it. We may solve some personal problems but not the problems of the world. I think the goal of Christian life is not simply to hold high ideals but to change the world.

If we refuse to suspend our faith, we may yet hear a word from the Lord on a 9-to-5 job. To some of us it may say, "Hang in there, bide your time, await your opportunity, but never forget the goal." To others the word may simply be "shake the dust off the soles of your feet, get out, even if you risk unemployment." And for all of us as Christians, there must surely be a word that says to us that we must constantly be looking for a way in which this church can play its role in changing, if not the world, at least the city. For instance, some of us this week began thinking of setting up a model health care delivery to shut-ins, to our own members who have such a hard time leaving home, particularly on a winter day like this, and to many others in this community who also have a hard time. With the volunteers we have in this church we could create a fantastic model for the city. I even know a doctor who makes house calls!

But now a final word. I fear I may have sounded a bit grim this morning. If so there really was no reason for it. It's interesting, it's fun to train to gain insight, to become sufficiently perceptive to see what lies behind a falling apple, or a dull number. I think Samuel had a good time ministering to the Lord. And certainly Moses had a more interesting life after the revelation that made him change his vocation. After all, when "Earth's crammed with heaven / And every common bush afire with God" who wants to sit around and pluck blackberries? Why not so change the world that all Christians everywhere every morning outside their offices, factories, studios, would take off their shoes, for the ground upon which they are about to enter is holy ground.

Continuing Conversion

JANUARY 28, 1979
Reading: Mark 8:27–36

Sometimes, in a discussion group, it's useful to be a bit disruptive by asking, "Is that a personal question, or is it just an academic one?" There is a difference, as we see right away in the two questions Jesus addresses to his disciples. "Who do people say that the Son of Man is?" That's the kind of question you are asked in school or college, a question about other people; it's an academic, not a personal question. It may be demanding—you have to listen hard, do a lot of asking around, research, to find out what others are saying; but it's not threatening. So we shouldn't be surprised to read that *all* of the disciples answered: "They answered, 'some say John the Baptist, others Elijah, others Jeremiah, or one of the prophets.'"

Then we read, "And you, who do you say that I am?" This time only one person answers.

Some years ago Arthur Miller came to Yale to give a "Miller on Miller" kind of seminar to some fifteen seniors. At their first meeting he assigned *Death of a Salesman*.

"What critics should we read?" someone asked.

"None," he said. "I know what they write. I am interested in what *you* feel. Have you fathers like Willie, brothers like Biff?"

"The next meeting," he told me, "I could see they had all been reading those critics."

Freshmen can still tell you what's on their minds. Seniors are more apt to know what's on everybody else's mind. As for graduate students—well, sitting around with them is like being at a bibliographers' convention. As they say, education kills by degrees!

An academic question may be demanding but only a personal one is dangerous, for a personal answer commits the person giving it.

When Peter says, "You are the Messiah," clearly he is commiting himself to being a disciple of the Son of God. And notice that he who was least objective is the most perceptive. Objectivity has its place; but not everywhere. Not all passion blinds. Some is absolutely necessary for insight. Love is visionary. Just as an ear attuned to music can hear things a tin ear can never catch, so a warm heart understands things a cold one can never grasp. Jesus insists that Peter's revelation comes from God, of whom elsewhere we read: "God is love."

"And you, who do you say that I am?" Going beyond what research could tell him, prompted by the findings of his own heart, one person takes the plunge: "You are the Messiah, you are the Son of God."

As all forty-eight of you new members said as much just a few moments ago, we can assume that up to this point you and Peter are pretty close. In identifying Jesus as the Messiah, the Son of God, you identified yourselves as Christians.

But we're only at the beginning of the story. For Peter, always the first to leap, once again finds himself beyond his depth. Earlier he leaps out of the boat to walk across the water to Jesus and promptly begins to sink. As I think I said once before, you can't help wondering if Jesus didn't call him "the Rock" then, not for his foundational but for his sinking properties; in this story, too, he quickly flounders. For when Jesus begins to make it clear that he has to go to Jerusalem, there to suffer at the hands of the elders, the chief priests and the doctors of the law, Peter takes him by the arm and begins to rebuke him. "Heaven forbid. No, Lord, this will never happen to you."

In response, Jesus is strangely harsh: "Away with you, Satan." Jesus never withholds the telling blow when only the telling blow will serve. But I myself am touched by Peter's obvious concern for his master's safety. Moreover, although I'm quite prepared to say that only a fool would deny the fact of sin, still I yearn with Peter to see human hearts stilled in the presence of holiness, to see goodness vindicated and emulated. And not all prophets are slain. So we are sometimes justified in our yearnings. Sometimes greatness is recognized while a person is still alive. And didn't the crowds follow Jesus? Doesn't Palm Sunday make you want to hope that somehow Good Friday won't be necessary?

But clinging to the age-old dreams of humanity is no excuse for not facing the ruthless facts of humanity. Human beings are fearful, and what they most fear is not evil in the world, nor evil in themselves; it is rather the good in themselves, the good being so demanding. So we repress the good. Never would we have crucified the best among us had we not first crucified the best within us. We are Christ killers because we don't want to be Christ bearers.

True it is the elders, the chief priests, the doctors of the law—it is those in power whose power is most threatened by Jesus. "Woe to you, scribes, pharisees, hypocrites." Jesus certainly did not withhold from them any telling blows. And they quickly prove that hell hath no wrath like that of power scorned. When that brave Quaker, Anne Hutchinson, several centuries ago stood up in Boston and said, "Truth is my authority, not some authority my truth," the authorities were not pleased.

But Peter of course hasn't seen all this—not yet. He hasn't even seen that his concern for his master's safety is also a concern for his own. For if this is going to happen to the Messiah, what's going to happen to his disciples?

Now I think we are beginning to deal with ourselves in realistic fashion. For better than Peter could know at the time, we know that the world did not reward Christ for being Christ. Yet we expect the world to reward us for being Christians. Like Peter we may recognize the Messiah, but, like Peter, we have yet to come to grips with what it means to be Christian. In other words, conversion continues after you have declared yourself a Christian. During the week after Palm Sunday, Peter's warm and optimistic view of life receives a blast of reality as harsh and cold as any one of this winter's storms. The events of Holy Week crush his illusions with a heavy and indifferent hand. And largely because he was so unprepared—should we say willfully so?—he himself crumbled. At the Last Supper Jesus says, "Tonight you will all fall from your faith on my account." Once again it is he who leaps in. "Every one else may fall away, Lord, but I never will." Yet before the cock crows up the sun, terrified at being included in the sea of hatred and bloodshed now beginning to envelop Jesus, Peter disowns his Messiah not once but three times.

Well, disciples of Jesus Christ, are we prepared to stand where Peter crumbled? Are we more realistic about the world and what Christianity demands of us? I think in all honesty we had better admit that we have probably disowned Jesus far more than three times.

But now comes the most important point—the good news. Despite Peter's total collapse, Christ never gives up on his disciple. When after the resurrection he meets him again, he doesn't call him Simon, he calls him Simon Peter, from "Petra" in Greek, meaning "the Rock." And here's what we need to understand: To whatever degree the church *is* founded upon Peter, it is founded on a second chance.

It is a long pilgrimage after you have declared your allegiance to discover and embody the true meaning of discipleship. That much we have seen in the story of Peter, of Peter who eventually went to Rome and, according to church tradition, at his own insistence, was crucified upside down. But the most important lesson—I underline it—is not the lesson of human weakness; it's the story of Christ's endless mercy. It is more than adequate to all our weaknesses. If we trust Jesus—as Peter never ceased to do—we will find, as he did, that Christ's strength, Christ's joy, Christ's freedom, his love, become more and more our own. So new members of the church, I welcome you to Peter's pilgrimage, the one he took after he stood up, as did you, and declared himself a disciple. Remember the words read earlier from Isaiah, a prophet who happily was not slain:

> They that wait upon the Lord shall renew their strength,
> They shall mount up with wings like eagles,
> They shall run and not be weary,
> They shall walk and not faint.
>
> Isa. 40:31

Remember that Jesus never waivered in his faith in Peter. He will not give up on any of us. So let us all continue on Peter's pilgrimage, singing joyfully as we did earlier, of what is always rewarding, if never easy to do. In fact we can sing it with new meaning. Take the hymnbooks again, number 367, and listen carefully as once again we sing the last two verses:

> Cast care aside, lean on thy guide;
> His boundless mercy will provide;
> Trust, and thy trusting soul shall prove
> Christ is its life, and Christ its love.
>
> Faint not nor fear, his arms are near;
> He changeth not, and thou art dear;
> Only believe, and thou shalt see
> That Christ is all in all to thee.
>
> J. S. B. Monsell

After Rocky's Funeral

FEBRUARY 4, 1979

"All this is from God who reconciled us to himself through Christ and gave us the message of reconciliation."
2 Corinthians 5:18

On Friday afternoon, a couple of hours after the captains and the kings had departed, I returned to the sanctuary to tell the maintenance crew how marvellous they had been—as had the audio and other engineers, the security people, everyone. Scattered throughout the church, seated in various pews were strangers, some just watching, some praying, one a nun. When I asked her if I could help, she said, "Oh, no. I just watched on television the funeral of Nelson Rockefeller and it was such a beautiful service I had to come over to this church and pray for a while. Is that alright?"

A few hours later a graduate student in theology gave me his reaction to the service. "Riverside was raped: there was no prayer of confession, no penitence, only one passage of scripture, and most of the eulogies carried the message to the viewing and listening thousands that the Rockefeller view of America was the right one, and that what's good for America is good for the world."

I knew exactly what he meant, while feeling largely as did the nun. I too was deeply moved by much in the service.

Many of you may not have been aware, but for days before the service there was a tremendous amount of back-and-forth among staff and certain members of the church. At a meeting attended by the entire staff the anguish in some prompted questions such as, "Why can't all the pistols at least be left at the door? Does the FBI really have to know the birthday of every last soprano, alto, tenor, and bass?" And most of all: "Is it right that one of the chief architects of the war in Vietnam should speak from the same pulpit as was purposely chosen by Martin Luther King Jr. to denounce the same war? And, if nothing can be done about that, why televise his presence and words?"

It's a good week when issues so important to a church can be raised with such feeling. I myself was quite prepared to put my foot down, but I couldn't see where! All of which made me want to wonder again what Paul meant by the ministry of reconciliation given to us by Christ. (I should add incidentally that at that staff meeting, probably the majority of the staff listened to these anguished questions in disbelief. As far as they were concerned it was a very simple matter: Nelson Rockefeller was once a member of this church; he had been four times elected governor of the state, and was a Vice President, it was right that he should have a state funeral, and wasn't it a wonderful thing?—the President of the United States was coming to Riverside Church.)

Clearly, Paul recognized what we often tend to downplay, namely that there are things that need to be reconciled. There are genuine trespasses, like that imbecile war in Vietnam, terrible evils that make it both hard and so necessary for us to be reconciled to God, to one another, and not least of all to ourselves. Paul, in other words, didn't try to smooth things over, which is important above all for ministers to remember. Most ministers—I should say senior ministers of large churches—are apt to tell you that they are pastors not prophets, their best gifts being those of reconciliation. Well and good. But you have to go on to ask them: "Whom are you reconciling these days?" Most have associates so little prone to name trespasses—which of course gets people riled up—that the senior ministers rarely get a chance to exercise their great gifts of reconciliation!

Back to St. Paul: "All this is from God . . ." All reconciliation starts, as it finishes, with God. And God in Christ is both prophet and pastor to each of us. The same hand that knocks you down lifts you up. Christ names the trespasses and forgives the trespassers, and most of what he has to forgive stems from that greatest of evils—indifference to evil. But once we are penitent, God does not want us to stay stuck in guilt, for guilt is to save us not to destroy us. It is to keep us honest and to point us toward the forgiveness which is always there, to reconcile hostile separated parts, ourselves from God, ourselves from each other, and ourselves from ourselves.

But to appropriate the forgiveness we have to be penitent. Recalling the two thieves hung on either side of Christ, St. Augustine wrote, "One was saved, do not despair. One was not, do not presume."

When we presume to be innocent, God's forgiveness cannot be appropriated. But, does God then in frustration turn his back on us? The answer is never more clearly given than in the communion service: "This is my body broken for you. This is my blood shed for you." The reason that we say that Christ suffered more than any other human is because it is finally what breaks the heart which is so intolerable. It's having so much love to give and so few to receive it. "O Jerusalem, Jerusalem, how often would I have gathered ye unto me as a mother hen her chicks, and ye would not." (How long can you keep resisting that kind of suffering love?)

Returning now to our own ministry of reconciliation, remembering that "all of this is from God," was there anything on Friday that we should have done differently? As I said, I was ready to put my foot down but couldn't find a place. To insist that no weapons be brought into the house of the Lord might have meant that the President couldn't come. And, personally, I felt the weapons were not so much a symbol of purity violated, as a reminder that we Americans belong to a nation that assassinates its presidents. The symbol was one of penitence. But I am not sure, I'm really not sure.

To deny the pulpit to Henry Kissinger seemed awfully judgmental, less rather than more Christian, particularly as the occasion was to deliver a eulogy for his beloved and longtime friend. In retrospect, however, I think I could have been more straightforward, without being judgmental. At the first meeting to plan the service, at the beginning of last week, I could have asked him whether he had had second thoughts about the war in Vietnam—"My people need to know." One way or the other we wouldn't have taken any action. We wouldn't have turned our back, but we might have cleared the air. We wouldn't have tried to smooth things over. Believe me, memories of the war were present in the room in which we planned the service, and they were troublesome. For what is destructive is less what's known and spoken than what's known and unspoken.

Of course, he could have said to me, "Did *you* win the Nobel Peace Prize?" *Two* winners of the Nobel Peace Prize, my friends, have been in this pulpit: Martin Luther King Jr. and Henry Kissinger. The world's a tough place to figure out!

"All this is from God, who through Christ reconciled us to himself." Sure, there are things that separate us, trespasses that need to be named, but only that we can be brought together again. That's the purpose of naming trespasses, not to keep us apart, but to facilitate our coming together in an honest loving way. Personally, I think the main message of Teng Hsiao-p'ing's visit is simply this: Weren't we Americans unbelievably silly to think that for twenty-five years we could cut ourselves off from one-fourth of the human race? It may be hard to overcome evil with good, but one thing is more difficult, trying to overcome evil with evil. And if all human beings belong to God then we all belong one to another. That's the way God made us. Christ died to keep us that way. Our sin is that we are constantly trying to put asunder what God himself has joined together. So somewhere we have to declare a moratorium on our differences, to recognize that we have more in common than in conflict, and where else if not at a funeral service, in the presence of God, and in the face of death. We were all very human I thought on Friday, and Ann, the older Rockefeller daughter, said a touching thing as she described seeing her father after his death. "His body seemed so small."

Well, none of us are larger than life, and that's not very large. What made the service beautiful for me was the feeling that we were there together, we were doing things together. Because the frailty of life was before our eyes we were seeing once again our need for one another and for God. "The Lord gave and the Lord hath taken away." The important part of that sentence is the first: "the Lord gave." What came through to me again in that service was that this is God's world. At best, we are guests. Even the Rockefellers are guests in this world. And for all of us that is a reconciling thought, and surely one to remember when in a few minutes we meet our host at the communion table.

It seems to me that reconciliation means naming our trespasses but only in order to bring us together. Reconciliation means recognizing and celebrating that we have more in common than we have in conflict. Reconciliation never calls for sentimentality, but it does call for unfailing love, for a movement toward one another. Our hearts stay open, our hands stay open, no matter whether the fist we meet is clenched, no matter whether the heart that comes to meet us is callous. It's not easy, this ministry of reconciliation, to avoid sentimentality, to be loving, and I am far from happy with the way I myself handled some of the problems that arose in the course of this rich and moving week. But of one thing I am certain: we must err on the side of generosity. My word, I don't know how it is in your life, but in mine God certainly has allowed his generosity to outstrip his judgment.

The Uses and Misuses of Suffering

FEBRUARY 18, 1979

The beautiful, but harsh and unforgiving weather (not for nothing did George Herbert say, "One mile is two in Winter"); this raging inflation that goes on, all unchecked, ravaging the cupboards of the poor; the coming of Lent and the reading of a sensitive book—all these have made me think again of the human uses and all too human misuses of suffering. How much suffering that is accepted should be indicted; how much that should be endured is avoided; and how much senseless acceptance and cowardly avoiding is done in the name of Christianity! Still, as Roman Catholics like to say, *abusus non tollit usum*—"misuse does not negate proper use." The suffering that we see in the life and death of our beloved Savior, *that* suffering, beyond anything else in the world, can clarify, console and so strengthen our lives that even the gates of hell shall not prevail against them.

So let's think a bit this morning about the uses and misuses of suffering, taking for our text the familiar line of the Psalm, "He that keepeth Israel shall neither slumber nor sleep" (121:4) and St. Paul's "All things work together for good to them that love God" (Rom.

8:28). The last phrase, I grant you, sounds at first hearing a little bit like the banal optimism of an American head of state, or should we say the official optimism of the established church! But, let's see . . .

The book I admired is Dorothee Soelle's *Suffering*, which starts with a description of a childless woman in a small Austrian and Catholic village, who stays on and on in a marriage, although the chief characteristic of her relationship with her husband is that he is constantly taking revenge on her for everything life has withheld from him. Physically he beats her, mentally he tortures her, she has no life of her own. This leads Dr. Soelle to ask whether we should term her continued suffering a reflection of Christian patience or just another typical example of Christian masochism.

Soelle goes on to ask the same question of suffering imposed by poverty and tyranny, but which poor people perceive as their personal destiny designed by a God they devoutly worship. That leads to the all-important question: What kind of a God are they worshipping, these poor people, this Austrian-Catholic woman? When Christians acquiesce in mute hopelessness to their destiny, when they abnegate life to the point of impotency, when at best, for their suffering, they can conceive only of a Heavenly reward, then clearly the God they are worshipping is the King, the Judge, the one who causes suffering, not the one who shares suffering. They are worshipping the hunter, never the quarry, the executioner and never the victim; in other words, a God who can only become great when he makes us small.

I suspect that there is some small masochistic streak in every one of us. It's that streak that drives us to worship a God who judges because we really want to be punished. It's that streak that makes us want God to be all-powerful so that we can be all-weak—forgetting that God became weak precisely so that we might become strong. So we have carefully to examine any suffering in our lives that tends to make us powerless, hopeless, any kind of suffering from which we learn nothing. For it may not be Godly courage but satanic cowardice that keeps us enduring it.

In my own life, I confess, I have sometimes found it easier to endure a hardship than to resolve it. When resolution was called for, I was not resolute, and when I prayed for patience in tribulation, my prayers were answered. Said God, "I am getting impatient with your prayers for patience. When are you going to do something about all your tribulations?" You see what I am getting at? Passive suffering, where pain doesn't strengthen us. It is not Christian. And it's not Christian to worship a God who is seen as all-powerful rather than all-loving, a God who causes suffering but never shares it.

But if there is one thing worse than suffering merely endured, it is suffering simply avoided. To most of us that perhaps is a greater danger. Let me read you one paragraph from Dr. Soelle's book. "One wonders what will become of a society in which certain forms of suffering are avoided gratuitously in keeping with middle class ideals. I have in mind a society in which a marriage that is perceived as unbearable quickly and smoothly ends in divorce. After divorce no scars remain. Relationships between generations are dissolved as quickly as possible without a struggle. Periods of mourning are insensibly short. With haste, the handicapped and sick are removed from the house and the dead from the mind. If changing marriage partners happens as readily as trading in an old car on a new one, then the experiences that one had in the unsuccessful relationship remain unproductive." And here comes the important sentence: "From suffering nothing is learned, and nothing is to be learned."

I think it is hard to learn anything important at all in this world without suffering. Growth entails growing pains. Love can be painful, Cupid has darts. Perception is painful when truth is harsh. So we set up defensive mechanisms to prevent us from suffering. In universities we do this by treating only those problems that the mind can solve. That avoids a lot of suffering. Perhaps the worst thing that can be said about private prosperity is that it obscures public poverty. In politics, the worst thing that we can say about American anticommunism is not that it is a punitive ideology, which it most certainly is, but that by depersonalizing the enemy it saves us from suffering. American anticommunism helps protect us from perceiving Vietnam as our Auschwitz.

As those who wish to suffer worship a God who punishes, so those who wish to be spared suffering worship a God whose goodness is mixed with a toleration of injustice. Theirs is the "honeysweet Christ," not the Christ crowned with thorns. And if it is unchristian to worship a God who inflicts suffering but does not share it, it is surely no less Christian to worship a God who spares us all the suffering necessary for the well-being of his world and for our spiritual survival.

It was Thomas Münzer in the 16th century, the man who led the peasant revolt in Luther's time, who first made the distinction between the honeysweet and the bitter Christ. Münzer saw how apathy flourished in the consciousness of the satiated. (Apathy is necessary for exploitation to run its course smoothly.) And Münzer foresaw the spiritual demise of the affluent when he wrote, "Whoever does not want the bitter Christ will eat himself to death on the honey."

So, that kind of God, too, has no place in the church; which brings us to atheism, as a legitimate answer to bad suffering and non-suffering. I myself have always been drawn to the atheism that is born in the suffering of a sensitive soul—the atheist for love's sake, the Ivan Karamazov for whom no sorrow is alien, and who rebels at the suffering of the innocent. But finally, it is not only God that Ivan rejects; it's the world too. Ivan says to his brother, "I want to give back my entry ticket." He can't affirm the world, any more than he can affirm God. Pain to him is not something that can be integrated, or bemoaned, or consoled. No, pain is only something that can be denounced.

If the only God I could believe in was the God of Ivan, the God of atheists like Nietzsche and Camus, I too would be an atheist. I could never believe in a God who didn't suffer—given the suffering of the world. I could never believe in a God whose chief characteristic was his power, not his goodness. And because my God *is* a God of goodness, his chief characteristic is not peace but pain. I only quote Scripture, "He that keepeth Israel shall neither slumber nor sleep." My God hangs upon a cross, a victim not an executioner; the quarry, not the hunter; and one who not only suffers *with* me but *for* me, seeking not only to console but, beyond consolation, to strengthen me. Such a God I can affirm and a world with such a God in it I can affirm too.

Metaphysically, I can't answer the problem of pain. I can only resolve it by sharing it—by holding hands with the dying, by protesting in the name of my crucified Lord against war, hunger, oppression, torture, against suffering inflicted by our own human injustice. I know that the worst of all evil is indifference to evil. Indifference is what makes stones endure for millions of years, but it does nothing but destroy the humanity of human beings. So, we musn't fear to suffer, if our suffering springs from love, if it is like that of the God we worship, who cares so much for his beloved earth.

To keep vigil with him who neither slumbers nor sleeps—that's the way to live. The tragedy of the disciples falling asleep in the garden of Gethsemane is not only the tragedy of Jesus once again deserted, but the tragedy of people who, like children, can't keep their attention when it drags on too long and so missed out on all that's going on. I think the only people who really understand the world are those who suffer. There is a kind of "community of sufferers" all over this globe, some we know, most we don't. They are the saints, the ones who keep the world moving, who understand what suffering love is all about.

One who so understood the world was Teresa of Avila. Here's what, across the centuries, she has to tell us: "Christ has no body now on earth but yours; no hands but yours; no feet but yours. Yours are the hands with which he is to bless us now."

Yea, indeed, we can see it now: "All things work together for good to them that love God."

Wrestling with the Devil

MARCH 4, 1979
Reading: Luke 4:1–13

One of the livelier Christological debates in the history of the church revolves around the question, "Was Jesus ever really tempted?" The sides line up as follows—if you will pardon a flourish of erudition. One group says: "*Non posse pecare*"—Jesus was not able to sin; while the other says: "*Posse non pecare*"—he was able not to sin. It boils down to this: if Jesus' will was so attuned to God's that he was not able to sin, then he obviously was not really tempted. On the other hand, if he didn't sin, while at the same time being perfectly capable of sin, then he was really tempted. In fact, he was tempted as no one else, for who better measures the strength of the temptor—one who immediately throws in the towel, or one who contends to the very end?

Personally, I see no point to the debate. If Jesus wasn't really tempted, then he wasn't really human, for what else is at the core of human life if not the agony of choice and decision? And if Jesus wasn't really tempted, then the story is, as they say, "sheer hagiographical imagination," or worse yet, a fraud. For the story could have come to the disciples from nowhere else but the lips of Jesus himself, he being the sole witness to his own struggle.

So, I suggest we accept the description of Jesus found in Hebrews, "one who in every respect was tempted as we are, yet without sinning." *Posse non pecare!*

The next thing to say is that this story has very little to do with temptations as we generally understand them. (Who was it who said, "Everything I like is immoral, indecent, or fattening"?) This is big time stuff and the Greek verb actually means "to test" rather than to tempt. This is a large scale attack that the Devil is mounting and, fiendishly enough, at the point of our greatest vulnerability, our identity.

Significantly, the story follows hard on the story of Baptism. When he was baptized, Jesus received, as we all do in baptism, his identity. In receiving his identity he received a special mission, knowledge of his special powers. In baptism he hears, "Thou art my beloved Son." Now in the wilderness across from the River Jordan, he hears, "*If* you are the Son of God." In other words, the Devil, as always, is testing our faith, our commitment, our compassion. He tests the best in us, and can't you just hear him casting doubt, "Come on, Jesus, how can you, a penniless, uneducated, Galilean carpenter, how can you possibly be the long-awaited Messiah? Who is going to believe you?"

Put yourself in Jesus' place. Wouldn't you have been sorely tested? Isn't it hard to hang on to your calling, when all odds favor your failure? Let us remember as well that the Devil—(Incidentally, I always forget that there are one or two people who don't believe in the Devil, so let me tell you very briefly about him, as one who contends with him regularly. The Devil is a person, because evil is experienced as an intensely personal power, in the same way that God is a person because God is experienced as intensely personal power. Also, the Devil has to have a separate existence not because evil exists outside of us, but evil is experienced as something within and greater than us. And, lastly, of course, we must remember that the Devil is a fallen angel. His attack is always from on high, corrupting our freedom)— the Devil rarely suggests that we do anything bad; almost invariably he suggests we do what appears to be good. Eve only took the apple when she saw that it was "good for food, pleasing to the eye, and much to be desired to make people wise." So, let's use a little imagination this morning, avoiding the usual interpretations. Let's assume that the first of the three temptations, to turn stones into bread, is not a temptation to use his powers selfishly, nor as is often suggested, to win followers by material gifts. Rather let's view it as the far subtler temptation to compromise one's calling by substituting the good in place of the best. How often we say that the good is the best possible.

Had I been Jesus, I think I would have begun to reason as follows: why shouldn't I give my people bread? God himself knows how poor they are, as do I, having been born into their poverty. Didn't God help Moses with manna? And isn't the Messiah expected to do no less than Moses, as proved by the fact that the most popular picture of the Messianic age is that of a great banquet? We heard it earlier described in the words of Isaiah: "On that day the LORD of Hosts will prepare a banquet of rich fare for all the peoples, a banquet of wines"—take note, Baptists—"a banquet of wines, well matured and richest fare, well-matured wines strained clear" (Isa. 25:6). So why shouldn't the Devil say: "You are running counter to all expectations, Jesus. And how are you going to say to a bunch of starving people, 'I am the bread of life; he who cometh to me shall never hunger.' That's unconscionable, and you know it."

As the good sounds so reasonable and especially so realistic, I think I would have capitulated. But Jesus—*posse non pecare*—was able to withstand the temptation, remembering perhaps that it was only after they were filled with manna that the Israelites rebelled. After their bellies were full, they doubted their high calling.

Here is a wise word from a Russian theologian: "When bread is assured, then God becomes a hard and inescapable reality, instead of an escape from harsh reality." When bread is assured, then the contrast between the good and the best becomes sharp. The contrast may be a little overdrawn here but let's end the discussion of this first temptation with these words from playwright Herb Gardner. Arnold who has made his no-questions-asked peace with the world for thirty-thousand a year speaks to his ne'er-do-well brother, Murray, who has rebelled against the deceits of conventional society and cares passionately about people:

> I have long been aware, Murray, I have long been aware that you don't respect me much. I suppose there are a lot of brothers who don't get along. . . . Unfortunately for you, Murray, you want to be a hero. Maybe if a fella falls into a lake, you can jump in and save him. There's still that kind of stuff. But who gets opportunities like that in midtown Manhattan, with all that traffic. I am willing to deal with the available world and I do not choose to shake it up but to live with it. There's the people who spill things and the people who get spilled on. I choose not to notice the stains, Murray. I have a wife and I have children and business, like they say, is business. I am not an exceptional man, so it is possible for me to stay with things the way they are. I'm lucky; I'm gifted. I have a talent for surrender. I'm at peace. But you are cursed, and, I like you so, it makes me sad, you don't have this gift; and I see the torture of it. All I can do is worry for you, but I will not worry for myself; you cannot convince me that I am one of the Bad Guys. I get up, I go, I lie a little, I peddle a little, I watch the rules, I talk the talk. We fellas have those offices high up there so that we can catch the wind and go with it, however it blows. But, and I will not apologize for it, I take pride; I am the best possible Arnold Burns. (*A Thousand Clowns*)

The Devil is always testing, urging us to be realistic, to be reasonable, to compromise the calling we received in baptism, to allow the good to usurp the place of the best.

The second temptation is like unto the first. The Devil takes Jesus up to a high place, shows him all the kingdoms of the world in a moment of time, and claims that they all belong to him—a very interesting assertion. Then he says, "Here, they are yours." Once again, with a little imagination, we can see the Devil suggesting that something good and tangible is probably better than the best, which is wildly utopian anyhow. Had we lived as Jews under the rod of Rome, we surely would have longed for political liberation. Many of our fathers, uncles, grandfathers would have been numbered among the 100,000 people who perished in the abortive rebellions between the years 67 and 37 B.C. Like almost everybody else, we would have been expecting a political messiah, to implement the word and will of God as prophesied by Zechariah: "The Lord will set free all the families of Judah. . . . On that day, I, the Lord, will set about destroying all the nations that come against Jerusalem" (12:7, 9).

Why not? Putting myself in Jesus' place, I think I would have continued to reason that just as you can't talk to starving people about bread from heaven, so you cannot in good conscience talk about the Kingdom of God to people whose kingdom is under alien and harsh rule.

So, I understand the temptation today, for instance, to listen to that devilish realism, which maintains that Americans must increase their military might lest they fall under alien rule. "It's too bad, but after all the Russians don't understand non-violence." Still, I am troubled, because while the Soviets may be able to define us as citizens of America, we receive our identity from the Son of God who refused worldly power based on violence. Therefore, the question is real: should American Christians pay taxes to support the Pentagon's rising budget? Or, should they rather heed their own prophet, who warned "through violence you may murder the liar but you cannot murder the lie, nor establish the truth. Through violence, you may murder the hater, but you do not murder hate. . . . Returning violence for violence, multiplies violence, adding deeper darkness to a night already devoid of stars. Darkness cannot drive out darkness, only light can do that. Hate cannot drive out hate: only love can do that" (Martin Luther King Jr.).

Again we must ask ourselves if the Devil has persuaded us that the good should usurp the best because it is more realistic. At the outset of World War II, I stood with the poet Charles Péguy: "People who insist on keeping their hands clean are likely to find themselves without hands." And forty years later, I am still fearful of putting purity above relevance. But much has passed in forty years, and in the nuclear age it may be that nothing short of the best is relevant. As God is not mocked we shouldn't be surprised that the day is dawning when the so-called ethics of perfection are becoming ethics of survival. When we live at each other's mercy, we then had better learn to be merciful. And if we don't learn to be meek, nobody is going to inherit the earth.

Finally we see the Devil suggesting that goodness should have its reward; reasonable enough. If the Son of God is not to rescue people from their poverty, nor to liberate them from their tyranny, if the Messiah is to disappoint so many Messianic expectations, then at least let him be vindicated. Let God prove that this is what goodness is all about. Let God at least shield his beloved Son from harm; it's only fair.

But to insist on fairness is like insisting on justice for the hungry and freedom for the oppressed. It's right, it's good, but it's not enough. God goes beyond fairness in his dealings with us—thank God—because we are not exactly fair with him. But he doesn't care about fairness, only about us; that we know that His love exceeds the demands of justice, and that his forgiveness never fails. So, the Son of God must needs bear His cross, be despised, rejected, crucified, so that God's heart can be laid bare for all to see. God does prove himself, but in the power of His love.

It's hard, isn't it? It is very hard to be a Christian. "Whither, relentless, wilt thou still be driving thy maimed and halt and have not strength to go?" It's very hard to be a Christian, but it's too dull to be anything less. It's very hard to bear the agony of choice and decision, but it's inhuman to refuse it. So, in this tough time of testing in the Christian year, let's see if we can't find a little more courage to stand against the insidious realism of the Devil, resisting what at first blush always appears so reasonable, refusing to allow the good to usurp the place of the best. And of one thing we may be sure: as to Jesus so to us, angels will come ministering when the struggle is over.

Wrestling with God

MARCH 11, 1979
Reading: Genesis 32:22–30

As last Sunday we wrestled with the Devil, why not today with God! I know it sounds exhausting—all this contending, the suggestion that all true servants of God have to be wrestlers. Yet ask yourself: what kind of serenity are you looking for—the protective serenity that lies on *this* side of conflict, or the genuine one that lies on the other?

Significantly, Jacob cannot go home without the hardest struggle of his life. He can't be blessed without being wounded. No struggle, no Promised Land; no laming, no naming; no cross, no crown.

We have to come to grips with God; we can't float indefinitely. We know also that our faith has to be tried, if only to have it strengthened. But we can be of good cheer. "God fights against us with his left hand and for us with his right." If you're lefthanded make the appropriate changes in this biased phrase of John Calvin, but don't miss Calvin's conclusion: "God becomes in us stronger than the power by which he opposes us."

But conclusions are for the end. Let's go back to the beginning where we find Jacob clearing a time and a space to be by himself. On listening to the story, were you impressed by this withdrawal? Had I been one of Jacob's wives, or one of his eleven sons, I think I might have been hurt, being sent on in this fashion, deliberately being excluded from a moment so important in the life of my beloved husband or my beloved father. Why couldn't he share his struggle with us?

It's an important question—is our privacy in competition with our life together? Or, does solitude in fact enhance family, or church life, any kind of communal life? To bring forth your own feelings let me simply ask you whether clearing time for yourself makes you feel guilty, because it is taking you away from others?

I think the question deserves a clear and twofold answer. In the first place, without solitude we simply cannot be true to our own lives which are, finally, "solitudes." We are born alone, we die alone, and in between we stumble along in the footsteps of lonely literary prototypes like Abraham, Ulysses, and Faust. Let us not be deceived. Our life together is as two separate hands raised in prayer, their fingertips touching. But beyond that, without solitude our life together is also doomed. Writing in the latest *Sojourners* magazine, Henri Nouwen insists that intimacy grows in solitude. We take each other with us when we enter solitude. In solitude, with no danger of misusing or over-using each other, our relationships can quietly deepen and grow.

All of which is to say that had I been one of Jacob's wives, I hope I would have concluded that his solitude was a threat only to my pride, not to the fabric of our family life. If he wanted to wrestle alone with God, that was his legitimate business. All I'd ask was that later he share with the rest of us what had transpired, which Jacob must have done else we wouldn't have the story.

"And there was one that wrestled with him until daybreak." That has to be one of the least clear sentences in all of scripture. Who is this person? And if his identity is unclear, so, too, is the outcome of the struggle. Who wins? In fact, the whole story is so full of incoherent diversities that all we can say with any degree of certainty is that it relates a nocturnal struggle in which a man is opposed by a mysterious power attempting to prohibit him from crossing a ford. Scholars tell us that the story belongs to that category of ancient sagas dedicated to the theme—the trial of heroes.

Yet in a strange way, the story is powerfully suggestive to our imaginations, whose task it is to see that the struggles of scriptural characters are also our struggles. So let us see how we can make Jacob's struggle our own. When, as we must, we try to picture a world in which we have successfully banned the institution of war as we have that of slavery—when we try to picture such a world it becomes discouraging to remember that of the first two brothers recorded in the Bible, one dies at the hand of the other. Since the beginning fratricide has been a central fact of human life. In fact, psychologically the first part of the Book of Genesis doesn't represent an Oedipal world, a world of the fathers, so much as a world of brothers, a world in which younger brothers—first Abel, now Jacob—get themselves in trouble with their older brothers by successfully displacing them. And one can feel a certain sympathy for Jacob, the second born of twins, because only uterine placement made him miss out on the primogeniture, the inheritance of the older brother. He missed it only by minutes! Graphically he is pictured as coming out of Rebecca's womb hanging on to Esau's heel. And we can say that he never let go of that heel, not at least until he had tricked Esau out of his birthright.

Then, following some bad maternal advice, he tricks his father into giving him the blessing poor blind Isaac thought he was bestowing on Esau. Not surprisingly, Jacob had to leave town, and it is years later that we now pick him up returning home. He is rich beyond the vain imaginings of his youthful heart, but still unreconciled to Esau through whose land he now must pass. He hears that Esau is coming to meet him with 400 men, and to placate him Jacob sends servants ahead with gifts of prize livestock—goats, ewes and rams, milk camels, cows, bulls, and asses, in incredible numbers. Nonetheless, Jacob fears for his life and for the lives of the members of his family.

But is it only to Esau that Jacob remains unreconciled? In the language of depth psychology, Esau may well have become Jacob's own shadow, that part of him that connives so ruthlessly, that part of him that condemns him as loudly as does the voice of the approaching Esau, that part of him which he fears to face altogether as much as he fears to face Esau himself. And just as the Devil appears in the guise of the good in order to turn good into evil, so the angel of God can appear in the shadows of our lives to turn darkness into light.

It's true that our greatest conflicts are internal. Our greatest enemies are within. Our deepest wounds are self-inflicted. So what is wrestling with God if not coming to grips with ourselves—with strength from God. It's facing what we prefer to flee, admitting what we'd rather deny, letting the long separated alienated parts of ourselves have it out with each other.

That night on the banks of the river, Jacob decides to deny his demons no longer, to wrestle them as long as it takes to bring them to light; to wrestle them until they yield him a blessing. You remember the ancient myths about dragons that turn into princesses? Dragons turn into princesses, demons turn into angels, an assailant in the night proves to be none other than God himself. I'm not being fanciful. For God wants us to become whole and holy, to be reconciled to ourselves so that we can be reconciled to others. That is the correct order, for we sin out of our hurts. We wound because we first have been wounded. We grasp for others' blessings only because we have never reached for and accepted the one blessing that each one of us needs, the blessing of God himself.

And why does Jacob limp? So that he can never run away from himself again; so that he can trust in God's strength that is "made perfect in weakness." Having gone through all that, Jacob is now free to return home. At peace with himself, he is ready to make peace with his brother, as he does. Having wrestled with God he is ready for the Promised Land, that serenity that lies not on the near but on the far side of conflict, the simplicity that lies on the other side of complexity. And having wrestled with God he is ready for a new name that will be carried proudly by descendants as numerous as the sands of the sea.

No laming, no naming; no struggle, no Promised Land; no cross, no crown. And one more thought: In that nocturnal struggle, who did win? The beauty about wrestling with God is that no one loses. Everybody wins. As I said, dragons turn into princesses, demons into angels, an assailant in the night into God. And fratricide ends. O that all individuals and nations would cease "raging so furiously together" and turn to wrestling with God. Then would the blessings of peace fall on the earth like the morning dew.

The Parable of the Last Judgment

MARCH 18, 1979
Reading: Matthew 25:31–45

It's simply not true that Christianity has been tried and found wanting. It's been tried and found difficult. So it's been diluted. As they say, the weekly miracle of the churches is that they turn the wine into water.

All the reasons for Christianity being so difficult are to me far from clear. Lord knows Christianity is not too complicated. It's devastatingly simple. Give food to the hungry, drink to the thirsty—what could be more straightforward? Yet, once again this week, I forgot to bring my cans of food and bag of flour to the ever-emptying bread pantry of this church. Clothe the naked—again a simple proposition. Yet while volunteers are rarely lacking to serve on almost any number and variety of committees of this church, where are the hands ready to help Ruth Herrmann sort and give out clothes to the shivering mothers of this city? (Eighty-seven percent of the recipients of public assistance are mothers and their children. There are 600,000 children, one-half eight years old or under.) And for some reason it's easier for almost everybody to serve on a task force on criminal justice than to visit those in jail. No, it's not complicated but it's devastatingly simple to be a Christian. And about as easy as for a camel to pass through the eye of a needle!

What else do we learn from the parable of the Last Judgment? In a time of uncertainty and anguish, I suppose we shouldn't be surprised at the rising number of church voices critical of the World Council of Churches, of Latin American Liberation theologians and of their North American counterparts, such as our neighbor, Robert McAfee Brown. These are voices that decry the "politicization of the faith," and urge upon us greater concern for the salvation of our souls, for private religious experience, a concern for "what is uniquely Christian." Yet "when the Son of man comes in his glory, and all the angels with him"—what prose in this parable!—he is not going to be concerned with what is uniquely Christian, but rather with what is essentially human—feeding the hungry, clothing the naked. Notice, these are not even specifically religious exercises. I think it a terrible idea to try to reduce Christianity, a faith which seeks to elucidate the whole human enterprise, to something that is uniquely Christian.

That's an absurd reduction. This parable seems to expect all Christians to live in two communities—a community of faith and a community of suffering. In the community of faith we celebrate what is unique to Christianity—Christ himself. But in the community of suffering we celebrate what is essential to all human beings—compassion, that great bridge that links all the sorrows of this world to whatever the world has to offer in the way of hope. And in the community of suffering we celebrate compassion with Jews, Muslims—everyone.

Not only is it absurd to try to reduce Christianity to what is uniquely Christian, it is downright selfish to seek to save your soul. Where in the Bible do you ever read that the goal of life is to save your own soul? I read the Bible to say that we are here in this world to transcend ourselves, which is very different. We are here to stay with the grain of suffering, to learn to pour out to and with each other all the love that God in his infinite mercy has poured into the hearts of each of us. Doesn't the parable make that clear?

To stay with the grain of suffering. Some months ago I received a visitor who moved me deeply. He was a minister sent to New York by a strictly fundamentalist church to open an urban mission. He believed in "credal righteousness," if you will, and didn't believe in dancing, drinking wine—all those things that they are always doing in the Bible. And of course he believed in the inerrancy of Scripture. (How you combine those two has always seemed to me a feat of interpretive gymnastics!) But more than most of us he was ministering to the outcasts of this city, to child prostitutes—boys and girls—to homosexuals who were happy with their homosexuality and to homosexuals who were not happy; to people who were on welfare and to people who just couldn't take the hassle any longer. (It's a full-time job to stay on welfare in New York City!) His complaint was that the literalistic and moralistic doctrines of his church had become more a hindrance than an aid in interpreting the human condition as he personally was experiencing the human condition. He loved his church, he didn't want to leave it; yet it was tearing him apart. Suddenly he stopped, then blurted out: "You know what my wife says? My wife says, 'When are you going to get out of Vietnam?'"

That man was following the grain of suffering, learning what this parable teaches, that the purity of dogma is second to the integrity of love. Creeds are signposts, but love is the hitching post.

We live in two communities, the community of faith, and the community of suffering. We follow the grain of suffering, remembering that "God is love, and he who abides in love abides in God, and God abides in him" (1 John 4:16).

What else can we glean from this parable? The obvious, that God is partisan to the poor. "To establish justice for the innocent who are threatened and the poor, the widows, the orphans and the strangers who are oppressed . . . God stands at every time unconditionally and passionately on this and only on this side; always against the exalted and for the lowly, always against those who already have rights and for those from whom they are robbed and taken away." So spoke the elder Karl Barth. And two things at least can be said about these words. In the first place, sadly enough, their truth is less obvious to the critics of the World Council of Churches than they would have been to members of the first Christian communities. For while in New Testament times it was obvious to all that the Messiah was coming to the poor, and the rich were properly nervous, now it is widely assumed that God comes with equal ease to presidents of corporations as to mothers on welfare. Let me say it again: We think the poor are a problem to the rich, but the Bible is crystal clear that it is the rich who are a problem to the poor.

The second thing to say explains the first. Barth is speaking of justice, not charity. So frequently have Christians sought to ease their consciences by acts of charity that critics have properly accused us of having a vested interest in unjust structures which produce victims to whom we can then pour out our hearts in charity. Mind you, this is not to belittle charity. I am hoping to fill the food pantry of Riverside Church. But it is to warn that giving without receiving tends to be a downward motion, and that efforts to alleviate the results of poverty are no excuse for not eradicating the causes.

Earlier we prayed, "Thy Kingdom come." The Kingdom of God for which we pray and work is surely something more than social justice, just as it is something more than the B Minor Mass or all of Rembrandt and Michelangelo together. But surely also it is nothing less. I am reminded of what Dietrich Bonhoeffer said in Hitler's Germany. "Only he who cries out for the Jews may sing Gregorian chants."

The point I am trying to make—in response to a fervent request from one of our number—is that because justice is so central a Biblical concern, all Christian theology explicitly or implicitly is political. All Christian theology reflects good politics or bad politics, never no politics. The growing number of Christians who disavow social action as a proper expression of the Christian faith are the willing or unwilling advocates of the status quo. And how they can reduce the ethical demands of the prophet to "Let justice roll down like mighty waters" to a matter simply of personal rectitude and nothing more defies comprehension.

The separation of church and state does not separate a Christian from his or her politics. Of course religion is "above" politics in the sense that the faith is not to be identified with any particular political blueprint. "Let justice roll down like mighty waters" doesn't tell us which is the best irrigation system. But to their credit, the World Council of Churches, and Liberation theologians, are at least concerned that today there is such hunger in the midst of plenty, and concerned that government efforts not nullify the church's own efforts to feed the hungry.

God is partisan to the poor. God is not neutral. And at this time of year we remember that the words and deeds of his son were so disturbing to both political and religious leaders that He was crucified by a combination of church and state.

I hope all this has been of some help to my friend, but I want to end, if I may, on a very different note. You remember it is the Son of Man who does the final judging. All our judgments therefore are provisional, not ultimate, and I've yet to see a goat who didn't look sometimes like a sheep. And I must say that it's the sheep who always get my goat! There's a bad jingle that makes a good point:

> There is so much good in the worst of us,
> And so much bad in the best of us,
> That it hardly becomes any of us
> To talk about the rest of us.

To avoid sentimentality, we have to make judgments. But the art of life is to remember that judgments are provisional, that we love the sinner while we hate the sin, and that it takes a sinner to catch a sinner.

And lastly, isn't the surprise of the righteous the most poignant touch in the whole parable? It suggests something important. In the life of faith we're apt to go through three stages: conscious, self-conscious, and unconscious. In the parable, the righteous are responding to the Son of Man in a totally unconscious manner. They're doing what they are doing apparently because it is simply a wonderful way to live. So they are genuinely surprised that they should be rewarded further.

Well, I like my Christians unconscious too, don't you?

No Room for the Holy Spirit?

MARCH 25, 1979
Reading: Matthew 7:25–34

I want to talk today of the Holy Spirit, and I want to take as a text the words of our Lord: "do not be anxious about tomorrow."

Twenty-five years ago, still a student at Yale Divinity School, I received a telephone call which did me honor. It was an invitation to join a group which, from time to time, gathered in Thornton Wilder's house to hear the playwright's first rendition of his latest play. (Wilder reading, or Wilder just talking, was always a magnificent production.) No one, however, explained the rules, so when he finished and asked for comments, I said, "I think the ending's a bit thin."

When no discussion whatsoever ensued from that remark, I assumed that I would never again be asked to join the group: and I was right. But as we were leaving Mr. Wilder detained me, and when everyone else was out of the house he asked, "Billy boy, would you like to throw down a few thimblefuls?" Naturally I answered, "As many as you like, Mr. Wilder."

So off we went to a neighborly tavern called Kaysey's. As we entered we were hailed by a genial drunk at the bar who said, "Shay, aren't you the great Thornton Wilder?" "Just a New Haven boy," replied Mr. Wilder and propelled me on to a distant booth. There, after several thimblefuls, interspersed with remarks like, "Remember, Billy boy, God has a hard time loving those who don't love themselves," he inquired earnestly, "I hear you're already preaching. Do you write out all your sermons?"

"Yes, Mr. Wilder, I do."

"Why?"

"Well, until I write something out, how do I know I'm thinking, not just mooning?"

"No room for the Holy Spirit?"

"Well, Mr. Wilder, I figure the Holy Spirit has Thursday, Friday, and Saturday to visit, even Sunday up to eleven o'clock."

But Mr. Wilder wasn't satisfied with that answer, and neither was I.

Yet, it was not until five years after I had become chaplain at Yale that I could ever depart from a text, let alone leave an opening. I was too anxious. Not that thereafter every time there was an opening the Holy Spirit rushed in to fill it; as often as not demons came. But at least I wasn't so fearful that I had to impose an absolute rational control on what I was going to say, with no room whatsoever for any disturbance, holy or unholy.

"Do not be anxious." It may be that the Holy Spirit is urging upon some of us greater control in matters of food, drink, clothing and shelter, not to mention gas and oil, and self-pity. But the control in one area of life is only to liberate us in another. Basically, the Holy Spirit seeks to expand rather than restrict our lives. The Holy Spirit urges us to depart from the texts we have so carefully, so meticulously and so boringly written for our lives; as if our lives were to be controlled only by ourselves and never by our families and friends, never mind the agenda of the world, or by God himself who made us.

"No room for the Holy Spirit?" The Holy Spirit is trying to crack open our armored life. Or, to change the metaphor: while we think it's a rational grip we have on life, in fact, it's a white-knuckled grip.

Consider for instance the mindscape of today's average university. It is the mindscape of scientific rationality. The only interesting facts are those that can be proved. Fit for the natural sciences, such a mindscape has only a limited use in the social sciences and humanities. Particularly in the humanities the most important truths are those that can never be proved. All human values are finally truths that the mind can defend but not discover. So we have to ask: Where does the heart go to school? Is there no room for the Holy Spirit in higher education?

It's no less irrational that church people should be so rigid about their behavior, and more especially the behavior of others, when according to their own songs and prayers, it's love—wild love—that makes the world go round. I exaggerate but a little for it is not he who controls but he who *loses* his life who finds it. "Yea, though I have enough self-discipline to satisfy every living parent and teacher in the world, but have not love, it profiteth me nothing!"

I'm for discipline in personal behavior. I'm for discipline in bringing up children—consistent discipline and body warmth. I'm for discipline when it comes to preparing sermons, prayers, papers, reports; and Lord knows I'm for discipline when it comes to organizing protests against nuclear reactors and the arms race. But discipline is for the sake of freedom, not freedom for discipline. What we forget is that discipline is from the word "disciple," and we are disciples of him who said, "Do not be anxious."

I have an idea. Why don't we give up anxiety for Lent? Then in school we wouldn't pursue only those safe truths that can be proved. Then in church we'd be truly concerned only with motivation. Then we wouldn't walk the streets, ride the subways, worrying so much about our dim defeats and shaky victories, our status or lack of status.

"Do not be anxious about tomorrow"—about getting what you want in life. For in fact there may be one thing worse than *not* getting what you want, and that is getting it! For what we so want is apt not to be what we so need. Sure, we need food, drink, clothes, shelter—let's not minimize them. But let's not maximize them either. Let's not get anxious about them. We don't need *that* much money. Nor do we need much power, prestige. What we *do* need is some few real friends. We need Jesus as our Lord and Savior. We need the love of God. We don't need degrees by the dozen but we do need to understand life. And we need music. And we need art, and exercise. And we need to do our damnedest and blessedest to knock some sense and goodness into the head of this crazy world.

In this Lenten season it is good to recognize the danger of elevating our wants to the status of needs, to think we really need money, power, prestige, when these are things we only want. "Do not be anxious" refers to our wants, not to our needs. The art of life is to want only what we need—love, curiosity, passion, vulnerability, courage, hope. And all these are ours by the power of the Holy Spirit, which restricts our wants, expanding and satisfying our needs.

All the signs are clear. Hard times are coming fast, times of great uncertainty. We can meet them in two ways. One is to shrink back, close up, participate in the social meanness which characterizes the country's climate. Or we can recognize what the poet Rilke meant in saying "Perhaps everything terrible is in its deepest being something that wants help from me." So the second way is to become helpful, to open up, become freer, more generous, to depart from our carefully prepared texts (which the world isn't going to listen to anyway), rejoicing in a vulnerability which even if forced upon us still makes us recognize that always the Christian life is living securely with insecurity.

The world does not give us what we want but the Holy Spirit gives us what we need—and what we really want anyway. In this spring season the Holy Spirit says to us, "You are skylarks; what are you doing in that canary cage? Fly out, drop everything, go down to 96th St. and Broadway to sing the B Minor in wall-to-wall Bach; go to Groton, Connecticut, to protest the "christening" (We know where that verb comes from!) of the Trident submarine. The Holy Spirit urges us to adopt a kid out of jail, or write a letter to the editor, or to a friend with whom we've lost touch.

And we can do it all. For

> Hast thou not known, hast thou not heard . . . ?
> They that wait upon the LORD shall renew their strength,

They shall mount up with wings like eagles,
They shall run and not grow weary,
They shall walk and not faint.

Isa. 40:28, 31

"Do not be anxious."

"No room for the Holy Spirit?" *Veni sancte spiritus.*

Come, thou Holy Spirit, come.

Peace Sunday '79

APRIL 1, 1979

"Neither shall they learn war anymore."

Isa. 2:4b

Sometime ago a psychiatrist went on a fishing trip with a friend affluent enough not only to fly but to own his own seaplane. The two went to the lake country in northern Minnesota where lake follows lake with only an isthmus between. As there are no villages, towns, let alone any industry, the water is remarkably clear. Flying low they could see forty feet into the depths and looking down, behold, no fish, but two fishermen, happily angling on a sunny day like today. They thought the only decent thing to do was to land the plane and tell them "no fish," which they did. As they flew off, the psychiatrist mused to himself, "I had anticipated their disappointment but not their hostility." But then he went on to think, "It wasn't as if we had said to them 'Come with us, boys, and we will take you home to your wives and you can take a week off some other time,' or 'Come with us boys and we will take you to another lake where you can let down your lines and pull them in like the disciples in the Sea of Galilee.' No, we left them there where there wasn't a blessed thing else to do but fish, so on they went, only now twice as angry, twice as frustrated as before."

And there you have America today, at least a large segment of the American population, who knows there are no fish; who knows that there is no military security in the nuclear age; who knows that the answer to crime in the streets is not simply to build bigger prisons; and who knows that there is apparently no solution to unemployment and inflation—not in our present way of conducting business. Yet these same people are experiencing the unacceptability of unpleasant truth. So, on they go, thinking the same thoughts, doing the same thing, only twice as angry and frustrated as before.

The nation needs help from men and women of faith who presumably are less conformed to the ways of the world, who are less impressed by the weight and power of riches and weapons while, at the same time, more and more assured of those truths that are "hid from the wise and prudent and revealed unto babes."

God is calling his people to be the salt of the earth, to take up the prophetic task, to become spiritual seismographs vibrating to the first faint tremors that herald the coming earthquake. For if the United States is not to become one with Sodom and Gomorrah "one with the glory of Greece and the grandeur that was Rome," we the American people are going to have humbly to confess our sins unto Almighty God.

It is true that the Soviets are behaving terribly in East Europe, and the Cubans questionably in Africa. Yet let us not point to the mote in the other person's eye and ignore the beam in our own. We too have passed from isolation into interventionism, without passing through internationalism. Since World War II we Americans have intervened in the internal affairs of other countries through military operations or major efforts on the part of the CIA, on the average of one every eighteen months: 1948, Greece; 1953, Iran; 1954, Guatemala; 1958, Indonesia; 1958, Lebanon; 1960, Laos; 1961, Cuba; 1964, the Congo; 1964, British Guiana; 1965, the Dominican Republic, and thereafter Vietnam, Cambodia, and once again Laos, for as you remember in order to withdraw from one country we had to invade two and bomb three. And finally 1973, Chile.

Our violence abroad was reflected in our violence at home. Between 1966 and 1972, while 42,300 Americans were dying in Vietnam, 52,000 Americans were killed in the United States by handguns.

Yet we still sell more handguns than ever—one every thirteen seconds; we build more and more prisons even though they represent higher education in violence, with the lights kept on all night to keep the students at their homework. We have announced our intention to intervene again if our energy supplies are threatened; and we continue to produce three nuclear bombs a day even though our present stockpile translates into kill-power sufficient to incinerate everyone in the world several times over. Ours is not a defense budget. Ours is an offense budget. If we were more honest, we would change the name of the Department of Defense back to its old name, the War Department. For while we are able to wage lethal warfare, our weapons are not able to do the very things for which weapons are designed—protect the nation. The Pentagon is not seeking military security so much as it is seeking to maximize military power—and at the expense of national security. Never in our history have we been so vulnerable.

If we and the Soviets continue to reset the nuclear balance at ever higher levels of terror, then predictably both sides will adopt what's called a "launch upon warning" strategy; and because it takes missiles only minutes to go door to door, the power of decision will be taken from human beings and turned over to the impersonal province of computers. So, picture the following: a Soviet computer misreads a Soviet radar screen and takes the blips for missiles coming in from the United States and releases the Soviet missiles; thereupon an American radar computer correctly reads the American radar screen and releases American missiles. Somewhere in the Stygian darkness of outerspace Soviet missiles descending hurtle past American missiles ascending and ten minutes later, without a single decision having been made by a single human being—ten minutes later, well, this is what is going to happen here in Manhattan alone if we are "lucky" to be hit by a "mere" 20-megaton nuclear bomb. (One hundred megatons are probably pointing at us this minute.) First of all, there would be an incredible flash of heat and light. In less than a second, the temperature would rise to 150 million degrees Fahrenheit—that's four times the temperature at the center of the sun. A roar would immediately follow, but in the center of the city no one would hear it. There would be nothing left but heat and dust.

The explosion would bore a crater in solid rock—Manhattan, as you know, is solid granite—deep enough to contain a twenty-storey building. The crater would be a mile and a half wide. At ground zero, in less than one second, everything—skyscrapers, roads, bridges, some million people—would instantly evaporate. Within three seconds the fireball would reach a height and breadth of about four miles, and its flash would be bright enough to blind the crew of an incoming airliner as far as a hundred miles away. After sixty seconds the familiar shape of the mushroom cloud would begin to form, expanding for ten or fifteen minutes, reaching a height of about 25 miles, and extending some 80 miles across the sky. The ozone layer in the upper atmosphere, which shields us from the sun's ultraviolet radiation, would be severely depleted by contact with the cloud, thus damaging the prospects for life in the entire planet.

To a distance of five miles from ground zero there would be—nothing. To a distance of ten miles winds up to 1,000 miles per hour would hurl flaming trucks into the air like grotesque Molotov cocktails, spewing gasoline, oil, and shrapnel everywhere in their path. Twenty miles away people's clothing would burst into flame. Forty miles away people would suffer first degree burns. A firestorm would soon rage beyond control. Fallout could cover an area of about 4,800 square miles, depending on the wind. Lethal radiation would contaminate the area for as long as two months, then subsiding to high but not immediately lethal levels for as long as ten months.

Picture similar scenes across the face of the land and, needless to say, the living would envy the dead. The need for medicine, food, housing would be a nightmare. Deformities would continue for generations, assuming that the ozone depletion did not make the earth uninhabitable.

The March 12 issue of *BusinessWeek* was a special issue entitled "The Decline of U.S. Power" and the cover shows the face of the Statue of Liberty, one great tear rolling down her right cheek. But this is the statue of *Liberty*, not the statue of power; and if our lady is weeping it must be because of this nation's obsession with military power—"We're number one; we're number one"; and because "the tempest-tossed," the "huddled masses yearning to breathe free" are no longer only across the ocean but right behind her back. They are the victims of unemployment caused largely by an arms race industry now so capital intensive that most of the taxpayer's money goes to supplying jobs for machines not for human beings. Profits rise, but jobs fall. And while profits rise for some, prices rise for all, for guns over butter, as everyone now admits, equals inflation.

It's time we turned the Statue of Liberty around. It's time to "seek the Lord and live, hate evil and love good." For not only are we pushed to a new way of thinking, we are drawn to a new way of doing things; drawn by the love and passion of our Savior who in this season wept not for himself but for the city, saying, "Would that even now you knew the things that make for peace."

It's a tough world, early and late. We all know that. But we are the salt of the earth, called to speak truth to power, to pray for peace, to think for peace, to suffer for peace. And it wouldn't be that hard to begin if only we didn't so fear to be humiliated by loss of power. (That's the basic reason why we hate the Russians. Hate is an automatic response to fear because fear humiliates.) As a first step we could ban all new weapon systems, as the Soviets have proposed. We could openly announce that we shall never use nuclear weapons as an instrument of national policy. The Soviets have proposed this too; let's see if they mean it. As a gesture of good faith without in any way endangering a single American life, we could unilaterally start to reduce our arsenal, because overkill is overkill. Superfluous weapons are just that—superfluous.

And through conversion legislation we could start beating swords into mass transit, low income housing, channeling the billions saved into jobs and services for the poor who in our day are rapidly becoming modern day lepers.

This week we shall recall the twelfth anniversary of the death of Martin Luther King Jr. I hope you will all come to the service on Friday—but not to honor him as a martyr, while trampling on everything he stood for as a prophet. The words that he spoke shortly before his death are more applicable now than then. Said Martin:

> We are faced with the fact that tomorrow is today. We are confronted with the fierce urgency of now. Procrastination is the thief of time. . . . Over the bleached bones and jumbled residue of numerous civilizations are written the pathetic words: "Too late." . . . We still have a choice today: non-violent co-existence or violent co-annihilation. We must move past indecision to action.

It's not that our nation or the time in which we live is more evil than any other. Ranke, the German historian, was probably right. "Every generation is equidistant from eternity." But ours is the closest yet to ultimate extinction. And we want other generations to follow. This is the year of the child and God wants, in return for his love our own, and not the ashes of our children.

The Peace Sabbath, Peace Sunday weekend, celebrated across the nation this weekend will put many new people on the road to peace. It's a stony road, long and oft-times lonely. But our shepherd leads us towards the promised time—that time when faith and hope shall be outdistanced by sight and possession, when we shall live in a world without famine, a world without borders, a world at one and at peace because "nation shall not lift up sword against nation, neither shall they learn war anymore."

Ride On, Ride On, in Majesty

APRIL 8, 1979
Reading: Mark 11:1–11

The text of the sermon comes from the story we just read, "And those who went before and those who followed cried out, 'Hosanna! Blessed is he who comes in the name of the Lord!'" (Mark 11:9).

I just love Westerns. For one thing they present a Victorian world—American style—a world in which good is good and bad is bad and never the twain shall get confused. For another, they nourish the great American myth of rugged individuality, suggesting as they do that society is but a figment of the socialist imagination. I'm not joking, because in the average Western the structures of society fail: the telegraph lines snap, the sheriff gets drunk, the cavalry rides off in the wrong direction. Then up speaks the *Lone* Ranger: "We'll head 'em off at Eagle Pass." The "we" never includes more than a monosyllabic Indian, and, sure enough, against overwhelming odds, they save the day. It's all very satisfactory.

But I have omitted an important feature: the great horse Silver, a steed almost as mighty as its master. The two are really inseparable, the courage of the one matched and enhanced by the magnificence of the other. In every sense both are heroic.

But the redeemer king, astride a lowly ass, linking humility of all things to victory, is, to the eye of the religious beholder, yet more heroic. In fact, for sheer courage, as for high drama, Jesus' entry into Jerusalem is in all history almost unparalleled. Enacting Zechariah's prophesy, he puts himself in a great prophetic tradition. For when words failed to move their hearers the prophets often acted out their warnings, as if to say, "If you will not hear, I will compel you to see." This is exactly what Jesus is doing. Having said what he had to say about the kingdom of God and the messianic age which he was inaugurating, he now puts his words into action.

And what a parade it is, that first Palm Sunday! It's a good deal more than a mere spontaneous acclamation on the part of Passover pilgrims. Pilgrims and citizens of Jerusalem all seem utterly convinced that the long-awaited man and day had come. Their enthusiasm is at flood tide. "And those who went before and those who followed after cried out, 'Hosanna!' (which means literally "save now!") 'Blessed be the Kingdom of our father David that is coming.'" There's the tip-off to their expectations.

What drama then, and what courage on the part of Jesus to come as the Messiah—but not as a king to shatter physically the yoke of oppression; rather *in* peace and *for* peace. What drama, and what courage on the part of Jesus to come as the Messiah—but not merely for patriotic and virtuous Jews, but for everyone, including whores and tax-collectors, the hated collaborationists of the Romans who, too, are part of the scheme of salvation. In other words, Jesus comes as the Messiah in deliberate contradiction to almost everything everyone expected and hoped for. Need it be added that anyone who undertakes to show people that their deepest yearnings are misguided is in for trouble, and in for deep trouble if he is trying to tear up by the roots a people's nationalistic dream.

Let us not, however, make the mistake so frequently made by Christians of believing that Jesus rode into Jerusalem on the back of a lowly beast to demonstrate that he was a spiritual *as opposed* to a political Messiah. Had Jesus been as apolitical as some of his followers try to be today, the nails would never have grazed his palms. As is so often the case in history, his enemies understood him better than many of his followers. He was executed for his politics which were correctly labelled treasonous. Jesus never retreated from the giant social issues of his time into the pygmy world of private piety. He was more than a prophet, but he was never less than a prophet. As firmly as any before him, he stood for the oppressed, against the oppressor, for the poor as opposed to the rich; and in true prophetic style, he saw that the real troublemakers of this world are not the ignorant and cruel, but the intelligent and corrupt. But to the evils of oppression, poverty and corruption in high places—evils he proclaimed so clearly that the common-folk heard him gladly—to these evils he added one more, which lost him their vote, the evil of violence.

As he saw it, the problem with violent revolution is not that it changes too much, but that it changes too little. Nonviolence is more radical than violence. The human nature that Jesus knew so well had taught him that violence leads to lies, just as lies need violence to defend them. In contrast, truth is naked. To be pure, truth has to be vulnerable, disarmed, its only weapon love. So the very love that found oppression, poverty, and corruption so intolerable, this same love rather than inflict suffering accepted suffering unto himself. So we can say that just as Jesus was more than a prophet, not less, so he was more political, not less, his politics being the "politics of eternity." He prayed not for the coming of the kingdom of David, as did the folk who followed him in that parade; rather he prayed, "Thy will be done on earth for all, Thy kingdom come, though in my own undoing."

Was he a mildly deluded sentimentalist? I think the most effective arguments for the truth of Christianity are not spun out by preachers but by the events of contemporary history. More than ever, don't they prove that Jesus, far from a sentimentalist, was a stern realist? More than ever, isn't he now truth in a world governed by illusions?

His politics were the politics of eternity. He was more than a prophet, not less than one. Another mistake to be avoided is the notion that physical violence is the only or even worst form of violence. As I read scripture, I am impressed that in Jesus' mind anything that violates the humanity of human beings is violent. That means that the spiritual violence that drives the poor to despair, this violence in which never a knife is bared, never a shot fired, is surely more reprehensible than the physical violence it causes in reaction to itself. And those who fail to protest this "*violencia blanca*" as it is called in Latin America, this "white violence," are accomplices to it, as we can surely see by the light of Holy Week. What's worse—having blood on your hands, or water like Pilate?

"And many spread their garments on the road"—an impressive demonstration of self-forgetfulness. People were really lifted that day on a tide of hope and joy. And there's nothing comparable to this kind of exhilaration. "Take all away from me, but give me ecstasy," cried Emily Dickinson.

But knowing what we know today, can we still join the parade? The answer to that is "Of course." For truth is not only more unbelievable than fiction, it's twice as compelling, twice as exhilarating. And let us not forget that Christ is unbelievable not because it's too hard to believe in him; he's too good to believe, we being strangers to such goodness. But I want, I need that goodness. I prefer the politics of eternity to all the politics of this world. And I prefer to see humility linked to victory, knowing how pride goes before a fall. So Silver, you and the Lone Ranger, I love you in my fantasy life. But in real life I prefer the ass and the lonely, incredibly courageous, nonviolent Messiah, who draws me to him with a love that can only emanate from God himself.

And if you feel the same way, what are we waiting for? Let's join the parade on the road to Jerusalem. Let's take up the cry of the people but this time with a difference. Let us take up their cry in a way appropriate to our king, the King of Kings, the King of all the human race. "Blessed be he who comes in the name of the Lord." For he opposes all forms of violence, classism, sexism, spiritual, psychological and physical violence. "Blessed is he who comes in the name of the Lord." For he did not inflict suffering but took it upon himself, being obedient unto death, yea, even death upon the cross. So

Ride on! Ride on in majesty!
In lowly pomp ride on to die!

. . . .

Ride on! Ride on in majesty!
Thy last and fiercest strife is nigh;

. . . .

Bow thy meek head to mortal pain,
Then take, O God, thy power, and reign.

Living the Truth in a World of Illusions

APRIL 15, 1979

Some of you will recall the discovery in 1959 of two Japanese sol-diers in the wilds of a Philippine island, two men who fired on anyone who approached their jungle redoubt. Either they had not heard or had refused to believe that World War II was over. For four-teen years they lived an illusion. For fourteen years no one could dis-abuse them of their misapprehension of a world in which killing on a national scale was still the order of the day.

Well would you believe that for over 1,900 years, no tiny minor-ity but the vast majority of the human race has lived a similar illusion? Either they have not heard or they have refused to believe that Good Friday is over. They still live in a world in which fear holds sway, and I say "fear" for hate is but an automatic response to fear—because fear humiliates.

It is of course a believable illusion, this continuing Good Friday world. For like Pilate, most political bureaucrats are still seeking to minimize their responsibilities. Like Peter, most of Christ's disciples still fear to confess the object of their devotion before a hostile world. Like the Sadducees and Pharisees, many religious leaders still deify not God but their virtue; while the majority of citizens, like those on Calvary, gather not to cheer miscarriages of justice, but also not to protest them. They go home beating their breasts, preferring guilt to responsibility.

It's not that many people aren't decent; following their best instincts they are. And it's not that they can't be hopeful; they can be. But their hope is primarily dependent on hopeful circumstances. If things get better, they feel hopeful. In fact, they will construct the flimsiest structures of optimism imaginable. But then when things go badly, the structures collapse and they lose heart. Nor do all Christians deny their Lord as blatantly as did Peter that day. But Meister Eckhart is right: "There are plenty to follow our Lord halfway, but not the other half." And all this is because we still live in a Good Friday world. We simply cannot believe that all that goodness which on Good Friday we saw scourged, buffeted, stretched out on a cross, that perfect love of God which alone can cast out fear, is again alive, as alive as any of us here today.

But—praise be to God—ever since Christ burst the bonds of death and transformed a huddle of dispirited frightened people into a band ready to dare and do anything—ever since that first Easter there has been a chain of saints, persuaded that the reign of fear is over. Fearless, they are never humiliated. Fearless they never humiliate. I think of Peter after the resurrection, ten times the person he was before. I think of St. Francis kissing the leper—full on the mouth. I think of that brave Quaker woman, Mary Dyer, executed in the early days of Boston for believing "Truth is my authority, not authority my truth." I think of the Danish pastor who said, "I'd rather die with the Jews than keep company with Nazis"—and the Nazis obliged him. And I think of countless unsung heros and heroines who knew that to be meant to be vulnerable, who knew that human beings are as they love. Not that they were blind to the towering problems, the awful facts. But they believed that the most momentous fact of all was that Jesus Christ lived, died—and rose again. Therefore it is He and not fear who reigns. I believe it is this minority who continue to live the truth in a world of illusions.

Was the tomb really empty? I am not going to press the factual question. I did that last Easter, and that sermon is still available. (If you can't afford the dime, be Riverside's guest.) I am not going to press the factual question because more and more I am convinced that the question of fact is only meaningful to those who have answered the question of its consequences. Tell me that Easter can be the most significant event in your life and we will talk about the question of fact.

But now let us ask what are these illusory fears that keep us in our own tombs, that humiliate us, that prevent us from living life fully, and bravely and beautifully?

One surely is the fear that life has passed us by, that life has lost its purpose. That is a terribly humiliating fear, as some of you know well. I think of all the "cast offs" in the world: the boat people no one wants; the Arabs no one listens to; the *campesinos* no one pays a decent wage; the blacks no one employs—all the folk who are unloved. And those

192   *April 15, 1979*

of us more fortunate are not immune. In fact the question of meaning is never more hard pressed than it is for the affluent, for as the Russian theologian Nikolai Berdyaev said, "When bread is assured, then God becomes a hard and inescapable reality instead of an escape from harsh reality." Every sensitive person here has known moments when life seemed pointless. But never, I submit, when contemplating the life of Jesus. That would be like listening to Beethoven's nine symphonies and concluding that the world might be a decent place if only there were some decent music around. Think of the meaning that Christ has affirmed simply this last past Holy Week: a messiah who preferred to be hated for what he was rather than loved for what he was not; a messiah who needed no more than God as his witness. (Augustine said, "Anyone who needs more than God as his witness is too ambitious.") What honesty, what humility, and what love that in the way to his own death Jesus could weep not for himself but for the people of the city: "O Jerusalem, Jerusalem"—read "New York, New York"—"how often would I have gathered ye unto me as a mother hen her chicks, and ye would not." And now according to the Resurrection faith, this same humble, honest, loving messiah is alive, calling to the cast offs, "Come unto me, all ye who are weary and heavy laden, and I will give you rest" (Matt. 11:28). In all our sundry distresses and turmoils he says, "My peace I give you; not as the world gives, give I unto you. Let not your hearts be troubled; neither let them be afraid" (John 14:27). In the Kingdom of our Lord no one is humiliated and no one humiliates another. Every life has its purpose, its meaning. No one is left out.

Tillich wrote, "We are slaves of fear, not because we have to die. but because we deserve to die." Our guilty fears humiliate us even more than our fears that life has passed us by. But let us on this Eastertide note how Peter was among the first to reach the tomb. Why, you would have thought that his denial of his master would have chased him clean out of Jerusalem, probably even driven him to contemplate Judas' suicide. But no, he stays to be forgiven. He stays to become a leader of the early church, the best kind of leader, a forgiven sinner, a man with no pretensions, no blind sides. He stays to demonstrate to future sinners that the entire Christian church is founded on a second chance. For in the Risen Lord there is no condemnation, only reconciliation. Once again no humiliation, and no humiliation of others.

And what about the fear of death, the fear that, like Delilah's shears, cuts at the very root of our strength revealing the underlying weakness? As a matter of fact, in the ancient days of Greece death was pictured as the scissors that cut the thread of life. But the image is inadequate. Death is really a thread woven into the very design of our lives from beginning to end. Death is an event that embraces all our lives. We don't need to be saved from death. We do need to be saved from our fear of death. We don't need to know what is beyond the grave. But we do need to know who is beyond. And Christ's resurrection tells us simply in the words of Paul, "whether we live or whether we die we are the Lord's." If death is of no consequence to God, dear friends, it need be of little consequence to us. With Paul we can say—and with his marvelous thumb-nosing independence—"Death, where is thy sting? Grave, where thy victory?" "For I am persuaded that neither death nor life can separate us from the love of God which is in Christ Jesus our Lord" (Rom. 8:38–39).

"Perfect love casts out fear"—fear that life has passed us by, fear that we deserve to die, fear that we are going to die. In the Kingdom of our Lord all fears are banished forever as illusions that we can live without. In the Kingdom of our Lord there is no humiliation, only dignity for all. We too are resurrected, in all senses of the word, for

> Made like him, like him we rise;
> Ours the cross, the grave, the skies.

One final Easter thought. The resurrection of Christ brought into being a church, a community. Salvation may be an individual thing but it is a corporate responsibility. Human nature is too frail; we need to support one another. We cannot change human nature—that is true. But we can change the nature of human relationships. In the 16th century Cromwell understood the point. In drawing up the laws of war he had to face the question: what to do with a man found with a wound in his back? The answer: find his friends and drum them out of the army and out of the church. Cowardice is a communal not an individual failing.

And so, dear Christians, we must pull together in the colony of heaven that is the church at its best. We must be available to one another just as Christ is available to us, if we are to affirm Easter in a Good Friday world, if we are going to live the truth in a world of illusions. To live fully, bravely and beautifully we have to live together, to live lovingly. Then never mind if we are only a small minority. There is no limit to what love can do. Love is a miracle. Love is a basket of five loaves and two fishes which is never enough, until you start to give it away. So, on this Easter day, let's not limp back to business as before, rather let's join the saints who feed the hungry with the bread of this earth, and, better yet, with the bread of heaven—the resurrected body of our Lord and Savior Jesus Christ.

But enough of words; a mystery can only be celebrated. And we never sing these Easter hymns enough. So let us take that last hymn and sing its first verse once again,

> The strife is o'er, the battle done,
> The victory of life is won;
> The song of triumph has begun.
> Alleluia!

Breakfast with Jesus

MAY 6, 1979
Reading: John 21:1–17

Basically, this story is about the rehabilitation of Peter, the three questions corresponding to the three denials that took place on Good Friday.

But the story suggests so many things besides. For instance: At the beginning of the Gospel of John, Jesus visits human beings in their joy, at a wedding feast in Cana. Whether you believe that he turned the water into wine (and I have seen Jesus turn beer into furniture!) it is clear that Jesus is coming down on the side of joy as hard as he comes down on the side of suffering. Joy and suffering in the Christian life are inseparable and both totally to be accepted. But if a wedding feast is a special and especially joyful event, what could be more routine than the occasion on which Jesus last visits human beings—breakfast: fish and bread beside Lake Tiberias. Breakfast: the same food in the same place at the same time, with the same people, and all of them at their worst. Some of you, I know, will tell me your breakfast is a spectacular event. But I'll stand by my description of breakfast as about as routine an event as you can find in the course of a day.

But breakfast with Jesus—that's like eggs benedict, or maybe Vermont maple syrup with fresh waffles. It redeems the routine. The disciples were so excited they didn't dare ask, "Who are you?"

Breakfast with Jesus redeems the routine. To make the point clearer let me recall two breakfast scenes from modern American literature. The second isn't exactly breakfast but it will come close enough, as you will see. The first scene is from the third Act of Thornton Wilder's "Our Town." Emily Webb has recently died at the age of twenty-six and against the advice of the older dead, she chooses to go back. It's allowed, but in reliving life one has to watch oneself doing it. That's the condition imposed by the stage manager, who sort of runs things in heaven and on earth. So Emily chooses to return on the morning of her twelfth birthday.

"Good morning, Mama."

Mrs. Webb: "Well, now my dear, very happy birthday to my girl and many happy returns. There are some surprises waiting for you on the kitchen table. . . . But birthday or no birthday, I want you to eat your breakfast good and slow; I want you to grow up and be a good, strong girl."

The whole thing is going too routinely, and Emily now says with mounting urgency—only of course her mother can't hear her: "Oh, Mama. I married George Gibbs, Mama. Well, he's dead, too. His appendix burst on a camping trip to North Conway. We just felt terrible about it, don't you remember? But just for a moment now, we are all together. Mama, just for a moment we are happy, let's look at one another."

But it isn't working, and finally Emily says to the stage manager: "I can't go on. It goes so fast. We don't have time to look at one another." She breaks down sobbing, "I didn't realize. So all that was going on and we never noticed. Take me back up the hill to my grave. But first, wait, one more look. Goodbye, world. Goodbye Grovers Corners, Mama and Papa. Goodbye to clocks ticking, Mama's sunflowers, food and coffee, and new ironed dresses, and hot baths, and sleeping and waking up. Oh earth, you are too wonderful for anybody to realize you." She looks toward the stage manager and asks abruptly through her tears, "Do any human beings ever realize life while they live it, every, every minute?"

Stage manager: "No. The saints and poets, maybe; they do some."

"So all that was going on and we never even noticed." But with Jesus around, we begin to notice things that heretofore we had only seen. The world doesn't lack for wonders; it only lacks a sense of wonder, the wonder that comes with the realization that "the earth is the Lord's and the fulness thereof; the world and they that dwell therein" (Ps. 24:1). And everyone therein is so special. "Mama, let's look at one another."

The second scene is from one of the tales of Sholem Aleichem, and it is about a man to whom befell every misfortune imaginable. His wife died, his children never called, his house burned down, his job disappeared, everything he touched turned to dust. Nonetheless, he always remained cheerful, always returning good for evil. Finally he died. Word of his imminent arrival at heaven's gate caused the angels to gather. Even the Lord was there, so great was this man's fame. And when he arrived and stood with downcast eyes, the prosecuting Angel arose and for the first time in the memory of heaven said, "There are no charges." Then the Angel for the defense arose and after he had rehearsed all the hardships and had recounted how in all these circumstances the old man had always remained cheerful, always returning good for evil, the Lord said, "Not since Job have we heard of a life such as this one." Turning to the man he said, "Ask, and it shall be given unto you."

The old man raised his eyes from the ground and said, "If I could start every day with a hot buttered roll. . . ." And at that the Lord and all the angels wept.

It wasn't so much the modesty of the request as the understanding of the preciousness of what he was asking for. I said once, there are two ways to be rich—one is to have lots of money, the other is to have few needs. Let me put it differently: We don't need all things to enjoy life, because we have been given life to enjoy all things. Happiness lies in discerning the value of things we have. And if we have fish and bread and Jesus, that's enough. The routine is redeemed!

Then comes the poignancy of the question: "Simon, son of John, do you love me more than all else?" and the infinite tenderness of the answer, "Feed my lambs." Not the sheep, not the first time. "Feed my *lambs*." Jesus is always thinking of children. Every year is the year of the child as far as Jesus is concerned. It is as if he is saying to Peter, "Simon, son of John, each new child that is born is sufficient reason for the whole universe's being set into motion." For every child that arrives on this planet is unprecedented, irrepeatable, and, in the divine dispensation, irreplaceable.

"Albert, William, Shirley, Juliette—put in your own name—do you love me more than all also? Then watch over the children of this world."

"A second time he said to him, 'Simon, son of John, do you love me?' He said to him, 'Yes, Lord, you know that I love you.' He said to him, 'Feed my sheep.'"

Now it's the grown-ups' turn. But from his words it is clear Jesus had first in mind those hardly less vulnerable than the children. "Feed my sheep." *Homo homini lupus*. Human beings are wolves to each other. It is against that understanding that Jesus is speaking. For those whom the world in its callousness tramples on Jesus reclaims and presents to us anew for our consideration—the sick, the frail, the old, the poor. "Ah," says Jesus, "if only after the Year of the Child you would proclaim the Year of the Poor, and enjoin the rulers of the world to pass only such legislation as would benefit the bottom 30 percent of the economic ladder."

President Carter his submitted his budget and the Congress must vote on it before May 15. The President likes to present himself as a populist yet his budget redistributes wealth by taking from the poor and giving to the rich. His budget says "Goodbye" to "meals on wheels" for the aged, to training programs for the young—yes, even as Continental Oil Company registers profits 443 percent higher than last year. The military budget, the highest on record, includes $400 million for two destroyers ordered by the Shah that the new regime wisely doesn't want and that our own Navy needs like it needs two rowboats. But we have to pay for them, not the Litton Corporation of Mississippi that produced them, not the Shah who could afford them, and not even the Pentagon with its $22 billion of unobligated funds and its $60 billion in unexpended funds.

"Joshua, Lou, Cynthia, Joyce—fill in your own name—do you love me? Then watch over the poor. Don't let the country become a greedy disgrace."

"He said to him yet a third time, 'Simon, son of John, do you love me?' Peter was grieved because he said to him the third time, 'Do you love me?' And he said to him, 'Lord, you know everything; you know that I love you.' And Jesus said to him, 'Feed my sheep.'"

The point is made. The story is for the restoration of all of us, for promise-making, promise-breaking Peter is all of us. Jesus says to all of us, "I know that you have denied me, but if you keep believing in me the way Peter did, then you will understand that I believe in you. I have full confidence in you. And you'll find joy in opening the doors of life to others. Your own life will be resurrected—if you feed my sheep."

We've talked of the disciples' last breakfast with Jesus—bread and fish. Today we again celebrate the Last Supper—bread and wine. It's the same idea. The simplest things in life take on infinite meaning when they are shared, blessed with the presence of our Lord and Savior.

"Do any human beings ever realize life while they live it—every, every minute?"

No, but with Jesus you can come pretty close!

Neither Male Nor Female

MAY 13, 1979

The text for this Mother's Day meditation is Galatians 3:28: "There is neither Jew nor Greek, there is neither slave nor free, there is neither male nor female; for you are all one in Christ Jesus."

Out of a window in my apartment on 125th Street, I can see, across the Hudson, several very large apartment buildings. When first I viewed them I didn't like them. They looked ugly, remote. Oversized and over there, they played into a prejudice I indulge on my bad days, which is to believe that life is discovering that the light at the end of the tunnel is New Jersey! Then I found out that in one of the endless apartments lived Maestro Fred Swann. Instantly, those large, ugly buildings began to appear friendly.

There's the secret to humanizing the world. Picture a friendly face in a faceless crowd, and a collectivity of individuals turns into a community of warm human beings. Therein, too, lies the secret of our mothers. They mediate between us and nature; they mediate between us and humanity. The world is large, terrifying even, to a baby or small child. But by rocking us in their arms, our mothers tell us, "It's O.K., you are going to make it." Mothers close the gap between a baby's hunger and the food he can neither prepare nor eat. Mothers close the gap between a baby's desire and the toys he cannot reach. Mothers bring us to the shore of the sea of life and put out the orange buoys so that we can wade in safely, taking on no more than we can psychologically encompass. And if they are wise as birds, our mothers know when we can fly and kick us out of the nest.

Well, I suppose that's reason enough for gratitude, and the many special flowers on the altar today reflect the sentiments of deeply thankful hearts. But this is Mother's Day 1979, and it seems to me that we should try to go beyond what we have said, and try to say something about today's changing attitude toward motherhood on the part of so many women, and a growing number of men.

Let's start with disturbing words found in the second chapter of St. Paul's first letter to Timothy. "Let a woman learn in silence and all submissiveness. I permit no woman to teach or have authority over men. She is to keep silent for Adam was formed first, then Eve. And Adam was not deceived, but the woman was deceived and became a transgressor. Yet women will be saved through bearing children, if they continue in faith, and love, and holiness, with modesty" (vv. 11–15).

What is disturbing is not the statement that women need salvation—who doesn't?—but that motherhood is singled out as *the* vocation through which women gain salvation; and that motherhood is directly tied to the subordinate position of women; and the subordinate position of women is tied in turn to the order of creation. First Adam, then Eve.

I like to think of the Church as a seminar in remedial living. Here in the Church we try to remedy racial relations. Here in the Church we learn that class is altogether as tough a nut to crack as race. And here in the Church we had better learn that in society and in the Church, the most deep-seated prejudice—not the one with the worst effects, but the most profound—is the one reflected in Paul's understanding of "First Adam, then Eve." One reason for its being deep-seated is because it is the most complicated form of prejudice. Where else does the victim say, "I've met the enemy and he loves me"?

"First Adam, and then Eve." Paul's view is a direct reflection of the Jewish milieu in which he was raised. Jewish society was patriarchal. From circumcision to burial rites only the male was the true Israelite in every sense of the word. The feminine ideal was that of a good wife and mother. Becoming a Christian didn't noticeably change Paul's attitude toward women.

Understandably, therefore, a lot of Christian women are feeling a lot of hostility toward St. Paul these days. For myself, I see no reason to excuse him, any more than I can find reason to excuse Sigmund Freud for his more Victorian than Christian view of feminine inferiority. But that a man as modern and as scientific as Freud could be so prejudiced makes the point. No prejudice is more deep-seated than the one we are talking about. And to remind myself I reread this week the history of all the scientific "truths" that have been offered right up to the twentieth century to prove the physiological and the mental inferiority of women. Black men, after all, voted in the United States long before women did, and long before women did in almost every country of the world. I think it fair to say that today men and women have more stereotypes about each other than do whites and blacks.

Still, I want to return to St. Paul. In the first place, what can't be condoned can be forgiven. And were we to throw out all the writings of every prejudiced writer, what would we read?

Specifically, I want to return to the text, for Galatians 3:28 represents a kind of breakthrough. For most of the following I'm indebted to Professor Krister Stendhal. It's interesting how a spiritual revelation can point beyond and even oppose the views of the person who receives it; can point beyond and even oppose the prevailing practices of the Church. For in Galatians 3:28, Paul says that all divisions are overcome, a new unity is created; there is "neither Jew nor Greek, there is neither slave nor free, there is neither male nor female, for you are all one in Christ Jesus." In Christ Jesus all nations, classes, races and sexes meet, as all rivers meet in the sea. Grace transcends the law, says St. Paul. "The law was our custodian until Christ came, . . . but now that faith has come we are no longer under a custodian" (Gal. 3:24–25). Grace even transcends the order of creation: "There is neither male nor female."

That raises an interesting question: Will this new status, this new freedom, this new unity, be confined solely to the realm of the heart, or will it be implemented outside the realm of the heart, in the social sphere? And Paul's answer is very interesting, because ambiguous. As regards "neither Greek nor Jew," he sees clear implications for the social realm. Earlier in the letter to the Galatians, he insists that Greeks should not have to become Jews in order to become Christians. They don't have to be circumcised, they don't have to obey Jewish law. Jew and Greek must sit down at table together, for all are one in Christ Jesus. But as regards "neither slave nor free," he seems less concerned with implementing this spiritual freedom in the social realm; and as regards "neither male nor female," not at all.

But let us ask ourselves who today in the Christian Church would confine the implications of "neither slave nor free" to an attitude of heart, totally divorced from social structures and legislation? If, when we read the Bible, we listen as well to the dictates of conscience, then we have to conclude that if there is no continuing revelation there is always continuing implementation of a once-and-for-all revelation. Quite rightly, we have abolished slavery as a social institution. Quite rightly, we seek to implement in the social realm the revelation given St. Paul that in Christ there is neither male nor female. In other words, what is authoritative for the twentieth-century Church is the *revelation* of the first-century Church, not the stage of implementation which that revelation may have reached.

Need I add that just as the emancipation of Blacks led to full equality, so the emancipation of women will lead to ordination—even in the Roman Catholic Church. Not even the Pope will escape the benefits of the seminar in remedial living which is the Church at its best.

And now having done that little bit of Bible study, let us return to where we started with mothers and motherhood. As to date there is no other way, and never, I dare say, will there be a better way to arrive on this planet than through a mother; motherhood is an important human enterprise. And the rearing of children is a vocation inferior to none, especially when it is freely chosen, no longer tied to the subordinate position of women. But just as women are becoming free to widen their thoughts, their activities, so inevitably are men. In fact, let us recognize, on this Mother's Day 1979, that the woman most in need of liberation is the woman in every man. If in Christ there is no male nor female, then androgyny can replace misogyny. Spiritually speaking, motherhood is not confined to mothers. The feminine ideal when not imposed but freely chosen, the ideal of fulfilling oneself in service to others is a fine ideal for everyone. Mothers feed hungry children. Why shouldn't we all? Mothers conserve human life. I believe in that kind of conservatism. Mothers humanize a forbidding world, a fitting task for all humanity.

So, dear mothers, on this your designated day, we salute you, and thank you, not by trying to repay your love but by passing it on. For the world needs mothering. Let all of us then be gentle, be kind. Let all of us gladden the hearts of children. Let us share their pleasure in the beauty and wonder of the earth. Let us tell them our love, tell it again, and tell it still again. Amen.

Baccalaureate Sermon

MAY 27, 1979
Colgate University
The University Chapel

Dear graduating seniors, faculty, your mothers and fathers (without whom, let us face it, none of us would be here) and your sisters, your cousins and your aunts; and those who are sitting downstairs and standing out there: I hope you don't consider yourselves in outer darkness; if I were running this place you would be filling the aisles, but unfortunately, I'm not. So you'll have to stand where you are.

What President Langdon said in his remarks about Harry Emerson Fosdick is absolutely true. As for the rest, I thought it was very nice of him to allow his generosity to outstrip his judgment.

Now I am going to do a bit of preaching today, I hope. But given the rich mix of persuasions in this chapel this morning, I think I won't try to preach a sermon in the more conventional, formal sense.

Tolstoy once said, "Certain questions are put to us not so much that we should answer them but that we should spend a lifetime wrestling with them." And I am going to put to you, to all of us, three questions this morning and wish you a lifetime of good luck and God's grace as you wrestle with them.

Number One: Who tells you who you are?

When I was Chaplain at Yale, it was natural that many graduating seniors should ask me to write letters of recommendation. And brilliant letters they were, the ones that I wrote. And to the deans of eminent institutions of higher education, such as the Dean of the Harvard

Law School, and the Columbia Law School, I would often write: "This candidate will undoubtedly be in the bottom quarter of your class. But surely the bottom quarter should be as carefully selected as the top quarter. And for what would a dean be looking in the bottom quarter of the class, if not for the sterling extracurricular qualities so eminently embodied in this candidate?" And then I would list them. Then I would show the letter of recommendation to the student. And would you believe it? invariably, the student was hurt.

"How do you know I'm going to be in the bottom quarter of the class?"

"Well, all the evidence is in, isn't it?"

"Well, you didn't have to tell them."

Never mind that this was a caring, conscientious, beautiful person. Never mind that this student was already in the ninety-eighth percentile. If this student was not in the ninety-ninth percentile, that student didn't rate!

You see the power of institutions of higher education. As a minister, I can stand before you and tell you, you are human beings who happen to be students. But believe me, the 40 percent of you who go on to graduate school, you are going to be told that you are students who then happen to be human beings.

Who tells you who you are?

When I was Chaplain at Yale, I didn't often get an invitation to address the Yale alumni. They feared I was too controversial. Which simply showed how far removed from controversy they were.

But once I received an invitation to address the alumni at Chicago. Afterwards the president took me to his very spacious home in Evanston, Illinois. And as we were entering this beautiful home, he allowed that he was a member of a group called Lux et Veritas. Well, that's a group of alumni, who are, shall we say, sullen but not mutinous. And I said to him, "I've always wanted to hear you out, your unhappiness about Yale, so why don't you pour us a drink and then pour out your heart, and I'll listen." (I suppose in a college that has Baptist roots, and in the presence of a Baptist minister and Baptist choir, I should explain that with Yale alumni, at least, drinking is important because the superego is defined as that which is soluble in alcohol.) After about thirty minutes of careful listening to what he was saying and most of all to what he didn't say (which is always the way you want to listen to other people, and to yourself) I thought I caught something. I said to him, "Now let me ask you an honest question to which I want an honest answer. When you were an undergraduate at Yale, you were a C student, weren't you?"

And he demurred, mentioned a few B-'s. But, finally, he allowed, "Yes. My average was generally a C, C+." He said, "Why?"

And I said, "I'll tell you why. I think you're unhappy. Not because of anything that President Brewster said, or anything I said or did. Not because your kids didn't get into Yale—they got into perfectly good colleges. I think what's really bothering you" (mind you, this is about thirty years later) "is that you think you can't get into Yale today. And you are absolutely right. You wouldn't have a prayer. But while I understand why Yale needs you, your moral support, your financial support, what I cannot understand is, why do you still need Yale to tell you who you are?"

Who tells you who you are? Is it going to be some institution? Some people need money to tell them who they are. Some people need power to tell them who they are. Some people need enemies to tell them who they are. When President Johnson resigned in March of 1968, half-a-million people in the peace movement in the United States lost their identity. They needed enemies to tell them who they were. President Nixon came along and it was restored.

So I ask you, who is going to tell you who you are? That's a very important question if this nation is not to become a nation of practicing cowards where moral integrity, or even common integrity will be made to look like courage. Is it going to be power? Is it going to be money? Is it going to be some institution, or is it going to be God? If I were preaching a more regular sermon, I'd tell you what a difference it would be if it were God. But I will say only this. If it's God who tells you who you are, you don't have to prove yourself at all. All that is taken care of. You are precious, you are unprecedented, you are irrepeatable, and in the divine dispensation, you are indispensable. So you don't have to prove yourself again. All you have to do is *express* yourself. What a world of difference there is between proving oneself and expressing oneself. What a different world it would be if all we felt called on to do was to express the beautiful selves that we are made and meant to be by God.

Well, that is question Number One: Who tells you who you are?

Question Number Two: Who is going to define the United States? Now I recognize that some of you are not citizens of this country. But if you will excuse me, I will concentrate on America because it is the beloved nation to most of us. And that is an equally important question. Who is going to define the United States for you?

Let us grant immediately that for years the Soviets have been behaving abominably in Eastern Europe, Poland, Hungary, Czechoslovakia, Rumania. And let us grant that the Cubans are behaving questionably in Africa.

But let us not see the speck in the other person's eye and remain ignorant of the beam in our own. For this was the first country after World War II that passed from isolationism into interventionism without passing through internationalism. Since 1945, the end of World War II, the United States of America has intervened in the internal affairs of another country by military effort, or by major effort on the part of the CIA, on the average of once every 18 months. Let's rehearse it: 1948, Greece; 1953, Iran; 1954, Guatemala; 1958, Indonesia; 1958, Lebanon; 1960, Laos; 1961, Cuba; 1964, British Guiana; 1964, the Congo, as it was then called; 1965, the Dominican Republic; and thereafter, Vietnam, once again Laos, and then Cambodia, because in order to withdraw troops from one country, we had to invade two and bomb three. 1973, Chile. We have just heard it sung, "sound the alarm on the mountain of God."

The alarm must be sounded.

On the front cover of the March 12 issue of *Business Week* it was announced that the entire issue would be dedicated to the decline of United States power. And the cover showed the face of one of my most favorite ladies in all this world, the face of the Statue of Liberty. And down one cheek of the Statue of Liberty was coursing one single big tear. Now when I was a kid, I was brought up to believe that that was the Statue of *Liberty*! . . . and not the Statue of American power. And if our lady is weeping, as I dare say she is, it is because of the irrational love of covetous power that fits this description: "We're Number One!"

That is the cry that is going up from almost every American heart, and not "Number One" in decency, mind you. We are the first in the world when it comes to military strength. And you listen to the debates that are about to take place on the SALT treaties. For every Senator who stands up and says, "Will this treaty make the world more safe for our children?", there will be ten Senators who will say, "Will this treaty still mean that we are second to none?" And if our lady is weeping, it probably is also because those teeming masses yearning to breathe free are no longer across the Atlantic Ocean but right behind her back: in New York City, and in all the major cities in this country, where the poor are being turned rapidly into modern-day lepers. So I ask you, Isn't it time to turn the Statue of Liberty around? Isn't it time we began to define the country in terms of something a little more human than simply being "number one" in the world in terms of military power?

Who is going to define our beloved nation?

And that leads to the third question. What kind of a world do you want the graduating class, let us say 20 years from now sitting here, to be looking at? What kind of a world do you want to leave your children?

Einstein, early on in the nuclear age, said: "The release of the power of the atom has changed everything except our way of thinking." And thus we drift toward catastrophe of unparalleled magnitude. Einstein had reason enough to know that the nuclear age was the antithesis of the prenuclear age. Most people still think it is merely the extension. Most people think nuclear weapons can serve the interests of the nation state. Einstein was prescient enough to know that nuclear weapons had in effect made the nation state obsolete.

If we don't learn to be meek, there will be nobody around to inherit the earth. We better learn to be merciful when we live at one another's mercy. The world is now too dangerous for anything but truth, too small for anything but love. Its physical unity needs to find reflection in the moral unity which is fundamentally ours anyhow.

Now if you are religious, you're all set. You rejoice that the only viable future is a global future. You rejoice that the only viable future is a just and global future because of your religious conviction—Jew, Muslim, or Christian—because you believe God made us that way. We all belong with one another: God made us that way. From the Christian point of view, Christ died to keep us that way. We should not put asunder what God himself has joined together. Am I my brother's keeper? No, I'm my brother's brother, or my brother's sister. Human unity is not something we are called on to create—only something we are called on to recognize.

But even as you graduate from Colgate, you must feel that a *liberal education* has *intimated* this moral unity. Because when you stop to think of it, what is more quintessentially British and at the same time universal than Shakespeare? What is more quintessentially Russian and at the same time more universal than Dostoyevsky? Quintessentially more Chilean, and at the same time more universal than the poetry of Pablo Neruda?

Our only viable future, from a religious, cultural, psychological, physical point of view is a global future. What is the survival unit right now in the world? It is not an individual nation. The survival unit in our time, right now, is the entire human race plus its environment.

We've made a world for *some* of us. I think it's probably time we made a world for *all* of us. But I leave you that question. What kind of a world do you want to leave to your children?

Some questions are put to us not so much that we should answer them but that we should spend a lifetime wrestling with them.

Dear graduating seniors, I leave you your continuing education, to wrestle with these kinds of questions: Who tells you who you are? What kind of a country do you want the United States to be? And how are you going to create a world fit for children?

So, may God bless you, perhaps by denying you some of the things you want and granting you all the things you need, so that you may become part of the solution and not the problem. Or in the words of that great Spanish philosopher, Miguel de Unamuno, in your personal lives at least, "May God deny you peace but give you glory." Amen.

A Message from Christians in Cuba

JULY 1, 1979

"Therefore, I tell you, the Kingdom of God will be taken away from you, and given to a nation that yields the proper fruit."
Matthew 21:43

"Happy the people who have the Lord for their God."
Psalm 144:15

As many of you know, for the last two weeks I was part of a small delegation of ministers touring Cuba as guests of the government. The island, incidentally, is a botanist's paradise with over 800 kinds of trees. Very few have as yet to compete with the high stacks of industry. So the skylines everywhere are superb, as are the extravagant colors of the flowers, the length and number of the beaches, and I don't even want to get started on the pineapples, papayas, oranges, lemons, limes, coconuts and guavas. Suffice it to say, all are as apples to the eye of Eve. Columbus mistakenly thought himself in the Orient that October Sunday in 1492 when he first saw the pastel greens and blues of the Cuban shoreline. But we should believe him when he wrote, "This is the most beautiful island my eyes have ever seen." Looking at it, in the company of our communist hosts, forced me to realize once again how the grandeur of God's creation overcomes human differences.

Although guests of a government which today is probably more a-religious than antireligious, we had no trouble contacting fellow

Christians: a morning service with Presbyterians on Sunday, a Wednesday evening fellowship with Baptists, an afternoon visit with faculty members of a Protestant seminary. And on the morning of our last day, we drove 2½ hours out of Havana to meet with twenty Baptist ministers looking for all the world like *campesinos* with their straw hats and machetes. They had volunteered to cut cane for two weeks, along with young communists, in order to prove that the best way for communists and Christians to get together is to work together for goals both consider important. We ended the meeting with my saying, "Why don't you all drop your machetes, we'll take each other's hands and you say the Twenty-third Psalm in Spanish, the rest of us in English." (Which we did.) Then I said, "*Hay que cantar algo*. We must sing something"! To my amazement they burst into "Onward, Christian Soldiers"; in those circumstances not too imperialistic a hymn to sing!

On each of these occasions, I asked the same question: "Dear brothers and sisters, What do you want me to say to my people at Riverside?" They said many things: "Give them our warmest greetings" (which I hereby do); "Ask them to pray for us" (which I trust you will). But two things, in particular, were striking, came through with clarity, and are worth reporting.

"Remind them of the parable of the two brothers," said Baptist pastor Suarez that Wednesday night when we sat around in the courtyard in a circle outside the church, the circle lit by gaslight. "The Cuban revolution of 1959 was like the second brother, the brother who denied his father, but did his will. Unfortunately, our churches before 1959, were more like the first brother, who said he would work in the vineyard but never went." And he went on, "Remind them how the chapter ends, 'Therefore, I tell you, the Kingdom of God will be taken away from you, and given to a nation that yields the proper fruit.'"

I thought that was a rather stunning commentary on more nations than just Cuba. Hardly had I begun to think about it, however, when the young pharmacist next to Suarez chimed in, "That's right. Before 1959, we Christians showed the face of a God of private property, the face of a God of money. We never showed the world the true face of God. As a result, we now have to earn the right to be heard."

At the seminary, we heard much the same thing. "It was the churches' practical atheism that promoted and justified the theoretical atheism of Marxists. Marxists still think that God has to be denied for the cause of humanity to be advanced. It is our job to show that this is not true." Even Fidel, over the years, has said in effect, "Our quarrel is not so much with Christianity as with the churches. Better yet, it is with those middle-class, rich church people who claim the faith but never practice its charity." In other words, atheism is more an ethical than an intellectual problem.

St. Ambrose said, "The world is given to all, and not only to the rich." Many centuries later, the riches of Cuba have been given to the poor in large measure—and by the revolution of '59. As many Christians said, "They, the non-Christians, have done the Christian thing." Medical services are everwhere, in the country as in the city, and all are free. The same is true of education. Nine percent of the work force in Cuba is engaged in education we were told. Illiteracy was practically wiped out in a campaign in which the whole country took part. Five hundred thousand adults are now engaged in continuing education.

I suspect that Cubans take a deeper interest in each other than do we. Often, of New York, I have thought two things: many of us are attracted to the freedom of anonymity, while at the same time we are repelled by the city's indifference. Well, in Cuba today, there's little freedom of anonymity and there's little freedom of the press, for the government, following Lenin's lead, views the press as an ideological instrument of the revolution. But, there's little indifference too. In myriad ways in small villages, on every city block, people are organized to take care of each other. The two ministers in our delegation who come from East Harlem were simply stunned to see before their eyes the kind of organized care they, for thirty years, have labored to bring into being with so little help from the city.

And of course, it's safe. You can go jogging at two o'clock in the morning, if that's what you like to do at two o'clock in the morning. And there are no more prostitutes, and no drugs.

Interestingly enough, now that the government has taken over the responsibility for "the social content of the gospel," Christians are now freer to pray, to concentrate on their inner spiritual development, freer to seek that love that goes beyond justice, and beyond each other. I'm thinking of love of enemy, love for the world. "We have to earn the right to be heard. We must show the world the true face of God."

I pray for their success, for the future role of the churches in Cuba will surely be that of Marxists in the old days—to "tell it like it is," to hold the government to its own stated ideals. (I'm always struck by the naivete of Communists. Said one high government official, "You can't be corrupted by a system that impedes avarice." If avarice were only the only way to be corrupted! And when I asked the Minister of Education, a very impressive man, to comment on a problem that has long vexed the churches—"How do you draw the line between education and indoctrination?"—the shallowness of his answer showed how little he had grasped the depths of the problem.)

But, once again, the degree of social justice that has been achieved in twenty years is deeply moving, and it does make a U.S. Christian ponder Christ's warning: "I tell you, the Kingdom of God will be taken away from you and given to a nation that yields the proper fruit."

The second thing they wanted me to tell you turns out to be something worth thinking about especially today, on the eve of the Fourth of July. The Baptists and Presbyterians were too tactful, and far too grateful to American missionaries to dwell on the sins of U.S. imperialism. But the truth of the matter is that, as much as anything else, these sins have shaped the history of twentieth-century Cuba. On the eve of our great national holiday, let me read you some words, loudly applauded at the time, words spoken by Senator Albert J. Beveridge in Washington, D.C. in 1898, two days before war was declared on Spain. Said Senator Beveridge, "American factories are making more than American people can use. American soil is producing more than they can consume. Fate has written our policy for us; the trade of the world must, and shall be ours. And we will get it as our mother England has shown us how. We will establish trading posts throughout the world as distributing points for American products. We will cover the oceans with our merchant marine. We will build up a navy to the measure of our greatness. Great colonies governing themselves but flying our flag and trading with us, will grow about our posts of trade. Our institutions will follow our flag on the wings of commerce. And American law, American order, American civilization will plant themselves on shores hitherto blooded and benighted, but by these agencies of God henceforth to be made bright and beautiful."

What still amazes me is how many times as a boy I sang, "From the halls of Montezuma to the shores of Tripoli," without once asking just what those marines were doing there anyhow! What I never learned in my high school history was that Teddy Roosevelt and the Rough Riders rode roughshod over the dreams for Cuban independence, dreams for which some seventy thousand Cubans had given their lives. Their colleagues in arms who survived them weren't even allowed to witness the signing of the peace treaty between the United States and Spain. True, we didn't keep Cuba the way we did Puerto Rico, the Philippines and Guam. But we built the Platt Amendment into the constitution of the Cuban Republic, established a permanent naval base at Guantanamo Bay, and withdrew our troops only after assuring the trade arrangements about which Senator Beveridge had spoken so eloquently. From 1905 to 1922 Cuba got 40 percent of her imports from the United States; after World War I, 65 percent; just before World II, 67.5 percent. And that's not to mention the number of banks, mills, sugar and tobacco fields that were bought by American capital.

What I was chastened to find out was the degree to which the 1959 resolution was a war of national liberation from my country, and not just a socialist revolution for Cuba. I had not realized the degree to which the Bay of Pigs must have been promoted by U.S. business interests. And then, when the invasion failed, the United States proceeded to punish Cuba—for defending itself!—by persuading the nations of the Organization of American States to impose a complete embargo on all trade with Cuba. Only Canada and Mexico had the independence to resist.

Eighteen years later we are the only nation to continue the embargo. The best cars in Cuba are made in Argentina. Franco Spain traded with Cuba. And of course we trade with every other communist nation except Vietnam, another small country where we were unable to impose our will.

It is the vindictiveness of these actions that troubled just about every Christian we met in Cuba. They said: "How can American Christians be quiet about this embargo? Tell your people we want to hear their voices. Carter's Christianity should be felt. Justice demands lifting the embargo."

They call it a "*bloqueo*" and spiritually speaking they are right. It is a blockade, one we've thrown around our own minds and hearts. Economically it has meant that Cubans have had to go thousands of miles away to Russia for medical supplies, tractors and trucks they could receive in greater quantity and quality from a country only ninety miles away. Politically, it has given Cuba an identity apart from the United States. It has been Castro's ace in the hole, always available to inspire nationalistic loyalty, added justification for sending Cubans to Angola. And the spiritual blindness represented by this blockade has spelled nothing but recurrent embarrassments, setbacks and failures in American foreign policies.

On the eve of our great national holiday, I have to confess that as an American I am embarrassed that whenever power changes hands in a third world country—Cuba, China, Vietnam, Iran, and now Nicaragua—we always seem to be caught by surprise. We seem to react defensively with an all too apparent lack of vision. Therefore, "Happy are the people who have the Lord for their God." Because if the Lord were indeed our God, if indeed we meant it when we sing, "Be thy strong arm, our ever sure defense," I cannot think our actions would reflect such narrowness and vindictiveness. So I pass on to you the words of our fellow church people in Cuba: "How can American

Christians be quiet about this embargo? Tell your people we want to hear their voices. Carter's Christianity should be felt. Justice demands lifting the embargo."

I'm going to do what I can, and I hope all of you will urge President Carter to affirm the Christianity that the Cubans have recognized in him.

May I wish all of you the finest of holidays, but one in which you will take a little time to ponder the two phrases that have served us as our text: "Therefore, I tell you, the Kingdom of God will be taken away from you, and given to a nation that yields the proper fruit," and "Happy the people who have the Lord for their God."

Abraham's Continuing Journey*

JULY 8, 1979

"By faith Abraham obeyed the call to go out to a land destined for himself and his heirs and left home without knowing where he was to go."

Hebrews 11:8

With everyone and everything that belonged to him Abraham set out to seek a new home, "a different sky." As the story is familiar, we take it for granted. But that was some move on Abraham's part, particularly when you stop to think that by this time his face was full of "the credentials of humanity," as Shaw once called wrinkles. He was seventy-five years old. And can't you hear the neighbors: "Abraham, where in the world do you think you're going?"

"I don't know."

"What do you mean you don't know? What is this—some wild dream? Have you thought of Sarah? And what about that promising nephew of yours, Lot? He's just getting started. And furthermore, probably in more ways than you know, Abraham, you're indispensable to all of us here in Haran."

Then Abraham gave one of the best answers in his life, one unfortunately not recorded in the Bible. He said, "No one is indispensable, except to God."

---

*This sermon was given after reading Robert Raines' *Going Home.*—WSC

How about that, mothers and fathers! None of us is indispensable, except to God. Our children need us, but not that badly. Only God does, because she is the creator and without us can't create. To be faithful then is to be creative.

We don't usually think of it that way, do we? Most of us think of religion not in terms of creativity, but in terms of right and wrong—mostly wrong. "Religion," said the small child, "is what you don't do." And to read that Abraham "obeyed the call" would seem to give credence to their belief. For obedience suggests discipline rather than discovery. Obedience suggests submission, punishment, rules to be followed, being what we ought to be, not what we want to be. Whoever thought of looking for God in his wants? Yet our wants may be a good place to look. Abraham here doesn't seem to be doing what he ought to be doing. If we read between the lines in Genesis, rather than heeding rules, he seems to be paying attention to some instinct deep within himself, an instinct a lot of us might deny, but one Abraham is intent on honoring. I've often said that the senior years can be the formative years. Abraham is a prime example. Some old people look for recreation, but he seeks a vision. Some old people live on memories, but he wants a dream. You see why I'm suggesting that faithfulness is tied up with creativity. Abraham's obedience has less to do with punishment than with promise. His obedience has less to do with what he ought to be doing than with what most of us, probably, in our hearts, really want to be doing—if only we had Abraham's courage.

Rather than be indispensable, applauded in Haran, he wants to be fulfilled, anywhere. You might say he wants to be real, rather than right. He wants to be responsible, "response-able," able to respond to the call to be creative which the creator has embedded in every last one of us. And it's a call which we all had better heed, if we want to add some measure of grace to the world, and not simply cheer it on in its present path to perdition.

To be faithful means to be creative. Something more: "By faith Abraham obeyed the call to go out to a land . . . without knowing where he was to go." Most of us, whenever we go somewhere, know where we're going. We go by knowledge, we have the answers, we're in charge. *But Abraham had fewer answers than questions, no map, only the promise of a presence.* He's not in charge, he can't make it happen. He has to let it happen the way it happened to those two travelers on the road to Emmaus, the way it happened to Paul on the road to Damascus. In fact, as Robert Raines writes, "A journey is biblical prime time for being apprehended afresh by God."

Well, why talk about all this this morning? Because summertime is also prime time for being apprehended afresh by God.

A reporter once asked Pope John XXIII how many people worked in the Vatican. Answered the dear old man, "Oh, about half I guess." That would seem to be true of most enterprises in New York in July—Riverside of course excepted! But summertime is time not only to deaccelerate; it's time to put our lives together before another winter. It's time to get back to basics, to realize that our lives are like Abraham's. They are a journey whose final destination perforce is unknown, and a journey which we have to keep pursuing if, spiritually speaking, we are to stay alive, if we're going to obey the call of God. And, incidentally, that's not supposed to be easy:

> The woods are lovely, dark and deep.
> But I have promises to keep,
> And miles to go before I sleep,
> And miles to go before I sleep.
> Robert Frost

Now let's be practical. There must be at least two people in church this morning whose journeys have come to a halt because they have reached a juncture in their vocational lives. In fact, in their heart of hearts a decision has already been made. But they haven't found the courage to acknowledge it. To obey the call would mean to them to honor and no longer ignore that decision.

Others who have spent much of last week in gas lines, have realized anew how we misconstrue our priorities. In fact, in the United States, I think almost all of us consistently adhere to creeds of questionable value so as to keep pleasure and deep joy continually confused! Our journeys would pick up again if we heeded the still small voice that says, "Take joy."

Or maybe we're stalled in our journey because we engage in unproductive nostalgia. We yearn for the good old days which seem to us better, only because we ourselves were better.

When I was Chaplain at Yale, I would find myself saying to students about to graduate, "Watch it, lest fifty years from now you look back on the springtime of your lives and say 'Ah, those were the days!'—and be right."

If we're still mourning a loved one long lost, maybe it's time to ask, "Is grief really the only way to hold a person close?" And if we're as old as Sarah and Abraham, it's time—high time—to accept in ourselves what can't be changed: our age, the increased cost of upkeep, our past errors and sins. Yesterday I heard of a man who took great pride in his lawn, but he found himself with a large crop of dandelions. He tried every method he knew to get rid of them; still they plagued him. Finally he wrote to the Department of Agriculture. After enumerating all the things he had tried, he closed with the question, "What shall I do now?" In due course came the reply, "We suggest you learn to love them."

One final thought: In Genesis we read, "The LORD said to Abram, 'Leave your own country, your kinsmen and your father's house and go to a country that I will show you. I will make you into a great nation'" (Gen. 12:1–2). That suggests that the purpose of our journey is not private escape but public responsibility. And nations, like individuals, can get stalled in their life's journey. Nations, like individuals, if they don't lift their eyes to something above themselves will sink to something below themselves. I suspect the United States is momentarily stalled, witness our President holed up in Camp David suffering the agony of indecision. But the direction our country takes will be our affair too, for democracy is a way of distributing responsibility. Before we go any further, we must again distinguish between patriotism and nationalism. "Patriotism is the love of one's native land, of one's soil, of one's people. Nationalism, on the other hand, is not so much love, as a collective egocentricity, self-conceit, the will to power and violence over others" (Nikolai Berdyaev).

Our recent actions and threatened future ones in Nicaragua suggest nationalism rather than patriotism, power, or maybe it is the arrogance of importance. We are told that we must not fail to meet a threat, but more important would be our failure to meet an opportunity. Now is the time for the United States, in its journey, to move into a day of new relations with nations of Central and Latin America, and not stay stuck in a past where there is so little anyhow of which we can be proud.

Here again the truly patriotic words of Isaiah,

> About Zion, I will not be silent.
> About Jerusalem I will not grow weary,
> Until her integrity shines out like the dawn,
> And her salvation flames like a torch.
> The nations then will see your integrity,
> All the kings your glory,
> And you will be called by a new name,
> One which the mouth of Yahweh will confer.
>
> Isa. 62:1–2

It's a funny thing: We know in our personal as in our national lives that change is inevitable. Yet consistently we deny it. We're like the caterpillar who said, looking up at the butterfly, "You'll never find me flying around in one of those crazy things."

Why can't we cooperate gracefully with the inevitable? Why don't we remember that butterflies are more beautiful than caterpillars. They have wings, they fly higher, further. Like Abraham, why can't we refuse to stay stuck in Haran being applauded for our indispensability, remembering that we are indispensable to no one, except to God, who needs us to continue the work of creation.

So let us obey the call that keeps us going, we know not where. Let us be faithful to the creator by continuing ourselves to be creative. I used to think the poet guilty of shallow optimism, but now that I understand Abraham better I realize that Browning was profoundly right when he wrote,

> Grow old along with me,
>   the best is yet to be;
>   the last of life for which the first was made.
> Our times are in his hand
>   who saith "A whole, I planned,
> . . . Trust God, see all, nor be afraid."

Amen.

"Neither Do I Condemn You"

JULY 15, 1979

"Early in the morning he [Jesus] came again to the temple; all the people came to him, and he sat down and taught them. The scribes and the Pharisees brought a woman who had been caught in adultery, and placing her in the midst they said to him, 'Teacher, this woman has been caught in the act of adultery. Now in the law Moses commanded us to stone such. What do you say about her?' This they said to test him, that they might have some charge to bring against him.

Jesus bent down and wrote with his finger on the ground. And as they continued to ask him, he stood up

*and said to them, 'Let him who is without sin among you
be the first to throw a stone at her.' And once more he bent
down and wrote with his finger on the ground. But when
they heard it they went away, one by one, beginning with
the eldest, and Jesus was left alone with the woman
standing before him. Jesus looked up and said to her,
'Woman, where are they? Has no one condemned you?'
She said, 'No one, Lord.' And Jesus said, 'Neither do I
condemn you; go and sin more.'"*

John 8:2-11

In the economy of literature, as in the economy of life, less is often more. By this, I mean that if you want to write well, or live well, you have to guard against spattering out in irrelevant directions. All of us have constantly to relearn simplicity. That's one reason I so love the story just read. With a minimum of words, it tells a tale that vividly portrays powerful truths.

At the very beginning, there is a small detail which doesn't seem to interest the commentators, but it does intrigue me. The woman, we read, was "caught in adultery." "Why," I ask myself, "was she caught?"

A well-known contemporary political figure did not graduate from college because in May of his senior year a professor opened up his senior thesis to read it, and out fell the bill. Doesn't that make you wonder if the student was so careless because in his arrogance he thought he could get away with anything; or whether he got caught because at least some small part of himself didn't want to get away with cheating.

Often in life when we find ourselves in binds we choose the path of least resistance, or rather, we refuse to choose. When we need to be most decisive, we go passive. I think you have to be good by choice and that much evil is simply a refusal to choose. In fact, most evil in this world probably stems from indecision. This is an important point to make in a country that makes much of freedom of choice. For what is freedom of choice if you've lost the ability to choose?

Many women get pregnant "by accident." In explanation they say, "I never thought it could happen." The very passivity of their language gives them away. If only they would say, "I didn't know *I* could get so drunk. I didn't know *I* could be swept away by passion." And the men, of course, in these instances are equally passive, albeit many think they are being very aggressive.

Over the years I've performed several "shot-gun" weddings, and I haven't minded when the couple appeared genuinely in love. But I was always troubled by the suspicion that they hadn't been able to make up their minds: "Shall we or shall we not get married?" So, in effect, they said, "Let's let nature decide."

The worst things in my life I've done by indecision. I've watched things happen that I could have prevented in myself or around me had I been more decisive. I've paid for it, and worse yet, others have too at a higher price. So it was with painful interest that in a recent issue of the *Atlantic* I read a short story of John Gardner. It began in this way, "One day in April—a clear blue day when the crocuses were in bloom—Jack Hawthorne ran over and killed his brother David. Even at the last minute he could have prevented his brother's death by slamming on the tractor brakes, easily in reach for all the shortness of his legs, but he was unable to think, or rather thought unclearly, and so watched it happen as he would again and again watch it happen in his mind, with nearly undiminished clarity all his life."

I think all of us have watched things happen that could have been prevented had we exercised our ability to choose. The war in Vietnam took place, not because the American people are genocidal by instinct. Too many are simply too passive, forgetting the warning of Burke that "All it takes for evil to flourish is for a few good people to do nothing." And I still wonder how many Americans have the ability to choose. A recent commentator said, "Most Americans like to find themselves in the front of the bus, in the back of the church, and in the middle of the road."

I say all this because I suspect that the woman in the story is a stand-in for many of us. She is a "half-saved soul." She means well— feebly. She is described in St. Paul's words about himself, "The evil I would not, that I do." I suspect she too, acted out of indecision, and part of her didn't want to get away with it. Like so many people who have extramarital affairs, and make transparent excuses for where they've been, and carelessly leave notes and letters and telephone numbers all around the place, so this woman made it easy for someone to catch her. And catch her they did.

Will Campbell, who has a fine distaste for the official church, likes to remind us that "Jesus Christ wasn't a churchman." Certainly he was the opposite of those religious leaders who brought the poor woman to him in the temple. Picture for a moment their faces. What do you see? I see starched faces. I see faces of people who have disapproved of too many things over too many years; faces of people who hate evil more than they love the good; faces of good haters. I see faces of sex-fearing and God-fearing Americans who know very little of the immutable love of the heavenly father. I see the puritanical faces of people haunted by the fear that somewhere someone might be getting away with something. I see the faces of those who deify not God, but their own virtue.

And they are smart as whips, using one victim as bait to trap another. Apparently they are hoping to bring against Jesus a charge of illegally inciting others to kill a woman, one that would get Him in trouble with Roman authorities; or a charge of condoning a sin so heinous in Jewish law as to discredit Him in the eyes of religious people.

It was the Pharisees' most subtly laid trap. And what did Jesus do? He "bent down and wrote with his finger on the ground." (What do you think he wrote?) "And as they continued to ask him, he stood up and said to them, 'Let him who is without sin among you cast the first stone.' And once more he bent down and wrote with his finger on the ground."

The Scribes and Pharisees are the "faithful" who need the infidel to confirm them in their fidelity. Insiders always need outsiders to confirm them in their status as insiders. And, of course, anti-establishment people need the establishment to confirm them in what they believe to be their superior position. Jesus on the other hand will have nothing to do with such a breakdown of society. "Let him who is without sin among you cast the first stone." If we are not as yet joined one to another in love, we most surely are in sin, and sin is a wonderful bond because it precludes the possibility of separation through judgment.

In Christ's sight, there are no insiders and outsiders, for we are finally of one nature and one flesh and one grief and one hope. And in Christ's sight, if we fail in love we fail in all things else, which probably means that faults of passion are less deplorable than the cooler faults we tend to minimize.

Miraculously, some of this thinking breaks through the guard of these religious leaders. For we read, "when they heard it they went away, one by one, beginning with the eldest."

Another bouquet for the elderly! Who says they're all mean and selfish? Not Goethe who wrote, "One need only grow old to become gentler in one's judgment." "Jesus looked up and said to the woman, 'Where are they, has no one condemned you?' And she said, 'No one, Lord.' And Jesus said, 'Neither do I condemn you; go and sin no more.'"

Jesus does not trivialize her wrongdoing, because to do so would be to trivialize her as a person. Sin is intimately related to meaning. If nothing counts against you, nothing counts. Unlike so many hopelessly sentimental people today, Christ never confused the virtue of compassion for the sinner with the vice of condoning his sin. But if Jesus will not condone our sin, and cannot relieve us of the consequences of our sin, he can relieve us of the consequences of being sinners. That he does: where others condemn, he forgives. And if you think you are unworthy of such forgiveness, you miss the whole point of Christian faith. God's love doesn't seek value; it creates it. *It's not because we have value that God loves us; it's because God loves us that we have value.*

It is the revolutionary premise and promise of Christianity that the predatory, the callous, the indifferent—the lost—can only be found by a love that reconciles them anew to God and their fellow human beings. "God so loved the world that he gave his only begotten Son, that whosoever believeth in him should not perish but have eternal life" (John 3:16).

To know that is to begin to recover and develop your ability to choose. You don't change your nature so much as you receive a way of dealing with it. God is "a very present help in trouble"—not to distract us from it but to help us deal with it. "Therefore will we not fear." Like this woman, we are always going to be caught in binds. *Our struggles toward things that are worthwhile are always going to be undermined by psychological doubts.* At best we are going to be "half-saved." But that's the half that Christ is going to strengthen, rather than condemn the other. "Neither do I condemn you, go and sin no more." With that assurance we can go on.

Late last Sunday afternoon I walked across the George Washington Bridge. Once again I heard the same message I always hear from the smallest stream to the mightiest river—"Keep going."

And I'm sure the woman in the story did keep going. And so will we!

The Real Renewable Resources

JULY 22, 1979

"Let justice roll down like mighty waters."

Amos 5:24a

"What is impossible with men / women is possible with God."

Luke 18:27

W hat is the use of a house if you haven't a tolerable planet to put it on?" asked Thoreau. He also declared, "I am a citizen of the world first, and of this country only at a later and more convenient hour."

"Salvation is for everyone—including me." Actually, we think of salvation as a package deal which can be neither untied nor negotiated, and which includes everyone and everything—including politics and economics. For while human beings cannot live by bread alone, they cannot live without it, and those who live with too much of it must heed the words spoken on the *Mayflower*: "We must abridge ourselves of our superfluities for the sake of others' necessities."

The Christ Christians worship was certainly something more than a prophet, but surely nothing less. He too wanted justice to "roll down like mighty waters."

Last Sunday, the President talked a good deal about politics and economics. Frankly, I was disappointed, although not as disappointed as by the comments suggesting that his speech was more like a sermon! Apparently if remarks are lofty in tone but somewhat empty of content they constitute a sermon. I thought his speech was lofty alright, but in the manner of a giraffe who is lofty up front but drags a bit behind. There was talk of a crisis of the spirit, but where was the re-examination of the deepest roots of our belief? The President implied that a new day had dawned, but I missed the re-conceptualization, the redesigning of our national life. He talked of the energy crisis, but then proceeded to use the OPEC nations as scapegoats, a time-honored escape for political leaders at bay. Why, I asked myself, couldn't he say simply that we Americans could cut out more flab without touching a muscle than any other country in the world, that we Americans consume twice as much energy today as we did in the mid-sixties, that the Swedes get by with one-half of our per capita energy consumption, and nobody there is living in trees?

Anytime a president wants to be moral, he has only to point out that ancient faiths are confirmed by empirical events. A crisis always means that morality has once again become pragmatic. We pay for our sins. What a golden opportunity he missed to proclaim the ethic of enough.

As for our failure to have confidence in our leaders, that may be a crisis for them but not necessarily for us. President Johnson used to extol the virtue of national unity. But what's the virtue of unity if it is unity in folly.

Still troubled by such thoughts, I journeyed on Wednesday to Lafayette, Indiana, to preach the opening sermon at the week-long quadrennial gathering of Presbyterian women. Fifty-four hundred wonderful women! Naturally, I was nervous, but also honored. In fact, I thought the angel had spoken to me too, "Blessed are you among women."

But the best part came the next morning when, after Bible study, up spoke an economist named Hazel Henderson. Without mentioning the President's speech, she clarified its inadequacy. Said Hazel Henderson, "Our politics demand a mature outlook, but our economics stimulate infantile, selfish states of mind."

There's a contradiction none of our top leaders want to confront! Elaborating the point Ms. Henderson continued, "We now have an economic system that operates on many of the seven deadly sins: greed, pride, sloth (labor saving technology), lust, selfishness." And as too many of us act as if our society exists for its economy—instead of the other way around—not enough of us wrestle with the really hard questions. Mistaking growth for progress, we don't ask, "What should grow, what decline, and what should be maintained?" Extolling efficiency, we don't ask, "Efficient for whom and over what time frame?" Greedy for profits, we don't ask, "Is there a profit without a loss somewhere, to someone, at sometime?" And the "sometime" has to include future generations for, when you stop to think of it, we do not so much inherit the world from our parents as we borrow it from our children. (Let those who want to proceed blithely with nuclear energy remember the uncounted cost of decommissioning nuclear reactors, which our children will pay for some twenty years from now.)

"Our politics demand a mature outlook, but our economics stimulate infantile, selfish states of mind." Then Ms. Henderson said another helpful thing: "Remember," she said, "economics are always politics in disguise."

Last Sunday I said that while we have freedom of choice many of us have lost the ability to choose. Well, to say that "economics is politics in disguise" is to say that nothing is inevitable—except choice. All these huge permanent war machines, these windfall profits, costly space ventures, not to mention the frivolous, unnecessary, and downright harmful goods we have come to expect as a birthright—all these are ours *by choice*. Now that the crisis is upon us, we are going to have to choose between hundreds of brands of headache and sleeping pills, and cigarettes, and hair shampoos for pets, and expensively advertised and packaged junk food—choose between these private goods, and public spending for decent housing, decent schools, decent health care, and other essential services for our poor people. "Let justice roll down like mighty waters."

And believe me, it would be a clarifying experience for most Americans to give up a large chunk of their egocentricity. "We must abridge ourselves of our superfluities for the sake of others' necessities." This is fundamentally what the crisis is all about, for if "economics is politics in disguise," politics is an expression of public morality. That's why, if we're concerned with the stewardship of God's creation, we have to include politics and economics in the scheme of salvation.

Greed and lust for power will always be with us. There's no question about that. The question is, do they have to be as structurally rewarded as they are in American society? And if you cannot change human nature, at least you can change the nature of human relationships, so as to encourage, say, cooperation, as opposed to competition.

"What is the use of a house if you haven't a tolerable planet to put it on?" Our nation is going to have quite a say about how tolerable this planet is going to be. And if it's as hard for a rich individual to get into the kingdom of God as it is for a camel to pass through the eye of a needle, you can imagine what it must be like for a rich nation!

What has come clearer and clearer over the years is that American foreign policy is dictated largely by domestic attitudes towards domestic problems. Had we our own racial house in order, we'd be a lot clearer about our policies in South Africa and Zimbabwe. If we did not neglect our own poor, we would not now find in the government and media a growing contempt for the third world. "They shouldn't have as many babies." I have yet to hear anyone in the media or the government say that from the point of view of resources, it's fifty times the disaster to have a white middle-class baby born in America than it is to have one born in Bangladesh.

Martin Buber wrote: "The real exile of Israel in Egypt was that they had learned to endure it." Has the new Israel, the church, been so corrupted by the fleshpots of Egypt that it is incapable of even contemplating another Exodus?

I am delighted we are going to do more for the boat people. But I grieve that we cannot see our own complicity in their disaster. Many are leaving Vietnam for economic reasons. Why don't we give a little bit of help to the country we almost totally destroyed? The nation most present at the destruction is most conspicuously absent at the reconstruction.

If we normalized relations with Vietnam and set up consulates, we would never have to rescue people in the water; we could rescue people on the land. The Vietnamese themselves invited us to fly planes to take people out. The press never talk about the 600,000 Cambodian refugees the Vietnamese are caring for, nor about what the Chinese are broadcasting to Chinese in Vietnam, all of which has a lot to do with their leaving. This is a complicated situation, and nothing is gained except self-righteousness, by reducing such a complex problem to a simple moral one.

"Let justice roll down like mighty waters." We trade with the big communist countries—China and Soviet Union. But if they're small enough—Cuba and Vietnam—we impose embargoes on them.

But enough of this negative thinking—although I believe in the power of negative thinking. Remember if you're at the edge of an abyss the only progressive step is backward! But let's consider the hopeful news of the Gospel; "What is impossible with human beings is possible with God." The church, for all its manifold weakness, is the salt of the earth, the light on the hill—anytime Christians want to get serious about Christ. And if we got serious about renewing our Exodus, there's no telling what Promised Land we might find, for "eye hath not seen, nor ear heard, nor the heart of men conceived the things that God has prepared for those who love him" (1 Cor. 2:9).

What liberation of resources await us, undreamed of to this day? I think of the sun and the wind and the wave—all renewable sources of energy. But one thing is clear; we cannot maintain our planet half fortunate, half miserable, half confident, half despairing. We've made a world for some of us. The crisis demands that we make a world for all of us. And that thought points us towards the greatest resources of all. The resources that can be liberated without being exhausted are inner resources; gifts of the Holy Spirit.

I'm sure God is looking down upon this nation and his question is, "I wonder if my people are going to tap my resources?"

In Praise of Rest

JULY 29, 1979

"So God blessed the seventh day and hallowed it, because on it God rested from all his work."

Genesis 2:3

"Come unto me all you who labor and are heavy laden and I will give you rest."

Matthew 11:28

I'm sure some mean-spirited fellow is already saying to himself, "Aha, he's about to take a vacation and needs to justify his goofing off." That fellow is too clever by half—and of course correct. Or almost so, for it's really not so much a matter of justifying as of reminding oneself of the importance of goofing off.

But before getting further into that subject, let's recognize two groups of people, both undoubtedly represented this morning. Some of you will this year not get the vacation you deserve, and some of you are on an undeserved forced vacation by reason of unemployment. Unemployment used to be called the "scandal of capitalism," and, although it isn't often called that anymore, it still is a scandal. People have a right to contribute to the public good and, moreover, to have their labor not only financially rewarded, but be personally rewarding. That means we have two scandals: unemployment, and unrewarding, monotonous toil. For we are blessed not only when life gives us something but also when it doesn't take something away. Gertrude Stein said of France, "It wasn't what France gave me—so much, it was what she *never took away*." Daily work should never take away our high spirits, curiosity, sensitivity, and that so much daily work does just that is a scandal as great as unemployment.

But those are subjects for another sabbath. I didn't mean to get carried away; only to note with sympathy those who don't get enough, and who get too much vacation. Now back to the subject—in praise of rest—and to the Genesis text: "God blessed the seventh day and hallowed it, because on it God rested from all his work." God didn't bless the day on which he made the beasts of the earth, the birds of the air, the fish of the sea, and "every creeping thing that creeps upon the earth"; he didn't even bless the day he made us "male and female." No, he blessed the day on which he did nothing.

You'll have to admit, it's dangerous theology to try to improve on God. Therefore, when God herself rested, why are there so many of us workaholics who can only let go when, dead from exhaustion, we drop off to sleep? Isn't there some terrible pride involved in all this?

Sometimes I think it's more blessed to receive than to give; at least it takes more humility. When you stop to think of it, resting is receiving, and I'd like to suggest that whatever it meant for God to rest, for us, his creatures, to rest spells the rebirth of humility. I hadn't really thought of this until yesterday, when trying to write out my thoughts—for until you write them, how do you know that you are thinking and not just mooning?—trying to write these thoughts I looked out the window at the people resting in Riverside Park. I love to watch people resting in Riverside Park, and suddenly I discovered a new reason for it: it's a marvelously non-competitive scene. Except for the pickpockets, and an occasional mean child, no one is trying to take anything away from anybody. The individuals reading on the benches, the lovers strolling down the sidewalks, the families sitting on the blankets—they all seem to be receiving something. For one thing, they are receiving back their health, as health is not simply the absence of sickness but the presence of vitality. They are also recovering their sense of well-being: from the sky and trees, from the sounds of the Riverside Carillon, from the sight of the Circle Line Ferry taking one of the most gorgeous trips any tourist can take anywhere in the world. (There's reason enough for the Riverside Disarmament Program—to save New York City.) Most of all they seem to be receiving something from each other, because they have time now.

Then something else struck me, prompted by a memory. Almost twenty years ago I nearly died from pleurisy and pneumonia. Afterwards my wife told me that I was never more lovable than at death's door when all I could do was rest and receive. Maybe I was so lovable because I was so humble. That would make sense, wouldn't it? So there's one good reason to rest: to recover humility.

Pushing that thought a little further, maybe I was lovable because I was so grateful, gratitude being so closely related to humility. As never before I was grateful for life itself. As never before I was grateful for the love of family and friends. Even in the midst of pain I could be grateful for the fact that God hadn't asked me to bear anything without at the same time giving me the wherewithal to endure it.

But let's go back to the people in the park. For the most part, what they are receiving and enjoying are the good things in life that are free. You don't have to pay for any of the pleasures in Riverside Park. And life is good to the degree that it means something for nothing. And people who are grateful are also lovable because when they are so aware of all the unearned, undeserved goodness in their own lives, they have no inclination to take anything away from your life. As a matter of fact, what Gertrude Stein said about France, Alice Toklas, her constant companion, said about Gertrude Stein, years later, after her death. "It wasn't what Gertrude gave me—so much, but it was what she never took away." Isn't that a lovely thing to say about someone? Put differently, it's a wonderful thing to be loved by someone who is not in psychological competition with you.

And that leads us directly to God, the only person in your life who will never compete with you, the person above all others who can give you both humility and gratitude. And like humility and gratitude, God too is best found in rest. "Be still and know that I am God." "Come to me all you who labor and are heavy laden and I will give you rest."

Perhaps the point is best made in the thirtieth chapter of Isaiah:

For thus said the Lord GOD, the Holy One of Israel,
"In returning and rest you shall be saved; in quietness
and in trust shall be your strength." And you would
not, but you said, "No! We will speed upon horses."
(Isa. 30:15–16a)

It's nearly impossible to feel the nearness and dearness of God when you're speeding upon horses, or cars or subways—when you're speeding, period! And that is why of course, some of us *do* keep speeding, are workaholics; in order to escape God, and one another, and humility and gratitude. Most of all, I guess, we want to escape from ourselves. We're afraid that if we ever stopped to pay a call upon ourselves, we'd find nobody home.

But that's crazy. We are home, even behind a locked door. At heart, we're dying to have someone pay a call. And God is always there, probably resting once again himself, and wishing we would slow down so we could get together.

God is fun, the best possible person with whom to take a vacation. And it is fun to be more lovable, because more humble, more grateful, the very qualities we recover in rest. Just look at it this way; Have you ever asked what's at the finish line of a rat race? Even if you win a rat race you're still a rat!

Two brief concluding thoughts. I've suggested that a vacation can spell the rebirth of humility, the rebirth of gratitude, the rebirth of our relationship with God. All of us can and should take a dozen or so minute-long vacations a day. Several times in the middle of work or in unemployment, whether the work is interesting or whether it's unbelievably boring, we should say with the psalmist, "Return unto thy *rest*, O my soul, for the Lord hath dealt bountifully with thee." Then we should count the things that God has given us, and not taken away from us.

And lastly, just as there's no work without rest, so there is no rest without work. God rested on the seventh day. Then, I assume he went back to work. It certainly wasn't very long before rescuing the human race was a full-time job! And of course, it is our job too, called as we are to be co-creators with God. About the chances of saving the human race, we can't be optimistic, but we can be persistent. And if we rest with God we can return to His tasks in good shape and find the yoke easy, the burden light.

So dear friends, try to find some rest, will you? As for me, when next you see me I'll be so humble you won't recognize me! Grateful too. May God be with you til we meet again.

"And Jesus Looking upon Him Loved Him"

SEPTEMBER 16, 1979

O ver the years, in times of uncertainty and stress, and for reasons never totally clear, one line of Scripture from the New Testament has continually come to mind. It is found in the story of the rich young ruler, in Mark: "And Jesus looking upon him loved him." As I say, I don't know why the line keeps coming to mind except perhaps as a reminder that it is *human* judgment that is so lacking in compassion, never the judgment of God. In any case let's take these words as a text for a sermon on "Homecoming" Sunday.

"And Jesus looking upon him loved him." What a difference there is between that love represented by Jesus, God's love in person on earth, and that symbolized by Cupid, an infant in diapers, blindfolded to boot. Cupid's love may be blind but God's love is visionary, piercing through every façade—or armor—to perceive the individual that each one of us is, an individual with a half that is repentant and with another that will never repent; an individual with a half that entreats the Lord and with another half that can't bring itself to entreat. God's visionary love sees not only the small strengths and small weaknesses which even our dim perceptions can grasp, but also great strength side-by-side with great weakness, something we generally have trouble understanding. And God's piercing love sees our persistent perversity—that we go through life shoving our best foot forward when it's the other that needs the attention! And yet, at the very moments in our lives when, like the young man, we are about to receive and refuse the finest offer a person can ever receive, "Come, follow me," that is, constant companionship with Jesus, at that very moment, Jesus looks upon us and loves us.

Sometimes I think God in her ways must be as perverse as we are in ours. Why should she keep pouring out so much love when the returns are so pitiful? Yet if we struggle with this question we come up with a clear answer.

In September of 1945, the then Secretary of War, Henry Stimson, suggested that the only way to avoid a feverish arms race with the Soviets was to share fully with them all our atomic secrets. He was then 84 years old, and he wrote: "The chief lesson I have learned in a long life is that the only way you can make a man trustworthy is to trust him, and the surest way to make him untrustworthy is to distrust him and show him your distrust."

That is wisdom from on high. And the only way to make a person lovable is to love him. So "Jesus looked upon him and loved him."

It is proper to call a church a "home" and a Sunday a "homecoming" Sunday, for when we stop to think of it this is one place where you are expected to come through the door shoving the best foot forward yes, but dragging the other one along too. This is a place you can come bringing both halves, the repentant and the other half that never seems to repent. Church is where you can come in sickness and health, in joy and in sorrow, knowing that you will be both seen and loved by God, by Jesus, and not least of all, by others. And that is such a momentous and heartwarming thought that I suggest we take a moment right now to cast a loving eye on our neighbors and to receive in return a loving glance!

Now things become more difficult as we turn from Jesus to the rich young man. Most of us are like him, in that when in distress we seek the guidance of some spiritual leader, we think we do so because we want change. Actually, as in the story, we want to remain the same and feel better about it. In psychological terms what we really want is to be more effective neurotics, "preferring the security of known misery to the misery of unfamiliar insecurity" (Sheldon Kopp).

Listen once again to what Jesus says to the man. Listen to the underlying essence behind the words: "You lack one thing. Go and sell what you have and give it to the poor, and you will have treasure in Heaven; and come, follow me." I hear Jesus offering the man his freedom, which is just another word for nothing left to lose. But instead of the excitement of freedom, the exhilaration of the constant companionship of Jesus, the rewards of truth and righteousness, the man chooses the security of his golden chains, no matter how pedestrian their possibilities!

How about you? Did you come to church today to change, or to seek a way to stay the way you are and feel better about it? Jesus is looking upon you and loving you, and saying "Come, follow me."

Come follow me. That's what Abraham Maslow would call the "growth choice," as opposed to the "fear choice" elected by the young man in the story. But of course the man was right to be fearful. Jesus gets us into altogether as much trouble as he saves us from. But it's good trouble, it's healthy trouble, it's useful trouble, the kind of trouble in which we ourselves live our lives and are not lived by them. That kind of trouble doesn't represent another bout of "unearned unhappiness," the blight of the American middle class.

We come to church to be loved, and that means we come to church to change. Now let me suggest two ways that we can help each other, those of us who wish to change. The first is to read and to study together. Don't tell me, "Nobody was ever changed by a book," and I won't tell you that books only change people for the good. As a matter of fact, since the invention of writing, books have won people over to both good and evil, to both revolution and reaction, to atheism and to the faith. That makes the point: books are potent. Think of Augustine, seduced by St. Paul's epistle. Think what Thomas Paine's tracts did for the French revolution, what that little book, *Uncle Tom's Cabin*, did for the American Civil War. And where would the Roman Catholic or any church be without St. Francis' *Canticles*, St. Teresa's *The Interior Castle*, or the verse of St. John of the Cross—to name but three saints of the Middle Ages?

Books are potent. And study is too, if by study we don't mean "intellectual volleyball"—"let's bat this one around." I mean the kind of reading and discussion that is personal, not merely academic, the kind that leads to and guides personal struggles, self-surrender, and profound religious experiences.

To indicate a second way to help each other change I want to read opening lines from a South African novelist and Christian, Alan Paton, who began *Too Late the Phalarope* in this fashion: "Perhaps I could have saved him with only a word, two words, out of my mouth. Perhaps I could have saved us all. But I never spoke them . . . For he spoke hard and bitter words to me, and shut the door of his soul on me, and I withdrew. But I should have hammered on it, I should have broken it down with my naked hands, I should have cried out there not ceasing, for behind it was a man in danger, the bravest and gentlest of us all."

There is no place in the church for the brutality that masquerades as frankness. There is such a thing as knowledge for destruction. But, as Paton indicates, there is also knowledge for salvation, and we must not withhold it from one another just because it's painful. Remember Jesus hurt the rich young man, just as he hurt many others, but he never hurt anyone without meaning to. And he spoke the truth only in love. Which is to say, dear brothers and sisters, if we are deeply Christian, we shall be both kind and candid, and so help one another change.

So we come to church to love, to be loved, to change, and to help change. We can't close, however, without recognizing that when Jesus said, "Come, follow me," he meant not only that the young man would be changed, but that as a disciple he would become Christ's fellow worker in shaping the world after his desire. Charity begins at home but it never stops there. It is not enough to walk around this city wearing a button that says "I love New York." What does it mean to love New York? Don't you have to study New York, struggle for New York, suffer for New York? And doesn't the religious community have a primary responsibility in trying to make this inhumane place more human? And not only New York. It is right that on "Homecoming Sunday" there should be once again in our midst some folk from Chile, once again because they are grief stricken by the latest actions of their government. May Riverside always be their home, too. It is also right that Admiral LaRocque should be here to talk about the arms race Henry Stimson so accurately predicted and which reminds us that we have to seek the welfare of all if there is to be welfare for any.

The church is our home. But, so is God's universe our home—a church without walls. Here we love one another intimately and intensely. Yet our intensity is never at the expense of universality. Christian hearts are as wide as God's universe. In praise of our beautiful home and in thanks for the blessings that membership here brings us, I want to end with an inscription found over the door of St. Stephen's Church in London:

> O God, make the door of this house wide enough to receive all who need human love and fellowship, narrow enough to shut out all envy, pride and strife. Make its threshhold smooth enough to be no stumbling block to children, nor to strained feet, but rugged and strong enough to turn back the temptor's power. God, make the door of this house the gateway to thine eternal kingdom. Amen.

The Pharisee and the Publican

OCTOBER 7, 1979
Reading: Luke 18: 9–14

Let us take as our text the prayers of the two men: "God, I thank thee that I am not as other men are"; "God, be merciful to me a sinner."

Last week in Moscow, after a day of strenuous conversations, our delegation was overjoyed at the announcement that the evening called for a visit to the circus, which like the Moscow subway, is one of the very best in the world. There, I recalled that every circus has to have two types of performers, for without the one, you have too much of the other. On the one hand, there are the heroes, the virtuosi, the high-wire artists, the gravity defying acrobats who catapult themselves off the ground to the top of human pyramids; there are lion and tiger tamers, the trainers of elephants and horses. And then there are the clowns about whom Henri Nouwen wrote, "The clowns are not in the center of the event; they're between the great acts. They fumble and fall and make us smile again after the tension created by the heroes we came to admire. Clowns don't have it together. They do not succeed in what they try. They are awkward, they're off balance but they are on our side. Of the virtuosi we say, 'How can they do it?' Of the clowns we say, 'They're like us.' The clowns remind us with a tear and smile that we share the same human weaknesses."

It is good that in each of us there dwells a bit of the virtuoso and a bit of the clown; just as in each of us there's something of the Pharisee and something of the Publican. Actually, in the parable, the Pharisee is quite a virtuoso. You might call him a virtuoso in virtue; and he's heroic too. Not a lion but an appetite tamer, he fasts not once a year but twice a week. He also tithes beyond any demands of the law, which is more than can be said for more than 600 members of the Riverside Church who don't even pledge! (But that was last year and happily opportunity will soon knock again.)

But it's hard to picture this Pharisee clowning. It's hard to picture him weeping or smiling; he's probably too tight-lipped for either. In fact, so caged is the clown in him, that he reminds me of the man in an old Jewish tale on whose unprotected head rains down all manner of misfortune. When he protests, "I've fulfilled every last one of the 613 laws laid down in Holy Writ. Why me?"—a voice from heaven answers, "Because you're a bore."

The Pharisee, however, is more than boring. He shows us that he who seeks his own virtue no longer seeks God or his neighbor. For to seek your own virtue is too self-seeking an enterprise. True, he goes into the Temple, but only as so many good Christians go to church, in order to make their last stand against God. True, he prays, but he praises not God but his own virtue. True, he worships, but I think he's worshipping himself worshipping. I think he sees God at best as some kind of corporation in which he's earned sufficient stock to warrant the expectation that any day now he'll be asked to join the Board of Directors.

Remember Jesus spoke the parable to "some who trusted in themselves that they were righteous, and despised others." Is that a necessary connection? In other words, can you be self-righteous without projecting unto others your inadequacy? Isn't pride essentially and not accidentally competitive? Notice only the Pharisee compares himself to others: "God, I thank thee that I am not as other men are." The Publican does not compare himself to anyone. But what strikes me most powerfully is that it is in the very act of praying that the Pharisee seeks to break the God-given unity he shares not only with that tax-collector but with everyone else in the world. I say "God-given," for according to the faith we are together before we come together. According to the faith there is a unity prior to all unifying action. According to the faith, community is not made by us but given by God. So it is the sin of the Pharisee, and of the Pharisee in each one of us, that he seeks to put asunder what God himself has joined together.

Let me repeat: there are good things about the Pharisee. Jesus doesn't criticize his fasting and tithing anymore than he justifies the tax-collector's way of life, which probably included graft and worse forms of thievery. But the Pharisee had everything, except the one thing necessary, while the tax-collector had nothing, except the one thing necessary.

Now let's turn to the tax-collector, this crook who may save us from the pretensions of our virtue. Last Wednesday during Bible Study, some of you were suspicious of his humility. So is Nietzsche who paraphrased Jesus' words. Said Nietzsche: "He who humbles himself *wills* to be exalted." Or maybe the man's breast-beating represents some kind of punishment that people resort to in order to avoid judgment. Once, like this tax-collector, you know that you are a sinner, the next thing to do is to escape judgment. And the best way to escape judgment is to seek punishment. For while judgment demands a new way of life, punishment, by assuaging a bit the guilt, makes the old way of life bearable anew.

Whether the tax-collector came into the temple for judgment or punishment, we really can't tell for there's no sequel to the parable. But my guess is that he was sincere, that after his experience in the temple he became as zealous as the Pharisee, only his zeal stemmed from that gratitude which in turn stems from the experience of forgiveness. In any case, Jesus' point is clear: Mercy can't come to those who think themselves flawless. God simply can't reach the self-sufficient.

On an individual level, I don't think this particular parable is all that timely. I suspect few these days are pharisaical in either the good or the bad sense, because we are too uncertain of ourselves, too insecure. Unfortunately, however, we're compensating for our personal insecurity by projecting power and virtue onto the nation. It is our national life that is threatened by our pharisaical spirit as our politicians, seeking election, seek to renew the Cold War. "God, we thank thee that our nation is not as other nations are: atheist, communist, imperialistic, understanding only force." Dwight Morrow once observed that we Americans are prone to judge other nations by their actions and our own by our ideals. Even as the bombs were destroying Vietnam, the Air Force continued to claim, "Peace is our profession."

It is consoling, of course, to view ourselves as models of rectitude and even more so perhaps as misunderstood models of rectitude. But simple honesty compels us to see that we *are* as other nations are. The trouble with saying that the only thing that the other side understands is force, is that you have to behave as if the only thing you understand is force. We have decided to show our strength in Cuba. How much smarter it would be, instead of sending Marines to Guantanamo Bay, to send businessmen ashore in Havana, to lift our embargo, to normalize our relations with Cuba. As John Knox said, "It is very difficult to alienate people and to influence them at one and the same time."

Listen again to the words of the Pope, not at Chicago, but at the U.N. where he spoke to all of us. Commenting on the pharisaical spirit in our national life, he said, "The ancient says, '*Si vis pacem para bellum!*' (If you wish to see peace, prepare for war.) Can our age still really believe that the breath-taking spiral of armaments is at the service of world peace? In alleging the threat of a world enemy, is it really not rather the intention to keep to oneself a means of threat in order to get the upper hand with the aid of one's own arsenal of destruction?" And the Pope understood that time no longer grants us the gift of indifference. If we don't do something now, the atom will.

So what should our prayer be? "God, I thank thee that my nation is as other nations are, for then I can view it as I would any other, empathetically from the inside, and realistically from the outside. God, I thank thee that my nation today is no more powerful than the Soviet Union, for equality allows us to freeze the arms race and to negotiate parity going down, instead of parity going up. God, I thank thee that my nation shares the weaknesses of every nation for if we are not yet bound one to another in love, at least we are in sin; and that's a previous bond because it precludes the possibility of separation through judgment."

After two weeks in Russia, I have to report that our suspicions of them are reciprocated. On both sides those who negotiate want to see all the cards before they make a move—never mind that humanity is on the brink of suicide. Both sides ask for proof of trustworthiness when what are needed are expressions of trust, be they ever so small.

I'm glad that today is Worldwide Communion Sunday. It is a day to celebrate that community is not made by us, but given by God. I'm glad that we shall soon sing, "In Christ there is no East or West, there is no South or North, but one great fellowship of love throughout the whole wide earth." And I'm glad for the publican and pharisee in each of us. Let the publican keep us humble, at one with one another. And because we can't be optimistic, may the pharisee keep us persistent.

The Parable of the Sower

OCTOBER 14, 1979
Reading: Mark 4:3–8

True parables, we are warned, seek to illustrate one point only, which is to say, that in their interpretation we must avoid the fanciful flights of imagination more appropriate to allegories. But when a parable is as singularly suggestive as that of the sower, Jesus will forgive us, I'm sure, if we mention some other points implied beyond the central one he clearly sought to make.

Incidentally, why do you suppose Jesus told these "earthly stories with heavenly meanings"? Why this method? In part, I'm sure, so that those who had ears to hear could understand. But I'm equally sure that Jesus told parables because he was pastoral enough to know that if you win an argument you may lose a follower. Who wants to be worsted in an argument? But where arguments alienate, parables disarm.

Let me suggest first how *not* to allegorize and interpret the parable: God is the sower, the seed is the word, spelled with a small or capital "W"; some seeds never get beneath the surface of men's minds, some get strangled by competing claims; only a few find the sustaining depths of soil good enough to bring forth the harvest God has in mind for the human race; and that, dear friends, well, that's life.

Not for a moment do I believe that the parable celebrates despair, albeit, the seeds for most part fall on an alien world. Most of you probably know the prayer that begins so wonderfully, "Dear Lord, the sea is so wide and my boat is so small." Well, Christians have been praying that prayer or prayers like it for centuries. But let us remember that God answers the prayer in words something like these: "Don't forget, dear child, that all the water in the world can't sink a boat until it gets inside. All the despair in the world can't sink one of my believers unless it gets in her heart."

I think the parable celebrates the boat that floats, the seed that sprouts, the prophetic minority that can never be silenced by the clamor of competing claims, the prophetic minority that always has more to say to a nation than any majority, silent or vocal. Politicians tell us what we want to hear; prophets tell us what is right. If we elect to office more politicians than prophets, that only shows that democracy is based not on the proven goodness of majorities, but rather on the proven evil of dictators.

So the parable celebrates neither fatalism nor despair. It celebrates hope. It also celebrates the mutuality that characterizes our relationship with God. The seed may be good but it is the soil that determines its success or failure. That is the main thrust of the parable, isn't it, its primary point? The parable celebrates hope, mutuality, *and human freedom*. It says that where there's a free will there's a way to break up the crust of self-satisfaction, to pull up the strangling thorns of corruption. There's a way for everyone of us to prepare our minds and hearts for the planting of God's word.

How do we do it? The parable tells us that good soil is deep soil, so I guess we can't be religious without being profound. What does that mean? I imagine that means that we have to give up everything that is shallow—innocence, illusions, and certainty; and embrace what's profound—the ambiguity, the insolubility, not to mention the inevitability of the human situation. Innocence is a false option for Christians, for in the sullied stream of human life it is not innocence but holiness that is our only option. To be "born again," according to the story of the Gospel of John, is to be baptized by water and by the spirit which I read to mean that you have to become as vulnerable as a child but not as innocent as a child. Yet many a twice-born American Christian is seeking just the opposite: to be as innocent as a child in order not to become vulnerable. The twice born Christian—too many of them—want their riches *and* their Jesus Christ *and* the MX missile. Psychologically speaking, they are trying to re-enter their mother's womb, the very thing the Gospel tells us can't be done. Or, in the terms of this parable, many twice-born Christians are like the seed that fell in shallow ground and immediately sprang up "since it had no depth of soil." Their evanescent enthusiasm is not the same as that deep-seated joy that can absorb all sorrow. They can't take the heat and soon they will wither away, for too many twice-born Christians in our land are the quintessential "uprooted" generation.

In the sullied stream of human life it is not innocence but holiness that is our only option. Holiness means no blind sides. It means a willingness to face the truths we've always fled. "You mean my marriage may not be as secure as I've always thought it to be? You mean I'm going to spend my life watching my child never grow up? You mean the United States might be as Castro portrayed us, the greatest purveyor of violence in the world?"

Faith takes off the blinders. If we have our security with the absolute then we can and must live with temporal insecurity, including intellectual uncertainty. When the mind is no longer plowed and made receptive by curiosity and wonder it becomes shallow and hard. Beware of Christians who have stopped thinking. Christianity makes good thinking possible.

Holiness means no blind sides. I think I once lamented the fact that Christians weren't more Elizabethan, less Victorian. What I had in mind was this: one of the truths we flee is the truth of our animal nature. Many of us want to deny our animal nature, which is too bad if only because to accept it might help break our pride. Many of us think our minds have always to be in the saddle exerting strict rational control over the rebellious mount that constitutes passions and instincts. It's an exhausting way to live! It's also a false way to live because the body with its passions and instincts also has messages that need to be heard. Of course, it is just as false to view ourselves as riderless horses. As God has made us mind and body together, the true view of ourselves is probably that of a centaur.

Most especially many of us want to deny our sexual instincts, which to some degree is possible because to some extent our sexual needs are expendable. We couldn't get away with denying hunger or thirst. But again it is too bad, because, when you stop to think of it, of all instincts sex is the only one that is fundamentally interpersonal. There must be a message there too, and one missed in part by the Roman Catholic Church. It is interesting that the issues at present tying up the Roman Catholic Church—with the exception of the issue of authority—all relate to sexuality: the ordination of women, the celibacy of priests, contraception, abortion, the treatment of homosexuals. If we are going to be profound, I believe that we have to see that God created sex not only as a means of procreation but as the honey and flower of life. And if Christians could accept that more positive view, more churches, I believe, could accept the ordination of women as well as the marriage of priests. Also homosexuals would be better treated. When a homosexual comes out of the closet, sex comes out of the closet, and that is what, to so many, is so intolerable. Our fear of homosexuality reflects a fear of our own sexuality.

So what have we said? Good soil is deep and if we want to be profound we must have no blind sides. We have to accept the world as it is—full of ambiguities and uncertainties; we have to accept ourselves as we are which includes our animal nature full of instincts and passion. In the words of Matthew Arnold, we have to "see life whole and see it steadily."

But what of those nasty little thorns that also grow in deep soil, choking God's seed? What are they? When I was a high school senior, as part of our course in American history, we had to read Madison's notes on the Constitutional Convention. I still remember vividly two suggestions made by Benjamin Franklin who by then was well into his eighties and well into his cups. (But let's not be too judgmental. Too many Christians confuse being sober with being profound!) The first suggestion was that the lawyers themselves choose the justices of the Supreme Court since they undoubtedly would select the best in order to divide up the trade after they'd gone. The second suggestion was that the President should receive no salary. Said Benjamin Franklin: (I paraphrase) "Gentlemen,"—for alas, there were no ladies—"Gentlemen, after long years of observation I have concluded that human beings are prone to two great weaknesses: one is for riches, the other for power. Should the two be combined in the high office of the President of the United States the results could only be mischievous."

Greed takes place when our possessions possess us. Greed is that which possesses us without fulfilling us. If God's seed is the flower, we have to uproot greed. Remember Christ's words: "No one can serve two masters; for either he will hate the one and love the other, or he will be devoted to the one and despise the other. You cannot serve God and mammon" (Matt. 6:24).

As for power, it is good only when it empowers others. What is evil is lust for power over others, and it makes little difference whether "others" are viewed as victims to exploit or wards to protect. If Jesus never exploited anyone, neither did he smother anyone with love. God really is the perfect parent who combines closeness with freedom, safety plus danger.

If Benjamin Franklin was right, then we shall probably not succeed in uprooting completely the thorns of greed and the lust of power. But evil can also be viewed as a kind of energy in need of transformation. What we can't uproot we can offer to God to transform. Didn't the prophet himself say: "Instead of the thorn shall come up the cyprus; instead of the briar shall come up the myrtle."

I said we need to accept the world as it is, ourselves as we are, and that is true. "He who loses his life shall find it" must never be used as an excuse to avoid the question, "Who am I?" But we need also to know that we are *more* than ourselves, and that, in Paul's words, "the universe itself is to be freed from the shackles of mortality and enter upon the liberty and splendor of the children of God." We are children of God because the seed of God is within us. That is the life that must not be aborted, this tender stem of Jesse that seeks to take root in our hearts and minds. Once he walked upon the earth, but today Christ has no feet but ours, no arms but ours, no lips but ours. I said the parable celebrated freedom, but it also understands that human beings are never freer than when they are free to will the will of God. So let us tend the stem of Jesse, heed the word within us, ever praying, "O Jesus Christ, take our minds and think through them, take our lips and speak through them, and take our hearts and set them on fire." So may it come to pass in a world far fairer than our own, that our children and grandchildren will look back and say, "Yes indeed, 'other seeds fell into good soil and brought forth grain, growing up and increasing and yielding thirtyfold, and sixtyfold, and a hundredfold.'"

The Good Samaritan

OCTOBER 21, 1979
Reading: Luke 10:25–37

The parable of the Good Samaritan is well worn, but wears well. Better than any other, and more lyrically than any statement, it makes the point that if you want to find God you need seek no further than your neighbor's need. It makes the point that love of God and love of neighbor are absolutely inseparable. And I think we could agree that nowhere in literature, religious or other, is there to be found a better definition of neighbor than the one given in this parable.

It all began in what we may assume was one of the many discussions that Jesus had with religious executives and seminary professors—I'm updating the titles—discussions in which the religious executives and seminary professors always seemed to end up on one side of the issue while Jesus alone stood on the other. There's a sobering Sunday thought for those who work at 475 Riverside Drive or teach across the street!

"And behold, a lawyer"—or "scribe," a religious leader—"stood up to put him to the test, saying, 'Teacher, what shall I do to inherit eternal life?' He said to him, 'What is written in the law? How do you read?'"

The way the story begins recalls the old joke in which the Gentile complains to the Jew: "The trouble with you Jews is every time someone asks you a question, instead of giving an answer, you ask another question."

Says the Jew, "Why not?"

Yet I dare say, in this instance Jesus would not have answered the lawyer's question with another had the lawyer been more like the rich young man, who, in another instance, asked the same question. But when *he* asked, "What must I do to inherit eternal life?" his question clearly came from a heart full of despair, reflecting a life empty of purpose.

In contrast, the lawyer was trying to score points, and Jesus must have caught the undercurrent of his motives moving counter to the surface current of his words.

Nevertheless, the lawyer answers Jesus well. He may have read the words—you remember Jesus said "How do you read?"—read them from the leather bands which pious Jews to this day still wear around their wrists. Or he may have known the words by heart. In any case he combined the so-called "Sh'ma" from Deuteronomy (6:5), "Thou shalt love the Lord thy God with all thy heart, and with all thy soul, and with all thy strength, and with all thy mind," with Leviticus 19:18, "Thou shalt love thy neighbor as thyself."

As far as I know, scholars are not certain when those two were put together, the two great commandments "upon which hang all the law and the prophets." In any case, it was a superb answer.

Now it is Jesus' turn to say words almost as fine as those quoted by the lawyer: "You have answered right; do this and you will live."

I thought we lived in order to love. But apparently not. We love to live. "Do this and you will live." Only by love do we escape the sarcophagus of the self! "Though I give my body to be burned but have not love—nothing." There is no more radical affirmation in the whole New Testament. Love alone is the expression of our aliveness. "We pass from death into life because we love the brothers and sisters" (1 John 3:14).

"But the lawyer, desiring to justify himself" (the undercurrent is now surfacing), "said 'And who is my neighbor?'" That joins the issue, doesn't it, and joins each one of us to the lawyer. For who among us doesn't seek to mutilate the meaning of neighbor? To the lawyer's Jewish mind, neighbor was "Jew" spelled large, just as it so often seems to be in the mind of Israeli Prime Minister Menachem Begin. I say nothing anti-Israel, for to American minds also the neighborhood is restricted, bound at best by the borders of the good old U.S.A. It's a universal phenomenon we are talking about, for hardly anyone in the world believes territorial discrimination to be as evil as racial or religious discrimination. But it is. Nationalism at the expense of another nation is just as wicked as racism at the expense of another race. In other words, it is a fact that no one's heart is as wide as God's love. Rather, each of us seeks to be an "insider" by seeking an "outsider" to confirm us in our insider status. So each of us is looking for a bad Samaritan.

Last week I said that where arguments humiliate—who wants to be worsted in an argument?—a parable can disarm, and win over. Here we see Jesus confronting one of the most deeply seated prejudices in the world, and instead of engaging the man in an argument, he tells a parable. What a pastoral touch! And one more thing: the lawyer is asking about neighbor as object—"Who is my neighbor?"; but Jesus will answer by defining neighbor as subject—"which proved neighbor unto the man." I can't think of anything in all Scripture that is more adroit than that turnaround from neighbor as object to neighbor as subject.

But now, let's get on with the parable: "A man was going down from Jerusalem to Jericho, and he fell among robbers, who stripped him and beat him, and departed, leaving him half dead."

Well, New Yorkers, gratuitous violence is apparently nothing new. Unfortunately, it has been going on for centuries, and especially, it seems, on that particular 20-mile stretch of road, a road lined with giant boulders behind which robbers can hide; a road full of hairpin turns as it drops from 2,300 feet above sea level at Jerusalem, down to 1,300 feet below sea level where Jericho is located hard by the Dead Sea. Four centuries later, according to Jerome, the road to Jericho was still being called "The Red, or Bloody Way." And as late as the nineteenth century, if you wanted to travel safely on that road from Jerusalem to Jericho, you paid off the local sheik.

After the mugging, we can picture the poor man, unconscious, face in the dirt, "half dead" we read, and probably looking totally so. Then, says the story, "Now by chance a priest was going down that road; and when he saw him he passed by on the other side." It is a mistake, I think, to write off the priest as merely callous. Hearers of Jesus—those same religious executives and religious teachers—would have known that in the nineteenth chapter of Numbers it is written: "He who touches a dead man is unclean for seven days" (v. 11). Had the man been as dead as he looked, and had the priest rolled him over in order to make sure, the priest would not have been able to perform his Temple duties for a week.

How many of us are willing to jeopardize our jobs? How many of us do things off duty that could affect adversely what we do on duty? I like to think of the priest as "a nice guy." He probably felt sorry for the man, and probably a little guilty about doing nothing—guilt being such a wonderful substitute for responsibility. In any case, it is clear that the claims of liturgy were greater than those of charity. A nice guy—but not a good man. So, instead of going to the inn, he goes to church!

"So likewise a Levite, when he came to the place and saw him, passed by on the other side." I like to think of the Levite as smart: he knew that robbers used decoys; so why take chances? But I may be wrong and you may be right, those of you who are thinking that the Levite was simply late to a meeting at "The Seaside Church" on the upper West Side of Jericho where they were going to discuss what additional security measures could be taken to protect travellers going from Jerusalem to Jericho! (I'm glad you laughed, because I did too when I wrote those words. And then I stopped, remembering a hospital call I hadn't made because I was too busy writing a sermon on the Good Samaritan!)

"But a Samaritan, as he journeyed, came to where he was; and when he saw him, he had compassion and went to him"—ah, how much more useful compassion is than guilt—"and bound up his wounds, pouring on oil and wine"—which he was probably carrying for his lunch—"then he set him on his own beast"—which made the Samaritan, now on foot, far more vulnerable—"and brought him to an inn, and took care of him."

And that's the heart of the parable, isn't it? Again and again we are brought back to the notion that "caring is the greatest thing, caring matters most."

Do you know what it was about Ignatius Loyola and his band of nine that finally turned Pope Paul III around in the sixteenth century so that he granted them permission to form the Society of Jesus? These men arrived in Rome glittering with degrees. Some were even doctors of divinity. But the Pope was unimpressed. And then came the winter of 1538, a terrible season, the worst in Roman memory. These ten people "took on themselves the burden of the city's destitute. They put the sick into their own beds, begged straw pallets and food for the rest, and at times had as many as three or four hundred crowded into a ramshackle residence which was all they could afford. So spectacular were their efforts that even the Pope could no longer ignore them, and in 1540 he granted them the right to term themselves a genuine religious brotherhood" (from *Saint-Watching* by Phyllis McGinley).

In other words, learning is so important and love is so much more important. The acquisition of knowledge is second to its use, or in the old Calvinist phrase, "Truth is in order to goodness."

And love is also so much more important than the laws which Jesus talked about in the beginning of the story. For love goes beneath the laws, reaching to the question of motives. Love goes between the laws, filling the inevitable gaps. And love goes beyond the law. Laws are more restraining but love is more demanding. Laws are more irritating, but love is more costly.

Love *is* costly. It is interesting that Jesus too was called a Samaritan. In the eighth chapter of John we read, "The Jews answered him, 'Are we not right in saying that you are a Samaritan and have a demon?'" (John 8:48). He denies having a demon, but not being a Samaritan. For "Samaritan" also signifies a spiritual outcast, a heretic, and of course half the time "heretic" signifies someone who is freer than we are. And when human beings see someone freer than they, instead of emulating his freedom, they generally seek to take it from him. They turn the Good Samaritans whom they fear into the Bad Samaritans they are looking for. Good Christians will often be viewed as Bad Samaritans, for if Christ was not rewarded for being Christ, it's a bit naïve to think that Christians will be rewarded for being Christian.

Let's see now if we can be very practical. While the Samaritan instinct may be constant, the expression of it invariably changes. If today, for example, you walked out of the church and let's say you went down 125th Street, or you went over to the East Side, let's say, 104th Street between First and Second Avenues, and you found somebody who had fallen among the thieves, you wouldn't pick him up and take him to an inn. In fact, you probably wouldn't pick him up at all, because you know that you might do him more harm than good. Today there are others more qualified to deal with people who are half dead in the streets. So what do you do? You take off your jacket or coat, you put it over the man to keep him from going into shock, you go to the nearest phone booth and call an ambulance. But now comes the problem. In a year or two there may be no Metropolitan Hospital on the East Side. If the Mayor's plan goes through, those two hospitals will be closed and the so-called "underserved" will be served even less, unless Good Samaritans come to the rescue. But how do we rescue these days? How can we make sure an ambulance gets there in time to save the man? We are talking about ambulances and city hospitals—city politics. We are talking about somebody who fell among thieves, because there were no police around—once again city politics. It is inevitable: to express fully our Samaritan instincts these days, we have to find public as well as private ways, act corporately as well as individually.

Fortunately we now have a religious coalition in this city that has designated this Sunday as "Health Crisis Sunday." Do read the insert, get in touch with Dr. Lowe, come to the interfaith service, get yourselves educated, for Samaritans now must offer helping minds as well as hands.

And next Sunday is Pledge Sunday. Riverside is a church whose building is rich but whose congregation is not. And even the church is not so rich that the cost of living won't outstrip the endowment. It will, in about a year. The programs of the church depend upon us, the members. Yet—would you believe—the average pledge in this congregation is only $262? That's not even a dollar a day. Fifty-one percent of the members pledge $100 or less. And 600 don't pledge at all!

Let me suggest $365 as the average pledge this coming year. A dollar a day. And to help you give it, let me remind you that to keep the Pentagon going, all of us Americans pay an average of $600 a year. Do you want to give less to the Riverside Church than to the Pentagon?

A word to the rich among you: It is very hard to enter the Kingdom of Heaven, but it can be done. Remember that just as the Good Samaritan added money to his good works so we have to add money to our labor. And you the rich have a special obligation, because there are so many folk in this church who simply cannot afford to pledge as much as you.

To the poor let me say that experience shows that the poor who pledge generously end up with more money, simply because they have become more cognizant of what money is all about.

Let us all remember that we are not supposed to do well, doing good. Let us all remember that we are not supposed to give until it hurts. We should feel the pinch because "the gift without the giver is bare."

Let's not let the ministry of this church suffer—not when people are hurting in this city as they are. And the worse the situation, the better we have to become.

It's time to close with a final thought. I have long felt that giving without receiving is a downward motion; whether it is church charity or foreign aid, it makes no difference. But in the parable, the Samaritan receives something in return—his identity. The other two fellows never found out who they were. But the Good Samaritan was called into being and accepted the invitation. Had there not been a man lying on the side of the road, he might never have found it. Ponder the fact that all those conspicuously "called" in the Bible— like Moses—were called through the voices, the sorrows of the poor. All the prophets responded to the voices of the oppressed. Think then of what we receive when we accept the invitation to become Good Samaritans. We receive our identity, we receive our life. Once again, "We pass out of depth into life because we love the brothers and sisters." Yes, indeed, as Saint Francis said, "It is in giving that we receive." Amen.

Without a Vision the People Perish

OCTOBER 28, 1979

As today is both Pledge and Reformation Sunday; and as The Riverside Church is even now in the early morning hours of her 50th anniversary; and as the whole world is on the brink—I am afraid the word is well chosen—of a new decade; and as it is true that without a vision the people perish—not to mention their clergy; let me try to set forth today a vision of where this hopefully ever reforming church might go in the coming decade. Never mind the details, nor even the ultimate destination; my interest is in the right direction.

Let me start with words of C.S. Lewis describing what can be expected if one is to become a Christian: "Imagine yourself as a living house. God comes in to rebuild that house. At first, perhaps, you can understand what he is doing. He is getting the drains right and stopping the leaks in the roof, and so on. But presently, he starts knocking the house about in a way that hurts abominably and does not seem to make sense. What on earth is he up to? The explanation is that he is building quite a different house from the one you thought of, throwing out a new wing here, putting on an extra floor there, running up towers, making courtyards. You thought you were going to be made into a decent little cottage. But he is building a palace. He intends to come and live in it himself."

Our God is too small, and for that reason alone it is perhaps a good thing that we worship in a building more like a palace than a cottage; a church whose ceiling is nine stories away, whose organ and whose choir, and whose congregation both in size and composition all remind us that if indeed we love the Lord with all our hearts, minds, and strength, we are going to have to stretch our hearts, open our minds, and strengthen our souls, whether our years are three score and ten, or not yet twenty. God cannot lodge in a narrow mind. God cannot lodge in a small heart. To accommodate God, our cottages must give way to palaces. Of St. Francis, a small man, it was said that where he stopped physically he was just getting under way. I like that, because it suggests that becoming a Christian is less exhausting than exhilarating. But "becoming" is the important word. We never are there. Hopefully we grow in the right direction.

As I think of this church, there is no doubt in my mind that it is primarily here, at the eleven o'clock hour, week by week that we become "Franciscan." It is here we learn anew what it means to live a normal life, "normal" meaning not average but that which operates according to the norm. This service is the heart of the life of this church. It is here that we are most forcefully reminded that bread and power cannot save humanity, that reason for all its importance can be perverse, that there is no security in science. No, our norm is Jesus Christ, God's love in person on earth. So normal life can be likened unto a triangle, an isosceles triangle, where the base angles are equal, with God at the apex, ourselves at one base and our neighbors at the other. And life is normal when around that triangle circles not greed, power, lust for consumer goods at the expense of goodness itself. No, life is normal when love courses around that triangle holding us all together.

To affirm that is of course to recognize that most of our days we live "subnormal" lives. And that's why we come here: to be forgiven, restored, to be converted not from life to something more than life, but, from something less than life to the possibility of full life itself.

I myself find this service week by week so restoring that I wouldn't change it much. But if we are to keep reforming, Council I should keep trying new non-sexist words in the hymns—and abandon those that don't work! Council I should also plan more Sundays, such as next Sunday's Latin American service. We should have more special services of the kind the Black Christian Caucus brings us; and from time to time, special services during the week with New York City's actors, dancers, singers contributing their talents to celebrate the glories and to recall the travails of education, of health, and other areas of the city's life. New York needs more services. Right now, for instance, could we not use a service on Cambodia? an interfaith service of reconciliation for Jews and Blacks *and white Christians* as we are the only ones who persecute both?

Turning to the pastoral side of the church, let me read some other words, this time of Henri Nouwen: "To care means first of all to empty our own cup and to allow the other to come close to us; to take away the many barriers which prevent us from entering the communion with the other. When we dare to care, then we discover that nothing human is foreign to us, that all the hatred and love, cruelty and compassion, fear and joy, can be found in our own hearts. We can participate in the care of God who came, not to the powerful but powerless, not to be different but the same, not to take our pain away but to share it. Through this participation we can open our hearts to each other and form a new community."

Of course we need a new pastoral minister and we shall have a new pastoral minister, as well as the services—God grant—of one or perhaps more retired ministers. And our counselling center is certain to expand in the 1980s its already marvelous work. But what I dream of, more than anything else, is some way for our caring to extend itself through the whole length and breadth of this enormous parish. I dream of the new communities of which Nouwen writes. I long to do Bible study in a newly formed house church somewhere on 30th Street, let's say, on the lower West Side. I would even go to New Jersey or darkest Westchester to do Bible study in a small church within this large church! New members need to be pointed towards some church within this large church, a place near where they live, a place where in smaller numbers than here people gather to sing, have a good time, pray, study, have potluck suppers, in warmer weather, picnics. I dream of house churches where joys are enhanced and sorrows diminished, for in general it's true, that a joy shared is a double joy, while a sorrow shared is half a sorrow. I envision in the years ahead a ministry of the laity which goes well beyond running this church. (We are overrun with people running this church!) I see more and more laity participating "in the care of God." Everyone of us is called to be pastoral. It is instructive to recall that the church got along without benefit of clergy for three whole centuries. And it's frightening to some of us to think how well that church flourished! So I see a day when strangers, more even than they do today, will want to come to Riverside because they've heard "how those Riversiders do care for each other!"

On the right kind of Bible and theological study we can never get enough, not if the expression "courage of your convictions" has meaning. I think it does, more than ever, in a day when common integrity is made to look like courage. But along with the old we need a new theology. On this Reformation Sunday let me state it this way: The first Protestant Reformation went hand in hand with an age of expansion that came in the sixteenth century after the rather static Middle Ages, static not stagnant. "The Protestant Reformation was a driving force behind the economic expansion of the West. Capitalist development, in turn, helped institutionalize the Protestant ethic as a world view. Together, Protestantism and capitalism transformed the planet." That, I think is probably a pretty fair statement.

But now we are finding out that there are limits to growth. This has to affect our understanding of the Biblical term "dominion." It is even possible that we have misconceived "dominion." For God doesn't exploit. God doesn't manipulate. It may well be in the coming decade, instead of exploiting we are going to have to conserve nature. Maintenance will have to replace the notion of progress. Nurturing will have to replace the notion of engineering. A new doctrine of stewardship will have to become more important than doctrines of ownership—that is, if we are to stop devouring our planet, spewing out wastes in all directions. And the new doctrine of stewardship will have to go hand in hand with the old doctrine of social justice, for in an age of scarcity the question of equity can no longer be deferred.

In an age of expansion we could see the rich nations of the world going down one track, the poor along a parallel one, and we could say, "Well, the poor may never catch up with the rich, but poor nations will one day reach that station called 'sufficiency.'" Now, however, fuel is scarce, so which locomotive is going to be serviced first?

What is true in the world is also true in the nation, and here in the city of New York where the poor are surely getting poorer, not richer. The system simply isn't working. So we need to think differently, and a second reformation could, in fact, be as profoundly influential as was the first.

To celebrate our fiftieth anniversary, among other things, we are planning a conference on the city. This is to be a conference to "revision" New York at the start of a new decade. The follow-up to the conference will hopefully be a "Center for the City"—never mind the exact title—a place where people who have new ideas for our beloved city can share them with others who want to hear them, and implement them; a place where, as it were, the community can instruct the community, with Riverside playing essentially the role of a broker.

And why is this so important right now? Because the nation, feeling humiliated through loss of power, and distressed by inflation, is beginning to resemble the Weimar Republic just before Hitler. It is important that our churches be courageous and creative, not sanctuaries for frightened Americans, which is to say recruiting grounds for authoritarian figures and movements which bear the earmarks of an emerging fascism.

Our task is not easy. But let's think of it as exhilarating, not exhausting. You'll notice that I haven't mentioned the theatre, the arts and crafts program, which I am sure will find new life in the '80s; and the Tower League, too, the "B's & P's", Maranatha, the Black Christian Caucus, Koinonia, the Outreach Task Forces, the "Reverse the Arms Race" program.

Nor have I mentioned evangelism. Properly understood, evangelism is not trophy hunting, "bring 'em back alive." No, evangelism is a beggar telling another where he found bread. And if here we have found the bread of life, and if we take friends to the movies, why shouldn't we bring friends to church?

I've gone on long enough. All I wanted to offer was an outline of a vision, one for you to fill in or modify. But we need a vision, and we need to support it. I hate to ask anybody for money to meet a need. But if a need can be translated into an opportunity then one need not be shy. So let me ask you to think about the church. How do you feel about it? Has it meant something to you in the past? Is it an opportunity for the future? Certainly the church has a mandate:

> I will appoint you as a covenant to the people
> As a light to the nations.
> To open blind eyes
> To bring prisoners from the dungeon.
> Isa. 42:6–7

Ours is a rugged, not a gilt, cross. But it's exhilarating. Who wants to stay a spiritual midget when like St. Francis we can grow day by day? And who would want to stay alone in isolation when it is possible to build a loving community? And who would wish that community to be restricted by these walls? On this Reformation Sunday, pledge as much of yourself as you can, to as much of this church as you believe in. Remember, Christ has no eyes but ours, no hands but ours, no feet but ours. He is calling us to be co-creators of a new age of surpassing beauty in the building of which Riverside, I hope, with modesty but with vigor, will play a worthy part.

The Twenty-third Psalm

NOVEMBER 11, 1979

First, let me say how wonderful it is to have the bellringers and you fourth graders with us. You can start opening your Bibles, fourth graders, to page 485 while I say two things to the rest of the congregation. Carelessly I left in the choir room an article from the Cleveland *Plain Dealer*, a review of a Riverside Church service, by the twenty-year-old daughter of the religious editor of the Cleveland *Plain Dealer*. She said I was a fine preacher but lost my direction about halfway through the sermon. Recalling the Sunday she was here, I was impressed! But the choir, she said, had to be the best she had ever heard, and the organist, too, came off very well. "He doesn't play too loudly," she wrote, "at least not for the congregation, which really sings." I thought you should hear that.

The second thing that I want to report is that the Every Member Canvas is, as they say, moving well. Some of you have been touchingly generous. But the main goal in my mind remains the same: everybody gives something. About 25 percent have yet to make their pledges. If you feel poor and are embarrassed to make a small pledge, read your Bible. What does it say about "the widow's mite"? A small donation from someone who can't afford it is in the eyes of Heaven twice as glorious as a large donation from somebody who says, "I think I can give that without feeling the pinch." So, be Christian; don't be worldly! The widow's mite is a beautiful gift. Let's all pledge.

Now I want to go back to the Twenty-third Psalm. You can't preach once on the Twenty-third Psalm, as I did about a year and a half ago, and not return to it. As finally there is only one hymn, "A Mighty Fortress Is Our God," so finally, there is only one Psalm, the Twenty-third. (Am I being sufficiently dogmatic?) Have you got page 485, over there? All right fourth graders: follow what I read. You won't follow everything I say but some of what I say you will be able to follow. And for the rest of you, who may not know the Psalm by heart, it's in the back of the hymnbook.

Let me say what I said last year: the greatest statements in the Bible are not the Commandments, the great "Thou Shalt Not's," nor even are the great "Thou Shalt's." Stirring, stunning as they are, the Commandments are not the greatest thing. The greatest statements in the Bible are in the indicative, not in the imperative. It is not what God tells us to do, but what God has already done for us that is the basis of the Christian faith. So the most important statements are such as these: "God so loved the world that he gave his only begotten son that whosoever should believe in him should not perish but have everlasting life" (John 3:16). "God is love, and he who abides in love abides in God, and God abides in him" (1 John 4:16). "Even though I speak with the tongues of men and angels but have not love, I am as a noisy gong and clashing cymbal" (1 Cor. 13:1). And from the Old Testament: "God is our refuge and strength, a very present help in trouble" (Ps. 46:1). And "The Lord is my shepherd, I shall not want" (Ps. 23:1).

Why is this so important? I've visual aids for us today. Everybody won't be able to see this picture, but the fourth graders can. Here is a shepherd carrying a sheep. The shepherd is Christ, and a black Christ, because Christ is Black, white, yellow, red, just as God is male or female. And here we see Christ carrying a small lamb, just the way a mother carries a small child. And what does a mother say to a child as she rocks the child in her arms? "Little child you are all right, you're going to make it, I'm going to protect you from the terrors of the day, and the darkness of the night." The child is being confirmed. We become who we are because we are loved. We are loved into being and that's what Jesus the shepherd does for us. The Shepherd says you are certified, stamped as it were, not made in the U.S.A., Korea or Japan, made in the mind of God. And nurtured in the arms of the Shepherd.

There is nothing more important than understanding that God really cares. Of course, when we grow up, like so many sheep, we go astray. That can happen even in the fourth grade. And we heard about that in the New Testament lesson. And then what does the shepherd do? He abandons ninety-nine sheep to get the one sheep that is lost. Actually, if you want to read a really moving chapter, read the three stories in the fifteenth chapter of Luke. It starts with a lost sheep; it goes on to a story of a lost coin, and it ends up with a story of a lost person, the Prodigal Son. But that story is not really about a lost person; it's about a bereaved father, who can't keep his son at home, but when his son goes astray, he stands on the road day after day, yearning, longing, hoping. No, more than that, in the New Testament God the father goes down the road to meet the son—a son for a son, a savior to save. God cares. That's the most important thing we can possibly say. So, "The Lord is my shepherd, I shall not want. He maketh me to lie down in green pastures." Green is generally considered the most comforting color. "He leadeth me beside the still waters." But now before we go on, listen to this, fourth graders, are you with me?

You probably don't see many sheep in New York, do you? And not many shepherds. But, let's pretend that right out here in the Park around Grant's Tomb, there's a herd of sheep. And wouldn't you picture two sheepdogs, probably running around keeping them all in line? And wouldn't you picture the shepherd with his big staff, behind the herd, sort of keeping them in line? But, look again at this picture. Where's the shepherd? behind the sheep? No, he's in front of the sheep. "He *leadeth* me beside the still waters." And "He leadeth me in the paths of righteousness." And see, I've got another picture here to make the same point.

This picture shows *how* he leads the sheep. Love draws, love calls us, love is ahead of us. Western shepherds may drive their sheep, but Eastern shepherds lead them. And that big staff is not to nudge the sheep, it's to beat off the wolves. Love leads us, draws us, calls us, God is always ahead of us. A pillar of fire by night and a cloud by day. God is ahead of us as much as above us, or in us.

I'll tell you something else about Eastern shepherds. A friend of mine went to India once and ran into a shepherd. He said to him,

"Have you gone to school?" The shepherd said "No." "Can you count?" Again, "No." "How do you know you haven't lost a sheep?" "Oh, I know them all by name."

Love individualizes. In Isaiah 43 we read: "But now thus says the Lord, He who created you, O Jacob, he who formed you, O Israel: 'Fear not, for I have redeemed you, I have called you by name. You are mine.'" That's what the Shepherd does. He leads us and knows each one of us by name.

Now let's take a look at where he leads us. We read that "he leads us beside the still waters," where he restores our souls, and that "he leads us in the paths of righteousness" and not for our sake, but for "his name's sake." He leads us in two places—"by the still waters," for rest, and "in paths of righteousness," for labor.

As I look around this church and recognize some of the workaholics among you, I wonder if you let the Good Shepherd lead you beside still waters. It is presumptuous to think that we can go without rest, just as presumptuous as it is to think that everything in the world should work out well without our having to walk in the paths of righteousness.

The book you fourth graders hold in your hands is not mostly poetry, like the Twenty-third Psalm; it is mostly history. And in English the word comes out rather well—"his story"—because God is the main character in the book. When you grow older, I hope you will study history. Most Americans don't. Most Americans think history began yesterday, and they forget what the Bible teaches: that we do not so much break the Ten Commandments as we are broken on them. We are not punished for our sins so much as we are punished by them. Life is consequential, for real. And life swings on an ethical hinge. If you loosen that hinge, history and even nature will feel the shock.

History is catching up with us in this country. Today our iniquities testify against us. We grieve over Cambodia, and grieve we should. But we cannot grieve over Cambodia without seeing our complicity in the very famine we abhor. The famine didn't begin with the invasion of Vietnam, or with the Pol Pot regime. It began at least when the United States helped overthrow Prince Sihanouk because he wanted no part in our war in Vietnam—ours, not his. Had he not been overthrown, there would have been no Khmer Rouge, no Pol Pot, probably no invasion by Vietnam, no famine. This Shepherd does not lead us in paths of violence, on warpaths; he leads us in the paths of righteousness. If we end up in blind alleys, we shouldn't blame the Lord, or anybody else. The sins of the fathers are visited upon the children. That's not a statement of justice, that is simply a statement that life is consequential. We are not all guilty, but we are responsible. Today we worry about Cuba. Had we not kept in power a cruel dictator named Batista, there would be no Castro. We worry about Nicaragua. Had we not kept Somoza in power, there would have been no Sandinistas. We worry today about Iran, and worry we should, and about Americans held hostage by angry students. But we forget that we helped kill their leader in 1953—Mossadegh. The CIA connived to put him out of office because he wasn't sufficiently sympathetic to us. And Mr. Allen Dulles, head of the CIA, personally escorted the Shah to Iran in 1953. Now the students tell us that the Shah killed 75,000 Iranians between 1953 and 1979. If that is true, can you blame them for being angry? We don't have to condone what they are doing, but come on, Americans, can we condemn their action without pointing at what produced it? I don't know why we admitted the Shah and why now we don't allow some non-American doctors to verify his illness. And if it is true he took some five billion dollars, it is only fair that he should return part of it.

"He leadeth me in the paths of righteousness." Thus says the Lord: "Stand by the road and look and ask for the ancient path, and where the good way is, and walk in it, and find rest for your soul." That's a beautiful line combining rest and righteousness.

Fourth graders: I'm talking history today. Sixty-one years ago today, World War I ended. That was supposed to be the war to end all wars. It was supposed to be the war to make the world safe for democracy. But today we have to wonder whether democracy, American-style, is safe for the world, and whether indeed the earth is any more peaceful around the globe than it was at the end of World War I. I don't think our generation has done very well. But I think your generation can do better. To encourage you, I brought you a present. Yesterday I was in Maine talking about the arms race, and I said to the people in the church: "seeing you are not going to pay me a nickel for my speech, the least you can do is give me that beautiful banner on the wall which I want to give to the fourth graders in our Sunday School." They protested, but lost. So here it is. I give it to you, and hope you will hang it in your classroom.

What you read is from another Psalm, the Thirty-third Psalm. And in your book, your Bible, it will read "The warhorse is a vain hope for victory, and by its great might it cannot save." I hope that your generation will succeed in abolishing war as a former generation succeeded in abolishing slavery. Be abolishionists, and study war no more.

Let's go back to the Twenty-third Psalm now, and on to the end. Here's my favorite part: "Yea, though I walk through the valley of the shadow of death, I will fear no evil." There's one of the great sentences in the indicative. Notice the way the psalmist underscores the sure presence of God at life's most difficult moment. Up to now, God the shepherd has been referred to in the third person singular. "The Lord is my shepherd, *he* leadeth me beside the still water, *he* restoreth my soul, *he* leadeth me in the paths of righteousness." Now as the psalmist refers to life's most devastating moments, he says, "Yea, though I walk through the valley of the shadow of death, I will fear no evil, for *thou* art with me." The first person changes to the second person singular, a statement to a prayer. And the prayer continues: "*Thy* rod and *thy* staff they comfort me, thou anointest my head with oil, my cup runneth over."

Something else has changed. God is no longer the shepherd, and we the sheep. God now is the host and we are the guests. What's being referred to here is the desert law of hospitality. Were I fleeing my enemies and I came to you for refuge, according to the law of desert hospitality, you would have to accept me for two nights and the day intervening, and my enemies would have to stay outside the circle of light cast by the fire. "Thou preparest a table before me in the presence of mine enemies. Thou anointest my head with oil, my cup runneth over." The psalmist ends by contrasting this limited hospitality with the hospitality that we can expect from God. "Surely goodness and mercy," and if you want those sheep to have sheepdogs, let's call them Goodness and Mercy because they "shall follow me all the days of my life; and I shall dwell in the house of the Lord" not for two nights and the day intervening, but "forever."

And all that, dear fourth graders, is only what you said yourselves earlier when you recited, "The Lord is good, his steadfast love endures forever, and his faithfulness to all generations." May you know God's love in your generation. May the world know your love in the next generation.

Now why don't we end this little homily by all of us saying together the Twenty-third Psalm. You read it out of your Bibles; some of us will read it from where it has long been written—in the soft places of our hearts.

John 3:16

NOVEMBER 18, 1979

B efore turning to the sermon, let me read you a statement just received by me, and sent, I would imagine, to many preachers. It comes from the White House.

"As we approach our traditional day of national thanksgiving, the hearts of all Americans are heavy with concern for the safety of those held hostage in Iran. We join with people of all faiths throughout the world who adhere to fundamental principles of human rights and international law. We are united with them in seeking an end to acts of terrorism against innocent people. On Thanksgiving Day and during the holiday weekend, I ask all Americans to make a special prayer at churches and synagogues and places of public meeting. Let us seek God's guidance in our search for peace and human brotherhood, and pray for the safe return of those whose lives are threatened. May we come with gratitude for our abundant blessings and humility before the heavy burdens of world responsibility that our blessings and power have brought."

I had not read the statement before. Hearing it, I wish it had included a little more penitence. Listen again: "We join with people of all faiths throughout the world who adhere to fundamental principles of human rights and international law." Let us not forget that it was the C.I.A. that overthrew Mossadegh in 1953 and none other than the head of the C.I.A. who escorted the Shah back in 1953. I hope the Shah and Henry Kissinger, the officers of the Chase Manhattan Bank, which did the biggest business in Iran from 1953 to 1979, and all of us will pray not only for the hostages, but also for forgiveness for our own complicity in the very events we condemn.

And now for the sermon. Let us take as our text John 3:16: "God so loved the world that he gave his only begotten son that whosoever should believe in him should not perish but have everlasting life."

Say to me, "the Heavens are telling the glory of God," and, remembering the clear vault of the sky these last few days, I will instantly agree with you. Tell me, "He spreads frost on the earth like salt, and icicles form like pointed stakes," and remembering New England winter scenes beautiful beyond description I will say, "It is true." But tell me, "As is His majesty so is His mercy," and my heart will demur. So too will the heart of many an honest non-believer. "Come on, Christian, what do you mean your God is merciful? God so loved the world that 2,000,000 Cambodians are now starving to death? God so loved the world that some 400,000,000 in some 32 countries the world around are not far behind? God so loved the world that the president of the disarmament center of the United Nations has to be here today to tell us how the world faces its own extinction? Aren't you Christians a bit fatuous to talk about an all-loving God, when almost every inch of the earth's surface is soaked with the tears and blood of the innocent?"

Such things can be said with some reason, for the suffering of the innocents is surely the greatest dilemma believers have to wrestle with. Of course, non-believers have a mystery of their own which they too must wrestle with, namely, the mystery of undeserved good. What did we ever do this week to deserve such fantastic weather? To be remembered also is that love is self-restricting when it comes to power. Every loving parent knows what I am talking about. Love is not powerless, but it seeks to empower, not overpower. And if love is the name of the game, then the primary rule of the game is freedom. It has to be. Freedom has to be taken with great seriousness. If we human beings are free to will the will of God, we are no less free to say, "Not Thy will but mine be done." We have the freedom and right to go to hell as it were. So every time we survey the troubles and dis- aster in which the human race has involved itself, every time we lift our eyes to Heaven and cry out, "How long, O Lord, how long?" it is precisely at that moment that the Lord himself is asking precisely that question of us, "How long, O children, how long?"

Love is self-restricting when it comes to power. God's love is most eloquent in its restraint. The central symbol of the faith shows us that we are going to be helped by God's weakness rather than by his strength. So it just may be true: "As is his majesty, so is his mercy."

But my heart demurs for another reason. Were I God viewing from Heavenly places this earthly mess, I would be tempted to wash my hands of the whole thing. And I think I know why. Gratitude is not gen- erally a profound emotion; but the expectation of gratitude most cer- tainly is. I can't see how God keeps up His interest in us when there seem to be so few returns. Yet God continues to pour out His heart for this wayward, wicked, sinsick world. Imagine God allowing himself to be spat upon, shouldered out of this world, hoisted upon a cross. Why, if I were mugged once, it would probably change my outlook on the world. But obviously, "My ways are not your ways," saith the Lord.

In myriad ways God continues to bless us: by the heavens, which we already mentioned; by the earth, "with its store of wonders untold"; by giving us neighbors with whom we can walk and talk, and love and laugh, and learn that in giving is taking. But most of all, "God so loved the world that he gave his only begotten son."

When we Christians think of Jesus, and remember Jews, and peo- ple of other faiths, I think we have to think carefully. In the first place we shouldn't be surprised that different people believe different things. More surprising, is how much is believed in common. None of the great religions of the world, for instance, admire cowardice. And in the second place, "God moves in mysterious ways his wonders to perform." His revelations are manifold. So I think as Christians we have to say God is not confined to Christ, only most essentially defined by Christ.

To Christians at least, Jesus is the Rosetta Stone of history, making meaningful the hieroglyphics of heaven and earth. To Christians Jesus is the main theme. Imagine for a moment that you heard Beethoven's Fifth, beginning in the fifth measure. It would be interesting, but puzzling. Something would be missing. Then all of a sudden you heard, "Da, da, da, DA . . . Da, Da, Da, DA." "Aha," you'd say, "so that's what it was all about." Or we can think of Jesus as a window to divinity, a window revealing as much of God as is given mortal eyes to see. When Christians see Christ empowering the weak, scorning the powerful, healing the wounded, and judging their tormentors, we are seeing transparently the power of God at work. What is finally important is not that Christ is Godlike, but that God is Christ-like. God is like Christ. That's what we need to know, isn't it? Then we know how to pray—through Jesus Christ, our Lord, who gives us the right and confidence to pray the way we do.

"God so loved the world that he gave his only begotten son." I think it important to catch something else at this moment. In the same third chapter of John we read: "No one has ascended into Heaven but He who descended from Heaven." I interpret that to mean that if we try to be otherworldly, we are presumptuous. But more than that: to rise above this world we will pass the young man coming down. God so loved the world that he wanted us to abandon it? No, the world is like the flag, don't burn it, wash it. Our quarrel with the world is a lovers' quarrel, not a grudge fight. Jesus is not *of* this world, but he is *in* this world, seeking to redeem it. He is God's love in person, on earth. He didn't come to lead us out of this world, but to show us how to live in it. And we are called on to live life after the fashion of Christ. It's that simple. And that difficult.

This is important, for how many times are we told, "You've got to be realistic." Of course you have to be realistic. What else would you be in any kind of world, ideal or corrupt? But what is reality? The Rosetta Stone that makes meaningful all hieroglyphics of this world, the main theme of the symphony, the window through whom we see that part of divinity that is given to mortal eyes to see—that is reality. Christ is our reality. He alone is for real. The rest is unreal. As I said, it's that simple, that difficult, and that important.

Let's go on to the last phrase: "God so loved the world that he gave his only begotten son, that whosoever should believe in him should not perish but *have everlasting life*." At first, those words seem more poetic than clear. Earlier this week in southern California, I met a woman younger than I, who was in a prayer group of women, mostly 80 or over. "God, Bill," she told me on the way to the airport, "I am learning so much from these women." What she is learning is that death has little sting for people who have heard the Word, for people who sing, as last night here we did, "Precious Jesus, Lead Me On." Death has no sting for those who believe with St. Paul, "No one lives unto himself alone, and no one dies unto himself alone. If we live, we live unto the Lord, and if we die, we die unto the Lord. So whether we live or whether we die, we are the Lord's" (Rom. 14:8).

Eternal life refers to a kind of life, not its length. Length is not the most important dimension. Here on earth it may be a long life; it may be a short one. The point is, the world can't destroy eternal life. The world can't even touch it. You may be pitifully poor and still have eternal life. You can be unemployed, on welfare, fighting inflation and several ailments all at once, and still have eternal life. Think of it this way, "all you who labor and are heavy laden": it is upon Calvary, when all seems lost, that Christ becomes most irresistible. So, too, when all seems lost to you, you become most irresistible to Jesus. "Come unto me, all you who labor and are heavy laden, and I will give you rest." "Not as the world gives, give I unto you, let not your hearts be troubled, neither let them be afraid" (John 14:27).

To avoid sentimentality, however, we have to add that Christ will give no rest to those who seek weapons to blast the world into annihilation. There is no eternal life for those who depose governments abroad. There is no eternal life for those who starve the poor. You can't be proud and Christian both. How God must despise the sounds of those who pray this day, "Thy kingdom come," and tomorrow bar its way. How God must despise the spectacle of Christians who climb upon the Cross to be seen from afar, thereby trampling on the one who has hung there so long.

Last week, we talked of the shepherd leading us beside the still waters *and* into the paths of righteousness. We see the same rhythm in Jesus' life. Now he is in the mountains praying, now he is in the valley healing; a rhythm of meditation and action. Eternal life, I imagine, knows both poles of life.

I am glad the Hunger Task Force and the Christian Education Department have gotten together to put on an amazing exhibit in the Assembly Hall. I was there for an hour before this service, sitting with children writing letters to Representatives, urging them to consider not only the hungry in Cambodia, but the underfed in our own country. And I'm glad to see all the cans piled up around the altar; a beautiful sight. Bread for ourselves may be materialistic, but it's spiritual, a gift of the spirit, when it's for the hungry. Soon, with other churches in the area, we shall have enough food pantries to see the hungry of this part of the city through the winter.

And what about the Cambodians? Let me suggest that tomorrow, those of you who are employed seek to call a meeting of your fellow employees. Suggest to them that between Thanksgiving and Christmas everyone give one percent of their income to be split between OXFAM, Catholic Relief Services, UNICEF, or other organizations. If that's too much, suggest a dollar a day, from Thanksgiving to Christmas. What's clear is that all of us should do something special.

Without God we can do nothing; without us, God won't do anything. That's the nature of our relationship. God's power is most eloquent in its restraint. We are going to be helped by her weakness. Her love does not overpower, it empowers; it empowers us so to love the world that others are drawn to God, the source of all power. When we understand how God's love and power comes, we can say with conviction, "As is his majesty, so is his mercy." Indeed, "God so loved the world that he gave his only begotten son that whosoever should believe in him should not perish but have everlasting life."

Iran[*]

DECEMBER 2, 1979

"... and the government shall be upon his shoulder ..."
Isaiah 9:6

I know it's hardly great music, but there is one hymn I love to sing: "What A Friend We Have In Jesus." In Jesus we have a friend like unto no other. No other friend can fill our lives with such a presence. No other friend can so gladden the heart, liberate the mind and stretch the imagination. But it is also true that no other friend is more demanding. Old man Simeon foresaw this when he said of the child Jesus in his arms: "Behold this child is set for the fall and rising of many in Israel, and for a sign that is spoken against . . . that thoughts out of many hearts may be revealed" (John 2:34–35).

[*]This sermon owes a great deal to Clarence Jordan.—WSC

It is often said that Christianity has been tried and found wanting. It would be more accurate to say that it has been tried and found difficult. It has been said that the weekly miracle of the churches is that we change the wine into water!

"And the government shall be upon his shoulder." I've never been clear as to what that means but let's listen again to what Jesus had to say about love and hate: "You have heard it said that 'you shall love your neighbor and hate your enemy.' But I say to you, 'love your enemies and pray for those who persecute you'" (Matt. 5:43–44). What does that say to us this morning if not, "You have heard it said 'You shall love America and hate her enemies,' but I say to you, 'Love the Ayatollah and pray for the students who persecute your fellow Americans in Tehran.'" Have you tried? It isn't easy, is it? Watching television we get the impression that it is easy to be Iranian and Muslim these days. I am not sure, but I am sure that it is very difficult to be American and Christian.

Let's go back to the Sermon on the Mount. "You have heard it said 'An eye for an eye and a tooth for a tooth'" (Matt. 5:38). Often that saying is misunderstood. Jesus is referring to a law which can be found in Exodus, Leviticus, and Deuteronomy, a law which underscores *one* eye for an eye, *one* tooth for a tooth. The law was necessary because the first method we humans devised to deal with our enemy was unlimited retaliation: "Kill my cat, and I'll kill your dog, your mule, and you, too." The father/mother of this unlimited retaliation is of course the idea that might makes right—a thoroughly uncivilized idea, although one that still governs many actions of civilized nations today.

To the early Hebrews, however, it was clearer than it is to many of us that the end result of unlimited retaliation is mutual self-destruction. So a better way was sought and there arose the notion of limited retaliation. In the twenty-first chapter of Exodus we read that in the event a person harmed another "then shalt thou give life for life, eye for eye, tooth for tooth, hand for hand, foot for foot, burning for burning, wound for wound, stripe for stripe" (vv. 23–25). Limited retaliation certainly is a step forward over unlimited retaliation. "Do unto others as they do unto you." "Get even, but no more." Limited retaliation is what most people have in mind when they speak of justice. It's the justification also most frequently used for capital punishment.

But Jesus then talks of a third stage, one that comes after unlimited and limited retaliation, one which we can call "limited love." "You have heard it said, 'You shall love your neighbor and hate your enemy.'" Actually in Leviticus 19:18 it is written: "You shall not take vengeance or bear any grudge against the children of your own people, but you shall love your neighbor as yourself."

Again, a step forward. Limited love is better than limited retaliation. But when the neighbor has been limited to one of one's own people, then limited love has supported white supremacy, religious bigotry, the notion of "Herrenvolk" and "America for Americans," which, of course, never meant the Indians. Limited love is more self-serving than generous, as Jesus recognized when he said: "If you love those who love you, what reward have you? Do not even the tax collectors do the same? And if you salute only your brethren, what more are you doing than others? Do not even the Gentiles do the same?" (Matt. 5:46–47).

Then comes the demand of which I spoke at the beginning: "You therefore, must be perfect, even as your heavenly Father is perfect" (v. 48). Without question the translation presents a problem. The Greek word really means "to be perfected," or "completed," "finished"; it's the same that Jesus used on the cross when he said, "It is finished." So perhaps we could translate the sentence: "You therefore, must be completely mature, even as your heavenly father is mature." In other words, unlimited retaliation is babyish, limited retaliation is childish, limited love is adolescent. Only unlimited love that applies universally to all races and nations is evidence of maturity. It is God's desire that her children be as adult as she. In Advent, to prepare for the heavenly child we must become mature adults.

How all this applies to the present crisis in Iran is surely not as clear as the sky above us today. Lord knows our judgments are always subjective. No one has all the answers. If anyone did it would simply mean he did not have all the questions! Nevertheless we must strive to think as Christians, and to help us do so let me add one more thought: "You have heard it said"—and then came a law; "but I say unto you"—and then came Jesus' understanding of the will of God. Jesus confronts the law with the will of God, insisting that the will of God is never something less and always something more than the law.

This is important because the United Nations' debate made clear last night that the great temptation today is not just to stay with limited love—think only of your own fellow Americans, your own fellow diplomats. There is also the temptation to think only of the law and its violations. There is no question about it: to invade an Embassy and take hostages is to be in total violation of the law and to be against about every diplomatic tradition you can think of. So it is natural for Americans, and it is natural for diplomats, to say as so many do: "The hostages have to be freed. That is the first and only really important thing."

But suppose the government is to be upon His shoulder, not ours? Suppose we go from limited to unlimited love? The first thing we would have to do would be to put ourselves into Iranian shoes. If the will of God goes beyond the law, so do human relations. Human relations are finally not contractual. Human relations are finally just that—human. So the question we have to ask is not only, "What is legal?" but "What is the human, moral, compassionate, imaginative thing to do for the good of all involved?"

Let's put ourselves in Iranian shoes. Clearly the Iranians think their moral, and even their legal, position is as strong if not stronger than ours. They think we are harboring a criminal, an Adolf Eichmann; only worse, because the Shah *gave* the orders, orders that imprisoned, tortured, and killed tens of thousands of Iranians. And they claim he absconded with millions of dollars. Some Iranians even think we are harboring him in the hope that we can put him back again on the throne. After all, it was not the choice of the Iranians but that of the CIA that put him there in 1953. So, if we try to move from limited to unlimited love, if we put ourselves in Iranian shoes, we can see that morally speaking we Americans appear to be living in a glass house, and people who live in glass houses shouldn't throw stones.

Two wrongs however don't make a right. They simply make two wrongs that need to be righted. Unfortunately, however, both the United States and Iran have sought to use the UN in an unprincipled way. Each side has sought to use the UN to right only the one wrong that has been done that side. But in a situation of unlimited love, both sides should try to rise above their present condition. Both sides, it would seem, should try to let the UN negotiate the release of the hostages and investigate the charges against the Shah.

There are two other things I think Christians should ponder. In the background of this problem is the broader one of tyrants deposed but not brought to trial. Since Nuremberg we have not tried any deposed tyrant. I am thinking of Idi Amin, Anastasio Somoza Debayle, Pol Pot, Emperor Bokassa I. And I am thinking that if we had a legitimate international tribunal—something better than victors sitting in judgment, as at Nuremberg—then two things: (1) people wouldn't have to occupy other people's embassies in order to get their tyrants tried; and, (2) tyrants might be less tyranical if they knew that one day they might be held not only morally but legally accountable for their misdeeds.

My final thought is this. I hope the Shah is tried, but it will not bother me one bit if he is tried *in absentia*. Cain killed Abel, but God, who doesn't believe in limited retaliation, does not kill Cain. God leaves Cain at the bar of history, a wonderful bar. I think that's where a ruler like the Shah should be left. I thought at the time how wonderful it would have been had the Israelis, after trying Eichmann, after putting the whole sad story before the whole world for the whole world to see—I thought it would have been wonderful had the Israelis turned to Eichmann and said, "OK, that's all, you can go. Like Cain you're marked; go wander the world." Because what is limited retaliation when it comes to an Eichmann, a Shah, an Idi Amin, a Pol Pot? And could there be justice without there being vengeance? And can justice without mercy ever be just?

I don't know. I do know that Jesus said, "Love your enemies and pray for those who persecute you," and I know that Advent is the time for unlimited love. This is the season in which we wait for Him who will bear the government upon his shoulder.

I guess we have a lot to think about, and a lot to pray about too.

Emmanuel

DECEMBER 9, 1979

"'And his name shall be called Emmanuel'
(which means, God with us)."

Matthew 1:23

In days like our own, when the currents of history once again are churning into rapids, threatening to overflow every restraining embankment and carry everything before them, everything decent and civilized; in times when only those of firm faith can stand firm, while others bend and are shaken like forest trees in the wind; in such times it is natural to want to cry out to seemingly empty skies, "Oh, Lord, how long, before you declare yourself with some mighty act; prove your existence, and so bring us to our senses. You are the savior, so save us."

It's a natural cry. We just heard from Isaiah, "He shall smite the earth with a rod of his mouth, and with the breath of his lips, he shall slay the wicked" (11:4). In Jeremiah, we read, "Is not his word . . . like a hammer that breaketh the rock into pieces?" (23:29). And yet I am sure that Isaiah and Jeremiah both knew as well as the next religious person that the Word of the Lord generally hits the world with the force of a hint. Most of the time the Word of the Lord comes as a question: "Adam, where are you?"—the eternal question, put eternally to each of us, or "Elijah, what are you doing over here?"—here, instead of "there, where you belong." In the story of Elijah, you remember, the Word of the Lord was not in the earthquake, wind, or fire, but in the still, small voice. And at Christmas the Word of the Lord is a babe in a manger. It's all very touching—and maddening.

Yet, how could it be otherwise? To say, "God prove your existence and so bring us to our senses," is really to pray, "Please, God, give us evidence to make intelligently selfish decisions. If you prove to me that I'm going to be punished, I'll be good. Talk persuasively to me of pie-in-the-sky-by-and-by, and I'll defer gratification." I'm tempted to listen to the evangelists who try to get me to invest in heavenly bonds that will pay off handsomely on the other side. But I know that God is not in the business of overcoming our selfishness by appealing to our selfish motives. God doesn't hit us over the head so much as he tugs at the sleeve, or heart. He is the Prince of Peace because he disarms us, coming to us as one of us, totally vulnerable, goodness unguarded, as fragile as a rose in winter.

Each of us, I guess, has her favorite Christmas carol. Likewise, each of us has his favorite Christmas story, many of whose heroes, not surprisingly, are children, like Tiny Tim or Amahl. But my favorite Christmas story is Søren Kierkegaard's story of the king and the maid. Kierkegaard didn't tell it as a Christmas story, but that's all right; "The Star-Spangled Banner" was originally a drinking song, and Dvorak's "Going Home" was played at twice the tempo it is played today. An author is entitled to everything the hearer hears in his work.

Once upon a time a king fell in love with a maid. It's an old theme, how love overcomes all barriers of class and of race, and of nationality. But for all its beauty, the king didn't see the matter easily resolved. Racking his mind and heart was the question: how to declare his love? Unable to answer it, he summons to his palace all the wise people of his kingdom and put the question to them. As one, they responded, "Sire, nothing could be easier. Your majesty has but to appear in all your glory before the humble abode of the maid and instantly she will fall at your feet and be yours."

But it was precisely that thought that so troubled the king. In return for his love, he wanted *hers*, not fears that would lead to her submission. He wanted *her* glorification, not his. What a dilemma when to declare your love means the end of your beloved, and when not to declare your love means the end of love. Night after night the king paced the floor of his palace pondering, until at last he saw love's truth: freedom for the beloved demands equality with the beloved. So late one night, long after his courtiers and counselors had retired to their chambers, the king stole out of a side door of the palace and appeared before the humble abode of the maid dressed in the garb of a servant.

He comes to us as one of us. Indeed, the Christmas story. And again it's touching—and maddening. This solution, so satisfactory to the king—and to Kierkegaard—had I been the maid, I am not sure that I would have found it satisfactory at all. I would have wanted to know more about this young man, about his future and mine. Were the two of us going to be stuck forever in this miserable hovel? Why couldn't he be more honest? I don't mind marrying a king.

What makes it so maddening is that while we want God to be God, He wants to be human. We want God to be strong, probably so that we can be weak. But He wants to be weak so that we can be strong. We want God to prove herself. But she answers: "Do you want proof or freedom?"

"God is love," as Scripture says, and that means the revelation is in the relationship. "God is love" means God is known devotionally, not dogmatically. "God is love" does not clear up old mysteries, it discloses new mystery. "God is love" is not a truth we can master; it is only one to which we can surrender. Faith is being grasped by the power of love. So the perfect self-expression of the Holy is in human form.

Late one night he stole out of the side door of his palace and appeared before the humble abode of the maid, dressed in the garb of a servant. Why should the maid, why should any of us, open the door? Because, although we behave like frightened virgins, we know that it is in self-abandonment, not self-improvement, that we find our self-fulfillment. We should open the door because we need to be set free, *from* fear, *for* love, from self, to God. We should open the door because we need to turn from the apparent to the significant. We should open the door because to deal rightly with earth's sins and needs we must look steadfastly at him who was sent from heaven. We should open the door because deep down we know William Blake was correct:

> And we are put on earth a little space
> That we may learn to bear the beams of love.

So as we near Christmas, dear sisters and brothers, pray to Jesus. Pray to Jesus several times a day this week. St. Thomas à Kempis said, "Let thy thoughts be always upward to God and direct thy prayer to Christ continually." But pray to Jesus, as to one who is more holy than upright; more beautiful than correct; less law abiding and more love abiding. Yet pray to him as to one who can make our souls steady, as well as ardent.

And we are put on earth a little space
That we may learn to bear the beams of love.

Like Kierkegaard's maid, we live in a little space and but for a lit-tle space. Yet, like St. Teresa who, taking her turn in the kitchen, found Jesus very easily among the pots and pans, so we can find him with us in the dreariest stretches of our experience. Will we be stuck forever in this miserable hovel? Who's to say? But we do know the transporting power of prayer:

With a folding of hands
There's a spreading of wings.

In a palace or in a hovel, we can, through self-abandonment, find self-fulfillment. "O Jesus thou art standing outside the fast-closed door." I hope the maid opened the door. And I hope we do, too; open the door and say "Yes, Jesus, yes, and always yes."

"Sinner Cryin', Come Here, Lord"

DECEMBER 16, 1979

For a text this morning we have strayed from the Bible, but in word only, not spirit. We heard it sung: "Sinner cryin', Come here, Lord."

There are those who deplore a commercialized Christmas, and they are right; it is in wretched taste. But a commercialized Christ-mas has one great virtue: it doesn't pretend to be anything else. Not so a sentimentalized Christmas, sentimentality representing those emotions that do not arise out of the truth, but which are poured on top. Sentimentality smothers the truth.

Here is an example of sentimentality. The smallest street in Paris is called *La rue du chat qui pêche* (The street of the cat that fishes). Leading off the Seine near Notre Dame, it extends no farther than a quarter of a block, and is so narrow that two bicycles could scarcely pass one another. Each year thousands of tourists, strolling down the quay, come to the head of the street, peer down, read the sign, and exclaim, "How picturesque, how quaint." Were they to venture down the street, however, and into the dark dank rooms that pass for habitation, they might conclude that "the street of the cat that fishes" is more suitable for cats than for human beings. It's picturesque all right; it's also horrible.

The same holds for the Bethlehem Christmas scene. We look at the ox and ass, we exclaim "How picturesque, how quaint," forgetting for a moment that these animals aren't there because they simply could not stay away. Unlike the shepherds, they are not guests. This is their home, and the unsentimental truth about Christmas is that he who was to be Bread of Life for human beings is laid in the feedbox of animals. The biblical account is clear: "He was in the world, and the world was made by him, and the world knew him not" (John 1:10–11). Man's humanity to man is surpassed only by man's inhumanity to God. At Christmas, as on Good Friday, human beings come off badly.

There would be no point in dwelling on all this except for one simple reason: while God would like to please us, He would rather save us. But He cannot save us—not until we feel the need to be saved. "Watchmen, tell us of the night": it's only when we recognize the surrounding darkness that we can also discern "that glory beaming star." Only in prison do we yearn to be rescued. "O come, O come, Emmanuel, and ransom captive Israel." And as usual, it's a Negro spiritual that puts it more succinctly, "Sinner cryin', Come here, Lord."

Last week I said that God will do anything for us, short of violence to his own gift of free will. He loves us, but he can't force our love in return. At Christmas he sends us a Savior; but do we want to be saved?

Ask me that question and I'll tell you frankly, that I'd rather be made happy, I'd rather improve myself; in fact I'd rather be almost anything than saved. For it takes a lot of humility to be saved. To be saved you have to allow someone to do for you what you can't do for yourself.

Occasionally, of course, we have the grace and humility to allow this to happen. Yesterday I did what ministers are so lucky to be permitted to do—I performed a wedding. For us, as for those getting married, it's a moving experience. Before us stand two ordinary mortals. But they are experiencing something extraordinary. The groom, were he not so nervous, would tell you he's "on cloud nine." But he'd hasten to add that he didn't get there by placing a ladder against the cloud and climbing up painful rung after painful rung. No, he'd be the first to admit that he was elevated by the power of the love of the woman at his side. Likewise, the bride would gladly admit that she's "walking on air," and that she too was levitated by the love of her lover.

Yesterday the bride wanted me to read words of the painter, Henri Matisse, which bear out what I was just saying: "Love wants to rise, not be held down by anything base. . . . Nothing is more gentle than love, nothing stronger, nothing higher, nothing larger, nothing more pleasant, nothing more complete, nothing better—in heaven or on earth—because love is born of God, and cannot rest other than in God above all living beings. He who loves, flies, runs, and rejoices. She who loves is free, and nothing holds her back."

What holds all of us back is of course self-love, a survival instinct without which, initially at least, we probably couldn't survive. But we can't *live*—that is, we can't love—until we get beyond survival. For only he who loses his life will find it. And we cannot *will* our way out of self-love. We need what that great theologian of the last century, Horace Bushnell, called "the expulsive power of a new affection." Only love of others can save us from love of self. And no sentimental love either. Weddings are beautiful, but if two people love only each other then we have "*égoïsme à deux,*" as the French would say. We have two slaves without a master. Matisse rightly discerned that only infinity can fill the abyss of the human heart. To have expulsive power, the new affection must be the love that is "born of God and cannot rest other than in God above all living beings."

"Unto you is born this day, in the City of David, a savior." Assuming the unassuming glory of a child, God comes to us as one of us. On Christmas a savior is born for us. On Good Friday the same savior will die for us. As I said, God will do everything for us, short of violence to his own gift of free will. But do we want to be saved?

Let's be as unsentimental as possible. If you think failure is final, you don't want to be saved. By this I mean that half the people who tell you their sins are not telling you straight. They tell you their sins are a problem; I tell you their sins are their solution. They want pity, they want sympathy, they want understanding, they want almost anything but forgiveness. "Sinner cryin'" but no "Come here, Lord." They don't want to let anybody else do for them what they can't do for themselves. Yes, guilt is the last stronghold of pride.

If you write benefits in sand, but injuries in marble, you don't want to be saved. In one of Arthur Miller's plays a character cries out, "Oh God, why is betrayal the only truth that sticks?" It's true, isn't it? Our lives are saturated with grievances. Why, some of us each morning, even before our eyes are open, remember that garden of grievances. We reach for the rake, the hoe, the watering pot. If you want never to be saved, concentrate on health, wealth, and status; but most of all concentrate on your grievances. As I said, write benefits in sand, but injuries in marble.

If you say of your job, "This is all, and everything else a distraction," you don't want to be saved. If you want the American flag to fly higher than the cross, you don't want to be saved. If you think it is not the fault of the poor that the city presently is in a financial crisis, but that the poor, nonetheless, should pay the heaviest price, you don't want to be saved. And if you're a champion of justice, but an enemy of mercy, you don't want to be saved.

But then—but then—who knows? I don't think there is a one of us who at some level of his or her being doesn't yearn for salvation. For the wheels of self-love never turn that smoothly, do they? There's always a bit of grit in the machinery, enough to make us feel uncomfortable. "Our hearts are restless until they find rest in thee."

I can't remember if it's this night, or some other this week, that "the Fonz" is going to play Scrooge. Many of you, I'm sure, will watch. But in your surprise at seeing Henry Winkler in a new role, don't overlook Dickens' point: Scrooge was saved, not improved, *saved*. I grant you that a ghost hardly represents "the expulsive power of a new affection." But a ghost is a good beginning, and my only fear is there are not enough ghosts around for all the Scrooges of the world!

But maybe the Lord has provided. Maybe this week some ghosts will visit us, as well as Henry Winkler. Perhaps some ghost, gentler than the ones visiting Scrooge, will appear to you and ask, "Isn't all that bitterness a bit boring? How does your garden grow—with flowers, or weeds?"

Maybe some gentle ghost will appear to you this week and ask, "Don't you think it strange that you should act as though comfort and luxury were the chief requirements of your life, when all you need to make you really happy is something to be enthusiastic about?"

Maybe some ghost will appear to you this week and whisper—because even a ghost wouldn't speak louder on this subject: "Isn't it conceivable that a decline in U.S. power might not be all that great a catastrophe?"

"He who loves, flies, runs, and rejoices. She who loves is free, and nothing holds her back."

Do you want to be held back? I don't. So why don't we too sing: "Sinner cryin', come here, Lord! O little did I think he was so nigh. He spoke and made me cry. O mourners, if you will believe, the grace of God you will receive. They seek God's face, but don't seek right. They pray a little day, and none at night. O sinner, you had better pray. For Satan's round you every day. Sinner cryin', come here, Lord!"

And Pray for Iranians, Too

As yesterday I told the choir, and as by now many of you undoubtedly are aware, Thomas Gumbleton, auxiliary bishop of Detroit, William Howard, Baptist pastor and president of the National Council of Churches, and I have been invited by the Iranian Foreign Ministry to celebrate Christmas with the hostages in Tehran. Christmas in tinsel may be more joyous but Christmas in captivity has to be more meaningful. So I feel happy, honored, and deeply grateful. Sobering the good news is the fact that I shall miss the "Mass for Cain" tomorrow night, Christmas Eve. But I shall think of you as I hope you will of me.

Beyond gratitude and happiness, I must confess to a little apprehension. I'm not the least bit apprehensive about any physical danger, nor really about the physical health of the hostages. I'd be surprised if we didn't find them in pretty good shape. I am, of course, worried about their psychological state. But also troubling me is the sure knowledge that we Americans are better talkers than listeners, especially when it comes to listening to people of countries smaller than our own, countries that have been unimpressed by our greater power, countries that have thwarted our national will. The descendants of Thomas Jefferson tend to make like George III. Two hundred years after our own revolution we don't listen easily to revolutionaries. Pray, then, that your pastor, who understands the problem, may overcome it. Pray that the preacher may recognize that it is more blessed to listen than to speak.

Apparently there were three long-time supporters of the Iranian human rights movement, three Kansas professors, who *did* listen, and listened well enough to play a sizeable part in the formulation of this invitation. As the State Department will probably not acknowledge this fact, let me. They are Muriel Paul, Clarence Dillingham, and Norman Forer. Clearly, private citizens like the three of them, or the three of us, cannot negotiate for our government, and there is a Logan Act to remind us. But when governments are having trouble talking to one another, private citizens can attempt to open up channels of communication. Whether they are thanked for this or not is unimportant. We understand that hell hath no wrath like that of a bureaucracy scorned! And we understand further that peace is too important to be left to the experts. And finally, from history—from Bethlehem itself—we learn that those furthest from the seats of

270   *December 23, 1979*

power are apt to be nearer to the heart of things. So let private citizens be humble, but not intimidated. Let them rather remember the fine words of President Eisenhower: "I like to think that people want peace more than governments. In fact, I think that people want peace so badly that one of these days governments had better get out of their way and let them have it."

As by now you've probably gathered, you're not going to get the Christmas sermon you so richly deserve. But believe me, dear parishioners, while it is possible—though not easy—to turn off the press, it is impossible to turn off the phone when parents and pastors, wives and sisters are all calling in messages to take to their loved ones in Iran. I have pages of tender notes. And on the chance that we would be allowed to take pictures, and record Christmas messages, several of us spent the afternoon yesterday collecting film and taping material. (I won't mention the time spent buying tickets, and wondering what you did with your passport.)

But before leaving, I do want to say a few words from the heart. Lord knows I appreciate the generosity of this invitation and I appreciate the importance of preaching Christ's deliverance to those who sit in captivity. And even though I *am* an American I can appreciate that to Iranians, their holding of my fellow Americans reflects decades of pain and anger. We scream about the hostages, but few Americans heard the scream of tortured Iranians. I appreciate that to Iranians, holding hostages may appear more an effect than a cause. Nonetheless, Christmas is a time for reconciliation, for the demonstration of that mercy that Muslims understand as well as Christians. Moreover, those who sit in captivity—at least the vast majority of them—are only symbolic representatives of the guilty parties. So days ago, when the invitation was still only a possibility, I told those kind enough to think of extending it that, yes, I would gladly go, but that in all conscience I would also plead for the return of all hostages. In fact, I expressed the hope that it might be possible for the three of us to return with, let's say, the three youngest, as a start.

But whether we do or not, we Americans must be patient. While there is such a thing as holy impatience, ours is only understandable, not holy. We Americans are not running out of time; we have all the time in the world. We are only running out of patience, and there is nothing Godlike about that. Christ who endured the manger and the cross, and so much in between, expects us to endure better than we are at present.

You remember the words of Simeon, "This child is set for the rising and falling of many in Israel . . . that thoughts out of many hearts may be revealed." Christ came to stand in deliberate tension with the way we live, the way we think. Therefore, as Christians, we must approach with grave skepticism the increasing cries for national unity. We must never cease asking, "What is the virtue of unity if it is unity in folly?" I happen to believe that the present proposal to impose sanctions is highly reminiscent of Lyndon Johnson's bombing of North Vietnam: it will only put iron up the spine of the other side.

Senator Kennedy spoke the truth about the Shah, and instantly drew fire from the White House, competing candidates, editorialists. His timing, he was told, was all wrong. What does that mean? Does it mean we lie on Monday, and only speak the truth on Tuesday? Of course timing can be important, and, as a matter of fact, his was excellent in that it helped save lives. At last, some American leader acknowledged the just grievances of the Iranian people. These grievances still have not been aired, and if not in a trial in Iran, then somewhere in the name of justice they must be aired. If that is true, we have a patriotic duty to ask of our government, "What in the name of justice are you doing to allow this process to go forward?"

Patriotism is a wonderful thing, but it must be based on morality, and not defined by the needs of a militant unity. Rather than rally around the flag let us gather around the Holy Child.

So, dear parishioners, pray for us. Pray for the hostages. And pray for the Iranians, too. Pray this Christmas that those who have offended may repent. Pray, in this holy season, that the darkness of our impatience may not overcome the light of compassion; that the darkness of growing violence may not quench the light of peace. Pray in the name of a child, the Prince of Peace.

Report from Tehran

DECEMBER 30, 1979

Dear parishioners:

I want you to know that wherever we flew—New York to London, London to Tehran, Tehran back to London and London back to New York—whenever we had to fill out those forms asking for a residence, I always wrote "490 Riverside Drive." It's good to be home.

You not only represented home to me, I represented you abroad, for as surely as this Church is committed to reversing the arms race, our trip was a mission of peace. Among the American captives and their Iranian captors, where there was hatred, we tried to sow love. Where there was doubt, faith; where there was despair, hope; where there was sadness, joy. And to go on with St. Francis' words, we sought less to be consoled than to console; to be understood than to understand; to be loved than to love. Never easy, it was never harder than in the conditions we found.

According to the January 1980 issue of *Life* magazine, the U.S. Embassy, situated in the middle of downtown Tehran (population some 4 million people), covers twenty-seven acres. It comes complete with several residences, tennis courts, swimming pools, parking lots. There is even a football field. A wall surrounds the entire compound. Only the size of this compound were we able to appreciate the night of our arrival, for we entered the grounds at about 11:15. It was Christmas Eve, two hours after our landing in Tehran.

Moving slowly down a back street toward a rear entrance, our chauffeur-driven car lent us by our host, the Ministry of Foreign Affairs, was suddenly surrounded by what appeared to be teenagers. They were heavily armed with American tommy guns, and American pistols. Peering in at us, as they ran along beside us, they shouted at the driver where he was to turn in. Finally we all stopped outside a small building. There we were escorted into a small crowded office, while the driver and his car were escorted out of the compound. For hours he waited in the street. Make no mistake about it, the students not only took that turf, they own it. No one tells them what to do, except, perhaps, the Ayatollah. As the deeply religious Muslim students who worked with me into the early hours of the morning were to say, "His whisper is our command."

There were four of us visitors, for, unknown to us, the Foreign Ministry had also invited Cardinal Duval of Algiers. At 77, the Cardinal is a man of extraordinary dignity. During the Algerian war, he sided with the Algerians against the French. After independence was won, the Roman Catholic Church, to its credit, asked him to remain. The Algerians consider him one of theirs. In businesslike fashion we were told that we would receive our hostages four at a time, in three different places, each group for a period of twenty minutes. In friendly fashion, we replied that the conditions were unacceptable. They said they were dictated by considerations of security. We said ours were dictated by the integrity of the religious services we had been invited to perform, and which they were now preventing us from doing. They said, we said, they said, we went on for two tense hours. And we ended up where they began.

So I got up and said, "There's no hurry, we'll come back in the morning and pursue the discussion." Bishop Gumbleton got up, too. Thereupon His Eminence came running around the table with surprising alacrity, and whispered into my ear, "Mon cher pasteur, we are going to get nothing more." At that point, I also heard Bill Howard of the National Council of Churches, say to the chief "non-negotiator," "Brother, I hear you." I realized we were now two against two. Gumbleton and I acceded. And in retrospect, I think Cardinal Duval and Bill Howard were right. We might not have gotten back into the compound. As we later found out, it had taken the Ayatollah to get the students to accept our visit.

I was then escorted into a van whose windows were papered over, and driven to the steps of the living room of what I later found out was the residence of the ambassador. It was a room with a fine grand piano, and was now decorated with Christmas ribbons, cards, sayings of Jesus, some few of the Ayatollah; and in the center stood a table laden with Christmas cookies, brownies, apples, and oranges. These, I am sure, were there both for the American captives and for the camera which filmed everything we did.

Let me say a word here about my host for the occasion, the same chief non-negotiator. He was not only hostile, he was intelligent, self-disciplined, a Muslim certain of the righteousness of his cause, definitely a student, not only by virtue of his age (and they all qualified age-wise), but by virtue of having studied electronics in the United States. ("If you didn't want us to be independent, you shouldn't have educated us.") He reminded me of the American students who occupied buildings in the late 1960s, only he was clearer about his reason. He reminded me also of religious fundamentalists I have known.

When I said to him, "Look, if we're going to be together for the rest of the night, I want to have a name I can call you," he replied, "Call me 'Mohammed.'" And when I said to the second student with us, "And what shall I call you?" he answered, "Ali."

To my added annoyance, there were two TV cameras in the room. I managed to get one out, but the second I was told had to stay. "Then see that it stays in the far corner," I said. Mohammed agreed, but every time I went to the piano the camera crept forward to get close-ups of the men.

The first four who came into the room were clearly marines. They were big, their fatigues were clean, and their boots shined. The last looked morose, the first rather cheerful. I recognized him immediately as Gallegos, the man made famous by NBC, and, as I suspected at the time he talked on NBC, he seemed in good shape. You may remember that after his appearance, Hodding Carter of the State Department stated with certainty that the man was brainwashed. I'm not saying he wasn't. But I am questioning Carter's presumption that he could tell so clearly, and his right to mark a man so that when Gallegos returns to Pueblo, Colorado and walks down the main street, folk will say, "Aha! He's the one who was brainwashed." I also want to report that an Iranian official told me that had Hodding Carter not said what he said, we would have returned with three hostages, including Gallegos.

When I gave him a big hug; he returned it. So did the others, which seemed a good sign. When we sat down on the couch, Mohammed sat between two of them, Ali between the other two. Forced now to improvise a service, I said, passing out the Riverside Carol books, "All right, Gallegos, you choose the first Carol." So he chooses the one that should have come last—"Silent Night." But he chose it, and I played it on the piano, and three of them sang it; not the morose one. We did the second verse without accompaniment because the camera was beginning to encroach, and I wanted to get in front of them to see what they looked like as they sang. They seemed to be doing all right, except for the tight-lipped one who remained tight-lipped.

Then I suggested we read the Christmas Story. "We'll take the second chapter in Luke and take turns reading, OK?" "Fine" they said. So we passed the Bible around, and they all read well. Again a good sign.

Then I tried to cheer them up by telling them how awful the first Christmas was. "It was cold," I said, "dark, dank, and lonely. Joseph must have been tired, Mary exhausted. We read, 'There was no room for them in the inn,' but of course there was. There was all the room in the inn for them but no one would move over for a pregnant woman. So they ended up in a stable and he who was to be bread of life for human beings is laid in the feedbox of animals. It was a terrible Christmas. But you see what I'm getting at? God's love can change no place into some place, just as the love of God changes a man who feels like a nobody into a somebody." I said, "This is certainly not the most joyful Christmas of your life. But it just might be the most meaningful."

After a little more of that kind of talk, we all took hands, Mohammed and Ali too, and as we held hands we prayed. We prayed that we might all experience a moment of grace, a moment when, as always in the sight of God, there would be neither captive nor captor, neither American nor Iranian. We prayed that the Christ Child might find hearts wide enough to lodge in, that rather than rally round any flag we would be able to gather around the Holy Child, as members of one family.

It began to get really moving. The men were beginning to respond. I could see Mohammed trying to fight back the tears. He couldn't wipe them away, what with his hands being held by a couple of big marines. Needless to say, I too was prepared to weep a bit. After all, that's why God gave us tears—to wash away all the bitterness, anger, and sorrow from our hearts.

Then we sang a couple of Carols more. Then I had them write brief Christmas messages which I promised to deliver to their families. Mohammed hadn't expected this but he didn't protest. Finally they all helped themselves to the cookies and to the batches of mail piled up on the floor, mail from their fellow Americans all over the country. I assured them they were not forgotten, neither at home nor in heaven. And they left.

With some variations that's the way the services went. I saw a total of sixteen men. Bill Howard saw twenty-one, and Bishop Gumbleton and Cardinal Duval saw four men and two women. We all had much the same feeling, that physically the hostages are doing alright. They looked adequately fed, and reported an hour of exercise a day. Psychologically the strain has to be great, and will be borne differently by different people. As regards, for instance, the marines: it's tough when you're trained to guard, to find yourself guarded. It's tough, when you're used to being very physical, to find yourself with hands tied, albeit fairly wide apart. After explaining that their hands were no longer tied, Mohammed went on, "It was a matter of security. These fellows are big, twice the size of most of us. We were afraid initially that they might try to jump one of us, and get shot. And at that time, we hadn't sorted out the hotheads among us. Now, we have all the hotheads far from the hostages, and the hostages are now beginning to accept their lot. We're into a routine. So we can untie their hands. But we don't let them get together in a group. It's a matter of security."

Security seems to cut two ways. Not only are the students afraid the hostages might try something silly; Mohammed, at least, remembers the San Tay raid. (The abortive attempt to rescue POWs in North Vietnam.) He thought a military rescue mission was not out of the question. What was reassuring to us was the apparent seriousness of the students' concern for the safety of the Americans. "If any harm comes to any hostage we know we've failed." It was also reassuring to be in a situation so Muslim that there was no danger of any guard getting drunk.

Of the many vivid moments of that evening, the one I shall probably remember best was the one when Barry Rosen came in. His wife, who lives in Brooklyn, and small child were the last people I saw at the church before leaving for the airport. Said Barbara to Alexander, who's about three I guess, "Kiss Reverend Coffin, and he will kiss Daddy for you." So, I got smooched with a big wet kiss from Alex, which was enough to melt me. Twenty-four hours later, and 8,000 miles away, I suddenly see—and recognize from a photo—Barry Rosen. He's the last man in the third group, and does he ever look downcast. But when I say, "I'm going to give you a big kiss from Alexander," it's as if the Christmas tree outside the White House had suddenly turned on in that man's head. Never have I seen such illumination. And needless to say, I brought back some kisses too.

On Christmas Day we went to see the Chargé d'Affaires, the Security Officer, and the Political Officer, the three who were making a routine visit to the Ministry of Foreign Affairs when the students attacked the embassy. They never made it back, and now live in high level captivity on the top floor of the Ministry of Foreign Affairs. For exercise they wear out paths on the most expensive Persian rugs you've ever seen. On the windowsill is a phone with which they call Washington several times a day.

Bruce Laingen, the chargé, is a dear and decent man whose anguish is that of a captain separated from his crew. I'm sure he wouldn't mind if I used him to illustrate the depth of the dilemma we found in Tehran. After we had told him as much as we could about all of the people we had seen in the embassy, we tried talking a bit about the situation as a whole. It soon became apparent that this very sensitive and intelligent man, quite understandably, was so totally absorbed in the illegality and immorality of Iranian students taking his people hostage that he simply was not able to think about, even less, feel any wrongs that Iranians might be experiencing. And on the other side we found exactly the same thing. Both sides feel so wronged, that they can't conceive of having done any wrong themselves. It was reminiscent of unhappy divorces. It was a classic case of polarization. When I said to Mohammed that it was wrong to have hostages, his reply was, "What's fifty-two days in captivity compared to twenty-six years under the Shah."

The students weren't alone in their feelings. After meeting with the Foreign Minister, and at his suggestion, we met with the leading Muslim clergy of Tehran. This took place in a small room in a seminary. To a man, they were burning with anger against the Shah. One man had been eight years in jail. And when the oldest one there, in the middle of an impassioned speech, began to weep, I interrupted to ask the interpreter what he had just said. "He was beginning to tell you how his son was imprisoned, tortured, and executed." All I could do was to reach out and take his hand.

When we asked why they were so angry at Carter, as opposed to Kissinger and Nixon, who had upheld the Shah so much longer, they reminded us that Carter had said that he and the Shah saw eye to eye on human rights. They reminded us that Carter had interrupted his business with Begin and Sadat at Camp David to telephone his support to the Shah. This was in September of '78, on the very day when thousands of Iranians were being killed. American tanks were used to disperse crowds. American arms killed bare-handed Iranians. When we pointed to the irony of the situation, that Iranians, by taking hostages, are helping to reelect Carter, they simply couldn't hear us. We were back to St. Francis' prayer. But where such hatred exists, how do you sow love? Where there is such injury, who is able to pardon?

If we want to get our fellow Americans back soon I think we should forget about any "hard line." It will only stiffen resistance. I think we should, first of all, follow a path of reciprocal gestures. It wouldn't be difficult for somebody in the government to say, "We appreciate the gesture made to our people in allowing three clergy to celebrate Christmas services with the hostages. And we would like to reciprocate. We have decided not to deport any more Iranian students. Let them stay at their studies." And if the government can't say it, let the government just quietly do it. Then, were three hostages to be released, we could stop deporting civil servants working here for the Iranian government. Such gestures would help cool the situation.

Beyond that, we have to think realistically, Biblically, if you will. We have to face the fact that "the sins of the fathers are visited upon the sons and upon their children's children." We cannot pretend that history began yesterday, that life is not consequential, that we do not have to pay for our sins. Somewhere, somehow the just grievances of the Iranians have to be aired.

Unfortunately, there seems to be no real acceptance of this fact on the part of our government. When I asked Cyrus Vance, "Have you told the Secretary General of the UN that if the UN went ahead with a tribunal, you would make available documents going back to 1953, to the overthrow of Mossadegh?" he replied, "No." When I asked, "Has anybody asked Congress for a hearing?" the answer again was "No."

The government's position seems to be: "Until the hostages are released we won't do anything." Such a stance makes legal sense. But as psychiatrists would say, it is "true, but not helpful."

If unity means, "Don't question," then I think we'd better have a little less national unity. I think we should have a little more of that good old American national debate. Unity is no more patriotic than debate. And debate is healthier, because, properly understood, unity is based not on agreement, but on mutual concern. When all hearts are one, all minds don't have to be one. And if the government won't support a hearing then let the churches start one. We care only about saving lives. We don't care about saving face. We understand the cleansing power of confession, the need for atonement—at-one-ment. One Iranian official said to me, "Only you clergy are going to be able to solve this." I think I understood him. I think he meant that Cyrus Vance has nobody to talk to in Iran. The Foreign Minister has no power over the students. Only the Ayatollah does, a deeply Muslim person, advised by a revolutionary council made up also of Muslims. Only these religious people seem at this moment to have the power to change the situation. So why shouldn't religious people here do what they can to move religious people there? While nothing is guaranteed, this path seems to promise the most, if once again it is lives we want to save, not face.

Twenty-seven acres is a lot of ground in a city. There used to be 45,000 Americans in Iran, including several thousand military experts. It wasn't the soft line that got us into this mess. It was the hard line. We armed the Shah as we have armed few people in this world, and we supported him after his own subjects deserted him. I don't think a hard line is going to get us out of this mess. I think we need to think of humbler, more gracious ways.

And I think we have to pray. Prayer is an act of empathy, not an act of self-expression. Prayer is thinking God's thoughts after him—hard as that is. Prayer is really meaning, "Thy Will be done, not mine." Prayer is really meaning, "Thy Kingdom come, not mine." If both sides truly pray to the one God they both believe in, both sides will rise above their present condition.

1980

All One in Christ Jesus

A new year, a new decade, a second 50 years, if not for the church at least for the building—how can the preacher not talk of the future, and of what I would call its God-ordained surprises? Here's what I mean: any authentic surprise, say at the end of a good "Who-dunit," is one which makes you gasp, reflect, and exclaim: "Of course." Surprise, in other words, is the discovery of inevitability. The future is bound to be full of such surprises.

But first, let's say a few words about change itself. I think it help-ful to remember that change is not only, as we like to say, "inevitable"; more positively, it is the will of God, the will of Him who declares, "now I create new heavens and a new earth," of Her who announces, "Behold I make all things new." Of course, it's one thing to quote these grand words and another to believe them; or shall we say, it is one thing to believe them intellectually, and quite another emotion-ally to appropriate the knowledge. For emotionally, most of us human beings hate change. Even when we know it to be inevitable, still we resemble the caterpillar who said, looking up at the butterfly, "You'll never find me flying around in one of those crazy things" (which reminds me of the old Episcopal saying: "Be we high or low, the sta-tus is quo").

Yet, if God be a God of history, of a history that has a beginning, a middle, and end, a history moreover that is characterized by an Exo-dus, and proclaims a New Testament, which hails a new heaven and a new earth, which describes a new Jerusalem, anticipates a new song, a new wine, and promises that we shall all become "new beings"—if all that's true, then surely it's a sin to try to put the freeze on history, whether the history we seek to put on ice be our own personal one, or that of our church, our nation, or world. And we should be chang-ing right to the very end, for "though our outer nature is wasting away, our inner nature is being renewed each day." Death itself can be the greatest moment of spiritual transformation if we heed the

ALL ONE IN CHRIST JESUS 283

injunction: "Don't die with the others, die with Christ." Good Friday is not Bad Friday but Good Friday, from the vantage point of Easter which says that the abyss of love is deeper even than the abyss of death. "Yea, neither death nor life can separate us from the love of God which we see in Christ Jesus."

For those of us who try to be serious Biblical Christians, I think we can see change in this way: If there is no continuing revelation, there is always continuing implementation of a once-and-for-all revelation. The Bible will always be authoritative but what will be authoritative, say in the 1980s, will be the revelation given to the First Century Church, and not the stage of implementation which that revelation may, or may not, have reached in the first century.

Let us this morning consider one of the great gifts of life, the relationship of the sexes, something certain to be creative and troublesome in the eighties, as it has always been in the past. I would suggest that the revelation that sheds most light on the relationship is given in Galatians 3:28, which we just heard, in which Paul you remember says that in Christ all human divisions are overcome and a new unity is created. "There is neither Jew nor Greek, there is neither slave nor free, there is neither male nor female, for you are all one in Christ Jesus."

Reading such a passage, it should occur instantly to Biblical Christians to ask: "Is this new status, this new freedom, new unity, to be confined solely to the realm of the heart, or is it to be implemented outside as well—in the social sphere?" As regards this particular passage, St. Paul's own answer, as Krister Stendhal points out, is most interesting because most unclear. Regarding "neither Greek nor Jew" Paul sees clear implications for the social sphere. Earlier in the same letter to the Galatians, he insists Gentiles don't have to become Jews in order to become Christians. They don't have to be circumcised, they don't have to obey the Jewish law. Without fuss, the two—Jew and Gentile—should sit at table together for the two are one in Christ.

However, as regards "neither slave nor free," Paul, for whatever reason, seems decidedly less concerned about implementing the spiritual freedom in the social realm; and as regards "neither male nor female," not at all. In fact, quite the opposite. The author of First Timothy, if he be Paul, is the author of these words: "I permit no woman to teach or have authority over men. She is to keep silent, for Adam was formed first, then Eve." (Isn't it wonderful how selective Anita Bryant is in her choice of Pauline passages?)

What are we to say about the contradictory sentiments found in Galatians 3:28 and First Timothy 2:12–13, if not that one is pure revelation, the other more a matter of implementation? More than that, I think we have to say, once again, that "God moves in mysterious ways his wonders to perform." For a genuine spiritual revelation can point beyond, and even oppose, the person receiving it. A genuine spiritual revelation can point beyond and even oppose the prevailing practices of the church. (Caterpillars *do* become butterflies, no matter what caterpillars think!)

Who today would hold that the implications of "neither slave nor free" should be confined to an attitude of heart divorced totally from any social legislation? The whole world has abolished slavery as an institution—and rightly. And rightly not only the nations, but the churches, the entire world should seek now to implement in the social realm the revelation given St. Paul that in Christ there is neither male nor female. Here is one God-ordained surprise the future has in store for us: just as the emancipation of slaves leads inevitably to their full equality, so women's liberation will lead to their full ordination in all churches, including the Roman Catholic.

That it should take the Roman Catholic Church—not to mention the Orthodox and some other churches—so long to realize the implications of their own revelation; that so many problems presently tying up the Roman Catholic Church should be so related to the relationship of the sexes—the ordination of women, the celibacy of priests, the rights of homosexuals, and to some degree even contraception and abortion—surely all this says something to all of us.

What it says to us men is very simple: it says our pride-swollen faces have closed up our eyes. But what is morally true can be better understood in psychological terms. One thing we human beings have found out is that the subconscious has no digestive tract. What goes down has to come up again, and usually does so in the form of displaced violence. There is an intimate relation between inner repression and outer suppression. *Those who are themselves repressed become themselves repressive.* Those, for example, who repress in themselves the dark, angry side of their nature will perforce show more reverence for law and order than reverence for life when it comes to the lives of those in Attica. Those who repress the "feminine" side of their nature will perforce be anti-feminine, and probably anti-gay. So, as we enter the 1980s, I think we can safely say that the woman most in need of liberation is the woman in every man, and the man most in need of liberation is the man in every woman. And I think we can safely predict another God-ordained surprise: when at last, those two are freed, androgyny will replace misogyny, and God will be pleased. For not only is it a matter of grace transcending the order of creation—"in Christ there is neither male nor female" transcending "first Adam, then Eve"—it is a matter of creation itself. For not only is the Creator beyond "male" and "female," it would appear that a bit male and a bit female created She every man and every woman! And that's what makes the relationship between the sexes so creative—and troublesome.

I hope in the coming decade the churches can also be more honest, and hence more helpful, in addressing the related subjects of sex and homosexuality. Progress has been made, but not enough. Too many Christians, for example, still say, "Homosexuals are promiscuous," which is a terrible thing to say, first of all because it's not true of all, and second, because that's more a comment on the wrongness of promiscuity than any statement at all about homosexuality itself. I also think it terrible that straight Christians read so little of what has been written by thoughtful and faithful scholars. And I would recommend, as a start, John McNeill's *The Church and the Homosexual,* which is out in paperback. Among other things, this Jesuit scholar points out that the tender, loving homosexual relations that patently exist—for those who have eyes to see—these relations simply are not addressed in the Bible, which also says nothing about lesbianism, which itself is very instructive. But most of all, I think it wrong that Christians should object to gays and lesbians coming out of the closet without recognizing that their deeper objection is to the fact that sex, once again, is coming out of the closet. I hope American Christians in the 1980s will become less Victorian, and more Elizabethan, less repressed, more irrepressible. And it would help if from our pulpits we heard more Gospel and less law, more about the virtue of love than about the virtue of abstention and chastity.

Like teetotaling, chastity is absolutely right for certain ages, and even for many people. Love on the other hand is indispensable for everyone, at all times, and in all places. Chastity is a matter of law, love is a matter of grace. And what law-abiding, as opposed to love-abiding, Christians must realize is that much chastity goes unaccompanied by love. It is not possible to interpret Jesus' parable about the virgins without oil in their lamps as an illustration of people more interested in being chaste than in being loving; an illustration of people fearful of that self-abandonment so necessary to self-fulfillment?

In any case, the guiding revelation in matters of sex and homosexuality seems clear. It comes on almost every page of the New Testament: "Though I speak with the tongue of men and angels—though I have all faith to remove mountains—and though I give my body to be burned"—and shall we add though I keep my body from any contact with any other human being—"but have not love—it profiteth me nothing." That's probably the most radical statement of Christian ethics in the New Testament. But there are others like it: "We pass out of death into life because we love the brothers" (and sisters) (1 John 3:14), and "God is love, and he who abides in love abides in God and God abides in him" (1 John 4:16).

The implementation of the revelation is, as always, less clear. But never mind. The ultimate destination is never as important as the right direction. And the 1980 signposts pointing down the straight and narrow way—as opposed to the broad way that leads to destruction—all read the same: "it is the inner worth and not the outer appearance of a relationship that determines its nature and quality." There may even be a signpost big enough to contain these words of the theologian Helmut Thielicke: "The primary moral problem is not sex within marriage versus sex outside of marriage, or sex within a heterosexual versus sex within a homosexual relationship. The problem is sex as a depersonalizing force versus sex as fulfillment of a human relationship." In answering that question in the 1980s, straight Christians will not only have to keep open their minds and hearts, read and study these things; they will have also to remember that the better part of the answer will have to come from Christian gays and lesbians themselves.

Dear sisters and brothers, already in the first month of this decade, the world is proving "too dangerous for anything but truth, too small for anything but love." And that means that if our personal beliefs about what is right and wrong separate us further from one another, then there must be something wrong about what we believe is right. Let me suggest that beliefs that keep us on the grain of love are truthful. Let me suggest that beliefs that keep us on the grain of human suffering are truthful. And the two are related, for those who see pain and remain unmoved are sure to inflict it.

I have talked a lot this morning about change. But there is also continuity. In fact, life is probably as T. S. Eliot once described it, the rediscovery of "that which has been lost, and found, and lost, again and again." That we are all one—all of us—in Christ Jesus, is surely a first-century revelation that we must never lose sight of, and one which, as never before, we must now seek to implement.

"Judge Not That You Be Not Judged"

JANUARY 27, 1980
Readings: Matthew 7:1–5; Hebrews 12:1–3

In the mid-fifties, at the start of the space age, the Soviets sent into orbit a dog named Laika; and, as the problem of reentry had yet to be solved, in about a week's time the dog died. The British, who seem to feel more strongly than most of us that such things shouldn't happen to animals, stormed the Soviet embassy in London with the fury of contemporary Iranian students. Others saw symbolic importance in the event. It so happened that day I was in the home of Professor Michael Karpovich, the great Russian historian of Harvard. The phone rang and someone must have asked "Mikhail Mikhailovich, how are you?" because I heard him respond, "All right, as well as can be expected in a world surrounded by a dead dog."

Well, how do you feel, twenty-five years later? It has been an emotionally strenuous week, hasn't it? I think it's good that many of us are scared. And I think it's good to remember that many of *them* are scared too. Last September, in the Soviet Union, some Russians told me they had solved the problem of a nuclear attack. "Find a white sheet, wrap it around yourself, and crawl slowly to the nearest cemetery."

"Why slowly?"

"So as not to create panic."

As I say, it's a good sign that they and we are scared. But are we scared to death, or are we scared to life? That's a question to which we shall have to return.

Less healthy than this feeling of fear is another I have observed this week. Watching it has reminded me of a comment I read this summer in Freeman Dyson's excellent book, *Disturbing the Universe.* Dyson, a physicist, recalls Robert Oppenheimer's famous "confession" published in *Time* Magazine in 1948, three years after the explosion of the first atom bomb whose production Oppenheimer had directed at Los Alamos. "In some sort of crude sense," wrote Oppenheimer, "which no vulgarity, no humor, no overstatement can quite extinguish, the physicists have known sin." Instantly, most of his former colleagues indignantly repudiated the confession. They had only done a necessary job, they insisted, one morally justified in a desperate war against Hitler's Germany and Hirohito's Japan. But, as Dyson comments, "They did not just build the bomb; they enjoyed building it. They had the best time of their lives while building it . . . That, I believe, is what Oppy had in mind when he said they had sinned. And he was right."

When President Carter this Wednesday evening was talking his tough military talk, I thought too many of his Congressional listeners, generals, and others were enjoying it. That bothered me, because I only trust sad soldiers, as I only trust sad revolutionaries. Happy ones are always out to get someone. And many of the President's listeners seemed eager to "get" the Soviets. The only ones I trust are the ones whose hearts are more full of compassion for the people of Afghanistan than of anger against the Soviets.

Also dangerous is a new view of ourselves, that we are being encouraged to enjoy, a view which says, "You don't have to examine yourself any more, America—your mind, heart and backbone—all those things which your preachers, and intellectuals have been talking to you about at least since the end of the war in Vietnam. No, it's all over. You are healthy. *They* are the ones who are sick. Five Soviet divisions crossing the Afghan border have restored you to perfect spiritual health."

"Judge not that you may not be judged." That suggests guilt. But, it's not guilt, it's *lessons* that God so wants his creatures to learn from history. Nonetheless, most of God's lessons are based on Augustine's insight that it is a mistake to fight evil as if it were something that arose totally outside of yourself. Not only the physicists, all of us have known sin. If not in love, all of us are one at least in sin, which precludes the possibility of separation through judgment. Therefore, "judge not that you be not judged" "Love your enemy"—yes, in part because you made him so.

Should we feel any sense of complicity in the very invasion we deplore? There is no question that the Soviets' invasion of Afghanistan was, still is, and always will be, a terrible thing. But the question we have to ask ourselves is, "Did we help them reach that decision?" Last week, after the service, Eqbal Ahmed pointed out that for years the Soviet government never allowed our American misdeeds in the Third World to interfere with détente. Even as we mined the Haiphong Harbor, even as we increased our bombing of North Vietnam, the Soviets allowed President Nixon to come to Moscow to talk of arms control. In contrast, over the last nine months, we have used their shenanigans in the Third World—even inventing a few, like their combat troops in Cuba (whatever happened to those combat troops?)—as a pretext to undermine détente. We raised the military budget five percent over inflation; we passed the MX as well as the Trident; we made it quite clear to them that we were not about to sign SALT II; and finally, ignoring their offer to negotiate and their removal of 20,000 troops and 1,000 tanks from East Germany, we went ahead and pushed hard so that NATO agreed to place in Europe 600 nuclear strategic missiles which the Soviets call "the '62 Cuban missile crisis in reverse."

Surely our undermining of détente must have helped saw off the limb on which their doves were precariously perched. Their hawks must have argued, "How can you urge détente when the Americans don't want it? And we don't want ayatollahs screaming across our 100-mile border with Afghanistan. It's bad enough that they scream across one thousand, two hundred and fifty miles in Iran. Our thirty million Muslims don't need to hear them. So we're going in."

"Judge not that you be not judged." Find your complicity in the very evil you abhor. Love your enemy, in part because you made him so. If you have to be a soldier, be a sad one.

The line that follows is more difficult: "And the measure you give will be the measure you get." That's hard to accept when we know the unmerited good as well as evil in this world. Yet it does seem to be the case, in the long if not in the short run, that life gives back what we pour into it. Those who consider the world unfriendly are apt themselves to be pretty unfriendly. When people know we love them, it's harder for them to hate us. And we know that if we say "The only thing the other side understands is force," then we shall have to act as if the only thing *we* understand is force.

We are told that we have been soft on Communists, the way we once were on Hitler. I think that's wrong. I don't think we have ever been soft on Communists, certainly not since the late forties, either at home or abroad. And I think it's not the soft but the hard, i.e., callous line that begets the callous line, that begets one crisis after another. It was the hard line that armed the Shah. It was the hard line that admitted the Shah to this country, despite warning telegrams from our own embassy, despite reports from the CIA. It was the hard line for thirteen days thereafter—before the students occupied the embassy—that made us deaf to the cries of one million Iranians demonstrating on the streets of Tehran, and deaf to the cries of Iranian students occupying our own Statue of Liberty (how quickly we forget!). And it's the hard line now that has us shopping for new dictators to arm, that terms restraint "unpatriotic," and all other approaches "Utopian." If one day we return God's creation to him in ashes, it will be because we marched towards annihilation under the banner of realism. And maybe we'll have deserved it, for "the measure you give will be the measure you get."

The Roman Catholic Church, whose glories we today celebrate, has given us a great insight. The first of the cardinal virtues is "*pruden-*

tia" or "*providentia*," which really means "darn good thinking." It means that if your heart is full of love, your head will be clear. It means that if your heart is not full of love, while you may be very clever you'll never be wise, because wisdom is rooted in compassion. And if your heart is set on power, you will be blinded by that power.

I find it very interesting that the two Goliaths of the world were totally taken by surprise by the discovery of a militant Islam. The Goliaths of the world don't know how to cope with the Davids. They don't think about slings. They don't even see them, until it's too late. The Goliaths never say, "I wonder what the kid's got in the bag." Today both Goliaths have been stunned. And what is so dangerous is not some Kremlin grand design, but the fact that the two giants of the world are stumbling around in a small area in the middle of which is a land mine they know about because they put it there.

Today we plead and pray for Christian unity throughout the world. I hope that in the 1980s Christians will unite to speak truth to power. I hope in the 1980s Christians will continue to remind our travailing world that there are two overriding imperatives. The first is to disarm the planet. And the second imperative is to feed the hungry, clothe the naked, house the homeless, find jobs for the unemployed, heal the sick.

The latter part of this week I kept remembering that 50 percent of all of God's children in this world in all their lifetime never so much as open their mouths to say "aaah" to a doctor. And I kept remembering that for black men born in the City of New York, the odds are that one out of twenty will be murdered. National security has become a matter of domestic politics. I hope Christians in the 1980s will unite to tell all citizens that it is just as patriotic to keep your country from dying, as it is to die for your country.

When that courageous man Andrei Sakharov was exiled this week to Gorky, I thought of these words his compatriot Alexander Pushkin once penned about himself:

> And long will I be lovingly remembered
> Because my poems kindled kindness,
> Because amid the cruelties of my century
> I called for freedom
> And sought compassion for the fallen victims.

For us to do the same, would be to honor Sakharov. For us to do the same would be to honor the memory of Justice Douglas. And for us to do the same would prove that we are not scared to death, but scared to life.

This world is surrounded not only by a dead dog; we are also surrounded by a cloud of witnesses, from churches and faiths the world around, who have shown us how with perseverance to run the race that is set before us. One of them, a Quaker, William Penn, wrote this:

> Love and persuasion have more force
> Than weapons of war.
> Nor would the worst of men
> Easily be brought to hurt those
> That they really think love them.
> It is that love and patience
> Which must in the end have victory.

As Christians, let us seek no other victories than that victory of love and patience which we see in Jesus, "the author and finisher of our faith." Rather than joining the bandwagons of renewed militarism and self-righteousness, let us rather "consider him who endured from sinners such hostility against himself, so that (we) may not grow weary or fainthearted."

Beating the Blues

FEBRUARY 3, 1980

"A cheerful heart is a good medicine, but a downcast spirit dries up the bones."

Proverbs 17:22

According to the Rev. Dr. Eugene E. Laubach, and he has been around long enough to know whereof he speaks, early February is when Riversiders get the blues. At Christmas, and as recently as Epiphany, they were on tiptoes of expectation. Now, however, they are simply standing around, flat-footed, wondering if there is somewhere for their feet to go, somewhere with a purpose for going.

If that is so, and if misery loves company, Riversiders, rejoice! You are one with many. For this is the time of year when the climate alone can cool the cockles of the heart. This is the time of the year when life seems to throw more stones, and it isn't easy to pick them up and build an altar, even though we know that what is worst for our morale is often best for our character. This is the time of year when children complain, "Why are all the vitamins in the spinach and not in the ice cream?" This is the time of year when their fathers and mothers recall G. B. (George Bernard) Shaw's definition of love: "a gross exaggeration of the difference between one person and everybody else." Yes, it was at this time of year that a shivering old New Yorker crept out of the cold and into the warmth of a "greasy spoon," there to be met by a big ugly waiter with a filthy apron. "OK, Mac, what's yours?"

"Two fried eggs, and a few kind words?"

Soon the big ugly waiter was back, slapped the eggs down on the table and started off.

"Friend, you forgot, the few kind words."

"Oh, yeah—Don't eat dem eggs!"

So what to do, when hope looks more like a candle about to burn out than a beacon blazing across the sky? What to do to beat the blues?

Of course we can pray for an encounter with God, for so overwhelming is that experience that Moses, you remember, took off his shoes, Elijah covered his face, Isaiah fell apart and broke into confession, while Peter dropped to his knees. But that might be to tempt the Lord. Besides, even for the prophets and saints such encounters are rare, and it's probably for the best;

> Go, go, go, said the bird: human kind
> Cannot bear very much reality.
>   T. S. Eliot

We can, of course, pray, and, even in New York City experience daily "the earth with its store of wonders untold." Living in the neighborhood, I spend a fair amount of time observing gulls. Some of the time, I confess, mostly when they are in the water, fighting and hollering at each other, they openly deepen my depression, reminding me of certain meetings I attend, and also from whence cometh the expression, "bird-brained"! But they have only to take off into the air and start gliding, diving, hovering, and I find myself talking to their Creator and mine, "O God, if only we humans could be who we are so effortlessly."

"Thy bountiful care, what tongue can recite; it breathes in the air, it shines in the light." "The world," said Chesterton, "does not lack for wonders, only for a sense of wonder." Human beings too, for all their gaucheries and downright wickedness, still are wondrous. Of course, if your desire is to control others they will appear smaller than they really are. But if you simply *wonder* at human beings—and the lonely among you can do this better than those who are too busy—wonder about their sensibilities, subtleties, and surprises, human beings will appear bigger than life. I never cease wondering at the courage that persists amid the fury of disease and pain. I never cease wondering at the way the human spirit survives in this city, despite poverty and persecution, insult and injury. My mind boggles at the amount of time, energy, imagination it took to build the place. I never cease wondering at New York!

Aristotle was right: we should approach the world with wonder; and then with doubt. If you are in the throes of the blues, see if you haven't gotten the order reversed. So if you aren't approaching the world with doubt first. Your sense of wonder would then be atrophying.

"The world does not lack for wonders, only for a sense of wonder." Kierkegaard said much the same: "The greatest miracles in this world take place there where people say 'I don't see anything so miraculous about that.'"

So for those trying to beat the blues, I have a very simple wish: between today and next Sunday have a "wonder-full" week.

If a sense of wonder can do wonders, so can anger. Of course depression and boredom are both linked to anger, but to anger that is repressed. So lethal is repressed anger that I want to pass on to you some good advice given me years ago: "Remember," said this friend, "a thought-murder a day keeps the psychiatrist away." She was drawing a very important line, the line between feelings and behavior. All feelings are valid; all behavior isn't. And her words reminded me of those of St. Paul: "Be angry, but do not sin." Actually, if we're never angry we probably *are* sinning. After all, Jesus was mad a great deal of the time, and for good reason. The world does not lack for things to be angry at; only for lack of anger! Jesus never tolerated the intolerable, and neither should we. In fact, I think anger is not only a good counter to depression; I am convinced that given the massive immoralities in which we are immersed, only a moral passion akin to Christ's can save our sanity.

Some years ago, an overly polite father, who had never been able to get near to his son, one day reported he and his son had ended up rolling all over the floor in a fight. He was horrified, but I confess I rather rejoiced. To be sure, that's not the best way for a father to get in touch with his son. But it *is* contact. And as every Black in this church knows, courtesy can be a barrier more devastating than a blow. (I dare say all of us have a few acquaintances with impeccable and very tiring manners.)

Some people are afraid of being angry for fear of losing friends. Well, isn't it better to be hated for what we are than loved for what we are not? Isn't a true friend one who risks friendship for the sake of his friend?

Thoreau was a great American because he never trimmed the truth. Like Jesus, he never tolerated intolerable hypocrisy. Jesus said, "Woe to you, scribes, pharisees, hypocrites." Thoreau said, "For every virtuous person there are 999 patrons of virtue." Jesus said, "Not all who say 'Lord, Lord' shall enter the kingdom of heaven." Thoreau wrote of the New Testament: "Most people favor it outwardly, defend it with bigotry, and hardly ever read it."

Unheeded and unpopular in his time, Thoreau is today honored because he put something of substance into the mainstream of American history that sustains us over a hundred years later. Like Jesus he never repressed his anger, but he did keep it focused. Like Jesus, he was willing to risk his friendships for the sake of his friends.

So, all of you who are trying to beat the blues: have not only a wonder-full week; have a feisty one. "Be angry, but do not sin."

Most of all, start loving someone. You know how it is, when psychologically you are on dead center, you cannot move. In moments like that, it's very important that you do something, if only to clean up your room. Well, when you're depressed you've got to start loving someone, you've got to do something for others. Visit someone in the hospital, write a fan letter, take someone to the movies, contribute to Cambodia relief, write to a Congressman today about hunger in America. Of course it won't save the world, but that's not your business; that's God's. Ultimately, we are not called upon to be effective. Ultimately, we are called on to do what's right; only penultimately, to be effective. How do we get *that* order also reversed! Imagine Socrates, as they handed him the hemlock, saying, "Wait a minute, boys, is Plato going to write me up?" Imagine Nathan Hale, just before his execution, saying, "Wait a minute, boys, are the 13 colonies going to win this war? And then, in this new country is every kid going to memorize the famous last words I am now about to utter?"

I know how easy it is to get depressed because the world seems to be going down the drain with a loud gurgle, and there doesn't seem to be anything any of us can do about it. Half of the time when I stand up in public and plead for a disarmed planet, I feel like Rocinante, a tired hack of a horse being ridden by a Quixotic idea. But who knows? Only God knows how effective any one of us is going to be in anything we do. But we do know that love is a necessity as well as a command. We know that love is like the loaves and fishes: there is never enough until we start sharing. And of Jesus Christ, our Lord and Savior, we know that "all the armies that ever marched, and all the navies that ever were built. . . . and all the kings that ever reigned, put together, have not affected the life of (humankind) as powerfully as has that One Solitary Life" (J. A. Francis).

That thought snaps me right out of it. It's enough to make me want to say again, "Bless the Lord, all his works, in all places of his dominion. Bless the Lord, O my soul."

Riversiders, have a wonderful, feisty, and loving week! God bless you.

To Savor *and* Save

FEBRUARY 17, 1980
Reading: John 2:1–16

To start us off, let me give you a quote which is lovely, and not surprisingly so, seeing it comes from the pen of E. B. White: "If the world were merely seductive, that would be easy. If it were merely challenging, that would be no problem. But I arise in the morning torn between a desire to improve (or save) the world, and a desire to enjoy (or savor) the world. This makes it hard to plan the day."

In the coming week it may get even more difficult to plan our days, torn as we shall be between those desires represented by Mardi Gras and Ash Wednesday. On Tuesday, we shall be encouraged to eat, drink, and be merry, for on Wednesday, and the 39 days thereafter, life is going to be grim. Conventionally conceived, that's the way the days ahead look: Tuesday we're gluttonous pigs, Wednesday abstemious prigs.

There must be something wrong with a view that encourages the notion that secular holidays are fun, while most things religious are anything but. As the small boy said, "Religion is what you don't do." To be sure, Ash Wednesday and Lent point to the cross and all the events leading to Christ's death. But do this, if you will: Think of some dear relative or friend whose death has left you with a great sense of loss. Now ask yourself, "Is the only way to hold that person close by grief?" and "Would that person want to be held close by grief?"

I certainly hope no one remembers me by grief, at least not by grief alone. And I don't think Jesus, who is not a memory but a presence, wants to be greeted daily in sorrowful fashion, not the Jesus who, in the Gospel of John, first visits human beings in their joy, at a wedding feast at Cana. Far from a grim do-gooder, Jesus is the life of the party. In fact, he saves the party. Think of that: Jesus not only saves individuals, he saves parties! In fact, nowhere in Scripture is there any indication that he ever turned down an invitation.

Too many of us I think have a picture of Jesus more suitable to John the Baptist, a great but grim man. You'd never catch him at a noisy reception like this. In fact, he'd ruin it. John drew the line at locusts and honey. John, really, was the patron saint of so many of our Puritan forebears, who, as I had reason to note this week in Connecticut, craved no recreation other than that of carving out of any unyielding wilderness towns by the name of Goshen, Canaan, Dan(bury), Bethel, and Bethany.

I'd like this morning to suggest to you that an accurate, if not adequate, description of our lives would be a party, a great big party at which the wine would run out were it not for Jesus who is always there to refill our cup.

By the looks of some of you, I see that the suggestion is going over real well! Well, Saint Teresa said, "There is a time for partridge and a time for penance." She knew that our Savior both saved *and* savored the world. She knew that in a world full of poor and hungry people, he was considered a glutton and a drunkard—something to think about. Teresa knew that "Joy is the serious business of heaven." The Hassidim in Brooklyn would also know what I am talking about, for in their tradition there is a stated commitment to "joy in the world as it is, in life as it is, in every hour of life in this world, as that hour is."

Isn't it a joy, simply to watch the Olympics? How many crazy wonderful things can human beings think up to do with their bodies? Isn't it a joy to watch the city blanketed in snow? And what about the prospect of the hostages returning soon? And having a neighbor with whom to walk and talk, and love and laugh, and learn that in giving is taking and all is grace? Every opening hymn of every church service is a hymn of gratitude, for the simple reason that life is basically something for nothing, a gift. Why not, then, a party?

Do you feel as if the wine has run out of your life? If so, I know how you feel. But perhaps you can do something about it. Maybe it's because you are engaging in unproductive nostalgia. Simone Signoret once said, "The art of life is to have a good memory and no nostalgia." Maybe it is because you feel you are a flop at forty. Forget it. Christ can take your defeat and turn it into the occasion for the victory God always had in mind for you. Maybe the wine has gone out of your life because on the contrary you are a success American-style—fed up at forty. If so isn't Jesus just the person to give you better wine?

Or, maybe you have forgotten that it takes more than one person to make a party. Alone with yourself you're in bad company! And if you think the world is unfriendly, it certainly is. But isn't that all the more reason not to be unfriendly oneself? And, finally, who or what is going to determine the joy or sorrow in your life? I haven't had many inspired moments, but years ago I had one. I had been arrested for aiding and abetting the draft resisters and was sentenced to two years in jail. I happened to be at the Yale Law School at a time when Ramsey Clark, who was still Attorney General, was standing in a reception line. (It was a little unfair, as he didn't know what was coming.) The dean, with a certain malice, said "And now, Mr. Attorney General, we present to you our beloved Chaplain." I saw Clark's lower jaw drop to his belt-buckle, and taking his right hand in both of mine, I said, "Mr. Attorney General, believe me, there are no hard feelings." "Well," he said, "I'm glad you can smile." And then the Lord spoke to me. I heard myself say, "Mr. Attorney General, would you hand over your high morale to the United States Government?"

Whose party is this? I stand by the suggestion that in a very fundamental way, life is a party at which Jesus makes sure the wine never runs out.

But to savor the world without at the same time trying to save it would surely be boring, more boring, even, than trying to save the world without savoring it. And life being what it is, if we don't make a difference by trying, we'll make a difference by not trying.

It is interesting how in this second chapter of John's Gospel the second story follows hard on the first. Right after being the life of the party, Jesus becomes the scourge of the temple crowd who have made of God's house a house of trade. And notice how unsentimental Jesus is. He knows that you can't help the powerless without directly challenging the powerful. You can't succor the poor without taking on the rich. Most of us, of course, prefer the risk-free sentimental route of helping the poor and powerless while avoiding any confrontation with those who make and keep them that way. Jesus savors *and* saves. He fills the cup of life, then strikes a blow, as it were, for the improvement of that life. I think we should do the same. I hope at the very least all of us before sundown will send President Carter a cable urging him to express regret over some past American actions in Iran, in part because to do so would bring home our hostages more rapidly, and in greater part because it is right so to do.

The playwright, Harold Pinter, once pointed out that what poisons life is not what's known and spoken, but what's known and unspoken. That's so true in our personal lives, isn't it? And in our public life, too. For instance, everyone now knows that the war in Vietnam was a mistake, and that we extricated ourselves from that war as callously as we waged it. Yet no American president, no national figure, has ever faced the American public on television and said, "My fellow Americans, we erred." Among other things, we waged the war with a chemical called "Agent Orange" which is now producing cancer in the American soldiers who used it. Can you imagine what Agent Orange has done to Vietnamese? Yet, once again, no one has said, "My fellow Americans, we must never do this again." Confession is good for the soul. But, we are told that to express regret will reduce our credibility. When that which we are being asked to regret is already in everybody's mind regrettable, how can that reduce credibility? And, furthermore, who is to express regret (note, I don't even talk of confession now) if not the most powerful nation in the world? I just don't understand how any diplomat worth his pinstripes can't understand that.

Mardi Gras and Ash Wednesday don't have to be poles apart. In fact, in a very profound way, they can merge. In the twelfth chapter of Hebrews, we read "Looking to Jesus the pioneer and perfecter of our faith who *for the joy* that was set before him, endured the cross . . ." For the joy that was set before him, he endured the cross. What finally makes life joyful? It's not the Olympics, it's not this beautiful snow-covered city; it's not even the glories of Bach and one another's company. It's not even the absence of pain. It's the presence of God, a sense of purpose so much larger than our lives alone could possibly provide. It's not the results that give satisfaction in this world so much as the sense of undeserved integrity that comes from being in the right fight. "Who for the joy that was set before him endured the cross." "I arise in the morning torn between a desire to improve (or save) the world, and a desire to enjoy (or savor) the world." Both are possible, if, for Lent, we gave up all indifference. And let me suggest that on Ash Wednesday, we meditate on how Christ indeed saved the best wine to the end, to the very end. "This is my blood which is shed for you." The cup of life poured out to fill the cup of each of us.

Nonconformity

FEBRUARY 24, 1980

"Do not be conformed to this world."

Romans 12:2a

"And all the multitudes who assembled to see the sight,
when they saw what had taken place, returned home
beating their breasts."

Luke 23:48

Six years ago, I was asked to tape and then publish in *Harpers* magazine a discussion with Jeb Stuart Magruder, at the time a Watergate defendant, and, 17 years earlier, a student of mine at Williams College, where I taught him Social Ethics! I suggested that the conversation could only be improved by the voice and thoughts of that great radio interviewer and author, Studs Terkel. "Studs," I said, "you'll see. It will be Hannah Arendt's 'banality of evil'—American style."

"No, no," he shot back, his hoarse voice rising over the phone, "what we'll see is the evil of banality."

As you can see I've never forgotten that line, which reminded me of another, equally shattering, a self-appraisal offered by a Peter De Vries character: "Deep down, I'm shallow." And I recalled, as well, Thomas Merton's insight, that it is always the individual conscience, as opposed to the mass mind, that best reflects the universal conscience of humanity. For the mass mind is always shallow. The mass mind is always banal. The mass mind always conforms to this world, because it reflects the mentality of those who have a greater sense of themselves when they are with others than when alone. This was fundamentally Magruder's problem, as he himself admitted.

Some people think that to do something truly evil, you have to be some kind of Bengal tiger. In fact, it is enough to be a tame tabby, a nicely packaged citizen, safe, polite, obedient and sterile. It's enough to be a nice guy, as opposed to a good man.

In this Lenten season, it is appropriate to ask, "Who killed Jesus?" And if we are to believe a late sermon of Harry Emerson Fosdick (and I can rarely find reason not to believe anything Harry Emerson Fosdick wrote), it was the combined forces of organized religion, organized business, and organized politics, organized—all three of them—in much the same way as they are organized today. That's a terrifying thought, and one to make you wonder if there isn't something evil with organization in and of itself. If bigness is a problem, therefore "small is beautiful"—maybe organization in and of itself aids and abets the mass mind.

I must confess, as I see masses of people drifting toward cheap military solutions to what are difficult political and economic problems, I find myself leaning more and more toward the political philosophy of anarchism. For sure, anarchism could never put a man on the moon. But it may be the only way to survive on earth. For sure, anarchists tend to be cranks. But as E. B. Schumacher wrote: "I would like to be known as a crank, because it is part of a small hand-operated machine which causes a revolution."

Clearly individuals cannot do great evil without the masses aiding and abetting. Listen again to Luke's description of the Good Friday scene: "And all the multitudes who assembled to see the sight. . . ." Luke doesn't say they came to cheer it, but Luke also doesn't say they came to protest it. They came to see—and went along. There's the shallowness of the mass mind conforming to this world. There's the evil of banality.

But at least on Good Friday their eyes were opened, for Luke goes on, "when they saw what had taken place, (they) returned home beating their breasts." Albeit too late, they saw their own part in the very crucifixion they deplored.

In these days of ABSCAM, we pretend to be mortally shocked that our elected representatives have been videotaped with the goods.[*] "Baloney," writes Meg Greenfield in the latest *Newsweek*, "we love it. Nothing so reinforces the scapegoating instinct in us as this. Nothing does more to bolster the pernicious idea that our economic and social troubles are due to the larceny of a few elected officials, as distinct from being largely the predictable consequences of our society's own actions and choices."

Good for you, Meg! And she might have added, that it is generally the listless who elect the lawless.

My dear fellow Christians, in this season of penance, of rugged honesty, let us put aside self-righteousness and self-pity which clings so closely, and recognize that to a degree far greater than that to which we would gladly admit, we get what we deserve in this world, both in our personal lives and in our public life. In this season of George Washington's birthday, let us recall that when we got started as a nation, we had only three million people, less than half the inhabitants of this city. Yet we turned out a generation of statesmen named Washington, Hamilton, Jefferson, Franklin, Adams—I could name a list as long as my arm. Today we are a population seventy times as great. But how many of those presently campaigning in New Hampshire would you say are of the caliber of that first generation of statesmen? And why are there not more? Because, as Plato said, "What's honored in a country will be cultivated there." We Americans have fantastic basketball players!

It may be hard for middle class folk to identify with the multitudes. But a multitude can be middle class as well as proletarian. Yes, a multitude can be a congregation of hymn-singing Americans just as it can

---

[*]ABSCAM was an FBI public corruption investigation in the late 1970s and early 1980s that led to the conviction of numerous national and state officials.

be a mob of Iranians shouting slogans on the streets. The multitudes around the Cross represent any group in which individual members have lost their capacity to judge individually, to act freely. And respectability and good manners and efficiency can be hallmarks of the herd mentality just as easily as bad manners and inefficiency. (Those among you who are public school teachers know that one reason it is so hard to teach the slow track is because, with little to lose, students are uncomfortably honest, while those in the advanced track, eager to succeed, will do almost anything to please.)

Lent warns against the herd mentality, the mass mind. Lent reminds us that human unity is based on mutual concern, never agreement. When all hearts are one, nothing else has to be one. But when agreement replaces mutual concern, when we start agreeing our way through life, "Look out!" For then "play it safe," "don't climb out on a limb," "don't rock the boat," these slogans become, as it were, the eleventh commandment on which are "hanged" all the law and the prophets! This is the commandment that drops the mask of dissimulation over the face of truth, the commandment that makes us turn our backs on screams in the night, makes us turn the other cheek—in order not to see the evil, that makes us hide behind our specialities pleading insufficient knowledge, and makes us collaborators in the very evil we deplore.

Here are some bitter but true words full of Good Friday overtones: "Don't be afraid of your enemies; the most they can do is kill you. Don't be afraid of your friends, the most they can do is betray you. Those you should be afraid of are the indifferent. They are neither friends nor foes, they neither kill nor betray, but because of their indifference there are so many killings and so many betrayals."

Those are the last written words of a Polish deportee in a concentration camp in World War II.

Now, however, we must be careful. I said that, albeit too late, the multitudes on Good Friday saw their complicity in Christ's crucifixion. They went home, as Luke says, "beating their breasts." Come to think of it, that's not a very constructive reaction.

In a dramatic moment in Arthur Miller's *Incident at Vichy*, Dr. Leduc, a Jewish psychiatrist, forces Prince Von Berg to recognize his complicity with the very forces of Nazism he deplores. He makes him see how he "went along." But the moment is as charged with danger as with drama. For now the Prince's concern begins to move away from the plight of the Jews in the police station about to be deported and sent to virtual death in concentration camps—away from their plight to his own, to feelings of remorse that are beginning to flood his soul. Sensing the movement of withdrawal, Leduc turns on him and says fiercely, "It's not your guilt I want, it's your responsibility."

The banality of guilt is that it is such a convenient substitute for responsibility. It's so much easier to beat your breast than to stick your neck out. Of course we must not repress but confess our guilt, particularly in this season, even momentarily be overwhelmed by it. But Christ will die in vain if his crucifixion doesn't bring home to each of us the message that there is more mercy in him than sin in us. That's the essential message of Lent. And more and more I am convinced the essential problem of the church is not to convict people of their sin; it is to persuade them of their forgiveness.

"Father, forgive them." Christians are not sinners; they are forgiven sinners. We are not permanently defeated folk whose contrite hearts have drained all the iron out of our spines. Rather, Christians are those who are rendered zealous by their forgiveness to translate their guilt into responsibility.

At the end of Miller's play von Berg succeeds in doing just this— translating his guilt into responsibility. As a Gentile he is given a pass by the police. But he slips the pass to Leduc, who escapes to freedom. As the curtain falls, a volunteer stands in place of the victim.

Like many of you, I've been moved by two stories in the papers of volunteers who took the place of victims: the young photographer in downtown Manhattan who came to the rescue of a man being mugged; and the young man in Los Angeles, who, amid the swirling floods, saw a child, and threw himself into the torrent. He saved the child but lost his life. I have also been moved by the dedication and energy of the Olympic athletes. Said our own Phil Mahre, after winning the silver in the slalom: "In Alpine skiing, it's you against the mountain and the clock. You can't ever hold back. It's all or nothing. No timeouts. No coasting."

If only we could "put out" that way off the snow, off the ice, in contests of greater moral import! But of course that's pure sentimental yearning, for the multitudes in such instances gather not to cheer their heads off, but at best to watch silently, and at worst to cry "crucify."

But that's what life is all about lived to the full. Von Berg, the young photographer, the man in Los Angeles—they understood. And he who needs more than God as his witness is too ambitious.

So, enough of banality: "No, no, what we'll see is the evil of banality."

Enough of shallowness. Who wants to say of herself, "Deep down, I'm shallow"?

Enough of the mass mind, for it is the individual conscience, as opposed to the mass mind, that best reflects the universal conscience of humanity.

"I appeal to you therefore, brothers and sisters, by the mercies of God, to present your bodies as a living sacrifice, holy and acceptable to God, which is your spiritual worship. Do not be conformed to this world but be transformed by the renewal of your mind, that you may prove what is the will of God, what is good, and acceptable and perfect."

The Sabbath Was Made for Man

MARCH 16, 1980
Readings: Psalm 115; Mark 2:23–27

First, I want to say a few words on behalf of the many of you who, like me, knew and loved Allard Lowenstein.

When I was a small boy I half believed John Wayne had invented the horse. Now in my old age, I'm still not sure that Al Lowenstein didn't invent the telephone. Even as he talked to me he was always talking to someone else on the phone. I think carrying on one conversation at a time simply wasn't challenging enough for Al. Yet it was his genius to make the two of us—the person on the phone and me—feel that we were his best friends; and at the moment we probably were.

Once I heard a man say, "I used to be an incurable optimist, but now I'm cured." Al was never cured. But, his optimism wasn't naive either. He was incurably intelligent. He combined moral passion with political sophistication. And he was the best standup orator I ever knew. I was on a David Susskind Show about two and a half years ago with him when Al was still a UN Ambassador. Halfway through the show Susskind turned to me: "For you, Bill, you're unusually quiet." "David," I answered, "when Lowenstein speaks on human rights, let the whole world keep silence before him."

What Al was doing that night really represented his life mission: to address and arouse and organize the better self in every one of us.

For a man as brilliant as he, he was remarkably loyal. It was not incongruous that Al should die at the hand of a former student. Under Al's influence Dennis Sweeney fought many battles for civil rights and became a casualty of the wars. But where others deserted, Al befriended. Had he survived the five bullets—which he almost did by spirit alone—the first person he would have gone to see was Sweeney in jail.

It is written in scripture, "Let the dead bury the dead," which means "and not the living." Al would not have wanted us to be buried with him. Al would not wish to be held close by grief. So I pray that God will fill the hollow in our hearts with his kind of passion and loyalty and love of decency. And if we can't share his optimism we can share his persistence.

God bless you, Al. You sure blessed us.

Now let's return to the New Testament story. The Pharisees turn to Jesus and say, "Why are they"—the disciples—"doing what is not lawful on the sabbath?" And Jesus answers "The sabbath was made for man, not man for the sabbath."

What a rare but brilliant "put down." It reminds me of the school teacher who sent a note home with a pupil informing his parents that he needed to develop habits of personal cleanliness. Before he was returned to school he was to be properly scrubbed and washed. What the teacher got, however, was a note in return: "Never mind about Joey's face and neck. Joey's no rose. But your business is to learn him, not to smell him."

That school teacher was prissy. So were the Pharisees, but worse: they were out there with their hostile, critical eyes, actually spying on Jesus and his disciples. What else would Pharisees be doing in the middle of a cornfield? They must have looked about as out of place as the FBI "birdwatchers" on Fisher Island closing in on Father Daniel Berrigan. It's bad enough to be tailed by the FBI, but imagine being followed by a bunch of bleak Pharisees. Had there been a Freedom of Information Act then, and had Peter later applied for his "scroll," what do you suppose he would have found written thereon?

Lest, however, we feel unduly superior, let us note that today the disciples would have been charged with stealing corn. But not then. Listen: "When you go into your neighbor's vineyard, you may eat your fill of grapes, as many as you wish, but you shall not put any in your vessel. When you go into your neighbor's standing grain, you may pluck the ears with your hand, but you shall not put a sickle to your neighbor's standing grain" (Deut. 23:24, 25).

Let's update that: "When you walk down Broadway, and you are hungry, you may eat fruit or vegetables off the fruit and vegetable stand of any chain store (we have to protect the small merchants), but you shall not put anything in a bag."

Wouldn't this city be better off were we able to resurrect that ancient understanding of the practice of mercy?

Had it not been Saturday, the Pharisees would have held their peace. But this was the Sabbath, and the Sabbath law was clear: no reaping, threshing, winnowing and preparing food. Technically it could be argued the disciples had done all four.

"The Sabbath was made for human beings, not human beings for the Sabbath." I wonder if any Biblical saying is more eternally relevant to almost any institution, any system, any law? Welfare is made for human beings, not human beings for a welfare system, particularly not one which shows a pervasive disregard for "the lives, fortunes, and sacred honor" of the people it presumably serves. Economics are made for human beings, not human beings to perpetuate an economic system no matter how entrenched by time and custom. National security is made for man not man for national security, any national security system, for they all tend to confuse security with secrecy, survival with superiority, responsibility with power. No *thing* is sacred. No property is sacred, not even private. No system is sacred, not even the American way of life. No institution is sacred, not even the Riverside Church. No law is sacred, not even the Sabbath law. The Sabbath belongs to man. *Only human beings are sacred.* And because they are sacred, they don't work for institutions; institutions work for them.

The Sabbath is made for man. So simple to say, those words are about as easy to believe in our hearts and to implement in our lives as for a camel to pass through the eye of a needle.

St. Paul once wrote words which for years nobody picked up. Nobody knew what to do with them. Today, they are clear: "We contend not with flesh and blood but with principalities and powers." Initially, however, these powers were probably benevolent. So often what ends up destructive originates as helpful. I'll illustrate from the animal world, but you make the human connection. Those of you who have been to the Natural History Museum must have stood at some point before those enormous elks, now extinct. With larger horns, these animals intimidated competitors, attracted more females and won the battle of survival by virtue of their self-enhancing, self-glorifying equipment. But with selective breeding over many generations the horns became ever larger and more elaborate until they were so complex and grand that they trapped the elks in the trees of the forest and slowly they began to die out. What had originated as helpful ended up destructive.

I think the headquarters of just about every bureaucracy in this city now has antlers so grand and complex that anyone of them that ventures forth outside the building gets trapped in the nearest tree.

March 16, 1980

One of my favorite insights in the Old Testament speaks to this point. The ancient Israelites, while still wandering in the wilderness, were persuaded that the grace of God not only had brought them forth from Egypt, but that once in the Promised Land only the grace of God could keep them from behaving like Egyptians. They had the insight to realize that with the passage of time, first things tend to get displaced into second place, third place, fourth place, not to say fourteenth place. So, according to the Israelites, every fifty years we should blow the whistle on the human enterprise. This was the Year of Jubilee. "You shall hallow the fiftieth year, and proclaim liberty throughout the land to all its inhabitants . . . each of you shall return to his property, and each of you shall return to his family" (Lev. 25:10). The understanding of property is the tip-off. "The land shall not be sold in perpetuity for the land is mine," saith the Lord (v. 23). Once again, no private property is sacred. But the point is this: a homeless person, unable to buy property, and without relatives to do it for him, could, during the Year of Jubilee, receive his original land back free of charge. Why? Because first things first; it is not the will of God that anyone be homeless. The Year of Jubilee proclaims that human relations are only penultimately contractual, a matter of law; ultimately human relations are human. People before anything. The Year of Jubilee reaffirms the preeminence of the person. Jesus is doing the same: "The sabbath is made for man, not man for the sabbath."

Unfortunately the Year of Jubilee was never observed. So the history of the world is a history of revolutions, many trying to accomplish by violence what the Year of Jubilee sought to achieve by peaceful means. But wouldn't it be glorious if we could proclaim a Year of Jubilee in New York City, or in this whole nation which, after all, was, and still is, the land of Jefferson and Lincoln, the land of Martin Luther King Jr., and a land that belongs to a world that itself embodies the warning that if we cannot help the many who are poor, we shall never save the few who are rich.

"The sabbath was made for man." Why is it so hard to affirm and reaffirm the preeminence of human beings in our personal life and in our communal life? Another Biblical insight tells us, "Thou shalt love the Lord thy God with all thy heart and with all thy soul, and with all thy mind, and with all thy strength, and thou shalt love thy neighbor as thyself; on these two commandments"—which really are one— "hang all the law and the prophets." Surely that is one of the great "Thou shalt's" of scripture, and what does it say if not that the art of life is to make an absolute commitment to the absolute and only a relative commitment to the relative. Consciously or unconsciously, however, again and again, we deny God and make an absolute commitment to a relative value. And this absolutizing of a relative is what the Israelites called idolatry.

Clearly the Pharisees in Jesus' mind had absolutized the Sabbath law, just as some patriots absolutize the "absolute sovereign power" of the nation, and others absolutize the importance of scholarship or athletics, or wealth, or power; anything almost can be absolutized in a person's life, or in the life of a nation. And now we come to the insight. Who worships—gives worth to—the Sabbath law? Sabbatarians, like these bleak Pharisees. Who worships scholarship? Scholars! Athletics? The athlete. Wealth? The rich, or the poor who think, "If only I were rich, then I would be someone." Who worships the United States of America? Americans! No Americans worship France—unless *il parle très bien le français*. Who worships cleanliness? The school teacher who sent Joey home—I'll bet he was squeaky clean!

When we absolutize a relative value we are only absolutizing ourselves. All idolatry is worship of the self—the self projected into objective form, the self writ large. In other words, "Thou shalt love the Lord thy God with all thy heart, and with all thy soul, and with all thy mind and with all thy strength—or thou shalt surely love thyself with comparable fervor." Idolatry, said the ancient Israelite, is the root of all evil, because at the root of all idolatry is pride.

What Jesus is really saying is, "The Sabbath was made for God, not God for the Sabbath; and you Sabbatarians are also made for God and for your neighbors, like my disciples here; and not made for your own self-enhancement and self-glorification." And that's what the Pharisees obviously heard. That's why by saying, "The sabbath was made for man" Jesus took two giant steps towards his death.

Dear Riversiders, what is the absolute in your life? What relative value from time to time surreptitiously slips into an absolute position to your selfish advantage, and to the great disadvantage of your children, your friends, your fellow citizens in this nation and on this planet? Is it cleanliness? is it wealth? is it chauvinism? is it Riverside Church? This Lenten season is the season to smoke it out, lest in answer to the question, "Were you there when they crucified my Lord?" you be forced to say: "You bet I was, hammer in hand."

Or maybe you are being dehumanized, depersonalized by some institution for which you work. Maybe, spiritually, you are starving and like the disciples need to eat. Maybe it's time you answered the teacher's letter with one of your own, straightening out the situation.

Listen again to the devastating words of the psalm:

Their idols are silver and gold, the work of men's hands;
They have mouths, but do not speak; eyes, but do not see;
They have ears, but do not hear; noses, but do not smell;
They have hands, but do not feel; feet, but do not walk, and
They do not make a sound in their throat.

Now listen to this:

Those who make them are like them. So are all who trust
in them.

Ps. 115:4–8

What a description of depersonalized, dehumanized, idolatrous, prideful life!

But faith wilts the need for pride. If God loves you—yea, dotes on you—you can forget yourself, believing joyously, praying faithfully, loving ardently, witnessing courageously. Yes, let each of us this week find some way to reaffirm in our personal lives, in our vocational life, in the life of this city and nation—let us find some way to reaffirm the preeminence of human beings; to make it clear to all around us that persons are precious, only persons are sacred, all else is relative. Let us find some way to witness this week to Jesus' words and to the actions of his disciples: "The Sabbath belongs to human beings, not human beings to the Sabbath."

The Rising Cost of Discipleship

MARCH 23, 1980

"As they were going along the road, a man said to him, 'I will follow you wherever you go.' And Jesus said to him, 'Foxes have holes, and birds of the air have nests; but the Son of man has nowhere to lay his head.' To another he said, 'Follow me.' But he said, 'Lord, let me first go and bury my father.' But he said to him, 'Leave the dead to bury their own dead; but as for you, go and proclaim the kingdom of God.' Another said, 'I will follow you, Lord; but let me first say farewell to those at my home.' Jesus

*said to him, 'No one who puts his hand to the plow and
looks back is fit for the kingdom of God.'"*

Luke 9:57–62

They are full of truth but they are harsh sayings, these "disciple sayings." They speak of the cost of discipleship, which rises as Jesus
nears his death. When common integrity is made to look like
courage, the cost of decent living rises. In days like ours, of general
world unrest and economic stress, feelings of tenderness tend to fade
in the human heart. It becomes that much more difficult to dissolve
fear and reestablish faith and rekindle a wider sense of kinship. So we
can talk, as someone recently wrote, of "discipleship inflation."

I think we can picture two aspects of Christian faith. In one, Jesus
faces us, beckons to us to come, or even comes himself to knock on
the door we so frequently shut on him. This aspect of the faith we can
call a "come-to-me" aspect. "Come to me, all ye who are weary and
heavy laden." All we need is need. If we confess our need to be comforted, our need to be strengthened, our need to be forgiven, Jesus
will meet these needs. "Come unto me, all ye who are weary and
heavy laden, and I will give you rest."

It's easy to exploit this aspect of the faith. The so-called electronic
church has little to do with preaching, or teaching, or praying, or
great music. But the ministers have mastered the art of the pastoral
visit by TV. One of them comes right into your living room, just after
you have concluded, "Bye bye happiness, hello loneliness" and he says
"Jesus loves you, and so do I." Very comforting!

But we mustn't forget, particularly in the Lenten season, another
aspect of the faith in which Jesus says not, "Come unto me" but "Follow me." Or, to put it differently, he says in effect, "I have ministered
unto you, now you must minister unto me." And we say, "When,
Lord, did we see you naked, or homeless, or hungry, and did not minister to you?" And of course he answers, "Inasmuch as ye did it not to
the least of these my brothers and sisters, ye did it not unto me."

It's the second aspect of the faith, the "follow me" aspect, that these
harsh disciple sayings address. Actually it was rather courageous of
Jesus, in effect, to rebuff the first man, for if we are to believe
Matthew's version of the encounter, the man was a scribe, an important person, a key person, one to impress others, to get support for
the cause. He was the kind of person every church generally is very
careful not to rebuff. And the man actually volunteers: "I will follow
you wherever you go." But Jesus puts him off: "Foxes have holes in the

ground, and the birds of the air have nests, but the Son of man has nowhere to put his head."

Was Jesus literally homeless? What about his house in Capernaum? By this time, he has probably left his home, and he is suggesting that the man not support him on his prophetic journey—which would be easy—but join him.

Now a scribe was the kind of person who had a house full of scholarly scrolls, the kind of person who could afford the comforts of home. Homelessness to him, say, as opposed to a fisherman like Peter, would have been tough. Yet, there was no compromise. Jesus didn't say, "Well, if you can't join me, at least support me."

Those of you who are thinking that Jesus must have been referring to a deeper homelessness are, I think, right. The scribe, we can say, was safe in his vocation. The scribe was safe in his traditions. He followed beaten paths. When Jesus says, "Follow me," he is saying in effect, "Do not follow where the paths lead. Rather come with me where there is no path, and we'll leave a trail."

I don't know how much time all of you spend deriving inspiration from these two hundred people on our altar screen. Any time at all reminds you they are there because they did not follow where the path led; they went where there was no path and left a trail. They abandoned their "low-vaulted past," to borrow a phrase from Oliver Wendell Holmes, and therefore are honored in our high-vaulted chamber. They were homeless in the sense that the universe was their home. They had no ceiling but the heavens, no floor but the "ground of all being." They are larger-than-life figures because they led larger-than-life lives. And it was tough for them, just as it is tough for any of us when we go where there is no path.

Yes, it's "follow me" that means "Bye bye happiness, hello loneliness" even "I think I'm going to die." It also means "I am going to live as never before. So, I am not only supporting, I am joining Jesus. And no handful of silver is going to buy me away."

"To another he said 'Follow me.' But he said, 'Lord, let me first go and bury my father.' But he said to him, 'Let the dead bury the dead.'" That is a truly harsh thing to say, because of all duties, none was more sacred than that of burying one's parents. You didn't even have to say the "Shma Israel" if you were burying your parents. Of course, the father may only have been aged and the son was only asking for time—"when my dear father dies, then I will come and follow you." But that would hardly soften the answer he received, "Let the dead bury the dead."

I think what Jesus is saying most fundamentally is "Let the dead bury the dead—and not the living." William Blake expressed the same thought: "Drive your cart and your plow over the bones of the dead," a hard saying, full of wisdom. In still another metaphor, we might say that in every time and country there are those, usually in charge, usually older, who face the sunset of a dying day. Others, more prophetic, usually younger, strive to turn their country around to face the dawn of a new day. I would suggest that in our time and country those who face the sunset think it's the end of the world to admit mistakes in Iran. Those facing the sunrise think to admit mistakes is the beginning of humanity, not the end of it. Those facing the sunset refuse public discussion of the possible consequences of a nuclear accident. Those facing the sunrise think human beings should not die like Pennsylvania sheep. Those facing the sunset want more arms and more men under arms. Those facing the sunrise want not military strength, but moral courage, the strength to face the fact that the whole world is weak to the point of helplessness in the face of nuclear peril. For the first time in history the end of the world is in our hands. And only God has the moral authority to end life on this planet. So, while those facing the sunset still talk of the national security state, those facing the sunrise speak of world order.

Of course, he would have been treated as dead had the man done as Jesus told him. His family would no doubt have not taken lightly his desertion. They would have known how to make him feel guilty. In fact, in the old days in India, some families carried a casket in public procession, as a sign of how they regarded someone who embraced Christianity. Will you still say, "I am not only supporting, I am joining Jesus and no loyalty will stand above my loyalty to him"?

"And the third one said, 'I will follow you, Lord, but let me first say "farewell" to those at my home.' Jesus said to him, 'No one who puts his hand to the plow and looks back is fit for the Kingdom of Heaven.'" It is not enough to drive our cart and our plow over the bones of the dead; we can't even look back. We can't even kiss our fathers and mothers farewell, as Elijah allowed Elisha to do a little later in the story we heard earlier. "Oh, Jesus, whither relentless wilt thou still be driving thy maimed and halt that have not strength to go?" That's what we are always saying, aren't we? Elijah said the same: "Lord, now take away my life, for I am not better than my fathers." Elijah is always feeling sorry for himself, and always with good reason. Later the Lord asks him, "What doest thou here, Elijah?"—"here" as opposed to "there" where he belonged. And Elijah answers (words that produced some of

Mendelssohn's greatest music): "I have been very jealous for the LORD God of Hosts, because the Children of Israel have forsaken thy covenant, thrown down thine altars, and slain thy prophets with a sword. And I, even I only, am left, and they seek to take my life. It is enough." To which the Lord answers, "Arise, go forth."

That's heavenly therapy for you! We hunger to lie down, and he gives us meat to go on. "Arise, and eat, because the journey is too great for thee." See how the "come to me" and the "follow me" aspects join? The electronic church thinks "come to me" comes first and then "follow me." But it may be the other way around. "Blessed are those who do hunger and thirst after righteousness, for they shall be filled."

"No one who puts his hand to the plow and looks back is fit for the Kingdom of Heaven." Actually, how can you plow a straight line looking over your left shoulder? "Follow me": the journey is always ahead. Ahead is the shepherd: "He leadeth me in the paths of righteousness." Ahead too is Horeb, the mountain of God. And the angel of God gives us in one meal, meat enough for forty days and forty nights.

Feeling sorry for yourselves? Are people forsaking God's covenant, overthrowing altars, slaying prophets? Has the cost of decent living gone up?

> Say not the struggle nought availeth,
> The labor and the wounds are vain;
> The enemy faints not, nor faileth,
> And as things have been, they remain.
>
> If hopes were dupes, fears may be liars;
> It may be in yon smoke concealed
> Your comrades chase, e'en now, the fliers
> And but for you possess the field.
>
> For while the tired waves, vainly breaking,
> Seem here no painful inch to gain,
> Far back, through creeks and inlets making
> Comes silent, flooding in, the main.
>
> And not by eastern windows only
> When daylight comes, comes in the light.
> In front the sun climbs slow, how slowly,
> But westward, look, the land is bright.
>
> Arthur Hugh Clough

The Politics of Eternity

MARCH 30, 1980
Reading: Luke 19:28–40

C an we let our "sweet hosannas ring," can we still celebrate Palm Sunday, knowing as we do, how the story ends?

I want to answer that question, but first let's set the stage. G. K. Chesterton has a poem in which the donkey speaks:

> When fishes flew and forest walk'd
>   And figs grew upon thorn,
> Some moments when the moon was blood
>   Then surely I was born.
>
> With monstrous head and sickening cry
>   And ears like errant wings,
> The devil's walking parody
>   Of all four-footed things.
>
> The tatter'd outlaw of the earth
>   Of ancient crooked will;
> Starve, scourge, deride me, I am dumb,
>   I keep my secret still.
>
> Fools! For I also had my hour,
>   One far fierce hour and sweet,
> There was a shout about my ears,
>   And palm before my feet.

If you've ever had an hour like that, when others thought you were foolish and you knew you were a fool for Christ's sake, you've had one of the greatest experiences in life.

As a matter of fact, however, in ancient Palestine the ass was a noble, not a despised or even particularly humble beast. Most of all, the donkey was the beast of peace. In war, kings rode horses; but not in peace time. So entering the capital city astride the colt of an ass signalled humility, but above all—*peace*. He came *in* peace *for* peace.

I couldn't help thinking about that last weekend when some of us were "marching"—loosely defined—around our own capital. In Washington, the statues enhance the valor of the men they exalt—

I've yet to find a woman—by placing them astride horses seemingly more mighty than their masters. Some few of these men, like Jefferson, stand pensively. But only one or two sit serenely. It's no accident, however, that one who does was the commander-in-chief who, in wartime, said "With malice toward none and charity for all."

Picture a capital city with statues of men riding donkeys! How different the history of that country would be. And how different our own history might have been had Ben Franklin's advice been heeded and the turkey been designated our national bird. I'll bet we'd have passed up Vietnam, and passed the ERA!

This was not the first time Jesus had been in Jerusalem. According to the Gospel of John he went there frequently for the great feasts. According to St. Matthew's account of the Passion story, Jesus at one point says poignant words: "O Jerusalem, Jerusalem, how often would I have gathered ye unto me as a mother hen her chicks, and ye would not" (Matt. 23:37). That "how often" suggests earlier unsuccessful visits, and explains, perhaps, the incident of the colt. Jesus had made previous arrangements with a friend who understood that the password would be, "The Lord needs it now."

By way of setting the stage, let me say one more thing. In the book of Kings, Ahijah the prophet takes a new garment and rends it into twelve pieces saying: "For thus saith the Lord, the God of Israel, 'Behold I will rend the Kingdom!'—which was then one—'because they have forsaken me'" When words alone failed to move the people, the prophets frequently acted out their warnings, as if to say, "If you will not hear, you must be compelled to see." Surely this is a compelling act. Jesus is compelling the authorities to take notice. Remember, he's a marked man; they want to destroy him. Prudence would have counselled that he enter the city in secret. Instead, he does it in the most public way possible, defying the authorities to do their worst.

But if he is provocative to the leaders of the city, he is even more so to the crowd, although at the time they don't know it. He deliberately fulfills the prophecy of Zechariah. He assumes all the trappings of the long-awaited Messiah, who indeed is the "Prince of Peace," but also the one who is expected to re-establish both the geographical borders and the glories of the ancient kingdom of David. "Blessed is he who comes in the name of the Lord" is from a conqueror's psalm, thought by many to commemorate the great battle of 163 B.C. won by Judas Maccabeus. And "Hosanna"—hosanna in Hebrew means "Save now"—went up not as a word of praise to Jesus but as a cry to God to break in and save his people through the Messiah.

If it is dangerous to defy the authorities, what about coming into the capital city of an occupied country as a king, in order to tear up, by the roots, a people's nationalistic dream? Was there ever courage like unto that?

But now let us look at the story more carefully. How are we to contrast Jesus' vision of things and the people's expectations? Are we to say he was a spiritual Messiah as opposed to a political one? Heaven forbid! That's the great Palm Sunday "cop-out" that will be proclaimed from pulpits all over the land today. Had Jesus been as apolitical as these pulpiteers, you can be sure the nails would never have grazed his palms. In the best prophetic tradition Jesus stood for the relief and protection of the poor and persecuted; for such use of the riches of creation that the world might be freed from famine, poverty and disaster. And in the best prophetic tradition, he saw that the real troublemakers were not the ignorant and cruel, but the intelligent and corrupt. In contrast to so many of today's pulpiteers Jesus knew that "Love your enemies" doesn't mean "Don't make any!"

But to the evils of oppression, poverty and corruption in high places, evils he proclaimed so forcefully that common people heard him gladly, he added one more which lost him their vote—the evil of violence.

The trouble with violent revolution is that it changes not too much, but too little. Nonviolence is so much more radical than violence. It is more truthful. Because of the perversity of human nature, violence always needs lies to explain it, just as lies need violence to defend them. By contrast, truth is naked, vulnerable; its only weapon is love. So the very love that found oppression, poverty and corruption intolerable, this same love, rather than inflict, takes suffering upon itself. What can only be said cynically of another—"it is better that one man should die than that an entire nation perish"—can be said in utter truthfulness about oneself—"It is better that I should die rather than a single other person perish."

Jesus was more, not less, than a prophet; more, not less political than others. Only his were the politics of eternity. And the politics of eternity insist not only on nonviolence—an affront to almost every revolutionary; they insist on "one world"—an affront to every nationalist. We shall begin to understand the politics of eternity, when we recognize that territorial discrimination is as evil as racial discrimination.

And that leads me to say one more difficult thing about the politics of eternity, one more beyond the two mentioned, that nonviolence and universality are cornerstones of these politics. You remember what I said about the statues of people astride horses? Show me "a man on horseback" and I will show you a person who represents rigorous idealism at the expense of self-knowledge. You remember what I said about the real troublemakers being the intelligent and corrupt? Reinhold Niebuhr wrote, "Ultimately considered, evil is done not so much by evil people, but by good people who do not know themselves." The scribes, the Pharisees, Robespierre, Lenin, were fierce idealists, people of great moral vigor. But they had little self-knowledge. They couldn't see the falsehoods in their own truths. They couldn't see what Pascal saw, that the world divides itself between saints who know themselves to be sinners, and sinners who imagine themselves to be saints. The Passion story this week will teach us the deepest lesson about political life. It is not that evil men triumph over good, that good is "forever on the scaffold, wrong upon the throne." It is that all people stand in need of a merciful God.

It has been said that the Kingdom of God is no more distant than our knees. That's where the politics of eternity begin—in confession and forgiveness. In political life, we think it's the end of the world to confess sins. But to admit mistakes is the beginning of humanity, not the end of it. And to know that under the skin we are all one—in sin and in God's love—is to know the most important thing about the human condition, the sole reality upon which we can build a decent political life.

Can we still celebrate Palm Sunday knowing how the story ends? Yes, because with a better understanding of what was going on, we have even more to cheer about. The cross of Christ says something terrible about us, but something wonderful about God. It symbolizes not only the defeat of a good man, or, if you will, the triumph in defeat of a good man. The cross of Christ represents the merciful action of a forgiving father "who knows our frame and remembers that we are dust." Jesus the Messiah, the Son of Man, the Son of God "did not come to be served, but to give his life as a ransom for many." "God was in Christ reconciling the world to himself."

"O Lamb of God, that taketh away the sins of the world, have mercy upon us. O Lamb of God, that taketh the sins of the world, grant us thy peace." Can we not say to our dear Savior:

> Ride on! Ride on in majesty!
> Thy last and fiercest strife is nigh;
> . . . .
> Bow thy meek head to mortal pain,
> Then take, O God, thy power, and reign.
> Henry Milman

"Father, Forgive Them, for They Know Not What They Do"

Good Friday
APRIL 4, 1980

As at the beginning so at the end of Jesus' life, we human beings come off badly. All of us do, but especially his own people, his disciples. Listen again to St. John's account of Christmas: "He was in the world, and the world was made through him, yet the world knew him not." That's everyone. "He came to his own home, and his own people received him not" (John 1:10–11). That's us. And on the eve of Good Friday "all the disciples forsook him and fled."

Generally when the day goes hard, and the cowards steal from the field, there are a few, just a few, who can be found where the fighting is fiercest. On any given moral issue, the majority will probably be wrong and a large minority indifferent. But a tiny minority will protest passionately, all the more so for not being heard. But not this time: "all the disciples forsook him and fled."

At his last supper with his disciples Jesus says, "Verily I say unto you that one of you will betray me." Scripture records that "they were extremely sorrowful and began everyone of them to say unto him, 'Lord, is it I?'"

In his *St. Matthew Passion*, Bach has the entire chorus ask the question in great agitation. Then, great theologian that he was, Bach has the entire chorus answer its own question, "It *is* I"—the so-called Chorus of Believers. And it's true: deliberately, or through fitful and lazy devotion, all of us betray our Lord.

But if our hearts swim in tears today, let these tears not be solely for our transgressions, manifold though they may be. Let gratitude mingle with sorrow, gratitude because he who himself so wanted to flee, who prayed, "Father, let this cup pass from me," and so fervently that "his sweat became as great drops of blood falling to the ground" this man ended his prayer, as we so rarely end ours, "nevertheless, not my will but thine be done." Let there be gratitude because he who could have summoned to his aid twelve legions of angels said, "Put your sword back into its place," healed the ear of the slave of the high priest, and became a lamb in the claw of a tiger. Let there be gratitude because he who was too good for the world never counted the world unworthy of his suffering.

There's a sequence in the Good Friday story that always leaves me "lost in wonder, love and praise." Falsely accused by the chief priests and scribes, and the whole assembly of elders, Jesus is brought before Pilate. For a few moments, for the first time, he has the ear of Caesar's own personal representative. Where else, if not before the highest authority in the land, would you state your case? Yet he says nothing. "Then said Pilate unto him: 'Hearest thou not how many things they witness against you?'" And he answered him never a word. Not until Pilate had washed his hands saying, "I am innocent of the blood of this just person"; not until the people had cried back, "His blood be upon us and on our children"; not until they had railed at him, "He saved others, himself he cannot save," and nailed him to the tree—only then did he speak. And what does he say? He presents to the highest authority in heaven and on earth not his case, but ours, and recommends a proper sentence: "Father, forgive them for they know not what they do."

It's the gentleness of the indictment that makes it so devastating. It's bad enough to do what we do, knowing what we do. But not to know—that's devastating. It's devastating for two reasons. First of all, our ignorance stems from our complacency which makes our ignorance a moral default, not an intellectual one. It's a willed ignorance. And secondly, and more fundamentally, we don't know what we do because we don't know who we are.

All of you, I'm sure, have heard the terrible stories about beggars in poor countries who maim and mutilate their children to prepare them for their future station in life. Well, spiritually, in the manner of these beggars, we maim and mutilate ourselves, we amputate the best, the most generous, loving part of ourselves, calling it "adjustment for life," "socialization," "realism."

The Greek writer, Nikos Kazantzakis, tells of a monk's dream in which the child Jesus is brought to him by Mary his mother who is convinced the boy needs healing.

"What's the matter, my son?" he asks.

"I don't know. I walk the streets, wrestling."

"With whom are you wrestling?"

"With God, of course. With whom else would you wrestle?"

So the monk takes the boy to his home, teaches him carpentry, takes him on long walks during which he talks to him of God as one might of a friendly neighbor who stops by of a summer evening to chat as everyone is enjoying the last rays of the sunset. In a few months the boy is cured; he goes home. Years later the monk hears he's doing well; in fact, he's the best carpenter in Nazareth.

Instead of saving the world, he becomes the best carpenter in Nazareth.

And we, instead of that salvation that could make us whole and holy, seek solutions to our lives that exclude salvation, and generally include the goal of becoming the best "splendid splinter" in town. We amputate the best in ourselves because its realization would be too demanding. We become complacent and fearful, fearful of dying, but no less fearful of living and loving. And when we see someone who is alive and well, free and loving, our instinct is not to emulate his life but to take it from him. We crucify Christ—but only after we have crucified the best in ourselves.

Yet all we hear from the victim of the greatest miscarriage of justice in the world is "Father, forgive." No sanctions, no denunciations, no new threats of exile and flood. Why? Because Jesus is after the fear below the surface, not the behavior that makes it visible. Instead of chipping away at the top of the iceberg he melts it from the bottom. We read in scripture, "Perfect love casts out fear." Forgiveness is perfect love, the never ending love that alone can overcome our complacency, that alone can melt our frozen fears of becoming who we are, that alone can melt our fear of shame, caused by our denial of our identity. In other words, more powerful than the denunciation of sin is the affirmation that the need for it simply does not exist. So Jesus dies to make that affirmation live.

> O Lamb of God that taketh away the sins of the world,
>   have mercy upon us.
> O Lamb of God that taketh away the sins of the world,
>   grant us thy peace.

Easter: Promise or Demand?

APRIL 6, 1980
Reading: Matthew 28

Last night at midnight, on 93rd Street, a congregation of Russian Orthodox believers streamed out of their darkened church, candles in hand, following the cross, the priest, their chanting choir. Had they owned enough real estate they would have walked slowly, three times, around the church, now become the tomb of Christ. Then the priest approached the closed doors, and knocked mightily. Suddenly they opened, and the congregation could see a church bathed in light and filled with the sweet smell of incense and Easter flowers. Turning around to the congregation, the priest said in a loud voice: "Christ is risen!" And they answered in an equally loud voice: "He is risen indeed!"

Let's do it: "Christ is risen."

(The congregation:) "He is risen indeed!"

The text for the morning sermon is from St. Matthew, "Full authority in heaven and on earth has been committed to me." Let me start by sketching a scene, not as fanciful as at first it might appear. Picture the disciples shortly after Good Friday. Grief-stricken they surely were, their hearts feeling that weight which is so real and physical when you have lost someone you dearly love. And the horror of the crucifixion must still have been vivid in their minds, and their own cowardice too, for although only one betrayed, all forsook Jesus and fled. But perhaps they were also beginning to experience that sense of relief that comes with resignation from the struggle. "Well, he won a lot of hearts but no election. We tried hard, Lord knows, but the Establishment, that trinity of organized religion, organized business, and organized politics, was too powerful. So, it's back to fishing, to business as usual."

Then comes the word: "He's back."

"Oh, no. Not again."

What I'm getting at is this: Had we exchanged the Easter greeting in the first century, as we just did now, every one of us would be liable to punishment by death.

On Good Friday organized religion knew what it was doing, organized religion being so much more law than love-abiding, preferring God's truth *in vitro* to truth *in vivo*. Organized business, too, knew what it was doing. "Why, didn't that man say 'It is harder for a rich man to enter the Kingdom of Heaven than for a camel to pass through the eye of a needle?' And, as if to prove it, didn't he die with a robe his sole possession?" As for the State—organized politics—it may not have been as convinced as organized religion of Jesus' crime. But Pilate had only to hear "Thou art not Caesar's friend," and away he fell like an autumn leaf, washing his hands, and thereby plaiting the crown of thorns, reflecting the official charge of treason.

How much better the enemies of Christ understand him than most of his followers. Moreover, if Christ's enemies knew what they were doing on Good Friday, they quickly came to understand what Christ had done on Easter. The resurrection of Christ means, in essence, you can kill God's love but you cannot keep it dead and buried. Hate kills, but love never dies, not with God, and therefore not with us either. The Easter message means that all that tenderness and strength, all that beauty and goodness, which on Good Friday we saw scourged, buffeted, stretched out on a cross, is again alive. "And be assured, I am with you always, to the end of time." Until all eternity, Christ will be alive, not as a memory that inevitably made fade, but as a presence. (A scholar who knows all about Jesus is as nothing compared to the humblest Christian who knows him.) And Christ is risen from the dead to put us back on our feet, to convert us, not from this world to some other, but from something less than life to the possibility of full life itself. Then, through our resurrected lives, Christ plans to assail and overpower all the forces of "death militant" that corrupt life, and bring ruin to the earth. No wonder the authorities felt threatened. No wonder they put Christians to death. It was an act, however, of desperation. For if love never dies, death has no dominion. The state has lost its ultimate power over us.

Still it would be small wonder if the disciples' very first reaction to the news of Christ's return was not "Oh, no; not again." Easter is anything but sentimental. It's hard. It's hard because Easter is a demand more than a promise, and a demand not for sympathy with the crucified Christ, but for loyalty to the resurrected one.

Sometimes I think we Christians are hopelessly sentimental. We pray for peace, and pay for war. We sympathize with the crucified Christ, but continue our loyalty to the institutions that crucify him. We know that the world did not reward Christ for being Christ, but we think the world should reward us for being Christians. But if it is not excusable, at least it's understandable, as understandable as "Oh, no, not again." As I said, Easter is a demand more than a promise.

Fortunately, the resurrection of Christ cannot be proved. I say "fortunately" because I think all of us are prone to seek evidence to make intelligently selfish decisions. As God is not in the business of overcoming our selfishness by appealing to selfish motives, no proof will be found for the existence of God, or for the resurrection of Christ. But if the resurrection of Christ cannot be proved, it can be known, it can be experienced, it can be trusted. Faith after all is not believing without proof; it's trusting without reservation. The resurrection faith is a willingness on the basis of all that we have heard, all that we have observed, all that we have thought deeply about and experienced at a level far deeper than the mind can comprehend (for there are truths that the mind can defend but not discover), the resurrection faith is a willingness to risk our lives on the conviction that indeed to Jesus Christ "full authority in heaven and on earth has been committed."

It was this conviction which made Peter after Jesus' death ten times the person he was before. It was this conviction that made St. Stephen under the rain of death-dealing stones cry out, Christlike, "Father, forgive." It was the resurrection faith that made that brave Quaker woman, Mary Dyer, say to the authorities of organized religion and organized politics in Massachusetts, "Truth is my authority, not authority my truth"; that made the Danish pastor say, "I would rather die with the Jews than live with the Nazis"—and the Nazis obliged. And it was faith in the resurrection of Jesus Christ that prompted Archbishop Romero of San Salvador, the Sunday before he was assassinated, to end his sermon in this fashion: After appealing to the men in the Army, the National Guard, and the police, to obey their consciences and not sinful orders to kill their very brothers, he said, "The Church is the defender of the law of God and of the divinity of the human person, and cannot remain silent before such an abomination. We want the Government to recognize that reforms are worthless if they are stained with so much blood. In the name of God, and in the name of the suffering people whose cries rise to the very heavens and become more tumultuous each day, I beseech you, I beg you, I order you, in the name of God, stop the repression." It was that order that sealed his martyrdom.

But the abyss of love is deeper than the abyss of death. The resurrection of Jesus shows us that God has made an unshakeable commitment to us—in our sufferings and joys, and on both sides of death. "For I am persuaded that neither death, nor life, can separate us from the love of God which is in Christ Jesus."

What then shall we say to these things? Shall we not with Peter and Stephen, with Mary Dyer and Abraham Lincoln, and Martin Luther King Jr. and Oscar Romero, declare our loyalty to the one to whom has been committed "all authority in heaven and on earth"? "The Church is the defender of the law of God and of the dignity of the human person." From St. Peter to Oscar Romero, the great souls of the church have always stood for the dignity of human beings and against the power that denies it. The great souls of the church have always made the distinction between the power to do something, and the right to do it. For instance, here in the United States, we have the power to continue to neglect the unemployed and the sick, the elderly and the uneducated; we have the power but not the right. We have the power to continue massive preparations for war, to make the world itself the target of war—just think, everyone lives on the target! But while we have the power to destroy the world, we haven't the right to take a single life, not unless we think God's right name is Satan. And each of us has the power to live superficial, supercilious, guilt-ridden, spiritless, boring lives, but we have not the right, not if Jesus Christ has been raised from the dead to put us on our feet again.

Now let's talk about the promise of Easter. It was Léon Bloy who said, "Joy is the most infallible sign of the presence of God." Joy is the most important Christian emotion. Duty calls only when joy fails to prompt. And Easter is the source of that joy. Because Christ is risen and is a presence in our lives, we can of every day say, "This is the day which the Lord has made, let us rejoice and be glad in it." Because Christ is risen and is a presence in our lives, we can say with Teresa of Avila, "All the way to heaven is heaven because Jesus said 'I am the way.'" Because Christ is risen, even the organized forces of religion, politics, and business can be redeemed, and the light of Easter can dissolve the shadow of a human-authored holocaust. Because Christ is risen, we can say with Paul, "Death, where is thy sting? Grave, where thy victory?" Death is only an horizon, and an horizon is nothing, save the limit of our sight. If we don't know what lies on the other side, we know who is there, and that's enough. Because Christ is risen, we too can rise: "Made like him, like him we rise, ours the cross, the grave, the sky."

"Oh, no, not again?"

"Oh, yes, again and again. Come, Lord Jesus, we follow."

The Russians do it three times: Christ is risen. (Congregation) He is risen indeed. Christ is risen. (Congregation) He is risen indeed. Christ is risen. (Congregation) He is risen indeed.

Rise up, O resurrected ones, and hug one another and wish one another a Happy Easter!

Living beyond Our Moral Means

APRIL 13, 1980

It seems appropriate that Peace Sunday, an idea launched two years ago from this church, should be celebrated today by thousands of churches on the Sunday after Easter. For this is the day when Jesus, reappearing to his disciples, says, "If you love me, feed my sheep." And that didn't mean "fatten them for the slaughter."

Yesterday I was in Salt Lake City. The citizens of Utah are beginning to see the true purpose of the proposed MX missile—that silo-busting, rocket-destroying system, with its 10,000 miles of missile roads, and 5,000 miles of access roads, and, most of all, its 4,600 so-called "aim points." In a moment of surprising candor, Air Force

General Allen said that the system is to act as "a giant sponge" to absorb the fire power of "five thousand Soviet missiles." In other words, the people of Utah are being led as sheep to the slaughter. They are to be victims of 70 percent of Soviet nuclear weaponry, so that American Minutemen elsewhere can survive. Said a Mormon lawyer: "I don't believe that the faithful remnant of Mormons should be only Spanish-speaking." Protesting the unthinkable results of a nuclear exchange, he rose to quote Isaiah: "The earth shall reel to and fro like a drunkard and shall be removed like a cottage; and the transgression thereof shall be heavy upon it, and it shall fall and not rise again" (Isa. 24:20).

So we are met in a moment of some historical magnitude. Prophets have proclaimed that the unity of humankind is less a goal than an obvious condition of biological survival. In the words of Raymond Aron, "This is the century of total warfare." Let us remember that the bomb whose effects were so vividly described just now by Mrs. Shibama—the bomb that destroyed Hiroshima is so small it is not even considered in treaty negotiations. And if World War III becomes a reality, it will embrace not only Osita, a male of draft age, not only Juliette Bursterman, a retired school teacher, not only Americans but everyone—friends, foes, the globe around. The world is now the target of war. All of us live on the target. To grasp the immorality of even plotting such a crime against humankind, we would have to multiply by ten the combined atrocities of Attila the Hun, Tamburlaine, Genghis Khan, the barbarians of the Dark Ages, and Adolf Hitler. And while some Germans could plausibly argue that they didn't know, we can't. We know exactly what's being planned.

Does that mean that we have all become moral monsters? I think the answer is "no." I think it true to say, as did the historian von Ranke: "Every generation is equi-distant from eternity." I think it fair to say that people in every generation have striven for power, the only difference being ours has achieved it. This is "the century of total war" because this is "the age of omnipotence." What has happened is curious. You know the expression, "A man's reach should exceed his grasp." That means our moral imagination should stretch beyond what we are able to do. Now the situation is reversed: what we are able to do is beyond the reach of our moral imagination. Our capacity to destroy is virtually unlimited. But our capacity to imagine, to feel, to respond, is, as always, limited. Thus we are able to do physically what we cannot grasp morally. We are living beyond our moral means. That is the heart of our problem. As one man said, it is possible to repent one murder but not a million murders.

These million murders we are plotting are a funny form of murder when the murderer remains thousands of miles away from his victims. His eyes never see the corpses. His ears are spared the screams of the dying. The stench of the burned flesh is untouched by his nostrils. Killing is so much easier when it is so far away, so impersonal, so anonymous.

John Bennett said, "Anything is permitted at a distance." That makes the point. The technological momentum of weapons has outstripped our moral imagination. We are not moral monsters, but we are living beyond our moral means.

Let me read you a story to illustrate the heart of the problem. It's a story of two "silo-sitters," told by Philip Berrigan. They are clad in spotless white overalls. Each wears a .45 automatic on his hip. Each wears a badge with a motto, "Aggressor Beware." Each has a key, which, at the command of authority reaching back to the president, can turn a lock in the silo to hurl out of the ground more explosives than have been fired in all the wars of history. Call them Smith and Jones. They command ten Minuteman missiles buried in eighty feet concrete silos in South Dakota, each of them capable of 500 times the explosive force which hit Hiroshima thirty-five years ago. The Minutemen are programmed by electronic computer for Russian cities. Jones, an air force captain, is asked, "How would it feel to receive the order to fire and to turn the key?" He smiles and says, "It's no different than going home and turning the key in the lock."

We are living beyond our moral means. So sharply has the cost of violence risen that we have to accept austerity in violence. In fact, in a century of total war, and in an age of omnipotence, the institution of war has to be abolished. The new "abolitionists" must abolish war.

Let no one say it will be easy. On the contrary, we shall have to develop a habit of heroism, the heroism of love, and patience, the kind of restraint displayed by King Arthur when he found that his dear friend, Lancelot, was having an affair with his wife. How hurt, how humiliated, how vengeful his feelings must have been. Yet he said what each of us has to repeat: "This is the time when violence is not strength, and compassion is not weakness. And we shall live through this together. May God have mercy upon us all."

This is the time to become the hero of the Talmud, the one who turns an enemy into a friend. For great nations can no longer afford the luxury of enemies. Russia may be our toughest adversary, but not an enemy. Our mortal enemy is war, war itself.

Let us not argue that we must go to war to defend selfish interests. They are not worth it. Nor let us argue that we must go to war to defend our democratic way of life. Such a way of life will not survive. And let us proclaim a new kind of patriotism, which takes as its object of ultimate loyalty not the nation-state, but the human race. (Didn't Margaret Mead say, "We have explored the entire planet and found only one human race"?)

"Son of man, I have made you a watchman for the House of Israel. Whenever you hear a word from my mouth, you shall give them warning from me." The people of Utah have heard the warning, and are proclaiming their opposition to the MX. The same Mormon lawyer who quoted Isaiah went on to quote from the play, "Rosencrantz and Guldenstern Are Dead." At some point Guldenstern muses to himself, "There must have been a time at the beginning when we still could have said 'no.'"

The citizens of Utah are saying "no," and asking that we join them. With Günther Gras we must beat our tin drums in order to drown out the idiocies we hear about us. We must act because of our faith, and in the face of our fears. We must press the Congress this coming week not to vote for registration, and before July, not to vote for the MX. It's time and past time that we got back to the primary agenda of this planet, which is to disarm it. Our government and the government of the Soviet Union have a major responsibility. So let's get on with Salt II, and Salt III, and Salt IV and V. Between us let us decide what parity looks like going down, instead of going up, and with all nations work to rid the world of the scourge of war. Then, and only then, the sheep may safely graze.

We must work as hard for peace as those who plan for war. We must breathe in thought and breathe out action. It's not enough to be a people of action; generals are that. We have to be a people of vision. More aware, we are finally more powerful. And then we must organize, because one and two and fifty make the million necessary to "see that day come 'round." We must engage in electoral politics, wear out letterpaper, stand in silent vigils, refuse to pay taxes—all enterprises as American as cherry pie, and honorable expressions of a deeply held religious faith. And if we trust in God's grace, and share of ourselves with one another, we shall prevail. That's why we are having a picnic today. No amount of pessimism and sorrow is going to cast our souls into despair. We shall prevail for the reason heard earlier: "Love never ends." Yes, love is a long-distance runner. Love has a longer wind than any other contestant in the race. Amen.

Thorns in the Flesh

MAY 11, 1980
Reading: 2 Corinthians 12:7–10

They are small things, thorns, like blips on a large screen. But as we all know, a small blip can sink you. In this world, nothing is easier than to have the experience and miss the meaning. And nothing, perhaps, is more difficult than to have the experience of a thorn in the flesh—and then to extract, not the thorn, but every ounce of meaning that is available in the experience.

As in St. Paul's case, a thorn in the flesh may be a physical disability. Those of us lucky enough to have been spared ornery genes, or tragic automobile and other kinds of accidents, can never, I think, show sufficient admiration (not pity, which is mixed with condescension) for those whose physical lives have been maimed, yet who survive spiritually intact. If this sermon is dedicated to anyone, it's dedicated to you for what you've shown the rest of us.

But Paul's "thorn in the flesh" may also be psychosomatic. Moses, it would seem, had a stammer. And a thorn can be totally psychological. I think in Jeremiah we sense a man who is constantly overcome by a sense of his insufficiency. Think of the thorns being borne right here, today, in this church. Some are thorns of grief—for a child, a husband, or a wife whose death was totally unwarranted. Others carry thorns of betrayal. One of Arthur Miller's characters says, "God, why is betrayal the only truth that sticks?"

A thorn can also be a divorce, long past, which still poisons the bloodstream of our lives. A thorn can be a child we think has disgraced us, or one we think we have disgraced. A thorn can be any lapse of judgment, or mistake. The way we treasure mistakes makes me think sometimes that they are the holiest things in our past!

You see what I'm getting at: in this world there are things hoped for, and things stuck with. The thorns are what we are stuck with. All of them cause pain, that real pain which is associated with loss: loss of health, loss of faith and hope, as when we somehow feel "unblessed"; loss of joy, loss of love, and certainly loss of power. To see how hurt we feel through loss of power we have only to recall the thorn in the flesh of the nation today—those 53 hostages we cannot seem to extract from Iran. So humiliated are we as a people through loss of power that today, in foreign affairs, almost any issue is turned into a test of strength. Didn't the aborted rescue mission of the hostages put the stature of the United States above the safety of the hostages?

So take a moment, will you, and pick out a real thorn in the flesh, a real "messenger of Satan" in your life. Pick one out and then we'll see if you and I deal with our thorns the way St. Paul dealt with his.

I must say I'd love to ask for a show of hands to see how many of you found no thorn! Maybe you are luckier than most. More likely, it's because as Pascal said, "Our wounds are too deep; we cannot examine them." If so, that's sad, because what's beyond recall is generally beyond redemption.

St. Paul, of course, is keenly conscious of his thorn, although we don't know whether it was epilepsy or something else. He "takes it to the Lord in prayer": "Three times I besought the Lord about this, that it should leave me . . ."

Generally, prayer is not an act of self-expression. Prayer is an act of empathy; prayer is thinking God's thoughts after him. Prayer is praying "*Our* father who art in heaven" when everything within us longs to cry out "*My* father," because "our" includes that horrible divorced husband, that wayward child; it includes muggers, rapers, the Iranian captors, all the people who jam thorns into our flesh.

But sometimes prayer *is* an act of self-expression. It was to St. Paul—"Three times I besought the Lord about this, that it should leave me." When we do express our feelings to God, we should, like Paul, be as specific as possible. Don't pray, "Lord, I'm in pain"; say, "Lord, feel the throbbing in my right knee," or "Lord, you know how heavy my heart is with grief because of the death of Johnny." There is too much dignity in too many prayers—dignity at the expense of specificity. It is really fake dignity, the kind that puts taste ahead of truth. So never mind how crude or how trivial your prayers may sound to you. There are no unimportant tears to God.

"Three times I besought the Lord. . . ." What do you suppose happened the first time, what happened the second time, and what happened the third time? It seems to me that the first time around Paul probably did not receive the answer he records in the letter to the Corinthians. It would make more sense if, by way of an answer he heard nothing, but rose from prayer a better person. That's no mean answer, in fact, answer sufficient in many cases. In other words, the first time Paul simply unburdened himself—all his anger, his grief, all his frustration. In this crazy, mixed-up world you have "to dump the mud." Don't be so proud to think that you don't have to; all of us do. I know a monk, probably the most saintly person I know. Someone told me two days ago that in a recent meeting, a stupid man was saying stupid things and suddenly this monk got up, walked across the room and punched him right in the nose. You see, even a saint has to dump the mud, although probably on the nose of another man may not be as good a place as in the lap of the Almighty. "Three times I besought the Lord." The first time I imagine, Paul simply wanted to unburden himself. And that's enough for at least a week or two.

Now what about the second time? It would be true to the essence of life if the second time around Paul received an answer that went something like this: "I hear what you're saying, Paul, but let me remind you that it takes both sunshine and rain to make one of my rainbows. You are a keen observer of the human condition. You know that people tend to live merely in the service of their own success. Those who know nothing but prosperity and pleasure become hard and shallow. Those whose prosperity has been mixed with adversity can be kind and gracious. And civilization, Paul, from a heavenly point of view, is only a slow process of learning to be kind."

I'm sure you would agree with me that tension is the pulse of life. As Blake said, "Without contraries is no progression." Moreover, I think you will agree with me that what makes us unhappy can also make us more alive. Often pain can bring more life than pleasure. But for this kind of life to sprout and flourish we have to stop denying and defying these thorns. We have to begin to accept them. More than that: we have to befriend the enemy. The Torah says the true hero is one who makes a friend of his enemy. Let's apply that insight to our own internal enemies. Each of us has a whole community of folk dwelling inside us; some are friendly, and others real enemies. When for the second time we take our thorn to the Lord, we have to begin to allow the Lord to help us begin to embrace the thorn. Finally, you must take your whole life in your arms, and allow your self and your life to be embraced by the almighty arms of God himself. That seems to me would be a good agenda for the second time.

Then—sometime later—comes the third time. My guess is that, the third time, Paul discovers the true mercy of failure. "Three times I besought the Lord about this, that it should leave me; but he said to me, 'My grace is sufficient for you, for my power is made perfect in weakness.'" Now that is one of the great lines of Scripture, but not one easy to understand.

I said that human beings tend to live merely in the service of their own success. I suspect that's true. And to individuals and nations alike, success tends to spell power. Then when we seek to exert power over others we lose it over ourselves. The reason for this seems simple. By nature we are neither humble nor reasonable. Freud said intelligence is weak, if persistent. And Isaac Bashevis Singer, in accepting his Nobel Prize, pointed out that he thought the Almighty was frugal when it came to the intellect, lavish when it came to passions and emotions. Among these passions and emotions are, of course, ambition, greed, the instinct to dominate, the needs of the ego, and a whole bundle of personal vanities and anxieties. Only when they are contained do reason and the Holy Spirit have a chance. That's why, I think, God's power is made perfect in weakness.

I am sure that many of you have read "Blessed are the meek," and wondered what that meant. Does that mean we are supposed to become doormats for people to walk all over us? Certainly a lot of Christians act as if that is what it means. But the word in Greek is "praos," and that word "praos," as a verb, refers to the channeling of energies, as in taming horses. Before they could be useful horses had to be "meeked." In Wycliffe's Bible we read "Blessed are the 'meeked' for they shall inherit the earth."

We are meeked by the thorns in our flesh. The mercy of our failures is that they point us toward true success, which reluctantly we have to admit is with God alone. So a "messenger of Satan" can become a servant of God. The Devil's subtraction can become God's addition. If you look at the Cross, you can see two great symbols: a capital "I," a powerful "I," crossed out; and you see a minus turned by God into a plus. "When I am weak, then I am strong."

So, dear friends, if you are up for it this week, take your Bibles. Read not only the twelfth chapter of 2 Corinthians, but read also the fourth chapter. Read "But we have this treasure in earthen vessels to show that the transcendent power belongs to God and not to us." Read "We are afflicted in every way but not crushed, perplexed but not driven to despair, struck down but not destroyed; always carrying in the body the death of Christ so that the life of Christ may also be manifested in our bodies" (2 Cor. 4:7–10). Then go to work. Describe to God in minute detail just how you feel about that thorn in your flesh. And make it sound as full of self-pity and anger, make it sound as trivial as you want. But make it specific; get it all out. And don't ask for answers: "Lord, just listen to me; I don't want to hear anything." A week later, try it again. Maybe you will have to do it several times, if you are as angry as I am about one or two thorns in my own life. But I'll tell you something: You get bored with your bitterness. After a while it gets boring just dumping the mud: "I said that last week, Lord; I am beginning to get bored with it this week." So the third time, you may find that you can begin the process of integration, begin to befriend the enemy. You can take what seems like a defeat at the hand of Satan and turn it into the occasion for the victory God always had in mind for you.

Let's listen once again to St. Paul: "And to keep me from being too elated, a thorn was given me in the flesh, a messenger of Satan, to harass me, to keep me from being too elated. Three times I besought the Lord about this, that it should leave me. But he said to me 'My grace is sufficient for you, for my power is made perfect in weakness.'" Then with a kind of nose-thumbing independence Paul says, "I will all the more gladly boast of my weaknesses that the power of Christ may rest upon me. For the sake of Christ then I am content with weaknesses, insults, hardships, persecutions, calamities." And he ends triumphantly, "For when I am weak, then I am strong."

"Suffer the Little Children . . ."

MAY 18, 1980

"Suffer the little children to come unto me and forbid them not; for of such is the kingdom of heaven."
                                                    Mark 10:14

As we all know, when somebody tells you how young you look, he is telling you how old you are! But there are other ways as well of finding out how old you are. One is to find yourself reading with greater frequency the King James Version of the Bible. But if you read it not because the words are familiar, but rather because they are unfamiliar and hence more powerful—you're still young in mind and heart. I prefer "suffer" to "let" the children come unto me. That word "suffer," which means "permit" carries a special kind of meaning for me. However it's the meaning of the whole text that we're after this morning.

On the very first page of what he calls his "Anti-memoirs," André Malraux recalls a conversation with a priest that took place during World War II when both of them were in the French Underground.

"Tell me, padre," says Malraux to the older man. "You've been listening for years to confessions. What have you learned?"

Without hesitating the priest answers, "People are not as happy as they appear; and finally, none of us grows up."

I was touched when I first read that exchange, and still am moved by the two insights of the priest. Both strike me as true, poignant, and finally comforting, After all, trouble is a great common bond between us all. Trouble is a great equalizer. Out of my own experience I would only add to the words of the priest that while people may not be as happy as they appear, most of us are happier than we know. But that's a big subject for another time. For the moment let's not worry how happy or unhappy we may be, although I continually pray for the happiness of all of you. Rather, let us ponder why it's true that we never grow up, and whether it's all that bad that we don't.

That we should grow up seems indicated by St. Paul's words, "When I was a child I spoke like a child, I thought like a child . . . when I became a man I put away childish things" (1 Cor. 13:11). But that we should remain childlike seems indicated by Jesus' words: "Suffer the little children to come unto me and forbid them not; for of such is the kingdom of heaven."

Those of you my age, or a few hours older, know how frustrating it is that somehow we never seem to get these childish things put away. And I am afraid it's true that the childishness of many Christians is fostered by misconceptions of the faith. Only this week I heard someone say that with all this talk about Christians being "children of God" and "born again," the church really ritualizes regression. Too many Christians seek an all-powerful God in order to gratify their longing to remain weak, refusing to recognize that in Christ, God Himself became weak that they might become strong. Still others— fundamentalists for example—longing to be spared the insecurity of uncertainty, engage in what psychiatrists call "premature closure." They misuse faith as a substitute for thought, when faith in fact is what makes good thinking possible. Still other church members suffer defeat at the hands of the world. But instead of turning their defeat into the occasion for the victory God always had in mind for them, they try to compensate for their defeat by seizing turf in the church and holding on to it for dear life.

Most of us smile when in Scripture we read of the silence of the disciples, too embarrassed to admit to Jesus that a dispute had risen among them as to who was the greatest. But do we ever stop competing with our parents, our children, among ourselves, even with God, although, when you stop to think of it, God is the only person in your life who will never compete with you? All these are childish things which bear out the priest's insight that finally none of us grows up. It's humbling. Often the best we can do is simply to laugh at ourselves. If, beyond that, you want to fight that childish aggressiveness in yourself, I have in hand a helpful tip from Snoopy: "Sometimes when I get up in the morning, I feel very peculiar, I feel like I've just got to bite a cat! I feel like if I don't bite a cat before sundown, I'll go crazy! But then I just take a deep breath and forget about it. That's what is known as real maturity."

But if it's immature to be childish, to remain child*like* may be a function of maturity, for as Jesus said, "whoever does not receive the Kingdom of God as a little child will not enter therein." Discussing this passage, Biblical commentators like to dwell on the natural humility, the basic obedient and trusting quality of children; and I have no quarrel with such emphasis. All of us could profit from being a little more humble, trusting and obedient, although Christians have to recognize that obedience to God has more to do with being love-abiding than law-abiding. But why, I wonder, don't these same commentators talk about the natural idealism of children? It's children who want to save the seals, save the whales, and all the rest of us to boot. It's kids who sell cookies for causes, bake bread for brotherhood, save pennies to fight pollution. It's kids who have walkathons against war. And of course we encourage them. We believe in their being generous. But it's also true that we encourage them to outgrow it, as though generosity were a pair of short pants. Do you think Jesus would bless that view of growing up?

This sermon was inspired by something I read in the *Boston Globe* by Ellen Goodman. She wrote, "We raise our children with ethical time bombs, built-in disillusionment alarms. We allow them their ideals until they are 14 or 18, or 22. But if they don't let go, we worry about whether they will be able to function in the real world. It's all quite mad. We regard toughness as adult, cynicism as grown-up.

"Adults *know* that clean air is all very nice, but it must be balanced against jobs. Adults know that helping others is neat, but it may take away their motivation. Adults know that peace is swell, but you may need annihilation to save your national security. Adults know that war is to be feared, but so is the fear of war."

Goodman suggests that this so-called realism, that adults devour, may be the true "junk food" of our time.

"Whosoever shall not receive the Kingdom of God as a little child shall not enter therein." Remember Christ was on his way to Jerusalem when he said that. (That's why the disciples tried to keep the kids out of the way; they figured he had other things on his mind.) He knew what was coming. There were no illusions in his mind. A realist, Christ knew the imperfections of the world. Only he protested and fought them, unlike "mature" adults who only deplore them, and then use them as an excuse to prolong them. Do you think Jesus would say to us, "Suffer these grown-ups to come unto me and refuse them not, for of such is the Kingdom of Heaven"?

To take on the imperfections of the world means of course that your heart will be saddened, your self-confidence impaired, your trust disappointed. You will know despair. But isn't maturity the ability to outlast despair? Isn't that what growing up is all about—learning to outlast despair?

The words that we heard earlier from the Psalms are very familiar, but if well worn, they wear well. "God is a very present help *in trouble*"—not to get us out of trouble or to spare us trouble. "Therefore will we not fear"—now listen to this—"though the earth be removed and though the mountains be carried into the midst of the sea." What do you think the psalmist had in mind? Why, the whole bottom of his world must have fallen out. And it's not just personal tragedy. "He maketh wars to cease unto the end of the earth, he breaketh the bow, and cutteth the spear in sunder; he burneth the chariot in the fire." That's—shall we say—long-term thinking. That's the hope that is born when optimism dies. The psalmist is "hanging in there," outlasting despair, knowing that "the LORD of hosts is with us, the God of Jacob is our refuge" (Ps. 46).

"In our most common parenting scenario, we instill ideals in our children, resent it when they challenge us for not living up to them, and then feel reassured when they give up their ideals, like sleds or cartoons" (Ellen Goodman).

Why don't we make *ourselves* guardians of our ideals, seeing that we grown-ups have the power to implement them? Now we're getting to the heart of the matter: I think Goodman is right in suggesting that we make our children repositories of our ideals precisely because they are powerless. That way we can have our ideals and ignore them, assuage our conscience while maintaining the status quo.

I think now I understand why even Biblical commentators don't talk much about the natural idealism of children. To remain childlike in respect to the idealism of our childhood would be to expose ourselves to ridicule, to hardship and suffering. So it's easier to call such idealism naive, cute, childish.

The world is full of the intricacies of wrongdoing. Not to recognize them is childish, as childish as to expect them to disappear. But to recognize them, and then to take them on, is childlike—and Christlike. Christ was on his way to Jerusalem to show us that to be is to be vulnerable. And on his way, he stopped to teach us the greatest loss in life is not death, but what dies within us while we live—the idealism of our childhood. "Suffer the little children to come unto me and forbid them not; for of such is the kingdom of heaven." May Christ teach us this Sunday, that we are never too old to become younger.

Babel and Pentecost

MAY 25, 1980
Readings: Genesis 11:1–9; Acts 2:1–18

Anyone who plunges into the sea of life and dives deep enough to come up all red-eyed, will, I think, come up also with the conclusion that the human race's capacity for self-deception is awesome. In fact, I don't think you and I could invent anything that could possibly be more unbelievable than what most of us already believe. This, of course, is no novel insight into the human condition. Already in the eighth century B.C., when the prophet Amos spoke the truth, the priest Amaziah said (correctly), "The land cannot bear his words." If the truth be abject and miserable, though it stare us in the face, we shall not see it until it hits us in the face. I ask you: In your own or in public life, how often is a crisis a crisis before it's validated by disaster?

Usually all this denial of truth takes place on a subconscious level. But it can take place consciously too. Surely all of you have known moments when all you wanted was to forget everything and face nothing, moments when you could have said with Edmund in *Long Day's Journey Into Night* (what a title!) "Who wants to see life as it is, if they can help it? That's what I wanted—to be alone with myself in another world where truth is untrue and life can hide from itself."

There's a reason for this. For most of us life is no sunny and secure place. In *Moby Dick* Melville wrote: "Man has lost that sense of the full awfulness of the sea which aboriginally belongs to it"; "and the sea," he reminds us, "covers two thirds of the fair world." That may be. But I don't think, subconsciously at least, we have lost that sense of the full awfulness of the world no matter how fair it may be on a day like this. The world is both lovable *and* horrible. We're terrified of death, of the fact that nature intends to get us, and in the end is going to succeed. We're terrified of fate: where is it going to strike next? We're terrified of guilt and of the possibility of final condemnation. We're terrified of meaninglessness—not of choosing the wrong values but of the possible bankruptcy of all our values and loyalties. So we try desperately to secure ourselves against our insecurity and that is where self-deception comes in.

For instance, what do you suppose those descendants of Noah thought they were doing in the Tigris-Euphrates Valley? Did they really believe in that unbelievable tower? (I beg you not to heed the crudeness of the attempt to account for the fact that different people spoke different tongues. You're right, the story of Babel is a myth. But you are wrong if you forget that the truth of a myth, as Thomas Mann once defined it, "is a truth that is and always will be, no matter how much we try and say it *was*.") Did these people really think they could build a from-here-to-eternity edifice, defying gravity, chance, human error, human sinfulness, God himself? Did they really believe that with enough furious activity they could at last triumphantly find for themselves a sunny and secure perch on top of their world?

Apparently they did, and if so they are no crazier than we. Besides, rather than something ungodly, isn't there something Godlike in thrusting against destiny, testing freedom to the limit? Human beings, to be sure, are a rich mix of marvelous possibilities and grievous limitations, but isn't there a real danger of trying to draw the line too soon? In my experience, some of the best things in the world have been done by people too stupid to know they can't be done!

Personally, I'm fascinated by these Babel builders. Without their kind of self-deception, the kind that always accompanies ambition, we'd have no pyramids, no King Tut's treasure, far fewer castles in the world, and less Greek thought. I say that about the Greeks because Plato too was trying to build a from-here-to-eternity edifice, only he tried to do it not with bricks but with ideas. And finally, as Woody Allen said, capturing the essence of creativity, "If you're not failing at something you're not doing anything!"

That being said, however, we have also to recognize that without this kind of self-deception we would not have had Adolf Hitler who, as some of you will remember, announced, "The Third Reich will last a thousand years."

"Come, let us build ourselves a city and a tower with its top in the heavens, *and make a name for ourselves.*" There's the real self-deception; we have to make a name for ourselves. We think we have to prove ourselves when God has already taken care of all that. A few minutes ago we baptized Mia. Baptism symbolizes the fact that God gives us a name so that we don't have to make a name for ourselves. Baptism symbolizes the truth that God has proved us by His love so that we have only to express ourselves, and what a difference there is between proving ourselves and expressing ourselves.

The story of the tower of Babel as you remember ends in confusion and the scattering of the races, which reflects another insight into the human condition. Activity rooted in pride can never unify, as pride is not accidentally but essentially competitive.

Before turning to the New Testament story of Pentecost I want to point out how much ambition there is in youthful idealism. This is important to recognize because when our ambition is thwarted we generally abandon the idealism and hang on to the ambition, when in fact we should abandon the ambition and hang on to the idealism. When we are young we think that we love virtue when what we are really in love with is the image of ourselves as virtuous people—at least in part. When we are young we think we want to give, but what we don't realize is that we need desperately to prove to ourselves and others that we have something to give. When the world does not reward our ambition—because virtue is its own reward, and reward enough—we abandon the virtue and redirect the ambition. We become cynical and self-seeking, and begin to deceive ourselves in a new way. We say, "One week's worth of world news is enough to prove how naive it is to try to save the world." Before we needed a moral sanction for our ambition. Now we need a rationalization to indulge ourselves in the petty greeds of everyday existence.

The real art is to graduate—to use a good metaphor of this season—to graduate from an instinctive, uninformed reaction to pain and frustration, to a condition of suffering in which we can contemplate pain and frustration, and learn from it. We need to suffer, for instance, our hostages in Iran—and learn. We need to suffer Miami's racial outbursts against a color-coded system of justice—and learn. We need to suffer the uprisings of the South Koreans. We need to feel ourselves naked, unaccommodated, alone; we need to learn to feel what wretches feel. We need to become part of the human condition. We need to experience the human condition without any deceptions, and not with fists raised in anger, or extended in greed. Rather we must learn to stand with palms up, empty-handed before God. Then we shall be ready for Pentecost. For only when the heart is empty of ambition can it be filled with the Holy Spirit. And when the heart is filled with that love which is the Holy Spirit, then the eye can see the truth, and the will can do God's work. Then we are free not to make a name for ourselves but to make manifest the love of God which is trying desperately to make itself manifest in the lives of each of us. And, of course, our strength without ambition will be as the strength of ten "for the zeal of the Lord of Hosts will perform it." We "shall mount up with wings as eagles." We "shall run and not grow weary!" Yes, we shall even "walk and not faint," which is so much harder than mounting up with wings like eagles. For "to walk and not faint" means you can plod along lifting love and laughter out of the mundane, find precious metal in the dirt.

Filled with the Holy Spirit we shall be united and not divided. We shall speak the language of the poor, understand the rich, listen to and

May 25, 1980

understand the voices of Iranians, Koreans, and all other children of a Father who loves all as if all were but one. And instead of seeking our own security, we shall learn to live in the midst of insecurity saying, "God is a very present help in trouble."

Instead of trying to storm the ramparts of heaven we shall allow heaven to take us by storm, and we too shall "dream dreams and see visions." May the Lord, on this day of Pentecost, bless us and keep us. May the Lord make his face to shine upon us. May the Lord take our minds and think through them; take our lips and speak through them. May the Lord take our hearts and set them on fire.

July Fourth

JULY 6, 1980
Reading: Matthew 14:22–33

At least since the bicentennial, I associate the Fourth of July with tall ships; and the association is a good one, especially for Americans like myself, who while in school, were invited to memorize:

Thou, too, sail on, O Ship of State!
Sail on, O Union, strong and great!

So on this patriotic weekend, let's see what meaning we can find in the New Testament story just read, which among other things is about a ship.

"Then he made the disciples get into the boat and go before him to the other side." It appeared a simple, straight-forward voyage. But then we read: "When evening came the boat was many furlongs distant from the land, beaten by the waves; for the wind was against them."

I think a parallel can be drawn. Two-hundred-and-four years ago, our Ship of State set sail, and while to Native Americans and Blacks the voyage did not appear promising, to others it appeared uniquely so. We weren't just another nation; we were a whole New World. With freedom and justice as our hammer and chisel, we were going to carve out a better life not only for our own people, but for the rest of humanity as well. The American dream was to dispel the world's nightmares.

As the years rolled by we seemed to be holding course, more or less. Lincoln called us "God's almost chosen people," and "the last best hope for democracy." We became the haven for Europe's "huddled masses yearning to breathe free"; and as recently as World War II, Churchill, in a grateful and encouraging cable to Roosevelt, quoted Longfellow at greater length:

> Thou, too, sail on, O Ship of State!
> Sail on, O Union, strong and great!
> Humanity with all its fears,
> With all the hopes of future years,
> Is hanging breathless on thy fate!

But nobody sends us telegrams like that anymore. Paradoxically, now that we've become the most powerful nation in the world, we haven't the same influence we once had when, as a people, we were weakest. The American way of life is not the automatic choice of other people, as frequently it has been fashioned, not to the enrichment but to the detriment of theirs. And at home the hammer of freedom is so frequently divorced from the chisel of justice that the common good, often as not, is identified with the good of those in power.

Like the boat of the disciples, our Ship of State has run into heavy weather. Like the boat of the disciples, our "Union strong and great" is losing headway. Rip Van Winkle fell asleep and awoke in the future. If we don't stay awake in this election year, we may wake up in the past!

And finally, as with the disciples so with us Americans, our troubles stem in large part from the fact that Jesus is not on board, but all by himself on a distant shore. I say that because the Christian faith is supposed to help us interpret storms. "God is a very present help *in trouble.*" But today, God is invoked less to interpret than to avoid the experience of trouble. God is invoked not to encourage us to face inevitable change, and the possible loss of what we most cherish, but rather to shore up what is most threatened.

Indeed there is a parallel. Listen again: "When evening came, he (Jesus) was there alone, but the boat by this time was many furlongs distant from the land, beaten by the waves; for the wind was against them."

As the curtain rises on Act II of our symbol story, we see one man preparing to abandon what appears to be a sinking ship. (And can't you hear the cries—there are so many on every sinking ship—"For God's sake, Peter, sit down, you're rocking the boat!") What do you suppose moved Peter and not the others to abandon ship? I think it fair to say that most of us "prefer the security of known misery to the misery of unfamiliar security" (Sheldon Kopp). That's why it's so hard to align feelings with reality; why new facts don't automatically alter old attitudes; why Picasso could truthfully say to Gertrude Stein, "No, I'm not ahead of my time, I'm with it. It is the others who are behind." But despite our fear of change, every so often one of us finds the courage to despair, the courage to revolt from evil doings, from the dullness of our lives, the banality of our culture. And it's not only *from* something that we revolt; you can "revolt into the sacred." That's what Christianity is all about, a revolt into the sacred. And when the time for the revolt comes, often in the fourth watch of the night, that miserable 2:00 a.m. to 6:00 a.m. shift, when you are most alone with yourself; and Jesus comes and bids you abandon the sinking ship and come to him, then like Peter, you may be ready for that most insecure of all steps, the leap of faith.

Peter, as you recall, having leapt, began immediately to sink. I wouldn't be surprised if scholars one day established the fact that Jesus called Peter "the rock" then, not for his foundational but for his sinking properties! For did not St. Paul say, "When I am weak, then I am strong"? When we realize that we can no more trust our own buoyancy than that of the ship we have just abandoned, then we truly give ourselves to Christ. And the more of ourself we surrender to Jesus, the more of ourselves he gives back to us. The more we pray for help, the more he reveals to us that we are not helpless.

That's the central meaning of the story that makes it so eternally true. Whether Jesus walked on the Sea of Galilee I really don't know; nor do I care. What I do know is that when I am sinking under waves of doubt, despairing of myself, my country, my church, and when, like Peter, I cry out, "Lord, save me," my Savior does. He saves me with a truth deeper than the mind can comprehend; with a love we ourselves can never express; with a beauty so lovely that it hurts. The central meaning of Christian life is this: Ask Jesus for but a thimbleful of help and you get an oceanful in return.

Wouldn't it be wonderful if the story stopped here? What happier ending for a troubled soul than to find rest, to find in place of doubt, certitude, and contentment amid pain?

I think it would be awful if the story stopped there. How would you feel if Peter had said to Jesus, "Now that you have saved me, Lord, let's walk off into the sunrise of a new day and forget all about those fellows in the sinking ship."

Having abandoned the sinking ship for Jesus, Peter returns with Jesus. "America, love it *and leave it*"—leave it for Jesus, and then come back *with* Jesus. That's how to love America—not with textbook pieties about how we are "the land of the free and the home of the brave," but with tough religious questions: Who's a Good Samaritan today, and where's the Judas selling Christ for coin?

How do you love America? Don't say, "my country, right or wrong." That's like saying "my grandmother, drunk or sober"; it doesn't get you anywhere. Don't just salute the flag, and don't burn it either. Wash it. Make it clean.

How do you love America? With the vision and compassion of Christ with a transcendent ethic which alone can rewed the hammer of freedom to the chisel of justice and so renew and fulfill "the patriot's dream that sees beyond the years her alabaster cities gleam undimmed by human tears."

"Behold I make all things new," saith the Lord. Our revolutionary forbears seemed to understand that. They didn't bestir themselves to salvage the past. Their political debate pitted one kind of future against another kind of future. They knew people were supposed to die *to* an old order and not *with* the old order. How ironic that their descendents should today be crushed by ancient outmoded structures because we prefer to be victims than to be rebels! How ironic that the descendents of Thomas Jefferson should make like George III! How ironic that there's hardly a youth in the land as radical and as reasonable as was Ben Franklin in his 80s, and in his cups!

When Peter returned to the boat with Jesus, the winds abated. I think our own ship could recover headway if more of us followed Peter's example. For we really do love America with all the ardor of Longfellow who ended his poem, as we shall this sermon:

> Sail on, nor fear to breast the sea!
> Our hearts, our hopes, are all with thee,
> Our hearts, our hopes, our prayers, our tears,
> Our faith triumphant o'er our fears,
> Are all with thee,—are all with thee!

The Lord's Prayer—I

JULY 13, 1980
Reading: Matthew 6:5, 6

It was Martin Luther who wrote, "The Lord's Prayer is the greatest martyr, for everybody tortures and abuses it." What he had in mind, I imagine, was the way Sunday by Sunday we repeat it mechanically and thoughtlessly. But "*abusus non tollit usum*," as the Roman Catholics like to say—"abuse does not negate right use." In an effort rightly to use the Lord's Prayer, I propose that this Sunday, and the remaining Sundays in July, we try to rediscover some of the excitement and meaning in the Lord's Prayer. For, in another Latin—and musical—phrase, the Lord's Prayer is the "*cantus firmus*" of the churches. It is the one prayer that for centuries has literally spanned the world; "the world of everyday trifles and universal history, the world with its hours of joy and bottomless anguish, the world of citizens and soldiers, the world of monotonous routine and sudden terrible catastrophe, the world of carefree children and at the same time of problems that shatter grown men and women" (Helmut Thielicke).

Why for so long has the Lord's Prayer meant so much to so many? The first thing I think we have to say, by way of an answer, is that it is because Jesus himself gave us the prayer. It is reliability of the source that gives authority to the words. In his Farewell Address, George Washington told us to "guard against the impostures of pretended patriotism." Thomas Paine warned us of "sunshine patriots," who shrink from service to their country in a time of crisis. Surely we should be no less vigilant against "sunshine Christians," against the "impostures of pretended Christianity." I, for one, simply cannot listen to God-talk from people too shallow to know that it is in the depth of hell that heaven is finally affirmed and life is sanctified. I cannot listen to God-talk from scared people who give quick Biblical answers because they are too frightened to confront tough personal questions. (Is there anything as irrelevant as an answer to an unasked question?) I cannot listen to God-talk from people who know perfectly well that the world did not reward Christ for being Christ, yet they feel they are going to be rewarded for being Christians. (I guess that takes care of just about every TV evangelist!) And I can't take God-talk from folk who are as joyless as the proverbial church soprano who looked as if she had been bred by a pair of tomahawks. I say that because no such sit in our choir loft (!) and to make Nietzsche's point: Christians, he said, would have to look more redeemed for him to believe in their redeemer.

In contrast, when *Jesus* says, "Our Father, who art in heaven," I listen. Even during my doubting days in college I listened, and carefully, because Jesus knew not only more about God than I did—that was obvious; he also knew more about the world. He could talk convincingly to me about a father in heaven because he took seriously the earth's homeless orphans. He could talk to me convincingly about living at peace in the hands of love because he knew that the world lived constantly at war in the grip of hatred. He could talk to me of light, and joy, and exultation, because I knew that he himself knew dark-ness, sorrow, and death. That's why, eventually, Jesus became for me too my Lord and Saviour, and that's why I think it right to say that the authority of the Lord's Prayer stems from the reliability of the source. Because Christ died for us, his words have authority for us.

One more thing by way of preface. In those same doubting days, I read the Bible not only for what it told me about God, but also for what it told me about myself and the human race. As a matter of fact, I was first attracted to Christianity because of what we might call "Biblical anthropology." When, returning home from World War II, I read in Scripture that of the first two brothers, one died at the hand of the other, I was impressed. That description of the human condi-tion reflected no chirping optimism. And you will notice, as we go along, that each phrase of the Lord's Prayer tells us just about as much about ourselves as it tells us about God. Take the first little word. "Our" in reference to a father makes everyone related. Therefore, it is dynamic, blowing into bits our favorite creedal, nationalistic, racial prejudices. How can we dare to say "our" when we have allowed our God-given differences to become blasphemously divisive? How dare we say "our" when the warning mark of Cain is on the brow of a frat-ricidal nuclear world?

We say "our" because Christ is not telling us what we are existen-tially; he is telling us what we are essentially. Essentially, we are all one. That's the way God made us. "Our" reminds us that Christ died to keep us that way. "Our" reminds us that our sin is that we put asunder what God himself has joined together. "Our" tells us that the answer to Cain's question, "Am I my brother's keeper?" is quite sim-ply, "No, you are your brother's brother." Human unity is not some-thing we are called on to create, only to recognize.

How much excitement, tension, there is in no more than the first word of the Lord's Prayer! And, of course, it confronts us with a hard choice: faced with an increasingly bellicose and exclusive form of patriotism that insists that the country be set above the rest of the world, will we become "sunshine Christians," or will we continue to pray with ever greater fervor "*Our* father."

Let's go on. God, of course, is no father in any literal sense, anymore than she is a mother. The "in heaven" signifies that God is beyond all human categories, as God is beyond the abyss of stars, immeasurable time, universal matter. But transcendent, God is also immanent, and how else, if not in personal terms, are we going to talk about a power which each of us experiences as a presence? It is absolutely right to call God "father" or "mother"—it matters not—when we meet God in our hearts rather than in our heads; when God is known devotionally rather than dogmatically. Let us not fear to exaggerate, to be imaginative. Just as the painter El Greco deliberately distorted physiognomic detail to get at the mystery of personality, so we need not fear deliberately to distort human relationships to get at the mystery of a power experienced as love. "God is love" means the revelation is in the relationship. So the psalmist uses the second person singular:

> Whither shall I go from *thy* spirit?
> Whither shall I flee from *thy presence?*

So Jesus talks of God as "Abba"—father. Anthropomorphism is indispensable to the believer; it is dangerous only to the literalist.

"Our Father who art in heaven, hallowed be Thy name." The last phrase recalls the first great commandment—"Thou shalt love the Lord thy God with all thy heart, and with all thy mind and with all thy strength." Idolatry is always enemy number one in Scripture, for idolatry is recognized to be the worship of the self writ large. Who worships power? The man of power, or the weak one who says, "If only I had power, I'd be someone." Who worships riches? The woman of wealth, or the poor one who says, "If only I had money, I'd have value." Who worships scholarship? The scholar. Athletics? The athlete. Who worships the United States of America? No American worships France—unless he speaks very good French. You see what I mean: idolatry is finally worship of the self projected into objective form. So it always comes down to, "Hallowed be *thy* name," or "Hallowed be mine."

But "Hallowed be thy name" can have another meaning (and another, and yet another). If God in heaven is like unto a father, then "as is His majesty, so is His mercy." "Our father, who art in heaven, hallowed be thy name, that thou dost forgive this idolatrous human race, and dost receive us unto thyself as the father the prodigal son." Incidentally that parable is all about the father, isn't it, so prodigal in his love?

Notice that nowhere in the Lord's Prayer, or anywhere else for that matter does Jesus teach us to pray, "Make me holy, make me dedicated." Holiness, dedication will come of themselves if we pray, "Hallowed be thy name." Luther once said that you don't need to command a stone lying in the sun to become warm. It becomes warm in the nature of things.

Today we have but to step out of this church and into a gorgeous July day to feel the warmth of the sun. And we have but to pray, "Hallowed be thy name" to say with Wesley, "I felt my heart was strangely warmed."

To become new men and women we do not start with ourselves; our good intentions, our well-meant moral activism. No, we start just as we end—with God. "Hallowed be thy name." If our relationship with God is right, we don't have to worry about our interior life; it will be just fine.

Helmut Thielicke, to whom I owe much in the preparation of these thoughts, once suggested that each of us is like a soldier in the night on sentry duty shouting into the darkness: "Who goes there?" Well, in the Lord's Prayer we get an answer—"a heavenly father" who with his love can scatter all the darkness of this world.

To a universal need there is a universal answer. Thomas Wolfe summed it up this way: "The deepest search in life, it seemed to me, the thing that in one way or another was central to all living, was man's search for a father, not merely the father of his flesh, not merely the lost father of his youth, but the image of a strength and wisdom external to his need and superior to his hunger, to which the belief and power of his own life could be united."

How lucky we are to be able to pray, "Our Father, who art in heaven, hallowed be thy name."

The Lord's Prayer—II

JULY 20, 1980
"Thy Kingdom Come"

Let's pursue the effort, begun last week, to recapture some of the excitement and depth of meaning which so easily get lost in the routine repetition of the Lord's Prayer. (T. S. Eliot suggests that life is always the rediscovery of that which has been lost and found, and lost, again and again.)

Those of you who were here last week may recall my describing "Our"—the very first word in the prayer—as explosive. In reference to a loving God, symbolized by the word father, "Our" means I live in you and you live in me, insofar as any of us live at all. Love alone is the expression of our aliveness. "We pass out of death into life because we love the brothers and sisters." "Our" means national boundaries are finally no more interesting than the equator. "Our" means territorial discrimination is as evil as racial discrimination. "Our" plus "father" taken together really tells the whole story; all the rest is commentary. For "Our father" suggests an isosceles triangle with God at the apex and you and I at the base angles, which are equal. The triangle works when love courses around it. (God has set up the circuitry; we have yet to turn on the circuits!)

I also said last week that anthropomorphism—attributing to God human characteristics—is indispensable. God is "father" or "mother" because God is experienced as a loving presence. Anthropomorphism is indispensable to the believer, dangerous only to the literalist.

To expand for a minute on the subject, we might recall that religious anthropomorphism is not the only form of anthropomorphism. Think of the university professors who project on to the world their own anthropomorphic expectations, insisting that the world be rational. Whoever said the earth was rational? Chesterton said, "The ego is more distant than any star." So too is God. At its depths, life is apprehended at a level deeper than the mind can ever comprehend. The most important truths in life are truths our minds can defend but never discover. One of the reasons I abandoned the academic world was because universities, by and large, have abandoned the all-important, unanswerable truths in favor of the answerable and unimportant ones! No less a logician than Ludwig Wittgenstein said, "When all the scientific answers are in, all the important questions remain untouched!"

And finally I said last week that we pray "Hallowed be *thy* name," because to hallow our family name, or the name of the institution for which we work, the name of the flag we salute, or the name of the church in which we worship—to call holy a name other than God's is idolatrous and divisive. It is divisive, for when you stop to think of it, an idol is any god that is mine but not yours. Idolatry is always the worship of the self writ large.

Well, today let's move on: "Thy kingdom come." Here at Easter, or wherever we sing the "Alleluia" chorus from the *Messiah*, we sing—piano—"The kingdom of this world is become." On that word, "become" there is a giant crescendo; then, with the basses coming in an octave higher, and the sopranos an octave and a third higher, everybody sings—fortissimo—"The kingdom of our Lord and of his Christ."

Handel knew what he was doing. He was affirming the difference between the kingdom of this world, and the kingdom of our Lord; he was affirming the vast superiority of the kingdom of our Lord; and he was affirming the fervor with which human beings must sing and pray for the coming of the kingdom because, Lord knows, it hasn't taken over yet!

In contrast to Handel, many people affirm something quite different. When things go badly in the kingdom of this world, as invariably they do, given the callous insensibility that turns human beings away from their neighbors in preoccupation with their own troubles, or dreams of aggrandizement—in such bad moments, many people turn from God, saying, "How could God permit such things to happen?" Instead of becoming alienated from their faith in God, wouldn't it make more sense for them to become alienated from their faith in human beings, alienated from shallow notions of automatic progress, from sentimental notions about the "nobility of man"? Of course we should live in and for one another. Not, however, because you and I are so lovable, but simply because that's the only way we are going to *become* lovable. Love one another, but *"in God we trust."* You couldn't come up with a phrase more suitable for the coin of a kingdom of this world than, "In God we trust."

But, like Handel's "The kingdom of this world is become the kingdom of our Lord," "In God we trust" is a hope, an aspiration, not an established fact. Both reflect the prayerful petition, "Thy kingdom come."

But *how* is the kingdom coming? Clearly in at least two ways; and in myriad ways, I'm sure, of which we know little or nothing. In the first chapter of Paul's letter to the Romans, we read this startling statement: "For this reason God has *given them up* to the vileness of their own desires" (v. 24). That passage confirms freedom of choice. It says: God who is slow to chide and swift to bless, will do anything for us short of violence to his own gift of free will. As there is no true and great love without freedom, we are free, if we so choose, to go to hell. But the passage confirms as well that true freedom is practically synonymous with virtue, as Abraham Lincoln understood so well when he talked about "a new birth of freedom." Freedom of choice is a small freedom. The freedom to understand and to love one another—that's the large freedom, the *"libertas maior,"* as St. Augustine called it.

"God gives us up." If there's one thing we learn in this world, it is that life is consequential. We were made and meant to love, and if we don't we suffer. "God gives us up." Paul is talking with God's judgment, which helps bring in the kingdom by preventing the final coming of any other. God's judgment is built into the nature of things. If you rend the bond of love, you will experience the loneliness, which is the experience of the bond of love rent. If you flee from God, you will be alienated from others also, and from yourself. You will be caught constantly between dream and reality, torn between what you think and what you do. You will have a divided heart: "Our hearts are restless until they find rest in thee."

I know of no passage in Scripture more devastating than the description in Psalm 115 of those who make and trust in idols. First the psalmist describes the idols:

> They have mouths, but do not speak;
> eyes, but do not see.
> They have ears, but do not hear;
> noses, but do not smell.
> They have hands, but do not feel;
> feet, but do not walk.
>
> Ps. 115:5–7

Then the psalmist says, "*Like them* are those who make them. *Like them* are those who trust them." (Remember T. S. Eliot's, "We are the hollowmen . . . headpiece filled with straw"?)

Life is consequential. We are punished not so much *for* as *by* our sins. We do not so much break the ten commandments, as we are broken on them. Consequential for us as individuals, life is even more so for the nations of this nuclear world. Hadn't we better learn to be merciful when we live at each other's mercy? If we do not learn to be meek, will there be any earth for anyone to inherit?

Life swings on an ethical hinge. If you loosen that hinge, all history, and even nature, will feel the shock. For God is not mocked, and the kingdom of God comes through God's judgment, which at least forbids the coming of any other kingdom.

But then there's another, more positive way, in which we can talk of the coming of the kingdom. Let me offer a very homely comparison. Once a week, in different parts of the city, four of us arise with the sun to come together for an hour and a half of very strenuous men's doubles. All of us play tennis fairly well, and some of us—not me—very well. Every now and then we put together a fantastic point. When that happens, one of our number sings out "tennis," expressing the exuberance we all feel that for a few brief moments it has been given to us to play the game the way the game is supposed to be played.

Likewise when, as happened this week, I listen to a middle-aged woman fighting off bitterness, trying to make of a sad divorce—and what divorce is anything else?—an enlarging rather than a diminishing experience—when that happens my heart sings out, "The kingdom." For on the rediscovery of her inadequacy, this woman is drawing on the strength of God. In the dirt she is finding precious metal. In the midst of catastrophe a door has been opened. The kingdom of God is coming into her life.

I think the kingdom of God is coming also into the lives of thousands of nineteen- and twenty-year-old Americans who feel that their country could not, in the immediate future, engage in a war that to them could conceivably be morally justified. Therefore, they are wondering today whether or not to register for the draft this week. If in their minds the conflict is between the demands of conscience and the demands of the state, and they are not fleeing but facing the conflict, the kingdom must be coming, for with Handel they affirm that there is a difference between the kingdom of this world and the kingdom of our Lord. In God they trust—at least the believers among them.

"Being asked by the Pharisees when the kingdom of God was coming, Jesus answered them, 'The kingdom of God is not coming with signs to be observed; nor will they say, "Lo, here it is!" or "There!" for behold, the kingdom of God is *within you*.'"

On the side of the mountain he said, "Blessed are the poor in spirit, for theirs is the kingdom of heaven" (Matt. 5:3). You can go right through the Beatitudes affirming that the kingdom is coming in those who mourn; in the meek; the kingdom is coming in those who hunger and thirst for righteousness; in the merciful; in the pure in heart; in the peacemakers; and the kingdom is coming in those who are persecuted for righteousness' sake—notice, not even for God's sake—"for theirs is the kingdom of heaven."

The kingdom of heaven comes through judgment rendered against all other kingdoms, and more positively when any of us pray, "*Thy kingdom come*." By the mercy of God the kingdom is ours to ring on. The kingdom can come in the lives of any of us. Don't forget: "God can carve the rotten wood, and ride the lame horse" (Martin Luther). The same One Hundred Fifteenth Psalm makes the same point: "He will bless those who fear the Lord both small and great."

"Thy kingdom come." To Christians the kingdom of God is where Jesus Christ is, and Jesus Christ is now within us. So we do not lose heart. Life is cause for frustration, but never despair. With all the saints in this world and the next, we repeat the words of St. Paul: "We are afflicted in every way, but not crushed; perplexed, but not driven to despair; persecuted, but not forsaken; struck down, but not destroyed; always carrying in the body the death of Jesus, so that the life of Jesus may also be made manifest in our bodies" (2 Cor. 4:8–10).

And now as our Savior has taught us, we are bold together to pray "Our Father . . ."

The Lord's Prayer—III*

JULY 27, 1980
"Thy will be done on earth."

Among the many and varied beasts of the field, whom the Lord God has created, cows happen to be favorites of mine; and many a farmer will tell you they're a lot smarter than horses. But smart as they are, cows still move in herds; it's in their nature.

By contrast, a herd mentality is not supposed to dominate human nature. Made "a little lower than the angels" puts us a little above blind instinct. So when we contemplate the mob-madnesses of which the human race is capable, when we see how most of us try to avoid trouble by agreeing our way through life, we are forced to conclude that instead of acting like human beings climbing toward heaven, we are behaving like cows being driven to market. You know how cows move along the road, their minds muddled, beaten now on this side now on that, always trying to avoid the stick and always running into it. Don't you feel like that sometimes? Even the poet Yeats experienced the feeling, describing it in a metaphor only slightly different:

> The years like great black oxen tread me down,
> And God the Herdsman, goads them on behind,
> And I am broken by their passing feet.

But is God really the Herdsman before whom we are as driven cattle? Is it God's will that we be as passive as cows? Today let us consider, "Thy will be done on earth," surely the most powerful phrase in all the Lord's Prayer, and also, I suspect, the most misunderstood.

Consider, for example, the following: Human beings go to war. Then if a close friend or family member is killed, likely as not, the grief-stricken will comfort themselves with the thought, "It is the will of God." But if it is not the will of God that anyone die at the hand of another, and if, as Jesus said, "inasmuch as ye have done it unto the least of these my brethren ye have done it unto me," then it is no exaggeration to say that in every war Christ is crucified afresh. It is no exaggeration to picture Christ between the warring sides, every bomb and bullet passing through his body. How dare we then say that when a person is killed in war it is the will of God? To say that is to confuse Christ with the cross.

*This sermon was greatly aided by Geoffrey Studdert Kennedy's *The Wicket Gate* (1923).—WSC

Another example: We fall desperately ill and say again, "It is the will of God," as if Christ did not spend a major part of his short life healing the sick! In other words, fate is one thing, God's will is quite another. Nothing, I suspect, in the mind of the believer, so confuses sound thought, and frustrates vigorous action, as the identification of God's will with fate. Faith and fatalism have nothing to do with each other. In fact, "faith and fatalism are like fire and water; the one is the death of the other" (Studdert Kennedy). It is Christ's fate, in a world that denies the will of God, to be crucified. It was his faith that triumphed over his fate. And we too can become "more than conquerors," in St. Paul's words, if we are persuaded that no fate—"neither tribulation or distress or persecution or famine or nakedness or the sword"—"can separate us from the love of God, which is in Christ Jesus our Lord" (Rom. 8:35, 39). But that triumph of faith over fate is possible only if we see that God is in the response to evil, not in the sending of it. A loving God can never will evil to anyone, anywhere, and at any time.

That leaves us with the question: If not from the hand of God, from whence come disease and disaster? It is a question we must answer carefully. I am quite prepared to say that evil must pass through the hands of God in the sense that God allows evil to exist. But "through the hands" is not the same as "from the hand." Let mystery remain mystery. Clearly the evils we *do* understand, more or less—wars, the terrible murder this week in the opera, the explosion in the borough of Queens—these evils stem directly from human sin, the misuses of human freedom. But the multiple sclerosis of Richard Queen, the returned hostage, the heat and the drought which have taken so heavy a toll in human life this summer—these are evils the causes of which we do not understand. So let us not pretend we do. Let us not say, "they are from God." We don't know that. Let us say simply, "We do not know." Two things, however, we do know about the mystery of undeserved evil, and the first is that it is more than matched by the mystery of undeserved good; and the second is that the primary task of Christians is not to explain evil but to destroy it, whether it be in the form of wars, droughts, or multiple sclerosis.

"Thy will be done on earth." God's will is not to be identified with evil in any form. God is in the response to evil, not in the sending of it. Nor let us Americans claim that it is God's will that human beings live in a democracy, as if freedom of choice, in and of itself, were a higher virtue. This week a well-traveled citizen of Barbados told me that in all the Caribbean he had not beheld slums like unto the slums of New York City. God didn't make these slums, we Americans made them—by choice. I think we can say democracy is a form of government that demands more virtue of its citizens than any other form of government, but I do not think we can say that democracy guarantees that the virtue will be exercised. So let us term freedom of choice less a virtue than a necessity, a precondition to the real freedom, which is the ability to make choices that are generous, loving and wise. Our wills are not free when they will what is bigoted, narrow, ungenerous. Our wills are only free when they can will the will of a loving God. "Thy will be done on earth."

And now we are come to one of life's deepest mysteries: our wills are never that free. Why, we do not know. Whole libraries have been written on the subject, but we know little more than we did before people learned how to write. All efforts to explain this mystery, simply explain it away. Fundamentally, know only that while intellectually we recognize that our neighbors are as important as we, emotionally we don't feel it that way. Immanuel Kant said once that there is something about the misfortune of even our best friends which is not altogether disagreeable. And St. Paul put the matter classically: "For the good that I would I do not; but the evil I would not, that I do." And he went on, "O wretched man that I am! who shall deliver me from the body of this death?" (Rom. 7:19, 24).

There is the anguished cry of every genuinely moral person who knows that human beings are not perfectible. People who think they are simply show how little they have tried to live out their own convictions. That's why moral people are driven to their knees—out of a sense of no other place to go. That's why we pray for help beyond our own. Knowing that it is really *our* will that we want done on earth, we pray, "*Thy* will be done on earth." Prayer is fundamentally an act of empathy. It is thinking God's thoughts after Him. Prayer is "letting go and letting God." And through prayer we reach St. Paul's conclusion: "Thanks be to God who gives us the victory through our Lord Jesus Christ." The victory is simply this: Christ accepts us even though we be unacceptable. Christ accepts us not because of our worthiness, but notwithstanding our unworthiness. Conscience, dear Christians, is a good servant but a bad master. Christians are not sinners; why even the heathen know they are sinners. Christians are forgiven sinners. "Thanks be to God who gives us the victory through our Lord Jesus Christ."

Will God's will ever be done on earth even as it is in heaven? What can we say, except once again, "We do not know." Were the matter left in our hands alone we would have to say, in the immortal words of Eliza Doolittle, "Not bloody likely." But in the words of T. S. Eliot: "We are only undefeated because we go on trying." We go on trying to kindle kindness in this world. Amid the cruelties of the century we go on trying to bind up the wounds of the fallen victims. We go on trying to destroy evil. "Aflame with faith and free," we allow our faith to triumph over our fate. When optimism dies, we live in hope. Yes, we live in hope even more than in memory, for God is ahead of us as much as within us, a cloud by day, a pillar of fire by night. He is no Herdsman driving his cattle; He is a shepherd who *leads* us in the paths of righteousness. He doesn't use sticks to keep us on the road; His rod and His staff protect us even in the valley of the shadow of death.

"What then shall we say to these things? If God be for us, who can be against us? . . . Who shall separate us from the love of Christ? Shall tribulation, or distress, or persecution, or nakedness or famine or the sword? Nay, in all these things we are more than conquerors through him who loves us. For I am persuaded that neither death nor life, nor angels, nor principalities, nor powers, nor height nor depth, nor things present nor things to come, nor any other creature can separate us from the love of God, which is in Christ Jesus our Lord" (Rom. 8:31, 35, 37–39), who taught us when we meet together to pray saying: "Our Father . . ."

Fiftieth Anniversary—1980

OCTOBER 5, 1980

"Work out your own salvation with fear and trembling."
Philippians 2:12

Gratitude is a much neglected virtue in the world, and even in the church. I say "even," because as every psalm and hymn-singing Christian should know, gratitude is the primary religious emotion. Duty calls only when gratitude fails to prompt.

So allow me also to thank God—and a few of his choice children—for this magnificent building. Call it "lyrical" or call it "an example of bewildered eclecticism"; call the quality of its exterior "more institutional than ecclesiastical," or call it a fitting counterpoint to the reassuring river on whose bank it stands—call it what you will. As for me, from the floor of its cool and serene nave to the lofty wind-blown observation deck above the 75-bell carillon including the largest tuned bell in captivity—*I love it*. Ten thousand times ten thousand people of every sort and condition it has served well, and will continue to do so—with a little more help from a few of God's choice children! So as the Poles cried out to their visiting Pope, I too would say on this fiftieth anniversary: "O wonderful Riverside Church building, may you live to be a hundred."

Now, I want you to "center down"—as the Quakers say, referring to God within us—center down to hear words said in prayer from this pulpit by the founding pastor of this church some years after his retirement. Be tolerant of his use of "brotherly," "mankind"—such words; remember they weren't considered sexist in his day.

(*Fosdick's voice on tape*) "But above all we pray that thou wilt not simply relieve our weakness, but will lay hold upon our strength. We bring to thee our minds. Fallible they are, yet rightly used they could give dignity and meaning to our lives and service to mankind. God forgive us that we so misuse them. Spirit divine, with great work needing to be done in this world, lay hold upon some minds here today that we may think more deeply, proclaim our faith in thee more intelligently, and work more wisely for the enrichment of mankind's life and the coming of thy kingdom. Lay hold upon our courage. We thank thee for the high gift of daring. For the bravery that human life exhibits, we are grateful. Forgive our misuse of this noble power. Lay thy hand upon it. May we fight well the good fight for righteousness, for personal character, for social welfare and for mankind's peace. Lay hold upon our good will. Forgive us that we use brotherly love so narrowly and poorly. Extend its domain, we beseech thee. Enlarge its reach over the bitter boundaries that often hem it in. Let no mean prejudice in us hold it back. Grant us good will toward all sorts and conditions of men of every color, every nation, every creed. Lay hold upon our faith, we pray. Faith can be the victory that overcomes the world. Yet see how we put our faith in small unworthy things. Lift our faith on high. May we believe afresh in thee, in the eternal purpose which thou didst purpose in Christ, in the infinite value of the human soul and in thy coming kingdom.

"O God, so often we have come to thee presenting our feebleness. Today we come presenting such strength as is ours. Take it and use it as thy graving tool to carve thy will in this world." (*end of tape*)

"Spirit divine, with great work needing to be done in this world, lay hold upon some minds here today." I hear Dr. Fosdick saying to us: "If you want to preserve your heritage, fulfill its promises." And how? Listen again: "that we may *think more deeply*, proclaim our faith . . . *more intelligently*, and work *more wisely* for the enhancement of human life and the coming of thy Kingdom." That appeal to our minds recalls a similar appeal of St. Paul's to the Philippians: "And this is my prayer, that your love may grow ever richer and richer in knowledge and insight of every kind, and may thus bring you the gift of true discrimination" (Phil. 1:10 NEB).

From Paul to Fosdick, all the great preachers of the Christian church have tried to engage the hearts *and* to inform the minds of their hearers. They have tried to link love with learning, piety with intellect, knowing that aroused but uninformed Christians are as dangerous as quack physicians. Think of the horrors associated with the church: inquisitions and holy wars, dogmatism and ignorance, book-burning, witch-burning, superstition, inhibition, morbid guilt, conformity, cruelty, self-righteousness, anti-Semitism. And I'm not associating those horrors with the uneducated alone. Hawthorne rightly warned that "the influential classes, and those who take upon themselves to be leaders of the people, are fully liable to all the passionate error that has ever characterized the maddest mob."

So on this historic occasion, in the name of the great preachers of history, I'm moved to address some of my fellow preachers in the land. I want to urge the prime-time preachers, the evangelists of the so-called "electronic church," the leaders of the so-called "moral majority" to "work out their salvation" with just a little more "fear and trembling." I agree that the Bible contains all the answers, at least all the significant ones. But I would insist that no one understands the Bible until he has seen and lived at least part of its contents. Like any book, the Bible is something of a mirror: if an ass peers in, you can't expect an apostle to peer out!

Preachers should be explorers as well as pulpit pounders. The energy which abounds in so many preachers, that glandular energy which so frequently is mistaken for the Holy Spirit—such energy is no substitute for wisdom; and wisdom abounds in Pascal's observation that a person "does not show his greatness by being at one extremity, but rather by touching both at once."

In other words, I would hope that preachers would dare to take on the ambiguities of our time. Change today is coming on apace. The currents of history are churning into rapids, sweeping before them all the familiar buoys which long have marked the channels of our lives. And when we look at the Ship of State, ours or almost anybody else's, all we seem to see—and hear—is canvas tearing, and cables parting. No wonder in such disorderly and frightening times people want their answers clear, clean and easy. But it is not the task of preachers to give their people what they want, but rather to give them what they need. And clearly what the American people do not need are answers that represent a rearrangement of the facts of life, simplistic answers that inevitably lead to disenchantment. For answers that begin by explaining all too much end always by explaining all too little.

The only security in life lies in embracing its insecurity. And faith in Jesus Christ, far from diminishing the risks, inspires the courage to take them on—all of them, including the risk of intellectual uncertainty.

The same holds for moral uncertainty. It's wrong for preachers on every issue to stand as if at Armaggedon battling for the Lord. I know that tolerance is a tricky business. Some people actually think that tolerance means being so broad-minded that your brains fall out. But I'm worried about growing intolerance in the church. I'm worried that the virtue of moral indignation is becoming the vice of moralism. Moralism is historically one of America's great defects. Moralism is intolerant of ambiguity, perceiving reality in extreme terms of good and evil and regarding more sophisticated judgments as soft and unworthy. The temptation to become moralistic is strong, for it is emotionally satisfying to have enemies rather than problems. It is emotionally satisfying to seek out culprits rather than flaws in the system. God knows it's emotionally satisfying to be righteous with that righteousness that nourishes itself in the blood of sinners. But God also knows that what is emotionally satisfying can also be spiritually devastating.

So, fellow preachers, let us heed St. Paul's injunction: "Let your magnanimity be manifest to all." Let us not sharpen our minds by narrowing them. Beneath the behavior deserving of censure let us see the frailty worthy of compassion. And most of all, let us never fight evil as if it were something that arose totally outside of ourselves.

And fellow Riversiders, my beloved, to what shall we pledge ourselves on this occasion? To the same things, I would hope, and to joy, for, like gratitude, joy too is a much neglected virtue, even in the church. And, of course, let us pledge ourselves to each other, to enrich our love for one another.

And let us pledge ourselves to what Fosdick meant when he prayed, "lay hold upon our good will." So often people of good will are people of no will. In the church they confuse "abiding in Christ" with "basking in Christ" (Horace Bushnell). They mean well—feebly. Listen again to Fosdick: "Forgive us that we use brotherly (and sisterly) love so narrowly and poorly. Extend its domain, we beseech thee. Enlarge its reach over the bitter boundaries that often hem it in. . . . Grant us good will toward all sorts and conditions of people of every color, every nation, every creed."

To me that means two things that we must keep high on the agenda of this church in the years to come. This church is rooted in the city, and its decency is at stake. I said I loved this building and I do. But a rich, proud building that is also a church cannot decently exist unless its preachers and members become humble before the poor, and bold on their behalf. There is something dreadfully amiss in New York City when a prestigious U.S. corporation offers St. Bartholomew Church on Park Avenue and 50th Street 100 million dollars for its property, and the mayor says he has no money to keep open a hospital on St. Nicholas Avenue and 124th Street. Dearly beloved parishioners, we have no choice, we must work for the redistribution of wealth. We must abridge our luxuries for the sake of others' necessities, in this city, in this land, and in the world.

Secondly, on this Worldwide Communion Sunday, let us pledge to continue to work for the abolition of war. Fosdick himself was a pacifist. Most of us are not, if by pacifist you mean one who believes that all war is always morally wrong, and always has been wrong. Nevertheless, I think most of us see war as an avoidable tragedy, and believe that the problem of solving international conflict without massive violence has become the number one problem of our time. It is unfortunate that the Soviets have so succeeded in identifying the cause of peace with the cause of the Soviet bloc that anyone who stands up for peace risks being called a fellow traveller. But we'll take that risk—in the name of Jesus Christ.

So may we preserve our heritage by fulfilling its promises. So may we work out our own salvation with fear and trembling. So, in other words of Paul, may we "shine like stars in a dark world, and proffer the word of life."

We gave the first word to Fosdick. Let's give him the last: "O God, so often we have come to thee presenting our feebleness. Today we come presenting such strength as is ours. Take it and use it as thy graving tool to carve thy will in this world."

On Humility

OCTOBER 12, 1980
Reading: Philippians 2:1–12

Humility is hard to handle; I mean just to understand, let alone to practice. For example, some people seem, in their mind's eye, to see a sort of ladder of humility, with themselves close to the top rung. Jesus said, "He who humbles himself will be exalted." But Nietzsche, watching Christians, said, "He who humbles himself *wills* to be exalted." Nietzsche linked the humility of Christians to lack of spirit, to self-abasement. Others associate humility with masochism. Surely you have seen them, these Christian masochists, who can't wait to turn themselves into doormats, eagerly awaiting the hobnail boots of the sadists. Of course, the smart sadist won't oblige them. The smart sadist knows that the smart thing to do to a masochist is nothing!

So, amidst all this confusion, what are we to say about humility? What does St. Paul mean: "have this mind among yourselves which you have in Christ Jesus—who humbled himself"?

The other day on television I watched a well-known TV preacher inveighing against sex education in the schools. He was part of a panel and, seizing the initiative, he turned to a fellow panelist, clearly not of his persuasion, and asked bluntly, "Are you for premarital sex?" Taken aback, the panelist began a "no-but," or "yes-but" kind of qualified answer when the preacher cut him off. "I am glad to say I am not, sir, and glad that you are not the teacher of my children."

I regretted that the panelist lost the initiative to the preacher. He might have answered, "Mr. Preacher, didn't your own Lord and Savior prefer adulterers and prostitutes to their judges?"

Thoreau said, "There are a thousand hacking at the branches of the tree of evil to one who is striking at the root." The root of evil is not lack of chastity but lack of charity. The root of evil has little to do with whether or not we are law-abiding, and everything to do with whether or not we are love-abiding. Chastity is a matter of the law. Love is a matter of grace. This is not to say that chastity isn't right for certain people at certain times, and maybe for their entire lives. But it is to say that love is indispensable at all times, that grace transcends the law. Why did Jesus prefer prostitutes and adulterers to their judges? He couldn't stand spiritual arrogance.

Why did he prefer the prodigal son to the one who stayed at home? He couldn't stand spiritual arrogance. Why did he prefer the tax collector to the Pharisee? Again, a matter of spiritual arrogance. Hans Küng described the God of our Lord as a God "who seemed to have abandoned his own law, a God not of the devout observers of the law, but of the lawbreakers, and even—we might say with very slight exaggeration—a God not of the God-fearing but of the godless."

We forget how truly scandalous is the teaching of Jesus for *our* time, as well as for that time. And so we miss the much needed consolation found in his reassuring descriptions of God as a woman, or shepherd, rejoicing at finding what is lost; as a magnanimous king, a generous lender, a gracious judge who forgives sins on the spot.

I say all this because humility comes from the Latin "*humus*," which means "earth." I think Christians should be more earthy—not only earthly, but earthy. Certain it is that we are earthbound. Those who think differently, who think we should head straight for heaven forget that on our way up we shall pass, on his way down, the Son of God himself. If Heaven comes to earth, why on earth should anyone head for Heaven? Isn't that spiritual arrogance? Isn't that saying with the Pharisee, "I thank God I am not as other people are"?

Besides, none of us can really rise that high. The moral profile of any human being resembles the silhouette of a giraffe: lofty up front perhaps, but dragging a bit behind! So humility has something to do with being earthly, and even earthy.

What else can we say? I said at the outset that humility is often associated with feeling guilty. Actually, guilt is more related to pride than to humility. In fact, guilt may be the last stronghold of pride. For guilt represents my opinion of myself, whereas forgiveness represents yours, or God's. I can make excuses for myself, but I cannot forgive myself; not if we can only forgive what we cannot condone. You can forgive me, and God can forgive me, but I cannot forgive myself. And it just may be that I am too proud to allow you or God to do for me what I cannot do for myself. Sometimes it is more blessed to receive than to give. At least it takes more humility. So, to be humble means to be earthy, and also to accept our forgiveness, remembering that our value is a gift, not an achievement.

One more suggestion. To be humble means that you are so busy thinking about others that you actually forget yourself. In other words, to be humble means to be loving, which sounds straightforward enough, but it isn't. In the first place, to love others you have to love yourself. Love is the gift of oneself, and how will you make a gift of that which you hate? (We are back to our last point about forgiveness.) Moreover, to love means to become vulnerable, to take risks. I wonder how many of us, for the sake of others, are willing to lose money. Quite a few I would imagine. But, let us ask how many of us, for the sake of others, are willing to lose our good reputation? Fewer, I would imagine. For even though we know that what counts is not how we look in the eyes of others, but how we look in the eyes of God and his angels, nonetheless, that knowledge emotionally is difficult to appropriate. And now suppose, for the sake of the world, we Americans were asked to give up our military supremacy. Would we give up power for love? W.E.B. Du Bois wrote: "How extraordinary, and what a tribute to ignorance and religious hypocrisy, is the fact that in the minds of most people, even those of liberals, only murder makes men. The slave pleaded, he was humble, he protected the women of the South; and the world ignored him. The slave killed white men, and behold, he was a man."

People today think the Soviet Union is a great power because it bristles with nuclear weapons. Well, I tell you the Soviet Union is not a great power; only a very large country. And I am afraid I often feel the same way about my own country, particularly when I think most Americans don't so much fear Communists as they fear appearing soft on Communists. (If true, that's pathetic.) In any case, I think it fair to say that neither the U.S. nor the USSR could properly be called humble. What then should Christian citizens do? Surely they should heed the words of Jeremiah, "Learn not the way of nations"; and at the very least, they should not "fall over one another to enlist in the Swiss guard of the power elite" (C. Wright Mills).

I cannot resist a fourth point, which I'll make briefly. Humility spells joy. It's fun to be earthy, it's joyful to be forgiven, and there is simply nothing like that sense of undeserved integrity which comes in moments of grace when we are truly able to love. But more: St. Paul wrote, "Not I, but Christ who dwells within me," and William Blake is reputed to have backed off from a finished and glorious picture, exclaiming, "Not I, not I." St. Paul, and Blake, both understood that whatever is of good is of God. It seems to me that to the degree you don't have to take credit for your talents, to that same degree you are truly free to enjoy them. I love to see somebody receive a compliment and hear her say "Thank you" with all the gratitude and joy that comes with not having to say, "Oh, well, it's nothing really, nothing much."

So, dear parishioners, my word for the week ahead is, "Be humble: i.e., earthy, forgiven, loving, and full of joy."

The Righteousness of Faith

OCTOBER 19, 1980
Reading: Philippians 3:2–11

If ever St. Paul wrote an earthy, meaty passage, it would have to be this one. However, let's make two things clear: "Look out for the dogs" sounds more offensive than it actually is. For "dogs" were what self-righteous Jews called Gentiles who did not observe their law. So

St. Paul is using the Jews' own term against them—fair enough—and in order to make what to him was a fundamental point: Gentiles didn't have to become Jews to become Christians. (Now the problem is to allow Jews to become Christian without becoming Gentile; and what an indictment of gentility that is!)

Nor is Paul as boastful as he may sound. "If any [person] thinks he has reason for confidence in the flesh, I have more." It's easy to mock wealth, power, lineage—any form of purely human achievement—if you yourself don't have any. Paul, I think, is trying to make clear that his reason for disparaging Jews and Judaism is not because he lacks status. After all, he is "a Hebrew born of Hebrews" and, as a matter of fact, of no less a tribe than that of Benjamin—which, though small, was the tribe that gave Israel its first king. Men from the tribe of Benjamin were traditionally the first into battle, accompanied by the war cry, "After thee, O Benjamin!"

In other words, Paul's criticism of Jews and Judaism is not that of an outsider. And I must say that I always prefer criticism from the inside. I like Roman Catholics who are "underwhelmed" by cardinals bristling with self-importance. I like Protestants who know there is no substitute for the Mass. I like socialists who grieve at the seemingly endless errors of the Left. I like capitalists who know that unemployment has always been the scandal of capitalism. And I like patriots who are occasionally moved out of love of country to write an honest confession, as did Smedley Butler, a former Commanding General of the U.S. Marines who said: "I was a gangster for Wall Street." (Isn't it amazing how as children we sang, "From the halls of Montezuma to the shores of Tripoli" without wondering what in the world our Marines were doing there?)

As all the first Christians were as Jewish as Jesus himself, Paul is not against all Jews, nor against all Judaism. He has no quarrel with the Prophets. But alongside the prophetic strain in Judaism was a legalistic, moralistic strain which in Paul's day had gained the upper hand. It is this legalism and moralism that he is attacking. "You cannot earn your salvation," he is saying. "Forget, O Philippians, any notion that would see any exterior sign as proof that your inner life is in good shape." For nothing external can transform selfishness into unselfishness. And if we fail in love, we fail in all things else. "Yea, though I give my body to be burned"—the very stuff of heroism—"but have not love, it profiteth me nothing."

Twenty centuries later, do we still tend to lean towards a religion that is legalistic and moralistic? You bet your life we do, and for the same old reasons: to prove to ourselves and everybody else that morally we're living alright, and to do so by avoiding the question of motivation.

But before going into that let us stay for a moment with Paul's first reason to have confidence in the flesh: his hereditary claim to status. Recently, an elderly lady of one of Boston's "first families" was asked by an earnest youth if she, like so many these days, had been born again. "Young man," she replied, "if you're born on Beacon Street, Boston, you don't have to be born again."

"After thee, O Benjamin!"

"After thee, O Beacon Street!"

> Boston, my Boston, the home of the bean and the cod,
> Where the Cabots talk only to the Lowells,
> And the Lowells talk only to God.

Or the updated version:

> Where the Kennedys get all the caviar
> And the McCormacks get nothing but scrod.

We laugh, but it's not so funny—this persistent claim to superiority through heritage. It accounts for the bombings of the synagogues in Paris, for the murder of eight Blacks in Buffalo, and the kidnapping of fourteen black kids in Atlanta. There was a long article this week on the troubles of the Metropolitan Opera. Adding to the discord, and complicating the negotiations is a class distinction: many of the 89 board members of the Metropolitan Opera come from old Eastern Anglo Saxon families, while ethnic names abound among the 93 orchestra members.

It is no accident that Shelley Winters, Jack Benny, Tony Curtis, Red Skelton and a host of other actors and actresses have perfectly good Jewish names, but don't use them. And it is clearly and sadly true that those who are persecuted discriminate against each other. I had a friend in New Haven, an old Jewish surgeon, who told me that he wasn't allowed to intern in one of the great Jewish hospitals of New York City because he was of Russian rather than German descent.

But "purity" of descent is only one reason for having "confidence in the flesh." The members of the orchestra of the Metropolitan Opera want the same hours and wages as members of symphony orchestras. They are keenly aware of the fact that they sit in a pit where people look down on them instead of on a stage where people look up at them.

Prestige, of course, has always been sought in wealth. At about the same time that my surgeon friend was having his troubles here in New York, in Massachusetts Anglican Bishop William Lawrence was giving his episcopal blessing to the ideal of the wealthy person: "In the long run, it is only to the man of morality that wealth comes . . . Godliness is in league with riches . . . Material prosperity is helping to make the national character sweeter, more joyous, more unselfish, more Christlike." And while we're not as blatant in our self-deceit as Bishop Lawrence, still the deception persists. Winners in America desperately want to believe that a system based on ruthless competition is somehow benign to losers.

But why, why is it so necessary for us to be winners? In our heart of hearts do we think we are losers? Sometimes I think so. Human beings are to anxiety born as the sparks fly upward. I think that on a scale of one to ten most of us see ourselves at minus three. So we seek to compensate, endlessly and vainly, for it is a fact of life that our capacity to reassure ourselves is outstripped by our need for reassurance. The higher we rise, the more exposure we experience. Michelangelo saw this: his powerful figures all bear the tell-tale sign of anxiety—dilated pupils.

We are to anxiety born as the sparks fly upward. And when purity of descent and wealth and power and nationalistic patriotism fail to reassure us, we're apt to turn to religion—but to a religion of legalism and moralism. Listen again to St. Paul's description of himself before his conversion: "As to the law, a Pharisee; as to zeal, a persecutor of the church; as to righteousness under the law, blameless."

Karl Barth wrote, "Most Christians go to church to make their last stand against God." I think he meant that they go to deify not God but their own virtue. They seek salvation through good behavior. That's moralism and legalism.

But in all honesty, we have to tell ourselves that such efforts don't work. The more you seek perfection the less you seek God and your neighbor, because seeking perfection is too self-absorbing an enterprise. That's why Luther said, "Good works don't make a person good."

So why do we keep on trying? One reason has to do with ambition and motivation. I think we fear that if we give up our ambition we'll lose our motivation.

Let me tell you a story, really an Easter story. It happened a good many years ago. A man was riding on a train in the mountainous region of Tennessee, where the train was curling around gorgeous mountains! Sitting next to him was a man lost in thought, of obviously not too pleasant a nature. He was restless and he became more and more agitated. So the first man asked him, "Is there something wrong?" The second man told him that he had been in jail for the last ten years, that he had just now been released and was going home to his farm in Tennessee. As he was practically illiterate, there had been little correspondence between him and his family over the course of the ten years. With the help of a fellow inmate, however, he had written a letter saying that he was going to be released, that he was coming home, but that he would understand it if they didn't want him back. If they *did* want him, they were to tie a white ribbon around the lowest bough of the last apple tree in the orchard, the one nearest the railroad tracks. He would see it before the train came into the station. If there was no ribbon, he would just go right on through and they wouldn't hear from him again.

As the train approached the station he was getting so nervous that the first man offered to watch for him. Suddenly he cried, "Hey, look, look." The second man did and saw that the whole tree was white with ribbons.

Now, let me ask you: Do you think that man lost his motivation? Do you think the prodigal son lost his motivation wrapped in his father's arms?

Listen to Paul one more time: "Indeed I count everything as loss because of the surpassing worth of knowing Christ Jesus my Lord. For his sake I have suffered the loss of all things, and count them as refuse in order that I may gain Christ and be found in him; not having a righteousness that is based on law, but that which is through faith in Christ, the righteousness from God that depends on faith." His motivation hadn't been lost, only transformed and strengthened.

Luther was right: "Good works don't make a person good, but a good person does good works."

"After thee, O Benjamin? After thee, wealth and fame? After thee, O virtue?"

No, "After thee, O Christ, and with thee forever."

Continuing Reformation

OCTOBER 26, 1980
Readings: Numbers 13:25–14:4; Philippians 3:13–16

Reformation Sunday is a good time to remember Paul's words: "forgetting what lies behind and straining forward to what lies ahead." It sounds exhausting, but it's really the only way to live, if we are to be lonely, fulfilled, not resentful. To be joyously and completely alive, we have to embrace change.

It's a funny thing: we know that change, like death and taxes, is absolutely inevitable, and we know that the art of life is to cooperate gracefully with the inevitable. Yet when it comes to deep personal change, or a change in our church or national life, most of us resemble the caterpillar who said, looking up at the butterfly, "You'll never find me flying around in one of those crazy things." Instead of "forgetting what lies behind and straining forward to what lies ahead," we turn our backs on what lies ahead and turn toward that which lies behind. We replace hope with unproductive nostalgia.

The Old Testament lesson makes this wondrously clear. After a long and tear-stained trek, the children of Israel finally make it to the borders of the Promised Land. Spies are sent out, and when they return they submit a majority report and a minority report. The minority report is prophetic, full of hope, which we can translate as "a passion for the possible." It urges the children of Israel to strain forward to that which lies ahead. By contrast, the majority report is "pragmatic," the caution it counsels reflecting the cowardice of those submitting it. It speaks of "giants in the land," descendants of Anak, "the long-necked one," and the key sentence reads, "We seemed to ourselves like grasshoppers, and so we seemed to them."

Predictably, the children of Israel accept the majority report, and we read that "All the congregation raised a loud cry, and the people wept that night, and all the people of Israel murmured against Moses and Aaron. The whole congregation said to them, 'Would that we had died in the land of Egypt.' And they said to one another, 'Let us choose a captain and go back to Egypt.'"

The "chosen people" refused to choose their destiny. Instead of straining forward to what lay ahead, they turned to what lay behind.

I said the key line was the fearful one: "We seemed to ourselves like grasshoppers." The story shows that while love seeks truth, fear seeks safety. And fear distorts the truth not by exaggerating the ills of the world—which would be difficult—but by underestimating our ability to deal with them: "We seemed to ourselves like grasshoppers." We human beings are always adopting what has been called "the protective strategy of deliberate failure." It goes like this: You'll never lose any money if you don't place any bets; you'll never fall out of bed if you sleep on the floor; you'll never fall on your face if you never stick your neck out; you'll never stub your toe if you don't take the first step. Furthermore, if you think other people, "giants in the land," make you into a failure, you don't have to feel badly about being one.

And finally, if you think those trying to wean you from your sense of failure—the Joshuas and Calebs, those who submit the minority reports—are only trying to push you around, then you can stone them with a good conscience, which is exactly what the children of Israel did at the end of the story.

Today we see a parallel. Today a prophetic minority is seeking to bear witness to ideas whose time has not yet come, while a "Moral Majority" seeks to bear witness to ideas whose time has passed. The Moral Majority wants to go back to when we owned the Panama Canal, back to when women were in the home and homosexuals in the closet, back to the time when a prayer in public school made this country Christian, back to a time when in terms of military power we were the Hertz of the world, Number One. Instead of pressing forward, God's children are holding back. Instead of seizing the time, we're losing our grip. Instead of straining forward to that which lies ahead, we are electing captains eager to lead us back to the flesh pots and spiritual slavery of Egypt.

Have American Christians forgotten that our nation was once famous for viewing its present, not in terms of the past, but in terms of the future? Of all nations, ours is founded not on geographical borders, but on an idea, a dream that seeks its fulfillment. Our forbears planted a seed of freedom they hoped would one day blossom like a mighty oak. But they knew that the true test of freedom is in its use. Freedom has no other test. "But the freedom in this sick and melancholy time of ours has become, not a thing to use, but a thing to defend" (Archibald MacLeish). And we're so busy defending it that we are subordinating the fulfillment of the American dream to the defeat of Soviet purposes, urged on by preachers declaring that our primary religious duty is not to love our enemies but to hate communists.

Of course, if not excusable, it's all understandable. Times are tough, and ahead *are* giant obstacles. But what is a giant obstacle if not a brilliant opportunity disguised as a giant obstacle? And are not Christians to say with Camus, "Even in the deep darkness of winter I knew in my heart an invincible summer"?

Ahead, there lies no more Promised Land for anybody, at least not on this planet. But I am convinced that for every member of the human family there lies ahead a Promised Time. I am convinced that all of us are on the border of that time promised by the prophets— "and it shall come to pass *in the latter days*"—a time when, by God's grace, we could create a world without famine, a world without borders, a world at last at one and at peace. But only if, "forgetting what lies behind we strain forward to that which lies ahead."

I hope Riverside Church will always seek to follow the prophetic minority, the Calebs and Joshuas, recognizing that it is always individual consciences, as opposed to the mass mind, that best represent the universal conscience of humankind. I hope that Riverside Church will always be a church in Exodus, for God is ahead of us altogether as much as above and within us. We are moved by memory, but even more by hope.

Having been this week on the West Coast, in Washington and also in Ohio, I can assure you many people look to this church as to a modest beacon of light in a rather dark night. They know of our efforts to try to persuade the country that to seek greater national security through more nuclear arms is nuclear nonsense; and more and more *are* persuaded. They have heard of our projected Conference on the City and are deeply interested, if only because they know that New York is today a "movable famine." And the preachers keep asking, "When are you going to have the next Fosdick convocation?" I hope Riverside will not let these people down.

"We seemed to ourselves as grasshoppers." It's our view of ourselves. Yet we know that God is always trying to make human beings more human. We know that we are not supposed to defend, but to use our freedom; and to do that, we need to nourish ourselves, educationally and pastorally. This church has yet to become the Upper West Side's spiritual New School! This church has yet to become a model of pastoral care for its own people and those outside its walls. And this church should commemorate the death of Virgil Fox, its great organist, by making sure that the kind of music he loved never dies in this place.

You know where my line of reasoning is leading—right into your pocketbook. For this is Pledge Sunday too, and Pledge Sunday and Reformation Sunday go pretty well together. God knows it's easy to be critical of money when it's used to keep score, a measure of the games we play much of our lives. But I'm sympathetic to those who say they want enough money to feel independent, and to do things for others. Well, that's what Riverside needs—money to be independent and to do things for others. We can't compete with Jerry Falwell, whose Gospel Hour on three hundred seventy-four TV stations brought in $56 million last year. But we can and must bring in half a million dollars, and when we do, my face will be as cherubic as Jerry Falwell's! So down with misanthropy and up with generosity. Make your pledges as close as possible to 10 percent of your income.

So, dear friends, let us continue with good hearts our Exodus from the old time to the new. The road is hard, but the future is bright. The

Promised Time is there ahead. Already we can dimly view its contours. The spies are back, the prophetic ones among them announcing that the Promised Time will be much better than the good old
days! Enough then of this "back to Egypt" talk. Enough of this talk
about seeming to ourselves like grasshoppers. We, too, can become
giants, Anaks, simply by sticking out our necks! Look at it this way:
We have made a world for some of us; it's time now to make a world
for all of us.

Those Stirring Saints

NOVEMBER 2, 1980
Readings: Wisdom of Solomon 3:1–9; Hebrews 12:1–4

In this season of spooks and spirits and shadowy shapes (many of
whom came creeping, crawling and flying into Riverside Church
last Friday), to calm my Halloween nerves this year I read a book
called *Saint-Watching* by Phyllis McGinley. I loved it. Ms. McGinley
watches saints as other people watch birds. She is fascinated by
saints—not because they are pious and sanctimonious, but because
they are stirring. It made me think: We should all be saint-watchers.
If people go to Italy to see great paintings of Michelangelo, and further yet to see large animals, if people go halfway around the world
to see Mount Everest, why shouldn't they be interested in the Mount
Everests of their own species?

It's not that saint-watching makes us saints. Watching birds doesn't
teach you how to fly. Nevertheless, when living in dark valleys where
hope and history seem never to meet, we must lift our eyes unto the
hills. As Tennyson wrote, "We needs must love the highest when we
see it."

Phyllis McGinley watches saints in part because she finds them as
varied and colorful as anything a birdwatcher could hope to see. St.
Francis, as we know, called the swallows his sisters, and once tamed
a wolf. But how many of you have heard of St. Dominic, who
preached to the fish along the shore when no one came to church to
hear his sermons? (Given the polluted state of the Hudson, I hope you
won't desert me.) Then there was Elisha, an early desert saint who
caroled like a thrush and wrote thirty thousand songs (so they say).
There was Nicholas the pilgrim, a shepherd who calmed his sheep by

singing the Kyrie Eleison. Fat and kind, St. Thomas Aquinas was called in school "the dumb ox." Then there was ever-so-generous Bridget of Ireland. There were Teresa of Avila and Catherine of Sienna, who, by writing like angels and by lecturing popes, gave women a respectable place in society. Saints founded the first free hospitals. Saints invented progressive education. (Said St. Philip Neri, "If you want to be obeyed, you must not appear to be giving orders.") Among the saints were whores, vagabonds, thieves, and even men who killed. Some were gregarious, like Philip of Seules; others were like hermits. Some loved beauty, and painted it, like Fra Angelico. And some, like St. Francis of Xavier, traveled through a dozen kingdoms with "no more eye for the scenery than a migrating bird." And let's not forget the first conscientious objector, St. Martin of Tours, a former officer in the Roman Legions jailed for his beliefs by Emperor Julian; nor the legendary St. Gothard, who, when he couldn't find a hook, hung his cloak on a sunbeam.

Phyllis McGinley considers a saint a sort of genius: "Like musicians, painters, and poets, saints are human beings, but obsessed ones. They are obsessed by goodness and by God as Michelangelo was obsessed by line and form, as Shakespeare was bewitched by language, Beethoven by sound. And like other geniuses they used mortal means to contrive their masterpieces."

Their masterpieces are, of course, their lives. Their lives are the only miracles; all the rest is commentary. And their lives differ from ours primarily because their hearts are stronger; the hearts of the saints can withstand the corroding effects of daily living. Fatigue and despair do not nibble away at the good intentions of the saints. Troubles in the office don't consume their kindness. As Phyllis McGinley says, "Saints master their environment, as we do not."

The secret of the saints is that they consider moderation a sin. Their dreams are wild, their ambitions filled with a kind of desperate vitality. Of course, today many of them would appear to us as crazy. But let us not forget: "It is the cracked ones who let the light through." What really sets them apart from us ordinary folk is the literal way they take the central imperatives of the Gospel. Does Jesus command us to feed the hungry? The saints feed the hungry. Does Jesus command us to clothe the naked? The saints clothe the naked. Does Jesus command us to sell all we have and give to the poor, to go forth and preach to all nations, to turn the other cheek, to return good for evil, to love God and our neighbor as ourselves? The saints do all these things, because saints believe these commandments mean exactly what they say.

Saints are lovestruck, God-intoxicated people; that's why they are stirring. That's why they are the Mount Everests of the species. That's why they master their environment. Saints are conquerors because it's not those who can inflict the most, but those who can suffer the most, who conquer this world. As one of them said, "Love bears all things, believes all things, hopes all things, endures all things" (1 Cor. 13:7). Ignatius Loyola was imprisoned eight times by the Inquisition. St. Teresa of Avila also ran afoul of it, as did a multitude of other saints. St. Paul was jailed, flogged, and perhaps even beheaded under Nero. And we know what happened to our Lord.

Now let's listen again to that passage from Hebrews: "With so many witnesses in a great cloud on every side of us, we too, then, should throw off everything that hinders us, especially the sin that clings so easily, and keep running steadily in the race we have started. Let us not lose sight of Jesus, who leads us in our faith and brings it to perfection: for the sake of the joy which was still in the future, he endured the cross, disregarding the shamefulness of it, and from now on has taken his place at the right hand of God's throne. Think of the way he stood such opposition from sinners and you will not give up for want of courage" (Heb. 12:1–4).

I think, dear fellow Christians, that most of us lead lives of quiet heroism, to paraphrase Thoreau. But today that may not be enough. It may be that some of us are going to have to train like marathon runners to be a little more saintly. I don't have to tell you that the upcoming election is far from inspiring (Tuesday's debate was called "the evil of two lessers"). I don't have to tell you that there is an ugly mood creeping over the country, that we seem to be pulling back from the frontiers of love and proclaiming a gospel of hanging on to what we have—never mind the deprivation of others in this and other lands. Let me just remind you that in "the race for which we have been entered," as St. Paul puts it, love is a long-distance runner. Love has a longer wind than any other contestant in the race. That's why St. Paul says, "Love never ends."

And finally, let me remind you that "The souls of the righteous are in the hands of God . . . slight was their affliction, great will their blessings be." That means that once you become a Christian, the worst that can possibly happen to you has already happened!

"The soul that on Jesus hath leaned for repose, I will not, I will not desert to his foes; That soul, though Hell should endeavor to shake, I'll never, no never, no never, forsake." Love alone makes us safe against all the assaults of death itself. "God is love, and he who abides in love abides in God and God abides in him" (1 John 4:16). That surely means our lives read from God, in God, to God again. Alleluia! The abyss of love is deeper than the abyss of death.

That is the blessed lesson we learn from the blessed saints—those stirring souls, those Mount Everests of the species. Let us pray God that a bit of their exuberance and stamina may rub off on us. Amen.

The Everyday Saints

NOVEMBER 9, 1980

It's a good aphorism: You have not lived if you have not lived in your time. This election week I imagine all of us lived in our time, and while the winners lived it up, some of the losers wondered if they would ever live it down! Said one, "I never thought I'd be proposing a toast to 1984." Several commentators compared the election to an earthquake—the whole country displaced to the right. But the simile I liked best came from William Safire, whose somewhat sour disposition has long allowed him to empathize with the resentment of those Americans who consider themselves overworked, overtaxed, and underappreciated. Safire's Wednesday column began: "Like a great soaking-wet shaggy dog, the Silent Majority—banished from the house during the Watergate storms—romped back into the nation's parlor this week and shook itself vigorously."

One fact has received little attention, but deserves much more. The stunning statistic was not the 51 percent who voted for Governor Reagan, or the 49 percent who voted against him. It was the 48 percent who didn't vote at all. It's especially striking when you think that from 1848 to 1896, during a period when, except for the Civil War, actions of government barely affected the lives of the majority of Americans, 75 percent, on the average, voted for presidents. Then from 1900 to 1960, when the actions of government began seriously to affect individual lives, the percentage dropped to 60 percent. By 1972 and 1976, the number was down to 55 percent. And on Tuesday, it hit 52 percent.

In other words, in this country—as in the Soviet Union—a great "internal emigration" is taking place. Like most emigrés, the majority in this instance are poor. But people can be deprived psychologically as well as economically. I think we face a deep spiritual problem, one alike for those who did and for those who did not vote on Tuesday. We'll come back to this a little later.

Last Sunday, All Saints' Sunday, I suggested that the saints have more stamina, more passion and less moderation than the rest of us. In Phyllis McGinley's phrase, they are "the Mount Everests of the species." To round out the picture, I want today to celebrate the less celebrated—those saints who may be sitting right here in these pews. First, however, let me emphasize that the great heroes of the church are always imperfectly heroic, as the Bible points out so relentlessly. Take David: David, a shepherd boy who became king; David, who performed feats of derring-do; David, "a yearning nation's blue-eyed pride," a shining figure of romance—in almost any other literature David would be remembered only by his deeds of glory. But the Old Testament includes his taking of Bathsheba and the murder of her husband—in contemptibility, a deed hard to surpass! So while every Hebrew child learned of the glorious deeds of David the King, the stories were told by parents and teachers so as to press home the point: "There is none that is righteous, no not one, save only the Lord God."

All heroes are imperfectly heroic. We should not be surprised to find great weaknesses side by side with great strength. And the same is true, of course, of the less heroic, the less celebrated. But they may be saintly in large part because they are less blind to their weaknesses than some of their more heroic counterparts. After all, power is rarely devoid of pride. It is our pride-swollen faces that close up our eyes.

So let us celebrate the saints who have few blind sides. Let us celebrate the saints who are free of self-deception. Let us celebrate an honesty that never comes painlessly.

Here's another good aphorism, this one from Pogo: "We have met the enemy, and he is us." In other words, don't complain about the way the ball bounces if you're the one who dropped the ball.

Cowards overflow with excuses. They always have, ever since that day in the uncertain mists of antiquity when Adam blamed it all on Eve—and Eve, in turn, blamed the serpent. The saints I want to celebrate today make no excuses, no more than did St. Augustine, whose *Confessions* alone would have qualified him for sainthood. All saints are fluent in the language of confession—not because they are sickly, self-abasing souls, but because they are hardy, good souls trying to keep their lives in perspective. They know their frequent lapses: their failure to follow through on good intentions, the devices they have used to keep at a distance needs they could have met, their tendency to label others according to their prejudices, their fear of the new, their unwillingness to change. And today, more than ever, we need to make their honesty our own if this country, spiritually and maybe even physically, is going to survive.

THE EVERYDAY SAINTS

Whatever their results I'm glad the political campaigns are over. I thought they exceeded the normal (and high) quota of truisms and untruisms. The moral posturing was appalling—and overblown expectations, like giant balloons, now float across the countryside. In the days ahead it's going to be very hard to keep our lives in perspective. It's going to be all too easy for the winners—and maybe even for the losers—to find fault, and to forget that faultfinding is not a minor vice, but a spiritual crime. Show me a faultfinder, and I'll show you a person who bears false witness against his neighbor. Even if what he says is completely true, it will not be truly complete. Hence, "Judge not, that you not be judged."

So here's to the saints among us in whom there is no detectable trace of eagerness for bad news. Here's to the saints who, by being fluent in the language of confession, will help this country to resolve conflicts rather than to fuel them.

Saints don't make excuses. By the same token, they don't excuse others; they don't confuse the virtue of compassion for the sinner with the vice of condoning his sin. The prophet Nathan didn't say to David the King, "I know you must be under a lot of pressure. It's lonely up there, making all those lonely decisions." No, he called a sin a sin. Dangerous though it was, he said, "Thou art the man!" Just as saints don't protect themselves from their own sins, so they don't protect themselves from the sins of others.

This week I had a wonderful experience. I ran into a friend, who was accompanied by a pleasant, ordinary-looking woman. He said, "Bill, meet the real Norma Rae." What could I do but hug her? She was the woman who said to J. P. Stevens, "Thou are the company!" Like Nathan, she spoke up clearly, but unlike him, she had to pay up personally. She's something of a saint.

At the end of that same day I went to hear Jacob Timmerman, the Argentine editor who was imprisoned, tortured, and finally exiled because he too refused to compromise. "Human rights is not a philanthropy," he said. In other words, it's a basic commitment. He understood that if we demean the humanity of others, we demean our own. He, too, is something of a saint. And both Norma Rae and Jacob Timmerman—and we could add Solzhenitsyn and Sakharov and a host of others, from all too many countries—know what Jesus meant when he said, "No one lights a light to put it under a tub; they put it on the lamp-stand where it shines for everyone in the house" (Luke 11:33). *Visibility is vital.* Lamps are not made to be concealed; they are to be positioned so that light may flood the darkness surrounding them.

I fear in the days ahead that as the world continues to do evil so overtly, we Christians will do good too covertly. I don't mind Ronald Reagan having been an actor. What I object to is the Hollywood view of the world (which is probably less his than that of some of his advisors). Hollywood is a feudal place where humans are considered to be property. In Hollywood there are stars, and the rest of the world; and the rest of the world consists of extras. That's the way so many of that 48 percent who didn't vote in this country feel: They are extras. They are going to be a deep spiritual problem, for themselves and for all of us, as long as they feel that their economic and social rights are a matter of philanthropy. That's the way much of the Third World feels. That the Panama Canal became such an issue in this election showed Third World people once again that the United States would rather dominate than help them.

So, here's to the saints who are both humble *and* bold, who are fluent in the language of confession, never finding faults in others they haven't first found in themselves. These saints know that visibility is going to be vital. Here's to the saints among us, some surely right here in this church, who in the days ahead will insist loudly that love is not a luxury; that wealth is acquired to share, and not to keep; that there must always be a star in the flag for America's destitute; and that Christ taught us to commit ourselves to humanity—to all of humankind, not just a portion of it.

"Give Us This Day Our Daily Bread"*

NOVEMBER 23, 1980
Reading: Luke 12:22–34

As today is Bible Sunday *and* World Hunger Sunday, the text for the sermon is the fourth, and, in some ways, the most modest of the seven petitions in the Lord's Prayer: "Give us this day our daily bread." It is important to see the training exhibit in the Assembly Hall prepared by the Sunday School, the Youth Department, and the Hunger Task Force. It is a powerful educational experience.

---

*This sermon owes a lot to three books: *Our Heavenly Father* by Helmut Thielicke, *The Wicked Gate* by Geoffrey Studdert Kennedy, and *Hunger for Justice* by Jack Nelson.—WSC

Some years ago a German novelist wrote: "In prayer we should reach for the hand of God, not for the pennies in his hand." That's a crucial *half*-truth. We can see what's true in the statement in what must have been a bitter experience for Jesus. All four Gospels record that after feeding the multitudes—the miracle of the loaves and fishes—Jesus withdrew from the crowd. (In the New Testament there's always that wonderful rhythm: up in the mountains to pray, down in the valleys to heal and preach and feed.) But St. John's account goes on to say that the crowd wouldn't leave him alone. They kept pursuing him, intent on making him king—by force, if necessary. When at last they caught up with him on the other side of the Sea of Galilee, they asked, "Rabbi, when did you come here?" And Jesus answered, "Truly, truly, I say to you, you seek me, not because you saw signs, but because you ate your fill of the loaves" (John 6:26). Can't you hear the sadness in Jesus' voice whenever the sentence begins, "Truly, truly, I say unto you"? In this instance he is saddened by the realization that the crowd that wanted to make him king wasn't reaching for God's hand, but for the pennies in his hand.

From firsthand experience, many of us know the truth of the saying, "There are no atheists in foxholes." But the new converts aren't looking for divine protection; they just don't want the bombs to land on their heads. And how many churchgoers go to find a little more security for their lives, instead of strength to withstand the trials of personal life, and the blandishments and threats of a perverse generation?

"Therefore, I tell you, do not be anxious about your life . . . And do not seek what you are to eat and what you are to drink . . . For all the nations of the world seek these things; and your Father knows that you need them. Instead, seek his kingdom, and these things shall be yours as well." We demean both God and our own humanity with our little desires, our little fears, our carking cares. So it's true: we should pray for strength alone; we should reach for the hand of God, not for the pennies in his hand.

Yet that is only a half-truth. The other half is that there *are* pennies, and for good reason. Like a mother interested in everything her children do, no matter how seemingly inconsequential, God is also concerned with all the trivialities of human life. "God was in Christ," which means that God is Christlike. And Christ, "whose eye encompasses in its boundless reach the first day of Creation and the last hour of judgment"; Christ, "whose outstretched arms enfold the oceans and the continents, because all authority in heaven and earth has been given to him"—this same Christ "occupies himself . . . with the grief of a mother who has lost her son, the predicament of a paralytic, the weariness of his disciples ('Come away by yourselves and rest awhile'), and he does not fail to notice that the people who followed him into the wilderness are hungry. He is even concerned about the wine at a wedding, and he bestows his special love upon the seemingly worthless experiences of those who are even more little than the so-called little people: the lepers, the mentally ill" (Helmut Thielicke).

"Seek ye first the kingdom of God and his righteousness." All well and good; but Christ, who spoke those words, also knows that just as foxes spoil a vineyard, so it is the little carking cares that generally undermine the spiritual foundations of our lives. After all, it was for only thirty pieces of silver, for five newly purchased oxen, for a mess of pottage in an hour of exhaustion, that three biblical characters forfeited their eternal birthright and blessing. And do we not ourselves do the same?

In his infinite compassion, Christ urges us to reach for God's hand *and* for the pennies in his hand. He tells us to pray, "Thy kingdom come," *and* "Give us this day our daily bread." Our little fears and desires may demean God and our humanity, but God's concern for such things as food, shelter, and clothing transforms trivialities. To God nothing is trivial. To God everything matters; even matter matters. Rightly it is said that Christianity is a materialistic religion, for you can no more separate food from faith than you can the body from the soul. One is the inside, the other is the outside, and God made them both. And that is why Christianity is also so spiritual a religion. The Roman Catholic Church knows what it is about when it conceives of the bread becoming the body of Christ; it is not to localize God's presence, but to show the sweep of the sacrament. In the sacramental view of the universe, everyone and everything matter to God. For "The earth is the LORD's, and the fullness thereof; the world and they who dwell therein" (Ps. 24:1).

So what does this tell us? It tells us that it is all right to pray for our daily bread. Further, it tells us that if Holy Communion doesn't lead to holy commerce, if bread for ourselves doesn't lead to bread for the world, the sacrament fails of its fruit. "And by their fruits ye shall know them."

Yet, how often we try to deny the sweep of the sacrament. How often—like today, in this country—we seek a false security, a false prosperity, by narrowing our responsibilities. "When, Lord, did we see *you* hungry, or naked, or in prison?" But the Lord, in responding, widens the responsibilities once again: "Inasmuch as ye did it not unto the least of these my brethren, ye did it not unto me" (Matt. 25:45).

There is malnutrition in South Africa today, and white South Africans want to narrow the causes to the drought. There's widespread hunger in the world, and most Americans think this is sadly the case despite our own best efforts to alleviate it. What white South Africans and most Americans forget is the lesson of Amos and all the prophets, who knew that hunger is never an historical accident. More fundamentally, hunger is the result of bad economics, the fruit of social injustices that exploit people at both ends of the food chain. Poor farmers, because of indebtedness, become landless serfs, and poor consumers—including poor farmers—can't fight the high prices of rich farmers and rich merchants. Once established, these structures of inequality tend to be self-perpetuating, and that's why the prophets are always inveighing against them. Reread the seventh and eighth chapters of Amos, and see if you don't agree with the conclusion he came to back in the eighth century B.C. In effect, Amos is saying, "Hunger is no private tragedy; it is a public crime." That's why instead of "World Hunger" we should call this Sunday "Hunger for Justice" Sunday.

Few of us know much about economics (including, I suspect, the economists), and I'm not one of the few. But I tremble when I read that President-elect Reagan wants to staff our government with people who, in his own words, "don't need the job." That sounds wonderful: dedicated people ready to become public servants. But doesn't that really mean people from the 99th percentile of income distribution? And don't such people, from biblical times to our own, generally come up with economic policies that heap more on the platter of the rich in the hope that bigger crumbs will fall to the poor?

In an age of scarcity, can that work? If rich Americans want Peruvian tuna for their cats, how will the Peruvian poor get that same fish for their children? If Latin American doctors are trained at the Hospital for Special Surgery here in New York, which training they can apply only to a few, won't amoebic dysentery remain endemic in the slums where the vast proportion of the population lives?

B.F. Schumacher, the author of *Small Is Beautiful*, once wrote, "The problem passengers on Spaceship Earth are the first-class passengers, and no one else." A few years ago, when the book *Limits for Growth* appeared, it reminded me of a famous scene from another book.

> "I wish you wouldn't squeeze so," said the Dormouse, who was sitting next to her. "I can hardly breathe."
>
> "I can't help it," said Alice very meekly, "I'm growing."
>
> "You've no right to grow *here*," said the Dormouse.

"Don't talk nonsense," said Alice more boldly. "You know, you're growing too."

"Yes, but *I* grow at a reasonable rate," said the Dormouse, "not in that ridiculous fashion." (*Alice's Adventures in Wonderland*, Lewis Carroll)

I think the biblical reminder is clear: Whatever our economic system the enemy is excess, not possessions. The battlecry is "Enough!" not "Nothing!" "Enough" so that we can all break bread together, so that the prayer of everyone can be answered—everyone the world around who prays, "Give us this day our daily bread."

Thanksgiving 1980

NOVEMBER 27, 1980
Readings: Deuteronomy 14:22–27; Luke 6:27–38

I can really "get into" Thanksgiving, the only victimless national holiday (if you can overlook several million turkeys). I love Thanksgiving because absent also from the day are the air-polluting, eagle-screaming orations, the well-shaped purple clouds of bombast that mar the blue of sunny skies on July 4, February 22, and even February 12 and January 15.

Not that Thanksgiving is without problems. Our spiritual forebears thought they had discovered America, or at least a new part of it. They believed—as their descendants continue to believe—that a country is "discovered" when the first white male sets foot on it! Moreover, this wasn't just another country: this was a vast, wild Eden waiting to be subdued, a New World with a new history that separated them from the past, connecting them only to the future—a future that would soon picture Americans as a new breed: "Stripped for the hardest work, every muscle firm and elastic, every ounce of brain ready for use, and not a trace of superfluous flesh on his nervous and supple body, the American stood in the world a new order of man." (These are the words of a man generally rather more bitter, albeit in an elegant way—Henry Adams.)

Nonetheless, after all the proper reservations have been registered, the story is a simple and stirring one. Persecuted in England and unhappy in Holland, the Pilgrims walked up the gangplank of the

Mayflower and sailed to a place they called Plymouth, near Cape Cod. Ten years after the landing, William Bradford, their elected governor, described how they felt at first: "They had now no friends to welcome them nor inns to entertain or refresh their weatherbeaten bodies; no houses or much less towns to repair to, to seek for succour . . . Savage barbarians, when they met with them, were readier to fill their sides with arrows than otherwise."

Soon it was winter, a winter filled with "cruel and fierce storms." Within seven months of their arrival, half the passengers of the *Mayflower* were dead. As today in so many towns of Southern Italy, so then in Plymouth: there was not one home where there was not one dead. Fortunately, in the spring, the Indians taught them how to plant maize (corn) and fertilize it with fish. And when the harvest was in, the Pilgrims invited the Indians to their feast of Thanksgiving, sharing the corn, beans, squash, and pumpkins the Indians had taught them how to grow, and the wild turkey the Indians had taught them how to hunt. They gave thanks to God for the new land, for their new life, and for the bounty God had given them.

What should their descendants say about them? I'm impressed that where the Pilgrims couldn't be optimistic, they were persistent. So too were their children and their children's children, who seemingly craved no recreation other than carving out of the unyielding wilderness towns by the name of Canaan, Goshen, Sharon, and Bethany.

Neither can we be optimistic as we pass through our particular stretch of history. Few believe the present recession will do anything but deepen, that unemployment and inflation will do anything but rise. Americans don't need the new divines, hot on the trail of national depravities, to tell them of the obscenity represented by the Forty-Second Streets of our cities. For there are worse obscenities, not mentioned by the new divines: the growing neglect of aliens, orphans, and widows; the rising cries to speed up the arms race; the threatened use of food as a weapon in foreign policy; the threats to desegregated education, to affirmative action, and even to civil liberties. A soon-to-be-published $100,000 study by the conservative Heritage Foundation in Washington urges President-elect Reagan to recognize "the reality of subversion and [to put] emphasis on the un-American nature of so much so-called 'dissidence.'" Recommending the removal of many specific restrictions on domestic intelligence work, the report says: "It is axiomatic that individual liberties are secondary to the requirements of national security and internal civil order." I've heard that last sentence almost verbatim from the lips of officials in Argentina and Chile, officials who never seem to get it through their heads that *injustice* is the major threat to internal civil order.

But if we can't be optimistic, do we have to descend into self-pity? I'm tempted to launch into an eagle-screaming oration in praise of Pilgrim persistence and Pilgrim ingenuity. The mayor of this city and maybe also state and federal officials certainly won't want to fund the transition of Sydenham into a community-owned hospital. But a Jerry Lewis-type marathon on Channel 5 might do the trick. Maybe the city will continue to cut back music programs in the public schools. But why shouldn't churches all over the city fill with concertgoers eager to hear famous musicians donating their services to keep music alive for the students? This week I talked to an exiled Argentine doctor who wanted other doctors to join him in offering his services *pro bono* one day a week. Why shouldn't rich lawyers do the same? Not that charity can go bail for justice, not permanently; but at least temporarily it can serve as a reminder of what justice demands.

It is certainly very American to think, as one citizen put it: "Americans believe there is nothing they cannot accomplish, that solutions wait somewhere for all problems, like brides." (Pardon his chauvinistic overtones!) I think it patriotic to strive to fulfill the dream "that sees beyond the years [God's] alabaster cities gleam undimmed by human tears." And I know it's Christian to believe what Paul wrote to the Ephesians: "We are God's work of art, created in Christ Jesus to live the good life as from the beginning he has meant us to live it" (Eph. 2:10).

Where they could not be optimistic, the Pilgrims were persistent. And with little else to sustain them, they persistently turned to God. As Bradford wrote: "What could now sustain them but the Spirit and His grace?" I think a time of scarcity is a time to recall that happiness lies in discerning the value of the things we have. I think the "limits to growth" concept reminds us that the only truly renewable resources are spiritual.

Lastly, and perhaps surprisingly, these Pilgrims knew how to have fun. H. L. Mencken once defined a Puritan as a person "haunted by the fear that somewhere someone might be happy." But the Pilgrims, in the best tradition of the Old Testament, tithed in order to throw a party. Here is the instruction in Deuteronomy that must have informed their first Thanksgiving:

> You shall tithe all the yield of your seed, which comes
> forth from the field year by year. And before the LORD
> your God, in the place which he will choose, to make

his name dwell there, you shall eat the tithe of your grain, of your wine, and of your oil, and the firstlings of your herd and flock; that you may learn to fear the LORD your God always. And if the way is too long for you, so that you are not able to bring the tithe, when the LORD your God blesses you, because the place is too far from you, which the LORD your God chooses, to set his name there, then you shall turn it into money, and bind up the money in your hand, and go to the place which the LORD your God chooses, and spend the money for whatever you desire, oxen, or sheep, or wine or strong drink, whatever your appetite craves; and you shall eat there before the LORD your God and rejoice, you and your household.

A spending spree, an orgy complete with whiskey or its equivalent, enough to make the upcoming Christmas commercials look like a Lenten fast! Such spontaneous, lavish celebrations of Thanksgiving are the very opposite of the greedy spirit of grasping, hoarding, and exploiting. I think the Thanksgiving feast some two hundred of you are going to have after the service right here in God's house is in the spirit of Deuteronomy, and I think the South Hall is going to be visited by the ghosts of Governor Bradford, Miles Standish, and Priscilla and John Alden.

Speaking of commercials, I'm sure you've all seen on television the extensive testing grounds maintained by automobile manufacturers, and have watched various vehicles prove themselves reliable under every adverse condition. I see the adverse times ahead as the Pilgrims obviously saw theirs—tiring, but a good proving ground for persistence and reliability. Frequently they must have read Job's words: "God knows the way I take; when he has tried me I shall come forth as gold" (23:10). And St. Paul's, too: "You can trust God not to let you be tried beyond your strength, and with any trial he will give you a way out of it and the strength to bear it" (1 Cor. 10:13).

I see adverse times bringing us closer to God and to one another. I see excess being replaced by a generous give-and-take that is the shining characteristic of that first Thanksgiving. Perhaps on that day the Pilgrims read what we earlier heard: "Give and there will be gifts for you: a full measure, pressed down, shaken together, and running over, will be poured onto your lap; because the amount you measure out is the amount you will be given back" (Luke 6:38).

Have a wonderful Thanksgiving!

Authority, Not Power

DECEMBER 7, 1980
Readings: 1 Kings: 8–14; Luke 3:1–15

Today is the second Sunday and the first Communion Sunday in Advent, the season that hails the coming of the Prince of Peace. Today is also the thirty-ninth anniversary of the attack on Pearl Harbor, an event that took place also on a Sunday, and which inexorably brought the United States directly into World War II. As war and peace seem never able to let each other go—while one is in bed, the other's at the board—we should not be surprised to find inscribed over General Grant's tomb the words "Let there be peace." Nor should we be surprised that those words spring more readily to the lips of the victor who wants to preserve what he has won.

In this nave tonight, "Let there be peace" will again be everybody's fervent prayer, but not to preserve what the world has won—an unparalleled arms race and its twin evil, global misery. Bishop Helder Camara of Brazil will deplore the fact that despite severe food shortages, developing nations use five times as much foreign exchange for the import of arms as for agricultural machinery. In developing countries, there is one soldier for every 250 inhabitants, one doctor for every 3,700. And Olof Palme, a former prime minister of Sweden, will undoubtedly repeat the sentiments of the late Lord Mountbatten: In the nuclear age, to repeat the old Roman precept, "If you desire peace, prepare for war," is "absolute nuclear nonsense."

Advent, the coming of the Prince of Peace *and* Pearl Harbor, recalls a contrast often made these days between authority and power. The word "power" has overtones of "naked." It suggests coercion, the use of force in some physical, psychological or spiritual form. Authority, on the other hand, with its overtones of "legitimate," is based solely on qualities worthy of admiration. A person shows authority when she shows understanding, compassion, wisdom. Obviously, authority and power mix in both individuals and institutions, but surely the *ideal* for people of power and for institutions of power is to embody the attributes of authority.

Consider how totally without power the Prince of Peace enters the world. He whom at Christmas we will hail as King of Kings and Lord of Lords will be born in a manger. He who will be the bread of life for all humanity will be laid in the feedbox of animals. Unsentimentalized, the manger is a symbol of powerlessness. That those in power will seek to destroy the child Jesus reflects an early recognition of his authority, but not of his power. At birth, he has no power.

Even more arresting is this: By the end of his life, Jesus has certainly gained spiritual power over certain people and especially over the lives of his disciples. But he refuses to exercise it. Judas is known to be a defector, but no action is taken. Peter three times denies his Lord—hardly the action of a submissive fanatic. How different is Jesus from the Reverend Jim Jones! In fact, would it not be fair to suggest that Jesus is authority incarnate, saying "No" to power?

Now let us ask: Is this the way God generally deals with human beings—purely through authority, never through power? Let's go back to the first sentence of the New Testament lesson (and I'm grateful to my colleague George Thomas for pointing this out to me): "In the fifteenth year of Tiberius Caesar's reign"—there's imperial rank and power for you—"when Pontius Pilate was governor of Judea"—again, power—"Herod tetrarch of Galilee, his brother Philip tetrarch of the lands of Ituraea and Trachonitis, Lysanias tetrarch of Abilene"—power upon power—"during the pontificate of Annas and Caiaphas"—now religious power is added to secular power—"the word of God came to John son of Zechariah, in the wilderness" (Luke 3:1–2).

And *how* did the Word of God come to John the Baptist? Did it come in power, or simply with authority? We don't know, because we are not told. What we *are* told, in the Old Testament, is that God revealed himself to Moses in a burning bush, that to many a psalmist he was in the wind: "He did fly upon the wings of the wind" (Ps. 18:10); "The voice of the Lord . . . breaketh the cedars of Lebanon" (Ps. 29:5). To others he was in the earthquake: "The earth shook and trembled, the foundations also of the hills moved because he was wroth" (Ps. 18:7). From the earliest of times to the loftiest of prophets—at least to their imaginations—God did manifest himself in physical power.

But, as Edith Hamilton points out, countering this idea in the Old Testament is another, one found perhaps for the first time in the story of Elijah. Here we read that God, who did indeed lay the foundations of the earth; God, who keeps the stars in their courses—this same God speaks to the soul of each of us in a still, small voice, beside whose authority the power of storm and earthquake and fire is as nothing.

The story of John the Baptist shows that those furthest from the seat of power are often nearer to the heart of things. "Power tends to corrupt," as Lord Acton said, "and absolute power corrupts absolutely." Or listen to these words spoken centuries ago by Rabbi Nachman of Bratislav: "Victory cannot tolerate truth, and if that which is true is spread before your very eyes, you will reject it, because you are a victor. Whoever would have truth itself must drive hence the spirit of victory; only then may he prepare to behold the truth."

The story of John the Baptist shows us that integrity springs from authority, not power. The same is true of fearlessness. Those men of power, the Pharisees, must have been outraged to be called a "brood of vipers." But the multitudes, when they heard it, must have loved John for the enemies he dared to make. Because he himself had no fear, they must have felt sheltered by him. His courage must have been contagious; they must have begun to sense that there was nothing they couldn't do, once they saw in him that there was nothing they need fear.

And the story of Elijah shows us, in the words of Athanasius, that "The road to God is in the *soul* of every human being."

In this of all seasons, dear Riversiders, in this Advent season, let us not seek our salvation in the trappings of power. I know how authority and power vie in the souls of each of us: in our roles as parents, in the way we conduct ourselves on the job, in the way we perceive our beloved nation. But is it not true that it is precisely to the *divorce* of power from authority that we can trace the darkness in our personal lives and in the life of our nation?

Therefore let us allow God to search for us as God did for Elijah, and to find us, as God found Elijah, there in the depths of our souls where we can distinguish true authority from illusory power. There, to the still, small voice of God, we can answer with our own: "Whom in heaven have I but Thee? and there is none upon earth that I desire beside Thee."

May the Word of God, which came to John, son of Zechariah, in the wilderness, come also to you. In this season of births and rebirths, may the Word that calls forth shoots from dead stumps, a people from dry bones, sons and daughters from the stones at our feet, babies from barren wombs, and life from the tomb—may this Word, which is stronger than strength, mightier than might, call forth from each of you a new creation.

"Unto Us a Child Is Born"

This week, a sensitive parishioner submitted a legitimate request. One of these days, he said, he wanted a sermon on how Abraham heeded God's call to leave his country for a land the Lord God would show him. In my all-too-fallible inner ear, I heard him saying he wanted a sermon on how Abraham could bring himself to commit the one unpardonable middle-class, middle-aged sin: With all signs pointing to "go" in every department of his life, how could Abraham drop everything and take off, with no idea what was in store for him; for his family, which was extended; for his servants, who were many; or even for his animals. (Fortunately, beyond a possible cat, our parishioner doesn't have to worry about animals, nor certainly about servants.)

"But why," I said to myself after reading his letter, "why do we have to wait for 'one of these days'?" Doesn't the Magnificat, always read at least once in Advent, talk of God's mercy to "Abraham and to his descendants forever"? Moreover, the risk Abraham took going out into the world the Lord God took—and more—coming into the world. And finally, doesn't one birth for us—"Unto *us* a child is born"—demand at the very least one rebirth for God? (I have nothing whatsoever against being born again. My objection is only to the stillborn, to the spiritual "preemies.")

"For unto us a child is born." From one point of view, I suppose we could say that the prophet was wrong to seduce us with the belief that one single person can put all things right. For what in the world, in a broken, bickering world, can a single little child do to resolve humanity's ancient conflict? I suppose it could be argued that Isaiah was irresponsible to predict that "all the footgear of battle" and "every cloak rolled in blood" would be consumed by fire. What would he say now—now that the footgear of battle can fly like Mercury's winged feet and roll in blood every last cloak of every last man, woman, and child? Why, even the Lord Himself seems no match for Mars, the demonic mover of this century, with his globe of sun-fire and his pillar of cloud.

Let's engage in an imaginative enterprise, if only to prove that the first little gray hairs of the mind have yet to show. Shortly before that first Christmas, after the rumors were heard repeatedly on the heavenly grapevine of what the Lord God had in mind to do, the angels must have gathered around in some concern. One must have found voice enough to say, "Lord, if they hear not Moses and the prophets, neither will they be persuaded though one rose from the dead." Maybe another ventured, "Lord, they'll laugh at your son, and those who don't laugh at him will weep over him. What's the difference? None will follow."

The same risk Abraham took going out into the world, the Lord God took—and more—coming in. In the gentlest of tones, Christmas carols frequently suggest the utter absurdity of it all. "Lo, how a rose . . ." A rose, in winter! How can the tender, slender stem of a rose crack the frozen misery of centuries?

But the Lord God must have remonstrated: "It is true they are diseased through their disloyalty. Still, I cannot part with them; I cannot give them up. So what, dear angels, would you have me do? Offer more laws? More creeds? That these are important I will not dispute; but important as they are they are not compelling. They are like the sticks that these inventive creatures of mine have devised for their heavy-fruited plants: without them, the vines would never rise from the ground. But there is nothing in those sticks to give life to plants; only the sun and soil in union can make a vine flourish. Only love from heaven made incarnate on earth can make a human being grow. So my mind is made up: No longer shall we say to them, 'Seek ye the way.' The way itself will come to them and say, 'Arise and walk.'"

"But, Lord God Almighty, not a carpenter; at least a king."

"Dearly beloved, when you live so close to me you would think my will would be more transparent to you. I do not wish the submission of my people. I do not want *my* glorification, I want theirs. I love my people, and in return for my love I want their love, freely given. And you know that freedom for the beloved demands equality with the beloved."

"But at least give them proof. Give them a miracle."

"Again, you are not being perceptive. These creatures of mine are very clever. They are always looking for evidence to make intelligently selfish decisions. That's why their evangelists, instead of the freedom they need, give them all the proofs they want. I have told these evangelists there are no proofs for my existence, only witnesses. Nevertheless they go on proving one ineffable mystery after another with all the ardor of orthodoxy stamping out heresy. But I am the Lord God, and will not seek to overcome selfishness by appealing to selfish motives. So, as the prophet promised, I will send my people a son. I will seek to captivate their hearts, not conquer them. I will seek to open their minds, not crack their skulls. They, of course, will continue to fight me as they always have, but the contest between us will not be one of power—only of endurance. I will show them that true conquerors are not those who can inflict the most, but those who can suffer the most. I will show them that love never ends."

Returning now to earth, to our time, and to the parishioner who wrote the letter: not only does love never end; by its very nature it never ceases to take risks. If our love for God and for one another is for real, don't we have to expose ourselves far more than we do? How many things there are that we never talk about and yet never stop thinking about! But I have in mind as well the love of life, in general, and the risks such a love demands. You, parishioner, are middle-aged and middle-class. So am I. So are many here. That means we know that after our education—which we stupidly pack into the early years of life—after our formal education is over, life at first continues to be stimulating, what with new loves, new jobs, marriage, relocations. We can even live without new ideas, for a while. Then many of us learn to live permanently without them, encouraged by professions that discourage new ideas as well as outside interests. It is sad, but true: for many the professional world becomes "a kind of Franz Kafka mansion where the rooms get spiritually smaller and grayer the further up the stairs you go, and this is known as promotion" (Wilfrid Sheed).

My grandfather used to say about people who don't read poetry, "Neither does a cow." My great-uncle used to say about people who don't listen to fine music, "Neither does a pig." My great-aunt used to say about people who never change jobs, "Neither do garbage-horses." (In her day, they didn't have Mayor Koch's new trucks.)

If we fail in love—and that includes the love of life—we fail in all things else.

"Unto us a child is born." The same risk Abraham took in going out into the world, God took—and more—coming in. So what shall we say this Advent: a risk for a risk, a birth for us, a rebirth for God? But let us be clear: the point of rebirth is not to stay young, but to grow up. The point of a rebirth is to claim, as did Abraham, his God-given freedom: the freedom, at last, to rise above the moral squalor of prevailing opportunism; at last, no longer to render everything to Caesar; at last, no longer to acquiesce passively in evil (an acquiescence we often dignify in private life with the word "patience," and in public life with the word "patriotism"). But passive acquiescence in evil represents only one thing: the sin of cowardice.

"Unto us a son is born." We come to the child *to become adults*. We come to the manger to leave routine and unrewarding ways. Dear parishioner who wrote the letter, dear parishioners one and all, the mercy God showed unto Abraham, God this Christmas is showing again to all Abraham's descendants forever. A single child to set everything right? The carols know the absurdity is only apparent. "Rejoice, rejoice, Emmanuel has come to thee, O Israel."

Christmas 1980

L ast week, in the space of no more than forty-eight hours, Handel's *Messiah* was sung twice in Carnegie Hall and once in Queens; and in Avery Fisher Hall three thousand people paid handsomely for the privilege of singing it themselves. It's perdurable, this oratorio, and one reason for its deserved popularity is the Biblical texts that Charles Jennens so brilliantly laid out for Handel. The very first of them sets the theme and the tone for the whole oratorio for Christmas and really for the whole life, death, and resurrection of the Lord. The words are from the prophet Isaiah, and they are sung by the tenor soloist. So simply, on three descending notes, he sings: "Comfort ye." Then the words are repeated with variations: "Comfort ye my people, saith your God."

What solace there is in both the words and the music! Yet, given the state of the world—in which the lot of so many lives is grief untold and unrelieved—it seems appropriate this Christmas to ask: "*How* are we to take comfort?" Since the time when Abraham argued with God over the fate of Sodom, God's people have remonstrated with their Lord, a practice which, according to the Torah, is justified—provided one argues not on one's behalf, but on behalf of all humanity. So let us not fear to attempt the same.

In *Messiah* the text continues: "Speak ye comfortably to Jerusalem, and cry unto her that her warfare is accomplished, that her iniquity is pardoned." But even as *Messiah* was being sung last week, did warfare end in the Middle East, in Iran, in Ireland? Has warfare ended in Buffalo, New York, where Blacks are killed, or in Atlanta, where Black kids are kidnapped, or in this whole country, when John Lennon is only the most notorious victim of ten thousand handgun murders every year? East of the Elbe, the Poles still await what before them the Czechs received in 1968, and before them, the Hungarians; and before them, the East Germans. And south of the border there is growing proof that Amnesty International was right to contend, already in 1974, that torture, which had long been no more than a historical curiosity, has developed a life of its own and become a social cancer. The world is riddled with suffering, and because almost as an act of self-preservation we have mobilized our defensive energies and grown hard, I feel that behind the travails, behind the torments that have seized and shaken the whole earth, there stands a terrible sentence of guilt. To be sure, millions are more sinned against than sinning, yet today's "gross darkness that covers the people" is there because those who could have decided otherwise chose to blot out the light. So how, in a world of warfare and iniquity, can we take seriously and without sentimentality the prophet's words, "Comfort ye my people"?

The answer, I think, is: "It's simple, but not easy"—like singing the opening notes at the beginning of Handel's oratorio. If you stop to think of it, most things really worthwhile in this world are simple, and very difficult—if by "simple" you mean the simplicity that lies on the far side of complexity.

Goethe wrote that one can understand only what one loves. If you approach someone with aversion, there will be things you will never see. Love is not blind; love is visionary. Love not only heals wounds, love discovers them. Because of this relationship of love to knowledge, our most profound understanding is often associated with a mother's love. Picture any painting, any statue, of a Madonna and Child. Two things unite the mother and the child: the mother's arms and the mother's eyes. And the understanding is there in Mary's eyes not because she has read Dr. Spock, but because she *adores* her child.

In like manner, God adores all God's children. God sees our wounds, feels our grief. God understands us so much better than we can ever understand ourselves, not because He has the whole world in His hands, but because She has the whole world in Her arms. Or, if you prefer the image of the prophet, so tenderly put to music by Handel, "He shall gather the lambs in his arms and carry them in his bosom." (You can just feel the rocking in the ⅝ time!)

What comfort to know we are so understood because we are so loved!—God is omniscient not because He is the grandest of Grand Inquisitors, with an intellect that nothing escapes, but because God's love is infinite for each and every one of us, His creatures. Still warfare and iniquity continue, don't they? So it's fair to ask if God so loves us, why doesn't God stop them?

You all remember, I'm sure, the parable of the Prodigal Son in the fourteenth chapter of Luke. The story is really about the father, a father so prodigal in his love that he respects his son's freedom; he will not force him to remain filial. If the son insists on leaving home, there is nothing the father can do but release him unto the storms of the world and then stand daily on the road, watching and waiting and hoping and praying for the son's return. All you who complain about God—what more do you want from a father so loving that He refuses to be paternalistic?

Well, there is one more thing the father can do. He can go down the road and find the boy. And that's exactly what God does at Christmas. Here again is what the prophet wrote, the excitement of which Handel understood so well: "For unto us a child is born, unto us a son is given and his name shall be called Wonderful, Counsellor, the Mighty God, the Everlasting Father, the Prince of Peace." In no uncertain terms, the Messiah will speak to us of our sin. He will never withhold the telling blow when only the telling blow will serve. But he will also show his understanding of the homesickness of those who live in a far country. And he will assure us that if only we will return home to our loving father, our warfare will be accomplished and our iniquity pardoned. Yes, it's that simple: warfare could disappear as quickly as does a fist when it turns into an open hand. It's that simple—and that difficult. But it could happen, if only we would "let go, and let God."

The answer to the sufferings of the world is not to ask God to do away with them; nor, I believe, is it to force ourselves to look at sights I'm convinced no human eye could long endure anyhow. The answer is to "look to Jesus," in whom all the sufferings of the world converge. He hears the sobs of the lonely, the sighs of the prisoner; he knows the cares of little children and the grisly hallucinations of the insane. His heart is pierced by every knife drawn, every bullet fired, every evil word spoken. Like the world, Jesus is riddled with suffering. "Surely he has borne our griefs and carried our sorrows. He was wounded for our iniquities: the chastisement of our peace was upon him." But listen to the prophet's promise: "And with his stripes we are healed."

That's why I say we must look to Jesus to see our warfare accomplished and our iniquity pardoned. The answer, once again, is to go, as did the shepherds and wise men, "even unto Bethlehem and see this thing which has come to pass." The answer is to look to him who humbled himself that we might be exalted, who became poor that we might be enriched, who came to us that we might return home to God. We *can* bear the sight of a loving Christ whose love for us and the world will melt our own hard hearts until they become vulnerable and loving as is his.

Not centuries, but millennia have passed since Isaiah wrote. But his words do not breed hopelessness, although the truth in them has yet to be made manifest. On the contrary, there is fire in those words to rekindle in us the desire that was in Isaiah to translate pain into joy, problems into challenges, crises into opportunities. For we know that while God can start Creation alone, God cannot finish it without us. Therefore we can say "Yes" to what the prophet wrote, which so inspired Handel. Yes, as the tenor goes on to sing, "Every valley shall be exalted, and every mountain and hill made low: the crooked straight, and the rough places plain." And the whole chorus sings, "And the glory of the Lord shall be revealed, and all flesh shall see it together: for the mouth of the Lord hath spoken it."

"Comfort ye my people, saith your God." May you all have a wonderful Christmas, and may "Blessing and honor, glory and power, be unto Him that sitteth upon the throne and unto the Lamb forever and ever." Amen.

1981

All the Way to the Manger

JANUARY 11, 1981

I would like particularly to welcome to the church today a special delegation from the Soviet Union here under the auspices of the American Friends Service Committee to talk about disarmament.

Let us take for a text this morning the line that comes at the end of the story of the Wise Men: "And . . . they departed . . ."

> Go, go, go, said the bird: human kind
> Cannot bear very much reality.

I keep returning to those two lines of T. S. Eliot, for it seems so true that human beings simply are not capable of sustaining moments of high intensity. And that, I conclude, is why the men who came all the way to Bethlehem—who simply *had* to come—had also to go.

"Humankind cannot bear very much reality." Either we can't sustain high moments, or they refuse to hang around. Some of you will remember how Faust in a moment of ecstasy cried out, "Moment, ah still delay; thou art so fair!" (*"Augenblick, verweile doch; du bist so schön!"*) But these "highs" take off; they don't delay. As a paratrooper in the Army I used to love to jump at night. Out the door of the plane you'd go into a wind whistling past at about a hundred and thirty-five miles per hour. For a time you'd be buffeted mercilessly. Then suddenly the chute would open. As the plane by this time was at some distance; as the stars on the horizon were below you, and as initially there was no sensation of falling, for one glorious moment you found yourself hanging silently among the stars. "Moment, ah still delay; thou art so fair!" But all too quickly the stars began to recede, and the earth to rise. Soon, with a rude jolt, you were returned to business as usual.

The first and only time I both saw and heard Toscanini conduct I walked the streets all night, unable to bear the thought of the moment passing so quickly into memory. Watching Nureyev dance or hearing Leontyne Price sing is also an unforgettable high. Lovers know the experience. And who will ever forget John Jefferson snatching footballs out of the autumn skies? Or years ago in springtime watching

Ted Williams at bat? (When catchers protested that balls were strikes, umpires responded, "Mr. Williams will inform us when the ball comes across the plate.")

But take all these experiences and multiply them by ten, and I still doubt whether together their excitement could compare to that of seeing God's love in person, "live," lying in a manger. Compared to Revelation, all else must be as the lightning bug to the lightning. And yet we read that the Wise Men departed. So today we can ask ourselves, "What difference did it all make? How different are we, now that Advent, Christmas, and Epiphany are all over?"

I think high moments play a very important role in our lives. I think they define the essence of things; they tell us what music, love, dancing, sports, are all about. Do you remember Wednesday morning this last week? The sky was cloudless. Every tree branch was covered with fresh snow, as were every street and park. The snow blurred the harsh angles of buildings, making the rough places plain and even the crooked straight. It was sheer magic outside. *And it was normal*—if by "normal" you mean not "average," but that which defines the norm. What defines New York City—its beauty, or its garbage? If New York lived up to its norm, lived true to its essence, New York would be magical at all times, everywhere, even without the snow. Don't say I'm mad! "Much madness is divinest sense/To the discerning eye" (Emily Dickinson).

The discerning eye sees the essential beauty amid the garbage, and sees that the only way to live in New York is unceasingly to try to make manifest this beauty.

Likewise, there is a discerning way to look at human beings. "The word became flesh and dwelt among us," to reconsecrate the human race, to remind us that each of us is a unit of God's grace. I know that's not the way we generally regard one another, but that's because we're blind, not visionary. We do not see each other with eyes of faith. But the Wise Men, after seeing God's love in person—a Savior sent to remind human beings of their essential humanity—I'll bet thereafter they saw every human being as unprecedented, irrepeatable, and irreplaceable. And I'll bet they did everything they could to reinforce, not deny, the dignity of every person they met. (A good point to remember after Epiphany and just before Martin Luther King Jr.'s birthday.)

When the astronaut Edgar Mitchell, returning from his high on the moon, spied through the window of his capsule his home—a small, distant planet—he claims to have had an intense visionary experience. He saw, he said, that one human race is more important than one hundred and sixty-three nationalities; that, to paraphrase Thoreau, we are citizens of the world first, and of our own countries at a later and more convenient hour. I was thrilled once to hear Mitchell tell the tale. But I couldn't help thinking, "You shouldn't have to go to the moon to have such an experience; it's enough to go to Bethlehem." For the message of Bethlehem is that all human beings are members of one family, brothers and sisters of the Holy Child. The message of Bethlehem has been captured so well in the Episcopal collect, which says, "God cares for each as if God had naught else to care for, and for all as if all were but one."

Did we go to Bethlehem this year—all the way? Or did we stop somewhere outside the city limits, or at least somewhere short of the manger? The presence in the church this morning of our Russian sisters and brothers reflects our "normal" relations, but, alas, not the average relations between Russians and Americans. And how will their children fare with ours? I fear the Cold War of the 1980s more than I did the Cold War of the 1950s. Then, Hiroshima and Nagasaki had rendered nuclear war unthinkable. Now, with a superabundance of weapons hundreds of times more lethal, nuclear war is again thinkable—even winnable, we are told. What we had begun to delegitimize we are now relegitimizing. We are putting a foundation back under a condemned building.

"God cares for all as if all were but one." Let us recall that wars begin in the mind. We have first to *think* others to death. You can't kill a brother. You can't kill a sister, a friend, a fellow human being. But you can kill a Marxist, a capitalist, a terrorist. You can kill a Red Menace, or a shark of Wall Street. And we further prepare the mind to kill by using such juiceless jargon as "acceptable damage" and "modernization of NATO."

Faith is the opposite of fear.

For years the Soviet Union and the United States have lived in mutual fear. Deterrence has been the watchword. But on both sides a tremendous error has been made in thinking that deterrence is a stationary state. Deterrence is a *degenerative* state (E. P. Thompson). The repressed violence backs up into each nation's politics, economics, ideology, and culture. Mutual fear only increases selfish loves. Mutual fear refines ever more hideous weapons. Fear enlarges the government's control over its population and client states. Dear Russian and American friends, the renewed Cold War is reinforcing the ugliest features in both our societies. And we must remember a psychological factor: expectation without action becomes boring; so psychologically we are always pushed to fulfill our expectations.

But have we the will, the courage to act against these perverse expectations, against our fears and for our faith? Yes, if with the Wise

Men, we go all the way to the manger. Because the difference between Christmas and parachuting at night and listening to Toscanini and watching Nureyev and John Jefferson—the difference between these highs and Christmas is the difference between a memory and a Presence. In leaving the manger, we really don't leave Christ. He who came to show us the way will also see us through.

There's a nice story told of Heinrich Heine, the German—or Jewish if you prefer—poet, who was standing with a friend before the Cathedral of Amiens in France. "Tell me, Heinrich," said his friend, "why can't people build piles like this any more?"

"My dear friend," replied Heine, "in those days people had convictions. We Moderns have opinions. And it takes more than opinions to build a Gothic cathedral."

There's no question that almost all Russians and Americans want peace. But peace in their minds is an opinion, not a conviction. They are hearers of the word, not doers; they wish for peace, but they don't *will* it. They want peace in their shopping baskets, along with military superiority and a few other things that make peace impossible. They are like Kaiser Wilhelm, who is supposed to have remarked, "We do not want war, we want only victory."

Said [former Secretary of State] Cyrus Vance last June at Harvard: "History may conclude that ours was a failure not of opportunity but of seeing opportunity; a failure not of resources but of wisdom to use them; a failure not of intellect but of understanding and of *will*."

If we had the experience of Christmas and did not miss the meaning, we *will* from now on regard every human being as sacred, created by God and redeemed by Christ. We *will* regard every human being as a sister or a brother—and as a Russian or an American, a Marxist or a capitalist, at a later and more convenient hour. And we *will* continue to do so, because the Messiah who came to show us the way will see us through.

The Wise Men departed. They returned to business, but not to business as usual—rather to business as never before.

Of Thine Own Have We Given Thee

JANUARY 18, 1981

". . . so that the life of Jesus may also be manifested in our mortal bodies."

2 Corinthians 4:11

L ast week the text read, "And they [the Wise Men] departed." The three good men who simply had to come had also to go.

> Go, go, go, said the bird: human kind
> Cannot bear very much reality.

But I myself can't seem to let them go. I cling to them, perhaps feeling that only their kind of wisdom is going to rescue us from the vanity and villainy of our times, not to mention the eternal cussedness of the human race. So forgive me if, for one more week, we stay with the Epiphany story. I want particularly to review the gifts they brought, and to ask: "What does it mean to offer up our gifts to Christ?"

Let's start with Caspar's gold. Over the last two days, as they prepared to hand over Iran's frozen billions (I have a hard time picturing the details of these transactions), the bankers of Chase Manhattan, Bank of America, Citicorp, and the rest, cited their obligation to protect their stockholders. Well, I'd like to cite our obligation to protect God's wealth. In many churches, when the offering is brought forward, the congregation stands to sing "All things come of Thee, O Lord, and of thine own have we given Thee." The gold Caspar brought to the manger was given to him by God. Were we as individuals and as a nation as wise as Caspar, we would do the same with our God-given wealth.

But that's not so easy. Robert Bellah, the sociologist, writes: "That happiness is to be obtained through limitless material acquisition is denied by every religion and philosophy known to humanity, but is preached incessantly by every American television set." In other words, there is an enormous discrepancy between what we are brought up to believe, and what American society rewards. Talk about the cussedness of the race! It's money that measures the success or failure of most of the games we play most of our lives. It's money that gives us our identity, compared to which our identity in God is but a footnote. We expect more from financial success than from our relationship with God.

But does financial success bring us the happiness promised by every American television set? Listen to this: "Middle class depression is the well-spring of the competitive enterprise system, which demands always that we surpass someone else and requires that there be losers as well as winners. Until we feel better about ourselves we will need poor people to kick around."

I can't measure the psychological truth of that statement, but I do know this: When we are intent on being, rather than on having, we are happier. And when we are intent on being, we don't take away from other people's being—in fact, we enhance it. But when we are intent on having, we create have-nots—and invariably lie about the connection.

For example, there is much talk these days about hunger, and in most people's minds it is due primarily to overpopulation, particularly in Central and Latin America. Few people cite World Bank reports that small farms are three to fourteen times more productive than large farms in Argentina, Brazil, Chile, Colombia, Ecuador, and Guatemala. Nor, for that matter, do most people in America know that every study made by the U.S. Department of Agriculture has found that the most efficient farms in terms of cost per unit of output are the one- or two-family mechanized farms, not the large corporate operations. In North and South America large landholders control most of the land, yet they are the least productive. God is not mocked, so we should not be surprised that inequality fosters inefficiency. And it is inefficiency, far more than overpopulation, that spells starvation for millions.

It's true that we're running out of fuel. But we're not running out of energy, only out of oil. And why haven't we developed solar energy? Labor leader William Winpesinger once explained it to me: "Reverend, you can't hang a meter on the sun." Wealth corrupts our perceptions of ourselves and of life.

How, then, do we bring our God-given wealth to Christ? When we say, and really mean it, "All things come of *thee*, not me, O Lord"; when we earn money to share it, to enhance our life together; when we realize that dedication is worthy only as its object is worthy; when we realize that the reward of wealth is the happiness of others.

But if it is so wonderful to share, and to enhance life, then everyone should have a crack at it. That's reason enough to work for justice more than for charity. So let us pray God for large hearts and robust social consciences, that we, like Caspar, may bring our God-given wealth to be consecrated by our God-given Savior, "so that the life of Christ may also be manifested in our mortal bodies."

When consecrated, our money makes us more vulnerable, not less. The same surely is true of consecrated minds. Melchior's frankincense, because it is a fragrance, is often taken to symbolize our innermost thoughts. If we bring our God-given minds to Christ, we certainly gain security—but it is the security of knowing we are going to be ferreted out of any hiding place. The greatest censorship is always self-imposed: it isn't what we are told to think, but what we don't allow ourselves to think. What's too painful to remember, we choose to forget. Our ability to disavow unwanted knowledge is prodigious. We use, or don't use, our minds mainly to protect ourselves.

Now that I'm no longer a university chaplain but a local pastor, I receive a lot more invitations to address my fellow clergy. Once in Enid, Oklahoma, a colleague rose to ask, "How do you get away with talking about homosexuality, the arms race, all these controversial things? If you were in Tulsa, they'd run you out of town."

"In the first place," I answered, "I never claimed that Tulsa was leading the nation. Secondly, the congregation at Riverside is not so stodgy as you think. But if you really want the answer, here it is: How many here have read two books on homosexuality and the Church?"

Out of some four hundred people about five raised their hands.

"How many have read two books on the arms race?"

This time there were about twenty hands.

"So there it is. We don't talk about these things not because our congregations are conservative, but because we don't know what to say. And furthermore," I said—very gently—"to the degree our ignorance stems from our complacency, it's an ethical and not an intellectual failing."

I hope that once the hostages return, we may have the moral courage to admit that the Shah's regime was in the interest of everybody outside of Iran, and that we supported him long after he had been deserted by his subjects. And maybe, with God's help, we will one day open our eyes to see that it was not a coincidence that the enemy people of Vietnam were yellow, and that a disproportionate number of the U.S. GIs sent to fight them were black.

We are beset by illusions. How could it be otherwise in a cynical, violent, materialistic world? But if we bring our minds to Christ, he can use them to unlock the manacles of our mind, to play the religious role of disillusionment. Too many "evangelists" help us not to think or to reason, but to accept authority generally theirs. But faith is never a substitute for thought; it's that which makes good thinking possible. Harry Emerson Fosdick was right: "Faith does not take reason by the throat and strangle the beast. Faith and reason are not antithetical opposites. They need each other. All the tragic superstitions which have cursed religion throughout its history have been due to faith divorced from reason."

And we could add, "or to minds divorced from hearts." Lack of compassion distorts the intellect. There is knowledge that is the fruit of reason and knowledge that is the fruit of love. It is the second, I think, that made Melchior wise. So let us, along with our gold, bring our minds to Christ. Take our minds and let them be consecrated,

Lord, to thee, "so that the life of Jesus may also be manifested in our mortal bodies."

Gold, frankincense, and finally, myrrh—a bitter perfume used in embalming, and hence a symbol of sorrow. It is easier to offer up our wealth and our minds to Christ than to offer up our sorrow, for generally we prefer the luxury of bitter protest. Why does sorrow melt the heart of one and harden the heart of another? Rainer Maria Rilke has a wonderful line: "Be patient towards all that is unsolved in your heart and try to live the questions themselves."

I've learned more from failure than from success, more from suffering than from pleasure. Some of the greatest blessings in my life are joyous—children—but some of the deepest can only be labeled "severe mercies."

Bitterness is a diminishing emotion. When we nourish our grievances, we starve ourselves. Bitterness represents the wrong kind of suffering, which may be what Eliot had in mind when he said, "To rest in our suffering is an evasion of suffering." Far better to offer up our grievances to Jesus, along with our wealth and our minds. For this is the beauty of making gifts to Christ: the more of ourselves we give to Christ, the more of ourselves he gives back to us.

Ordained to Unrest

FEBRUARY 1, 1981
Reading: Matthew 10:34–39

This week, more tears of joy came to more eyes, more lumps to the throats of more Americans than in any week I can remember. It was marvelous that in times no one can rightly embrace with unrestrained enthusiasm, we could so unreservedly express our joy and gratitude. The hostages certainly deserved the fun and every drop of love poured out to them across the nation. As the cop at Battery Park said, "Nothing like a good time to make up for time lost." And what better means than a rain of ticker-tape to wash clean the heart of bitterness, that bitterness with which each hostage now must contend. May God grant them strength beyond their own, for from those few who had put on garments of vengeance, we could see how diminishing an emotion bitterness is. ("'Vengeance is mine, I will repay,' saith the Lord" means "Vengeance is *mine*—not yours.")

Addressing the multitudes at City Hall, Moorehead Kennedy was pleased to note that Americans seemed "much more comfortable with their feelings about their country—much more united." I think he was right. And what's wrong with unity? What's wrong with loving your country? Obviously nothing, absolutely nothing!

And yet . . .

And yet it was too bad the celebrations didn't make more of diplomacy's significant victory, of the fact that a lot of people—in Algeria, France, Germany, and Egypt, not to mention Iran and the United States—lost a lot of sleep bringing a dangerous confrontation to a peaceful conclusion. The abortive rescue attempt last April put the stature of the nation above the safety of the hostages. But this time, the American negotiators seemed more interested in saving lives than saving face. I thought that was worth celebrating, especially in a nation more self-assured about its military power than confident of its diplomatic skills.

And here's something else that was—and still is—too bad. Jesus said, "I have come not to bring peace, but the sword" (Matt. 10:34). That much-disputed statement recognizes that next to love, pain is necessary for growth. We've all learned that from our personal lives. In personal life, from failure we learn so much; from success so little. Not all pain, to be sure, results in growth; but there is no growth without pain. So pain is not the absence of grace; it's a means of grace.

It's too bad that we can't carry that insight about pain and failure from our personal lives into our national life, too. To admit error is not the end of the world, it's the beginning of humanity—a means of grace for a nation to grow in decency. Just as God, despite our manifold transgressions, still loves us, so we too can love the United States while at the same time admitting our mistakes in Iran, confessing our complicity in crimes far worse than any committed against the hostages.

"You corrupted your wisdom for the sake of your splendor" (Ezek. 28:17). In Iran, as in Vietnam, and now in El Salvador, we simply cannot accept the fact that nations have destinies not designed in Washington. And when we insist that they're designed in Moscow, it's often to give us the excuse to redesign them in Washington.

I love America, but not her presumptions of power. I love America, but I also know that her secure presumption of righteousness is her greatest sin.

"Woe unto you, scribes and Pharisees, hypocrites!" Jesus never hurt anyone, except deliberately. He hurt them only because he loved them, and wanted to save them rather than please them. And in true prophetic fashion he attacked none more than the nation's leaders, because their one-sided righteousness was the source of such blindness to themselves and the source of such suffering to others.

When politicians tell us only what we want to hear, prophets must tell us what is right. "Cry aloud, spare not, lift up thy voice like a trumpet, and show my people their transgressions" (Isa. 58:1). Even as the hostages were returning home, President Reagan and Secretary of State Haig were returning to Cold War politics with all the passion of sinners returning to the fold. Both, in this first week of their office, linked arms control to Soviet good behavior—as if the world might not perish before the Soviets ever behaved well, and as if our own house were in order, as if our own sphere of influence weren't littered with the corpses of democracies. To say, as did Mr. Haig, "The greatest priority in human rights today is the problem of rampant international terrorism" is to give the back of the hand to that which causes so much violence in the world: repression and exploitation. The violence of the oppressed, be it in Miami or El Salvador, may be a distortion of charity, but the complacency of oppressors is the essence of egoism. What's worse, Mr. Haig, having blood on your hands—or water, like Pilate?

It's remarkable how the descendants of Thomas Jefferson make like George III. How quickly we forget how, in primary school and at our parents' knee, we Americans learned all about our internal subversion against our lawful sovereign, George III, and we all thought it was wonderful. And weren't we taught that the external subversive help we received from France represented foreign aid for freedom?

For every complex problem there's a simple answer, as H. L. Mencken said, and they're all wrong.

Where there's doubt, there's more considered faith. Likewise, when citizens doubt, patriotism becomes more informed. For Christians to render everything to Caesar—their minds, their consciences—is to become Evangelical nationalists. That's not a distortion of the Gospel; that's desertion.

It's wonderful to love one's country, but faith is for God. National unity, too, is wonderful—but not unity in one-sided righteousness and folly.

There is joy and pain in being an American citizen. The latter American Christians must accept as part of Christ's yoke: "Take my yoke upon you and learn of me." We are ordained to unrest, in deceptive times to reach for truth that seems to many like madness; in the darkness of the world's hatred and prejudice to keep the small flame of love alight. For the world is now too dangerous for anything but truth, too small for anything but love.

Amo, Ergo Sum

FEBRUARY 15, 1981
Reading: John 21:16–19

I want to introduce some very welcome guests in our midst this morning. You will remember the saga of Richard Stevens, minister in South Africa jailed for his views, who finally got out of jail and out of South Africa by ways we are not told. For the last few weeks there has been much excitement about whether or not he was going to get his family out of South Africa as well. I'm happy to say that on Friday of this week, they did get out. Richard is here this morning with Mrs. Stevens and their four boys. Life in exile is never easy; we hope they will let us know if there is anything we can do to make it easier.

Last Sunday, Ernie Campbell eloquently differentiated between believing in Christ and following Jesus: "You can believe in Christ," he said, "without following Jesus, but you can't follow Jesus without believing in Christ." Today I want to continue his line of thought, which is why I read from the last chapter of John the passage ending, "When he [Jesus] had said this, he said to Peter: 'Follow me.'" The passage makes clear that before any of us can presume to follow Jesus, we have first to face him, and to answer the question he put three times to Peter: "Simon, son of Jonas"—substitute your own name— "do you love me?"

The question makes us realize that human beings are less what they've learned and more what they've learned to love. "*Cogito, ergo sum*"—I think, therefore I am? Nonsense! "*Amo, ergo sum*"—I love, therefore I am. We eat, sleep, breathe, and bleed, so we are part animal. The life of the mind also plays an enormous part in our lives. But most fundamentally, we are as we love. Love is the name of our journey. Love measures our stature: the more we love, the bigger we are. There is no smaller package in all the world than that of a man all wrapped up in himself! Yes, even though I have faith to move mountains, knowledge to understand all mysteries, and though I give my body to be burned—the very stuff of heroism—but have not love, I am nothing. You couldn't make the point more powerfully. Thank God St. Paul made it, for if, as Ernie Campbell suggested, there is little following of Jesus, there is much *loveless* following. Many followers of Jesus have just enough religion to make themselves miserable! Their following represents a premature submission, a facade for repressed rebellion. So we can see the importance of first answering Jesus' question, "Simon, son of Jonas, do you love me?"

Actually, the full question put to Peter was, "Do you love me more than these?" It's possible that the question was accompanied by a sweep of the hand indicating Peter's boats, his nets, his possessions. It's possible that Christ was challenging Peter to give it all up for the preaching of the Gospel. On the other hand, "more than these" could signify "more than these other disciples." In that case, Jesus would not be putting down the others, but rather reminding Peter of his own put-down of his fellow disciples. At the Last Supper, he insisted, "Though they all fall away because of you, I will never fall away."

Isn't it comforting to recall that to whatever degree the Church is founded on Peter, it is founded on a second chance? So often the church is derisively called a "crutch." So what makes you think you don't limp? The church is made up of forgiven sinners, people who need two, three, four, and more chances. (Christ told Peter to forgive "seventy times seven.") Three times Peter betrayed Christ—betrayed him as surely as did Judas. But in contrast to Judas, Peter returned. The real tragedy of Judas is that he never did. Judas bears witness to the truth that guilt is the hardest idol to overthrow (Bonhoeffer).

Three times Christ asks, "Do you love me?" as if each answer of Peter would wipe out each betrayal. And after each answer come, with only slight variations, the same instructions: "Feed my sheep."

Now what do those instructions mean? In life we have always to steer a course between an order that is repressive and a freedom that is chaos. The loveless followers of Christ quite naturally are law-and-order folk. They generally interpret "Feed my sheep" to mean "Fill them with religious scruples. Don't let them have their own way; oppress their natural liberty." Horrified at that extreme, other people rush to its opposite. To them, "Feed my sheep" means "Let them graze where they want, let them do their own thing."

In the Book of Lamentations we read, "The daughter of my people is become cruel, like the ostriches in the wilderness" (4:3). Job, too, depicts the ostrich as an example of un-motherhood:

> She leaves her eggs on the ground,
>   with only the earth to warm them;
> Forgetting that a foot may tread on them,
>   or a wild beast may crush them.

> Cruel to her chicks as if they were not hers,
>   little she cares if her labor goes for nothing.
>   Job 39:14–16

Surely "Feed my sheep" is just the opposite of such indifference. "Feed my sheep" means caring is the greatest thing, caring matters most. It recognizes how horrible is life where all is not well between people, where things are known but never spoken. It recognizes how horrible is life where reigns a love of the world, pride, ambition, all that is earthly, nothing that is heavenly. To me, "Feed my sheep" means, as regards children, lots of body warmth and consistent discipline; as regards the rest of us, lots of heart-to-heart, as Jesus went face-to-face with Peter. Does Christ forgive us our betrayals? So we should forgive in others what we can neither condone nor excuse. Forgiveness sows a Godly seed, which is why Abraham Lincoln said, "With malice toward none and charity for all," words that place him at the spiritual center of American history—if only Americans would join him there!

Let us also remember that shepherds in the East don't drive their sheep. "He *leadeth* me beside the still waters . . . he *leadeth* me in the paths of righteousness." Example is still the best form of leadership, which suggests that being a life-loving presence, being something for others, is finally more important than doing something for them. Luther put it well: "Doing good things doesn't make a person good, but a good person will do good things." Job was a good man.

> I was eyes for the blind,
>   and feet for the lame.
> Who but I was father of the poor.
>   The stranger's case had a hearing from me.
> I used to break the fangs of wicked men,
>   And snatch their prey from between their jaws.
>   Job 29:15–17

"Feed my sheep." Be a life-loving presence. Love always finds a way; "the readiness is all," as Hamlet said—a true prescription for Christian living.

But if love finds a task, it also brings a cross; at least it did to Peter, as before him to Christ. "'Truly, truly, I say to you, when you were young, you girded yourself and walked where you would; but when you are old, you will stretch out your hands, and another will gird you and carry you where you do not wish to go.' (This he said to show by what death he was to glorify God.) And after this he said, 'Follow me.'"

Why is goodness forever on the scaffold, wrong upon the throne? Because what human beings seem most to fear is not the evil in themselves, but the good—the good being so demanding. Never would we have crucified Christ, the best among us, had we not first crucified the best within us. But never mind! Don't follow the crowd. Follow Christ, cross and all. Say to yourself, with Kris Kristofferson, "Freedom's just another word for nothing left to lose." And where there's nothing left to lose, there's so much more to give.

Or think of this: At the time of Jesus' trial, "in the chaos of accusation and timidity, garment-rending and hand-washing, individual betrayal and mob-mania, there is one point of self-control: *Jesus is the only one who is acting freely*" (Jerry A. Irish).

Death is the common meeting place of all that lives. But while death—a common death—changes only the self, martyrdom is dying in order to change the world. So the cross is a symbol of life. One must truly have lived to be selected as a target for martyrdom. Martyrs don't die with their boots on; they live with their boots on!

So let us not fear to follow Christ, even though being open to love means being open to suffering. After all, we are made for love, not greed. We are as we love.

Let me conclude with a story that reinforces this Christian view, all the more so because it comes from another tradition. An old man in India sat down in the shade of an ancient banyan tree whose many roots stretched far away into a swamp. Presently he discerned a small commotion where the roots entered the water. Concentrating his attention, he saw that a scorpion had become helplessly entangled in the roots. Pulling himself to his feet, he made his way carefully along the tops of the roots until he came to the place where the scorpion was trapped. He reached down to extricate it. But each time he touched the scorpion, it would lash his hand with its tail, stinging him painfully. Finally his hand was so swollen he could no longer close his fingers, so he withdrew to the shade of the tree to wait for the swelling to go down. As he arrived at the trunk, he saw a young man standing above him on the road laughing at him. "You're a fool," said the young man, "wasting your time trying to help a scorpion that can only do you harm." The old man replied, "Simply because it is in the nature of the scorpion to sting, should I give up my nature, which is to save?"

Burn-Out

MARCH 8, 1981

T wo Sundays ago I moved myself almost to tears telling you the story of the old Indian getting stung trying to rescue the trapped scorpion ("Simply because it is in the nature of the scorpion to sting, should I change my nature, which is to save?"). Immediately after the service two of our ever-alert choir members came up to register their protests. Said a soprano of invincible practicality, "Why didn't the old man use a stick?" (I'd like to hear her sing a song about a stick getting stung.) Said the second: "What happens when your hand gets so infected it falls off? We need a sermon on burn-out."

Well, here it is, a sermon on burn-out, dedicated to a young soprano and to all others who still believe progress is an arrow, not a pendulum; that points once proved should stay proved; that wars once won should stay won. Perhaps it may even help codgers old enough to know that iron does more than mercury to prevent weariness in well-doing.

Tyrannies are most secure when their victims feel most alone. So let's not be victimized alone. More than ever we Christians need the Church, and particularly a church with a clear vision of the faith, a clear understanding of Christ's concern for the world. Christians are like spokes in a wheel: the closer they come to the center, the closer they are to each other.

So for Christians who are afraid they are going to have to fight again for turf they thought they'd won; for Christians who thought that on such issues as the environment, peace, civil rights, and human rights, they had built something solid on hard rock, and now fear the rock was sand—as a remedy for burn-out, let me offer three images of the Church.

The first is a Biblical image: a pilgrim people, who have decided never to arrive. I'm exhausted at the thought. But it's true to life, where change is as insistent as death, sin, and taxes. And it's true to our faith. Ours is a God, after all, who declares, "Behold, I make all things new." Ours is a God of history—a history characterized by an Exodus; one that proclaims a New Testament, which hails a new heaven and a new earth; one that describes a New Jerusalem, anticipates a new song, and new wine, and promises that we shall become new beings. God is ahead of us, as much as within us. God gives us the "growth choice," as opposed to the "fear choice," to use Abraham Maslow's terms; God gives us a present with a future, and a future right up to the very end of life, for "though our outer nature is wasting away, our inner nature is being renewed each day." Even death is only a horizon, and a horizon is nothing save the limit of our sight. "Weep not, I shall not die. And as I leave the land of the dying I trust to see the blessings of the Lord in the land of the living."

Yesterday I returned from Virginia, land of Jerry Falwell. It occurred to me that Jerry offers everyone a present that has only a past. Like the ancient children of Israel, the Moral Majority seeks to elect captains to lead us back to the fleshpots of Egypt. Theirs is the fear choice, not the growth choice. They want to go back to the time when the United States owned the Panama Canal; back to the time when we were the undisputed military power of the world; back to the time when women were in the kitchen and gays in the closet. Back, back, back! Why, they're so backward that out in California they're all worried about teaching children the origin of the species, instead of worrying about whether any of our children have a future other than that of a nuclear ash.

In contrast, let us look forward with the courage of our conviction that the Church at its best is always in an exodus. We are a pilgrim people, a people who have decided never to arrive, a people who live by hope, energized not by what we already possess but by that which is promised: "Behold, I create a new heaven and a new earth."

Sure, it's exhausting; and it's tough. Imagination comes harder than memory, and faithfulness is more demanding than success. But so what if we fail? Didn't Christ? And aren't Christians defined as "those who can afford to fail"?

We'll come back to that, but let's move on to a second Biblical image, that of a prophetic minority. The Bible knows nothing of a moral majority. It assumes that the individual conscience, as opposed to the mass mind, best reflects the universal conscience of humankind. And the Bible insists that a prophetic minority always has more to say to a nation than any majority, Silent, Moral, or any other. As a matter of fact, majorities in the Bible generally end up stoning the prophets, which suggests that democracies are based less on the proven goodness of the people than on the proven evil of dictators.

What must a prophetic minority do? Essentially, as did Jeremiah and all the prophets, speak truth to power. For governments are like individuals: they oversimplify the things that make them angry, and their ideological commitments distort their perceptions and deaden their moral sensibilities. We've seen this for years in the Soviet government.

But communism is not the only ideology in the world. In fact, when it comes to sacred symbols, unexamined slogans, and presuppositions, the most powerful ideology in the world may not be communism but anticommunism. I have in mind the anticommunism reflected in Latin American dictatorships and in past and present regimes in Washington. We have seen so many legends and lies lead to so many unnecessary deaths. The Gulf of Tonkin Resolution that brought us into Vietnam in a big way was based on a legend. What took us into the Dominican Republic in 1965 was a lie. Both times our anticommunism proved our worst enemy. Both times we oversimplified things that made us angry. Both times we saw red—in both senses of the word.

And now we have a White Paper on El Salvador that dwells once again on communist guns, but never mentions the fact that four-fifths of the weapons supplied to the guerillas come from free-enterprise gun runners in Florida, Texas, and California. The paper overlooks the forty-odd other organizations—aside from the communist party—that make up the Front in El Salvador; it mentions guerilla contacts in Havana, Moscow and Hanoi, but never the more extensive ones in Bonn, Paris, Stockholm, London, Caracas, and Mexico City. It ignores Archbishop Romero's plea to Washington to stop supplying weapons to a dictatorial regime despised by its own people. Finally, there is no grasp of the elementary fact that you simply can't have a revolt without revolting conditions. When a government tries to educate its people with a paper that couldn't pass a freshman course in political science, a prophetic minority cannot keep silent. In the name of God, and for the sake of God's children who are going to be needlessly slaughtered, a prophetic minority must speak truth to power, even as did Archbishop Romero, who not only spoke up clearly but paid up personally.

This is Lent, a time when we follow Jesus not around Galilee but when he sets his face toward Jerusalem. This is also a time to do more with the poor when the government clearly is doing so much less. We need extra hands, more minds and hearts. So I hope the members of Riverside Church will seek out others to become part of a pilgrim people, of a prophetic minority. And let us also pray for grace to contend against wrong without becoming wrongly contentious, to fight pretensions of national righteousness without personal self-righteousness.

I said I had three images of the Church. The last is non-Biblical, and it's really a bit cute, but here it is. There's an ad for a bubble bath for children that reads, "Makes getting clean almost as much fun as getting dirty." That strikes me as a good ad for a church, for while it recognizes a certain fun in wrongdoing, it also acknowledges that it is a joy to scrub one's mind and soul of dirt. It really is a joy—a bubbly joy—to be with irrepressible people who are so precisely because they know and love the Lord. It is a joy to be loved. It's a joy to love others. Sure, it's hard to keep going, but what do you want—lifetime membership in the Bystanders Association?

"*Que Diós no nos dé paz, y sí, gloria*." ("May God deny us peace, but give us glory.") I'm glad Unamuno put it in the plural, for *together* we can continue. (You remember the story of the blind man carrying the lame one.) And here's an even better answer to burn-out: In *Waiting for Godot*, Vladimir asks, "Where are you going?" And Pozzo gives the Christian answer: "ON."

Alone, Yet Not Alone

MARCH 29, 1981
Reading: Luke 4:1–13

$\mathbf{A}$nd Jesus, full of the Holy Spirit . . . was led by the Spirit . . . in the wilderness." There, a very young man, he was all by himself for forty days.

Yesterday I witnessed the opposite kind of scene. Early in the morning I flew back to New York with forty "Happy Hookers," as they called themselves, this band of lady knitters. They were headed, all of them together, to Saks Fifth Avenue, then to two shows, a restaurant, and then back home again to Charlotte, North Carolina. It was a good day's outing (and a good deal, as Eastern had offered them half-fare).

Still, watching and listening to them, I was reminded how many of us Americans feel more ourselves when with others than when alone. It's as if we were afraid of being alone, afraid that once alone we might have to pay a call on ourselves and find nobody at home. It's a pity, this fear of solitude, for ultimately aren't we all loners? We're born alone, we die alone, and in between—if we lead our lives rightly—we stumble along in the footsteps of lonely prototypes the likes of Abraham, Ulysses, Lincoln, Thoreau, King—and Jesus.

What are two lovers, strolling down Riverside Drive on a gorgeous spring Sunday afternoon, but two loners reaching out to each other—like the two opposite banks of the Hudson, enjoying the river that unites them? What is the Church but a community of solitudes united by their love of Christ?

Solitude is good for the soul, for ultimately we *are* alone. Moreover, it's when we're alone that being tested like Jesus, we come to know our inmost heart. It's when we're alone that we realize, "Yes, the life has gone out of my marriage and my job bores me to death." It's when we're alone that we realize how much money we *don't* need to make. It's when we're alone that our instincts for self-preservation confront convictions about integrity and self-sacrifice. At the end of his ministry Jesus was again alone, praying, "Father, if Thou art willing, let this cup pass from me! . . . and his sweat became like great drops of blood falling upon the ground" (Luke 22:42, 44). Solitude is tough, but good for the soul; for it's when you're alone that you get to know who you really are. (No wonder the philosopher Whitehead said, "Religion is what you do with your solitude.") "And Jesus, full of the Holy Spirit . . . was led by the Spirit . . . in the wilderness."

He was alone, yet not alone: "Think not thou canst sigh a sigh and thy maker is not by / Think not thou canst weep a tear and thy maker is not near" (Blake). God was never far; neither was the Devil. Now you may have trouble believing this, but in a congregation of this size, there are bound to be one or two people who don't believe in the Devil! So let me give a brief introduction to this person whom I have come to know so well.

We call the Devil a person because evil is experienced as an intensely personal power. We also call the Devil a person because while evil arises within us—not outside us—it is experienced as something larger and more powerful than we are; hence the rightness of ascribing to it a separate existence. (St. Paul put the matter classically: "The good that I would I do not, and that which I would not, that I do.") But easily the most important thing to say about the Devil is that the Devil is a fallen angel. Evil does not arise in our so-called lower nature—in, for instance, our sexual instincts. That's a Greek idea, and a very bad one. It was the Greeks who said, "*Soma sema*"—the body is a tomb. To Jews and Christians, the body is more a temple than a tomb. According to our understanding, evil arises in our higher nature, in that which is most God-like—our freedom. That is not to say that our higher nature can't misuse our lower nature; it certainly can. But the source of the trouble is our freedom. The Devil knows that, and is always saying, "Give me your freedom and I'll invest it for you." And when the Devil talks, it's like E. F. Hutton: everybody listens. Even Jesus couldn't help but listen, tempted as he was in all respects even as we are. And if he was tempted, dear sisters and brothers, we can be sure the temptations were serious.

After forty days, Jesus was hungry—desperately so. Then the Devil said to him, "If thou art the Son of God, command this stone to become bread." And Jesus, using Scripture as a sword to parry the thrusts of the Devil, answered (quoting Deuteronomy), "Man shall not live by bread alone."

All too often the important word is understood to be "bread," while the truly important word is "alone." Jesus never said bread wasn't important—"Give us this day our daily bread"—and, in fact, he did everything he could to feed the poor. With Mary, his mother, he believed that God "has filled the hungry with good things, and the rich he has sent empty away." How angry he must be with the way our government is now filling the rich with good things, and sending the poor empty away. How he would scorn an economic theory that says we must heap more on the platters of the rich, for only so will more crumbs fall to the poor. Never has a government climbed off the backs of the middle class so fast to tap-dance on the backs of the poor. Never in recent history have we had so blatant a plutocracy: a government *of* the wealthy, *by* the wealthy, and *for* the wealthy.

But maybe these hard, iniquitous times are the very best to realize that there are two ways to be rich: one is to have a lot of money, the other is to have few needs. Looking ahead to Good Friday, let us remember that Jesus—who influenced history more than any other single person, institution, or nation—died, his sole possession a robe. Even if these were the best of times in terms of distributive justice, we still would have moved from an era of growth to an era of limits, an era when all foreseeable energy resources are dwindling. So isn't this an appropriate time to realize that the only truly renewable resources are spiritual? I'm glad we're studying more at Riverside, meditating more, organizing more house churches, for all of these show us that God's riches are inexhaustible, and that to know God is to be at peace in the hands of love. And love—among people who are solitudes—is a basket of loaves and two fishes; it is never enough until you start to give it away. Perhaps barbarous times are the best to learn that civilization is but a slow process of learning to be kind.

But just as Jesus went up in the mountains to pray and then down to the valley to heal, so we must leave the highlands of the spirit for the lowlands of service. Bread for ourselves may be materialistic, but not when it's for others. As the tide of federal aid ebbs, church initiatives are going to be essential. In this church we now offer food and clothing and the English language. But, doctors, could we not offer medical services one night a week with physicians volunteering one night a month? And, lawyers, could we not, in conjunction perhaps with the Columbia Law School, offer legal services on the same basis?

We cannot ask God to make a stone into bread for us, for "man does not live by bread alone," but by every word that proceeds from the mouth of God. But we can heed God's word to share what God has given us, especially when those in our nation whose stomachs are empty are the very ones being asked to tighten their belts.

"And the devil took him up, and showed him all the kingdoms of the world in a moment of time, and said to him, 'To you I will give all this authority and their glory; for *it has been delivered to me* [a remarkable assertion!] and I give it to whom I will. If you then will worship me, it shall all be yours.'" And Jesus again picks up his sword and parries with, "It is written, 'You shall worship the Lord your God, and Him only shall you serve.'"

Three years ago, after reading this passage, I took a piece of paper and on one side wrote "Service to God" and on the other "Service to the Devil." Then I asked myself, "What's the bottom line on both sides? What's the sine qua non, the one thing you cannot be without if you're serious about serving God on the one hand, and the Devil on the other?"

On God's side the answer was easy. Even though I have faith to move mountains and knowledge to understand all mysteries, and even though I give my body to be burned—the very stuff of heroism—but have not love . . . nothing. As far as God is concerned, if we fail in love we fail in all things else.

But what about the Devil? What must we never be without if we're serious about serving Satan? The story suggests power, for the temptation seems to be to seek status through power. "To you I will give all this authority and their glory."

Then it hit me. The Devil has taken two hundred and twenty million of us Americans up to a high place, has shown us "all the kingdoms of the world in a moment of time." And the Devil is saying: "Let's see, Americans. You now have enough nuclear arms to kill everyone in the world several times over, and you're still turning out three warheads a day—terrific!—maybe you can bounce the rubble. And it only takes missiles some thirty minutes to go door-to-door, so that soon you and the Soviets will adopt what your Pentagon calls a launch-upon-warning strategy and give over the decision-making power to the impersonal province of those imperfect computers that make all those mistakes—it sounds marvelous! And you and the Soviet Union are both going for a first-strike capability. Wonderful!—that should make everyone as nervous as a cat in a room full of rocking chairs. Yes, just think! You and the Soviet Union one of these days might destroy all the kingdoms of the world in a moment of time—*by accident*."

And we sit there, transfixed, like bunnies looking at a cobra, because the one thing we will not give up is power. It's not national security, it's military superiority we want. And we're going to be militarily superior even if it kills us—and everyone else.

Let's look ahead again to Good Friday and hear Jesus' words: "Daughters of Jerusalem, do not weep for me, but weep for yourselves and for your children. For behold, the days are coming when they will say, 'Blessed are the barren, and the wombs that never bore, and the breasts that never gave suck' . . . For if they do this when the wood is green, what will happen when it is dry?" (Luke 23:28–29, 31).

Finally, the Devil "took him to Jerusalem and set him on a pinnacle of the temple, and said to him, 'If you are the Son of God, throw yourself down from here; for it is written, *He will give his angels charge over you to guard you*' . . . And Jesus answered him, 'It is said, *You shall not tempt the Lord your God.*'"

This is the kind of temptation that comes to a person who has renounced the struggle for worldly well-being, for worldly power. Instead, she has committed herself to God only with the secret expectation that God will now do all the work. So much so-called spirituality is pure laziness—reminiscent of the story of the priest who went golfing with the rabbi. Before putting, the priest crossed himself. By the ninth hole he was nine strokes ahead. Asked the rabbi, "Do you suppose it would be all right, Father, if before I putted I too crossed myself?" "Sure," answered the priest. "But it won't do you any good till you learn how to putt."

God *will* take care of us. She hears our prayers. When Jesus prayed so fervently in the garden of Gethsemane, his prayer was answered: he was delivered from his fear of death. God makes everything possible. Those who can see the invisible can do the impossible. So, paraphrasing a famous speech, let us not ask what God can do for us, but rather what we can do for God—for God, not the Devil.

"It is the solitary person," Thomas Merton wrote, "who does humankind the inestimable favor of reminding it of its capacity for maturity, freedom, and peace."

And so, fellow Christians, let us confound the Devil by confronting him. Let us not be afraid to go eyeball-to-eyeball with him on the basic temptations of our lives. Do we really want to sell our freedom for material well-being? Do we as individuals or as a people want to sell our capacity to love for loveless power? Do we really want to ask God to take care of us when we should be caring for others?

In Matthew's account of the story we read, "Then the Devil left him, and behold, angels came and ministered to him" (4:11). No doubt there are still a multitude of angels ready to do no less to us.

Your God Is Too Big

APRIL 5, 1981
Reading: Colossians 1:15–20

"For in him all the fulness of God was pleased to dwell, and through him to reconcile to himself all things, whether on earth or in heaven, making peace by the blood of his cross."

Colossians 1:19–20

Of the seven last words of Christ (spoken from the cross), only the fifth could have been said by any one of us. In the Gospel of John we read: "After this, Jesus, knowing that all was now finished, said 'I thirst'" (19:28).

Not even Martin Luther King Jr.—whose death we recalled with such renewed sorrow this weekend (how the nation could today use that voice!)—not even King would have cried out, "My God, my God, why hast thou forsaken me?" For in the eyes of almost all both at home and abroad, this Nobel Prizewinner died a just man, a prophet of God. It was the heathen who rejected Martin. But Christ was rejected by the religious (at least by their leaders), rejected in God's name as godless, in the name of holy law as a lawbreaker. That's real rejection—religious rejection. That's what creates doubt and prompts the heartfelt cry, "My God, my God, why . . ."

In contrast, any one of us could have said, "I thirst," for the words reflect sheer physical need. They have nothing to do with God; nothing to do with love, with faith. Yet on the lips of the crucified Son of God—is it not true?—they have everything to do with God; everything to do with love, with faith.

Let me ask you: When you think of God, what image comes to mind? Is it the grandfather figure of your childhood? Is it Michelangelo's powerful figure come down from heaven, surrounded by cherubim and seraphim, hand outstretched to Adam's hand upraised? (What a picture in those two hands alone!) One thing only we know for sure:

when we think of God we don't generally think of a bleeding, dying figure, pleading for someone to moisten his cracked and burning lips.

Several years ago a man named J. B. Phillips wrote a book called *Your God Is Too Small*. It was a good book, making the often forgotten point that God is not only our God but *their* God, as well, not a God of the few or of the many, but the God of all. She is also the God who laid the foundations of the earth and scattered stars in the heavens greater in number than all the inhabitants of the world. Yes, *"Pleni sunt coeli,"* "Heaven and earth are full of thy glory; glory be to Thee, O Lord most high."

But now, in Lent, is the time to say, "Your God is too big": too big to worry about every fallen sparrow; too big to worry about each fallen child in Atlanta; too big to worry about each child in the world—and there are millions of them—most of whom never so much as open their mouths to say "Aaah" to a doctor; too big to worry about every food stamp ($2 billion worth) about to be cut. What is the perfect expression of a loving God? "I thirst" on the lips of the Son of God. There is "the image of the invisible God" (Col. 1:15). For these two words from the cross lay bare the heart of God for all to see. They show us how God shares the lot of the least of us—handicapped children, lonely old people, the sick, those on welfare, the dying. He suffers with us; more, he suffers for us. "I thirst" on the lips of the Son of God: there's the perfect expression of God; for as St. Paul says, "In him all the fulness of God was pleased to dwell."

What's the matter with us? Why do we normally reject such an image, accepting instead images that really do not accord with a loving God? Is it because we want ourselves to be immune from such suffering and contempt? Maybe we want to think of God as powerful so that we can be like God, feeling as we so often do that only power impresses, only success succeeds. So we dehumanize ourselves by idolizing power, thereby making it necessary for God to come to earth in human form, to take our inhumanity upon himself in order to make us human again.

Or maybe we like to think of God as powerful so that we can be weak, whereas God wants to be weak so that we can be strong. Or maybe we want to keep God up there in the heavens where we can praise Him, far away from where we might have to follow Him.

In any case, Lent is the time to realize anew that we are not going to be helped by God's power, only by God's weakness. For power can only force us to do things. Power affects only behavior. Soviet tanks can affect Polish behavior; they can force the Poles into line; but Soviet tanks can never touch the hearts of the Polish people, except with fear. Only love can move us to do things. And nothing on earth so moves the heart as suffering love. That is why the perfect expression of God's love for us is a dying figure pleading for someone to moisten his burning lips.

And someone does. Someone runs to soak a sponge in sour wine and hold it up, on the end of a cane, to Jesus' lips. In Matthew the act is recorded as a gracious one, perhaps the only act of human mercy in the whole Passion story. And it has a special significance. Whenever we celebrate the Lord's Supper, as we do this morning, we receive the cup of Christ. Christ puts wine on our lips. But whoever puts wine on the lips of Christ understands the mutuality of Communion. We need our Lord, our Savior, but he also needs us. There are thirsty figures on crosses all around this globe, and "inasmuch as ye did it unto the least of these my brethren [and sisters], ye did it unto me" (Matt. 25:40). To find Jesus we need look no further than our nearest neighbor's need.

That is why we are asking you to heed the food stamp alert. That is why, inspired by the cup of Christ—"This is my blood, shed for you"—I would hope that we might not only moisten the lips but cut down the crosses of hunger and thirst on which millions of our fellow human beings are being crucified. And let us strive to cut down the cross of racism on which scores of our children and other fellow citizens have been crucified; and to cut down the cross being prepared by an arms race that threatens to crucify us all.

"Were you there when they crucified my Lord?" Of course you were—all of us were, hammer in hand. But let us lay down the hammers, and take up the sponge, and put wine on the lips of our suffering Savior. For in him we see the perfect expression of our loving Father. He is "the image of the invisible God," "For in him all the fulness of God was pleased to dwell, and through him to reconcile to himself all things, whether on earth or in heaven, making peace by the blood of his cross" (Col. 1:19–20).

Heroes and Heroines for God

Palm Sunday
APRIL 12, 1981
Reading: John 12:12–19

As any writer will tell you, the essence of good writing is drama, and the essence of drama is conflict. That's what makes the Palm Sunday story so dramatic. In the whole of the Bible—Calvary not excepted—there is no scene in which the people taking part have more conflicting ideas about what is going on. The Pharisees, of course, think they have a heretic on their hands, a peculiarly obnoxious one, for Jesus is saying, in effect, that the real troublemakers in this world are not the ignorant and cruel, but the intelligent and corrupt, like the Pharisees themselves. Naturally they resist him, and will do so all the more vigorously when he "cleanses" the temple by chasing away the money-changers, symbols of that oldest form of corruption—religion become subservient to profit-making. Yet these same religious leaders, who, goaded on by this affront to established power, later will see to it that he is arrested, are today powerless. "The Pharisees then said to one another, 'You see that you can do nothing; look, the world has gone after him'" (John 12:19).

Indeed, the world in the form of the Jerusalem multitudes did go after him that day, which is why Palm Sunday is so festive an occasion. Yet were they cheering a religious leader, who had searched their consciences, convinced their minds, and won over their hearts? Or were they following a political leader whose power was proved by the story circulating through the streets of the city that he had raised one Lazarus from the dead? True, they carried palms, symbols of peace; but then they were not allowed to carry spears. True, they were praising God; but they were also hailing the King of Israel. Some no doubt remembered the prophecy of Zechariah: "Behold, your king is coming to you, humble, and riding on an ass." But I'll bet the majority had Saul and Solomon in mind. They were hailing a new national leader come to help throw off the hated Roman yoke. You can't blame them for wanting their political independence, but you can't equate such a political leader with "the Lamb of God that taketh away the sins of the world."

With different perceptions go different emotions. The Pharisees are sullen, the crowd ecstatic. But the greatest contrast is between the crowds and Jesus. Wildly they shout, "Hosannah! Blessed is he who comes in the name of the Lord, even the King of Israel." And the king—instead of smiling and acknowledging the cheers—weeps. Reading now from Luke: "And when he drew near and saw the city he wept over it, saying, 'Would that even today you knew the things that make for peace! But now they are hid from your eyes. For the days shall come upon you, when your enemies will cast up a bank about you and surround you, and hem you in on every side, and dash you to the ground, you and all your children within you, and they will not leave one stone upon another in you; because you did not know the time of your visitation'" (19:41–44).

Had Jesus wept for what he had earlier predicted would befall him, that would be poignant enough. Instead he weeps for what he is sure will befall the very people who today are urging him on, and who tomorrow, because of their blindness, will be shouting "Crucify him!"

I suppose all this confusion is to be expected. Each of us is a walking civil war. We are so confused that Augustine could say of the Church that there are as many wolves within the fold as there are sheep without; and Pascal could say of the world that it divides itself between saints who know they are sinners and sinners who imagine themselves to be saints. The Passion story this week will teach us the deepest lesson about political life. It is not that good is "forever on the scaffold, wrong upon the throne"; it is that all people stand in need of a merciful God; it is that all politics should begin with repentance and forgiveness.

Fundamentally, what we all need to confess is that all of us are creatures trying to deny our creatureliness. Every human being is a creature trying to overcome a false sense of insignificance. I'm glad the shuttle got off this morning. It was a stirring sight, and it's a stunning realization that our earthbound days are coming to an end. But I was troubled by the president's message of last Friday to the spacebound astronauts: "You go in the hand of God." That's modest enough. But then: "Through you today we all feel as giants once again. [Catch the sense of insignificance?] Once again, we feel the surge of pride that comes from knowing we are the first and we are the best and we are so because we are free."

Not only Americans, every people wants to feel they are the first and the best and free, and every space shuttle and every missile, every bomb and every human edifice—be it constructed of brick or of ideas—all are attempts, in part, to defy our underlying helplessness and the terror of our inevitable death. In order to feel that sense of significance we have to scapegoat others into insignificance—into being second and not so free—for that surging pride of which the president spoke is not accidentally but essentially competitive. "Everybody has his Jew," said Arthur Miller; "even the Jews have their Jews," someone to degrade, to humiliate, to raise us above the status of creature. All humanly caused evil is due to our attempts to deny our creatureliness. It is based on heroics. We want to make the world what it can never be: a place free from accident, a place free from impurity, a place free from death.

So is the answer to avoid all heroics? No, the answer is to be a hero or a heroine for God—for the sake of no one less than God, and in such a fashion that only the eyes of God need see. Anyone who needs more than God as a witness is too ambitious! Isn't the perfect illustration of that kind of heroism the story of Jesus riding into Jerusalem on Palm Sunday? He could have stayed in Galilee where it was safer, but he chose instead to take his words and deeds into the capital, into the very heart of entrenched religious and political power. He could have come on a horse, as a wartime king, but chose instead to come *in* peace, *for* peace. He could have saved Israel, but chose instead to save the world. He could have come with violence, but rather than inflict suffering he chose to take suffering upon himself. What can only be said cynically of another—"It is better that one man should die than an entire nation perish"—can be said in utter truthfulness about oneself: "It is better that I should die rather than a single other person."

There is nothing wrong in being heroes and heroines for God. The danger is always that we combine great moral vigor with little self-knowledge. Reinhold Niebuhr wrote: "Ultimately considered, evil is done not so much by evil people, but by good people who do not know themselves." But if we start on our knees, we can rise to great heights, "rise and shine and *give God the glory*." The Gospel of John is full of heroic language. Christ himself speaks in tender but heroic words, proving once again that only the truly strong can be tender. "In the world you have tribulation, but be of good cheer, I have overcome the world" (John 16:33).

And listen to these words spoken in Jerusalem just before his death: "Father, the hour has come; glorify thy Son that the Son may glorify Thee, since thou hast given him power over all flesh, to give eternal life to all whom thou hast given him. And this is eternal life, that they know Thee the only true God, and Jesus Christ whom thou hast sent" (John 17:1–3).

There it is—the whole goal of life: to know God as the only true God, and to know Him through Jesus Christ, the King of Kings and Lord of Lords, riding into Jerusalem on the back of a donkey.

On that Palm Sunday and on the days that follow in Jerusalem, in Jesus' words and deeds we see the transparent power of God at work, empowering the weak, scorning the powerful, healing the hurt, taking upon himself the sin and suffering of the world. And just as Christ's knowledge still lights our path, and his faith lives on in our hearts, so his tasks have now fallen to our hands. Our hands are important. Without us the glorious space shuttle will surely turn into another inglorious weapons system. Without us, humanity will come to judgment not before God but before the atom. Without us, the poor will continue to get poorer, the rich richer. New York will never become that "golden city with milk and honey blest." But with reason, with restraint and faith that God can endow our lives with significance, we may yet see the world around "alabaster cities gleam undimmed by human tears," hear again the words of the Pharisees: "Look, the world has gone after him."

Can we still celebrate Palm Sunday knowing how confused the scene was, and how the story ends? Yes, because with a better understanding of what was going on, we have even more to cheer about. The cross of Christ says something terrible about us, but something wonderful about God. It symbolizes not only the triumph in defeat of a good man. It also represents the merciful action of a loving Father: "For God was in Christ reconciling the world unto himself."

> Ride on! Ride on in majesty!
> Thy last and fiercest strife is nigh;
> . . . .
> Bow thy meek head to mortal pain,
> Then take, O God, thy power, and reign.
>   Henry Milman

Rending the Bond of Love

Good Friday
APRIL 17, 1981
Reading: The Good Friday Story, especially Luke 23:39–43

"Surely he hath borne our griefs, and carried our sorrows . . . he was wounded for our transgressions, he was bruised for our iniquities . . . ; and with his stripes we are healed."
                                   Isaiah 53:4–5

St. Augustine observed: Two criminals were crucified with Christ, one on the right, one on the left. One was saved; do not despair. One was not; do not presume.

Let's think for a moment of the one who was saved. About him and his crimes we know virtually nothing, but about criminals and crime in general we know a great deal. We know, for instance, that most criminals are in jail by virtue of their poverty rather than their criminality; rich criminals are rarely imprisoned. We also know that all crimes ultimately are one and the same, because all criminals, whether or not they go to jail, conform to Raskolnikov, hero of *Crime and Punishment* and the prototype of all criminals. More convincingly and poignantly than any other literary figure, Raskolnikov demonstrates that crime is only superficially, legally breaking the law; more profoundly, morally, it is rending the bond of love. And the punishment for crime is not the physical isolation imposed by barred windows and thick walls so much as the spiritual isolation imposed by the walls of hearts grown so thick with anger, bitterness, guilt, and hate, that love can barely break in and enter. Crime is rending the bond of love. Punishment is experiencing the bond of love rent.

That makes Raskolnikov the prototype of all of us, for which of us has not rent the bond of love? And which of us has not known the ensuing loneliness? Those of us who have experienced the deepest sin know that to speak of its loneliness in terms of a cross is to exaggerate but a little. So some of us, at least, can identify not only with Raskolnikov, but with the thief on the cross whose physical suffering is an outward and visible sign of an inner and spiritual agony.

What else do we know about crime? We know that crime hurts not only the criminal and his victims. For every Raskolnikov there is a Dounia (his sister), a Sonia (his girlfriend). For countless criminals there are countless mothers, fathers, wives, friends, who are wounded for their transgressions, bruised for their iniquities. And with their stripes they heal their loved ones; to restore a criminal to the society he has abandoned, those already deeply hurt must continue to pour out their love until the walls of isolation are swept aside and hearts are washed clean of all bitterness, guilt, and hate. Who said love costs nothing? It costs everything. We're talking of forgiveness, and forgiveness is suffering love.

Consider now the immeasurable love of God, and against such a love measure the pain that must be God's whenever we rend the bond of love. Never think of sin as breaking some law; think of it rather as breaking God's heart. Yet despite the hurt God continues to love us, knowing that only by so doing can She heal and restore us. When we begin to understand that, and only then, can we begin to understand the person and work of Jesus Christ. "God was in Christ *reconciling* the world unto himself." "God so *loved* the world"—not was offended by it, angry at it, the way we so frequently are—no, God is divine and therefore "so *loved* the world that He gave his only begotten Son that whosoever should believe in him should not perish but have eternal life"; be reunited—that's what atonement is, at-one-ment—be made at one again with God, his neighbor, and himself.

There are many physical sufferings in Jesus' life, for his was a restless ministry, so peripatetic that it was no hyperbole to say, "Foxes have holes and birds of the air have nests, but the Son of man has nowhere to lay his head." The unbearable suffering, however, is not that which breaks the body, but that which breaks the heart. It's having so much love to give and so few to receive it: "O Jerusalem, Jerusalem, how often would I have gathered ye unto me as a mother hen her chicks, and ye would not" (Luke 13:34). Still Jesus continues to pour out his love. Even as the nails are being driven into his hands his cry is, "Father, forgive . . ."

It is at this moment that Jesus meets the thief. The thief is on his cross because he cannot love; Jesus is on his because he can only love. The thief is in spiritual pain because he has isolated himself; Jesus is in spiritual pain because he cannot separate himself from others. Then he whose heart is full of guilt sees that of all people Jesus is the most innocent, and hears, of all things, the innocent praying for the forgiveness of the guilty. Such suffering love proves too much: his own heart begins to melt. He cries out, "Jesus, remember me," and Jesus does. Christ performs his last miracle when from his cross he heals another on his.

On the ceiling of the Sistine Chapel Michelangelo has painted his vision of the bond of love as it was first established, so easily, so naturally. God simply reaches down from the heavens to touch the finger of Adam's upraised hand. But once rent, the bond cannot so easily be restored, for sin has its punishment and forgiveness its cost. The bond is forged anew only in the agony of two crosses, when we from our cross stretch out our arm to Christ and he, from his, stretches out an arm to us.

"Jesus, remember me!"

"Truly I say to you, this day you will be with me in Paradise."

Not as a Memory

APRIL 19, 1981
Reading: Matthew 28

Don't you just love it when, after four months in cold storage, energy comes pouring out of the ground and into every blade of grass, every flower, bush, and tree in sight? The robins join the pigeons, the sky is full of the thunder of the sun; overhead and underfoot and all around you can see, hear, feel the juice and joy of spring.

But suppose for a moment April had never come. Suppose the earth had somehow spun out of orbit and was headed for the immensities of space; suppose it was to remain there gripped forever in the cold of winter? That, I submit, would be not only a terrible prospect, but a proper analogy of the human world without Easter—at least according to St. Paul. Not one to hedge his bets, St. Paul puts all his Christian eggs in one Easter basket: "For if Christ has not been raised," he writes the Corinthians, "your faith is futile."

There is no question about it: Christianity stands or falls by the Resurrection, and we shall have to consider the actual event, the empty tomb. But later, not now, for it is a common and bad mistake to view Easter in too individualistic a light. Easter is concerned essentially not with one man's escape from death, but with the much larger victory of seemingly powerless love over loveless power. The Easter lantern swings not over some narrow, empty grave, but over the thick darkness covering the whole earth.

On Good Friday, the darkness was all but complete. And today the wintry smile on the face of Truth tells us that by and large ours is still a Good Friday world. Goodness incarnate stretched out on a cross, bequeathing its spirit to the oncoming night, is all too apt a symbol for a century that has planted more senseless crosses than any other in history. In the twenty-five years following World War II there were ninety-seven wars in the world—international and civil—with losses greater than the fifty-two million killed in World War II. And we can imagine the carnage by century's end if this insane arms race is not slowed, stopped, and reversed.

But by the light of Easter morn we can read a "Yes, but" kind of message. Yes, fear and hatred kill, but love never dies—not with God, not even with us. The Easter message says love is stronger than death. The Easter message says God is never driven out of human life. The Easter message says that all the strength and tenderness that on Good Friday was scourged, buffeted, and stretched out on a cross, all that goodness incarnate is once again alive. "And lo, I am with you always until the close of the age." Until all eternity Christ will be alive, in the form of the Holy Spirit, trying to bring about our own spiritual resurrection—"the glory of God is a human being fully alive"—and through us to bring to naught all the principalities and powers that spell distress unending to our fellow human beings and ruin to our beautiful earth.

That is why Easter was so decisive an event to St. Paul. It makes a difference whether we live in a Good Friday or an Easter world. And Easter should be no less decisive for us, asking as it does not sympathy for the crucified Lord, but loyalty to the Risen One. And oh, my fellow Christians, what a travesty of the faith it is that so many of us can at one and the same time profess sympathy for Christ crucified and continued loyalty to the people and powers that crucified him! There's sentimentality at its worst. And that's what keeps us in a Good Friday world. If truly we believe Christ is risen, that he is loose in a world where neither Roman nor Jew, Soviet nor American, can stop his truth, then ours today would be the loyalty of St. Peter that made him after Christ's death ten times the person he was before. Ours would be the loyalty of St. Stephen, who, under the rain of death-dealing stones cried out, Christlike, "Father, forgive"; ours would be the loyalty of the early martyrs who with their blood watered the seed of the Church until it became the acorn that broke the mighty boulder of the Roman Empire.

Paul draws a second consequence from Christ's Resurrection. He writes the Corinthians that had Christ not been raised, not only would their faith be futile, they would still be "in their sins." What does he mean? Paul knows perfectly well we're all sinners, the more so the more we try to deny it. But that's not the issue. The question is whether there's more mercy in God than sin in us. And, according to Paul, just as love is stronger than death, so forgiveness is stronger than sin. The Resurrection proves it. Peter denied Christ as surely as Judas betrayed him: the difference is that Peter came back to receive his forgiveness; the tragedy of Judas is that he never did.

Easter proclaims we are all forgiven. Brezhnev is forgiven, Arafat is forgiven, Begin too, Reagan, Stockton, Watt. All those who plot Marxist takeovers in Central America are forgiven, as are those in Washington who can't wait to start another Gringo war. White, black, yellow, and red, smart and stupid, starved and stuffed—all are forgiven. Even the members of Riverside Church, who have God in their mouths but not always in their hearts (like their senior minister)—all of us too are forgiven. And what does that mean? It does not mean that God relieves us of the consequences of our sin; it does mean that God relieves us of the consequences of being sinners. We are not sinners—we are *forgiven* sinners. And oh, how quickly a Good Friday world could become an Easter world if we accepted our forgiveness! For then we would be less concerned with what we can do for ourselves and more concerned with expressing ourselves as "trophies of God's grace," as followers of our beloved Lord, who became what we are to make us what he is.

And now perhaps we can deal with the empty tomb, the Resurrection event. St. Paul was the earliest New Testament writer, and it is clear that his Resurrection faith, like the faith of the disciples, was not based on the negative argument of an empty tomb, but on the positive conviction that the Lord had appeared to him. It is also clear that Christ's appearances were not those of a resurrected corpse, but more akin to intense visionary experiences.

Not only Peter, but all the apostles after Jesus' death were ten times the people they were before; that's irrefutable. It was in response to their enthusiasm that the opposition organized, and it was in response to the opposition, as many scholars believe, that the doctrine of the empty tomb arose—as a consequence, not a cause, of the Easter faith. The last chapter of Matthew *may* be literally true—I do not want to dispute it—but don't let it hang you up indefinitely. The chances are it is an expression, rather than a basis of faith.

Convinced by his appearances that Jesus was a living Lord, the disciples had really only one category in which to articulate this conviction: the doctrine of the resurrection of the dead. To Paul, the events of the last days had been anticipated, and God, by a mighty act, had raised Jesus from the dead. To Paul, the living Christ and the Holy Spirit are never differentiated, so that when he says "Not I, but Christ who dwells within me," he is talking about the same Holy Spirit that you and I can experience. I myself believe passionately in the resurrection of Jesus Christ, because in my own life I have experienced Christ as a presence, not as a memory. So today on Easter we gather not to close the show with Bob Hope's "Thanks for the memory," but rather to reopen the show, because "Jesus Christ is risen today."

There remains only to say a word about the final consequence Paul draws from the Resurrection. "If Christ has not been raised then those also who have fallen asleep in Christ have perished. If only in this life have we hope in Christ, we are of all people most to be pitied" (1 Cor. 15:17–19). What then are we to say of those who "rest from their labor"? How are we to anticipate our own death?

The Bible is at pains to point out that all life ends: "All mortal flesh is as the grass" (Isa. 40:6). But St. Paul insists that "neither death nor life . . . can separate us from the love of God which is in Christ Jesus our Lord." If death, then, is no threat to our relationship to God it should be no threat to anything. If we don't know what is beyond the grave, we do know who is beyond the grave. And Christ resurrected links the two worlds, telling us that we really live only in one. If, spiritually speaking, we die to ourselves and are resurrected in Christ, before us lies only the physical counterpart of this spiritual death. And physical death need not terrorize us, if fear of the unknown and fear of final condemnation lie behind, not before us.

April 19, 1981

Then we can proclaim with St. Paul's marvelous freedom, "Now this I say, sisters and brothers, that flesh and blood cannot inherit the Kingdom of God; neither doth corruption inherit incorruption. For this corruptible must put on incorruption, and this mortal must put on immortality. So when this corruptible shall have put on incorruption, and this mortal shall have put on immortality, then shall be brought to pass the saying that is written, Death is swallowed up in victory. O Death, where is thy sting? O grave, where thy victory?" (1 Cor. 15:50, 53–55).

So, sisters and brothers, what's it going to be—a Good Friday or an Easter world? God has done God's part: Resurrection has overcome crucifixion, forgiveness sin; and if love is immortal then life is eternal and death is a horizon, and a horizon is nothing save the limit of our sight. Can we do our part to make this an Easter world? Of course we can. It has been written, "If there should arise one utterly believing person, the history of the world would be changed."

The Practice of Peace

APRIL 26, 1981

Professor Siman:[*]
In his open letter of February 1980 to President Carter, Monsignor Romero said:

> It disturbs me deeply that the U.S. government is leaning toward an arms race in sending military equipment and advisors to "train three Salvadorean battalions in logistics, communications, and intelligence." In the event that this news is accurate, your government, instead of favoring greater peace and justice in El Salvador, will undoubtedly aggravate the repression and injustice against the organized people who have been struggling because of their fundamental respect for human rights.

I want to thank you for expressing your concern for the people of my country, for other human beings. That is, I think, one of the most

My remarks owe a great deal to a splendid speech given by Sargent Shriver at Notre Dame.—WSC

[*]Prof. Jose Jorge Siman, Former President, Commission of Justice and Peace of the Archdiocese, Catholic Church of El Salvador.

fundamental of the Christian characteristics. Let me ask you to continue to show your care for the fate of other human beings in this cosmic village we live in. Need I remind you of Christ's words in Matthew: "I assure you, as often as you did it for one of my least brothers and sisters, you did it for me" (25:40).

To talk about my country, El Salvador, is to talk about a very complex and at the same time very simple subject. It is to talk about life, human suffering, hope, the right to survive as a human being, the basic needs of human life. Most of the people of my country live on a horizon of death, instead of a horizon of life. This horizon of death is not due to "natural" conditions, but is imposed upon the Salvadorean people for reasons of power, domination, egoism, and structural conditions. How can you have a horizon of life if all the avenues that lead to it, that have been pursued with honest hope, have been cruelly closed? If there is not even a small ray of light for the future, if there is no opportunity to have even the basic requirements met for yourself or for those you love, how can you have a horizon of life? How can you believe that life has some meaning or some sense to struggle for, if the only alternative is a struggle to escape from a horizon of death?

What saddens me most is that my country's internal tragedy has been reduced artificially to a confrontation of competing ideologies, to a struggle for supremacy between the world's superpowers. It is sad to see the costs ordinary human beings have to pay for the struggles of others for power. The concern and respect that any human being merits is not taken into consideration. The desire to live a humane life is not valued, and the real sufferings of hunger, sickness, and death become subsidiary to doctrinaire ideological values. Within such a context, how can human beings struggle to be real members of the human race?

There was a man in my country who clearly represented the struggle of the people—Monsignor Romero. He was a profound Christian who acted according to Jon Sobrino's characterization of a human being: one who believes in God and has faith. The God he believed in was not the God of the powerful, nor an undisturbing and domesticated God, but the God that one finds in life and history. Monsignor Romero's humility was expressed in his willingness to learn. He was real. He dealt with violence, even though violence is so sickening. For him it was important to deal with the things of life. He did not decide what they were; he went to life and *found out* what they were—and that made the whole difference. The story of Romero is so simple: everybody thinks they know what life is about, but whenever you try to control life, you will never know anything about life. He realized that God was bigger than he was, so he would be humble and ready to do whatever God asked him to do.

In his homilies he would talk about real life, even if it was controversial. When people would criticize him for being political, he would answer, "Brothers and sisters, do not mistake the mission of the Church, preaching the Gospel and working for justice, for a subversive campaign. It is very different. Unless you want to call the Holy Gospel subversive, because it truly challenges the basis of an order that should not exist because it is unjust."

For the Salvadorean people, in a land where the relation between population and resources is so unfavorable, a long military conflict will only perpetuate a profound human tragedy. Consequently, only a genuine search for a negotiated political solution, taking into account the participation of all sectors of society, offers a pragmatic and ethical alternative. Monsignor Rivera y Damas, the present apostolic administrator, said this month in his visit to the United States:

> Your solidarity with the Church of El Salvador is greatly appreciated. Your concern is not just in words. You have sent your own sons and daughters to work among the poor and oppressed in my country. You have even spoken out against the policy of your government of sending military supplies to El Salvador that can only be used for more violence and bloodshed. I beg for your continued concern. El Salvador asks only to be allowed to settle its own problems.

Dr. Coffin:

Once again we are called to pray for the dead and fight like hell for the living. And, as always, we must start with the smallest, most needful thing we can do: give money to provide shelter, food, and medicine for the thousands of refugees who are clustered in groups everywhere from Honduras to the United States, and for those still in El Salvador who have been internally displaced by the terror. At times and in situations where seemingly there's so little we can do, it's heartening to remember Emily Dickinson:

> If I can stop one heart from breaking,
> I shall not live in vain:
> If I can ease one life the aching
> Or cool one pain, . . .
> I shall not live in vain.

Thank God for the work of Church World Service, and to the trustees of this church for giving us permission today to take a very special offering.

But Americans—*Norteamericanos*—can do more, and Christians have no choice, unless, like Soviet Communists of the most abject variety, we are willing to go along with every twist and turn of our own party line. Imagine being told that if you want to understand the present discontent of Blacks in the United States, you don't have to examine its roots in slavery, or to analyze what survived slavery—personal and institutional racism; no, it's enough to look for outside agitators who came into our country to make trouble and where possible to seduce naive Blacks, like Paul Robeson, into becoming Communists. Why, even the most bigoted segregationists couldn't be brought to swallow that line today. Yet regarding the Third World, a comparable line is being swallowed by almost all Americans. "Let's not delude ourselves," says our president. "The Soviet Union underlies all the unrest that is going on in the Third World. If they weren't engaged in this game of dominoes there wouldn't be any hot spots."

In Scripture we read: "The sins of the fathers are visited upon the children unto the third and fourth generation" (Deut. 5:9). It's not a statement of fairness, only a statement of fact—declaring that our actions have consequences, not only laterally across the face of one generation, but also vertically down the march of generations. That means, concerning violence in our ghettos, that you can only understand it by understanding the original injustice that puts people in the ghettos and keeps them there. With respect to the Third World it means that if you want to understand Castro, go back and look at Batista. If you want to know what happened in the Dominican Republic, check out Trujillo. If you want to know what happened in Vietnam, remember the French, Emperor Bao Dai, and Ngo Dinh Diem. If you want to know what happened in Nicaragua, look at Somoza. And if you want to know what's going on today in El Salvador, mention Cuban guns if you like—because in some quantity they are there; say the Soviet Union is imperialistic—it most definitely is; but don't say "the Soviet Union underlies all the unrest."

As early as 1932 (all but ignored by our press and forgotten today by the American public) Salvadorean peasants, artisans, and workers, armed only with machetes and stones, rose up against their misery. Within a month 30,000 of them had been slaughtered. Since then, as we have heard, conditions have improved but little. So let us indeed not delude ourselves: You cannot have a revolt without revolting conditions. Let us indeed not delude ourselves: Communism has never come to a nation that took care of its poor, its aged, its youth, its sick, and its handicapped.

So what should we do? The administration has a prescription that logically fits its diagnosis. Not only the president and secretary of state, but the CIA, the Senate, the House, the Committee on the Present Danger, all say that we must arm ourselves and our allies. To the poorest of the poor in the world, the poor of El Salvador, they say—going Marie Antoinette one better—"Let them eat guns." Our present answer is: ship arms to El Salvador, to Saudi Arabia too, and more to Israel and Europe; unleash the CIA in Angola, clasp South Africa to our bosom, strengthen Pinochet's power in Chile; tighten our belts, batten down the hatches, throw down the gauntlet! Didn't the voters cry, "*De*-fense! *De*-fense!"? Can't those peace-mongers see the enemy has the ball on our one-yard line?

Christians have to remember that the cross is higher than the flag. And Christians have to question whether it is peace they are creating in Washington. Augustus Caesar built a Temple of Peace, but only after he had gained absolute power. Deus, Imperator, Rex—God, emperor, leader—Caesar had it all. But did he have peace? Christ said "No" and was executed. The early Christians said "No" and either went underground or ended up, as did Paul, ambassadors in chains. Let's not delude ourselves: peace has more enemies than war, with its delusions of dominion and glory; and let's not delude ourselves, Washington at present is not creating peace, it's creating power—and loving it.

Fortunately, there is another way, as indicated by the psalmist: "The war horse is a vain hope for victory, and by its great might it cannot save." There is another way for those whose feet are shod "with the equipment of the Gospel of Peace." If it is true that Communism has never come to a nation that took care of its poor, its aged, its youth, its sick, and its handicapped, then why can't we say to the Junta in San Salvador, "We'll help you take care of your poor, your aged, your youth, your sick, and your handicapped, but we will not help you find a military solution to what is not a military problem"?

In Nicaragua, where Catholic priests are in the ruling cabinet, where Jesuits manage the nationwide literacy campaign and are nominated for the Nobel Peace Prize by more than one hundred members of the British Parliament, why shouldn't we help the Sandinistas in the same way we helped Somoza for forty years without blinking an eyelash? I thought we believed in coexistence. Can't we coexist with socialist regimes in the New World?

In Cuba, why shouldn't we lift the blockade of twenty years, and instead of sending Marines to Guantanamo Bay, let businessmen wade

ashore in Havana? That's what Castro wants, that's the way to coun-
teract Soviet influence, and that's the way to practice peace. The cure
is caring, not killing; serving people, not power. Caring for others is
the practice of peace. Dear Riversiders, enough of delusions. Peace
does not come through strength; strength comes through peace.

The Road to Emmaus

MAY 3, 1981
Reading: Luke 24:13–35

Once upon a time, I heard a clerk in a department store tell a
prospective customer, "We have compasses for drawing circles,
lady, but none for going places."

On that first Easter day, although literally headed for Emmaus,
these two disciples were really going in circles. But they ended up
going places, thanks to the finest compass God has ever seen fit to
present the world. Or, headed West at sunset, these two were going
toward a night that was falling, until Jesus turned them around to face
a dawn that was breaking. It's a suggestive story, one of singular
charm and grace, whose origins in the oral tradition are apparently
lost beyond recovery; and while the story appears in no Gospel other
than Luke, still its impact on early Christian communities was as
powerful as it is today in churches around the world.

I don't know what to make of their failure to recognize Christ. It
was too unexpected; he looked different; they were blinded by the
brightness of the setting sun, by intense preoccupations—such speculations seem farfetched, especially as Luke's intent seems clear. He
wants us to believe that their senses were supernaturally dulled: "their
eyes were kept from recognizing him." I myself can only really get into
the story when in answer to Jesus' question, "What is this conversation
which you are holding with each other?" they say, "Are you the only
visitor to Jerusalem who does not know the things that have happened
there in these days?" In effect, "Where have you been, man?" A real
put-down: they make Jesus the outsider, themselves the insiders. Playing along, the outsider asks ingenuously, "What things?" And then the
insiders tell him, "Concerning Jesus of Nazareth, who was a prophet
mighty in deed and in word before God and all the people."

That description I like—wouldn't it be wonderful to be described
as "a prophet mighty in deed and in word before God and all the peo-

ple"? And I like their description of what happened: "Our chief priests and rulers delivered him up to be condemned to death, and crucified him." "Our chief priests and rulers"—not these Romans, and not the people; although we must never forget how Pilate washed his hands and thereby plaited the crown of thorns, and that only the passivity of the ruled makes possible the terrible things rulers do. Edmund Burke wrote, "All it takes for evil to flourish is for good (people) to do nothing." On Good Friday, you remember, the crowd gathered not to cheer, but also not to protest; and "when they saw what had taken place, they returned home beating their breasts" (Luke 23:48). Big deal! Remorse comes easier than responsibility.

The description of Good Friday given by the two disciples ends with the touching line, "But we had hoped that he was the one to redeem Israel." Touching, yes; but the words also angered Jesus, and why not? For what in the name of God was he doing on Calvary if not redeeming Israel, and these two disciples still hadn't caught on! These insiders have no inside track at all. No wonder they were going in circles, heading toward the falling night. So does Jesus say gently, "Well, gentlemen, if I might venture to suggest . . ." ? No, Jesus never withholds the telling blow when only the telling blow will serve. He never hurts anyone—except deliberately. "O foolish men, and slow of heart"—what a phrase!—"slow of heart to believe all that the prophets have spoken! Was it not necessary that the Christ should suffer these things and enter into his glory?"

Romans, people, priests, rulers—on this score we are all alike: when the world takes a stand against God, we all think God should come on strong and set things straight. We all think in terms of power plays, whether in our own private theatrics or in the public arena. Pilate wanted to see proof of kingship, Herod a sign, and when Jesus was crucified the rulers scoffed at him, saying, "He saved others; let him save himself, if he is the Christ of God, his chosen one." Soldiers naturally expect power plays: "If you are the King of the Jews, come down from the cross." And the best remark that day came from the criminal who railed, "Are you not the Christ? Save yourself and us"—when that was precisely what Jesus was doing (Luke 23:35–40).

"Was it not necessary that the Christ should suffer these things?" Yes, because there are two things God is never going to do. When Adam fell, He could have canceled Adam; likewise Abraham, when Abraham lied; Jacob, when Jacob stole; David, when he committed adultery. But God knows such expedients are finally futile, for the world needs compassion even more than censure, and the kind of compassion that costs, that does not count the scars. Someone in this wicked world has got to become the lightning rod that grounds evil, that says, "Evil stops here." Hence, "turn the other cheek," "repay no one evil with evil." If you fight fire with fire you end up with more ashes. Instead of engaging in power plays, God ties his hands behind his back and comes to us saying, "I want my love for you to excite yours for me and for one another. Therefore, I shall not use my power but rather put myself in yours."

Was it not necessary that Christ should suffer these things? Put yourself in the shoes of those headed for Emmaus, and you answer the question.

Not only will God not engage in power plays; She will never take shortcuts. These two on the road to Emmaus are sad because, like us, they think that what doesn't get done now won't get done, period. "We had hoped that he was the one to redeem Israel." What kind of short-lived hope is that? Good things take time, and evil can't wipe them out just like that. You won't believe this, but I actually lie awake at night wondering how I'm going to keep Riverside going, when the fact of the matter is that were I to set out deliberately to stop Riverside, I couldn't succeed in a hundred years!

I'm not arguing, mind you, for passivity, for complacency; far from it. But I am arguing for trust in God, for that deep-down hope rooted in God rather than the shallow optimism rooted in us. "In a dark time the eye begins to see." So wrote the poet. And the saint reminds us that love not only bears all things, believes all things, endures all things—love *hopes* all things.

"Was it not necessary that the Christ should suffer these things?" Yes, because no power plays, and no shortcuts. Surely Jesus must have talked in some such vein to these disciples when, "beginning with Moses and all the prophets, he interpreted to them in all the Scriptures the things concerning himself."

Still, they did not recognize him, for the word, even the Word of God, is always preliminary to the deed. And here the deed typically is the simplest, most fundamental act of all, that which makes life possible. "When he was at table with them, he took the bread and blessed, and broke it, and gave it to them. And their eyes were opened and they recognized him."

This ordinary loaf in an ordinary room in the extraordinary presence of the risen Lord changed the direction of their lives. Like Jesus himself before them, they "set their faces toward Jerusalem," away from the night and toward the dawn of a new day that was breaking.

Mother of Us All

MAY 10, 1981
*Readings: Isaiah 66:7–13; Matthew 10:34–37,
12:46–50; John 19:25–27*

The way it's celebrated in churches around the country you'd think Mother's Day had become a religious holiday, the way "I'm Dreaming of a White Christmas" has almost reached the status of "Lo, How a Rose." But rather than buck the tide, let's go with the flow. Let's hail the designees of this day. Let's hail their wisdom in bringing us into the world, the time, energy, and patience poured into the development of every limb, every idea, every inch of our growth. And if you're free enough to realize that your mother didn't always measure up to the demands of the job, remember she was in a no-win situation. (A freshman once complained to me, "Reverend, I had a terrible childhood. My parents understood me.")

Then, as if this *were* a religious holiday, let us hail the greatest mother of them all—not only because she was the mother of our beloved Lord, but because, according to Orthodox and Catholic theology, she is the mother of every one of us. I believe that. I say my *Ave Marias.* But I hail Mary for her maternity rather than for her virginity.

The last words Jesus spoke to his mother, and to his disciple John about his mother, are full of concern for Mary's well-being. Yet they contrast sharply with what he said earlier in his ministry. In Matthew we read that once, inside a synagogue, he was "dividing the Word of God"—in the old Calvinist term for preaching—and "they came to him saying, Your mother and your brothers are outside asking for you." And Jesus replies: "Who are my mother and my brothers? . . . Whoever does the will of God is my brother, and sister, and mother" (Matt. 12:46–50).

Those are pretty harsh words, but this is not the first time Jesus has been disrespectful of his mother. When still a boy, he was taken to Jerusalem to the temple and afterwards rebuked by his father and mother for staying behind in order to preach to the elders. Affronted, the twelve-year-old Jesus said, "Wist ye not that I must be about my Father's business?" (Luke 2:49b).

From the very beginning of his life Jesus showed a healthy disrespect for respectability, a healthy mistrust of parental pleas. It was as if he realized very early that such protective slogans as "play it safe" and "don't climb out on a limb" constituted, as it were, the eleventh commandment on which are "hanged" all the law and the prophets.

What *were* his mother and brothers doing outside the synagogue? Why did they want to call him out? Why didn't they go in and listen to him? We know that because of the words he said and the miracles he performed, the Pharisees were after him. So it's safe to guess that his family had come not to open themselves to what he had to say, but to try to persuade him to stop all this wild-eyed, radical preaching and come home. Wasn't there a backlog of carpentry orders to be filled in Nazareth?

We offer our children advice to spare them suffering in the hope that it will prevent their making the same mistakes we made. But how did we get to be so smart except by making mistakes, through suffering? Can't we allow them the privilege of learning something on their own? If our children heeded our counsel they'd quickly get mired in a bog of sterility.

Lord knows the churches are equally remiss in their desire to keep things orderly. Rarely do they realize that "it is the cracked ones who let the light through." I love the story the novelist Kazantzakis tells of a monk's dream in which Mary comes to him with the boy Jesus, who needs to be cured.

"What's the matter, son?" asks the monk.

"I don't know. I just seem to wander the streets, wrestling."

"With whom are you wrestling?"

"With God, of course. With whom else would you wrestle?"

So the monk takes the boy into his home, where he teaches him carpentry. Together they go for long walks, in the course of which the monk talks to him of God as if God were a friendly neighbor who stopped by of a fair summer evening for a chat. Soon the boy is cured. He goes home. Years later the monk hears he's doing well; in fact, he's become the best carpenter in Nazareth.

Had Jesus heeded both his parents and the religious authorities of his day, instead of saving the world he would have become the best carpenter in Nazareth. Were our children to heed us and the religious authorities of our day, they'd all become nicely packaged citizens, polite, obedient, safe—and sterile.

Yesterday many of us were here for a wonderful wedding. If, in marriage, a man will leave his father and mother and cleave unto his wife, will he not also leave his father and mother—and if need be his church—and cleave unto God? That's why Jesus said, "He who loves father and mother more than me is not worthy of me."

All of us know, or should have experienced many times in our lives, the conflict between a narrow and safe loyalty, and loyalty to God—the conflict between loyalty to our family and loyalty to the world, our larger family. For Jesus the conflict was apparently so intense that it could finally be resolved only at the very end of his life, and only on a cross: "Woman, behold your son. Son, behold your mother."

That in this moment of pain Jesus could be so filial is indeed deeply moving. Apparently Joseph is dead; Mary is widowed, and Jesus is providing for her physical and economic well-being. But beyond that, he is providing for her spiritual well-being, in a very interesting way. Now Mary too leaves her family, goes to John; and by urging her to join his disciple, Jesus includes her in his mission, thereby resolving the conflict between loyalty to her and loyalty to God.

Where do you suppose were Mary's other children, those who had been with her that day outside the synagogue, those brothers to whom a dying son would normally commend his mother? Probably they were still in Nazareth, cursing the fool to whom misfortune had related them. Never would they allow themselves to feel the tension between narrow and larger loyalties.

But not so Mary. Clearly her son has reached her. Something has happened to change her mind. (Who was it who said, "Once an idea has stretched a mind it can never return to its original shape"?) We read that Mary is standing by the cross, standing, mind you, not fainting; perhaps in a distress too deep for tears, but also—at last—in all the legitimate pride of motherhood. Maybe she is remembering old man Simeon's words: "Behold, this child is set for the fall and rising of many in Israel, and for a sign that is spoken against (*and a sword will pierce through your soul also*) . . ." She is beginning to understand how inevitable is this terrible, glorious end to her son's life.

And notice that Jesus is not the least bit protective. Mary has to suffer his sufferings, and to translate them into the pangs of childbirth that will result in a new and larger family. For she will take care not only of John, but of countless souls, including millions today who in many languages will call her "Mother" because they consider themselves sisters and brothers of Christ.

"'Shall a woman bear a child without pains? Shall I bring to the point of birth and not deliver?' says the Lord. 'Shall I who deliver close the womb?'"

Every child is born of God as well as of woman. Every birth brings into the world not only another child of another mother and father but also another son or daughter of the Most High. Each of us has dual citizenship, here below and in the City of God; dual parentage, our earthly mother and father, our heavenly Father/Mother; dual membership in our narrow loving family and in the world, our larger family so desperately in need of love.

At the wedding yesterday the preacher said these ringing words: "Whom before God has joined together let no one put asunder." God has created of one blood all the nations of the earth. We all belong one to another, every one of us on this planet. That's the way God made us; Christ died to keep us that way; our sin is that we are always putting asunder what God has joined together.

So hail to thee, O Savior, whose heart on Good Friday was as heavy as the world of sins and miseries that it bore. And hail to thee, O Mary our mother, whose love and example nourishes us all. Standing—all of us now—with Mary and with John at the foot of the cross, we can hear Jesus' words:

> "Mother, behold all your sons and daughters;
> sisters and brothers, behold your mother."

The Hostility Stops Here

MAY 24, 1981
Readings: Hosea 11:1–9; Matthew 5:43–48

"When Israel was a child, I loved him, and out of Egypt I called my son."

Hosea 11:1

Our personal lives, the life of our nation, the life of our beloved planet—these lives are not tales told by fools, full of sound and fury, signifying nothing. These lives have purposes, at least in the sight of God and in the eyes of those who see God, and who therefore sing with conviction the lines of the closing verse of Newman's great hymn:

> So long thy power hath blest me, sure it still
> Will lead me on.
> O'er moor and fen, o'er crag and torrent, till
> The night is gone.

But as Newman's reference to night suggests, as surely as there are purposes for more lives, just as surely we thwart them. "The more I called them, the more they went from me," cries the prophet Hosea in the name of the Lord. And why do we thwart these purposes? Are we talking of ignorance awaiting enlightenment, human imperfection awaiting completion? No, we're talking of the pride that rules our wills, of greed and indifference, of the bondage in which we are held by *ME*—the great jailer of us all. The world's not imperfect, it's diseased, as we have reason enough to recall this weekend, which commemorates the 9.8 million killed in World War I (in church we count the losses on both sides) and the 52 million killed in World War II. To that almost inconceivable number we can add the far greater number who have died since World War II in well over one hundred more wars, civil and international. If we've learned one thing from the twentieth century, it is that progress is no mechanical necessity. The world can go, as did the life of Napoleon Bonaparte, from a high-hearted beginning to a mean and squalid ending.

So we have a thesis: ". . . out of Egypt I called my son"; life has meaning, full as it is of divine purposes. And, in Hegelian terms, we have an antithesis: "The more I called them, the more they went from me." What is the synthesis, the Christian answer to all the wrongs we do one another, the answer to the beastly, bloody actions we commemorate this Memorial weekend? It's hard to believe, but here it is: the Christian remedy for all the evils in the world is forgiveness of sins. "'My heart recoils within me, my compassion grows warm and tender. I will not execute my fierce anger,' saith the Lord."

Listen to St. Paul. "God was in Christ reconciling the world to himself, no longer holding our misdeeds against us" (2 Cor. 15:19). And in Ephesians: "Be generous to one another, tenderhearted, forgiving one another as God in Christ forgave you" (4:32). Listen as well to St. Augustine: "Our very righteousness . . . is yet in this life of such a kind that it consists rather in the remission of sins than in the perfecting of virtues. . . . Witness the prayer of the whole city of God and its pilgrim state"—what a definition of the Church!—"for it cries to God by the mouth of its members, 'Forgive us our debts as we forgive our debtors'" (*City of God* XIX: 27).

And once again these words of Jesus: "You have heard it said, 'You shall love your neighbor and hate your enemy.' But I say to you, love your enemies . . . You must be perfect as your heavenly father is perfect" (Matt. 5:43–44, 48)—which can be translated, "There must be no limit to your goodness, as your heavenly father's goodness knows no bounds."

Most of us don't believe these words of Jesus, not for a single minute. Why, if we didn't punish crime, how could we be said seriously to oppose it? If criminals knew they would be forgiven, how could we protect their future victims? And wouldn't it be a betrayal of our country and of every other decent country not to threaten the Russians if they make another move outside their borders? In other words, "With all due respect, Jesus, you are soft in the head." Or, on a higher level of argumentation, "With all due respect, Jesus, we feel you're treating wrongdoing with less than ultimate seriousness."

But is that true? Has anyone hated sin more deeply and consistently than Jesus? Has anyone made it clearer that all forms of sin—murder, thievery, extortion, adultery, greed, oppression of the poor, religious hypocrisy, and spiritual pride—fall under the judgment of God? And to Jesus isn't the repentance of the sinner always seen as the precondition to the acceptance of forgiveness? (Not to the *offering*, but to the *acceptance!*)

I think it's impossible to argue that Jesus treats wrongdoing less seriously than do we. What then *is* the difference? I think it is simply that most of us are more eager to bring judgment against sin than to bring healing to the sinner. I know that's true as regards the Soviet Union. I know that's true as regards those we incarcerate; as the riots in Michigan proved once again, our jails are more punitive than curative. And while we may be slow to judge ourselves, aren't we even slower to heal ourselves?

But God is not like us. Sin estranges us from God but never God from us, for "God is not only the moral judge of the world; he is even more the moral restorer of the world" (Donald Shriver). "For I am God and not man, the Holy One in your midst, and I will not come to destroy."

Sin estranges us from God and from one another. Sin walls us in and others out. But "Something there is that doesn't love a wall, / That wants it down." (Robert Frost). Only forgiveness of sins can topple the walls that make bad neighbors.

Some people argue, "Forgiveness can't bring a single victim back to life, so let's forget about forgiveness, not dwell in the past, but rather move on toward the future and try not to repeat the same mistakes." The trouble with that viewpoint is that it overlooks William Faulkner's truth: "The past is never dead, it's not even past."

Can you un-son or un-daughter yourself? Which of us travels unencumbered by the memory of misdeeds or grievances? (I ran into a woman not too long ago who said she was making progress in therapy. When I asked her how she knew she said, "It's easy—I can now say 'Shut up' to my M-o-t-h-e-r.") And what of our collective life? Clearly in Ireland today a penny of reason is outweighed by a ton of history. In the Middle East too the past overwhelms the present, as it does in South Africa, and even in our own country. (I'm thinking of racism.) The consequences of the past are always with us, and half the hostilities tearing the world apart could be resolved today were we to allow the forgiveness of sins to alter these consequences. Let's go further: all the hostilities in our personal and planetary life could be ended were we to allow the forgiveness of sins to act as a lightning rod grounding all these hostilities, if we were to say of ourselves, "The hostility stops *here*."

Well, if forgiveness is ethically right and so eminently practical, why are we so loath to be forgiven and forgiving?

It takes humility. It takes humility to acknowledge our need for forgiveness—and even more to accept it, because guilt is the last stronghold of pride: it represents my opinion of myself. Forgiveness is not something I can do for myself. It is something only God or you can bestow on me, and I may be too proud to allow you to do for me what I cannot do for myself. Put it this way: forgiveness offers me my value as a gift, but I may prefer to view my value as an achievement.

It also takes courage. If the forgiveness of sins is a lightning rod grounding all hostility, then forgiveness of sins signifies in its fullest sense the destruction of evil. Forgiveness of sins means saving the world, and the trouble with most of us is that we're too worldly to save the world. To save the world you have to split with the world, but by that I don't mean you have to become "anti-establishment." Had anyone asked Jesus if he considered himself "establishment" or "anti-establishment," I don't think he would have understood the question; he never recognized the authority of the establishment in the first place. And that's what I mean: like Jesus, Christians have God as their authority, and no authority as their God—and the authorities don't like that.

If we truly believe as did Jesus in the forgiveness of sins, then like Jesus we have to proclaim a new order of things, an order dedicated to grounding, not perpetuating hostility; an order dedicated to trust, not suspicion (simply because there is no other way to make a person trustworthy than to trust him); an order dedicated to love, not fear; to peace, not war; an order determined that the men and women we commemorate today shall not have died in vain.

I believe in the forgiveness of sins because without it my own life would be a wilderness of unyielding despair. And I believe in the forgiveness of sins because I see no other way to end hostility than to ground it. I believe that "God was in Christ reconciling the world to himself, no longer holding our misdeeds against us"; I believe God will not execute his fierce anger because God so loves the world that

He wants to heal it. So I think St. Augustine was absolutely right: "Our very righteousness . . . is yet in this life of such a kind that it consists rather in the remission of sins than in the perfecting of virtues. . . . Witness the prayer of the whole city of God in its pilgrim state, for it cries to God by the mouth of its members, 'Forgive us our debts as we forgive our debtors.'"

Dearly beloved, "Be generous to one another, tender-hearted, forgiving one another as God in Christ forgave you."

Competitors for the Throne

MAY 31, 1981
Reading: Acts 1:6–11

It is hard, to say the least, for modern, scientific minds to grasp what actually happened on Ascension Day. All we really know for sure is that the Church has hailed the fortieth day after Easter as a feast day, for it marks the time when Jesus, having been crucified and resurrected, assumes his glory and power. Henceforth, in rich Biblical imagery, we picture Christ "seated at the right hand of the Father." This, then, is the Sunday when we "enthrone" Jesus, singing,

> Jesus shall reign where'er the sun
> Does his successive journeys run;

or,

> Crown Him with many crowns,
> The Lamb upon His throne.

Surely one of life's more depressing features is the inordinate amount of time we spend unlearning things we learned so well. As small children we more or less blindly obeyed our parents; we had to, or we'd have disappeared under a speeding car, or drowned, or gone up in smoke. To some degree we also had to become what they wanted us to become, for without some support or approval on their part we couldn't have become anything at all. But what's depressing is how from then on we seem to spend our lives seeking the approval of others, becoming what sells, trying never to get burned, and at best only testing the water, never plunging in—and this even though we know that when the children of Israel reached the Red Sea and Moses stretched out his hand, nothing happened—until the first Israelite leaped into the waves!

This Ascension Day I spent in Salina, Kansas, with Kansan Methodists gathered for their semi-annual conference. While there, I went to visit a real agricultural "nut" who lived and worked on the outskirts of town. "Bill," he said as we tramped around the twenty-eight acres of his Land Institute, "I want you to realize that next to the sword, the plowshare is the greatest threat to humanity. While it is true that each year there is more produce from these fields, there is less soil in these fields." He waved at the Smoky Hill River, thick with mud. "Each year there is more production, but the soil becomes increasingly poisoned from farm chemicals and salts from irrigation. I tell you, Bill, this fossil-fuel chemotherapy is giving everyone a false picture of the health of our agriculture. And the trouble is not only petrochemicals, oil versus soil; more basically, Preacher, it's this: Nature teaches enterprise and patience, but human beings have learned only enterprise. The result is that we have a monoculture of annuals instead of a polyculture of perennials. Now either you preachers are going to have to teach Homo sapiens patience, or I'm going to have to teach these perennials to become more enterprising." And he proudly showed me the more than fifty-seven varieties of perennials he and his disciples were trying to coax into greater activity.

Wes Jackson has a Ph.D. in genetics, and the frequency and naturalness of his Biblical allusions attest to his religious upbringing. Yet he has quit the university, and the Methodist Church. In both, he claims, the more important the problem the less the chances of its being studied. He's bored with both. So he feeds his family and students on what he grows; and who knows, they may yet teach the patient earth to reward a balanced yet more enterprising ecosystem.

What I like about Wes Jackson, Amory Lovins, David Brower, and conservationists of their ilk is first of all their understanding, learned through agriculture, of sin: it's our saying "Yea" to God's "Nay." But more than that—they're not afraid of getting burned, of plunging in, of being considered nuts. And if we are seriously going to enthrone Jesus in our lives this Ascension Sunday, like them we are going to have to be willing to risk something big for something good.

And what is it we're going to have to risk? Consider this: Jesus never said, "It is impossible for a harlot or a drunk to enter the Kingdom of

Heaven." But he did say, "It is easier for a camel to pass through the eye of a needle than for a rich man to enter the Kingdom of God" (Matt. 19:24). And he might have said, "an educated person"—for wasn't he always arguing with the scribes and Pharisees? Or "a patriot"—for the Zealots, the nationalists of his day, turned from him and against him in bitter disappointment.

Wealth, education, patriotism: it's the positive, good things, not the bad things in life, that most effectively separate us from Christ on his throne. Luther understood this, for in the last verse of his great hymn, "A Mighty Fortress Is Our God," he doesn't say "Let lust and gluttony go"; he writes instead of the things most loved in our lives—

> Let goods and kindred go,
> This mortal life also.

These are the real competitors for the throne of Christ.

What Martin Luther wrote about, Albrecht Dürer drew. In his famous engraving *Knight, Death, and the Devil*, he shows all the tempters: toads and salamanders, symbols of our baser instincts; death, the specter that undermines our faith; and also the homelike castle in the background, signifying all that to the knight is dear and familiar.

Years ago I listened to an honorable headmaster explain why there were as yet no Blacks in his private school: "I have to wait for a rich, and unfortunately bigoted, trustee to die; we need his money for scholarships." Money for scholarships—a good thing.

Years later when we used to stand outside factory gates pleading with workers to quit their jobs, to stop making guns to kill Vietnamese, rarely were we told, "But they should be killed; they're Commies." Almost always it was, "Listen, Reverend, I have a wife and two children." A family—the best life has to offer. How true are Jesus' words, "A person's enemies will be those of his [or her] own household." The only time I began to falter just a little in my opposition to the war in Vietnam was when the hate callers began to get hold of my children, then very small, and say, "Tell your father we're going to kill him."

Body, child and spouse, goods, fame, riches, education, love of country—we must clear the throne of all these good things. *Around* the throne they belong, but *on* the throne they distort our perspective and ruin our relationship to them. The body is a temple—that keeps the body in shape! If we dedicate our minds to Christ, the more important problems of life will be studied, not studiously ignored. If we dedicate our wealth to Christ, what a harvest of blessings will be reaped for the sake of the many. And if we reconnect nature to nature's God, and our nation to the family of all nations under God, then we shall have an agricultural and a foreign policy fit for children.

Limitations*

JULY 5, 1981
Readings: Genesis 2:5–9; 1 Corinthians 3:18–23

L ife is limitation": it can never be said too often. Nor can the positive side of that statement be sufficiently stressed, for just as a stream has no chance of running deep until it finds its banks, so we, until we discover our limits, haven't a prayer of becoming profound.

Of all life's limitations, the greatest, of course, is death, the Grim Reaper, who intends to get us and in the end will succeed. But consider for a moment the alternative—endless existence. Why, without death, life would be interminable! Like that little bit of Ireland a Spanish priest once told me about. It reminded him of home, so deaccelerated was the pace. He asked an Irish friend of his if in Gaelic there was an expression of "mañana." Answered his friend: "Ah, we have many such expressions, but none that carry the same sense of urgency."

If we had all the time in the world, we'd never use any of it. We'd become, in Thurber's phrase, "blobs of glub." We'd be as bored as the old Greek gods and no doubt up to the same frivolous tricks. Moreover, for some people life is cruel; they have a right to see it end. And if life is good, as fundamentally it most surely is, then we should be willing to get out of the way and let others have a crack at it.

I don't mean to make light of death. Whether life is good or bad, death is awesome and terrifying; and as death is an event that embraces all our life, the sooner we use our faith to come to terms with it, the better off we are. But finally, death is more friend than foe. Thank God that "no life lives forever, that even the longest river winds somewhere out to sea." Praise be to God for our brother/sister Death.

Another kind of limitation has to do with our ambitions. When we are young we dream big. We're going to sing like Jussi Björling, dance like Patricia McBride, write like Maya Angelou, have the courtroom career of a Louis Nizer or the lash-like left of a Ron Guidry. (Oh, that

---

*This sermon owes much to John Claypool's sermon, "You Can't Have It All."—WSC

this season of diamond doldrums would end!) It's all very hot and heady. But then, say at age thirty-five, comes the cold shower, the sharp contrasts between the dream and what became of it. Suddenly we realize we're not going to sing, dance, write, orate, or pitch like anyone else but ourselves. It's discouraging, but also creative—another important crisis of faith, for the art of Christian life is to take our defeats and turn them into the occasions for the victories God always had in mind for us. Like St. Paul's thorn in the flesh, any defeat can become a severe mercy. For as the Lord said to Paul, "My strength is made perfect in weakness."

Then there's a third kind of limitation. I think we bump into it hardest in summertime; warm weather seems to favor fantasies. We want to be Jussi Björling *and* Patricia McBride *and* Maya Angelou *and* Louis Nizer *and* Ron Guidry. *We want it all*—just the way we did as small children the first time we stood in a cafeteria line; as did Adam and Eve in the Garden; as did Jesus in the wilderness when the Devil promised him the whole world for a seemingly small price.

Here's how a modern writer, Sam Keen, put the matter for himself, for me, and, I'm sure, for many of you.

> There are so many lives I want to live, so many styles I would like to inhabit. In me sleeps Zorba's concern to allow no lonely woman to remain comfortless ("Here am I, Lord, send me!"), Camus' passion to lessen the suffering of the innocent, Hemingway's drive to live and write with lucidity, and the unheroic desire to see each day end with tranquility and a shared cup of tea.
>
> I am so many, yet I may be only one. I mourn for all the selves I kill when I decide to be a single person. Decision is a cutting-off, a castration. I travel one path only by neglecting many. Actual existence is tragic, but fantastic existence (which evades choice and limitation) is pathetic. The human choice may be between tragedy and pathos, Oedipus and Willy Loman. So I turn my back on small villages I will never see, strange flesh I will never touch, ills I will never cure, and I choose to be in the world as a husband and a father, an explorer of new ideas and styles of life. Yet perhaps Zorba will not leave me altogether. I would not like to live without dancing, without unknown roads to explore, without the confidence that my actions were helpful to some.

I like that passage, and I agree with Keen that life is either tragic or pathetic. But again, how could it be otherwise? Choice is at the core of life. Without choice, without the hard choices that Adam and Eve refused to make and that Jesus accepted, life wouldn't be human at all. Why do I bring all this up? Because I don't think most of us have really accepted the notion that life is limitation. We don't really accept death, or the limits of our talents, or the hard choices we have to make just to be the best we can be. Or let's say the knowledge of these things stays stuck between our ears; it doesn't work its way down. The longest, most arduous trip in the world is often the trip between the head and the heart. Until that trip is complete, we remain in pain, at war with ourselves. And, of course, those at war with themselves are those who make casualties of others, of friends and loved ones.

What is true in personal life is equally true in national life. Nations at war with themselves, like the Soviet Union and the United States, displace their violence abroad in promiscuous interventions. Nations don't live forever either; there are limits to their talents, and no more than individuals can they have it all. Primarily they can't be at one and the same time the most powerful and the most virtuous. It is gratifying for Americans on this weekend to recall that ours is the longest-lived revolution in the world, maybe even the most successful. But it would be a mistake to forget that our influence as a people was greatest when as a nation we were weakest. We rallied far more hopes and energies when we had no rockets and no muscle. The other day I read words of Alexander Hamilton more pertinent perhaps to our time than to his: "To be more safe the nations at length become willing to run the risk of being less free." Today our danger may lie in becoming more concerned with defense than with having things worth defending.

"Actual existence is tragic, but fantastic existence (which evades choice and limitation) is pathetic." I said I liked that, and I do. But it sounds a bit too negative. As I said at the beginning, it's a good thing that life is limitation. Without death, we'd never live. Without discovering the limits of our talents, we'd never discover who we are. And finally, hard choices have a potential for riches beyond any reckoning, "For eye hath not seen nor ear heard nor the heart of man conceived the good things that God hath prepared for those who love him" (1 Cor. 2:9). Deserted by his disciples, in agony on the cross, barely thirty years old, Christ said, "It is finished." And thus ended the most complete life ever lived.

So, dear friends, we need not endlessly grieve the distant villages we'll never see, even the fact that we never got out of New York this

Fourth of July weekend. We need not grieve the strange flesh we'll never touch, the wrongs we'll never right, the ills we'll never cure. Contentment lies in discerning the value of the things we have. I think I've lived just long enough to begin to discern what St. Paul meant when he wrote, "For all things are yours, whether Paul or Apollos or Cephas or the world or life or death or the present or the future, all are yours; and you are Christ's; and Christ is God's" (1 Cor. 3:21–23).

Homosexuality

JULY 12, 1981
Readings: Isaiah 1:10–17; Acts 10:1–20

Aside from their extraordinary contributions to human progress and happiness, what did the following have in common: Erasmus, Leonardo da Vinci, Michelangelo, Christopher Marlowe, King James I of England, Sir Francis Bacon, Thomas Gray, Frederick the Great of Germany, Margaret Fuller, Tchaikovsky, Nijinsky, Proust, A. E. Housman, T. E. Lawrence, Walt Whitman, Henry James, Edith Hamilton, W. H. Auden, Willa Cather, and Bill Tilden, the greatest tennis player of his time?

Some of you, no doubt, have the answer. They were all homosexual. And why do I bring up this subject, probably the most divisive issue since slavery split the Church? Because the once unmentionable has become unavoidable. Christian ministers are claiming as coming from God the judgment that gay men and women are not only different, but sinfully different; gay men and women are being physically and psychologically abused; they are being excluded from their families and frozen out of churches; and on June 18, the House of Representatives voted to bar the Legal Services Corporation from pressing cases where homosexuality is at issue. We have no choice but to bring up the issue. Straight and gay American citizens, and especially American Christians, can remain neither indifferent nor indecisive.

What's hard, of course—and hard for many gays too—is to approach the subject with open minds rather than with fixed certainties, with hearts full of compassion rather than repugnance. That's why we just heard read the Biblical account of Peter's struggle to abandon his own fixed certainties, to overcome his own repugnance. Three times he protests when in his trance he hears the Lord order him to rise and kill and eat birds and reptiles and pigs. Hardly surprising, when you remember that ever since he was a tot he has had it drilled into him: "Every swarming thing that swarms upon the earth is an abomination; it shall not be eaten. Whatever goes on its belly, and whatever goes on all fours, or whatever has many feet, all the swarming things that swarm upon the earth, you shall not eat for they are an abomination." That's Holy Writ, part of the holy Levitical Code (Lev. 11:41–42), the Word of God as Jews understood it. And now God suddenly is telling Peter just the opposite: "Kill and eat. . . . What God has cleansed, you must not call common." Moreover, all his life Peter has been instructed not to associate with Gentiles. Nevertheless, when the three men arrive he accompanies them to Cornelius' house where he later confesses, "Truly I perceive that God shows no partiality, but in every nation anyone who fears him and does what is right is acceptable to him."

So the question is whether those of us who were drilled, as was Peter, to think a certain way are as willing as he to risk reexamining what we were taught. Moral judgment has a progressive character, criticizing the present in terms of the future. Could it be that the Holy Spirit in our time is leading each of us to a new conviction, a new confession: "Truly I perceive that God shows no partiality, but *in every sexual orientation* anyone who fears him and does what is right is acceptable to him." (We'll have a "talk-back" session after the service so you can give me the benefit of your thinking on this issue.)

Several years ago James B. Nelson, a professor of Christian ethics, suggested that there were four primary theological stances toward homosexuality. The first was a rejecting-punitive position; the second a rejecting-nonpunitive position; the third a conditional acceptance; and the fourth an unconditional acceptance. I think these four positions reflect the differing attitudes of most church members today.

The Jerry Falwells of the land obviously take the rejecting-punitive position. To them homosexual acts are perverse, repugnant, and sinful. Like Peter's argument with God, theirs too is based on Levitical law, in this case, "You shall not lie with a man as with a woman; it is an abomination" (Lev. 18:22).

What they never point out is that "abomination" (*toevah* in Hebrew)—the word used in reference to homosexual acts—is also used in reference to eating pork, to a misuse of incense, and to intercourse during menstruation. Generally it does not signify something intrinsically evil (like rape or theft, which are also dealt with in the Levitical Code), but something that is ritually unclean. So like Peter we may be called to recognize the distinction between intrinsic wrong and ritual impurity.

Here are some other things never mentioned by the Jerry Falwells. To avoid idolatry, the Israelites went to great lengths to separate their worship of God from the fertility cults of their neighbors, whose rituals involved male as well as female prostitutes. But their primary concern was with idolatry, not homosexuality. Likewise they rejected the practice widespread at the time in the Middle East of humiliating captured foes by forcing them to submit to anal rape in a fashion similar to what goes on in prisons today. But again the emphasis was not on prohibiting homosexuality but on not dishonoring a fellow human being. It was also widely believed—and by the Israelites as well in this case—that the male seed alone carried life; women provided only the incubating space. Hence any ejaculation outside of a woman's body was a form of abortion, and procreation was mighty important to a very small nation in a sea of hostile ones. Most of all, what we need to remember is that while homosexual *acts* are condemned, nowhere does Scripture address a homosexual *orientation*. Biblical writers assume that homosexual acts are being committed by people whose basic orientation is heterosexual. The problem they are addressing is, in modern terms, perversion rather than inversion. The Bible says nothing directly one way or another about the loving, lasting relations known by so many of the people I listed at the outset, the loving, lasting relations that patently exist today between so many gay people in this country, this city, and this church.

As for Sodom and Gomorrah, scholars are far less clear about what happened there than are most contemporary evangelists. Said one: "God dropped an atomic bomb on Sodom and Gomorrah because they were perverts." If, however, we allow the Bible to illumine its own cloudy passages, we find that the destruction of Sodom and Gomorrah had little if anything to do with homosexuality. In Ezekiel we read: "This was the iniquity of your sister Sodom: she and her daughters had pride of wealth and food in plenty, comfort and ease, and yet she never helped the poor and the wretched." In the first chapter of Isaiah, where Judah is rebuked through a comparison with Sodom, homosexuality is never mentioned among the specific sins, which again include a failure to pursue justice and to champion the oppressed. The most likely other sin of Sodom was a failure to show hospitality to strangers—a possibility indicated by Jesus' words to his disciples: "When you enter a town and they do not make you welcome . . . I tell you, it will be more tolerable for Sodom on that day than for that town." How ironic that because of a mistaken understanding of the crime of Sodom and Gomorrah, Christians should be repeating the *true* crime every day against homosexuals.

Clearly, it is not Scripture that creates hostility to homosexuality, but rather hostility to homosexuality that prompts certain Christians to retain a few passages from an otherwise discarded law code. The problem is not reconciling homosexuality with Scriptural passages that appear to condemn it, but rather how to reconcile the rejection and punishment of homosexuals with the love of Christ. I don't think it can be done. I don't see how Christians can centrally define and then exclude people on the basis of sexual orientation alone—not if the law of love is more important than the laws of biology.

The rejecting but nonpunitive stance, while condemning homosexual acts, strives not to condemn the homosexual person. According to this second view, homosexuals are not criminals or sinners so much as victims of arrested development or some other form of psychic disorder, because fundamentally homosexuality is "unnatural." The problem with this position is that most gay people assert that they did not choose their orientation, they discovered it; and scientific research supports the assertion. Psychology professor John Mooney, a leading authority on character development, claims that it is not possible to force a change from homosexual to heterosexual "any more than it is possible to change a heterosexual into a homosexual." If that's the case, then the offer to "cure" gays of their "sickness" carries the danger of raising false expectations, and then guilt when the cure doesn't work. Besides, how sick *are* gays? I was impressed when in 1973 the American Psychiatric Association voted to remove homosexuality from its list of mental disorders. The association didn't deny that many homosexuals were disturbed, it only acknowledged that many were not. And what is the meaning of "natural" and "unnatural"? I come back to the law of love and the laws of biology. If we as Christians judge what is natural according to the law of love, and if we can affirm that gays can be as loving as straights, then why is homosexual love contrary to human nature? Shouldn't a relationship be judged by its inner worth rather than by its outer appearance?

That brings us to conditional acceptance. Many sensitive straight Christians have struggled to reach this position. They now believe that all rights should be accorded gay people. They believe in the ordination of avowed gays, if only because they see the hypocrisy involved in supporting job opportunities outside the church only to deny these same opportunities within. But they can't picture a gay spouse in the parsonage; they're uncomfortable with public displays of gay affection. In their heart of hearts they feel that homosexuality is not really on a par with heterosexuality.

I have tended to lean toward that position, but I think it's untenable. Consider Jewish-Christian relations. Most Christians will insist that Jews should enjoy the same rights as Christians because they're as good or as bad as we are; we're all equal. Nevertheless, in their heart of hearts they think Judaism is inferior to Christianity. But can you champion equality while nourishing the theological roots that make for inequality? Finally, doesn't Judaism have to be not inferior, not superior, just different? There are dilemmas, major ones, particularly for Christians who feel that Jews never recognized God's love in person on earth. But dilemmas we can live with, and even find creative. And the worst thing we can do with a dilemma is to resolve it prematurely because we haven't the courage to live with uncertainty.

I think straight Christians have to reach the same position vis-à-vis gays. They're different—that's all. What I've come to recognize is that just as "the Black problem" turned out to be a problem of white racism, just as "the woman problem" turned out to be a problem of male sexism, so "the homosexual problem" is really the homophobia of many of us heterosexuals. I know gays have hang-ups; so do straights, and I leave these hang-ups to the psychologists. I'm appalled at the promiscuity of some gays, but no more appalled than are many other gays. Promiscuity is cruel and degrading in any sexual orientation, but straights bear a special responsibility for the promiscuity of gays. Just as Blacks used to be labeled shiftless by whites who made sure there would be no reward for their diligence, so straights call gays promiscuous while denying support for overt gay stable relationships—the spouse in the parsonage.

So enough of these fixed certainties. If what we think is right and wrong divides still further the human family, there must be something wrong with what we think is right. Enough of this cruelty and hatred, this punitive legislation toward gay people. Peter widened his horizons; let's not narrow ours. It has been said that a mind once stretched by a new idea can never return to its former shape. Let's listen, let's learn, let's read and pray—none of this is easy—until with Peter's conviction we can make a similar confession: "Truly I perceive that God shows no partiality, but in every sexual orientation anyone who fears him and does what is right is acceptable to him."

What St. Augustine called the duty of the preacher is the obligation of every one of us: "to teach what is right, to refute what is wrong, and in the performance of that task to rouse the careless and to conciliate the hostile."

May God grant us success in this ministry of reconciliation. Amen.

The Courage to Be Well

JULY 19, 1981
Reading: Mark 2:1–12

In childhood, after a summer shower, didn't you love to go puddle-gazing—to wander from one puddle to the next, wondering how so much of the sky, so many treetops and buildings, could be reflected in such small bodies of water? With similar amazement I continue to wonder how so much of the story of earth and heaven can be captured in small Biblical tales such as the story of Jesus and the paralytic. Here we see the eternal dispenser of freedom confronting the eternal paralysis of the human will. Here we see the eternal dispenser of life healing a man whose life has become one long suicide.

Precisely what was wrong with the man neither scholars nor doctors can say. Jesus' words, "My son, your sins are forgiven," indicate an illness related to feelings of guilt. We know that at the root of every emotional disorder there is some paralyzing fear. Hospital wards are filled with people scared to death—literally, like the paralytic, scared stiff (sometimes in a fetal position, that being the last in which they experienced any semblance of security). And we know it was widely believed in the Biblical world that misdeeds caused misfortunes, sin caused sickness—this despite the psalmist's claim, "My *help* cometh from the Lord" (Ps. 121:2; not "my tragedy"); and despite Job's profound dissatisfaction with all the learned, clever attempts to explain tragedy in this simplistic fashion. Throughout Scripture, alongside Job's skepticism are pious assertions such as, "No ills befall the righteous, but the wicked are filled with trouble" (Prov. 12:21). Wisely, we side with Job, but it would be a mistake to rule out altogether a causal connection between sickness and sin. All of us know of sicknesses, and especially of cures, that to some mysterious degree are matters of the will. So let us assume that whatever the paralytic's illness, it was, as we say, psychosomatic.

Turning now to Jesus: He is to Christians God's love in person on earth. What a difference there is between the love symbolized by Cupid—an infant in diapers, blindfolded to boot—and the love of God. Far from blind, God's love is visionary. It penetrates the armor we don the moment we're out of diapers, and perceives an individual full of hurts and joys of every size and nature, an individual unprecedented, irrepeatable, and, in the divine dispensation, irreplaceable. God's love is also creative: it doesn't seek value, it creates value.

Christians recognize their value as a gift, not an achievement. It is not because we have value that we are loved, but because we are loved that we have value. Jesus says, "My son, your sins are forgiven," his visionary love recognizing a need for spiritual, not physical, mending. Jesus' creative love restores the man's sense of worth, cleansing his heart of the fearful, guilty thoughts paralyzing his will.

Which of us is not at least partially paralyzed? Whose hands are free to be extended to anyone? Whose feet are free to walk any path of life, free to walk out of that tight little protective circle of friends? Whose eyes are not fixed on some status symbol or other? It is inevitable: before the awesome terrors of the world every human heart quakes. Every human being tries desperately to secure herself against her insecurity—by gaining more power, more money, more virtue, more health. But the effort is vain; our need for security always outstrips our ability to provide it (a failure understood by Michelangelo, all of whose powerful figures bear the telltale sign of anxiety: dilated pupils). This anxiety is the precondition of our paralysis, which in turn produces more anxiety as we realize how we have stunted our growth, denied our destiny. Hence there's not one of us who doesn't need to be converted—not from life to something more than life, but from something less than life to the possibility of full life itself. "The glory of God is a human being fully alive": to become fully alive is undeniably possible, for to each of us as to the paralytic come the words, "My son"—my daughter—"your sins are forgiven."

What follows in the story is to me its most dramatic moment. Obviously the man must have wanted to be cured altogether as much as his four friends wanted to see him cured, because when Jesus says "Your sins are forgiven," the paralytic believes him. When Jesus tells him to stand up, he does.

With no difficulty I can picture myself lying on the pallet, the center of the crowd's attention. I can imagine myself enjoying the ability to use my distress to manipulate my friends. I can imagine the comfort I would draw from the words, "My son, your sins are forgiven." But when, following the indicative of forgiveness, I heard the imperative of responsibility—"Rise, take up your pallet, and walk"—I think my inclination would have been to murmur, "Oh, no, Jesus, I think I'll just stay here on the stretcher."

I'm driving at what I think is the central problem of the Christian church in America today: most of us fear the cure more than the illness. Most of us prefer the plausible lie that we can't be cured to the fantastic truth that we can be. And there's a reason: if it's hell to be guilty, it's certainly scarier to be responsible—*response-able*, able to respond to God's visionary and creative love. No longer paralyzed, our arms would be free to embrace the outcast and the enemy, the most confirmed addict, the reddest of Soviet communists. No longer paralyzed, our feet would be free to walk out of any job that is harmful to others and meaningless to us, free even to walk that lonesome valley without fear of evil. Everything is possible to those whose eyes, no longer fixed on some status symbol or other, are held instead by the gaze of him who can dispense freedom and life in measures unheard of.

But as the hand of love freely extended always returns covered with scars (if not nailed to a cross), it is not dumb to refuse the cure; it is not dumb to remain paralyzed, stuck on the pallet; but it is *boring*. And alas, whether they occupy pulpits or sit in the pews, most American Christians are still on the pallet. Like the paralytic they know they are sinners, at least in a vague sort of way. But lacking his will to be cured, lacking the courage to be well, they do not seek the forgiveness that offers a new way of life; instead, they seek punishment—which, by assuaging the guilt, makes the old way of life bearable anew. And they find this punishment not only in boring sermons and services, but also in a religion of legalism and moralism that turns people who could be free and loving into mean little Puritans, into blue-nosed busy-bodies.

Let's switch images for a moment and see how we're like the rich young ruler who eagerly sought out Jesus only to go sorrowfully away. When, in distress, we seek guidance, we think we want to change when actually we want to remain the same—but feel better about it. In psychological terms, we want to be more effective neurotics, "preferring the security of known misery to the misery of unfamiliar insecurity" (Sheldon Kopp). But, dear friends, is it not unbelievably boring—this secure, paralyzed life, this deliberate retreat from the mysterious to the manageable, from freedom to bondage? Isn't it dull as dishwater to live life to the minimum? And is it not dishonest to call ourselves Christians and then to pretend that Christ is not the healer, the eternal dispenser of freedom, the eternal dispenser of life? Nor can we pretend that God's love in person on earth doesn't say as much about what we are to become as about what God has become.

The courage to be well is a crucial virtue. Once again the currents of history are churning into rapids, threatening to carry before them everything we have loved, trusted, looked to for pleasure and support. We are being called upon to live with enormous insecurity. The churches could become centers of creative and courageous thinking. They could also become sanctuaries for frightened Americans, recruiting grounds for authoritarian figures and movements, some of which already bear the earmarks of an emerging fascism.

Will we be scared to death or scared to life. It all depends on where we find our ultimate security. In Leipzig, Martin Luther was asked, "Where will you be, Brother Martin, when church, state, princes, and people turn against you?" Answered Brother Martin, "Why then as now, in the hands of Almighty God."

"My son, your sins are forgiven. . . . Rise, take up your pallet, and walk." Where the man went we do not know. Jesus healed with no strings attached. But the paralytic did respond to God's love with his own, so we needn't worry, "For eye hath not seen nor ear heard nor the heart of man conceived the good things that God hath prepared for those who love him" (1 Cor. 2:9).

"The glory of God is a human being fully alive."

Abortion

JULY 26, 1981
Readings: Genesis 2:1–7; 1 Peter 2:1–5, 9–10

Here is some first-rate advice: Think thoughts that are as clear as possible, but no clearer; say things as simply as possible, but no simpler. And remember the physicist Werner Heisenberg, who asked, "What is the opposite of a profound truth?" and answered, "Another profound truth."

I offer this advice, because I want to discuss abortion, which is not only a complex, controversial, and pressing problem; to my way of thinking it is an unyielding dilemma. Or, more accurately: Abortion is a dilemma that yields but a little, and only to those who accord it the respect due an unyielding dilemma.

Consider, for instance, some of the phrases commonly heard in the abortion debate. The phrase "sanctity of life" can be invoked in favor of fetal rights, in favor of the right to self-determination on the part of the mother, and in favor of the human species' right to survival, threatened as we seem to be by overpopulation. Or take the phrase, "God forbids the taking of innocent life." Patently true, and another reason for abolishing warfare in the nuclear age; but that still leaves us human beings to define "innocent" and "life." Or, "We cannot play God." Agreed again. But God himself doesn't play God, as that phrase is generally understood. God doesn't intervene directly in our affairs as the primary causative agent of our births and deaths. God doesn't marry us, take us to bed, go around seducing us, any more than God goes around firing every murderer's pistol, sitting behind every steering wheel, and smoking every cigarette. Of course we can't play God, but we also cannot pretend we ourselves are without choice, without responsibility, mere passive victims of whatever befalls us. For we are "a chosen race, a royal priesthood, a holy nation, God's own people."

What we *can* say is that God wants us to affirm and protect life, more and more of it. God must have been pleased with the social consciousness that finally grew sufficiently sensitive to abolish slavery. God must be pleased today with our long-overdue recognition of the rights of women, the rights of prisoners, soldiers, poor people, children, even whales. Why shouldn't we talk of the rights of the unborn? I think it's fine that we do. Still I see no final, lasting, satisfactory-to-all-sides solution until medical technology becomes so advanced and society so enlightened that abortion is no longer necessary.

Is there any ground for moral consensus? And if not, are there grounds at least for legal consensus? On the moral aspect, I think we can agree that the right to life of a human being is fundamental, and that innocent life should not be taken. If so, the crucial question is, "At what point, if at any stage, can unborn life be called human?"

The Roman Catholic Church certainly has clear thoughts on this matter. The Catholic Hospital Association of the United States and Canada has specified: "Every unborn child must be regarded as a human person, with all the rights of a human person, from the moment of conception." That statement commends itself for its clarity, for its desire to affirm and protect more and more of life, and for its honesty in making the assertion a moral, not a medical judgment. Medicine cannot tell us when unborn life can be called human. Medical science can tell us when a heart starts beating, just as it can tell us when a heart has stopped beating. But science cannot say when it is morally right to cease all artificial supports of a dying person, because science is not in a position to declare: "This is no longer a human person." That's a moral, not a medical judgment. The business of science is only to make clear the facts of natural life, not the values of human life.

But is that clear assertion of the Catholic Hospital Association just a little clearer than clarity warrants? There was a time, centuries ago, when the Church was less clear on this matter, a time when theologians tried to distinguish between a fetus that was "formed"—"ensouled"— and one that was as yet "unformed," without soul. Writing in the twelfth century, Gratian declared, "He is not a murderer who brings about abortion before the soul is in the body."

That sounds fairly Biblical, doesn't it? "Then the Lord God formed man of dust from the ground, and breathed into his nostrils the breath of life; and man became a living soul." The purely physical aspects of life are metaphorically portrayed as dust. But a living soul is more than dust; a living soul is nature-plus! A living soul speaks, reasons, judges between right and wrong. Certainly a fertilized egg in a woman's uterus is human in origin and human in destiny, but is that enough to make it an individual human being with full human rights? Doesn't the older and less clear developmental view of life make at least as much sense as the contemporary one, which erases all distinctions between *potential* life and *actual* life? In fact, don't Roman Catholics, along with all the rest of us, act as if there were a difference between potential and actual life? When a fetus aborts spontaneously, we grieve for the parents, hardly at all for the life no one has seen. We don't have funerals for unborn children. And I've never heard anyone urge the same punishment for a mother who aborts a fetus as for one who murders a grown child.

Troubling too in the standard Catholic view of abortion is the divorce of motive and action. I always have trouble with a moral methodology that has so worked out its principles in advance that the specifics in any given case are irrelevant. Suppose a mother in the slums of New York or Caracas, with more children than resources to keep them alive and well, decides on an abortion for the sake of the children she already has. Can her motive have "the moral malice of murder"? If every doctor who in good conscience performs an abortion is a murderer, then so is every conscientious soldier. Obviously such labelling is unfair, simplistic. Obviously you can never totally divorce actions and motives. It's not that the end justifies the means, but that ends give meaning to means.

And finally, there is simply insufficient evidence to bear out the claim so frequently made that abortion is dangerous because it threatens the meaning and value of life generally. Japan has the most permissive abortion system in the world, but is life less sacred there than, say, in Argentina or Chile?

Turning now from the moral to the legal aspect of abortion, I think we have to say that the legal position generally taken by Roman Catholic bishops is consistent with their moral position. At their best the bishops are not trying to infringe on our religious liberties by imposing Catholic beliefs on non-Catholics. Their opposition to the legalization of abortion is based on their belief that "any law that

imperils the right to life of innocent human persons is a social evil."
If abortion is murder, then it is a crime; it's that simple. Therefore it
makes little sense for Jews, humanists, and Protestants to say to
Catholics, "Call abortion a sin, but not a crime." How would you like
it if someone came up to you and said, "Call genocide a sin, but not a
crime; call a pre-emptive strike on Russia a sin, but not a crime."

But again, it's not that simple, and the best of the bishops know it.
We are at the heart of the dilemma, but here the dilemma does yield
just a bit. In Roman Catholic jurisprudence, for a law to be good it
must be shown—among other things—to be enforceable, for unen-
forced laws tend to bring all law into disrepute. Recognizing that
there has been little will and probably no way to enforce anti-
abortion laws, some Catholics, like Father Robert Drinan in Boston,
have brought traditional Catholic legal points to bear in order to
lessen traditional Catholic opposition to liberalized abortion laws.
The moral position of these Catholics remains the same, but they recognize the lesser of two evils. They know that legalized abortion
means more legal abortions. But it also means fewer deaths of women
from illegal abortions. Father Drinan has even suggested the removal
of abortion from the field of legislation, provided there was an understanding that Catholic doctors would not be forced to perform operations to which they were conscientiously opposed.

I've tried to suggest the right to life of a fetus, from the moment
of conception on, is too narrow a basis for determining the morality
of abortion. Such a view doesn't differentiate sufficiently between
biological and human life, between potential and actual life; it leaves
out altogether the question of motive; and it links abortion to the
devaluation of all life in an unpersuasive manner. Now I want you to
consider one more statement: "Whether or not to have an abortion is
a medical question to be decided, like all other medical questions, by
the patient and her doctor."

Like the earlier statement of the Catholic Hospital Association, this
one too commends itself for its clarity. But unlike the statement of
the doctors, it shows no desire to affirm and protect more and more
of life, and—ironically—reduces the moral judgment of the doctors
to a mere medical one. Abortion is certainly a medical procedure, but
is it a medical question? If science is in no position to decide when in
the womb natural life becomes human, so science is in no position to
decide that unborn life is never human. That's a moral judgment; and
it's a bad moral judgment, in my view, to make the value of a fetus
solely dependent on whether or not the mother wants it. To be sure,
a fetus is part of a woman's body, but it is also not part of a woman's

body. If a man participated in its origin, and its destiny is to live on its own, how can it be considered merely a woman's property, like an ear, and its removal no different from the removal of any other tissue of a woman's body?

It has even been said that a woman's right to an abortion is an absolute right. Whether that means a legal or a moral right is not always clear. What is clear is that, whether legal or moral, an absolute right—one right taken out of the framework of all other rights—is what gets us into trouble. What is the opposite of a profound truth? Another profound truth. What is the opposite of a human right? Another human right. These are genuine dilemmas, and as I said a couple of weeks ago, the worst thing we can do with a dilemma is to resolve it prematurely because we haven't the courage to live with uncertainty. On this issue, as on the homosexual issue, I think we have to listen and think and read, pray hard, and reason together, all of us. I'm looking forward to the day when technology will be so advanced and society so enlightened as to make abortion unnecessary. In the meantime, I'm with everything said and implied in Margaret Mead's statement: "Abortion is a nasty thing, but our society deserves it."

If we follow Father Drinan's line of reasoning I think we may yet reach a widely acceptable legal position. I also think that, in the final analysis, it is the women themselves who have to make the decision whether or not to have an abortion. In other words, the legal question is to me relatively clear. But the moral question—under what circumstances to have an abortion—appears to me a complicated one. As to the question at what point, if at any stage, can unborn life be called human—I can't answer that. And if I remain as religious as I have been thus far, I may never be able to do so. In God's world there are mysteries known only to God. We may be "God's own people," but we shouldn't play God.

Being Called

SEPTEMBER 27, 1981
Readings: Exodus 3:1–12; 1 John 3:17

The call of Isaiah took place twenty-seven centuries ago, and Moses' even earlier. Obviously God has been calling a wide variety of people for a long time. Yet today confusion reigns. Today only clergy are "called"—generally at a slightly higher salary—which leaves doctors, lawyers, merchants, artists, social workers, teachers, Mom and Dad, people who have made their peace with society, people who have fled it, and still others who have vowed to overthrow it. Have none of them a calling? Aren't we all called? What exactly do we mean by a call from God?

If "God is love," then in responding to God we respond also to one another: the other members of our family, of our church, and of our circle of friends. But is that enough? Jesus said, "Inasmuch as ye have done it unto the least of these my brethren (and sisters) ye have done it unto me" (Matt. 25:40). To be converted by Christ is to be converted to the poor: to lives bleak and merciless, to people for whom there seems to be neither past nor future, only a meaningless present. There is no way that Christianity can be spiritually redemptive without being socially responsible. A Christian can't have a personal conversion experience without experiencing at the same time a change in social attitude. "Inasmuch as ye have done it unto the least of these . . ." God is always trying to make humanity more human. But without us he won't, just as without him we can't. So every time we lift our eyes to heaven and cry out, "O Lord, how long will the wicked flourish? How long will they utter and speak harsh things?" at that very moment you can be sure God is putting precisely the same question to us. So our calling is simply to help God protect, affirm, and dignify life—more and more of it.

To see how all this works out, let's turn to the opening twelve verses of the third chapter of Exodus. Here we read of God's well-known call—"Moses, Moses"—and Moses' reply, "Here am I." Moses has been playing essentially a spectator's role. In his youth he had been part of what today some would call "the struggle," but only impulsively; after killing the Egyptian guard he had fled. Then he entered what psychologists like to call "a period of consolidation." He went to Midian, married, had a fine boy, entered his father-in-law's business; he settled down. Suddenly in the midst of all that security he hears, "Moses, Moses . . . Come, I will send you"—right back into the thick of everything he had tried so hard to escape.

Let me offer a modern-day analogy. During the years I lived and worked in New Haven, Connecticut, I frequently took what was euphemistically called "The Express" to New York City. It was easy, I noticed, to remain a spectator as outside the window Fairfield and Westchester counties went by. But then the train slowed and pulled into the first New York stop, the 125th Street station. Now, outside the window, in place of Long Island Sound, gentle hills, and manicured lawns, was Harlem at its harshest—burned-out buildings, shabby signs, and on the streets truncated, embittered human life. Suddenly I felt myself drawn out of my spectator's role. I felt myself coming under some strange kind of judgment as I began to sense my own complicity in the evil I saw and abhorred. So it was a great relief when finally, instead of all those sad, passive, or angry faces, I saw my own reflected back as the train—thank God—entered the tunnel.

"Then the Lord said, 'I have seen the affliction of my people who are in Egypt, and have heard their cry because of their taskmasters; I know their sufferings and I have come down to deliver them out of the land of the Egyptians.'"

Even in far-away Midian, Moses could not turn a totally deaf ear to the cry of his own people. (That fine boy of his he had named Gershon, which means "I live as a sojourner in a foreign land.") His feet were in Midian but his heart was still in Egypt. In other words, God's call to Moses was embedded in a cry of pain, and it was a call to alleviate that pain by sharing it.

The same is true of the call that came to Samuel, to Elijah, Amos, Jeremiah, and Jesus as well—Jesus, who arose that day in the synagogue to read from Isaiah, "He sent me to proclaim release to the captives and recovery of sight to the blind" (Luke 4:18). Jesus delivered people from paralysis, insanity, leprosy, suppurating wounds, deformity, and muteness. But time and again in word and deed he returned to the plight of the poor—whose poverty, in true prophetic fashion, he considered no historical accident but the fruit of social injustice. What would he say in our hard and uncertain times, in a world one-half of whose children never so much as open their mouths to say "Aaah" to a doctor; a world in which almost every nation, our own included, is robbing the poor to feed the military? And what would he say to our spiritual deprivations, the poverty of our aspirations and expectations? The world with its triumphs and despairs, its beauty and ugliness, has today moved next door to every one of us. Therefore only spiritual deafness can prevent our hearing the voice of God in the clamor of the cities. Only blindness of a willful sort can prevent our seeing the face of Christ in the faces of the suffering poor.

But let us not be paralyzed by guilt. To our comfort let us recall that when Moses first received his marching orders he was not happy. Far from falling on his knees he reared up on his hind legs: "Who am I that I should go to Pharaoh, and bring the sons [and daughters] of Israel out of Egypt?"

How I love that cry of protest; it rings so true. We forget that a relationship that makes no room for anguished argument leaves little room for honesty either. We forget that premature submission is but a facade for repressed rebellion—which may be why so many Christians are so hostile!

And Moses wasn't the only prophet initially to resist. "Ah, Lord God," implored Jeremiah, "behold I do not know how to speak for I am only a youth"—words a modern-day prophet could well have repeated, for Martin Luther King Jr. was all of twenty-seven-years old when in the front of that bus in Montgomery, Alabama, "Rosa Parks sat down and all the world stood up."

But if there are reasons to resist, there are yet stronger ones to accept the call of God. In answer to Moses' objections, God says, "But I will be with you." Could God have been with Moses in the same way had Moses elected to stay stuck in Midian? Could Moses have become Moses? Jeremiah, Jeremiah? The Good Samaritan, the Good Samaritan? Just as the call of God is embedded in a cry of pain, so the acceptance of God's call is at one with our self-fulfillment. We give, but in return we receive so much—our whole identity. *"Cogito, ergo sum"*— "I think, therefore I am"? Descartes could not have been more mistaken. "I care, therefore I am." Caring is the greatest thing, caring matters most. In these hard and uncertain times, in a world as always so full of busy sinners and lazy saints, we are as we love. "We pass out of death into life because we love the brothers and sisters." Love is the name of our journey. It is love that measures the human stature. Deny it, beat it down, stifle it—still it lives, that love, in each and every one of us as a tiny spark that will not die; although of course it tortures terribly because all the odds are against its continual burning.

And we can go further: *"We* care, therefore we are the Church." What finally defines the Church is not the purity of her dogma but the integrity of her love. Remember the New Testament story of the paralytic: how four men—who moreover remain nameless—carry their desperately ill friend to the fount of all healing. In all of Scripture is there a finer symbol for the Church at its best? If Christ is God's love personified, the Church is God's love organized.

Essentially every church and every personal vocation represents love in search of form. As I read the lives of the Berrigan brothers, the message is not that everyone should do as they have just done (although Lord knows there is much to recommend civil disobedience as the only answer to the mad momentum of the arms race); the more enduring message is that we should not make our peace with the world as it is, but rather move to the creative edge of whatever estate we happen to occupy. In this city, for example, there are community organizers, doctors, teachers, politicians, cops too, Moms and Dads in wretched neighborhoods who are viewed by the inhabitants as bright lights in their dark streets. I know of a church in a run-down part of Philadelphia that has organized a community bank, and bought a radio to be a voice for the voiceless. I know businessmen whose money speaks, proclaiming literally the recovery of sight to the blind. And at their best these individuals and these churches are championing justice, seeking not only to alleviate the results of poverty, but more importantly to eliminate its causes.

What is worth living for is also worth dying for. Moses knew he'd be lucky to get out of Egypt alive. Martin Luther King Jr. wasn't lucky. And neither, more recently, was Archbishop Romero of El Salvador, who in a nationwide broadcast took on the junta of his long-suffering country: "I implore you, I beg of you, nay, I order you, in the name of God, stop the repression!" Within a week he was shot dead in a church. It is sad, terribly sad, when a good person dies, but is it tragic that people do not count their own lives dear and lay them down for their friends? "By this we know love, that he laid down his life for us and we ought to lay down our lives for our sisters and brothers" (1 John 3:16). Death is the meeting-place of all that lives, and while a natural death changes only the self, a martyr dies to change the world. The cross of Christ is more a symbol of life than of death, for it takes a lot of living to be selected as a target for martyrdom.

"Moses, Moses" . . . "Mary" . . . "John" . . . "Our Lady of Sorrows" . . . "Riverside Church"—fill in your own name and church. There is no question but that the air is full of calls, for the city, the nation, the world is full of pain. The only question is which of us, and which churches—after some stout resistance—will find the courage, imagination, and grace to reply, "Here am I" . . . "Here are we."

The Broken Body

OCTOBER 4, 1981
Readings: Isaiah 53:1–6; 1 Corinthians 12:12–24

A ll the members of the body, though many, are one body"—this is Paul's famous metaphor for the Church. On this World Communion Sunday, it is good to remember that there are many "bodies," metaphorically speaking, and that one of them is more important even than the Body of Christ, the Church: the world itself, which the

Church exists only to serve. It is a spiritual fact that all humanity is one. We belong to one another, on every continent and isle, all of us—black, white, yellow, and red, starved and stuffed, smart and stupid—all three billion of us, "though many, are one body." That's the way God made us. Christ died to keep us that way. Our sin is only that we are constantly trying to put asunder what God himself has joined together.

And furthermore, as St. Paul says elsewhere, "God is not mocked." It is a spiritual fact that all humanity is one, and it is a pragmatic fact that the survival unit in our time is no longer a single nation or a single anything; it is the entire human race, plus its environment. When I was young, people used to worry that one part of the world wouldn't be able to protect itself from another part. Now it's the whole that can't protect itself from the parts. So either we affirm our oneness by putting an end to war, or just as surely as the sun illumines the eastern sky, war will put an end to us.

But the body of humanity is broken not only by warfare. This weekend we at Riverside began our fall focus on racism, and all day yesterday we heard from the lips of one member after another the word "exploitation"—racism being "prejudice plus power." As I listened I thought of Procrustes, the legendary Greek brigand whose habit it was to lay his victims on a bed. If they were too short, he stretched them to fit. If they were too long, he lopped off their limbs. It occurred to me that not only American society, but the whole body of humanity is today stretched out on an economic Procrustean bed, economics these days being the primary measure of human stature. And having been declared expendable, the marginalized millions of the world are being lopped off. The ghettos are not a problem; they are a solution. Prisons are not a problem; they are a solution.

Are we having trouble balancing our American budget, given our insatiable desire for more and more weapons? Then by all means let's cut off a few more inches from society's legs—the improvident old, the unemployable young, the uninsured sick. "But," you protest, "the head cannot say to the foot, 'I have no need of you.'" Oh, yes it can, if the profit motive runs not only our banks but our hearts and heads as well. Small wonder that the Pope this week zeroed in on capitalist as well as communist economics; or that, at the meeting of the Commonwealth nations, when (Canadian Prime Minster) Trudeau counseled, "wisdom, compassion, cooperation, and patience," Nyerere (President of Tanzania) responded with a call for a new economic order.

As every African leader knows, that continent and others are being torn apart by exploitation. So if the Christian Church worldwide is to become what it is meant to be—strong at the broken places—then it is going to have to remember that the love of which it speaks (sometimes too glibly) lies always on the far side and never on the near side of justice. To Christians, justice is not a human option; it is a divine imperative.

We also talked yesterday of the Body of Christ, the Church; and specifically of Riverside Church. I think the consensus was that we were not vicious one to another so much as neglectful. Over 350 years ago George Herbert wrote: "For want of a nail, the shoe was lost; for want of a shoe, the horse was lost; for want of a horse, the rider was lost." Commenting on these words, Ben Franklin concluded, "A little neglect may lead to great mischief."

We are neglectful, for one thing, of the genuineness of our differences: whites still tend to view pluralism as assimilation. As one Black member said, assimilation means "trying to make Black people again invisible." "In sociological terms," said another, "assimilation declares whites the norm, and Blacks the deviants." We are also neglectful of the balance of power. If racism is prejudice plus power, then Blacks can only be bigots, not racists, because they lack the power of whites to oppress. Unwittingly, perhaps, the whites in this church have neglected to share their power sufficiently with Blacks. And there was a lot of talk of cultural differences. For instance, the vast majority of the hymns and anthems we use in the services were written by white males. Again, we unwittingly impose restrictions that rob us of the cultural riches of true pluralism. We agreed that we are all in cultural captivity, tending to love our forms more than we love our Lord. Will Kennedy told of visiting a modern church in Connecticut in which every architectural line was circular or curved—the architect being convinced, after much consultation, that the congregation was a genuine community, vulnerable and searching. The only right angles in the whole church were over the altar on the cross. Professor Kennedy asked the minister showing them around, "How do the members respond to their new building?" After a long pause the minister answered, "People sure love right angles."

While trying to be strong at the broken places of the world, we are not going to neglect the stresses and strains caused by racism in our own church, for every member is as a piece of paper on which a precious signature is written. And we will "hang in there," because he who came to show us the way will also see us through. The one broken body glorious to behold is the body of Christ himself, for while the cross reflects the power of sin it also lays bare the heart of God. Jesus is God made poor. Jesus is God made weak. Jesus is God become a martyr, because martyrs die to change the world.

The power of a suffering love, the "expulsive power of a new affection" (Horace Bushnell), Christ's love for us drives out our selfish loves and fears. We heard earlier how the one broken body mends all others: "He was wounded for our transgressions, bruised for our iniquities . . . *and with his stripes we are healed.*"

The Gospel hymns record the truth:

> Rock of Ages, cleft for me,
> Let me hide myself in thee.
> Let the water and the blood
> From the riven side which flowed
> Be of sin the double cure,
> Save from wrath, and make me pure.

Concerning communion services, there will always be talk of transubstantiation and consubstantiation. But don't look for Christ in the nouns; find him rather in the verbs: "This is my body *broken* . . . this is my blood *shed.*"

Then the peace of God which passes all understanding will cause all wars to cease within you, and make you one with the world. Then will the spiritual fact of human oneness have a chance of becoming the pragmatic fact of the nuclear age. Then the looted of the world may be restored their just deserts. Then will the head say to the foot not "I need you" but "I love you," with all the love with which we all are loved, even the love of God which we see in the broken body of Jesus Christ our Lord.

The Ultimate Form of Slavery[*]

OCTOBER 11, 1981
Readings: Isaiah 43:16–21; Acts 4:18–35

At two a.m. the other morning I looked through my apartment window down on 125th Street, which Maya Angelou once claimed was to Harlem what the Mississippi was to the South, "a long traveling river always going somewhere, conveying something." I saw a bunch of teenagers carrying batteries they had just liberated from

---

[*]This sermon owes much to Jim Wallis' *The Call to Conversion.*—WSC

parked cars. As they approached my car, I felt that surge of helplessness familiar to those of you who have been robbed.

But I had the wry satisfaction of registering their disappointment when under my hood they discovered no battery—because another crowd had beaten them to it about an hour before, which was why the car was sitting out there on 125th Street—a poor Rabbit become a sitting duck.

The next day I told the tale to a friend. He answered, "That's nothing. You know that old Buick of mine? Well, I blew the right rear tire the other night. So I pulled over to the side of the street and jacked up the rear. I was rolling the tire around when I saw the car start to shake. I looked up and saw a fellow had raised my hood and was going for my battery. 'Hey, what are you doing?' I cried. 'Easy, friend,' he said. "You work the rear and I'll take care of the front.'"

The city, the whole nation, is rapidly dividing into two camps—the anxiety-ridden and the poverty-stricken. The anxiety-ridden are increasingly possessed by their possessions, faced as they are with the increasing prospect of losing them, while the dispossessed, shut out of the good life, want desperately if only for a few hours to step right into the middle of the television commercials they see every night and help themselves. And when they fulfill such desires they don't feel that guilty. Most outlaws—the poor among them—carry in their hearts a sense of justice outraged; others have committed worse crimes and flourish. So they don't feel (as society likes euphemistically to describe them) "disadvantaged." They feel robbed. And in a way they're right, for the primary question facing every society is not how much the rich should give to the poor, but when they will stop taking from the poor.

It's not that street criminals are starving; the really starving people haven't the energy to rob. It isn't a question of nothing to eat, but of nothing to do, nothing that will provide alienated teenagers the excitement and self-esteem they get from looting, and then showing off their loot. I'm not trying to justify criminals; that's not the point. The point is that street crime is but the seamy underside of American consumerism. The point is that "the looting by the poor mirrors the looting of the poor" (Jim Wallis). The point is that street criminals share with boardroom managers and a lot of other people a common reverence for the supreme value of money and what it can buy, and that selfish acquisition is the common method—the only differences being the accepted rules of the games and the degree of success achieved by the players. The point is that almost all of us Americans—rich, poor, and in-between—are consumers *in excelsis*, holding the values of a consumer system without recognizing our subservience to it—which is, of course, the ultimate form of slavery.

This bondage is not new. Cyprian, the third-century Bishop of Carthage, described the rich of his time in this fashion:

> Their property held them in chains . . . chains which shackled their courage and choked their faith and hampered their judgment and throttled their soul. . . . If they stored up their treasure in heaven, they would not now have an enemy and a thief within their own household. . . . They think of themselves as owners, whereas it is they rather who are owned; enslaved as they are to their own property, they are not masters of their money but its slaves.

So when I plead with you, as I do now, to make a generous annual pledge to the church, I am not saying that the pledge represents the price you have to pay to be a member; it's the opportunity you have to declare yourself a child of God and proud of it, to declare some independence from the values of a consumer society by storing a part of your treasure somewhere outside it. And what part of your treasure should that be? Take one dollar a week and multiply it by the number of thousands of dollars in your annual income. If your annual income is $10,000, that's 10 times 52, or $520—5 percent of your income. That is what we're aiming for—5 percent of everyone's income. If it's $40,000, then 40 times 52 equals $2,080, or 5 percent. The most important thing, however, is that everybody give, and that nobody be ashamed they can't give more.

Is our goal of $600,000 realistic? If the average income in this church were the same as the average for New York City—that's $9,000—and every member pledged 5 percent, we would receive $1,033,375. Our goal is eminently reachable.

Almost all of the deacons and trustees have pledged, as has the collegium—for a grand total of $54,259, an increase of 21 percent over last year. Only in this instance would I plead with you to follow the leaders.

"The whole group of believers was united, heart and soul; no one claimed for his own use anything that he had, as everything they owned was held in common" (Acts 4:32). They were really together, those first Christians, one in heart, soul, *and money*. And they were far poorer than are we. But knowing that Christ had shed his blood for them, they were willing to water his vineyard with the sweat of their brows. May we, their descendants—in a time when faithful Christians are in short supply—be willing to do no less.

God is urging us toward care and compassion, not away from them. He wants us to affirm and dignify life, more and more of it. She wants us to create communities "aflame with faith and free," if consumed by the cleansing fire of the Holy Spirit, free from the need to consume everything from car batteries to each other's lives.

"Yes, I am making a road in the wilderness, paths in the wilds." By God's grace and with a little help from God's faithful we might indeed hail the day when 125th Street will be as a long and traveling river; and on both its banks will gleam an alabaster city undimmed by human tears.

Will the Every Member Canvass workers please come forward.

Sisters, brothers: I charge you to take your work with utmost seriousness, and yourselves with something less. Be diligent, but sensitive too; see souls, not just pocketbooks. Go for gratitude, not guilt. I hope this will be a process whereby we are once again knitted together by a sense of common cause, because never before in my lifetime have I seen compassion and generosity so threatened by mean-spiritedness. It is so important that we as Christians appeal to the generous self that is present in every one of God's children. Pledge generously yourselves, and then—may God bless your outstretched hands.

Single and Christian

OCTOBER 18, 1981
Readings: Psalm 27; Ephesians 4:25–31

What to talk about with so many things to celebrate: the 50th anniversary of the George Washington Bridge, whose structure is "so pure, so resolute, so regular that here, finally, steel architecture seems to laugh." So spoke Le Corbusier, who wasn't alone in considering the George Washington Bridge the most beautiful in the world. Then there's the 200th anniversary of the Battle of Yorktown, which completed in Virginia the work begun in Massachusetts five years before, when by "the rude bridge that arch'd the flood" the embattled farmers stood and fired "the shot heard round the world." And if your blood doesn't race and your eye grow dim at the very thought of what's going to happen in our town on Tuesday next, then you have either no youth left in your heart to renew or an undying hatred of the New York Yankees.

On the more sober side we might consider the first UN proclamation of Food Day, reminding us of all the preventable deaths we don't prevent; or we could recall the melee that took place only a few blocks away on Thursday when two thousand New Yorkers turned up to apply for 126 federally subsidized apartments. (How dramatically the pressure in New York is rising for decent, affordable housing!)

But I'm only going to signal these events, not dwell on them, because a few days ago a woman, young (by my standards) and divorced, made the suggestion that I say something about being single and Christian.

The woman, of course, could have been old and widowed, or younger and not married. She could have been any one of the 57 percent of our church members who are presently single. And maybe we shouldn't stop there but include everyone; for, finally, which of us is not a solitude, forced to bear the burden of freedom that makes it possible for each of us to be unique? Each of us is born alone and dies alone, and in between we stumble along in the footsteps of lonely literary prototypes like Abraham, Ulysses, and Faust. Jesus himself was only acting out this basic truth of human life when he forsook the safety of family, friends, and the ties of small-town life to live amidst his enemies and die deserted by every last one of his followers.

Surely then the first thing to be said about being single is that none of us should seek to escape the reality of our solitude. We shouldn't thrash around, grabbing for relationships. Be careful when you feel more yourself in the presence of others than when you are alone.

But if you're single *and Christian*, you have more to affirm than your solitude; you have yourself whom you must love as one made lovely through the love of Christ. That's not as easy as it sounds. Said Sigmund Freud: "It's a good thing people do not love their neighbors as themselves. If they did, they'd kill them"—which is what we're doing much of the time.

Do you really love yourself? I wonder if you'll cringe or say "Amen" to this quote of Maya Angelou: "I think it is wisdom itself to be good to oneself when things are going well, and absolutely imperative when things are going badly." How can you live alone with yourself without being good to yourself? And how can you love others without love for yourself—for love is the gift of oneself, and how will you make a gift of that which you hate?

"Love vaunteth not itself, is not puffed up" (1 Cor. 13:4). Paul makes the point: loving yourself with the love with which Christ loves you has nothing to do with being vain. There's a world of difference between loving yourself, being good to yourself, and being endlessly preoccupied with your self-worth. As bullies are really cowards, so people who are narcissistic are insecure. The original Narcissus, endlessly regarding his image in the pool, was responding to a sense of unworthiness with defiance.

Loving yourself with the love with which Christ loves you is what theologians call justification by grace, which is not the same as self-justification. Dietrich Bonhoeffer put it well: "Self-justification and judging others go together, as justification by grace and serving others go together."

I want to press a little further. Do you love yourself when your eyesight, your hearing, and your memory begin to fail, when you're arthritic and frail? Or do you feel humiliated by the weaknesses of old age? It's a test of faith to grow old without resentment, free of defensiveness, to lose power without an increase in self-pity. Remember that perfectionism can apply to age as well as sin, and that if God can find something noble in the ruins of a life ravaged by sin, how much more noble in Her sight are lives when "crooked eclipses 'gainst (our) glory fight, and time that gave doth now his gift confound."

Dear old people, you will remember what many today never learn, the song that starts "Believe me, if all those endearing young charms," and how it ends:

> Thou woulds't still be adored
> As this moment thou art,
> Let thy loveliness fade as it will;
> And around the dear ruin
> Each wish of my heart
> Would entwine itself verdantly still.
> Thomas Moore

That, dear old people, is a love song to you from God himself! To be single and Christian is to love oneself at all stages of life with the love with which Christ loves us.

But how really alone are we? Each of us is supported by memories as important to our personal lives as is the memory of Yorktown to our national life. We are today summoned by the sights and smells of an Indian summer and the sound of a Rachmaninoff anthem, as well as the laughter from the steel of the George Washington Bridge. And if we are spiritually alive and well we can anticipate joys of greater depth and duration than even the World Series. "Yea, I had fainted unless I had believed to see the goodness of the LORD in the land of the living" (Ps. 27:13). Daily we see, hear, feel, touch, taste this goodness.

And then there's the community of which Paul says we are members one of another. Paradoxically it is in church that we learn how to live alone—to be free, strong, and mature—just as it is when we are alone that we realize how properly to live with others. There is an interesting relationship between being alone and being in community: "Let him who cannot be alone beware of community. . . . Let him who is not in community beware of being alone" (Bonhoeffer).

Church is where all hearts are one so that nothing else has to be one. Church is where there's such a climate of acceptance that each of us can be his or her unique self. Church is where we learn to be free, strong, and mature by sharing with one another our continued bondage, weakness, and immaturity. Church is where we so love one another that it becomes bearable to live as solitudes. So when we are in church let us remember Paul's words: "Let all bitterness and wrath and anger and clamor and slander be put away from you, with all malice, and be kind to one another, tenderhearted, forgiving one another, as God in Christ forgave you." And when we're apart let us remember that we are never alone, for as the psalmist wrote:

"Wait on the LORD: be of good courage, and he shall strengthen thine heart: wait, I say, on the LORD" (Ps. 27:14).

I think we're going to make it—we who are single and Christian. I think we're all going to make it, we Christian solitudes, who love ourselves as those made lovely by the love of Christ.

It's a Sin to Build a Nuclear Weapon[*]

NOVEMBER 22, 1981
Readings: Psalm 9; John 7:53–8:11

> *"The nations have sunk in the pit*
> *which they made;*
> *In the net which they hid*
> *has their own foot been caught."*
>
> Psalm 9:15

And to those words from the Ninth Psalm let us add these of Winston Churchill: "The Stone Age may return on the gleaming wings of science, and what might now shower immeasurable blessings

[*]This sermon was delivered in Amsterdam, Holland, at the World Council of Churches Hearings on Nuclear Weapons and Disarmament, on November 22, 1981.

upon mankind, may even bring about its total destruction. Beware, I say, time may be short."

Time *is* short. Only yesterday we worried that one part of the globe couldn't protect itself from another part; today it's the whole that can't protect itself from the parts. Only yesterday nations at war targeted one another; today the whole world lives on the target. Our world has become a constantly wired and rewired, ever-ready bomb, and every day we wake up could well be the day it goes off—by accident. Yet Americans and Soviets continue to build weapons like the Trident submarine we Americans launched ten days ago, a ship which in an hour can kill many times more human beings than the six million Jews killed during the six years of World War II. It makes common sense blush. We're like alcoholics who know that liquor is killing them, yet always have a good reason for taking just one more drink.

"The Stone Age may return on the gleaming wings of science." Always tragic, war has now become preposterous. It is ridiculous to talk of a "defense" budget, a "Defense" Department, when there is no defense; to talk of national security when every attempt to enhance security by accelerating the arms race has inexorably diminished it. Neither the United States nor the Soviet Union is superior one to another; rather, both sides are weak to the point of helplessness before the threat of a nuclear holocaust. To stay the return of the Stone Age we have to realize that nuclear war simply isn't war—it's suicide. Hence it is a matter not for statesmen and generals to plan but for citizens to prevent. As for those who talk of a limited nuclear war, they are like a person walking into an ammunition dump, lighting a match, and saying, "Don't worry, I'm just going to blow up a few mortar rounds."

But Christians have more to say, something quite simple: God alone has the authority to end life on the planet—but human beings have the power. Since this power is so clearly not authorized by any tenet of the faith, Christians have to say that it is a sin not only to use, not only to threaten to use, but to *build* a nuclear weapon. The building and owning of nuclear weapons must be in the sight of the Almighty an abomination comparable to the buying and owning of slaves. Therefore in repentance lies our hope, the hope that we can recognize the crisis before it is validated by disaster. Repentance would give us two great insights not available to the unrepentant. The historian Herbert Butterfield wrote: "In the kind of world that I see in history there is one sin that locks people up in all their other sins, and fastens men and nations more tightly than ever in their predicaments, namely the sin of self-righteousness."

Self-righteousness concentrates all attention on the sins of others. Self-righteousness fights evil as if evil were something that arose totally outside of oneself. We Americans tend to think the sins of the Soviets so heinous that—by the standard illogic of comparison— their wickedness confirms our goodness. We are like the exultant Pharisees, who were prepared to stone to death the woman caught in adultery. Interestingly enough, Jesus doesn't dispute the sin, nor even the sentence of death. He simply suggests that it would be questionable for a person worthy of the death sentence to condemn anyone else to death: "Let him who is without sin among you cast the first stone" (John 8:7). He takes a conspicuous example of wrongdoing and uses it not to nourish our cherished self-righteousness but rather to bring awareness of the sin common to all human beings, and of the need we all share for repentance.

Today Jesus would not be "soft on communism," nor on capitalism. But I can hear him saying, "Let the nation without sin among you aim the first missile." Were we Americans truly to hear Jesus' words we would see that if we are not one in love with the Soviets at least we are one with them in sin—which is no mean bond, for it precludes the possibility of separation through judgment. Were we truly to hear Jesus' words, Soviet missiles would remind us of nothing so much as our own; Soviet threats to rebellious Poles would call to mind American threats to rebels in El Salvador; and Afghanistan would prompt us to remember Vietnam. Saved from self-righteousness by a vision of our common humanity and sin, might we not, like the Pharisees in the story, lay down our weapons?

"Ah, yes," some will protest, "but the Pharisees had nothing to fear from the woman; she was disarmed." The objection is valid, but it makes the point—fear is what arms us, not what disarms us.

For this reason deterrence is finally a disastrous policy. To induce fear is not the best but the worst possible way to avoid conflict. Here are the words of a far-seeing diplomat: "Fear begets suspicion and distrust and evil imaginings of all sorts till each government feels that it would be criminal and the betrayal of this country not to take every precaution, while every government regards the precautions of every other government as evidence of hostile intent." Spoken by British Foreign Minister Sir Edward Grey in 1913, those words describe a similar double standard today: *they* arm, it's evil; *we* arm, it's necessary for national security.

Deterrence is a disaster because "deterrence is not a stationary but a degenerative state" (E. P. Thompson). The repressed violence backs up into each nation's politics, economics, ideology, and culture. Fear increases selfishness. Fear refines ever more hideous weapons. Fear enlarges the government's control over its population and client states. Without doubt, the renewed Cold War of the 1980s is reinforcing the ugliest features in both American and Soviet societies. And we must remember a psychological factor: expectation without action becomes boring, so psychologically we are always pushed to fulfill our expectations.

Self-righteousness and fear—these are the twin enemies pushing us ever closer to the return of the Stone Age, the masters whom we cannot serve if we are to serve God as well. That is why I liked George Kennan's proposal—"an immediate across-the-board reduction by 50 percent of the nuclear arsenals now being maintained by the two superpowers." It makes the point that Enemy Number One is not the Soviet Union nor the United States but the weapons themselves. Would that our government were prepared with such a proposal when U.S. and Soviet representatives meet in Geneva on November 30.

But let us at least rejoice that during his speech of last Wednesday President Reagan's tone was less polemical than heretofore, that he talked of parity, not of superiority, and that he uncoupled arms control from Soviet good behavior. At the same time we must regret that he did not start the negotiations by taking action. The problem is not the stated willingness of both sides to negotiate; rather it is that neither side has demonstrated its readiness to disarm. How fine it would have been had President Reagan ordered suspension of work on the neutron bomb, or called home two hundred of the American bombers he did not mention in his speech and whose importance will now become the subject of endless and childish dispute. How fine it would be if tomorrow, from Bonn, President Brezhnev were to order the dismantling of some SS-20s. Given the devastating firepower that would remain, neither nation would be threatening its security, for let us never forget how totally false is the popular idea that nuclear deterrence only deters when it is precisely balanced at every level. (Whatever happened to the notion of sufficiency?)

It is also regrettable that negotiations are about to begin with the principal parties concerned not present. After all, it was the marching of European feet that produced these negotiations. I hope they will not rest, these feet—joined shortly by more American and Russian feet too—not rest until their peace-loving owners are properly represented in the negotiations, not until every last nuclear device has been removed from European soil, nay, from the face of the earth. Said President Eisenhower, "I like to think that people want peace more than governments. In fact, I think they want it so badly that one of these days governments had better get out of the way and let them have it."

It is a sin to build a nuclear weapon. In repentance lies our hope, the hope that we will recognize the crisis before it is validated by disaster. Either we quickly end the arms race or the arms race will surely end the human race. Of one thing only can we be more certain—of God's far-reaching mercy. To us today, as to that sad and lonely figure of long ago, come similar words of assurance and admonition: "Neither do I condemn you. Go and build nuclear weapons—no more."

The Greatest Hope

DECEMBER 6, 1981
Readings: Psalm 46; Romans 15:4–13

"May the God of hope fill you with all joy and peace in believing, so that by the power of the Holy Spirit you may abound in hope."

Romans 15:13

But how, we may well ask St. Paul, are we to abound in hope when hope and history seem destined never to meet? As just one example of this cruel and seemingly permanent divorce, consider the way this great, exciting, fun-loving city "trashes" its elderly poor. Sydney Shanberg described it poignantly in yesterday's *New York Times*—how rapacious landlords eager to mine the gold that lies in building luxury high-rise apartments hire goons to break down doors and smash furniture in order to drive out the "throw-away" people who occupy single-room occupancy hotels. All this I saw with my own eyes late Friday night on West 85th Street, where the rising tide of "gentrification" surges up Amsterdam Avenue, flooding every low-income apartment and small store, forcing dwellers and shopkeepers to flee ever further north.

And what of the rising tide of unemployment, crime, drug abuse—not to mention the inordinate number of recent deaths in our own parish? How are we to abound in hope when we remember that it is forty years almost to the day that the Japanese bombed Pearl Harbor, and that the bombs they dropped were as the lightning bug to the lightning compared to the two that ended the war—which in turn have paled into insignificance compared to the bombs that await us all at the end of the present countdown to destruction. I haven't mentioned the starving millions, the Soviets' shabby treatment of dissidents, the unleashing yesterday of the CIA. (When will the world ever realize that freedom's primary defense lies in its use?) If, then, hope and history seem destined never to meet, perhaps we should abandon the incorrigibly hopeful Paul and side with the person who said, "I used to be an incurable optimist, but now I'm cured."

Beset by similar unelevating thoughts, I entered last Sunday morning the Cathedral of Notre Dame in Paris. Immediately the organ reminded me of Riverside. The voices of the choir, I must say, were not comparable, but the rose windows were incomparable, enough to lift any sagging heart. When finally I was able to lower my eyes, they fell on a poster tacked to a bulletin board, on which was written words of that mystical paleontologist, Teilhard de Chardin: "The world will belong tomorrow to those who brought it the greatest hope" ("*Le monde appartiendra demain à ceux qui lui ont apporté la plus grande espérance*").

Since that moment hardly an hour has passed that I haven't thought of those words, for what can we bring to the world if not hope? If you ask me why I go to church, it is out of longing. I long to see myself, and you my friends, and this city, this country and earth fulfilled. My most insistent feeling is, "There must be something more." I don't search for truth wondering if it's there; I *know* it's there—if only I could find it. I *know* there's more light—if only the scales would fall from my eyes. I *know* there's more love—if only I could "let go and let God." I don't want Riverside to be an institution for those interested in things religious. I want it to irrigate the community with hope, because without hope we are all literally hopeless, creatures of despair. If we cannot feel something more, we become something less, just as if we cannot look to something above us, we will surely sink to something below us. So I'm with Teilhard de Chardin: "The world will belong tomorrow to those who brought it the greatest hope."

But who these days qualifies as a harbinger of hope? Given the pervasive injustice in the world, the Che Guevaras and the Camilo Torreses—dedicated, selfless revolutionaries who long to release "a second flood to wash the cities of the world"—are surely eminently qualified. But the hope they offer, though real, is limited, for so often those who say they want change really mean "exchange," as we have seen all too often in this century of revolutions gone sour.

Rightly, we continue to look to education as a source of hope. But again the hope has to be deemed limited, for again (as our century has also demonstrated), if a little education is dangerous, a great deal can be lethal. Only a Ph.D. can build a neutron bomb; and the brightest and the best brought us Vietnam. The moral and spiritual impulses that originally spawned institutions of higher education, like those that spawned hospitals, have somehow atrophied.

Disenchanted with secular humanism and with the political left, many these days in Christianity and Islam are joining the religious right. Our best hope, they say, lies in recapturing old-time values. It is a seductive belief in a chaotic world. But with old-time values go old-time structures of religious authority, and it was precisely the repressive dogmatism of these structures of religious authority that gave rise to secular humanism and the political left. It would be intolerable to return to the religious intolerance under which so much of humankind suffered and bled for so long—and suffers and bleeds today in Iran. Moreover, to demand, as do fundamentalists, individual obedience rather than individual thinking is to advocate a return to the nursery, rather than to a religion worthy of the name.

In undogmatic caring lies the hope of the world. It is the hope we celebrate every Advent, for, as St. Paul so clearly saw, embodied in that child is God's undogmatic caring for Jew and Gentile alike. Every Advent I'm stunned at the boldness of God's thought. Then, as now, the rich were greedy, the nations crazed with power; then as now, truth was on the scaffold, wrong upon the throne; and as the problem was clearly planetary, what any one individual could do was clearly limited. Then, to bring that person into the world in a place even dingier than an SRO hotel—it's scarcely credible.

But it's not really too hard to believe, just too good to believe, we being such strangers to such goodness.

Put yourself in God's place. What were the choices? How else would you bring hope into the world except through a person? How else would you make a statement about love, except through a person? And if you were God, how else would you disarm the power-crazed nations except by becoming yourself as disarming as a child? There is no strength in weakness—but what strength there is in a clearly voluntary renunciation of power! Isn't that the Godlike restraint the superpowers need today to understand and emulate? Just think: a little-by-little renunciation of power in order to defeat the great enemy of our day, distrust.

How else do you make a person trustworthy except by trusting her? It's a risk to trust the Russians, the Americans, but not a great risk, not compared to the risk God took in trusting all of us to respond to His voluntary renunciation of power, to His undogmatic caring. And that perhaps is the most hopeful thing we can say about the human race—that God is still willing to trust it, knowing that Christ today is real in the world through the bodies of ordinary men and women, or he is no more than a voice in the wind. The Incarnation says as much about what we are to become as it does about what God has become.

Shall we then not be hopeful?

There *is* more truth, and we can find it. There *is* more light, and we can see it. There is more love, and we can bring it everywhere, for that is what the Holy Spirit is here to help us do. We can bring love to education, for "even though I understand all knowledge and all mysteries . . . but have not love . . . I am nothing." We can bring love to dedicated revolutionaries, for "even though I give away all I have and give my body to be burned"—the very stuff of heroism—"but have not love, I gain nothing." And to the religious right, what can we say if not that the integrity of love is more important than the purity of dogma?

The Advent hope is that love, the long-distance runner, will outlast all competitors. The Advent hope is that love will never die—not with God, and therefore not with us. "Let the nations rage, the kingdoms totter . . . the LORD of Hosts is with us; the God of Jacob is our refuge" (Ps. 46:6–7).

A Habit of Caring

DECEMBER 13, 1981
Readings: Psalm 67; Matthew 3:1–12

Last Sunday the Advent banner read "Hope," and with Teilhard de Chardin we affirmed that the world tomorrow will belong to those who brought it the greatest hope. Not an easy affirmation to make then, it is even harder now amid the piling garbage, an all-too-obvious symbol of an age of municipal decay. But even outside the city, in suburban and rural settings, apprehension grows with the feeling that there is a storm approaching. As the snow buried New England last week, I remembered Robert Frost's poem "Storm Fear":

> I count our strength
> Two and a child,

Those of us not asleep subdued to mark
How the cold creeps as the fire dies at length,—
How drifts are piled,
Dooryard and road ungraded,
Till even the comforting barn grows far away,
And my heart owns a doubt
Whether 'tis in us to arise with day
And save ourselves unaided.

This Advent more than most our hearts own the Baptist's warning, "Even now the axe is laid to the root of the trees"—and Mighty America picking on Little Libya won't stay the progress of the blade for a moment. Nevertheless, "The world tomorrow will belong to those who brought it the greatest hope," for without hope, we become creatures of despair.

This Sunday we have a similarly difficult task—to proclaim love in a city and a world where people are being unloved to death. Here's a thought for evolution-denying Creationists: "The most shocking fact about evolution is not that we descend from something we probably wouldn't like to meet alone in a forest at night, but that something descends from us which we certainly wouldn't like to meet even at noon in a crowded street" (Ashley Montagu).

Today the banner reads "Love"—meaning love, Biblically understood. So much talk of love is wretchedly sentimental, lacking depth. It's all froth and no beer, sizzle but no steak. In thinking of God's love, what we forget to our peril is the absolute precondition to love, which is human freedom. No freedom, no love. In other words, God's love—all love—is self-restricting when it comes to power.

Let's look at some examples of this. Earlier we heard, "You brood of vipers! Who warned you to flee from the wrath to come?" These harsh words are addressed to the Pharisees and Sadducees, who share two common traits with all rulers, religious, political, and educational. In the first place rulers prove that while gratitude may not be a profound emotion, the expectation of gratitude most certainly is. (Parents too have that problem.) In the second place, rulers have a remarkable ability to flee responsibility when things go badly. After World War II people blamed God for the Holocaust. They should have been in the courtroom at Nuremberg where the high-and-mighty super-efficient Nazi overlords who ran the war and the Reich were busy blaming the next Nazi above them. Who warned them to flee from the wrath to come? As a terrible tribute to the *Führerprinzip*, it was only dead Hitler at the top who was guilty.

These Nazis, of course, were only repeating the oldest story in the world: "The woman thou gavest me, *she* gave me the fruit." And did not the woman say, "The *serpent* beguiled me"?

After experiencing the horrors of the Vietnam War, certain American veterans proclaimed they couldn't believe in God any more, as if it had been the will of God that they should have been over there in the first place. It is not the will of God that any human being die in a war, on a battlefield, and it is no exaggeration to picture Christ between the opposing lines, every bullet missile passing through his body.

Why does God let these things happen? Because God can't prevent them, love being self-restricting when it comes to power. If these human disasters grieve us, we can imagine how they break God's heart. But human disasters are the responsibility of human beings, not God. We can blame God only for giving us the freedom that, misused, makes these disasters inevitable. Often, I confess, I do blame God. I rail at God, saying, "Look, God, if you give an expensive watch to a small child, and the child smashes it, who's at fault?" But I have to recognize that if love is the name of the game, freedom is the absolute precondition. God's love is self-restricting when it comes to power. The Christmas story, more than any other in the Bible, shows us that we are going to be helped by God's powerlessness—or God's love—not by God's power. The Christmas story shows us that God *had* to come to earth as the child of Joseph and Mary, because freedom for the beloved demands equality with the beloved.

But is the choice really as I have set it up, between loveless power and powerless love? What did God hope to accomplish by coming to earth, a babe in a manger?

The other morning on the Phil Donahue Show, I listened to Ashley Montagu make one wonderfully outrageous remark after another. (In his pearly Oxfordian tones he said, "Psychiatry, you know, is the search for the id by the odd.") This seventy-eight-year-old anthropologist was on the show to promote his twentieth book, *Growing Young*, in which he contends that adulthood is our undoing. As long as we are young, says Montagu, we are "loveable, open-hearted, tolerant, eager to learn and to collaborate." We "can even be induced to play with one another. Most adults, however, are mortal enemies."

When adults become unloved and unloving, is it not because, like the Pharisees and Sadducees and other rulers, we have become defensive? So many of us are hardly out of diapers before we don suits of armor. Like our rulers, we believe that security comes through greater defense (show me a person who is in favor of bigger defense budgets and I'll show you a person who is personally defensive!). Yet at the same time, as Montagu recognizes, part of us longs to be more vulnerable, more childlike. I think one reason we so love babies is that their very helplessness is disarming. In primitive societies, children are almost never out of someone's arms—their parents' arms, the arms of older children—always being loved into being. When you hold a child in your arms, don't you feel *dis*armed? Close your eyes for a moment and picture yourself as one of the shepherds around the manger. Suddenly Mary says to you, "I'm cold, I have to find another shawl. Here, hold the baby for a moment." And there you are holding all that unguarded goodness in your arms. Don't you want to respond to God's vulnerability with a little vulnerability of your own?

But we can't become more vulnerable until we get rid of the guilt that helps make us so defensive. It is often scornfully said that the Church is a crutch. Of course it's a crutch. So what makes you think you don't limp? We confessed earlier, "We have talked a better game than we have played, judged others more harshly than we have judged ourselves." If this is true, isn't it a good thing we confessed it? But guilt is there to save us, not to destroy us. The point of guilt—which comes from the freedom we have misspent—is to direct us to forgiveness. Forgiven, we can become vulnerable. Unforgiven we can't. Forgiven, we're free to love again. Unforgiven we can't love, for love is the gift of yourself, and how will you make a gift of that which you hate?

What did God hope to accomplish?

This week a chief resident took me on a tour of a city hospital. In a bed in the intensive care unit lay a man in a coma, every imaginable tube stuck into him. On the bed was the familiar tag, another symbol of municipal decay: UBM—Unknown Black Male. (Just as often it's W for White or F for Female.) I asked how long the man had been there. "Almost three weeks now," a nurse replied. "No one has spoken for him. The police came yesterday to take fingerprints, but they still haven't been able to identify him." I asked the nurses how they felt about the stranger for whom they'd been caring without a word being exchanged. One of them said, "In a funny way, I've come to love this man. That's why I'd like to see the life supports removed." Later, at Grand Rounds, I asked the interns if they didn't get angry at having to get up in the middle of the night to take care of these indigents. They all recognized the problem; but, as one intern said, "We get mad all right, but we try to keep the anger focused on society, not on its victims." I thought, "Even in the mud and scum of things / There's always always something sings"—like love.

On Tuesday a frequent attender of this church had a massive heart attack on 43rd Street, and when he fell over backwards, a young man caught him, laid him down on the sidewalk and gave him mouth-to-mouth resuscitation. The police were there within five minutes, and in less than ten minutes the paramedical unit arrived. They took him to the hospital, where the emergency team tried to get his heart started again—but to no avail. When I went to see his wife later on, she told me, "You know, they all waited for me at the hospital. The young man who caught him wanted to tell me that he was absolutely sure my husband was totally unconscious, and that he didn't hit the sidewalk. The paramedics wanted to tell me that everything that could be done had been done. The doctors wanted me to know that he was dead before he reached the hospital. The police wanted to make sure I was all right, and to see if I needed a ride home." She said, "You know, in a funny way, Bill, I think in this last hour I have seen some of the finest people I have seen in ten years in New York."

"The world belongs tomorrow to those who will have brought it the greatest hope" because they showed it the greatest concern. In both cases the people who had helped were strangers, but they had a habit of response, a habit of caring. Who knows how many of these people believed in God—off the top of their heads. But from the bottom of their hearts they were responding to the kind of love embodied in Christ whom we await in two weeks.

Made vulnerable and forgiven, we are also empowered by the love that is of God. Love is not powerless: on the contrary, "for I tell you God is able from these stones to raise up children to Abraham." We could stay the axe from being laid to the root of the trees were we to allow the glory-beaming star to illumine our night; were we to cease crying, "I want mine, now, more," and start building, not a more competitive, not permissive, but a loving society. And what else but that should we be about this harsh but promising Advent season?

If we fail in love, we fail in all things else. The world tomorrow will belong to those who brought it the greatest hope, because they showed it the greatest love.

The First Fruit of Love

DECEMBER 20, 1981
Readings: Isaiah 53:1–5; Matthew 1:18–23

Two weeks ago we celebrated hope, in a world in which hope and history seem destined never to meet. But *biblically* hope is not the same as optimism; its opposite is not pessimism, but despair. Hope is the sole precondition for a new and better life for all—but without any guarantee that such an existence will come into being. As hope is totally independent of results, we can always go on being hopeful, always undefeated, if only because we go on trying. Just as all the water in the sea can't sink a boat unless it gets inside, so all the despair in the world can't sink you unless it seeps into your soul.

Then last Sunday we celebrated love—not the sentimental kind symbolized by Cupid, an infant in diapers, blindfolded to boot; but the unguarded goodness of the child Jesus that disarms us, God's vulnerability that makes us want to respond with some of our own. Like hope, love too doesn't depend on results; fortunately so, for to the question "Why do you continue to knock yourself out when no one responds?" the answer is, "I figure God's got the exact same problem with every one of us."

Today, the last Sunday in Advent, the banner reads "JOY." Of the three, joy is perhaps the easiest to affirm, because the joy that is of God unites most easily with pain. Two years ago in Tehran I suggested to our American hostages that the only good thing to be said for that worst of all possible Christmases was that it most nearly resembled that first Christmas. Were they up for it, they were in the best position to grasp the real meaning of Christmas joy. That first Christmas was miserable for everyone involved. The Christ child, we read, was in the manger "because there was no room for him in the inn." But that, of course, is nonsense. There was all the room in the inn for him, only no one—or so thought the innkeeper—would make room for a woman about to give birth. The ox and the ass we tend to view as picturesque guests who, with the shepherds, just had to come along and see what had happened. But they were not guests at all. This was their home; he who was to be bread of life for human beings was laid in the feedbox of animals.

Nevertheless, "Joy to the world," because our inhumanity to one another and God notwithstanding, "the Lord is come." At the beginning as at the end of Christ's life, human beings come off badly. But God comes off wonderfully, giving each of us the first and finest Christmas present of them all—himself, wrapped in swaddling clothes. As all the joy of Christmas comes from on high, it is quite proper for "Joy to the World" to start on a high D and come down the scale until it reaches us, a full octave lower.

Let's look at our text: "Now all this took place to fulfill the words spoken by the Lord through the prophet: 'A virgin [or young woman] shall conceive and bear a son, and his name shall be called Emmanuel' [which means, God with us]" (Matt. 1:22–23). More specifically, how does divine joy unite with human pain? Try to recall in your own life moments of great pain, suffering, terrible confusion. You know that at such moments there is nothing more important than the simple presence of someone who cares. It is not necessary that the person give you advice or try to cheer you up. In fact, it's better that they *not* try to give you advice and cheer you up, because that advice and cheer is usually experienced as a refusal to enter into the sadness of your situation. Nor is it desirable that the person should fall apart, simply because you may well have fallen apart. Doctors tell you they are afraid of becoming too emotionally involved with their patients, but the fact is they're identifying more with their patients' diseases than with the patients themselves.

Twenty-one years ago I almost died of a combination of pleurisy and pneumonia, and for days was barely conscious. Every day my predecessor, the former chaplain of Yale, a man then in his seventies, quietly entered the room, pulled up a chair, and said, "Don't say a word, Doctor. I'm just going to sit here a few minutes." And he'd take my hand without himself saying another word. It was consolation itself.

That's the way it is with Emmanuel, God with us. Christ is always with us, sensing our suffering with perfect sensitivity. Only of Jesus can you say, "He knows exactly what I'm going through." Not necessarily giving advice or even saying a word, he is simply present to us in the most intimate possible way, transforming situations of sorrow into sources of joy.

How else does divine joy unite with human pain? Earlier we sang:

> Come, thou long-expected Jesus,
> Born to set thy people free.
> From our fears and sins release us,
> Let us find our rest in thee.

We also heard, "You shall call his name Jesus, for he will save people from their sins." Perhaps the worst form of psychological pain is the guilt that comes with sin. I imagine some of you here are suffering some terrible guilt for an action you consider totally unforgivable. But that word "unforgivable" is itself totally unforgivable, because it is precisely what cannot be condoned that *must* be forgiven.

Emmanuel is God with us, not only to comfort us in tragedy but also to forgive us in our sin. Jesus doesn't approve our sins, nor does he relieve us of the consequences of our sins. But he does relieve us of the consequences of being sinners. Through forgiveness he gives us a new beginning, another chance to love, and if you've ever had the humility to be forgiven, then you know that like unto that joy there is none. It's so totally a gift, something for nothing. If you are feeling desperate about a deed you consider unforgivable, let God this year make you a Christmas present of forgiveness. So of joy, divine joy, we can say that whether it is experienced in tragedy or in sin, it is that which survives when all your worst fears have been realized. Joy is that which still burns brightly when the sorrows of the world sweep over you like a sea. What Scripture says of love can as well be said of joy: "Many waters cannot quench it; neither can the floods drown it" (Song 8:7a). That's the real joy of Christmas, the kind the hostages could still celebrate in a faraway country in captivity—if they were up for it; the kind we too—if we are up for it—can all celebrate in whatever captivity is ours today.

But joy can also unite with happiness. Far from denying happiness, joy is its true foundation, infusing pleasure with meaning. It's easy, particularly for preachers, to take off after the happy drunk and say, "You're not really happy," when obviously he's feeling no pain. But fundamentally, pleasures that are an escape from reality lack meaning. They lack purpose. The joy that is of God, on the other hand, infuses earthly pleasures with a foundation of meaning. The Emmanuel we await is not a John the Baptist dedicated to locusts and honey in the desert. Jesus will be called "a glutton and a drunkard." In the Gospel of John, which depicts Christmas so starkly—"He was in the world and . . . the world knew him not. He came unto his own home and his own people received him not" (John 1:10–11)—Jesus first visits human beings at a wedding feast. He visits them first not in their sorrow but in their happiness. And whether you believe he turned the water into wine is not as important as the understanding that Jesus believes in happiness. He is full of joy as well as sorrow, for the greater one's capacity for sorrow the more one is capable of joy.

Believe me, if you know some gloomy Christians they are gloomy not because they are Christian but because they are not Christian enough. It's amazing how many people have only enough religion to make themselves miserable! Let us recall that "the poor are called blessed not because poverty is good, but because 'theirs is the kingdom of heaven'; the mourners are called blessed not because mourning is good, but because 'they shall be comforted'" (*Compassion*, by McNeil, Morrison, and Nouwen). In the same fashion we can say, "Blessed are the guilty, for they will not be destroyed but saved from their guilt"—if they understand what forgiveness is all about.

All of which suggests that finally joy really has little to do with happiness or unhappiness, pleasure or pain, and everything to do with meaning and self-fulfillment. Didn't Paul write of Jesus that "for the joy that was set before him, he endured the cross"? How paradoxical, and how true. And that brings us back to the love embodied in that child in the manger, the love that "bears all things, believes all things, hopes all things, endures all things," the love that is the name of our human journey. Because it is in loving that we find life's deepest meaning, a meaning that can be affirmed this very day in the face of tragedies we cannot fathom and in the face of human stupidities we cannot fathom and in the face of human stupidities we can understand all too well. The highest purpose of faith is to make people loving— by choice. And the first fruit of love is joy, the joy of self-fulfillment.

So, dear Riversiders, may your Christmas be joyful and hopeful and loving. May our Christmas be one in which we can be present one to another in tragedy, sin, and happiness as God is present to each of us in Emmanuel.

> Come, thou long-expected Jesus,
> Born to set thy people free.
> From our fears and sins release us,
> Let us find our rest in thee.

Extending Christmas

DECEMBER 27, 1981
Readings: Isaiah 40:1–5; John 1:1–17

Let's hear again that opening statement of the prophet (generally referred to as Second Isaiah) whose name is unknown, but whose words work their way powerfully each Christmas into the hearts of believers and nonbelievers alike—especially when they're accompanied by Handel's music.

> "Comfort ye,
> Comfort ye my people," saith your God.
> "Speak ye comfortably to Jerusalem,
> And cry unto her that her warfare is accomplished,
> That her iniquity is pardoned."

Whenever a suffering person or a sick world cries out in anguish, few words, I imagine, offer greater comfort. Spoken over twenty-five centuries ago, they speak still of a joy that can heal all scars, of a hope that can absorb all rebuffs, of a future that can be so much better than what we know at present. The words go straight to the heart of each of us because they seem to come straight from the heart of God, affirming what's always so hard to believe—that the power that set the stars in orbit knows you by name, that He who knows all cares most.

Of course, what makes that so incredible is only that our ways are not God's ways, nor our thoughts hers. According to our way of thinking, the higher the boss the less time he or she has for the little folk down below, for little ol' me. Therefore God at best must be remote.

But that's the human way of thinking. By contrast, in the divine dispensation "the very hairs on your head are numbered." In the divine dispensation, God cares for all as if all were but one. In the divine dispensation, the higher the boss the more he cares about little ol' you.

And here's another reason why God is so close to you, closer than any human being: God is the only one in your life who will never compete with you. Earlier we heard the choir sing, "Love came down at Christmas / Love all lovely, love divine." And all of us have sung the words of Charles Wesley: "Jesus, thou art all compassion / Pure unbounded love thou art." But we human beings are all competition—or almost all. We define ourselves by our differences, by the distinctions we achieve, by the trophies we win or don't win. Just to say we want to be rich is nonsense. We want to be richer, smarter, more talented, better-looking. We even develop complexes along competitive lines, such as the "more radical than thou" complex that vexes the peace movement. And let us not overlook the "guiltier than thou" complex, of all complexes surely the most insufferable. In other words, in defining ourselves by our differences, we define ourselves in ways that require us to maintain a distance from each other. And that is why God is so much closer to us than we are to each other: compassion erases the distance competition has to maintain.

At the Riverside staff Christmas service last Wednesday, I quoted what Hubert Humphrey told three Catholic priests who came to see him in his senate office shortly before his death. They asked him to talk about compassion. The Senator picked up a long pencil with a small eraser at its end. "Gentlemen," he said, "look at this pencil. Just as the eraser is only a very small part of the pencil and is used only when you make a mistake, so compassion is only called upon when things get out of hand. The main part of life is competition; only the eraser is compassion."

The beauty of Christmas is that it is all eraser. Christ comes to erase our mistakes, to rub out our sins. And the beauty of Christmas is that we get the message. We remember—if only for a little while—that the world from which we usually take things for ourselves is also a place where we can find happiness in bringing happiness to others. Sometimes we actually do deeply Christian things, as when those who have offended repent, and those who are offended forgive. In short, at Christmas we comfort one another with the love with which we are comforted by God. "'Comfort ye, my people,' saith your God." Less competitive and more compassionate, we draw closer to one another at Christmas than at any other time of year.

Now—two days after Christmas—the challenge is to extend that time, to lengthen the eraser. Going back to Second Isaiah, you remember that the first voice cried that our warfare is ended, our iniquity pardoned. But now, "A voice cries in the wilderness" (it is not going to be easy), "prepare ye the way of the LORD. Make straight in the desert" (where the sands are always shifting) "a highway" (no small way) "for our God. Every valley shall be lifted up and every mountain and hill made low. The uneven ground shall become level and the rough places a plain, and the glory of the LORD shall be revealed and all flesh"—not just you and I and a few others, but all flesh—"shall see it together for the mouth of the LORD has spoken it."

With the comfort from God comes a calling to us, a calling to be witnesses to God's design. And what God has joined together let no one put asunder. So enough of this false quietism we see around us that tries to pass itself off as piety, this otherworldliness that watches the world go to hell while we Christians prepare to go to heaven. Let us not forget that the love of God represents no sentimental readiness to give us what we want, but rather a passionate yearning to raise us up to Christ's own likeness. The Incarnation we celebrated two days ago speaks to what we are to become, as much as it says about what God has become.

When I was chaplain at Yale, what most put me off was the way professors and parents patronized youth. A father once said to me, "You know, my son is really the perfect sophomore, asking all these big questions." I couldn't help answering, "And when did you stop?" (Tolstoy once said: "Certain questions are put to humankind not that people should answer them, but that they should spend a lifetime wrestling with them.")

Today I feel much the same way. So many people my age disparage youthful dreams as if we old codgers know better. We don't know better, we know worse! Having imbibed despair, or just grown lazy, or having lost the art of removing the "daily" from living, we accept the gloom of the present as a permanent condition. We've abandoned the dreams of our youth and embraced a yet greater foolishness—the belief that all there is is all there is to be.

Let's turn now to the New Testament lesson for its extraordinary realism. The Apostle writes, "The true light that enlightens (everyone) was coming into the world." And then come these two devastating sentences: "He was in the world, and the world was made by him, yet the world knew him not. He came to his own home, and his own people received him not." But that's not the end of it. "To all who received him, *who believed in his name*, he gave power to become children of God." What an extraordinary balance: faith, despair, pessimism, hope.

Look at the way people all over the world are responding to what's going on in Poland today.* I'm sure it's partly because it's Christmastime, and they've gotten the message. They're not just cursing the darkness, they're lighting candles as symbols of the unquenchable light of Polish freedom. They're sending food and clothing to Poland and to the more than fifty thousand refugees in hospitable Austria.

It's infectious, this Christmas spirit, this spirit of compassion rather than competition. Four of us the other day were discussing how wrong it feels to see Polish hams for sale all over New York City, while Poles are starving in their own country. So we cooked up a scheme. Tomorrow we're going to try to get through to the presidents of some big supermarket chains, and ask them if they would announce that during the first week of January all the profits from the sale of Polish hams to American people would be converted into money to buy food for the Polish people. If any of you have any good ideas or want to help, do come forward after the service and meet with C. J. Everitt in front of the pulpit

"But to all who received him . . . he gave power to become children of God." Half the time I suspect things are much more complicated than we think and the other half I'm convinced that if we get the Christmas message, everything is really quite easy. We could even end the arms race—easily. At the hearings of the World Council of Churches in Amsterdam last month the Kennan proposal came up—a 50 percent cut across the board in all nuclear weapons by the United States and the Soviet Union. When the church leaders inquired how that proposal could be implemented, given the asymmetrical nature of parity, a cheerful Italian scientist said brightly, "Just adopt the archaeologists' principle." He was pressed to explain. "When archaeologists

---

*On December 13, 1981, the government of the People's Republic of Poland imposed martial law on the country.

undertake digs in another country, they must agree to leave behind 50 percent of what they dig up. But how do you determine 50 percent of a batch of assorted pottery, fragments of parchment, and scraps of fabric? It's easy. You ask the archaeologists to divide their find into two piles. Then the customs official looks them over and says, 'I'll take that one.' Since the Soviets and the Americans each know full well what the other has, they could easily do the same. One side could make two piles, and the other could choose." It's not that difficult, once you get the Christmas message. Then you're more interested in compassion, which stimulates imagination, than in competition, which shuts off all kinds of creative thought.

It's infectious, this Christmas spirit, this finding happiness in bringing happiness to others. We saw it so beautifully symbolized in the candlelight service last Sunday, when the light from the main candle on the altar was passed from candle to candle throughout the choir and down to the congregation. We saw that as one light lights another, nor grows less, so love enkindles love.

On Christmas the "true light that enlightens everyone" came into the world. We don't want to be part of the darkness that to this very moment has not overcome it. No, we want to be part of the light, to become children of God. So let's continue to stay close, be less competitive and more compassionate, erasing one another's sins as God has pardoned our own iniquity. Having freely received so much comfort, let us also freely receive our calling. And let's see if together, in the wilderness of our time, we can prepare the way of the Lord.

1982

What Made the Wise Men Wise?

JANUARY 10, 1982

Henry David Thoreau once claimed that for every virtuous person there were nine hundred and ninety-nine patrons of virtue. Let me suggest that for every person who is truly wise there are at least nine hundred and ninety-nine who are merely clever. And I could add that the world is in its present mess in large part because of that clever person so many of us see in the mirror. As the difference between wisdom and cleverness is crucial, let's see if we can find it by asking, "What made the Wise Men wise?"

Certainly they were educated, but it is just as certain that education alone can't make a person wise. In this city it's all too obvious that the wisdom of those who are not educated is matched only by the folly of those who are. In fact, in the rarefied reaches of today's scholarship, wisdom is often lost in knowledge, as knowledge is lost in information. A poet, exceedingly well educated, wrote:

> All our knowledge brings us nearer to our ignorance,
> All our ignorance brings us nearer to death;
> But nearness to death, no nearer to God.
> Where is the life we have lost in living?
>
> T. S. Eliot

That's the business of the wise—to rediscover that which has been lost and found and lost again and again: the meaning and deep purposes of life. These are not automatically uncovered or even sought for in today's education, which is so often for a living, not for life. In school you can find out everything about the world, except "Why?" For "Why?" is a religious question, whether or not you give it a religious answer. A wise person, then, is always looking for the meaning and deep purposes of life. She may doubt the quality of the bread but she doesn't kid herself that she isn't hungry. She knows that the surface of life is just that—superficial; and she knows that life's meaning and purposes are embedded deep in mysteries, as real as they are uncertain. A wise person knows that the meaning of life is apprehended on a far deeper level than it is comprehended; that there are truths in the presence of which the mind can play an all-important legislative role, but not a creative role. A wise person knows there are truths the mind can indeed grasp, but there are other, more important ones before which human beings can only bow down. Those Wise Men did not come to study the child, but to worship. So let us say they were wise, first of all, because they recognized the importance of a religious question and were willing to go a long way to find the answer.

Of course they weren't the only ones seeking the child. King Herod too was interested, if for very different reasons. He wanted to kill, not worship, the child. Herod was certainly clever, but nobody has ever accused him of being wise. So perhaps we can go on to say that as opposed to cleverness, wisdom is always rooted in compassion, a definition that doesn't make the latest moves of the Reagan administration appear wise. (I have in mind cutting thousands more off welfare; counting food stamps as income; and, reversing a policy of eleven years, giving tax relief to schools that discriminate against Blacks and Orientals in the name of Scripture. Someone should remind Mr. Reagan of Pascal's assertion: "People never do evil so cheerfully as when they do it from religious conviction.")

Wisdom is rooted in compassion. Someone once asked Gandhi, "What do you think of Western civilization?" He answered, "I think it would be a good idea." His answer suggests that civilization is but a long process of learning to be kind. Here's what Norman Cousins wrote recently: "The highest expression of civilization is not its art but the supreme tenderness that people are strong enough to feel and show toward one another." I like his recognition of the fact that only the truly strong can be tender. And I like his conclusion: "If our civilization is breaking down, as it appears to be, it is not because we lack the brainpower to meet its demands but because our feelings are being dulled. What our society needs is a massive and pervasive experience in resensitization."

Rooted in compassion, wisdom always respects the importance and fragility of individual life, and cares for all individuals, in the manner of Christ, as if all were but one. According to tradition, the Wise Men came from different countries, and they came, of course, to worship him who was to be the light of all nations. A wise person, then, knows that the most significant thing you can say about human differences is that they are not that significant. What *is* significant, and needs desperately to be made manifest, is the oneness of humanity.

As we read on the first page of the order of worship, "Epiphany is the service in which the theme of light reaches a climax." But the light we remember and celebrate today was no blazing sun but a more distant, fainter light, glowing in darkness.

> The bright light blinds
> The half-light dulls the edge of things
> But darkness challenges the eye.
>
> Peter Weiss

A wise person accepts the challenge of the darkness and develops a catlike ability to see at night. Not much of significance is clearer in our world than it was in the world of the Wise Men. Good and evil continue their incestuous relationship. As always, nothing is easier than to denounce the evildoer, and nothing is more difficult than to understand him. It is of course emotionally satisfying to denounce enemies. God knows it is emotionally satisfying to be righteous with that righteousness that nourishes itself in the blood of sinners. But God also knows that what is emotionally satisfying can also be spiritually devastating. And it is spiritually devastating to claim more light than is shed by God upon the human situation, to project a brief, narrow vision of life as eternal truth. Life doesn't sit around to have its portrait painted, and besides, who could ever catch its shimmering depths? Said F. Scott Fitzgerald: "Show me a hero, and I'll write you a tragedy."

The wise don't pretend to know it all. They know that you don't have to think alike to love alike. The message they read from the Star is that only love makes sense, and not much else makes any difference.

So here's to a new crop of wise men and women, who will go to great lengths to find life's meaning and deep purposes; who will never forget that wisdom is rooted in compassion; and who, instead of cursing the night, will develop a catlike ability to see in the dark, in order to follow that God-given light that no darkness can overcome.

Leaving Home

JANUARY 17, 1982
Reading: Mark 1:1–11

It would warm my heart to preach a sermon that would honor those who have already been baptized, honor those who in a few minutes will be joining this church, and honor as well the memory of Martin Luther King Jr., whose fifty-third birthday we celebrated Friday. Let's take as a text this sentence from the first chapter of the Gospel of Mark: "In those days Jesus came from Nazareth of Galilee and was baptized by John in the Jordan" (Mark 1:9).

I never cease to marvel how Mark's simple, straightforward sentences turn out to carry enormous spiritual freight. Measured by miles, the distance from Nazareth to Jordan was short. But measured spiritually, the journey must have been incredibly long and arduous. For thirty years—as best we can tell—Jesus had lived at home. For at least half of those years he must have been helping his father fill orders in the carpentry shop. Then suddenly he decided to be baptized, but not to reinforce this filial piety so often held up to Christians as an admirable thing. No, he wasn't planning to return home at all, which suggests that adult baptism or joining a church means not so much renouncing your wild oats and settling down as abandoning your parents and home town (a suggestion not made in our churches with great regularity).

Marriage services generally include this statement: "Our Savior has declared that a man will leave his father and mother and cleave unto his wife." It's the kind of statement that makes psychiatrists who are atheists leap to read the Bible, for as one confessed, "There are more psychological insights in the Bible than in the collected works of Freud." The insight here is profound: "A man will leave his father and mother and cleave unto his wife" means that the bride, in marrying the groom, should not be marrying her future mother-in-law or father-in-law. In marriage counseling nothing is more important than establishing the freedom of the bride and groom to make their own decisions independent of their parents. This doesn't mean that they are defying their parents. Defiance may be a first step toward freedom, but it is not freedom achieved; you're only free when you no longer have to defy. When from the cross Jesus says, "Father, forgive them for they know not what they do," that's not defiance, that's freedom. When under a death-dealing rain of stones St. Stephen cried out, "Lord, do not hold this sin against them," that's freedom. When Jan Hus at the stake in 1415, observing an old peasant bringing yet another stick to throw on the pile, murmured "*O sancta simplicitas!*" (O holy simplicity!), that's freedom. Martin Luther King Jr. loved white folk because he didn't have to hate them; that's freedom.

Actually in the traditional marriage service the father of the bride is asked to act out this separation of parents and children: "Who giveth this woman to be married to this man?" Standing behind the bride, the father steps forward, takes his daughter's hand, gives it to the minister (symbolizing the church) and then takes his place in the congregation with everybody else. To preserve the symbolism and avoid the sexism, you have only to change the service so that the groom too is given away.

If a man and a woman leave their parents when they decide to join each other in marriage, should they do less when they decide to join Jesus?—which is what joining a church and adult baptism is all about. Didn't Jesus himself insist with seeming cruelty, "He who loves father and mother more than me is not worthy of me"? It seems to me that in joining a church you leave home and home town to join a larger world. The whole world is your new neighborhood and all who dwell therein—black, white, yellow, red, stuffed and starving, smart and stupid, mighty and lowly, criminal and self-respecting, American or Russian—all become your sisters and brothers in the new family formed in Jesus. By joining a church you declare your individuality in the most radical way in order to affirm community on the widest possible scale. That's what we learn not only from the baptism of Jesus but from the life of every prophet from Moses to Martin Luther King Jr.

Why did Jesus choose that particular moment? We can only guess. No doubt long months of preparation preceded his decision, and probably John the Baptist had something to do with it. While God sometimes speaks to us directly, as to Moses, God's voice also reaches us through the actions of other people, as God reached Martin Luther King Jr. through Rosa Parks, who in 1957 in the front of a Montgomery, Alabama, bus "sat down, and the whole world stood up."

I can't even remember the name of the student who in April of 1961 late at night in a kitchen in North Carolina told me his story of a sit-in at a Greensboro lunch counter: "The five of us came in and sat down on what empty stools there were. Pretty soon the man behind the counter slipped out. In the mirror I could see the crowd begin to gather on the sidewalk outside. Then the other folks on the stools began to go out whether they had finished or not, and without paying, seeing there was no one left to pay. The five of us moved together for a little warmth. Then in the mirror I was relieved to see the police. But no sooner had they appeared than they disappeared, deliberately. That was the signal. The crowd began to come in. You could just smell their anger. Some of them began to shout insults into one of my ears while from the other side a guy starts to blow cigarette smoke into my eyes. I'm gripping the counter. Then the guy with the cigarette puts it out on the back of my hand. I think I'm going to faint. Then I feel a knee in the middle of my back, then an arm around my neck. Someone is pulling my hair, hard. Pretty soon I'm on the floor, trying to stay curled up in a ball. They were really kicking us. When we were practically unconscious, the police reappeared and arrested all five of us lying on the floor for disturbing the peace. In jail they roughed us up some more, just for good measure. Then came the best part. When I got out I called home and my mother told me, 'Good Negroes don't go to jail.'" I can't remember his name, but he made it easy for me to go on a freedom ride the following month.

God calls so many of us through other people. When Bishop Matthiesen of Amarillo, Texas, told the press he thought the neutron bomb immoral, I called him immediately. "What prompted you to say that?" I asked. "A good question," he replied, "seeing I've been here for twelve years and never opened my mouth. But a man who worked in the Pantex factory came to me awhile back for spiritual advice. 'Bishop,' he said, 'I think this bomb we're assembling here in Amarillo is immoral.' That put the matter on my conscience. Weeks later I figured he was right and that I ought to say so publicly."

In adult baptism and in joining a church we assert our individuality in the most radical possible way in order to affirm community on the widest possible scale. And throughout our lives we are called by God to repeat this action, sometimes directly, sometimes through other people. James Russell Lowell wrote a hymn about this.

> Once to every man and nation
> Comes the moment to decide
> In the strife of truth with falsehood
> For the good or evil side.
> Some great cause, God's new Messiah . . .

Actually it's not once but twice, three, four, or fourteen times these moments come, but Lowell understood what happens when they do:

> Then it is the brave man chooses
> While the coward stands aside
> Til the multitude make virtue
> Of the faith they had denied.

In *Julius Caesar* Shakespeare says much the same:

> There is a tide in the affairs of men
> Which, taken at the flood, leads on to fortune;
> Omitted, all the voyage of their life
> Is bound in shallows and in miseries.

Martin Luther King Jr. deserves a national holiday because he rescued the American people from the shallows and miseries where they had chosen to live their lives. He deserves a national holiday because more than any other public figure in this century he asserted his individuality in order to affirm community on the widest possible scale; because better than any other public figure he understood the nature of compassion, that it did not exclude confrontation. It was Martin's message that it is not enough to suffer with the poor; we must confront the people and systems that cause poverty. It was Martin's message that you cannot set the captive free if you are not willing to confront those who hold the keys. Without confrontation compassion becomes merely commiseration, fruitless and sentimental.

Likewise King understood the difference between defiance and freedom. Confrontation to him did not mean the ruin and humiliation of opponents. Nonviolence to him represented conquest without the humiliation of the conquered. Nonviolence to him represented an effort to give visibility not to our own poor powers but to God's everlasting love. "Not unto us, O Lord, not unto us, but unto thy name be the glory." Nonviolence represented a chance for all parties to rise above their present condition.

Measured by feet, it was a short distance from King's pulpit to the streets of Montgomery. Measured spiritually, it was a long journey. But he took it, in the name of him who "in those days . . . came from Nazareth of Galilee and was baptized by John in the Jordan."

In our day we have a similar journey—all of us—which is why we come to be baptized and to join a church.

One-Talent People

JANUARY 24, 1982
Readings: Genesis 4:1–16; Mark 2:15–17; Matthew 25:14–29

No doubt some think we should say something today about the mercenary mayhem that is about to take place in Pontiac, Michigan—symbolically, in a giant pleasure dome shielded from the rigors of Michigan life outside: the cold, and Pontiac's 24 percent unemployment. Actually I thought about it: about what that Roman statesman Cincinnatus might have to say—or St. Francis; about how gracefully to drop back and punt when life seems to present to you an unending sequence of fourth downs with ten yards to go. But I didn't get very far. So I decided to leave the whole matter up to the players themselves, those several tons of discourteous gristle, in the fond hope that none by nightfall will find themselves in that End Zone in the Sky where, one day, the Great Quarterback will throw to each and every one of us a touchdown pass.

I also thought of talking about Christian unity, but I decided the best way for Christians to get together is to work together. Actions speak louder than explanations. Besides, we've already sung and prayed for unity, and our brother Garcia has demonstrated that Christians from any denomination and in every tongue have more in common than in conflict. So let's go back to some words he read from Mark: "*Los sanos no tienen necesidad de médico, mas los que tienen mal*" ("Those that are whole have no need of the physician, but they that are sick") and "*No he venido a llamar a los justos, sino a los pecadores*" ("I came not to call the righteous, but sinners to repentance").

Those words raise the question: who is sick and who is healthy? Who are the sinners, and who are the righteous? Christian teaching on this matter is very clear: the world is made up of sinners who think they are saints, and saints who know they are sinners. The great discovery of adolescence is not sex, but that none of us is a Boy Scout or a Girl Scout. "All we like sheep have gone astray, . . . every one in his own way" (Isa. 53:6). Actually, saints—biblically understood—are *forgiven* sinners, which is what gives us hope to be in their number. It's quite simple: the one person for whom Jesus can do nothing is the person who thinks herself so good that she needs nothing done for her, while the person for whom Jesus can do everything is the person who knows he is sick and wants a cure. So it's clear why Jesus said, "Those who are well have no need of a physician, but those who are sick; I came not to call the righteous but sinners to repentance" (Mark 2:17). A sense of need is the passport to Christ's presence.

Both the Old and New Testaments take a strong stand against those who think they need nothing done for them. In Jeremiah we read: "Behold, I will bring you to judgment for saying, 'I have not sinned'" (Jer. 2:35); and in the letter of James, "God opposes the proud, but gives grace to the humble" (Jas. 4:6).

But if the Scribes and Pharisees attacking Jesus for dining with sinners are counterattacked by Jesus for thinking themselves superior, let us not for an instant suppose that it is better to feel oneself inferior. Consider the story of Cain and Abel, which suggests that a person with feelings of inferiority toward his brother tends to think of himself as less loved and appreciated by God. But that's pure projection. God is not the judge Cain imagines. Instead of accusing, God asks him in friendly fashion. "Why are you angry, and why has your countenance fallen?" God is like a patient therapist with an aggressive patient, questioning him in order to help him gain some insight.

But Cain doesn't want any insight. So God warns him of the danger: "If you do ill, sin is couching at the door; its desire is for you." What a description! Now God is urging Cain to control, not to submit to, the situation. But Cain ignores the warning and continues to nurse this dark feeling of his own inferiority, until one day in the field he strikes out blindly and bitterly against the supposed superiority that shames him. Of the first two recorded brothers in the Bible, one dies at the hand of the other. Such a true and tragic insight!

After the killing, God is angry. Fortunately so; for a God without wrath would be a God without pity—and a world without meaning. Still God continues to urge Cain toward some kind of insight: "Where is your brother Abel? What have you done?" But Cain continues obstinate—"Am I my brother's keeper?" and rebellious—"My punishment is greater than I can bear"; and insecure with the insecurity of the guilty—"Whoever finds me will slay me." Cain is such a stand-in for so many of us. I would go so far as to suggest that the egotism of those who feel inferior may be even more all-embracing than the self-regard of those who think themselves superior.

To bear this out we have the New Testament parable of the talents. At first reading, Jesus seems to be saying what the world seems so intent on proving, that the big time always wins and the small fry always lose. Jesus seems to be joining the already all-too-numerous citizens of almost every nation who are intent on attacking the vulnerable instead of the powerful. But maybe Jesus is only trying—once again—to break through our defenses, to unearth something most of us would prefer to keep buried. The parable, in fact, does not discriminate: the two-talent man enters into the same joy of his master as the five-talent man. I think the deep-down message of the parable is that *small is beautiful*; *God loves one-talent people*. That's why he made so many of us. And that's why his son comes down so hard on this particular one-talent person—because he refuses to believe it. What can you do with someone who insists that he is inferior, who refuses to believe that she is loved just the same as anyone else?

The one-talent man is much like Cain, only shrewder. Deciding that the best defense is offense, he says, "Master, I know you to be a hard man, reaping where you do not sow and gathering where you do not winnow." In effect, what he's saying is, "You see, Master, you shouldn't be like that. Look where it gets you. Now if you had slipped me five, or even two talents, things might today be different."

As opposed to Cain, this man is a *passive*-aggressive, but with a punishing instinct, like Cain. Overcome by his sense of inferiority he digs—shall we say?—his own hole, then tries to punish the master for putting him in it, and for not rescuing him from it. It's really surprising that he didn't present the master with the bill for the shovel!

The ultimate weapon of those who feel themselves inferior is to try to hold everyone back. (Cain did it with a vengeance.) As opposed to the Pharisees, they know their weaknesses but don't try to live their strengths. They lean on their swords, catching their breaths—all their lives. They don't make history; they suffer it. And God is not their hope, but their excuse.

And it's true to say "to everyone who has will be given" when what's being given is not money, but love. For love begets love, its power more power.

Which brings us to the first disciples—the fishermen and Matthew the tax collector—sitting at dinner with Christ, and Lord knows who else, enjoying his company. Of them we can say that they were among the sick who wanted to be cured, the repentant sinners ready for forgiveness. They were one-talent people (with the possible exception of Matthew, who may have had more) entering into the joy of their Master. They knew their weaknesses but were prepared to live their strengths. They had leaned on their swords long enough; they were prepared to move on. They had the will to live bravely, even dangerously, in following Jesus—especially Matthew, who had burned all his bridges behind him. He couldn't go back to tax-collecting as could the others to fishing. They had much still to learn, these disciples, but at least they had shaken off any lethargy of the spirit.

In these Falwellian times, these cruel days of Reaganomics and American and Russian chauvinism, I occasionally think of Eric Sevareid's description of the human race. There are three kinds of human beings, he said: life-enhancers, well-poisoners, and lawn-mowers. Few of us here are well-poisoners. But there's a danger that we become lawn-mowers, going endlessly back and forth doing the same thing in almost the same pattern. I like those Polish intellectuals who yesterday put themselves in danger opposing martial law in their country. I like the old people and other sufferers who took themselves down to the Police Plaza Auditorium on Friday to protest their unnecessary suffering, caused by Reaganomics. I like the Salvadorans who will start a fast this week here in the church to protest the enforced repatriation of their fellow citizens. (Just think: we arm the junta that kills people and makes refugees. Then we send the refugees back; we can't give them asylum, because we're supporting the junta. So we forcefully repatriate about two hundred of them a week, back to almost certain death in El Salvador.)

I like all these people because I believe life loves those who live it to the full, and because I believe they are true disciples of him who came to set the captives free. In these confusing times, if we cannot see what lies dimly at a distance we can do what lies clearly at hand. With St. Teresa we can remember that Christ has no body now on earth but ours, no hands but ours, no feet but ours. Ours are the eyes through which Christ's compassion looks out on the world, ours the feet with which he is to go about doing good, and ours are the hands with which he is now to bless all humanity.

True ecumenicity is remembering this; it is worshipping together in the highlands of the spirit and then entering together into the lowlands of service. The toughest battle of life is not fought in Pontiac, Michigan, but in the heart of every one of us when we hear Christ's call, "Follow me," and another voice that says, "No, I'm too superior for that" or "I'm too inferior." Let's forget those categories, for they are meaningless. Let us strive to be life-enhancers, which we can become simply by recognizing that we are the sick who look to Christ to be made well; we are the sinners who look to Christ for forgiveness; we are the one-talent people who know that "this little light of mine," dedicated to Jesus, can be fanned into an unquenchable flame that will shine, shine, shine.

The Extra in the Ordinary[*]

FEBRUARY 7, 1982
Readings: Psalm 104:1–13; Matthew 13:13–16

In our opening hymn we sang what we shall later sing again in the Sanctus—"Holy, holy, holy." We sang, "All thy works shall praise thy name in earth and sky and sea," and we shall sing, "Heaven and earth are full of thy glory. Glory be to thee, O Lord most high."

Christians believe all that. They believe that "the earth is charged with the grandeur of God," that "There lives the dearest freshness

---

[*]This sermon was based on the book *Mystery of the Ordinary* by Charles Cummings (Harper & Row, 1982).—WSC

deep down things"—to quote Gerard Manley Hopkins—and that therefore even in the deep darkness of winter we can know in our hearts an invincible summer. But it isn't easy to feel perennially green, not in the first week of February, nor in a world of war and want and waste—nor even in the church, which, alas, so often plays the role of Judas, or Cain. So for a few minutes let's consider some of the ways to live as if that truth were true—"The earth is charged with the grandeur of God." Let us consider a few of the ways to take the "daily" out of living.

"Blessed are your eyes, for they see, and your ears, for they hear." Implied in these words is the suggestion that the most extraordinary things in life take place where people say, "I don't see anything so extraordinary about that." In other words, it is not outside but inside ordinary, everyday things that the richness of life is to be found and celebrated. St. Teresa of Avila said, "I believe that in each little thing created by God there is more than what is understood, even if it is a little ant." It's that "more than" we're after, that "more than" we must hear and see if in a wintry world our hearts are not to grow dull.

"Blessed are your ears." Hearing is a faculty but *listening* is an art. In one of his songs John Denver speaks of listening "for the sound like the sun goin' down." I like that—the idea that if we really listen we can hear the inaudible, what Plato called "the music of the spheres." To St. John of the Cross, God was "music without a sound, sonorous solitude." Prayer really is listening more than speaking, an act of empathy rather than of self-expression. And if we really listen not only to God but to one another, we will again hear the inaudible— what was not said, which is altogether as important as what is said. We shall hear in every question the silent statement behind it. We shall hear in every statement the unspoken cry for help, the invita- tion, the command. The heart of a good listener is perennially green, always awake. To a good listener, life is perpetually renewing. "Blessed are your ears, for they hear."

And "Blessed are your eyes." Sight is a faculty, but *seeing* is an art. "Nothing is profane for the one who knows how to see," said Teilhard de Chardin. Biblical prophets were also known as "seers." They were the men and women of moral passion sufficient to heat the blood and race the pulse and prompt the vision of a world that swings on an eth- ical hinge; they knew that if you tamper with that hinge all history and even nature will feel the shock. Any Biblical seer could tell you that the United States has just been presented a budget of want and waste and war. Any seer could tell you that those more concerned with dis- order than with injustice will invariably produce more of both, that in places like El Salvador it is those who made peaceful evolution impossible who now have made violent revolution inevitable.

Poets too are seers. They are the ones who see that "the earth is charged with the grandeur of God," who write of God as one "who hast stretched out the heavens like a tent, who hast laid the beams of the chambers on the waters, who makest the clouds thy chariot, who ridest on the wings of the wind, who makest the winds thy messengers, fire and flame thy ministers" (Ps. 104).

That is why, if we want to take the "daily out of living," we should read poems as regularly as newspapers. You won't believe this, but there are people who actually go through a whole day without reading a single poem!

And finally painters are seers, which is why museums are such lifelines, particularly in the cold of February when it's hard to be inspired by nature. I've heard that in all his life Van Gogh sold all of two paintings. But recently one of his oils was auctioned for five million dollars. Why? Because he used color quite arbitrarily to awaken insight, because he saw the extraordinary in things as ordinary as an old pair of miner's shoes, as his own bedroom at Arles. A painting called simply "The Potato Eaters" tells us so much about the mystery of a shared meal. Blessed were his eyes, for they saw.

To seers, to listeners, there is too much of beauty and interest for hearts to grow dull. The seers, the listeners—they are the "saunterers" of the world.

Writing in *Atlantic Monthly* in 1862, one of America's great walkers, Henry David Thoreau, wrote that the word "saunter" is beautifully derived from idle people who roamed about the country in the Middle Ages and asked for charity under the pretense of going "à la Sainte-Terre," to the Holy Land. Children exclaimed, "There goes a *Sainte-Terrer,*" a Saunterer, a Holy Lander.

The true saunterer in this city knows the truth of the poster that reads: "You have to be crazy to live in New York, but you'd be nuts to live anywhere else."

It is in ordinary, everyday things that the richness of life is sought and celebrated. True of our blessings, this is no less true of our afflictions—not that suffering itself is good, but that it can be put to good use. Said Simone Weil, who never made it all the way to Christianity, but who certainly understood it: "The extreme greatness of Christianity lies in the fact that it does not seek a supernatural remedy for suffering but a supernatural use for it." Obviously she read the Bible: "The Lord is close to the brokenhearted, and those who are crushed in spirit he saves" (Ps. 34:18). "This poor man cried, and the Lord heard him, and saved him out of all his troubles" (Ps. 34:6). "Blessed are those who mourn, for they shall be comforted" (Matt. 5:4).

Which brings us to communion and to the "more than" that is in the ordinary bread and wine. "On the same night on which he was betrayed, Jesus took bread, and when he had given thanks, he broke it, and gave it to his disciples saying, 'Take, eat, this is my body which is broken for you.' And in the same manner also he took the cup, after he had supped, saying, 'This is the new covenant in my blood.'" The new covenant tells us that there is a loving, long-suffering heart as well as grandeur at the center of this universe, that we live not only under the commandments of God but within the love of God. I tell you, if you believe that, to you will be fulfilled the promise made to the disciple Nathaniel: "Truly I say to you, you will see heaven opened and the angels of God ascending and descending upon the Son of man." If you believe that there is more mercy in God than sin in us, never again will you turn a deaf ear or a blind eye to any of God's works or creatures, never again will life be dull to you, for "eye hath not seen nor ear heard nor has it dawned on the hearts of human beings what God has prepared for those who love him."

"Blessed are your eyes, for they see, and your ears, for they hear. Truly I say to you, many prophets and righteous people longed to see what you see, and did not see it, and to hear what you hear, and did not hear it."

"All thy works shall praise thy name in earth and sky and sea."

> Holy, holy, holy, Lord God of hosts,
> Heaven and earth are full of thy glory.
> Glory be to thee, O Lord most high.

There by the Grace of God Go I

FEBRUARY 21, 1982
Reading: Luke 18:9–14

I have enormous admiration for scientists who see the ocean in a drop of water, for poets who "see a world in a grain of sand / And a Heaven in a wild flower," and for psychiatrists who see in the dropping of a handkerchief a whole law of human behavior. So I marvel at the way Jesus, in one small parable, can tell so much of the story of heaven and earth. I also appreciate the special value of parables: they shift responsibility from the teller to the hearer, suggesting that God leads with a light rein, giving us our head. And regarding this particular parable, it makes me admire anew the courage of Jesus, who surely must have known that telling a story so devastating to a Pharisee— albeit all Pharisees weren't arrogant, nor were all tax collectors repentant—such a story could only hasten his death. As the parable prepares us well for Ash Wednesday, let's take a closer look at it.

"Two men went up into the temple to pray, one a Pharisee" (which these days you can translate as a "church executive," or, if you prefer, "the senior minister of a large urban church") "and the other a tax collector" (which these days you don't have to translate at all). "The Pharisee stood and prayed thus with himself, 'God, I thank thee that I am not like other (people).'"

Whatever in this world is worthy of censure is also deserving of compassion: who would pump up his ego in this fashion unless it was rapidly losing pressure? The man does deserve censure however, when he resorts to the odious way of comparison. But that is always the way of pride, pride being not accidentally but essentially competitive. We cannot inflate our own egos without deflating others. Usually, of course, we do it with greater subtlety than did the Pharisee, starting with a show of mock grief: "Joe's such a wonderful guy, too bad . . ." Too bad my eye! By pushing Joe down we can now rise in our own eyes. It's standard operating procedure: we all want to be insiders, but insiders need outsiders to confirm them in their insider status. Christians want to be counted among the faithful, but the faithful need infidels to confirm them in their fidelity.

The Pharisee further typifies us by listing the vices from which he abstains: "I am not like other people, extortionists, adulterers . . ." Without doubt the easiest way to feel virtuous is to concentrate on wrongs you don't commit and avoid at all costs examining your motives for abstention. Contrary to popular belief, most good behavior is due to the weakness of our passions rather than the strength of our character. "Prudence," said William Blake, "is a rich, ugly old maid courted by Incapacity." Most people who bemoan the sins of their youth are really regretting their lost capacity to repeat them. But then the Pharisee goes on to list what he does do, proving he is a veritable virtuoso in virtue: he fasts not once a year but twice a week; and he tithes—dare I say it?—far more than do most of us.

Yet there is something skewed in his virtue; he comes across about as warm as February in Moscow. He is a cold hilltop where no flowers grow. People should be a special blend of tenderness and outrage, but this man is too cold for either. And boring, too, so studiously controlled he doesn't realize that our animal nature can help break our pride. I'll bet in him there was a murderous antagonism between feeling and thought, heart and mind, an antagonism once described in this fashion by e. e. cummings: "along the brittle treacherous bright streets / of memory comes my heart singing like / an idiot, whispering like a drunken man / who (at a certain corner, suddenly meets) the tall policeman of my mind."

This Pharisee is pious and sanctimonious, but hardly stirring and compelling. He seems to view salvation as something you achieve and keep, rather than something you live out, more committed to the going than to the getting there.

But Jesus' point is not as complicated as all this. He is saying simply that our secure presumption of righteousness is itself our greatest sin. If you stop and think about it, anyone seeking to be virtuous is no longer seeking God or neighbor, for the enterprise is too self-seeking. True, the Pharisee goes into the temple, but only as do so many Christians—to make their last stand against God. True, both pray, but deify not God but their own virtue. Both worship, but worship themselves worshipping. And their view of themselves obviously conditions their view of God. To pharisaical Christians, God appears as a corporation in which they've earned sufficient stock to warrant the expectation that someday soon they'll be asked to join the Board of Directors.

And finally—once again—the Pharisee's view of himself conditions not only his view of God, but his view of others. In his eyes the tax collector is an abstraction, an enemy really, an ant to be stepped on. With spiritual arrogance goes the itch to destroy. He may have been a virtuoso in virtue, this Pharisee, but history warns that the best is always a hair's breadth from the worst, and that heartless moralists in the corridors of power are those who start inquisitions.

Perhaps the most ironic feature of the story is that it is in the very act of praying, which is a form of union, that the Pharisee seeks to break the God-given unity he shares not only with the tax collector but with everyone else in the world. I say "God-given" because according to the faith we are together before we come together. According to the faith, community is not made by us but given by God. So it is the sin of the Pharisee, and of the Pharisee in each of us, that we seek to put asunder what God himself has joined together.

Now let's turn to the tax collector, that hated symbol of those days and ours, often in those days a crook—but a crook who may save us from the pretensions of our virtue. Of course we have a right to be skeptical of him too, a man who "would not even lift up his eyes to heaven, but beat his breast saying, 'God be merciful to me a sinner.'"

If I've learned anything, it's to beware of the helplessness gambit of chronic victims. And I remember Nietzsche's warning: "He who humbles himself *wills* to be exalted." It may have been that this tax collector was looking for punishment in order to avoid judgment. For while judgment demands a new way of life, punishment, by assuaging a bit the guilt, makes the old way bearable anew.

Whether the tax collector came into the temple for judgment or punishment we can't tell, for there's no sequel to the parable. But if we can assume his sincerity and his recognition of that basic tenet of the faith, that there is more mercy in God than sin in us, then we can go on to assume that he became as zealous as the Pharisee—except that his zeal was an expression of his gratitude, not an effort to prove himself. In any event, Jesus' point is clear: mercy and forgiveness can come only to those who seek it. There is no way God's love can reach the self-sufficient.

It would be nice to stop here; we've given a pretty good interpretation of a perfectly marvelous parable. But to do so would be to miss the terrible relevance of that parable today. To quote Blake one more time: "The strongest poison ever known / Came from Caesar's laurel crown."

We're in for turbulent times, dear Christians, as our leaders become ever more spiritually arrogant. There was a time when nations were judged by their treatment of the poor, but today the poor have become modern-day lepers. There was a time when ghettos and prisons were considered problems; today they're solutions, places to keep our expendable poor. And in El Salvador, where 2 percent of the population owns 60 percent of the land and nearly 50 percent of the children die before the age of five, the poor are little more than ants to be stepped on. Our leaders tell us that the Salvadorans' destiny is being designed in Moscow, but that's only so that they can redesign it in Washington. Moscow probably has about as much to do with what's going on today in El Salvador as does Washington with what's going on in Afghanistan. And last week, here in our own church, we could see all kinds of connections between the poor at home and abroad when the Salvadorans were fasting next to our Food Pantry, where for two hours a day we give food to the city's needy. Twenty-seven million dollars was the initial price tag for military aid to El Salvador. Twenty-seven million dollars was also taken out of the welfare budget of New York City. So what are our leaders doing? Taking money from the poorest people in our land to buy helicopters and weapons to kill people who are even poorer in Central America—while praying, "God, we thank thee that our nation is not as other nations are: atheist, communist, imperialistic, understanding only force."

The future is bleak. History teaches that policies founded on error multiply, they don't retreat; and that at the very moment these policies are most bankrupt those responsible for them can least afford to admit it. That is why I'm so happy that this month is Black History month. For Black History not only opens windows into long-ignored anterooms, it challenges the secure presumptions of righteousness of white history, exposing "the lies agreed upon," and calling for a new venture based on greater truth. In February's *Ebony* magazine, historian Lerone Bennett Jr. writes: "If truth is 'the look in the eyes of the poor,' if truth is what the poorest of the poor experience, if it is the reality the least of these have lived, then Black history is the essence of the American experience."

In white history the dominant voice belongs to the victors, but I tell you all victims of racial pride and blindness have passed through Glory's morning gate and walk today in Paradise, "for everyone who exalts himself will be humbled, but he who humbles himself will be exalted."

What is so sad is that our leaders think that to admit error is the end of the world. To admit error is not the end of the world, it's the beginning of humanity. Looking at the tax collector the Pharisee said, "There but for the grace of God go I." He should have said, "There *by* the grace of God go I," a fallible human being capable of error, sinful yet forgiven. The Pharisee had everything except the one thing necessary; the tax collector had nothing except the one thing necessary—trust in God's saving grace. "God be merciful to me a sinner." Those are words that can change worlds.

Insidious Realism

FEBRUARY 28, 1982
Readings: Isaiah 55; Luke 4:1–13

You are young only once, but you can be immature indefinitely. And when we ask, "When dawns the day of maturity?" the answer is "Never." Finally, none of us grows up. But there are promising signs along the way: We are approaching maturity when we no longer need to be lied to about anything. We are approaching maturity when we realize that God hides things by putting them next to us. We are approaching maturity when we realize that the line between good and evil cuts right through the heart of every human being and stays there because no wants to destroy a piece of his or her honor. We are approaching maturity when we realize that "necessary evil" can become so necessary that it's no longer evil—the lesson learned yesterday from slavery and today from nuclear weapons. And we are approaching maturity when we realize that rarely does the devil suggest that we do anything bad. Eve, after all, only took the apple when she saw that it was "good for food, pleasing to the eye, and much to be desired to make people wise."

So let's be imaginative, avoiding the usual (perfectly sound) interpretations of Jesus' temptations. Let's assume that the first, turning stones into bread, is not a temptation to use his powers selfishly, a temptation to win a following by material gifts. Rather it is the far subtler temptation to compromise his high calling by substituting the good in place of the best.

Had I been Jesus I think I would have argued: "Why shouldn't I give bread to my hungry people? God knows they're poor, and so do I, having been born into their poverty. Didn't God help Moses with manna? And shouldn't God do at least as much for the Messiah himself, particularly when, urged on by the prophet Isaiah, everyone pictures the messianic age in terms of a banquet: 'On that day the LORD of Hosts will prepare a banquet of rich fare for all the peoples, a banquet of wines, well matured and richest fare, well-matured wines strained clear.' How, dear God, can I run counter to all these expectations? And most of all, how can I stand before a crowd of hungry people and say 'I am the bread of life'? That's unconscionable!"

The Russian theologian Nikolai Berdyaev has written: "When bread is assured, God becomes a hard and inescapable reality, instead of an escape from harsh reality." Of course we are to feed the poor, just as did Jesus. In the phrase "Man does not live by bread alone," the important word is not "bread," but "alone." Human rights are an essential part of the Gospel. But they don't exhaust it, and when bread is assured God does become a hard and inescapable reality. When bread is assured the contrast between the good and the best becomes sharp, and the temptation to compromise one's high calling becomes great. Listen to playwright Herb Gardner's character Arnold Burns explaining himself to his ne'er-do-well younger brother Murray:

> I have long been aware, Murray, I have long been
> aware that you don't respect me much. I suppose
> there are a lot of brothers who don't get along. . . .
> Unfortunately for you, Murray, you want to be a
> hero. Maybe if a fella falls into a lake, you can jump

in and save him; there's still that kind of stuff. But who gets opportunities like that in midtown Manhattan, with all that traffic. I am willing to deal with the available world and I do not choose to shake it up but to live with it. There's the people who spill things and the people who get spilled on. I choose not to notice the stains, Murray. I have a wife and I have children and business, like they say, is business. I am not an exceptional man, so it is possible for me to stay with things the way they are. I'm lucky; I'm gifted. I have a talent for surrender. I'm at peace. But you are cursed, and, I like you so it makes me sad, you don't have this gift; and I see the torture of it. All I can do is worry for you, but I will not worry for myself; you cannot convince me that I am one of the bad guys. I get up, I go, I lie a little, I peddle a little, I watch the rules, I talk the talk. We fellas have those offices high up there so that we can catch the wind and go with it, however it blows. But, and I will not apologize for it, I take pride; I am the best possible Arnold Burns. (*A Thousand Clowns*)

Aren't we all tempted constantly to be realistic and reasonable, to make a no-questions-asked peace with the world? And yet it is true— we are filled but unfulfilled, for when bread is assured God becomes a hard and inescapable reality. Our unlived lives poison our existence. If we are sufficiently mature to know that God hides things by putting them near us, then let us heed Isaiah's plea, "Seek ye the LORD while he may be found, call ye upon him" while we compromise our high calling by substituting the good in place of the best.

The second temptation is like unto the first. The devil, you remember, takes Jesus up to a high place, shows him "all the kingdoms of the world in a moment of time," and makes the remarkable claim that they all belong to the devil. Then he offers them all to Jesus. Once again, with a little imagination, we can see the devil suggesting that something good and tangible probably beats something that is wildly Utopian. Had we lived in Jesus' time, as Jews under the rod of Rome, we surely would have longed for political liberation. Many of our immediate family would have been among the 100,000 Jews who perished in a series of abortive rebellions against the Romans between the years 67 and 37 B.C. Like everyone else we would have been expecting a political messiah to implement the word and will of God as prophesied by Zechariah: "The LORD will set free all the families of Judah. . . . On the day, I, the LORD, will set about destroying all the nations that come against Jerusalem" (Zech. 12:7, 9).

God *will* set free all the captive people of the world, whether they live in Poland, Afghanistan, Cambodia, South Africa, El Salvador, or Mississippi, for free people will always rise up against tyranny. Once again: human rights are an essential part of the Gospel, but they do not exhaust it; and when political freedom is assured God becomes a hard and inescapable reality, instead of only a moral force to overcome a harsh and unjust reality.

We are approaching maturity when we realize that the line between good and evil cuts through the heart of every human being; and because that is so, every revolution "ends in the reappearance of a new ruling class" (Sébastien Faure). Moreover, whoever said the nation-state would forever be worth defending? Not Jesus. And historian Henry Commager in the March edition of *Atlantic Monthly* argues that nationalism "is as much of an anachronism today as was States' Rights when Calhoun preached it and Jefferson Davis fought for it . . . None of our global problems can be solved within the largely artificial boundaries of nations—artificial not so much in the eyes of history as in the eyes of Nature." And he could have added, "artificial always in the eyes of God."

In politics and economics, solutions always cause problems. Beyond that, we cannot equate the Kingdom of God even with bread, even with freedom, precious as those two are. So our unlived lives will poison our existence, if we heed the devil and compromise our high calling by substituting merely the good for the best.

The last temptation is eminently reasonable. If the Son of God is not to rescue people from poverty, nor to liberate them from tyranny, if the Messiah is to disappoint so many Messianic expectations, then let him at least be vindicated! Let God prove that this is what goodness is all about by shielding the Son of God from harm.

There is only one thing better: for the Son of God to prove what God is all about by becoming totally vulnerable. There is only one thing better: to take up your cross so that God's heart can be laid bare for all to see. There is only one thing better than providing God's power and that is to prove God's love.

It's so hard to be Christian. We glory but also groan in our Christianity: "Whither relentless wilt thou still be driving thy maimed and halt that have not strength to go?" But if we are approaching maturity, we know that it's hard to be Christian but it's dull to be anything else. If we are approaching maturity, we know that it's hard to bear the agony of decision but it's inhuman to refuse it. So in this tough time of testing in the Christian year let's see if we can't find energy sufficient to resist the insidious realism of the devil and not compromise our high calling by allowing the good to usurp the place of the best. And of one thing we may be sure: In Matthew's account we read, "Then the devil left him, and behold angels came and ministered to him." No doubt there are still a multitude around, ready to do no less to us.

We Know Not What We Do

MARCH 7, 1982
Readings: Psalm 130; Luke 5:1–8

Had you to summarize the events of Holy Week, to put in a nut-shell the meaning of Palm Sunday, Maundy Thursday, Good Friday, and Easter, you'd be hard pressed to find a phrase more apt than the one Paul used writing to Christians in Rome: "Where sin increased, grace abounded all the more" (Rom. 5:20). When religious leaders plot to destroy the Son of God and the State washes its hands, when one disciple betrays and all others desert, when the crowd makes March weather look like a model of reliability—then sin increases, and the cross becomes the foremost sign of sin, providing our inhumanity to one another is exceeded only by our inhumanity to God. Yet that which makes the blood run cold also warms the heart, for the foremost sign of sin is also the chief symbol of God's grace. The cross tells us that you can kill God's love but you cannot keep it dead and buried; that there are more important tragedies than the tragedy of death and no victory more important than the triumph of love. The cross tells us that where sin increases, grace abounds all the more.

I want to give a series of sermons of Christ's words spoken from the cross, starting today with the first, which speaks most directly to this triumph of love. Even as the nails are being driven into his hands Jesus prays, "Father, forgive them for they know not what they do." To me, it's strange how people get all flustered about the Immaculate Conception, the Virgin Birth, the physical resurrection of Jesus, his changing the water to wine, and all the other miracles; in some ways, I find it far harder to stand up and say, "I believe in the forgiveness of sins."

Let's start by asking, "Who is the 'they' in 'Father, forgive them for they know not what they do'?" Unlike too many New Yorkers, Jesus didn't die at the hands of muggers or rapists, Mafia leaders or other thugs; he fell into the well-scrubbed hands of ministers and lawyers, statesmen and professors—society's most respected members. So when we ask ourselves, "Were you there when they crucified my Lord?" I think we have to answer, "You bet I was, hammer in hand." The "they" is us, and we know not what we do—the most devastating comment ever made on the stupidity of self-respecting folk—because we know not who we are.

It's not that our information is poor, but that our hearts are hard, our wills are weak, and our imagination is almost nonexistent. We think that to do evil in the world we have to be some kind of a Bengal tiger, when in fact it's enough to be a tame tabby. In a memorable passage in *Wind, Sand and Stars,* Saint-Exupéry, the French poet-aviator, muses to himself as he rides in a bus with government officials and clerks:

> Old bureaucrat, my comrade, it is not you who are to blame. No one ever helped you to escape. You, like a termite, built your peace by blocking up with cement every chink and cranny through which the light might pierce. You rolled yourself up into a ball in your gen-teel security, in routine, in the stifling conventions of provincial life, raising a modest rampart against the wind and the tides and the stars. You have chosen not to be perturbed by great problems, having trouble enough to forget your own fate as man. You are not the dweller upon an errant planet and do not ask yourself questions to which there are no answers. You are a petty bourgeois of Toulouse. Nobody grasped you by the shoulder while there was still time. Now the clay of which you were shaped has dried and hardened, and naught in you will ever awaken the sleeping musician, the poet, the astronomer that pos-sibly inhabited you in the beginning.

It's as if we settled for this horrible March weather, forgetting the riotous outburst of beauty that lies just ahead. It's as if we listened to Liberace and thought we were hearing Horowitz; as if we read the chirping optimism of the *Reader's Digest* and thought we were getting the heights of Dante's *Divine Comedy.* No wonder we crucify Christ. We crucify the best among us because we crucify first the best within us—and don't want to be reminded of it. Death is not tragic; it's the good things in us that die while we yet live, the "little deaths" that are so tragic. I said there were no victories more important than the triumph of love. But we constantly defeat ourselves by fearing failure more than we love life. We deny our faith by not daring to live beyond self-concern. And then when someone like Jesus does shake us by the shoulder—forcing us to face the bitter fruits of caution, the vacant years, the ugly altars to ourselves, our nation's lunatic lust for place and possession—either we crucify, in the time-honored tradition of ancient kings who killed the bearer of bad news, *or* we repent and confess: "Out of the depths I cry, Lord, hear my voice. Let thine ear be attentive to the voice of my supplication" (Ps. 130:1–2). When Simon Peter saw the beauty and power of Jesus in the miraculous catch of fish, his first reaction was to fall on his knees and cry, "Go, Lord, leave me, sinner that I am."

A kneeling person is one who knows how tall human beings can stand. A kneeling person is a victor, victorious over his pride; a seeker, looking above herself to find herself. A kneeling person is one who finally comes to see that forgiveness is not too hard to believe, only too good to believe, we being strangers to such goodness.

Dear Christians, we need to kneel because we are tied in knots by a chain of past mistakes, because we are dominated by what we have been rather than by what we could be. We need to kneel because we need new chances and the grace to make those chances good. We need to kneel because if we don't save our souls we'll never save the world.

The world can only be saved by those who know that there are more important tragedies than the tragedy of death, and no victories more important than the triumph of love. The world can only be saved by those who become as Christ can make us, who will allow their cross to become a lightning rod to ground the world's hate, determined that where sin increases grace will all the more abound. The world can only be saved by those who can say, Christlike, even from a cross, "Father, forgive them for they know not what they do."

The Grace of Dependency

MARCH 14, 1982
Reading: Luke 23:32–43

Here's a reminder from St. Augustine guaranteed to warm the heart and chill the blood: "Two criminals were crucified with Christ. One was saved; do not despair. One was not; do not presume."

About these two, we know absolutely nothing, a fact that hasn't prevented pious speculation from building whole biographies about the one whose eleventh-hour discovery of Christ allows us to say of him, in the words of Shakespeare, "nothing in his life became him like the leaving it."

But I'm not one to slight the other criminal. Perhaps he was an associate of Barrabas, the revolutionary hero released that same morning at the behest of the mob. Perhaps he was a freedom fighter determined to see Israel's independence, or to see Rome leveled by his attempt to gain it. In any case, in his harshest hour, he shows spirit—that's what his taunting of Jesus reflects—a defiant spirit similar to what Dylan Thomas wanted his father to show even as his life expired.

> Do not go gentle into that good night,
> Rage, rage against the dying of the light.

He raged all right, this thief; no whiner, he was a fighter to the end.

That being acknowledged, we have to recognize that defiance is only a step on the way to freedom, not freedom itself; and that the human best tends always to be at odds with the holy best. In a sensitive spiritual autobiography, *The Sacred Journey*, Frederick Buechner writes:

> to do for yourself the best that you have in you to do—to grit your teeth and clench your fists in order to survive the world at its harshest and worst—is, by that very act, to be unable to let something be done for you and in you that is more wonderful still. The trouble with steeling yourself against the harshness of reality is that the same steel that secures your life against being destroyed secures your life also against being opened up and transformed by the holy power that life itself comes from. You can survive on your own. You can grow stronger on your own. You can even prevail on your own. But you cannot become human on your own.

In other words, to be human is not to be self-sufficient but to know the grace of dependency. The defiant thief couldn't be saved because a clenched fist cannot accept a helping hand.

Although we ourselves tend to whine more than fight, many of us can identify with this thief—as many of us are a bit too self-sufficient, defiant, presumptuous. But can we also identify with the one who asked for a helping hand? Let's recall another criminal, the most renowned perhaps in all of Western literature, the hero of Dostoyevsky's *Crime and Punishment*, Raskolnikov. As all textbooks are quick to point out, *raskolnik* in Russian means a split personality. What few add—their authors blinded perhaps by their secularism—is that a *raskolnik* is also a heretic. In Russian *raskol* means heresy, and heresy is derived from the Greek verb meaning "to seize," as for example a town. Not for nothing did Dostoyevsky give his hero a name not found in any Moscow telephone directory, a name with a double meaning.

Contrary to what most people consider heresy to be, Dostoyevsky did not believe it an intellectual matter, but rather a psychological and moral one. It was not the position but the motive for having it that he counted important. (Generally you "seize" a town for yourself and at somebody else's expense.) Likewise, to Dostoyevsky crime was only superficially breaking the law. More profoundly it was rending the bond of love. And the punishment for crime was less the isolation imposed by barred windows than that imposed by thick walls of hardened hearts. The punishment for rending the bond of love is experiencing the bond of love rent. It doesn't matter the form the egoism takes: it can be self-exaltation, as with Raskolnikov, or self-abasement—an equally Russian phenomenon. (I'm sure Dostoyevsky would have loved what a modern Russian, Eugenia Ginzburg, wrote: "The egotism of those who suffer is probably even more all-embracing than the self regard of those who are happy.") In all its forms egotism has one punishment—split off from one another and from God, we are also split off from our loving selves. Egotists are heretics and heretics have split personalities—*raskolniki*.

Access to God—salvation—is never acquired through repression or self-mutilation. (If only Jews and Christians could get over the notion that the way to have religion is to make themselves miserable!) Access to God is access to wholeness; the words "whole" and "holy" have the same root. To see how all this works out, let's return now to the scene on Calvary. Using our imaginations, we can see that the criminal is on his cross because he has rent the bond of love. Jesus is on his because he can *only* love. The criminal is on a cross of isolation, Jesus on one of vulnerability. The criminal is experiencing the agony of sin, Christ the cost of devotion. Then he who is guilty hears the one who of all people is the victim of injustice pray for the forgiveness of his executioners: "Father, forgive them for they know not what they do." Such love proves too much. His own defiant heart breaks. Instead of seeking, as did his fellow criminal, to prevail, he becomes human. He cries out, "Jesus, remember me." And in his last hours, on a cross, Christ performs his last miracle.

In portraying the myth of creation on the ceiling of the Sistine Chapel, Michelangelo pictures the bond of love as it was first established—so easily, so naturally. Surrounded by cherubim and seraphim God simply reaches down his arm from heaven to touch Adam's upward-turned hand. But the bond, once rent, is not so easily restored. Sin has its price; and so has forgiveness. Restoration takes place on two crosses when a human being in agony stretches out his or her hand to Christ and says, "Jesus, remember me," and Christ from his cross stretches out his hand and says, "Today you shall be with me in Paradise." That's what atonement—at-one-ment—is all about.

But there's more: "Today you shall be with me in Paradise." What the thief conceived as a future promise Christ offers as a present possibility. And of course those same words could have been exchanged had they both still fifty years to live, for Paradise is the presence of God, just as hell is God's absence. Heaven and hell—they begin here, now.

All this strikes me as terribly important to us, here and now. Many of us Americans are deeply distressed, feeling today that ours is a large country ruled by small minds, by leaders too eager for power to be trusted with it. Abroad, they sound global alarms over local fires; their solutions exceed the problem. At home the reverse is true: the problems of poverty are never going to be solved by the crumbs that fall from the tables of the rich. More and more our country seems to resemble ancient Rome, of which Livy wrote that it could neither bear its ills nor the remedies that might have cured them. And the personal lives of many of us have taken a turn for the worse: we're nervous, we're tense, we're getting poorer, closer to unemployment, to divorce—you fill in the particulars.

The temptation in bad times is to steel ourselves against the harshness of reality. But listen again to Buechner: "The trouble with steeling yourself against the harshness of reality is that the same steel that secures your life against being destroyed secures your life also against being opened up and transformed by the holy power that life itself comes from. You can survive on your own. You can grow stronger on your own. You can even prevail on your own. But you cannot become human on your own."

In inhumane times, we must stay human. Rather than become defiantly self-sufficient, we must learn the grace of dependency. Once again, a clenched fist cannot accept a helping hand. Are you on a cross of pain—whether of society's making or your own? Then stretch out your hand to Jesus on his cross right next to yours. Say, "Jesus, remember me. I want to stay whole, vulnerable, tender, loving, human." And he will reply, "Today, you shall be with me in Paradise. I'll drain your heart of fear and bitterness, filling it instead with that joy that can absorb all sorrow, with my peace that the world can neither give nor take away. For lo, I am with you always—cross by cross—unto the end of the age."

This atonement, at-one-ment, is not a future promise, it's a daily possibility. "Jesus, remember me." "*Today*, you shall be with me in Paradise." Instead of being in hell, we can live in heaven, even while we are still on earth!

The Good Friday Crowd

MARCH 21, 1982
Readings: Romans 12:1–2; Luke 23:18

I'd like to welcome to the service the Venerable Sato, who has come to this country to organize the arrival of thousands of Japanese who are coming here for the demonstration during the U.N. Special Session on Disarmament on June 12. They will then fan out throughout the United States, representing the one nation that has suffered a direct nuclear attack, helping to convert all the rest of us to their ways of peace.

A warm welcome also to Monsignor Bruce Kent, who runs the Campaign for Nuclear Disarmament in London; and to Pastor Volkmar Deile, the person who had most to do with organizing the demonstration last fall in Bonn, West Germany, where more than 250,000 people turned up.

I'm eager to continue our series of sermons on Christ's last words from the cross, but I can't until we deal with the Good Friday crowd. The eighteenth-century philosopher Edmund Burke said, "All it takes for evil to flourish is for a few good people to do nothing." In other words, the lawless need the listless, and the multitudes gathered around the cross that Friday afternoon epitomize this fact. They're not a mean crowd. They didn't come to cheer the crucifixion, as did their religious and political leaders; but they failed also to protest it.

The majority may even have been on Jesus' side, but they didn't realize that compassion without confrontation is merely commiseration, fruitless and sentimental. And finally "they returned home," according to Luke, "beating their breasts," demonstrating once again how much easier it is to be guilty than to be responsible.

Not all crowds, of course, are listless. Undoubtedly many of these same people around the cross were also present on Palm Sunday—in a very different mood. Twenty-two years ago to the day in Sharpeville, South Africa, a very vigorous crowd gathered peacefully to protest the so-called pass laws, laws that determined where Black South Africans could and could not work and live, laws that separated families and denied freedom of choice and security to the vast majority of South Africa's citizens. They *had* to protest these inhuman laws or lose their own humanity, for you lose your humanity when you tolerate the intolerable. And they had to take to the streets, for only the well-heeled can afford to walk the corridors of power. The barefoot and ill-shod have only the streets in which to petition for redress of grievances. On that day twenty-two years ago the police killed sixty-nine of the demonstrators, and today we Americans in particular need to remember them, for the whole world knows that in South Africa the United States is taking sides by pretending not to.

No less vigorous have been the protests led by our guests Pastor Deile, Monsignor Kent, and the Venerable Sato. It's good that hundreds of thousands in Europe and Asia have demonstrated against nuclear madness. It's good that we'll all be demonstrating together in even greater numbers here in New York on June 12. For as terrifying as are the nuclear weapons themselves—they can nail all humanity to a cross—they are no more terrifying than the ability of most citizens to abide their production and deployment. What Hannah Arendt said of Eichmann could be said of most of the human race: we are "terribly and terrifyingly normal." Like the multitudes on Good Friday, we tend to be listless, standing around while abuses and new infamies are added to old.

Here's an example of listlessness: a *New Yorker* cartoon shows an executive type saying, "I've learned a lot in sixty-three years, but unfortunately almost all of it is about aluminum." Put enough of those executives together and you have a Good Friday crowd.

Over the years military people also learn a lot, but unfortunately almost all of it is about technological and tactical problems, not moral and political ones. When I was at West Point I reminded the cadets of their motto, "Honor, duty, country." Then I asked, "What is duty in a wrong war?" When no one wanted to answer that one, it was clear that we had another Good Friday crowd.

Striking closer to home, consider intellectuals we have known—ironic, cerebral, smooth as vintage port. Are they any less listless than the students and faculty of Jerry Falwell's college, where presumably no hint of intellectual freedom threatens their religious and political ignorance? I've noticed that where country folk take refuge in narrow righteousness, city folk do the same in shallow cleverness.

Here are some words full of Good Friday overtones: "Don't be afraid of your enemies; the most they can do is kill you. Don't be afraid of your friends, the most they can do is betray you. Those you should be afraid of are the indifferent. They are neither friends nor foes, they neither kill nor betray, but because of their indifference there are so many killings and so many betrayals." Those are the last written words of a Polish deportee in a concentration camp in World War II.

Now, however, we must be careful. Albeit too late, the multitudes on Good Friday saw their complicity in Christ's crucifixion and returned home, "beating their breasts." And I suggested that their reaction typified a lot of us who find it easier to be guilty than to be responsible.

In a dramatic moment in Arthur Miller's *Incident at Vichy*, Dr. Leduc, a Jewish psychiatrist, forces the Austrian Prince Von Berg to recognize his complicity with the very forces of Naziism he so deplores. He makes him see how listless he was, how he "went along." But the moment of recognition is as charged with danger as with drama. For now the Prince's concern begins to move away from the plight of the Jews with him in the French police station, who are about to be deported to almost certain death in German concentration camps—away from their plight to his own, to the feelings of remorse now flooding his soul. Sensing Von Berg's withdrawal, Leduc turns on him fiercely and says, "It's not your guilt I want, it's your responsibility."

It's so much easier to beat your breast than to stick your neck out, to be guilty rather than responsible. The essential problem of the Christian Church is not to convict people of their sin, but to persuade them of their forgiveness.

"Father, forgive them." The Good Friday crowd either didn't hear those words from the cross or didn't believe them; they went home beating their breasts. We must go forth from this place convicted of our sin, yes, but even more persuaded of our forgiveness. We must not go forth as defeated folk whose contrition has drained all the iron from our spines. We must go forth as *forgiven* sinners, rendered zealous by our forgiveness to translate our guilt into responsibility.

At the end of Miller's play, Von Berg succeeds in doing just that—translating his guilt into responsibility. As a Gentile he is given a pass by the police. But he secretly slips the pass to Leduc, who escapes to freedom. As the curtain falls, a volunteer stands in place of the victim.

"Do not be conformed to this world but be transformed by the renewal of your mind." Political leaders are always seeking to conform us to this world by extolling the virtues of national unity—generally, we might add, when the unity they promote appears to be unity in folly! Wrote Barbara Tuchman of this tendency: "Nor should we be paralyzed by fear of exacerbating divisions within this country. We are divided anyway, and always have been, as any independently minded people should be. Talk of unity is a pious fraud and a politician's cliché. No people worth its salt is politically united. A nation in consensus is a nation ready for the grave."

The same is true of the churches. When all hearts are one, nothing else has to be one. Christian unity is based not on agreement, but on mutual concern. And the Good Friday crowd is a standing reminder of what happens when agreement replaces mutual concern: "play it safe," "don't climb out on a limb," "don't rock the boat"—these slogans become, as it were, the eleventh commandment on which are "hanged" all the law and the prophets. These are the slogans that drop the mask of dissimulation over the face of truth, the slogans that make us turn our backs on screams in the night, the slogans that make us turn the other cheek (in order not to see the evil), the slogans that make us hide behind our specialties—behind narrow righteousness and shallow cynicism—pleading insufficient knowledge until, like Von Berg and the Good Friday crowd, we become collaborators in the very evil we deplore.

So, dear Christians, let us not this year seek a place in the Good Friday crowd, a place among the listless who aid and abet the lawless. Let's come to church to remember God's triumphs more than our own failures. There is too much focus on our peccadillos at the expense of a joyous and vigorous faith. Sorrow is not forever; love is. And "joy is the infallible sign of the presence of God."

This is the first day of spring. Not many of us have gardens, but we know enough about them to know that if you want flowers in your garden you have to bend your back and dig. Let's get some flowers blooming in this world—flowers, in place of crosses.

Our Father's Business

MARCH 28, 1982
Reading: Luke 2:41–49

It is good that we should consider Jesus' Third Word from the Cross on Youth Sunday, for it raises a thousand poignant questions about the right relationship between children and parents. In the nineteenth chapter of John we read: "Now there stood by the cross of Jesus his mother, and his mother's sister, the wife of Cleophas, and Mary Magdalene. When Jesus therefore saw his mother, and the disciple standing by, whom he loved, he said unto his mother, 'Woman, behold thy son.' Then said he to the disciple, 'Behold thy mother.' And from that hour that disciple took her unto his own home" (John 19:25–27).

Full as they are of concern for Mary's well-being, these words can't help but affect us deeply, particularly when we remember that they are said in the throes of an agonizing, degrading death. But what are we to make of the contrast between these words, so full of tenderness, spoken at the end of Jesus' life, and the harsh ones spoken earlier in his ministry? "While he yet talked to the people, behold, his mother and his brothers stood without, desiring to speak with him. But he answered, and said unto him that told him, 'Who is my mother? And who are my brothers?'" (Matthew 12:46, 48).

And this is not the first time Jesus has been disrespectful to his family. According to Luke, when still a boy—twelve to be exact—he was taken by Mary and Joseph to celebrate Passover in Jerusalem. When the festivities were over, assuming him to be among their kinfolk and friends traveling together back to Galilee, his parents did not miss him until the end of a full day's journey. And after what must have been a frantic search, they finally discovered him back in the Temple preaching—of all things—to the elders. Understandably annoyed, they rebuked him. But with not so much as a single word of apology for the hours of worry he had caused everybody, Jesus rebuked right back: "Wist ye not that I must be about my Father's business?"

In this instance, most of us would side with Jesus, sensing the larger destiny that claims him. And we recall his own words spoken years later, "Suffer the little children to come unto me and forbid them not, for of such is the Kingdom of Heaven" (Mark 10:14).

Not that children are superior in every respect, as St. Paul recognized: "When I was a child, I spoke as a child, I understood as a child, I thought as a child; but when I became a man, I put away childish things" (1 Corinthians 13:11). But if there's nothing commendable about being immature and childish in adulthood, it is absolutely indispensable to remain, throughout all of life, child*like*. "Whosoever shall not receive the Kingdom of God as a little child shall not enter therein" (Mark 10:15).

God knows, we'll never fathom the depths of that extraordinary statement. But in my own all-too-fallible and subjective judgment, Jesus is referring not only to the humility, the trusting quality of children, their glorious capacity to wonder; he's also referring to the natural idealism of youth. Idealism is childlike. It's kids, after all, who sell cookies for causes, bake bread for brotherhood and sisterhood. It's kids who want to save seals and whales, and even the rest of us. And we, their parents, encourage them. But we also expect them to outgrow their idealism, as if idealism were a pair of short pants. In her syndicated column Ellen Goodman once described "our most common parenting scenario": "We instill ideals in our children, resent it when they challenge us for not living up to them, and then feel reassured when they give up their ideals, like sleds or cartoons."

And why do we make children the repositories of our ideals? Because, says Goodman, children are powerless to implement them. That way we can have our ideals and ignore them, assuage our consciences while maintaining the status quo.

Returning to the Bible: Mary was only being a typical parent when she stayed outside the synagogue, not venturing in to hear what her extraordinary son had to say. And no doubt she brought her other sons along to put added family pressure on Jesus to stop all this idealistic, wild-eyed, radical preaching. They came to take him back to sensible life in Nazareth where there must have been a backlog of orders waiting to be filled by a good carpenter like Jesus. Mary thought Jesus was being childish when, in fact, Mary had failed herself to remain childlike.

Back to Ellen Goodman: "We raise our children with ethical time-bombs, built-in disillusionment alarms. We allow them their ideals until they are 14, or 18, or 22. But if they don't let go, we worry about whether they will be able to function in the real world. It's all quite mad. We regard toughness as adult, cynicism as grown-up.

"Adults *know* that clean air is all very nice, but it must be balanced against jobs. Adults know that helping others is neat, but it may take away their motivation. Adults know that peace is swell, but you may need annihilation to save your national security. Adults know war is to be feared, but so is the fear of war." Goodman suggests that this kind of realism adults so love to devour is the true junk food of our time.

"Whosoever shall not receive the Kingdom of God as a little child shall not enter therein." It was on his way to Jerusalem to die that Jesus stopped to say these words. He knew what was coming. He had no illusions about the world's imperfections. But he protested and fought them, unlike "mature" adults who only deplore them, and then use those imperfections as an excuse to prolong them. No wonder Jesus never said, "Suffer the grownups to come unto me."

When Jeremiah wrote, "I [the Lord] will put my law within them, and I will write it upon their hearts; and I will be their God, and they shall be my people" (31:33); when the psalmist wrote, "He maketh wars to cease unto the ends of the earth, he breaketh the bow and cutteth the spear . . . he burneth the chariot in the fire" (46:9)—these people also knew the imperfections of the world. They knew what the world can do to you—disappoint your trust, impair your self-confidence, break your heart with its follies and tragedies. They knew despair. But they also knew the hope that is born when optimism dies. They learned to "hang in there," knowing that maturity is the ability to outlast despair. That's what growing up is all about—learning to outlast despair.

"Wist ye not that I must be about my Father's business?" Already at age twelve Jesus was experiencing the conflict between a narrow and safe loyalty to his earthly parents Joseph and Mary, and loyalty to God; the conflict between loyalty to family and loyalty to the world, our extended family. And how did he resolve this conflict? Apparently he never did, not until the end of his life, and only then on a cross: "Woman, behold your son. Son, behold your mother."

That in this moment of pain Jesus could be so filial is, as we said at the outset, deeply moving. Apparently Joseph is dead; Mary is widowed, and Jesus is seeing to her physical and economic well-being. But beyond that, he is also providing for her spiritual well-being. Now Mary too leaves her family.and goes to John; by urging her to join his disciple Jesus includes his mother in his own mission, thereby resolving the conflict between loyalty to her and loyalty to God.

Where do you suppose were Mary's other children, those who had been with her that day outside the synagogue, those brothers to whom a dying son would normally commend his mother? Probably they were still in Nazareth, disavowing the one to whom misfortune had related them. Never would they allow themselves to feel the tension between narrow and larger loyalties.

But not so Mary. Clearly her son has reached her. Something has happened to change her mind. We read that she is standing—not fainting—by the cross, perhaps in a distress too deep for tears, but also—at last—in all the legitimate pride of motherhood.

And notice that Jesus is not the least bit protective. He doesn't say, "Take her away, John, this is no sight for a mother's eyes." No, she has to endure his sufferings, and to translate them into the pangs of child-birth that will result in a new and larger family. For she will take care not only of John, but of countless souls, including millions today who in many languages will call her "Mother" because they consider them-selves sisters and brothers of Christ. What is important about Mary is not her virginity, but her maternity.

"Wist ye not that I must be about my Father's business?" When you stop to think of it, any parent could say that to a child, just as easily as any child to a parent. "The business of America is business," said Calvin Coolidge. Well, the business of every Christian is our Father's business. That is the business common to us all, young and old. Every child is born of God as well as of man and woman. Every birth brings into the world not only another child of another mother and father but also another son or daughter of the Most High. Each of us has dual citizenship, here below and in the City of God; and two families, our smaller and hopefully loving family, and the world, our larger one so desperately in need of love.

So, all you young people who today have been baptized and con-firmed: Go ahead and outgrow your childishness, but never cease to be child*like*. And how will you keep your idealism? By remembering that love is a long-distance runner. And one more thing: suffer the grownups to come unto you, so that we may learn that we are never too old to become younger.

And together let us hail our Savior whose heart on Good Friday was as heavy as the world of sin and misery that it bore; and let us hail Mary too, for her shining example to all of us. In fact, we can picture ourselves standing at the foot of the cross, listening to Jesus' words: "Mother, behold your sons and daughters; sisters and brothers, behold your mother."

Palm Sunday 1982

APRIL 4, 1982
Readings: Zechariah 9:9–10; Luke 19:28–46

I think I know some of the reasons why Americans, and for that mat-ter people the world over, just love Westerns. Most people don't want war, they only want victory, and in a Western the losses generally are minimal while the victory is total. Secondly, in a typical Western, good is good and bad is bad, and never the twain shall get confused. Everybody likes that. And finally Westerns revive, if only for a moment, that rapidly fading myth of rugged individualism.

Normally in a Western the structures and institutions of society fail: the telegraph lines snap, the bridges are washed out, the sheriff gets drunk, and the cavalry rides off in the wrong direction. Then up speaks the Lone Ranger: "We'll head 'em off at Eagle Pass." Sure enough, with no more than a single companion, an Indian as brave as he is monosyllabic, he does; together they save the day.

But we've omitted an important feature—the "cloud of dust," the "horse with the speed of light"—a steed as mighty as his master. The two are really inseparable, the magnificence of the one enhancing the courage of the other.

Yet I would submit that the redeemer King astride his lowly colt, entering Jerusalem unarmed, fighting alone for God's grace and truth as he understands it, never giving up, about to die, killed by the violent and the indifferent, masters and servants alike—compared to the courage of the redeemer King, the courage of any Western hero is as the lightning bug to the lightning. For not only is he unarmed, he is alone. Nobody believes what he believes; nobody sees what he sees. Not even his disciples see him as he sees himself. Alone in a sea of misunderstanding, he is experiencing the worst possible kind of loneliness.

To the "chief priests and the scribes and the leaders of the people," he is of course a heretic, and a peculiarly obnoxious one at that, for all along Jesus has insisted that the true troublers of Israel's peace are not the ignorant and the cruel, but the intelligent and corrupt—people like the chief priests and the scribes and the leaders of the people themselves. And oh, how they will hate him for "cleansing" the temple, chasing away the money changers, symbols of that oldest form of corruption—religion become subservient to profit-making.

In contrast, the crowd has found a new leader. But what kind of leader are they cheering—religious or political? True, they carry palms, symbols of peace; but then they were not allowed to carry spears. True, they are praising God; but they are also hailing the King of Israel. Some no doubt remember Zechariah's prophecy, "Behold, your King is coming to you, humble, and riding on . . . the colt of an ass." But chances are the majority have Saul and Solomon in mind.

With different perceptions go different emotions: the chief priests and scribes are sullen, the crowd is ecstatic. But the greatest contrast of all is between the emotions of the crowd and those of Jesus. While they shout, "Blessed be the King who comes in the name of the Lord," the King weeps. Instead of acknowledging the cheers with a smile, as would any political leader, Jesus quietly sobs. And were he weeping for what he had earlier predicted would befall him, that would be poignant enough. But no, he weeps for what he is sure will befall the very people who are ecstatically and blindly urging him on. "And when he drew near and saw the city he wept over it, saying, 'Would that even now you knew the things that make for peace.'"

Would he, through comparable tears, say the same of us this Palm Sunday? Nineteen centuries later, have we learned anything more about the things that make for peace? I think we have to say "Yes": we've abolished slavery, we're talking about the rights of women, of children, of the unborn, even of whales and seals; we even talk of the rights of field mice—for heaven's sakes—when we propose to build a new Piggly Wiggly shopping plaza. All this is good. God has always wanted human beings to affirm life—more and more of it—and history has a way of driving home such ancient religious truths. But in all honesty we also have to answer "No." Speaking of human beings centuries later, Robert Louis Stevenson wrote: "Our frailties are invincible, our virtues barren; the battle goes sore against us to the going down of the sun." Could he have had in mind all the crises in history that are never recognized as such until they are validated by disaster?

Yes, we can sympathize with those Jews cheering Christ on because they so yearned for political independence. Colonialism at best can promote law and order, but never peace. But if, particularly in our century, we have learned a lot about the limits of colonialism, we have as yet learned little about the limits of nationalism, even though nationalism "as we have known it in the nineteenth and much of the twentieth century is as much of an anachronism today as was States' Rights when Calhoun preached it and Jefferson Davis fought for it." So recently wrote that grand old historian Henry Steele Commager, who went on to conclude: "None of our global problems can be resolved within the artificial boundaries of nations—artificial not so much in the eyes of history as in the eyes of nature." And he might have added "artificial, always, in the sight of God."

Will we never get beyond national sovereignty? Territorial discrimination has always been as evil as racial discrimination. For we all belong one to another, every one of us on this planet. That's the way God made us; Christ this Friday will once again die to keep us that way. Our sin is only that we are constantly trying to put asunder what God Herself has joined together. Will we see that truth that stares us in the face before it hits us in the face? Will this crisis finally be validated by one last, terrible disaster? "Would that even now you knew the things that make for peace."

Yes, we can sympathize with those Jews cheering Christ on because they saw in him—and rightly so—a prophet of justice. In the best prophetic tradition Christ stood with the poor against the rich. He knew that "Compassion without confrontation is merely commiseration—fruitless and sentimental" (Henri Nouwen). In contrast to many a preacher today Jesus knew that "Love your enemies" doesn't mean "Don't make any." But to the evils of oppression, poverty, and corruption in high places, evils he proclaimed so forcefully that the common people heard him gladly, he added one more, which lost him their vote—the evil of violence.

In this century that has seen millions die in ghastly wars, and with nuclear annihilation hanging over our heads; in this century that has seen every revolution end in the reappearance of a new ruling class (which is not to say the old was better); on this fourteenth anniversary of Martin Luther King Jr.'s death; and on this Sunday in which we hail our Lord with palms, let us remember that the trouble with violence is that it changes not too much, but too little. Nonviolence is more radical because it is more truthful. Violence always ends up calling on lies to defend it, just as lies call on violence to defend them. By contrast, truth is naked, vulnerable as Christ on the colt of an ass, its only weapon Christ's own, God's love. So the very love of God that found oppression, poverty and corruption intolerable, this same love, rather than inflict suffering—even on those imposing it on the poor—took suffering upon itself. What can only be said cynically of another—"It is better that one man should die than that an entire nation perish" (ah, the demands of national security!)—can be said in utter truthfulness about oneself: "It is better that I should die rather than a single other person perish." That's finally how truth disarms the defensive, and finally there is no other way.

"Would that even now you knew the things that make for peace"— the limits of nationalism, the limits of violence.

We started out talking of Westerns. If only life were so simple. If only there were evil people insidiously committing evil deeds, and our job were only to separate them from the rest and destroy them. But "Ultimately considered, evil is done not so much by evil people, but by good people who do not know themselves" (Reinhold Niebuhr). The chief priests and scribes may have been like Robespierre, Lenin, John Foster Dulles: fierce idealists, people of great moral vigor. But they had little self-knowledge. They couldn't see the falsehoods in their own truths. They couldn't see what Pascal saw, that the world divides itself between saints who know themselves to be sinners, and sinners who imagine themselves to be saints. The Passion story this week will teach us the deepest lesson about political life. It is not that "good is forever on the scaffold, wrong upon the throne." It is that all people stand in need of a merciful God.

So let's get off our great white horses, as individuals and as a people, and let's walk, palms in hand, blessed with the hindsight of history, by the side of him who rides today on the colt of an ass.

To him alone can we sing:

> Ride on! Ride on in majesty!
> Thy last and fiercest strife is nigh;
> . . . .
> Bow thy meek head to mortal pain,
> Then take, O God, thy power, and reign.
> Henry Milman

The Human Race Fully Alive

Easter Sunday
APRIL 11, 1982
Reading: Matthew 28

Suppose last week's storm was not the season's last. Suppose, for a terrible instant, that somehow the earth had spun out of orbit and was headed for the immensities of space; that we were forever to be lashed to the rack of winter, those ice-caressing winds not our passing but our constant companions. In the mind of St. Paul that would be a proper analogy of the human world without Easter. Not one to hedge his bets, St. Paul puts all his Christian eggs in one Easter basket: "For if Christ has not been raised," he writes the Corinthians, "your faith is futile" (1 Cor. 15:17).

I love the way St. Paul lays it on the line. He'd never make it in that fudge factory we call the State Department. He knows that human beings need convictions to live by—deep moral convictions, including the conviction of tolerance—that we can manage with opinions only if we want to die comfortably. And I like the way St. Paul insists on the consequences of the faith, which are little less than cosmic. To Paul the light of Easter is no lantern swinging over a narrow, empty grave, but a light capable of dispelling the thick darkness covering the nations. Paul never tries to explain the resurrection of Jesus. He knows that to explain the ways of God in the light of human experience is like trying to explain the sun in terms of a candle. It's the sun that makes sense of the candle. Likewise we don't prove the Resurrection; the Resurrection proves us. The Easter faith doesn't ask us to believe without proof, but to trust without reservation. Don't think your way into a new life, but live your way into an entirely new way of thinking.

And what is this new way of thinking we call the Easter faith? It says that we live in an Easter, not a Good Friday, world. It says that you can kill God's love, but you cannot keep it dead and buried. It says that all the strength and tenderness that on Good Friday we saw scourged and stretched out on a cross, the gorgeous life that kept alive the strains of hope even as they were being drowned out by orchestrated evil, the love of God incarnate is again alive, "and lo, I am with you always, even to the close of the age." The Resurrection faith says that until all eternity Christ will be alive, now in the form of the Holy Spirit trying by any road, and at any cost, to bring about our own resurrection, for "the glory of God is a human being fully alive."

The fact of the matter is that none of us is fully alive. Many of us are scared to death, our lives one long suicide. We are too fearful: we fear the past, the future, our children, our friends. We fear death and are fearful that we deserve to die. Like the guilty paralytic carried on a pallet to the feet of Jesus, all of us are at least partially paralyzed. Whose hands are free, free to be extended to anyone? Whose feet are free to walk any path of life, free to walk out of that tight little protective circle of friends? Whose eyes are not fixed on some status symbol or other? It is inevitable; before the awesome terrors of the world every heart quakes. Every human being tries desperately to secure himself against his insecurity—by gaining more power, more money, more virtue, more health. But the effort is vain: our need for security always outstrips our ability to provide it (a failure understood by Michelangelo, all of whose powerful figures bear the telltale sign of anxiety, dilated pupils).

It is this anxiety that is the precondition of our paralysis, which in turn produces more anxiety as we realize how we have stunted our growth, denied our destiny. Hence there is not one of us who does not need to be converted—not from life to something more than life, but from something less than life to the possibility of full life itself. "The glory of God is a human being fully alive." And to become fully alive, to be resurrected, is undeniably possible, for if Christ is risen, then to us, as to that sad, guilty, lonely figure on the pallet centuries ago, come the words, "My son"—my daughter—"your sins are forgiven. Rise, take up your pallet and walk."

If Christ is risen, we too can rise. No longer paralyzed, our hands are free to be extended to the outcast and the enemy—the most confirmed addict, the reddest of communists. No longer paralyzed, our feet are free to walk out of any job that is harmful to others or meaningless to ourselves, free even to walk that lonesome valley without fear of evil. If Christ is risen, we too can rise. Everything is possible to those whose eyes, no longer fixed on some status symbol, are held instead by the gaze of our risen Lord who is himself the eternal dispenser of freedom, the eternal dispenser of life.

But Christ is not only a healer of individuals. He is also a prophet to the nations. While he walked the earth Jesus delivered people from paralysis, insanity, leprosy, suppurating wounds, deformity, and muteness. But again and again in word and deed he returned to the plight of the poor, whose poverty, in true prophetic fashion, he considered no historical accident but the fruit of social injustice. What would he say and do in our hard and uncertain times, in a world of thirteen million refugees, a world one-half of whose children never so much as open their mouths to say "aah" to a doctor, a world in which almost every country is robbing the poor to feed the military? And would he not pronounce our own nation a greedy disgrace? Whole cities could live on the garbage from our dumps, on the luxuries we consider necessities. The world with its triumphs and despairs, its beauty and ugliness, has today moved next door to every one of us. Only spiritual deafness can prevent our hearing the voice of God in the clamor of the cities. Only blindness of a willful sort can prevent our seeing the face of the Risen Lord in the faces of the suffering poor. The glory of God is the human race fully alive, and that means minimally fed, clothed, housed.

And spared the threat of nuclear holocaust. Oh, how our Risen Lord must scorn the insolence and arrogance of our leaders: the surmises that pass as dogmas, the prejudices they call solutions, the speculations on nuclear war they suck out of their thumbs. The poor may suffer the degradation of poverty, but the leaders of the United States and of the Soviet Union are threatened by degradation through power.

What irony, that our Lord should rise in a world about to become one vast burial ground. Talk about living in sin! God grant that on this Easter day we recognize that it is a sin merely to build a nuclear weapon. In the sight of our Risen Lord the mere possession of nuclear weapons must be an abomination comparable to the possession of slaves 150 years ago. And just as the object then was not to humanize but to abolish the institution of slavery, so today it is our Christian duty to abolish from the face of the earth every last nuclear weapon. Thank God we have the beginning of an abolitionist movement.

Thank God, too, that we have seen the last of winter. Soon energy will be pouring out of the ground and into every blade of grass, every flower, bush, and tree in sight. Soon the robins will join the pigeons, the sky will be filled with the thunder of the sun. Overhead, underfoot, and all around we shall see, hear, and feel the juice and joy of spring. That's the natural world, and it's wonderful. The human world could be like unto it, if we mean it when we sing, "Made like him, like him we rise / Ours the cross, the grave, the skies." The glory of God is a human being fully alive. The glory of God is the human race fully alive. We can all be resurrected, converted to the possibility of a full life, if today we give our loyalty to the Risen Christ. Easter does not call for sympathy for the crucified Lord, but loyalty to the Risen One, the same loyalty that made Peter after Jesus' death ten times the person he was before; the loyalty that made St. Stephen under the rain of death-dealing stones cry out, Christlike, "Father, forgive"; the loyalty of the early martyrs who with their blood watered the seed of the Christian Church until it became the acorn that broke the mighty boulder that was the Roman Empire. Not for nothing has it been written, "If there should arise one utterly believing person, the history of the world would be changed." Well, dear friends—let's change it!

Where the Heart Is

APRIL 25, 1982
Readings: Isaiah 65:17–25; Luke 1:46–55

A short while ago I received a request from a representative of the Riverside Housing Task Force: "Please give us a sermon on 'the theology of domicile.'" A rather highfalutin' subject for a humble parish minister like myself—something the scholars at Union Seminary across the street are better equipped to tackle. But as I almost always do exactly what my parishioners request (please think twice before asking!), here goes.

Consider the word "home." With the exception of "homework," everything the word suggests is positive. "Home" suggests breathing space, comfort, warmth, dignity, grace and identity. And take the expressions "home free," "that hit home," "a home run" (something the Tigers seem to know more about these days than the Yankees), and "home is where the heart is." Or the adjective "homey." Or even "homing pigeons." Viewed positively death is "going home": "I'm a-goin' home"—we all sang that as kids. And when I was in the eighth grade in Carmel, California, our grammar school chorus sang words of Robert Louis Stevenson I can still remember:

> Under the wide and starry sky,
> Dig the grave and let me lie.
> Glad did I live and gladly die,
> And I lay me down with a will.
> This be the verse you grave for me:
> "Here he lies where he longed to be.
> Home is the sailor, home from sea,"
> And the hunter home from the hill.

In contrast, the word "homeless" is devastating, suggesting neither comfort nor companionship, dignity nor grace, and precious little identity. To have no place is to be no place. Homelessness is nowheresville—whether you're one of the world's 14 million refugees, a boat person from Indochina, one of Calcutta's 400,000 semi-starved sidewalk dwellers, or one of the 36,000 who in New York City spend so much of their time huddled in doorways, wrapping themselves in the *Daily News.*

Surely one of the hardest things for all of us is to keep first things in first place. Whether in our personal lives or in our public, national life, with the passage of time first things invariably tend to slip into second, third, fourth, not to say fourteenth place. Recognizing this, Moses proclaimed every fiftieth year a year of Jubilee, a year to blow the whistle on the human enterprise, a year for human beings to get first things back into first place, mostly in their relationships with each other. "You shall hallow the fiftieth year and proclaim liberty throughout the land to all its inhabitants; . . . each of you shall return to his property and each of you shall return to his family" (Lev. 25:10). By American standards, this understanding of property is nothing short of sensational. "The land shall not be sold in perpetuity for the land is mine" (saith the Lord). Homeless people, unable to buy property and without relatives to do it for them, could, during the year of Jubilee, receive back free of charge their original land. Why? Because first things first: it is not the will of God that any one of

God's children be homeless. Human relations are finally not contractual, a matter of law; finally human relations are just that—human.

We Americans often act as if private property were sacred. But, Biblically considered, no property is ultimately owned by anyone but God (something Native Americans understand far better than we do). "The earth is the Lord's and the fullness thereof," says the psalmist. "The land shall not be sold in perpetuity for the land is mine," saith the Lord. When I was chaplain at Yale, I used to suggest to economics professors that they ask students entering their classes to answer the question, "To whom does the earth belong?" because obviously the answer determines how one approaches economics. But don't think for a moment any of them took me seriously—despite the fact that all scholarship is based on presuppositions; despite the fact that the seas, the "high seas," are considered the common heritage of all humanity, so why not the land?

In the Bible there *is* private property, but the question of ownership is always subordinate to the question of use: "They shall build houses and inhabit them . . . They shall not build and another inhabit" (Isa. 65:21–22). And if it is the will of God that none of God's children be homeless, then we are dealing with a divine imperative, not a human option. This isn't a matter of charity, but of justice. Just as to the slaves freedom was not a gift but the restoration of a right no one had any business taking from them, so a home is a right; the homeless are being robbed. Also robbed of their rights are those who live in rundown, rat-plagued firetraps, or in rural communities— some thirty thousand—that are still without water or sewage systems. It's hard for New Yorkers to believe, but it is a fact that 60 percent of substandard housing in the United States is in rural areas.

We Americans tend to think that in recent years Washington has heavily subsidized housing for the poor. But we forget that the largest housing subsidies come through income tax deductions, the principal deduction being for interest on mortgages. Add these indirect subsidies to all the direct ones, and it turns out that 25 percent of all government expenditures for housing helps people with household incomes of over $50,000; just short of 50 percent of all government expenditures for housing helps those with incomes between $20,000 and $50,000; only 14.7 percent aids those with incomes between $5,000 and $20,000; and 14.1 percent of all government expenditures for housing helps those with household incomes below $5,000.

These 1981 statistics compiled by the National Low-income Housing Coalition are enough to mar the blue of sunny skies on a beautiful spring day.

A recent Presbyterian study indicates that over 6 million families pay more than one-half their income for housing; that the national stock of available low-rental housing is not expanding, but shrinking; and that new production of low-income housing is at its lowest level in two generations.

As all New Yorkers know, suburbia's children are returning to the city in droves, and the blockbusters of twenty years ago—who pressured whites to move out of the inner city to make room for Blacks and to make profits for themselves—have now been reincarnated as redevelopers, and are forcing out poor Blacks, poor everybody, to earn for themselves the profits to be made from the influx of the young and affluent. For fiscal reasons, the city aids and abets the process, for as property values increase so will the city's tax base. Meantime, where are the poor? They are pushed into ever-smaller subdivisions in ever-older buildings. As the Presbyterian study vividly states: "The amount of floor space available at affordable rent shrinks with each move, with each new partitioning of each old parlor or bedroom, in a cycle that reduces breathing space, comfort, dignity, and grace with the quiet inexorability of a salami-slicing machine."

In 1949 Congress declared the housing policy of the United States to be a "decent home in a suitable living environment for every American family." The aspiration was noble; its implementation is a national disgrace. It's time to get first things back into first place, once again to blow the whistle in the field of housing, as in so many other fields. The Riverside Housing Task Force has some people ready to dedicate our own energies, and today have letters for us to sign and literature to read in the cloister lounge after the service.

Almost a year ago, the National Council of Churches sent out what I thought was a perceptive message to all the churches in the country. In it they suggest that America has always been torn between two philosophies, two visions of itself.

> From the first, there were those who saw America as a rich treasure waiting to be exploited for the benefit of those daring enough and strong enough to take it. . . . In this vision of America, the fittest survive and prosper, and there is little room for public purpose since it interferes with private gain. Compassion is a weakness in the competitive struggle of each against all, and charity is the voluntary option of individuals. Government is at best a necessary evil which must be strong enough to protect privilege from assault but

kept too weak to impose public responsibility on private prerogative. In this vision, America is seen principally as Empire—"Manifest Destiny," "54–40 or fight," "Remember the *Maine*"—with a mission to extend its power and commerce throughout the continent, the hemisphere, the world.

But, as the Council points out,

another vision of America has been present from the beginning also. This second alternate vision has deep roots in religious faith and biblical images of divine intent and human possibility. The precious possession of pilgrims and padres, it was a vision of creating in the New World a new model of human community—the New Jerusalem—free from the oppression and misery that entrenched power and privilege perpetuated in the Old World they had fled.

In this America, it was envisioned, government would promote the common welfare and secure the blessings of liberty for all. The dignity and worth of each person would be respected and protected as a matter of policy as well as piety, and each person's potential would be developed to the fullest. Justice and compassion would reign in alabaster cities that stretched from sea to shining sea, and the bountiful resources of a favored land would be thankfully received and gladly shared with the whole human family, as the nurturing providence of the Creator meant them to be. This America would be known in the world for its compassion, its deep desire for peace and justice, its commitment to human rights and decency. It would stand as a beacon and a model, a city set on a hill, its power stemming from the irresistible example of a just, caring and peaceful people sharing life and treasure generously with all the people of earth.

Never realized, this second vision of America has never been abandoned. I submit this is the real America, the essential America, the one with first things in first place. And if today we as a people are torn apart, it is because people are whole only when they know what is essential. So let us address once again the generous self in everyone that gets addressed so seldom; let us indeed lift up our hearts and urge our nation *toward* care and compassion, not away from them; let us lift up our hearts to the God who exalts those of low degree. We have created a world for some of us; it's time now to create a world for all of us, a nation and a world in which everyone will feel at home and "none shall make them afraid."

"They shall not hurt nor destroy in all my holy mountain, saith the LORD" (Isa. 65:25).

Mother's Day 1982

MAY 9, 1982
Reading: 1 John 4:7–12

What to say on this fifth Sunday after Easter, which also happens to be Mother's Day? As the art of life is to cooperate gracefully with the inevitable, let's talk of mothers, starting with those no longer among us. Compared to us, they are doing just fine. "For to me life is Christ, and death gain . . . what I should like is to depart and be with Christ, that is better by far" (Phil. 1:21, 23). These ancient words of St. Paul find an echo in the sentiments of a modern poet.

> It is not dying hurts us so,
> 'Tis living hurts us more;
> But dying is a different way,
> A kind, behind the door . . .
> The southern custom of the bird
> That soon as frosts are due
> Adopts a better latitude.
> We are the birds that stay,
> For whose reluctant crumb
> We stipulate, till pitying snows
> Persuade our feathers home.
> Emily Dickinson

If our dear parents are in "a better latitude" (or altitude—wherever God is, which is everywhere); if our dear parents no longer have to pay the cost of upkeep, no longer have to worry about poverty, pollution, the Middle East, and the South Atlantic—not to mention us, their children; if they are with Jesus who "shines fairer than all the angels heaven can boast," then surely it is pure self-indulgence on our part to try to hold them close by grief. Grieve we must, for ourselves, for a while. But after a while, it seems right to remember less what we have lost and more the things that can never be taken away. It seems right to pray God to fill the hollow in the heart not with grief but with that joy that can absorb all sorrow, that hope that can overcome despair, that love that binds all in mortal and immortal life. Then we are free to return—as our parents would have us do—to "fight the good fight," to endure unto the end, "till pitying snows persuade our feathers home," and like them we are made partakers of God's eternal Kingdom. I like these last words of Edward the Confessor to those around his deathbed: "Weep not, for I shall not die. And as I leave the land of the dying I trust to see the blessings of the Lord in the land of the living."

But perhaps I have been proceeding on a wrong assumption. I have been implying that our departed mothers were all nourishing, comforting—all those good things we describe as maternal. Clearly that's not the case. What then shall we say of mothers—and fathers too—who on balance were not good parents, or good, perhaps, to everyone's children but their own?

This is a delicate and complicated matter, but a very important one. As William Faulkner noted, "The past is never dead; it's not even past." We human beings are shaped by our memories as much as we are shaped by our genes. And some people are their memories—their bad memories, mostly of their parents.

In my experience, there is no worse monkey to carry around on your back than that of a father or mother no longer alive, but not yet forgiven. People who walk around with such burdens rarely realize that it is precisely what cannot be condoned that has to be forgiven. What you can excuse, you don't have to forgive. What you can't excuse, what is "unforgivable"—that's what you have to forgive, even as our heavenly Father/Mother forgives the unforgivable in us. It's a crisis of faith we're talking about, because you can't appropriate God's forgiveness of you unless and until you forgive your parents—alive or dead. Harsh, but true.

Because the past is never dead it can be redeemed. Bad memories can be "befriended," as it were, and so changed. So let us pray God to fill the hollow in the heart with that forgiveness that can transform all anger and resentment.

And also banish guilt. For if some of us feel anger when we recall our parents, more of us, I suspect, feel guilt. We feel we failed them more than they us. (And often they help us to feel that way!) Again we are talking of a crisis of faith; God's forgiveness surely covers our failures toward our parents. Just as we have to forgive what we can't possibly condone, so we have to accept forgiveness when there is no possibility of amends. I imagine the latter may be even harder. Sometimes it is more blessed to receive, than to give; at least it takes more humility.

Perhaps all this can be summed up in Christ's injunction. "Let the dead bury the dead." I interpret that to mean, "Let the dead bury the *dead*, and not the living." Grief, resentment, guilt—good for the short run, in the long run those three emotions can bury the living.

Let's move now to the mothers still among us. For whatever they have given us of nourishment, comfort, all those good things we call maternal, we shall, of course not only be grateful but tell them of our gratitude, today—Mother's Day—and every day, for God knows we all need encouragement.

And if they are a pain in the neck we should probably inform them of that as well. Recently I was asked to perform an interracial marriage. (The term is sociological, all marriages in the church being strictly interpersonal.) The mother of the groom, who was white, was not behaving well. Finally the groom saw what he had to do— take her to task: "You brought me up right, Mother, to be decent, caring, without prejudice. I expect no less from you. So I don't want to hear another word of objection. Is that clear?" Somewhat to my amazement, the mother promptly shaped up.

I'm not saying we should always speak the truth to our mothers. The difference between a Boy Scout and a Christian is that a Boy Scout is always enjoined to speak the truth, while a Christian is enjoined—by St. Paul—to speak the truth in love, when it is good for edification. The son recognized the truth of Jesus' words, "He who loves father and mother more than me is not worthy of me"; and the mother recognized that if parents have the right to expect things of their children, children have the same right vis-à-vis their parents. The deal is clear: parents shouldn't treat their children as if they were too young, and children shouldn't treat their parents as if they were too old. We say we want to spare our parents' feelings, but that usually means we want to spare ourselves the unpleasantness implied in "He who loves father and mother more than me is not worthy of me." (That great gangster Al Capone hit on a great truth when he said, "We don't want no trouble!")

We've talked of parents, dead and alive. Let's try now to say a final word about ourselves, those of us who are parents. Even though it is

Mother's Day I want to include fathers, for just as the woman most in need of liberation is the woman in every man, so the parent most in need of encouragement is the mother in every father. A maternal father—what a beautiful person, tender as only truly strong people can be tender.

Let's face it: Being a parent is a no-win situation. I remember a college freshman telling me, "I had a terrible adolescence; my parents understood me." That suggested to me that if there's one thing worse than banging your head against a closed door, it's banging it against an open one—you lose your balance.

By the same token, being a parent is also a no-lose situation. Millions of children who had no right to turn out well are today doing just beautifully. Let's remember Margaret Mead. Let's remember Harold Pinter: "It's not what's known and spoken, but what's known and unspoken that sours human relations." Most of all, let's remember that our children are on loan from God. Children are *loaned treasures*. They belong to God before and after they belong to us. We should know that, and we should make sure they know that. Finally, we parents should not expect too much gratitude. (In my experience, gratitude is not as profound an emotion as the expectation of gratitude!) We shouldn't expect to see our love returned; we should hope to see it passed on.

So here's to our parents—and ourselves. If our parents are dead, let us try to recall them with gratitude rather than grief, with forgiveness rather than resentment. And if we failed them—and which of us didn't at some point or other?—then they can forgive us even as we forgive them and God forgives us all. If our parents are living, and we are adult, let's try treating them as peers; it's more interesting. And if we ourselves have children, let's enjoy them more than we worry about them. For they are indeed loaned *treasures*.

Let's listen once again to the New Testament lesson, which sums up all human and divine relationships so well:

> Dear friends, let us love one another, because love is from God. Everyone who loves is a child of God, and knows God; but the unloving know nothing of God, for God is love, and his love was disclosed to us in this, that he sent his only Son into the world to bring us life. The love I speak of is not our love for God, but the love he showed to us in sending his Son as the remedy for the defilement of our sins. If God

thus loved us, dear friends, we in turn are bound to love one another. Though God has never been seen by anyone, God herself dwells in us if we love one another.

Good Names for a Church

MAY 16, 1982
Reading: 2 Corinthians 4

In a very few minutes we shall be celebrating—and I hope the verb is well chosen—our annual church meeting. So, to put us in the mood, let's try to describe a church—any church—at its best, and let's do so in reference to three Biblical characters.

The first is the familiar figure of the Good Samaritan, whose story, more lyrically than any statement, makes the point that to find God you need seek no further than your nearest neighbor's need. To know God is to care for your neighbor.

To a great many institutions this is a foreign notion. Most institutions don't bleed when they hurt; they know no shame. But churches bleed for the world; in the mind of their Master, as the story of the Good Samaritan makes clear, caring is the greatest thing. Caring matters most—caring for the world too, for as the story demonstrates, global is essential, national is optional; or if you will, ecumenical is essential, denominational is optional.

To Christ, who told the story, the integrity of love is more important than the purity of dogma. Mirroring Christ, St. Paul could insist that even "if I . . . understand all mysteries and all knowledge"—academics take note—"if I give away all I have"—radicals, pay attention—even "if I deliver my body to be burned"—the very stuff of heroism—"but have not love I gain nothing." I doubt if in any holy writ of any religious faith there is a more radical statement of ethics.

So a church—any church—at its best represents not dogma in search of obedience, but love in search of form. Everything we do in this church—from the Chain of Prayer to the meeting of the trustees, from theological reflection to the daily teaching of English to hundreds of refugees—we do for one reason alone: to manifest the love of God that we see in the face of Jesus Christ.

Not that dogma isn't important. "Dogmatic" is bad, and so is being doctrinaire. But dogma and doctrine are good, even essential, as long as they are considered signposts, not hitching posts. Only love is absolute. The story of the Good Samaritan says to us that just as Jesus is God's love personified, so the Church is God's love *organized*.

Of the second Biblical character we know only his name: Gershom, which means "a stranger in an alien land." This is the name Moses gave his first-born. To me Gershom is a name that could be stamped on the lives of every one of us in the Church. I know that makes the human enterprise sound desolate, but that's not what I intend. I want only to pose the question: To whom finally does this earth belong?

Over thirty years ago, in my more-or-less unbelieving days, a friend of mine, my age, was killed in an automobile accident. I was terribly upset, and furious. I took his death as just one more bit of evidence to prove how fatuous is the Christian claim that God is all-powerful and all-loving, when any sensitive soul can see that the surface of the entire earth is soaked with the tears and the blood of the innocent. The funeral service was conducted by an Episcopal bishop. To my sour way of viewing things, he looked like a typical representative of the Church—a soft face over a hard collar. As he started down the aisle he began unctuously to intone Job's famous words: "The Lord gave, and the Lord hath taken away; blessed be the name of the Lord." From my aisle seat I could have stuck out my foot and tripped him up, and almost did so, had not a still small voice, as it were, suddenly arrested my attention by asking, "To what part of Job's sentence are you objecting?" I thought it was the second part—"the Lord hath taken away; blessed be the name of the Lord." But then it hit me: it was the first part. For the first time in my life I felt the full impact of "The Lord gave." The world, very simply, is not ours. At best we're guests. That's why I say Gershom, a stranger in an alien land, is a name that could be stamped on the lives of all of us. That's what St. Paul means by writing, "we have this treasure in earthen vessels, to show that the transcendent power belongs to God and not to us."

But if the Lord gave, if "the earth is the Lord's and the fulness thereof; the world and they that dwell therein" (Ps. 24:1), then we can talk of another stamp on our lives, which reads, "Made in Heaven." If you drove into the garage this morning you may have seen the sign one of the attendants posted. It shows a kind of human Snoopy saying, "I'm somebody—because God don't make no junk." That's a terrific sign, insisting as it does that we're precious, every one of us, "treasures in earthen vessels," treasures because God made us and not we ourselves. More than that: if the earth is the Lord's and the fulness thereof, then

we don't have to live possessively; and if we don't have to live possessively we are free to live gratefully. William Blake got it right:

> He who bends to himself a joy
> Doth the winged life destroy.
> But he who kisses a joy as it flies,
> Dwells in eternity's sunrise.

So Gershom finally is a good name for church members, a name with
positive connotations. A church—any church—should exude gratitude.

And also be full of divine discontent. No church that understands
itself as a stranger in an alien country can be for the status quo. Too
many churches preach Christ separated from the Kingdom that Christ
himself preached. Too many Christians will today pray, "Thy Kingdom
come," and tomorrow bar its way. Those who attack the status quo,
contrary to popular belief, are not mixing religion with politics. It's
those who support the status quo who are doing that. Two years ago in
this church, Dom Helder Camara, Bishop of Recife, Brazil, a friend of
the poor and therefore at serious odds with his government, was asked
by a reporter if he wasn't mixing religion with politics. Answered the
bishop: "When the Roman Catholic Church is in bed with the government, no one says, 'The Church is mixing religion with politics.'"

And of course churches should quarrel far more with the governments of their own countries. The prophets of Israel dwelt on the sins
of Assyria, which were manifold, as little as did Jesus on the evils of
Rome. Likewise in this church we shouldn't dwell on the sins of the
Soviet Union, which also are manifold. None of the terrible things
done by the Soviet government are done in the name of a single
American, whereas the American government can do nothing except
in the name of every American.

The Good Samaritan, Gershom—good names with good "vibes"
for a church—any church.

Finally, how about Isaac, which means "laughter"? And if you
remember the story, it's laughter—under the knife! Why not? It's
true that we are entangled in the web of life, bewildered by its vicis-
situdes, submerged by its demands, harassed by its haste and waste;
still, in the church, we do not hand over our high morale to the safe-
keeping of any but the Lord Almighty. The psalmist stated our case:
"Lord, by thy favour thou hast made my mountain to stand strong. . . .
Weeping may endure for a night, but joy cometh in the morning" (Ps.
30:7, 5). "Yea, though I walk through the valley of the shadow of
death, I will fear no evil: for thou art with me" (Ps. 23:4).

And so did St. Paul. "We are afflicted in every way, but not crushed; perplexed, but not driven to despair; persecuted, but not forsaken; struck down, but not destroyed; always carrying in the body the death of Jesus, so that the life of Jesus may also be manifested in our bodies."

"So we do not lose heart," not in the Church: "Though our outer nature is wasting away, our inner nature is being renewed every day." Faith puts us on the road, hope keeps us there, and love is the name of our journey. I can't imagine any institution to which I would rather pledge loyalty than to the Church. Like each of us, it's an earthen vessel—but it has the treasure, the light that shines in the darkness, the light of the knowledge of the glory of God in the face of Christ.

And belonging to Riverside Church I feel exceptionally blessed, as miraculously lucky as that legendary fellow in the Salvation Army who was playing the bass tuba the day it rained gold!

By Fire or Fire

Peace Sabbath
MAY 30, 1982
Readings: Selections from Acts 2

Let me extend on behalf of this congregation a most cordial welcome to the representatives of twenty-three delegations to the United Nations: Gambia, German Democratic Republic, Federal Republic of Germany, Iran, Peoples Republic of Benin, Peoples Republic of Bangladesh, Socialist Republic of Vietnam, Democratic Republic of Afghanistan, Madagascar, United States, Republic of Zimbabwe, Democratic Republic of Kampuchea, Lebanon, El Salvador, Union of Soviet Socialist Republics, Nicaragua, Guinea-Bissau, United Republic of Tanzania, Cuba, Bulgaria, Kenya, Belorussia, and Czechoslovakia. May I also extend a special welcome to the members of the United Nations Center for Disarmament, Ms. Ingrid Lehmann and Mr. Ogunsola Ogunbanwo, and to Mr. Jan Martensen, Assistant Secretary of the United Nations for Disarmament. I think we ought to recognize these representatives from many countries, some of which are not now at peace with one another. Let us hope we are all here to affirm that all people have more in common than in conflict.

(There followed thirty seconds of sustained applause.)

Several years ago, an outstanding American, John Gardner, wrote this of his country: "The nation disintegrates. I use the phrase soberly:

the nation disintegrates." Substitute for "nation" the "world" and you have the reason for Peace Sabbath. Today it is celebrated in about ten thousand churches nationwide—many more than last year, because in many more minds such questions as these are becoming increasingly urgent: Can humanity be saved from the doom of nuclear war? If the nations of the world do not reverse the arms race, who will have grandchildren? There is another question, whose answer depends on the answer given the arms race question: Can 500 million people the globe around be spared the agonizing death of starvation?

Last summer I read *Clowns of God*, Morris West's latest novel. It is about the approaching end of the world, and what is so eerie about it is that West's description of the last days of the human race mirrors so closely our own days: food shortages not only in the southern sphere but also in Poland and Russia, a worldwide shortage of fuel, and no apparent antidote to the ever-escalating arms race. Indeed the world disintegrates. I use the phrase soberly: the world disintegrates.

Nevertheless, no Christian can say, "All hope is gone"; only "All hope—but one." And that hope is the Pentecostal claim that, God willing, a heavenly fire will yet contain the flames of hell. But as the story of Pentecost underscores, "God willing" is insufficient: we too must be willing; the choice is always ours, all of which the poet understood so well when of Pentecost he wrote:

> The dove descending breaks the air
> With flame of incandescent terror
> Of which the tongues declare
> The one discharge of sin and error.
> The only hope, or else despair
>   Lies in the choice of pyre or pyre—
>   To be redeemed from fire by fire.
> T. S. Eliot

I quote T. S. Eliot because poets and artists best grasp the essence of mystery. Exactly what happened on that first day of Pentecost no one knows. Once again, as is so often the case in the Bible, it is the invisible event that counts. One fact alone is certain: heretofore hanging around at loose ends, the disciples now become ten times the people they were during Jesus' life on earth. Heretofore waiting and watching for God, they begin now to be moved and used by God. So the question to us on the Peace Sabbath and day of Pentecost is, can we too be so moved and used by God, that God's heavenly fire *in us* may yet contain the ever-advancing flames of hell?

More and more I'm convinced that the first thing that needs to be ignited by heavenly fire is our imagination. More and more I'm convinced that the revolution most needed by citizens of every country is a revolution of imagination. Shelley called the imagination a great instrument for moral good, and in all of George Bernard Shaw there is probably no line more poignant than that in the epilogue of *St. Joan*: "Must a Christ die in every generation to save those of no imagination?" In the first place, an ignited imagination makes us feel what we know. Almost everyone knows that "all men" (people) "are created equal." But how many *feel* the monstrosity of inequality? Another illustration: we all *know* that we live in the nuclear age. But how many *feel* the impact of that statement? Among other things, it signifies that "the arm of technology has grown by a factor of a million within the lifetime of one generation," words of physicist Victor F. Weisskopf to his colleagues in 1978. Anyone with an ignited imagination will realize that the nuclear age is not the extension of the pre-nuclear age, but in many ways the antithesis of it. All the explosives in all the wars of this century amount to something like sixteen megatons. The United States' nuclear arsenal today has in the neighborhood of seven thousand megatons, as does the arsenal of the Soviet Union. You can't persuade me that anyone who not only knows but *feels* those statistics would urge us to continue to build, plan, invent and buy such weapons—and for the sake, mind you, of national security. Such a person would have to have a stone for a heart.

I keep hoping there is at least the ghost of a smile on the lips of those who tell us that we need nuclear weapons to guard "the ethical traditions of the free world with their special respect for individual life." Compare those totally unimaginative words with these, spoken in Rio de Janeiro in 1960, by no less a military figure than President Eisenhower: "War is now utterly preposterous. In nearly every generation the fields of earth have been stained by blood. Now war would not yield blood—only a great emptiness of the combatants, and the threat of death from the skies for all who inhabit the earth."

Is it farfetched to see a little tongue of flame over President Eisenhower's head when he uttered those words—words which could be understood in any language by those who had ears to hear? He was being moved and used by God because he felt so deeply what he knew so well, which makes for a qualitatively different kind of knowledge.

But as Eisenhower's words suggest, an imagination ignited not only feels more deeply; it sees more clearly. What is this insanity in the South Atlantic if not—among other things—a failure of imagination? On the part of the British, it was a failure to foresee what was coming, given the way almost all Latin Americans feel about Las Malvinas. Would not diplomats with 20/20 vision long ago have negotiated some treaty whereby these islands could be to Argentina what Greenland is to Denmark, or the Cook Islands to New Zealand—an autonomous, self-ruling region under a distant flag?

And what a failure of imagination it is for President Reagan not to see that with regard to nuclear weapons the tightening noose around our necks is the requirement for speed. If those Pershing 2s are ever deployed in West Germany, the United States will be capable of destroying Soviet command, control, and communications systems after a flight of only six minutes. It sounds great to unimaginative Americans who never ask the all-important question, "*Then* what?" The answer was given by Arthur Macy Cox in Thursday's *Times*: "Since no human decision-making system can be responsive in six minutes, the Russians will have to rely on computers. Their computers are not as advanced as ours, and ours make errors."

Finally—so the Democrats won't feel left out—it is certainly a failure of imagination that we Americans seem to have the only democracy in the world with a nonrepressed, nonfunctional opposition. Julius Nyerere, President of Tanzania, once remarked, "Yes, we have one party here. But so does America. Except, with typical extravagance, they have two of them."

The heavenly fire ignites our imaginations so that we can feel more deeply, and see more clearly. How does all this apply to the United Nations, so many of whose members have graciously come to be with us today? Years ago a Latin American diplomat observed, "At the U.N., things tend to disappear. If there's a conflict between two small nations and we deal with it, then the conflict disappears. If there's a conflict between a small and a large nation, the small nation disappears. And if it's a conflict between two large nations, the U.N. disappears."

The U.N. disappears for a very simple reason: none of the absolute national sovereign powers has surrendered to it one iota of its absolute national sovereign power—and this at a time when, as any ignited imagination can see, nationalism is as irrelevant as was States' Rights when Calhoun preached it and Jefferson Davis fought for it. As the Falklands/Malvinas crisis shows, problems can be solved; it's national pride that is intractable. But in the nuclear age, when the whole can't protect itself against the parts, when all major problems are both international and interrelated, we have to think and feel globally. Responsible national citizenship has to give way to international citizenship. For the survival unit is no longer a single person, a single nation, or a single anything; the survival unit in our time is the entire human race, plus its environment.

And the first order of global business is disarmament. Four years ago we observed the first special session of the U.N. for disarmament. In honor of that occasion, and to commemorate the 100th anniversary of Harry Emerson Fosdick, we set up the Riverside disarmament program. Today we are here together from many nations, some warring with one another, because we know the fuse is shorter than it was four years ago and because we want God's heavenly fire to ignite all our imaginations as it did on that first day of Pentecost. So that inside the walls of the U.N. you diplomats may feel our support, hundreds of thousands of us—also from every continent—will march by on First Avenue the full length of the U.N., from 47th to 42nd streets, on Saturday, June 12.

We will march because the nuclear arms race is madness. We will march because people beg and starve, which they shouldn't have to do, and because in no country should a person's hardest job be to find one. We will march as victims of the forces of history and the forces of destiny, compelled by indignities of days gone by and by aspirations of generations yet unborn. We will march because we believe with the general that "war is preposterous," because we believe with the poet that our only hope lies in the choice between "fire or fire." We will march because we want to heed the injunction and know the promise of Scripture: "'Cast away from you all the transgressions which you have committed against me, and get yourselves a new heart and a new spirit! Why will you die, O house of Israel? For I have no pleasure in the death of anyone,' says the Lord GOD, 'so turn, and live'" (Ezek. 18:31–32).

The Human Century

JUNE 13, 1982
Reading: Ephesians 4:25–32

In the fourth chapter of St. Paul's epistle to the Ephesians is the provocative, engaging line he lifted from the Psalms: "Be angry but do not sin." It's the kind of line that you would gladly find in a Chinese fortune cookie, the quality of whose wisdom has so lamentably deteriorated over the years.

But perhaps some of you are wondering, "Why be angry at all?"—remembering God's words to Jonah, "Do you do well to be angry?" Because, for a starter (and this thought too should find its way into a fortune cookie), "A thought-murder a day keeps the psychiatrist away." In that wisecrack lies great wisdom, for it recognizes that while all behavior is not valid, all feelings are valid; and it perceives the true danger to lie not in having evil thoughts but in denying them. It says, "Deny your evil thoughts and you will crack up." I would add, "Deny your evil thoughts and you deserve to crack up for presuming to be above the human race." Deny any feelings, comforting or discomforting, worthy or unworthy—and you will live out your days incognito, your true self concealed, even from yourself. Once again: all feelings are valid, even if all behavior is not.

But there are other even more important reasons for being angry, other more important ways in which anger maintains our sanity. It is not sane to tolerate the intolerable. That's the way to lose your humanity, and perhaps the world as well. Two weeks ago I suggested that all of us would gladly repeat, and believe it, "All men [people] are created equal." Yet how many of us feel the monstrosity of inequality? How many whites feel the horror of racial inequality that continues to scar Blacks in this city, in this country, in—God save us—this church, and seemingly forever in South Africa? Or how many of us read with feeling the statistic that 50 percent of all children in the world never so much as open their mouths to say "aah" to a doctor?

Yesterday upward of half a million people gathered on the Great Lawn of Central Park because in our time the Declaration of Independence can be paraphrased to read: "All men are *cremated* equal." I was particularly moved by the Japanese witnesses pleading, "No more Hiroshimas, no more Nagasakis." Yet what Hiroshima and Nagasaki had begun to delegitimize, we are now, with our talk of limited or prolonged nuclear war, beginning to relegitimize. We are putting a fresh foundation in under a condemned building. We are once again thinking the unthinkable, accepting the unacceptable, tolerating what in the eyes of Almighty God must surely be intolerable. The reason? Indifference. Until recently disarmament has been low on the agendas of governments because disarmament has been no higher on the agendas of their citizens. That great Black prophet Frederick Douglass was right: "Find out just what any people will quietly submit to and you have found out the exact measure of injustice which will be imposed upon them."

So it's right to be angry about continued inequalities, and about nuclear madness (which today seems to involve a process of arms control by which one superpower says to the other, "You reduce what we don't like, and we'll reduce what we don't need"); about a national pride that is producing four senseless wars at a time when nationalism is as obsolete as was States' Rights when Calhoun preached it and Jefferson Davis fought for it. It's wrong to tolerate the intolerable. So lest we lose our humanity and the world—and betray our Lord and Savior—let us be angry.

"But do not sin." What had the psalmist and St. Paul in mind?

Sin is essentially separation—separation from God, from others, and from ourselves. All forms of separation connect: we can't get close to others as long as we are so far from ourselves. So "do not sin" means "do not disconnect," not from God, from others, from yourself. Whatever you do, let it be prompted by love, starting with love toward yourself. There's a lovely line in a book by Georges Bernanos, *The Diary of a Country Priest*: "How easy it is to hate oneself. True grace is to forget. Yet if pride would die in us, the supreme grace would be to love oneself in all simplicity—as one would anyone of those who themselves have suffered and loved in Christ." I'd like to engrave those lines on every church door because they make the point that sometimes it is more blessed to receive than to give; at least it takes more humility. So God grant that we might be humble enough to accept all the love that comes our way from God, parents, children, friends. Lord knows we need it. Most of us who behave like the Pharisee feel like the tax collector (if you know your New Testament parables). Or we're like the one-talent man who buried what little he had—which was enough—because the world seemed too big for him, or he too small for the world. It's wrong to refuse love. And this too we must remember: if we hate ourselves we can never love others; for love is the gift of oneself, and how will you make a gift of that which you hate?

"Do not sin." Do not disconnect from God, from yourself, or from others. And do not disconnect from your country. Yesterday in Central Park, ours was hopefully a lovers quarrel, not a grudge fight. Of course we must contend against wrong—but without becoming wrongfully contentious. Of course we must fight national self-righteousness—but without personal self-righteousness. "America, love it or leave it." I believe that. The trouble with that slogan, which found its way to endless bumpers during the Vietnam War, was that it didn't mean what it said. It meant, "America, obey it or leave it," as if national unity were more patriotic than national debate, especially when that unity seems based on folly. If the American people are worth the salt I think they're worth, they will never be politically united, for as Barbara Tuchman recently wrote, "A nation in consensus is a nation ready for the grave." Love of country, like love of parents, is never to be equated with blind obedience, as Jesus himself in both cases so poignantly demonstrated.

"Do not sin." If it is right not to disconnect from your country it is equally important not to disconnect from the enemies of your country: "But I say to you, love your enemies." At a very minimum that means recognizing that it takes a sinner to catch a sinner. If we are not one with the Soviets in love, at least we are one with them in sin, as both countries have passed from isolationism into interventionism without passing through internationalism. And sin is no mean bond, for it keeps us connected. Sin precludes the possibility of separation through judgment: "Judge not that ye be not judged." It may well be that the recognition of bilateral sin is the precondition for bilateral disarmament.

Jesus wasn't "soft" on the sins of Israel, or on those of any other nation. So love is not "soft" on communism any more than it is soft on capitalism. But love is universal. "All men are created equal." The root word for "equal" in Greek is one—"All men are created one." All have more in common than they have in conflict, and it is precisely when they have so much in conflict that love must maintain what they have in common.

Four hundred years ago Galileo looked into the telescope and saw that Copernicus was right: the earth is not the center of the universe. It was a costly truth for many to accept, and Galileo was made to pay the price. Today there is another harsh truth that needs to be faced: No country is at the center of this planet—no matter how glorious its past, how brilliant its future, how mighty its arms, or how generous its people. This is not the American century—Henry Luce was shortsighted. Nor is this the Russian century; nor will there be a Chinese century. Today, pragmatically, as eternally in the sight of God, there is only one century—a human century. Coming as they did from every continent on the planet, it was the human century that people were really affirming and celebrating yesterday in the park. And the first order of business of the human century is to freeze nuclear weapons before they burn the people.

Lastly, "Do not sin" means "Do not mean well—feebly." Yesterday was only a start, not an end, the first step in a long and stony road.

And how do we stay on a long and stony road that is really only a metaphor for life itself? Christians persevere because there are always two sets of footprints on the road—ours and those of our Lord and Savior. No, that's wrong: when the road gets unbearable there is only one set of prints, those of Jesus, because at those moments he carries us.

"Through many a danger, toil, and snare we have *already* come." With Christ at our side, for Heaven's and the future's sake we can go through many another danger, toil, and snare—provided we don't conceal ourselves through repression, or lose our humanity through indifference. We must become insistently and inimitably ourselves, so much so that at journey's end it can be said of us, as the poet put it: "They added forever to the sum of reality."

Just remember: "Be angry but do not sin."

Sail On, O Ship of State

JULY 4, 1982
Reading: Matthew 14:22–23

Should modern scholarship one day establish that George Washington never even attempted to throw the silver dollar across the mighty Rappahannock—or that the dollar had, in fact, splashed— George Washington would still remain, as we were taught in grammar school, "first in war, first in peace, first in the hearts of his countrymen." For the story of the silver dollar is an expression of faith, not a basis of faith. It's the kind of story that followers of Washington would love of a winter's night, having stoked up the fire, to tell about him.

And if Jesus never walked on the Sea of Galilee, to Christians he is still their Messiah. For Christ is not God's magic but God's love incarnate. He was not one to go around—Houdini-like—breaking the laws of physical nature, but rather one who, beyond all limits of *human* nature, loved as none before nor after him has ever loved. In the face of such awesome love surely even the waves must rise up and the winds bow down, even as at his birth a star stood still, and at his death the earth quaked, rending rocks and splitting graves wide open.

And what is the meaning of the story? If you ask a crowd straining their necks to look up at the ceiling of the Sistine Chapel what they are seeing, or ask an audience listening to Beethoven's Ninth Symphony what they are hearing, no two answers will be the same—such is the evocative power of great works of art. Biblical stories stimulate the imagination even more, so none of you should be surprised if I see in this story a perfect three-act drama for a Fourth of July sermon.

As the first act opens, the disciples are boarding a boat for what appears to be a routine crossing. But at some distance from the shore they find themselves buffeted by an unexpected and terrible storm. Their boat begins to sink, and not only because the winds are high and against them, but also, as it turns out, because Jesus is not there.

Well, were we not also taught in grammar school: "Thou, too, sail on, O Ship of State! / Sail on, O Union, strong and great!"? And in the middle of World War II, didn't Churchill send Roosevelt a morale-building telegram quoting that Longfellow poem more fully:

> Thou, too, sail on, O Ship of State!
> Sail on, O Union, strong and great!
> Humanity with all its fears,
> With all the hopes of future years,
> Is hanging breathless on thy fate! . . .

But nobody sends us telegrams like that anymore. We too seem at sea, caught in a storm with no compass to point us toward a promising future. That we've come a long way there's no denying. Even though we were a white nation founded on the genocide and bondage of other races, and though we've a long way to go in our treatment of Blacks and Indians, ethnic minorities and women (what's one woman on the Supreme Court but hollow symbolism when death comes to the Equal Rights Amendment?) still, ours is the longest-lasting revolution in the world, 206 years old today. And the liberties established way back then in a remote agrarian backwater of the world have miraculously survived and at times flourished.

But today something has happened to our understanding of freedom, to our notion of democracy. Our eighteenth-century forebears were enormously influenced by Montesquieu, the French thinker who differentiated despotism, monarchy, and democracy. In each he found a special principle governing social life. For despotism that principle was fear, for monarchy honor, and for democracy—take heed!—virtue. "It is this quality," he wrote, "rather than fear or ambition, that makes things work in a democracy."

Samuel Adams agreed: "We may look to armies for our defense, but virtue is our best security. It is not possible that any state should long remain free where virtue is not supremely honored."

Freedom, virtue—these two were practically synonymous in the minds of our revolutionary forebears. To them it was inconceivable that an individual would be granted freedom merely for the satisfaction of instincts and whims. Freedom, virtue—they were practically synonymous a hundred years later in the mind of Abraham Lincoln when in his Second Inaugural Address he called for "a new birth of freedom." Freedom and virtue embrace one another in perhaps the greatest of all American hymns, written by Julia Ward Howe:

> In the beauty of the lilies Christ was born across the sea,
> With a glory in his bosom that transfigures you and me;
> As he died to make men holy, let us die to make men free!
> While God is marching on.

But today we Americans are not marching in the ways of the Lord, but limping along in our own ways, thinking not of the public weal but of our private interests. Today tax-cutting is more popular than social spending, even for the poorest Americans. And because we have so cruelly separated freedom from virtue—because we define freedom in a morally inferior way—our "Union strong and great" is stalled in a storm, in what Herman Melville called the "Dark Ages of Democracy," a time when, as he predicted, the New Jerusalem would turn into Babylon, and Americans would feel "the arrest of hope's advance." America today is a cross between a warship and a luxury liner, with all attention concentrated on the upper decks. But below the water line there are leaks. Our ship is sinking.

But on to Act II, which opens with one person preparing to abandon ship. And can't you hear the cries—there are so many of them in every sinking ship: "For God's sake, Peter, sit down—you're rocking the boat!"

What do you suppose moved Peter, and not the others, to abandon ship? To most human beings there is something fundamentally unacceptable about unpleasant truth. Most of the time we seek to bolster our illusions, to protect ourselves from our fears. But in our more courageous and honest moments, some of us are willing to face the shallowness of our personal relations, the barbaric ladders on which we climb to success, the banality of our culture, the cruelty in our foreign policy (which leads us today to back the cruelty in Israel's). And when in the fourth watch of the night—that miserable 2 to 6 a.m. shift when we are most alone with ourselves—Jesus bids us come, some of us—like Peter—are ready for that leap of faith.

Peter almost immediately begins to sink, and modern scholarship may one day establish that Jesus called him "The Rock" not for his foundational but for his sinking properties. And why not? "In my weakness is my strength," said St. Paul, who had the vision to see that "God's power is made perfect in weakness" (2 Cor. 12:9). It is only when we realize that we can no more trust our own buoyancy than we can that of the ship we have just abandoned, that we truly give ourselves to Christ. Then the true miracle takes place, the one that makes this story eternally if not literally true. "Lord, save me," cries Peter, and Jesus does. There's the central miracle of every Christian life, which should take place on an average of about every other day. When, sinking in our sense of helplessness, we reach out for a love greater than we ourselves can ever express, for a truth deeper than we could ever articulate, for a beauty richer than we ourselves can ever contain, when we too cry out, "Lord, save me," He who died to make us holy does indeed transfigure you and me. Cry out for a thimbleful and you receive an oceanful of help.

Many people wish the story ended here. What greater relief to an unhappy soul than to find stability in a world of turmoil, certitude in a world of doubt, contentment amid pain? But the goal of the Christian life is not to save your soul but to transcend yourself, to vindicate the human struggle of which all of us are a part, to keep hope advancing. Peter doesn't say to Jesus, "Now that you have saved me, Lord, let's walk off—just you and me—into the sunrise of a new day and forget all about those fellows in the sinking ship." No, having abandoned the sinking ship for Jesus, Peter now returns *with* Jesus.

There is our Fourth of July message, our Fourth of July example for patriots who call themselves Christians: "America, love it and leave it." Leave it for Jesus, for America's sake as well as your own, and then return with Jesus. That's how to love America—with Christ's wisdom, with Christ's compassion, with a concern for the whole, fusing once again freedom with virtue in order to renew "the patriots' dream, that sees beyond the years, her alabaster cities gleam, undimmed by human tears!"

When Peter returned to the boat with Jesus the winds abated. I think our own ship could once again recover headway and direction if only more American Christians followed Peter's example. With faith in God, it's right to love one's country, love it as Jesus did Israel.

Longfellow may have been a bit triumphant in his view of America, but he was right in the fervor of his love. So let the more prayerful words he addressed to our nation at the end of his poem be the last words of this Fourth of July sermon:

> Sail on, nor fear to breast the sea!
> Our hearts, our hopes, are all with thee,
> Our hearts, our hopes, our prayers, our tears,
> Our faith triumphant o'er our fears,
> Are all with thee,—are all with thee!

The Prospect of Death

JULY 11, 1982
Readings: Psalm 90; Romans 14:7–9

The Riverside parish this week suffered a terrible tragedy: thrown from a horse in summer camp and killed was a nine-year-old, an only child, a golden boy. Then, on Friday, outside New Orleans, 143 people perished aboard a Boeing 747 and several more died on the ground when the big jet crashed. Not long before that in Gravesend, Brooklyn, a very different kind of tragedy occurred when a Black transit worker was murdered—or should we say lynched?—by a gang of whites. And all week long in Lebanon, South Africa, the Sahel, and Central America, in the form of starvation or terrorism—guerrilla or government style—death was again working overtime. So let's talk of death—once more—and start not with the death of others, but with the prospect of our own.

Dr. Johnson observed that the prospect of death wonderfully concentrates the mind. That is because the thought of death, or rather the fear of it, never leaves us—although we do repress it, which is why Scripture is at pains to resurrect it: "All mortal flesh," says the prophet, "is as the grass, and all the glory man would gain is as the grass and flower" (1 Pet. 1:24). And didn't we just read in the 90th Psalm, "The years of our life are threescore and ten, or even by reason of strength fourscore; yet . . . they are soon gone, and we fly away"—words paraphrased in Isaac Watts' great hymn, "Time, like an ever-rolling stream, / Bears all its sons away; / They fly forgotten, as a dream / Dies at the opening day." If we are to take more fully into account the true state of affairs, we had best recognize that nature intends to get us, and in the end will succeed.

But basically, that's all to the good, as we can swiftly recognize if we but consider the alternative—endless existence. Why, without death life would be interminable; we'd be as bored as the old Greek gods and probably up to their same frivolous tricks. Without death, there would be hedonism but no heroism; and not only would there be no heroism, but precious little wisdom either ("So teach us to number our days that we may get a heart of wisdom"); in fact, there would probably be no creativity of any kind. For the fear of death may well be the mainspring of human conduct. Not only does the prospect of death stir our instincts for self-preservation; it also starts and sustains the search for self-esteem. It makes us want to count, to stand out a little, to do something—write, paint, have children—something that might possibly outlive or outshine death and decay. Finally, to the human race death is more friend than foe.

But now comes the painful paradox, caught by Shakespeare in the sonnet's line: "And time that gave doth now his gift confound." The prospect of death that makes us create then goes on to undermine all creativity. Ernest Becker was dying of cancer when he wrote his great book, *The Denial of Death*. Among many great passages is this one:

> A person spends years coming into his own, developing his talent, his unique gifts, perfecting his discriminations about the world, broadening and sharpening his appetite, learning to bear the disappointments of life, becoming mature, seasoned—finally a unique creature in nature, standing with some dignity and nobility and transcending the animal condition; no longer driven, no longer a complete reflex, not stamped out of any mold. And then the real tragedy, as André Malraux wrote in *The Human Condition:* that it takes sixty years of incredible suffering and effort to make such an individual, and then he is good only for dying. This painful paradox is not lost on the person himself—least of all himself. He feels agonizingly unique, and yet he knows that this doesn't make any difference as far as ultimates are concerned. He has to go the way of the grasshopper, even though it takes longer.

In other words, death makes life itself the insurmountable problem. No revolution, no matter how sweeping, will ever do away with our fear of death. Death will always remain "the worm at the core" of human happiness, the skull grinning at the banquet. But death is also faith's most glorious opportunity. Without faith, fear of death can lead to boundless megalomania or make us feel no bigger than worms. But if we live in faith—that is, fully in this world on its terms, and wholly beyond the world in our trust in God; if we live in faith—that is, astride the visible and invisible worlds—accepting life finally as a matter of grace, not of human effort, then we can live hopefully, courageously, saying with St. Paul, "O death, where is thy sting? O grave, where thy victory? Thanks be to God who giveth us the victory, through our Lord Jesus Christ" (1 Cor. 15:55, 57). Or, "Whether we live or whether we die, we are the Lord's" (Rom. 14:8). To live in faith is really the only way to deal with death—and to do so is about as easy as for a camel to pass through the eye of a needle!

But what about the nine-year-old, and the 143 who perished on the Boeing jet? And let's not forget that pyramid of bodies—fifty thousand of them annually—killed on the highways of America. What we must never do is rationalize away our own responsibility for so many deaths. If we human beings insist on riding cars, airplanes, even horses; if we insist on erecting cities in Italy next to volcanoes (I'm thinking of Pompeii) or in California along the San Andreas Fault; if we insist on drinking to excess, taking drugs, making weapons capable of murdering one another in Brooklyn or in Lebanon, then the responsibility for the consequences of all these acts is ours, and ours alone. Let no one dare say angrily, "Why did God let it happen?" Or worse yet, piously, "It must be the will of God." The will of God my eye! Could it be the will of God that a small child be killed, that an airplane crash? And in Lebanon, it would be no exaggeration to picture Christ standing between East and West Beirut ready to absorb the bullets through his own body.

It is the will of God, who numbers every hair on our heads, that we his children forgive and forbear, that we love one another—and return her love with our own. And if love is the name of the game, and freedom the precondition to love, then we can't expect God to ground planes, slow down cars, tame horses, and deflect bullets, because God is not going to take away human freedom. Fault God for giving us the freedom in the first place, but understand that it was for the sake of love. God has the power to do anything, but God's love, like all love, is self-restricting when it comes to power. It's startling, but true: we are going to be helped more by God's weakness—a still, small voice, a babe in a manger—than by God's power.

All of which is not to say that God doesn't suffer with and for us. You remember the story of the Prodigal Son? It's really the story of a prodigal father, prodigal with gifts that the son abuses. But every day the father is out on the road, watching, waiting, hoping for his child's return. No, even more: In Jesus Christ, God goes down the road—not to force, but to lure through his love his wayward children home.

Of course there are many tragedies that remain genuine mysteries: why should it happen to a nine-year-old boy and not to a grownup? Why are there maimed and retarded children? Why does cancer exist at all? If we can find no meaning in the mystery, we have to trust where we cannot see, not curse what we do not understand, recognizing that the mystery of undeserved good is even greater than the mystery of undeserved evil, and that Christ himself was always about the healing ministry of his people.

In him we have our shining example of how to deal with death. While accepting his own death, albeit not easily ("Father, if it be possible, let this cup pass from me"), he did all he could to prevent the deaths of others. Let us do likewise. But let us recognize that preventing the deaths of others is like accepting our own: both are about as easy as for a camel to pass through the eye of a needle. In yesterday's *Times,* discussing the lynching in Brooklyn, Gardner Taylor didn't let any of us off the hook: "Polite racism cloaked in coded language, lily-white municipal government at policy-making levels, and Federal signals that the most disadvantaged are fair targets for fiscal punishment all lead to such lynchings." In similar fashion, Robert McAfee Brown writes of starvation in the world: "No American corporation executive . . . says to himself, 'Let's see now: How can I devise a way to increase profits that will make children starve to death?' And yet, abhorring the notion of children starving to death, he may be forced to institute a company policy in a Third World nation (refusing to let workers bargain collectively, for example) that will have precisely the result that because of labor conditions in the country children *do* starve to death. He doesn't even have to institute the policy; acquiescence will be enough."

Accepting the prospect of our own death, doing all we can to prevent the deaths of others—whatever is worthwhile in this world seems to be difficult. The psalmist had no illusions: "The years of our life are threescore and ten, or even by reason of strength fourscore; yet their span is but toil and trouble." Yet he doesn't ask for a life free of toil and trouble (which would be boring), he only prays the more fervently, "Let the favor of the Lord our God be upon us, and establish thou the work of our hands upon us, yea, the work of our hands establish thou it."

Accepting the prospect of our own death, doing all we can to prevent the deaths of others—the only way to deal with the worm at the core, the skull grinning at the banquet, the painful paradox of death, is to live in faith. For "none of us lives to himself, and none of us dies to himself. If we live, we live to the Lord, and if we die, we die to the Lord; so then whether we live or whether we die, we are the Lord's."

The Habit of Heroism

JULY 25, 1982

Readings: Isaiah 40:27–31; Philippians 2:1–13

I'd love to hear the reaction of every one of you to a sentence from that great moral philosopher William James: "[Humanity's] common instinct for reality . . . has always held the world to be essentially a theater for heroism" (*Varieties of Religious Experience*, p. 281).

I can imagine reactions ranging from skepticism to downright disbelief. I can hear the protests: "The world, a theater for heroism? God save us!" Heroics are doing us in in our century, be they the destructive heroics of Israel, of Iran and Iraq or of the Falklands caper, whose initiation was so demeaning to Argentina and whose conclusion prompted Britishers to boast, "Great Britain is great again" (at least until the intruder got into the Queen's bedroom); or be they the ignoble heroics of piling up privilege, money, and power in an acquisitive society—communist or capitalist, it makes little difference. Even baseball, a natural theater for heroics, is today "embroiled up to its batting helmet in greed and skullduggery," and in the mind of at least one observer, the flamboyant owner of the New York Yankees represents a "larger-than-life symbol of the get-rich-quick and let-morality-and-even-legality-be-damned America that's in such a rush to get somewhere that it has forgotten why it wants to" (Alan Wolfe).

And yet, and yet . . .

The Roman Catholics have a saying, *Abusus non tollit usum* (misuse doesn't negate right use). Turn a switch in your mind and instead of George Steinbrenner III think of the heroism of gnarled hands guiding a family through hunger and disease in Guatemala. Or think of that classic hero, Socrates, heroic not because he was intellectually brilliant—others have been his equal—but because he believed something worth living for was also worth dying for. The same was true of Nathan Hale, and eminently of Jesus, who "humbled himself and became obedient unto death, even death on a cross. Therefore"—one of the great Biblical words—"Therefore God has highly exalted him." And so do we highly exalt Jesus, because the folly of the cross, inexplicable to the intellect, has its own indestructible meaning. In our heart of hearts, all of us feel that a high-hearted indifference to life and death would somehow expiate all our shortcomings.

So William James may be right: the urge to heroism is natural, and to admit it honest. Everyone wants to feel secure in her self-esteem, to count, "to leave a stain on the silence" (Samuel Beckett). "What we now need to discover in the social realm," said James, "is the moral equivalent of war: something that will speak to people as universally as war does, and yet will be compatible with their spiritual selves as war has proved itself to be incompatible."

It is incompatible with our spiritual selves to live without heroics, tranquilizing ourselves with trivia and lulling ourselves with daily routines, satisfied by their rewards, glibly talking of freedom as an ideal while in the same breath we willingly give it up. Because we only toy with the idea of what we really might be, too many of us today resemble that "real man" described more than a hundred years ago by another moral philosopher, the lonely Dane Søren Kierkegaard:

> He is a university man, husband and father, an uncommonly competent civil functionary even, a respectable father, very gentle to his wife and carefulness itself with respect to his children. And a Christian? Well, yes, he is that too after a sort; however, he preferably avoids talking on the subject. . . . He very seldom goes to church, because it seems to him that most parsons don't know what they are talking about. He makes an exception in the case of one particular priest of whom he concedes he knows what he is talking about, but he doesn't want to hear him for another reason, because he has a fear that this might lead him too far. (*Sickness unto Death*, p. 196)

Tolstoy summed up the life of Ivan Ilych: "most commonplace, most ordinary and therefore most terrible."

It is not in accord with the Christian faith and it violates our spiritual selves to live without heroics. And, until we New Yorkers develop a kind of habit of heroism, this city will continue to be "the youth unemployment capital of the nation," vying to be the homeless capital as well. Unless the inhabitants of earth develop a little more heroism, all that will be left of all the cities of the world is the wind blowing through their streets. Barely a month has passed since more than 750,000 people voted with their feet in Central Park, only to have Congress this week vote to fund the MX.

Not that there is anything new in all this. You remember the Lord's answer to Jeremiah's bitter complaint about Israel: "If you have raced with men on foot, and they have wearied you, how will you compete with horses? And if in a safe land you fall down, how will you do in the jungle of the Jordan?" (12:5). And remember Jesus' warning: "For if they do this when the wood is green, what will happen when it is dry?" (Luke 23:31).

The answer to ignoble heroics is not no heroics, but decent heroics.

Of all the T-shirts I've bought (or been given in lieu of honoraria!), my favorite has "Picasso" written across the chest. Picasso is a hero to me, in part because art and faith have, to my way of thinking, so much in common. I think of a Christian as a struggling artist, her life her canvas. And all of us, according to the Jerusalem Bible translation of a passage in Ephesians, are "God's works of art."

Another of my heroes is Cézanne, who after he completed *Les Grandes Baigneuses* found he had made a picture so large that he couldn't get it through the door of his studio, nor through the windows. So he knocked out a panel in his studio wall.

Both artists and Christians should heroically go beyond the limitations of their surroundings, breaking conventions to satisfy deeper yearnings. We forget how much familiar art and music was initially hard for the public to take. Beethoven's Second Symphony was called a "crass monster" in 1804, and some years later someone put up signs in concert halls: "Look for the nearest exit in case of Brahms." Tchaikovsky's Piano Concerto was called "difficult for popular apprehension" in 1875. That's funny to us now, but maybe it's a commentary on us that today we find this music more comfortable than challenging.

Yet despite their groundbreaking, both art and the faith are rooted in tradition. All art has a point of departure in other art, and contemporary Christians only seek to reinterpret the faith of former generations.

Art and the faith break through conventions. They also have similar and heroic missions. The goal of art, according to André Malraux, is to remind people of the neglected grandeur that lies within them. That certainly describes the spiritual call to arms of every Biblical prophet. I love today's slang use of the word "beautiful," for rather than simply oppose "ugly" it implies a certain moral quality, something that lifts people out of everyday existence. When artists and Christians are heroic, that's what they are—"Beautiful!"

They break conventions, they are rooted in tradition, they have a mission. And both artists and Christians have to be fools. There's a saying in France, *Il faut être bête pour être un bon peintre* (you have to be dumb to be a good painter). Some of the best things in this world are done by people too stupid to know they can't be done. When I say "stupid" I'm not thinking of a mind as empty as yesterday's cloudless sky, but of fools who take enormous risks, who leave themselves wide open. Picasso, Pollack—they were great gamblers. Of Picasso it was said, "He knows that his faith in the accidental, the so-called laws of chance, is his best guarantee of continued creativity." So with Christians: they must become "fools for Christ's sake," they must willingly acquire vulnerability. Career-driven, emotionally remote American men unable to abandon the facade of total control may become church officers, but they are simply not vulnerable enough to be truly heroic. How much less can we call heroic our own nation, so determined not to become vulnerable that it does all it can to prevent revolutionary change in the Third World, while ignoring the fundamental changes that already have taken place in our relations with Europe and Japan.

Two more points of comparison: in art what is called "original" is very often "a tiny, tiny drop that is added to something that has been there before" (Alexander Liberman). That's all it takes to make a human canvas original. And lastly, neither in art nor in faith do we live alone. The Impressionists, beleaguered by their critics, hung together, and Cézanne took the long view: "I'm on a long road," he said. "Others will come." Christians are alone only as spokes in a wheel, and the closer they come to the center of their faith, the closer they come to each other. When in a few moments, upon receiving new members, we rise to sing, "Blest be the tie that binds," we won't be singing of some artificial, sentimental bond, but of solid connective tissue. "There is neither Jew nor Greek, there is neither slave nor free, there is neither male nor female; for you are all one in Christ Jesus" (Gal. 3:28).

We have said that our spiritual selves crave heroics, and so does the world if it is to be made safe for itself. The answer then to ignoble heroics is not no heroics, but decent heroics. To be heroes and heroines for Christ we must, like artists, be traditional yet always ready to break conventions; like artists, have a mission; like artists, be vulnerable, and yet together. Examples of such heroism abound—in this church I see it every day—but our eminent example is in Christ Jesus who "did not count equality with God a thing to be grasped but emptied himself . . . and became obedient unto death, even death on a cross."

And from whence comes the power to be so creative, to leave such a "stain on the silence"?

> Hast thou not known? Hast thou not heard, that the
> everlasting God, the LORD, the Creator of the ends

of the earth, fainteth not, neither is weary? . . . He giveth power to the faint; and to them that have no might he increaseth strength. Even the youths shall faint and be weary, and the young men shall utterly fall: But they that wait upon the LORD shall renew their strength; they shall mount up with wings as eagles; they shall run, and not be weary; and they shall walk, and not faint. (Isa. 40:28–31)

Backing away from a finished—and glorious—canvas, William Blake exclaimed, "Not I, not I!" Likewise St. Paul: "Not I, but Christ who dwells within me." Every hero and heroine for Christ with every breath says, "Not unto us, O Lord, not unto us, but unto thy name be the glory."

God's First Love

Homecoming Sunday
SEPTEMBER 26, 1982
Reading: John 3:16, 17

First let me say that I'm glad to be back—and to find that nobody's in my uniform! In particular I'm happy to be back in a community of believers that is profoundly serious, but not deadly serious; that "weeps with those who weep, and rejoices with those who rejoice," striving always to remember that the fact that human beings are human beings is more important than what they believe, or that they are black, white, yellow, or red, Palestinian, Israeli, Russian, or American. And yes, I'm glad to be back in New York City, "in whose conglomerate soil every wanton, ignoble, crack-brained idea flourishes like a weed" (Henry Miller), and the best of everything blossoms like a rose. So, dear Riversiders, New Yorkers, visitors—as Saint Paul would say, "Grace to you, and peace."

In all the Gospels you won't find a line more familiar than the one I've chosen as a text for our Homecoming Sunday sermon: "God so loved the world that he gave his only begotten Son that whosoever should believe in him should not perish but have eternal life" (John 3:16).

That God loves the world has either to be the ultimate truth or, after the massacres in Lebanon, the last straw. It's the latter to many a sensitive nonbeliever who can't help shaking a finger—or a fist—charging, "You believers are incredibly fatuous to keep on talking of the love of God when not only Lebanon, Cambodia, El Salvador, and South Africa but almost every inch of the earth's surface is soaked with the tears and blood of the innocent!"

The nonbeliever is right: the oppression of the weak by the strong is as worldwide as it is age-old, and the suffering of the innocent is surely the cruelest dilemma facing the conscience of any sensitive believer. But what nonbelievers can't seem to grasp is that God could no more stop those massacres in Beirut—or Babi Yar, Lidice, Auschwitz or Sharpeville—than could the father of the Prodigal Son keep his son from going prodigal. Jesus, who told the parable—which is really about the prodigal love of the father—knew better than anyone that love has to be self-restricting when it comes to power. Jesus knew that God's very act of Creation was an act of loving self-restriction, that God's love provides support, but never protection. It's a strange and wonderful thing how love is at once the most and the least powerful of all the powers in the world: "It is the most powerful because it alone can conquer that final and most impregnable stronghold which is the human heart. It is the most powerless because it can do nothing except by consent" (Frederick Buechner).

So to the nonbeliever we must answer: "The world continues to be God's first love; it is we his children who do not share that love. But because God cannot prevent massacres doesn't mean He's absent from them. You can be sure Christ was at Sabra and Shatilla just as he was at Babi Yar, Lidice, Auschwitz, and Sharpeville—and every bullet passed right through his body."

God's love for the world is the ultimate truth that needs to be shouted from every rooftop, particularly when, as now, the world seems hell-bent on denying it. So convinced was the German mystic, Angelus Silesius, that love was the very essence of God, he dared to write: "If God ceased to think of me he would cease to exist."

I love the gall, the absolute certainty it took to make a statement of faith like that. But that so few of us would have dared to write it points to a tragedy far deeper than the world's denial of God—the denial of God's love by believers themselves. How many of us look redeemed? have fun? are good company? I've said it before, and shall undoubtedly repeat it: Most Christians have only enough religion to make themselves miserable. Ask yourself: Is God more associated with law or with love? Is God experienced as a presence or as pressure? People who deny God's love can't look redeemed, for the simple reason that they aren't. They can't have fun because they're feeling too guilty. Commendably, they may be trying to pay for their sins, but they have yet to realize the vanity of the effort. If you've ever tried seriously to pay for your sins you realize you can never pay enough. As a modern Roman Catholic theologian has written, "Guilt is the currency of love, gone into inflation" (Sebastian Moore). This means that guilt quickly turns into dislike. We tend to think ill of people we have failed. In *The Brothers Karamazov* one character says of another: "I did him a bad turn years ago and I've had a grudge against him ever since." That's the way most of us feel about God: we've done God endless bad turns, She knows it, She judges us, She can't possibly like us, so we dislike her back. "Love God? I hate God," confessed Martin Luther.

Wrongdoing spawns guilt; guilt inspires further wrongdoing and turns love to hate. All this Jesus understood perfectly. Listen to what follows John 3:16 (both verses now from the New English Bible): "God loved the world so much that he gave his only Son, that everyone who has faith in him may not die but have eternal life. *It was not to judge the world* that God sent his Son into the world, but that through him the world might be saved." Jesus is not denying or decrying guilt, but simply saying that the purpose of guilt is not to destroy but to save us, by pointing to the forgiveness we need.

It is clear that we can no more forgive ourselves than we can sit in our own laps. It is clear that forgiveness is something we can never get but only be given, and that Jesus Christ is this gift to each of us. "God so loved the world that he gave his only begotten Son" to forgive us, one and all. I know you have to swallow your pride to accept forgiveness, but so does God in offering it. I know such love is too good to believe—we ourselves being strangers to such goodness. But look at it this way: maybe God's love is too good *not* to be true. Surely God's love is never anything less than human love as we know it at its best, and at its best human love includes forgiveness. So how much more forgiveness can we not properly expect from God, whose love compared to our own is as the lightning to the lightning bug? And finally—dear guilt-ridden Christians—how much more can we ask of God? Does Jesus Christ have to be crucified in every generation, live without a penny in the bank or a friend to his name, because we his professed followers are too proud, too obtuse, or too whatever to accept our forgiveness?

Homecoming Sunday proclaims we are coming home as prodigal children to the prodigal love of our Father/Mother. Homecoming means we are glad once again to live in our own skin and in the presence—not pressure—of God. For if guilt is the abyss we create between us and God, forgiveness is the bridge. Home free, no longer uptight, we are good company, we can have fun—or, as Jesus said, we have eternal life.

Eternal life is not what happens when life ends; it's what happens when life begins. Like heaven, eternal life begins here and now. "Eternal life is to be with God as Christ is with God, and to be with each other as Christ is with us" (Buechner). Those words are enough to indicate that eternal life is not life as it is generally lived. Often these days we hear that the Gospel is irrelevant to modern men and women, a contention I would dispute. The Gospel is always the answer; it's the Church that's the problem. But even the irrelevance of the Church—which is breathtaking—is little compared to the irrelevance of modern culture to the hapless human beings imprisoned in it. Think of the consumerism abroad today whose bottom line reads, "You are worthless in yourself; you need our product"; the Marxism that makes of our spiritual nature an economic epiphenomenon; or the psychology that sees religion merely as a coverup. Think also of higher education, which exalts the freedom of the individual over any sense of obligation and in so doing exalts the ability to do anything over the desire to do good. And what of the victims of American intervention in Nicaragua, the political prisoners all over the world, and the victims *by denial* of an arms race that now spends a million dollars a minute?

So homecoming means home to the prodigal love of God, which is celebrated in the Church. Homecoming does not mean home to the world. We are in the world, yes, but not of it. As W. H. Auden put it, we go native in all ways—except faith and morals.

But whatever we do, we do for the sake of the world, "For God so loved"—not the Church, but the world. Paraphrasing Silesius we can say, "If the Church ceased to think of the world, the Church would cease to exist." The world is God's first love, and it is our job to make God the world's first love.

It's good to be back. It's good to be home, to sing of God's prodigal love, to share the eternal life that is ours by God's grace, and to remember that the Good News needs sensitive and dedicated messengers.

The Hundredth Monkey*

Worldwide Communion Sunday
OCTOBER 3, 1982
Readings: Genesis 3:1–9; 1 Corinthians 12:24–26

I want to introduce the sermon for Worldwide Communion Sunday with a remarkable story.

The Japanese monkey, *Macaca fuscata*, has been observed in the world for a period of over 30 years. In 1952, on the island of Koshima, scientists were providing monkeys with sweet potatoes dropped in the sand. The monkeys liked the taste of the raw sweet potatoes, but they found the dirt unpleasant.

An 18-month-old female named Imo found she could solve the problem by washing the potatoes in a nearby stream. She taught this trick to her mother. Her playmates also learned this new way and they taught their mothers, too.

This cultural innovation was gradually picked up by various monkeys before the eyes of the scientists. Between 1952 and 1958, all the young monkeys learned to wash the sandy sweet potatoes to make them more palatable. Only the adults who imitated their children learned this social improvement. Other adults kept eating the dirty sweet potatoes.

Then something startling took place. In the autumn of 1958, a certain number of Koshima monkeys were washing sweet potatoes—the exact number is not known. Let us suppose that when the sun rose one morning there were 99 monkeys on Koshima Island who had learned to wash their sweet potatoes. Let's further suppose that later that morning, the hundredth monkey learned to wash potatoes.

THEN IT HAPPENEDI

By that evening almost everyone in the tribe was washing sweet potatoes before eating them. The added energy of this hundredth monkey somehow created an ideological breakthrough!

*This sermon was inspired and greatly informed by Michael Nagler's *America Without Violence*.—WSC

But notice. The most surprising thing observed by these scientists was that the habit of washing sweet potatoes then spontaneously jumped over the sea—colonies of monkeys on other islands and the mainland troop of monkeys at Takasakiyama began washing their sweet potatoes![*]

It is the high calling of every Christian to be, if not the first, at least that hundredth monkey—the one that provides the breakthrough, that shows things can change for the better, that dispels a destructive lie by replacing it with a life-enhancing truth, demonstrating the amazing phenomenon that if enough of us become aware of something, all of us will become aware of it.

What in our world today is the equivalent of the unwashed sweet potatoes? I suggest that it is a bad model for human relations—separatism. We habitually perceive and act toward one another out of a deep feeling of separateness, illustrated by Cain's question to God, "Am I my brother's keeper?" with its implied answer, "No, I am *not* my brother's keeper—let alone a brother to some stranger." Separatism is "me-ism" in its individual, corporate, and national forms. (After all, what is a "credible retaliatory posture" but a sophisticated version of a primitive caveman brandishing a club?) Separatism sees nature "red in tooth and claw," and war as the natural state of human affairs. Separatism is a gladiatorial view of the world, for the line from separateness to violence is short and direct. As the story of Cain and Abel illustrates, all violence stems from seeing others as alien, from counting the interests of others inconsequential compared to the importance of our own. James Baldwin saw it clearly: "It is a terrible, an inexorable law, that one cannot deny the humanity of another without diminishing one's own." And St. Augustine put the matter even more vividly: "Imagine the vanity of thinking that your enemy can do more damage to you than your enmity." It is no accident that as the incidence of murder rises, so too, as a rule, does suicide, for all forms of alienation—from God, from neighbor, from self—are related. Need I add that most of us are still eating dirty sweet potatoes?

The clean sweet potatoes are St. Paul's very different model of human relationships. Far from denying kinship, as in the question "Am I my brother's keeper?" St. Paul affirms it in a glorious metaphor: "The eye cannot say to the hand, 'I have no need of you,' nor again the hand

[*]From *Lifetide* by Lyall Watson (Bantam Books, 1980); quoted by Ken Keyes in *The Hundredth Monkey*, published by Vision Books.

to the feet, 'I have no need of you'" (1 Cor. 12:21). Far from a gladiatorial view of the world, Paul's model is a *holistic* way of seeing things. It's not me *against* you, but me *and* you against whatever evil seeks to divide us. Are we husband and wife? Then it's you and me against the intruder, estrangement. Are we black and white? Then it's you and me against the lie of segregation. It's not nation against nation, but nations together against the common enemy, war. According to the holistic view, we appear separate, but in fact are one. Einstein described this unity: "A human being is a part of the whole called by us the 'universe,' a part limited in time and space. He experiences himself, his thoughts and feelings, as something separated from the rest—a kind of optical delusion of his consciousness. This delusion is a kind of prison for us, restricting us to our personal desires and to affection for a few persons nearest to us. Our task must be to free ourselves from this prison by widening our circle of compassion to embrace all living creatures and the whole of nature in its beauty."

The holistic view is not softhearted. It doesn't deny that nature is "red in tooth and claw," but neither does it exaggerate the ruthlessness of nature. Like the family of Adam and Eve, the whole world can go from a high-hearted beginning to a mean and squalid ending. But that one of the first two brothers dies at the hand of the other doesn't make the two any the less brothers. The fratricide of Cain demonstrates that any time any of us commits violence it is "a wound in the very order of being," a reminder that what we are existentially is not what we are essentially. As Robert Browning wrote, "Life is an aspiration; man is not man as yet." In an interview with Flora Lewis this week, after calling what happened in Beirut a "pogrom," President Navon of Israel recalled Judaism's belief that one who saves a soul is as if one had saved the world, and one who kills a soul is as if one had slain the world. That is an expression of the holistic view of life. In olden times Jews used to be careful never to step on a piece of paper lest the name of God be written on it. Likewise we must be careful not to tread on a single soul, for we know there is that of God in every person.

The hundredth monkey showed that things *can* change for the better—fortunately so, for unfortunately the most prosperous nation in the world is also among its most violent. The incidence of murder in San Francisco is four hundred times greater than it is in Tokyo; and the 60 million citizens of Great Britain kill each other less often than do the 1.5 million inhabitants of Manhattan. All this violence stems from alienation, in all its forms, for which we all bear some responsibility. I'll leave it to you to make the connections between domestic violence and our violence abroad. Isn't it time we Americans started washing the sand off our sweet potatoes? Isn't it time we abandoned "me-ism" in all its forms and started to promote peace in the most fundamental fashion possible by affirming in all people their God-given dignity?

Let's listen again to Einstein: "Our task must be to free ourselves from this prison by widening our circle of compassion." Worldwide Communion Sunday is a reminder that salvation may be personal, but it is never private or exclusive. Salvation is for everyone—including you and me. It's a reminder that the divisions in the church are sinful, for only Christians united in love can show a divided world how to live in peace. Worldwide Communion Sunday answers Cain's question. "Am I my brother's keeper?" "No, you are your brother's brother." Human unity is not something we are called on to create, only to recognize. God made us one, and Christ died to keep us that way. So let's stop trying to put asunder what God has joined together. Rather let us gather now around Christ's table, so that "having supped with him and with each other, with hearts made warm and wills made strong again through bread and cup," we may resolve to be, if not the first, at least that hundredth monkey, who dispelled a destructive lie by replacing it with a life-enhancing truth, and showed the others what a true feast life has in store for all of us.

Rooted and Grounded in Love

OCTOBER 10, 1982
Readings: Psalm 46:1–7; Isaiah 43:1–3; Ephesians 3:14–21

Leonard Bernstein once wrote of Beethoven that he "broke all the rules, and turned out pieces of breathtaking rightness." Often I feel the same way about St. Paul: he broke all the rules of syntax and turned out sentences that are imperishable, so powerful, that at times the words seem already to have become deeds. Listen again to this sentence that covers six verses:

> For this reason I bow my knees before the Father, from whom every family in heaven and on earth is named, that according to the riches of his glory he may grant you to be strengthened with might through his Spirit in the inner [person] and that Christ may

dwell in your hearts through faith; that you, being
rooted and grounded in love, may have power to
comprehend with all the saints what is the breadth
and length and height and depth, and to know the
love of Christ which surpasses knowledge, that you
may be filled with all the fulness of God.

I turn to this sentence because it includes something of great
importance that I left out of last week's sermon. I quoted Einstein's
contention that our task is to "widen our circle of compassion to
embrace all living creatures and the whole of nature in its beauty."

No one will gainsay that sentiment as an ideal. But in reality, how
can you embrace all living creatures when you're among the country's eleven million unemployed? Or a member of [the Polish trade
union] Solidarity, now officially declared defunct? Or when you are
on the verge of losing, not only your job but your spouse as well? Or
when you're over eighty and your lower back is deteriorating? The
point is this: you cannot widen your circle of compassion until first
you widen your circle of security. Why do we so hate death and taxes
when death unites us with all nature and taxes with all humanity?
Because we're insecure. We admire Mother Teresa's selfless embrace
of the poor, but we're more apt to see ourselves reflected in this chilling picture of one man's isolation, a picture drawn by the man's own
son only days after his father died.

His legacy was like a huge mound of ice with him
balanced on top of it. It raised him above other people, but it trapped him at the same time. If he ever
felt any impulse to get down off it, one look at the
steepness, slipperiness, and height of his perch discouraged him. If he tried to come down, he would
break his neck; and if, by some miracle, he got down
unharmed, he would be helpless, because all he
knew how to do was to sit tight. There was nothing
he personally could do to retain his preeminence.
That was out of his hands. All he could do was pray
for the cold and darkness that would keep his mountain intact and curse the warmth and sunlight that
kept melting it away. (Robert Kimber)

We're not going to widen our circle of compassion until first we
widen our circle of security. How are we going to do that? The other

day I read that the Mbuti Pygmies, who still hunt and gather in the rain forests of Central Africa, nurture their children in such fashion that the security the children first experience in their mother's womb is carried forward throughout all their later growth. "From the moment of birth onwards everything is done to enable that sense of security to be transferred in steadily widening and inclusive circles from the sphere that is limited to the mother's body to the *endu* (leaf hut), to the *hopi* (playground), to the *apa* (camp) and finally to the most inclusive sphere of all, *ndura* (the forest)" (Colin Turnbull). The result is that the Mbuti Pygmies are among the least violent folk in the world.

It is a basic function of the Christian faith to give precisely that kind of security in the successively more complicated circles in which we live and move and have our being. In St. Paul's words: ". . . that Christ may dwell in your hearts through faith; that you, *being rooted and grounded in love*, may have power to comprehend with all the saints what is the breadth and length and height and depth . . ."

All great religious leaders have understood the relationship of security to compassion. "A mighty fortress is our God," the sole bulwark which faileth never—which is to say, "A mighty fortress is not my job, nor my trade union, nor my spouse, nor even my life." Yes,

> Let goods and kindred go,
> This mortal life also;
> The body they may kill;
> God's truth abideth still,
> His Kingdom is forever.

If you seek your security in the Eternal then you can live with all the insecurities of this temporal life, go on loving amid a sea of hatred, go on living joyfully when everything around you seems to be deteriorating. When in 1520, at Leipzig, Martin Luther was asked, "Where will you be, Brother Martin, when church, state, princes, and people turn against you? Where will you be then?" Replied Luther, "Why, then as now, in the hands of Almighty God." It was nine years later, when the prediction at Leipzig had proved true, in the darkest hour in the history of Protestantism, that Luther in Coburg sat down to write what Heine called "the Marseillaise of the Reformation." Since then, "A Mighty Fortress" has been sung by poor Protestant exiles on their way into exile, by martyrs on their way to death, by whole armies before battle, by those gathered around deathbeds in hospitals, and by the inhabitants of countless prison cells. Those of you who went to jail in the Sixties and Seventies will bear me out: rarely did Christians in jail not sing "Amazing Grace" and "A Mighty Fortress."

But to avoid all sentimentality, let us notice the second line of the hymn: "Our helper he *amid* the flood." This reflects the 46th Psalm on which the hymn is based: "God is our refuge and strength, a very present help *in* trouble"—not to spare us trouble. And remember what we heard in Isaiah 43: "But now thus says the LORD, he who created you, O Jacob, he who formed you, O Israel: 'Fear not, for I have redeemed you; I have called you by name, you are mine. When you pass through the waters I will be with you; and through the rivers, they shall not overwhelm you'"—words that inspired another great hymn, whose third verse reads:

> When through the deep waters I call thee to go,
> The rivers of woe shall not thee overflow;
> For I will be near thee, thy troubles to bless,
> And sanctify to thee thy deepest distress.

In other words, God's security provides support, but never protection. How often we who are parents confuse loving our children with protecting them, and when they reject our protection we withdraw our support! How often we are like the disciples who occasionally sought to make life easier for Jesus but lacked the discrimination to know what was significant. But Paul never confuses support with protection: "For this reason I bow my knees before the Father, from whom every family in heaven and on earth is named, that according to the riches of his glory he may grant you to be *strengthened with might through his Spirit in the inner [person]* . . ."

God is not going to keep our jobs for us—as eleven million Americans know—nor even our spouses. God is not going to indulge our narcissism by prolonging our youth, nor in old age mend our deteriorating backs. But if there is no God-given protection *from* suffering, there is God-given support *in* suffering, and a God-given use for *all* suffering. Einstein saw it precisely: our task is "to widen our circle of compassion to embrace all living creatures and the whole of nature in its beauty."

The only form of suffering that can't possibly put us in closer touch with nature and all living creatures is the suffering of a bruised ego. Always self-centered, pride is never more so than when it is hurt. But other forms of suffering produce selfless courage. They can widen our circle of compassion, putting us in closer touch with those who suffer as we, and far more, the world around, provided our own lives are rooted and grounded in the secure knowledge of God's love for us. Only by knowing "the love of Christ which surpasses knowledge" can we at all times and in all places pass on the riches of that love.

We've heard words from the psalmist, from the first Christian theologian, and from one of the greatest of all reformers. Let's give the last word to an artist who seems to have experienced something akin to what Paul and Luther experienced. This is what Henri Matisse had to say about being loved and being loving:

> Love is . . . the greatest good, which alone renders light that which weighs heavy, and beats with an equal spirit that which is unequal. For love carries weights which without it would be a burden, and makes sweet and pleasant all that is bitter. . . . Love wants to rise, not to be held down by anything base. . . . Nothing is more gentle than love, nothing stronger, nothing higher, nothing larger, nothing more pleasant, nothing more complete, nothing better in heaven or on earth—because love is born of God and cannot rest other than in God, above all living beings. They who love, fly, run, and rejoice; they are free and nothing holds them back.

Love's True Return

OCTOBER 24, 1982
Readings: Exodus 25:1–8; 2 Corinthians 9:6–12

"The Lord said to Moses, '. . . from every man whose heart makes him willing you shall receive the offering for me.'"

"Each one must do as he has made up his mind to do, not reluctantly or under compulsion, for God loves a cheerful giver."

The attitude of American churches to money is ambivalent, to say the least. They desire it, they go for it, yet at the same time they resent it, and some even pretend to scorn it. All would consider conspicuous consumption obscene, but most would not consider great wealth itself to be wrong. They are concerned with how people spend their money but remarkably indifferent as to how they make it in the first place. All of which confusion makes Pledge Sunday a very interesting day. I know that in the hearts of some of you there is great anxiety, and in a few even indignation. To some the mere announcement each fall of the Every Member Canvass is like receiving the famous Jewish telegram: "Start worrying. Letter follows." And Sunday by Sunday the hardest thing to consecrate in this service is the money—even though we call it an offering, even though after it we sing the Doxology, even though we place it up on the altar next to the Bible, where we put nothing else except the bread and wine. So we have a few things to talk about.

In a speech by John Gardner, former president of Common Cause, I came across these sentences: "One cannot discuss fundraising without some reference to the state of the economy. There's a country proverb that says 'No one tests the depth of a river with both feet.' That was before President Reagan launched his economic program. That concludes my discussion of the economy."

As times get harsher, the jokes get wryer. Now it is said that an optimist is one who believes that whatever happens, no matter how bad, is for the best; the pessimist is the person to whom it has happened. That makes for a lot of pessimists these days, including many here in this church, whose cars—if they still have them—sport the bumper sticker, "If you think the system is working, ask someone who isn't."

While deeply sympathetic to the despair of these people, I want to reinforce their pessimism. I don't think our economic troubles are temporary. Even if we had a compassionate administration in Washington, we would still be bumping our heads against the ceiling of limited resources. Resource constraints is a worldwide phenomenon, withering welfare in many countries which, like our own, have not justly distributed their wealth. So the future we face is hard—not necessarily bleak, but certainly hard.

What does that say to the ministers and officers of Riverside Church? If someone could find it, I'd love to pin on the wall of my office the old cartoon of Charlie Brown, looking around him from the pitcher's mound, saying, "How can we lose when we're so sincere?" In the harsh times ahead the officers and ministers of Riverside Church will have to become very tough-minded about our institutional effectiveness, resource allocations, priorities. And we have to raise money outside the membership of this church. Having realized that institutional vanity feeds on the illusion of self-sufficiency, we have—at long last—hired a strong and skilled fund-raiser, Richard Preston (who has to be strong and skilled because, given the competition, the art of raising money is rapidly becoming one of the martial arts). In short, we'll do our part, the ministers and officers of this church.

But now let me ask you: When times are hard, and the national administration is heartless, don't people have a right to turn to the churches for help of the most practical kind—food, clothing, shelter, day care, nursery-kindergarten, paramedical and paralegal help, and English-language instruction for immigrants? Lord knows, I hate to see the churches become havens in a heartless world and, by caring for the victims of such a world, reinforce its heartlessness. I hate to see charity go bail for justice. But what choice have we, until we in this country find the decency to distribute our wealth more equitably? Christians can't countenance people dying before their time, becoming, as the poor are rapidly becoming, exiles in their own land. "Inasmuch as ye have done it to the least of these . . ." Doesn't Christ say to us, "I'll know how much you love me by how much you love them"?

Furthermore, isn't it precisely when economic resources are scarce that the only truly renewable resources, the spiritual ones, are most needed? In the days ahead, more than ever the citizens of this land will need what the Epistle to the Hebrews calls "the assurance of things hoped for, the conviction of things unseen." Maybe, for the first time, Americans will be in a mood to contemplate why affluence hasn't bought morale, why the frantic search for happiness has only increased the profits of the tranquilizer industry, why the deepest truth about America may be our poverty of spirit, for the values of the Kingdom of God stand the present values of America on their heads. Maybe for the first time Americans will realize there are two ways to be rich: one is to have lots of money, the other to have few needs.

In other words, while Riverside Church has surely known glorious days, it has seen none more important than those that lie ahead. That is why it needs your support, and more now when that support is harder to give.

Which brings us to the concluding question: When times are hard, and therefore it is harder to give, can you give more and still do it cheerfully? Frankly, I can't. But I am instructed by the story of the widow's mite, which insists, first of all, that what counts is not how much you give but how much is left after you give. The story does not record, however, that having given her all, the widow then jumped up and down for joy. Maybe she simply figured that some things are so important that you have to go ahead and do them regardless of motivation.

Let me tell you what I did when, at a deacons meeting, we were all handed our pledge cards. I promptly lost mine, and forgot all about it—a clear case of "blocking." But when, this Friday, Richard

Preston confronted me with the fact that I was the only member of the collegium who still hadn't filled out a pledge card, I immediately—although I have lots of obligations, some fun, some not, to a lot of people—I immediately pledged ten percent of my salary, which is high for a minister. I pledged to give to the church $100 a week, $5,200 a year, and I did so instantly because I didn't want to stop to think. Boxers say, "If you have to think, it's too late." So with Christians: we need habits of the heart that work automatically. But I didn't feel cheerful, although I would have felt worse had I pledged less.

Gradually, however, I expect good cheer to come upon me, and for these bedrock reasons. Motives affect actions, but so do actions motives. We can act despite our motives, then watch our motives change. Furthermore, I'm convinced that we should never be afraid lest by our liberality we impoverish ourselves; it's hard to believe, but it's a basic tenet of the faith that God will supply our need. I also believe I am not giving to Riverside Church, nor even, finally, to others; I made my pledge to God, who has given her all for me, nothing less than the gift of herself. But even that description is not correct. In pledging, I wasn't giving, I was *lending* to God, who will repay the loan a hundredfold. For love's true return is not the return of love, but an increase in our capacity to love. The reward of generosity is not gratitude but a more generous heart.

Good cheer, then, will be mine when I realize anew that in giving we are not impoverished, but enriched; in giving we receive, and nothing less than our entire identity; that's the story of the Good Samaritan, who in giving received his truest self, his entire identity. The tragedy of the priest and the Levite is that they never found out who they were. Already, as I say these things, I can feel good cheer coming upon me for, with Paul, I am convinced that "Eye hath not seen, nor ear heard, neither have entered into the heart of man, the things which God hath prepared for them that love him" (1 Cor. 2:9).

"Who Do You Say That I Am?"

NOVEMBER 7, 1982
Reading: Matthew 16:13–23

I love the exchange that takes place in the first verses of this passage. Jesus asks the disciples a perfectly straightforward question: "Who do [people] say that the Son of man is?" It's an impersonal question whose answer will not reveal much about the person answering beyond establishing whether or not that person is observant. So we read, "And they [presumably all of them] said, 'Some say John the Baptist, others say Elijah, and others Jeremiah or one of the prophets.'" But then Jesus asks a personal question, the answer to which will reveal the very soul of the person answering: "But who do you say that I am?" This time no one speaks, except one, Simon Peter, who says, "You are the Christ, the Son of the living God."

To Jesus, of course, both questions were intensely personal, crucial to the success of his life. For this exchange with his disciples does not take place in the bright morning of his career, when all wondered and many bore testimony to him. No, it takes place in the long evening shadows, in the grim twilight. Jesus has to know who has understood him, for who is going to carry on the work after he's gone? Earlier, in the wilderness, he had rejected all methods for inaugurating the reign of God that would be incompatible with it—miracles, power. But years of teaching and healing later, who has understood the Kingdom? Who has understood that his matchless royalty can only be won by a matchless suffering?

From one point of view the answer the disciples gave to the first question is very complimentary. "Some say John the Baptist"—whose return from the dead many anticipated, and Herod, in particular, feared—"others say Elijah." To the prophet Malachi, God had promised, "Behold I will send you Elijah the prophet before the great and terrible day of the Lord comes." To this day Jews, at Passover, leave a seat vacant for Elijah, and if Elijah comes, can the Messiah be far behind? "And others Jeremiah or one of the prophets." Some Jews at the time believed that before their forebears had gone into exile, Jeremiah had taken the Ark and the altar out of the Temple, had hidden them in a cave, and before the coming of the Messiah would return and produce them so that once more the glory of God would descend on all the people. So to be called John the Baptist, Elijah, or Jeremiah was high tribute—but also crushing, for to make Jesus only a prophet among others, even to honor him as the first among all the teachers of all history, is to empty his life of its central meaning, his death of its efficacy, and the church of his authority.

So it must be with some relief that Jesus hears Peter's confession, "You are the Christ, the Son of the living God." Then a wonderful thing happens, a wonderful thing that has happened since a billion times over. No sooner does Peter tell Jesus who he is than Jesus tells Peter who *he* is. "Blessed are you, Simon Bar-Jona! For flesh and blood has not revealed this to you." There are truths that the mind can defend but never discover. "And I tell you, you are Peter, and on this rock I will build my church."

Let's not get embroiled in the controversy swirling around that passage. For our purposes, let's say simply that Jesus, in effect, said to Peter, "On such a faith as yours I can build a church. And because you are the first to grasp who I am, you are the first stone, the foundation stone; and in ages to come everyone who discovers me as you have just discovered me will become another stone added to the edifice."

Whenever like Peter we tell Jesus he is the Christ, he tells us who we are. Think for a moment: who—or what—tells you who you are? Some people need money to tell them who they are, or power; take both away, and they think they're nothing. Some need scholarship or athletic ability, and no few need enemies to tell them who they are. I have in mind anticommunists who need communists, or whites who need Blacks, or vice-versa. In March 1968, when President Johnson announced he would not stand for reelection, half a million people in the peace movement were left without their identity. Fortunately, Richard Nixon came along and restored it to them! Some people need their sins to tell them who they are. The way some of us treasure our failures, you'd think they were the holiest things in our lives. But the moment you tell Jesus, "You are the Son of God, you are the Christ," he says to you, "Blessed are you, Mary, John, Jason, Emily, for you are no longer defined by money, power, scholarship, your enemies, your sins, or anything else in all creation. Praise be to God, you are now as you love; you are as you receive my love, and return that love by loving others." When we tell Jesus who he is, he tells us who we are. He becomes the mirror to our humanity.

But more importantly, he is a window to Divinity, the window through whom we see as much as is given mortal eyes to see of God's gracious power and mercy. When we say, "You are the Christ, the Son of the living God," we are not saying that God is confined to Christ, only most essentially defined by Christ. Christ, if you will, is the Rosetta Stone that makes intelligible the hieroglyphics of history, the main theme that makes understandable all the variations of it in our lives. There is much needlessly complicated talk about Christ's deity. Finally, what is important is not that Jesus is Godlike, but that God is Christlike, that God is akin in purpose and method to Jesus. What is important for us to know is that when we see Christ at work succoring the sick, empowering the weak, and scorning the powerful, we are seeing transparently the power of God at work. What is important is for us to be able to pray to God, and everything we ask or affirm of God, we know we can say, "Through Jesus Christ our Lord."

Whenever with Peter we say, "You are the Christ, the Son of the living God," Jesus tells us not only who we are but who God is. He is the mirror to our humanity, and a window to Divinity. Whenever, with Peter, we say, "You are the Christ, the Son of the living God," we become another stone added to the edifice of the church, which, as Christ says, is finally invincible. How could he make such a claim? Because, as one Christian wrote centuries later, "All the empires and kingdoms have failed, because of this inherent and continued weakness, that they were founded by strong men. . . . But this one thing, the historic Christian Church, was founded on a weak man, and for that reason is indestructible. For no chain is stronger than its weakest link." But this weak Peter confessed Jesus as "the Christ, the Son of the living God," and became The Rock. And whenever Christians do as Peter did they become part of that community against which the wages of sin, the mortality of human beings, the corrosion of the centuries, and all the powers of death militant in the world cannot prevail.

As Paul would say, "Thanks be to God who gives us the victory through our Lord Jesus Christ."

Singing to the Lord

NOVEMBER 21, 1982
Readings: Psalm 95; 2 Corinthians 12:7–10

The Psalms, as all the fourth graders in the service today know, are poems, but poems with a particularly Hebrew characteristic called "parallelism." You say things one way, then you say the same things in a different way. It's like a country dance: three steps to the left, three to the right. You can find parallelism in English verse, whether in the childishly simple form of "The Cherry Tree Carol" ("Joseph was an old man, / An old man was he"); or in far more sophisticated form in some of the great poems of Christopher Marlowe: "Cut is the branch that might have grown full straight, / And burned is Apollo's laurel bough."

But the pattern is peculiarly Hebrew, so it is no surprise to find it throughout the Psalms: "He that dwelleth in heaven shall laugh them to scorn; the LORD shall have them in derision" (Ps. 2:4); "He shall make thy righteousness as clear as the light; and thy just dealing as the noonday" (Ps. 37:6). And when the fourth graders read (so beautifully!) the

95th Psalm we heard parallelism again in the opening verses: "O come, let us sing unto the LORD; let us make a joyful noise to the rock of our salvation."

And what poetry in these Psalms! Noise is an unwanted sound, but "make a joyful noise to the rock of our salvation"—wouldn't you have liked to have written that line? At best I would have written, as indeed it is written in the 100th Psalm, "We are his people, and the sheep of his pasture." But how dull compared to "For he is our God, and we are the people of his pasture, and the sheep of his hand."

Actually the Psalms (the word in Hebrew means "praises") are hymns, the sacred songs of Israel. The Israelites must have sung them with extraordinary intensity, for in so many of the psalms the only thing that appears disciplined is the writing. The feelings—whether of joy, rage, compassion, or awe—seem almost ungovernable. Like Moses' bush, the psalms blaze with color. Their authors are "aflame with love and free."

Not so all poets. Some live in their art more than they live in their lives, and many of *us* lead lives of precious little poetry. We live, but are dead inside. We are victims of lapsed intensity, people committed to loyalties we no longer feel. But the psalmists, whoever they were, clearly lived both in their lives and in their art. And, of course, they listened, ears glued to the sounds of two worlds, the eternal world and the world of time. They didn't walk the streets of Jerusalem or the country lanes of Judea with radios at their waists and earphones tightly pressed against their ears, tuning out the pain and anguish of the world. That's why their feelings occasionally ran away with them in a way that tends to shock us today. So deeply did the psalmists allow the injustices to penetrate their souls that occasionally they reacted with hatred and vengeance. But no matter. No flame is pure, and the impurities are not of its essence.

One thing more about the Psalms in general: "To everything there is a season . . . a time to weep and a time to laugh; a time to mourn and a time to dance." There is a time to be subtle, skeptical, sophisticated; a time to pursue truth as elusive as a fox that can be chased in the hills or chased in the bush, but that can rarely be caught in the open. And there is a time *not* to pursue, or even to defend the truth. There must be a time in all our lives to feed on the truth. The Psalms nourish not our doubts but our convictions. They tell us that if you lose your spine, you can't walk. And they're right: we need convictions to live. We can manage with opinions only if we want to die comfortably, and no psalmist would want to live a life so boring!

Let's turn now to the 95th Psalm. Like the five psalms that immediately follow it, the 95th is one of almost uncontainable joy: "O come, let us sing unto the LORD; let us make a joyful noise to the rock of our salvation." Those invited to sing seem to be entering the temple at a time of feasting much like the time that lies ahead of us this week. "Let us come into his presence with thanksgiving; let us make a joyful noise to him with songs of praise!"

At such a festive time it's natural to sing and dance and praise the Lord, and maybe the psalm should be read only in festive moods. But I, at least, want to know if it's possible to make a joyful noise unto the Lord while we're busy facing down our daily demons. Some of us here have cancer, no few are without a job, many are old and tired of paying the cost of upkeep, and all of us, if we look around, can see millions starving in squalor because of the well-fed disinterest of the rich.

I'm sure many of you have shared my experience of waking up some mornings feeling like nothing so much as a sensitive grain of wheat called on, once again, to face the millstone. All you can think to say is, "Hi, millstone, whom are you grinding up fine today?" And if you read the paper, you're convinced that if the world didn't have bad luck, it wouldn't have any luck at all. In such depressing times, can we still sing a song to the Lord?

Of course we can, provided we remember that those who accuse the times do but excuse themselves. God, after all, doesn't make poor people; the rich do that. God doesn't try to persuade the American bishops that nuclear deterrence is moral, that good will and mass killing go hand in hand; government representatives do that. St. Augustine notes that in the 95th Psalm we are invited "to a great feast of joy, of joy not unto the world, but unto the Lord"—and that's the key that unlocks the heart to sing its song to God no matter what the circumstances, for it is finally only in the depths of hell that heaven is found and affirmed and celebrated. Do you have cancer? Then cancer becomes a part of your life, but it doesn't control your life, because you and all cancer patients are "the people of his pasture and the sheep of his hand." Are you unemployed? The unemployment becomes a part of your life, but it doesn't tell you you're no good, for "the Lord is a great king above all the gods," including those of employment and unemployment, and will not empower them to tell us who we are. Are you just plain old and tired? Then maybe you'll want to listen to one of the most beautiful arias ever written, "*Ich steh mit einem Fuss im Grab*" (I stand with one foot in the grave)—beautiful because Bach wrote it knowing that death is more and other than oblivion, that "neither death nor life can separate us from the love of God," that the church above and the church on earth are one. And if you suffer, as all of us should, because of the world's violence and madness, then in the name of the suffering, crucified Christ you can protest that pain and anguish without going under, for God is with us when we suffer not only to console but to strengthen us.

So let us sing to the Lord first of all because of God's suffering love. As Christians, we know that Christ represents a beautiful life about ugliness, a life that keeps the sounds of hope alive even as they are being drowned out by orchestrated evil. But long before the advent of Christ and Christians, the psalmists too knew of God's suffering: "Behold, he that keepeth Israel shall neither slumber nor sleep" (Ps. 121:4). Maybe it's not God's peace but God's pain that passes all understanding.

And then let us sing to the Lord because of our own suffering. Elie Wiesel has written: "You can hold yourself back from the suffering world; this is something you are free to do . . . but perhaps precisely this holding back is the only suffering you might be able to avoid." Job is right: "Man is to trouble born as surely as the sparks fly upwards." Much political apathy arises from a desire to be free of pain, but apathy, being unnatural, requires a lot of emotional effort. Likewise anti-communism is an ideology designed to produce defense mechanisms against contact with suffering, but defense mechanisms demand an awful lot of maintenance. As for the suffering-free religion being huckstered by false prophets, those apostles of the Aspirin Age, it never makes it, except as a tool for exploiters, for exploitation needs apathy to run its course smoothly.

No, the tragedy is not that we suffer. What is tragic is the suffering where nothing is learned. What is tragic is the pain that somehow doesn't get converted into strength. What is tragic are the protests against needless suffering that do not lead to greater love. What is tragic is to have the experience and miss the meaning.

Some people think roses have thorns. Others prefer to remember that thornbushes grow roses. St. Paul came to realize that a thorn in the flesh could be a severe mercy: "For when I am weak, then I am strong," because God's power "is made perfect in weakness." Certain it is that if nothing can separate us from the love of God, neither death nor life, nor tribulation, nor famine, nor nakedness, nor peril, nor the sword; and if God is with us when we suffer not only to console but to strengthen us; and if while we were yet sinners Christ died for us, to prove that there is more mercy in God than sin in us, then it is possible to find heaven anywhere—even, and maybe especially, in the depths of hell; to say to one another not only in festive but in all circumstances, "O come, let us sing to the LORD; let us make a joyful noise to the rock of our salvation!"

Christian Obedience

DECEMBER 19, 1982
Readings: Isaiah 9:6–7; Luke 2:8–12

There are at least two versions of Christianity so out of step with Christmas that one of these years Christmas is just going to put them out of business. The first, rather obvious kind is joyless Christianity. When you stop to think of it, there are not that many Christians who look, feel, and act redeemed; and there are an awful lot who have just enough religion to make themselves miserable! The joyless Christians tend to be Victorian rather than Elizabethan. They tend to deify not God but their own stuffy respectability: pretending to be upright, they are really uptight, and that's what makes joyless Christianity no laughing matter. For as we all know, those who are themselves repressed become themselves repressive.

A second kind of Christianity that comes out all wrong at Christmas is authoritarian Christianity, as opposed—Erich Fromm says— to humanitarian Christianity. To the followers of authoritarian Christianity, God's power is much more important than God's love, and self-abnegation is much more important than self-realization. In authoritarian Christianity the cardinal sin is not a refusal to love, but disobedience to fixed norms of thought and behavior—fixed by someone else in some other time. And the followers of authoritarian Christianity tend naturally to be reactionary, for the goal of life as they see it is not to change the world but to reproduce it, generally according to an earlier and presumably simpler model.

Let's think for a moment about the Christian understanding of obedience. Was the poet Schiller correct in writing, "Courage can be shown by any fool / Obedience is the Christian's jewel"?

Surely there is a difference between discerning obedience and blind obedience. Discerning obedience I can understand as a legitimate religious concept, but blind obedience is anathema. Abraham's willingness, for example, to sacrifice his son Isaac I find totally incomprehensible, not to say reprehensible. How could Abraham have conceived God's love to be something less than human love as he knew it at its best? Actually there is an interpretation in the Midrash that says that God was so disgusted with Abraham's blind obedience to what he misconceived to be God's will that God hastily dispatched a ram to save Isaac's life, and swore never to speak to Abraham again, which in the Bible God never does.

In a book as provocative as its title, *Beyond Mere Obedience*, German theologian Dorothee Soelle confesses she too has trouble with the notion of obedience, and on three counts: she is German; she is a Christian; and she is a woman. (Let no American feel superior, for we too have fought, killed, and died in blind obedience to wrong causes.) Soelle has seen too many instances of people giving over their reason and conscience to someone else. She asks a telling question: Can you require unquestioning obedience to God, and then criticize the same stance when it comes to other people, institutions, and one's own nation? She makes her point powerfully by quoting the following lines:

> I was brought up by my parents to give due respect
> and honor to all adults, particularly older persons,
> no matter which social classes they belonged to.
> Wherever the need arose, I was told, it was my pri-
> mary duty to be of assistance. In particular I was
> always directed to carry out the wishes and direc-
> tives of my parents, the teacher, pastor, in fact of all
> adults including household servants, without hesita-
> tion, and allow nothing to deter me. What such per-
> sons said was always right. Those rules of conduct
> have become part of my very flesh and blood.

After a strict Christian upbringing, the author of those lines, Rudolph Höss, became for three years in World War II the director of the Auschwitz concentration camp.

I think we have to question whether obedience is indeed a Christian's greatest glory. At least we have to know what kind of obedience to what kind of power we're talking about, and I think this point is beautifully addressed at Christmas. At Christmas the Word of the Lord hits the world with the force of a hint: he who was to be the bread of life for human beings is laid in the feedbox of animals. The Christmas rose of which we sing grows not in summer's warmth nor in the splendor of the fall, but rather is brought to bloom by a chastening frost, and opens petal by petal into one winter storm after another. Why would an all-powerful God ever want to come to earth in this fashion?

The answer is suggested by the fable of the king who fell in love with a maid. To the question, "How shall I declare my love?" his counselors answered, "Your majesty has only to appear in all the glory of your royal raiments before the maid's humble abode and she will instantly fall at your feet and be yours."

But it was precisely that thought that so troubled the king, for he wanted *her* glorification, not his. In return for his love he wanted hers, freely given; what he did not want was her submission to his power. What a dilemma, when not to declare your love spells the end of love, and to declare it spells the end of your beloved! But finally the king realized love's truth, that freedom for the beloved demands equality with the beloved. So late one night, after all the counselors and courtiers of the palace had retired, he stole out a side door and appeared before the maid's cottage dressed as a servant.

Indeed, the fable is a Christmas story. But before we get carried away by this imaginative, loving king, let us realize that the fable, so satisfactory perhaps to its hero, and to its author, Søren Kierkegaard, might well have been anything but satisfactory to its heroine. Had I been the maid, I would have wanted to know more about this stranger who appeared at my door, about his future and mine. Was I to be stuck forever in the servants' quarters? Come to think of it, I don't mind a little submission. I don't mind marrying a king!

Likewise, before we gush any further about the King of Kings born among beasts in a stall, let us recognize that we too would have preferred it had God remained God, rather than becoming the frailest among us. We want God to be strong so that we can be weak, but here God is at Christmas becoming weak so that we can be strong. We want God to be all-powerful, to guide, direct, and protect us. I know how Isaiah felt when he cried out, "O that thou wouldst rend the heavens and come down, that the mountains might quake at thy presence—as when fire kindles brushwood and the fire causes water to boil—to make thy name known to thine adversaries, and that the nations might tremble at thy presence!" (Isa. 64:1–2). But no: At Christmas God puts himself at our mercy. Why, we could "crack that baby's skull like an eggshell or nail him up when he gets too big for that" (Buechner). Imagine: God is not safe from us, we have to protect *him*. I think I see it now: God had to come to earth as a child so that you and I and all of us might finally grow up. That's the Christmas message that one of these years is going to put authoritarian religion out of business.

The trouble with the usual notion of obedience, whether in relation to our parents, our husbands or wives, our nation, or to God, is that it represents an impossible balance of power. In relation to God, it makes God's power so much more important than God's love. It overlooks the truth grasped finally by the loving king that—again— freedom for the beloved requires equality with the beloved. The trouble with the usual notion of obedience is that it represents a childhood model of living. Fearing confusion and chaos, a child naturally desires supervision, control, direction. A child wants a superior power to provide order, to direct its destiny, and so do childish adults—which is to say, most of us. But let's face that desire and call it what it is, a temptation to disobedience, for we are called to obey not God's power but God's love. Christian obedience is not a childish acquiescence to fixed norms of thought and conduct, norms fixed by somebody else in some other time. God wants not submission to his power but in return for God's love, our own.

God comes to earth as a child so that you and I and everyone else might grow up. The other night I saw, once again, *Amahl and the Night Visitors*. Amahl, the crippled boy, is miraculously cured, you remember, when he himself gives to the infant Jesus his crutch. That's the Christmas present we should all bring to the manger: our crutches— so that like Amahl we might "run and not grow weary, walk and not faint"; so that like Amahl we might grow up and live joyfully and freely, free from the fear of death, free from the longing to be recognized and accepted, free, completely free for one another as God's love in Christ is so freely poured out for us.

Dear sisters and brothers, may you be truly obedient, and have a lively and loving Christmas.

The Beauty of Holiness

New Year's Eve
DECEMBER 31, 1982
Readings: 2 Corinthians 4 (selected passages)

The waning minutes of an old year seem naturally to bring to mind truths that are well worn, but that also (it is to be hoped) wear well. So, for you and yours, for all of us on Spaceship Earth, I have two very unoriginal wishes. The first is that in 1983, in spite of all, we find the world beautiful.

That we live in ugly times no sensitive soul will dispute. With a bit of luck we shall never look back on 1982 as the good old days. I hope we are passing through times that are transitional, though to what is less clear than from what; and I'm well aware of Adam's famous line to Eve, as both were being ejected from the garden: "Not to worry, darling; it's only a transitional period."

But it is precisely when times are ugly that we must find the world beautiful. When times are deadly we live by beauty. This is no new insight. Listen to this still-ringing voice of the last century:

> Spite of despondence, of the inhuman dearth
> Of noble natures, of the gloomy days,
> Of all the unhealthy and o'er-darkened ways
> Made for our searching: Yes, in spite of all
> Some shape of beauty moves away the pall
> From our dark spirits . . .

And Keats (you guessed it!) concludes that these things of beauty that are a joy forever, be they "the sun, the moon, trees old and young," or be they wrought by human hand—these things of beauty

> Haunt us till they become a cheering light
> Unto our souls, and bound to us so fast,
> That, whether there be shine, or gloom o'ercast,
> They always must be with us, or we die.

When times are ugly we live by beauty, or spiritually speaking we die.

It is a crime to live in New York City and not regularly experience the beauty of its skyline, its proud buildings, its parks, rivers, monuments, museums, and music. It's a crime, wherever you live, to let a day go by without reading a poem. (Don't worry about today; I've already read you the better part of one!) It's a crime to visit someone who is dying and not admire the beauty of courage. And if you're religious—and everyone is—it's a crime not to spend daily a minute or two in some place, inside or outside, with or without sight and sound, where you can experience beauty in its greatest depth, what Scripture calls the beauty of holiness. I grant you can't ask the night to pick its favorite star, nor a sunrise its favorite color, but I would contend that of all forms of beauty there is none like unto the beauty of holiness. As it is written in the psalms: "In thy presence is the fullness of joy." Just as half of human sorrow is for the inscrutable sorrow of the world, so half of our joy stems from the depth of its ineffable beauty, which is the beauty of holiness.

The second wish goes with the first: May we find the world beautiful—and try to make it more so. Now we are talking not only of parks and monuments, museums and music, and courage in adversity; we're also talking of justice. Said Dietrich Bonhoeffer in the late 1930s: "Only those who fight for the Jews can listen to Gregorian chants." We can update that for ourselves in 1983: Only those who hear the cries of the city's needy can enter its concert halls. Americans are only allowed to admire the statue of Simón Bolívar on 57th Street who also heed his words, "The United States seems destined by Providence to plague the Americas with miseries in the name of liberty." In other words, finally there can be no beauty if it is paid for by injustice; there can be no truth that passes over injustice in silence; nor can there be any moral virtue that condones it. The moral order may not exhaust the beauty of holiness, but it is an essential part of it, for in the grandeur of the prophets' vision the whole world swings on an ethical hinge. Disturb that hinge and all history and even nature will feel the shock.

And what individually and collectively can we do in 1983 to make the world more beautiful? Individually we can refuse to rationalize any more, we can refuse to justify any longer any form of injustice. This won't be easy, for as Ruth Benedict once noted of one form of injustice, "War is an asocial trait. . . . If we justify war, it is because all peoples always justify the traits of which they find themselves possessed, not because war will bear an objective examination of its merits."

No form of injustice will bear an objective examination of its merits. All forms—unemployment, malnutrition, homelessness—like war reflect asocial traits that we first must recognize within each one of us. Let us not deceive ourselves: Justice upsets the ordering of our individual lives before it shakes the Establishment. Then, having individually refused to tolerate the intolerable, we can individually and collectively talk about these things. Nowhere, except in the parables, is it recorded that Jesus talked about the weather, whereas always and everywhere he urged people to realize that God was trying through them to make this world more beautiful. "Blessed are the peacemakers, blessed are those who hunger and thirst after righteousness, blessed are they who are persecuted for righteousness' sake." If all of us, in our places of work alone, would urge our co-workers to put upon the mind and heart of the mayor the plight of New York's homeless, those spoken and written words would render a little less ugly the lives of some 36,000 of our fellow citizens.

As for the arms race, I know a Buddhist priest who has vowed for one month to remind everyone he meets—on the bus, subway, everywhere—of its evils and its madness.

As these are things all of us can do, the question is not whether we can make a difference, but whether we *will*. I'm sure we will, and the right kind of difference, too, if we keep these two wishes in close alliance. I would not want one fulfilled without the other. So allow me to repeat them: In 1983 may you and yours, may all of us on Spaceship Earth, find the world beautiful, and try to make it more so.